SIXTH EDITION

The Structure of Argument

Annette T. Rottenberg

Donna Haisty Winchell
CLEMSON UNIVERSITY

Bedford/St. Martin's
Boston ◆ New York

For Bedford/St. Martin's

Senior Developmental Editor: John E. Sullivan III
Production Editors: Kendra LeFleur and Karen Stocz
Production Supervisor: Jennifer Peterson
Senior Marketing Manager: Karita dos Santos
Editorial Assistant: Alicia Young
Copyeditor: Lisa Wehrle
Text Design: Claire Seng-Niemoeller
Cover Design: Sara Gates
Cover Art: Soonae Tark, *Kiss #2*, 2006, acrylic on paper, 29.5 x 21.5 inches
Composition: Achorn International, Inc.
Printing and Binding: RR Donnelley & Sons

President: Joan E. Feinberg
Editorial Director: Denise B. Wydra
Editor in Chief: Karen S. Henry
Director of Marketing: Karen Melton Soeltz
Director of Editing, Design, and Production: Marcia Cohen
Assistant Director of Editing, Design, and Production: Elise S. Kaiser
Managing Editor: Elizabeth M. Schaaf

Library of Congress Control Number: 2008925887

Manufactured in the United States of America.

3 2 1 0
f e d c b

For information, write: Bedford/St. Martin's, 75 Arlington Street, Boston, MA 02116 (617-399-4000)

ISBN-10: 0–312–69215–3
ISBN-13: 978–0–312–69215–5

Acknowledgments

Charles Adams. "Lincoln's Logic." From *When in the Course of Human Events*, pp. 193–211. Copyright © 2000 by Rowman & Littlefield Publishing. Reprinted by permission of the publisher

Advocates for Youth. "Will the Politics of Teen Sex Stop a Cancer Vaccine?" From *Advocatesforyouth.org*. Reprinted by permission.

Kevin Alexander. "MySpace Not Responsible for Predators." From *The Battalion*, June 28, 2006. Reprinted by permission.

Preface for Instructors

PURPOSE

Argumentation as the basis of a composition course should need no defense, especially at a time of renewed pedagogical interest in critical thinking. A course in argumentation encourages practice in close analysis, use of supporting materials, and logical organization. It encompasses all the modes of development around which composition courses are often built. It teaches students to read and to listen with more than ordinary care. Not least, argument can engage the interest of students who have been indifferent or even hostile to required writing courses. Because the subject matter of argument can be found in every human activity—from the most trivial to the most elevated—both students and teachers can choose the materials that appeal to them.

Composition courses using the materials of argument are, of course, not new. But the traditional methods of teaching argument through mastery of the formal processes of reasoning cannot account for the complexity of arguments in practice. Even more relevant to our purposes as teachers of composition is the tenuous relationship between learning about induction and deduction, however helpful in analysis, and the actual process of student composition. The challenge has been to find a method of teaching argument that assists students in defending their claims as directly and efficiently as possible, a method that reflects the way people actually go about organizing and developing claims outside the classroom.

One such method, first adapted to classroom instruction by teachers of rhetoric and speech, uses a model of argument advanced by Stephen Toulmin in *The Uses of Argument.* Toulmin was interested in producing a description of the real process of argument. His model was the law. "Arguments," he said, "can be compared with lawsuits, and the claims we make and argue for in extra-legal contexts with claims made in the courts."[1] Toulmin's model of argument was based on three principal elements: claim, evidence, and warrant. These elements answered the questions, "What are you trying to prove?" "What have you got to go on?"

[1] Stephen Toulmin, *The Uses of Argument* (Cambridge: Cambridge UP, 1958), p. 7.

"How did you get from evidence to claim?" Needless to say, Toulmin's model of argument does not guarantee a classroom of skilled arguers, but his questions about the parts of an argument and their relationship are precisely the ones that students must ask and answer in writing their own essays and analyzing those of others. They lead students naturally into the formulation and development of their claims.

In this text we have adapted—and greatly simplified—some of Toulmin's concepts and terminology for first-year students. We have also introduced two elements of argument with which Toulmin is not directly concerned. Most rhetoricians consider them indispensable, however, to discussion of what actually happens in the defense or rejection of a claim. One is motivational appeals—warrants based on appeals to the needs and values of an audience, designed to evoke emotional responses. A distinction between logic and emotion may be useful as an analytical tool, but in producing or attacking arguments human beings find it difficult, if not impossible, to make such a separation. In this text, therefore, persuasion through appeals to needs and values is treated as a legitimate element in the argumentative process.

We have also stressed the significance of audience as a practical matter. In the rhetorical or audience-centered approach to argument, to which we subscribe in this text, success is defined as acceptance of the claim by an audience. Arguers in the real world recognize intuitively that their primary goal is not to demonstrate the purity of their logic but to win the adherence of their audiences. To gain this adherence, students need to be reminded of the necessity for establishing themselves as credible sources for their readers.

We hope *The Structure of Argument* will lead students to discover not only the practical and intellectual rewards of learning how to argue but the real excitement of engaging in civilized debate.

ORGANIZATION

In Part One, after four introductory chapters, a chapter each is devoted to the chief elements of argument—the definitions that lay a foundation for shared understanding, the claims that students make in their arguments, the support they must supply for their claims, and the warrants that underlie their arguments. Popular fallacies as well as induction and deduction are treated in Chapter 9; because fallacies represent errors of reasoning, a knowledge of induction and deduction can make clear how and why fallacies occur. Chapter 10 deals with the power of word choice in arguing effectively.

We have provided examples, readings, discussion questions, and writing suggestions that are, we hope, both practical and stimulating. The examples include essays, articles, speeches, news reports, editorial opinions, letters to the editor, excerpts from online sources, cartoons, and advertisements. They reflect the liveliness and complexity of argumentation that exercises with no realistic context often suppress.

The selections and advertisements in Part One support in several ways the discussions of argumentation. First, they illustrate the elements of argument; in each chapter, one or more essays have been analyzed to emphasize the principles of argument explained in the chapter. Second, they are drawn from a range of publications and cover as many different subjects as possible to convince students that argument is a pervasive force in the world they read about and live in. Third, some of the essays are obviously flawed and thus enable students to identify the kinds of weaknesses they should avoid in their own essays.

Part Two takes up the process of writing, researching, and presenting arguments. Chapters 11 and 12 explain how to find a topic, define the issues that it embraces, organize the information, and draft and revise an argument. They introduce students to the business of finding sources and using and documenting those sources effectively in research papers. Part Two includes two annotated student research papers: one that employs the Modern Language Association (MLA) documentation system; the other that represents research in the social and natural sciences and uses a modified American Psychological Association (APA) documentation style. Chapter 13 provides guidelines for presenting arguments orally.

NEW TO THIS EDITION

Although the principles and concerns of the book have not changed, the new material in this edition should enhance the versatility of the text, deepen students' awareness of how pervasive argument is, and increase their ability to think critically and communicate persuasively.

We have revised many of the Writer's Guides and have added a new Writer's Guide on annotating a text. We have also added more help for understanding and working with the elements of argument: "Practice" assignments within each chapter ask students to apply what they've learned right away, and end-of-chapter assignments now include both discussion and writing prompts to help students move from informal to written response. New "sentence forms" templates help students understand the structure of summary and response in argument as they construct arguments of their own. And because working with visual texts has become increasingly important, all of Chapter 3, "Reading Visual Texts Critically," is devoted to that topic. It includes seven new visuals (photographs, advertisements, and Web pages) for illustration and analysis.

There's now also more help for researching and writing argumentative papers. A new Chapter 4, "Writing about Argument," includes more help with summary, paraphrase, quoting, documenting sources, and avoiding plagiarism. In Part Two, we've included new sample MLA and APA papers to provide updated models for students. We've also added new "source maps" diagrams to Part Two—a feature popular in many of our grammar handbooks—to help show students how citations spring from sources, illustrating both the mechanics and practical realities of citation. Finally, half of the readings are new to this edition.

ANCILLARIES

The instructor's manual, *Resources for Teaching* THE STRUCTURE OF ARGUMENT, provides additional suggestions for using the book as well as for finding and using the enormous variety of materials available in a course on argument.

A companion Web site at bedfordstmartins.com/rottenberg includes annotated links for students and instructors looking for further information on controversial topics, debates, and rhetorical theory. It also includes exercises for students on fallacies and warrants.

Mixed media and everyday arguments can be both more accessible and more challenging for students to examine. The i•claim CD-ROM offers a new way to visualize argument. It features six tutorials and an illustrated glossary. The i•claim CD-ROM can be packaged for free with *The Structure of Argument*. To see a sample tutorial, visit bedfordstmartins.com/iclaim. For ordering information, contact your local sales representative or e-mail us at sales_support@bfwpub.com.

Also available is *Teaching Argument in the Composition Course,* by Timothy Barnett. It offers a range of perspectives, from Aristotle to the present day, on argument and on teaching argument. The twenty-eight readings—many of them classic works in the field—present essential insights and practical information. For ordering information, contact your local sales representative or e-mail us at sales_support@bfwpub.com.

ALSO AVAILABLE

A longer edition, *Elements of Argument,* Ninth Edition, is available for instructors who prefer more readings. It presents not only Parts One and Two and the appendices, but also eight Multiple Viewpoints chapters, which include a total of sixty-eight selections and six cartoons.

ACKNOWLEDGMENTS

This book has profited by the critiques and suggestions of reviewers and instructors who responded to a questionnaire. We appreciate the thoughtful consideration given to previous editions by Kathryn Murphy Anderson, Kathryn Benander, Bill Bolin, Karen D. Bonnar, John Bradford, Kristina D. Busse, Alice Cleveland, Martha Goodman, Jean E. Graham, Jean E. Jost, Paul D. Knoke, David A. Kossy, Rebecca Lartigne, Madeleine Marchaterre, Judith Q. McMullen, Judith Mikesch, Don Miller, Rachel V. Mills, Theresa R. Mooney, John D. Musselman, William Provost, Karen L. Regal, Dr. Arthur T. Robinson, Diane Schlegel, Thomas F. Suggs, Elaine C. Theismeyer, and Jeffrey W. Vance. I would also like to thank those instructors who took the time to complete a questionnaire for the fourth edition: Lori Adolewski, Thomas Atwater, Victoria Lynn Ausland, Kim H. Baker, Kate Benzel, Edward H. Bloomfield, Ken A. Bugajski, Lisbeth Chapin, Patrick Clark, Irene P. Fass, Betsy Gwyn, Karen C. Holt, Steven R. Mohr, Meg Morgan, L. J. Palumbo, Pedro Pence, Peggy L. Richards, Meisha Rosenberg, Joseph Sigalas, Micheline M. Soong, Kim Stallings, Arlo Stoltenberg, and Marguerite Tassi.

We are also grateful to Patricia DeMarco, Daniel Gonzalez, Laura Hope, David Kaufmann, Kimberly Manner, James Romesburg, Tracy Schrems, and Jennifer Stromer-Galley.

We would also like to thank those who have reviewed and responded to questionnaires about the longer text from which this one developed, *Elements of Argument,* through its previous editions: Nancy E. Adams, Effrosini Piliouni Albrecht, Timothy C. Alderman, Yvonne Alexander, Kathleen Allison, John V. Andersen, Lucile G. Appert, William Arfin, Alison K. Armstrong, Karen Arnold, Angel M. Arzán, Mark Edward Askren, Michael Austin, David B. Axelrod, Jacquelyn A. Babush, Peter Banland, Carol A. Barnes, Tim Barnett, Marilyn Barry, Marci Bartolotta, Dr. Bonnie C. Bedford, Frank Beesley, Don Beggs, Martine Bellen, Bruce Bennett, Maureen Dehler Bennett, Chester Benson, Robert H. Bentley, Scott Bentley, Arthur E. Bervin, Patricia Bizzell, Don Black, Kathleen Black, Stanley S. Blair, Jim Bonnet, Nick Boone, Laurel Boyd, Mary Virginia Brackett, Robert J. Branda, Dianne Brehmer, Alan Brown, Megan Brown, Paul L. Brown, Bill Buck, W. K. Buckley, Alison A. Bulsterbaum, Eleanor Bunting, Clarence Bussinger, Deborah N. Byrd, Gary T. Cage, Karen Caig, Ruth A. Cameron, Dr. Rita Carey, Barbara R. Carlson, Eric W. Cash, Donna R. Chaney, Gail Chapman, Linda D. Chinn, Roland Christian, Gina Claywell, Dr. John O. Clemonts, Paul D. Cockeram, Tammy S. Cole, John Conway, Dr. Thomas S. Costello, Harry Costigan, Martha J. Craig, David J. Cranmer, Edward Crothers, Jennifer Cunningham, Sara Cutting, Jo Ann Dadisman, Sandra Dahlberg, Mimi Dane, Judy Davidson, Dr. Cynthia C. Davis, Philip E. Davis, Stephanie Demma, Loretta Denner, Cecile de Rocher, Julia Dietrich, Marcia B. Dinnech, Felicia A. Dixon, Jane T. Dodge, Ellen Donovan, L. Leon Duke, P. Dunsmore, Bernard

Earley, Carolyn Embree, Carolyn L. Engdahl, Gwyn Enright, Stephen Ersinghaus, David Estes, Kristina Faber, Lester Faigley, Faridoun Farroth, B. R. Fein, Delia Fisher, Philip L. Fishman, Catherine Fitzgerald, Evelyn Flores, David D. Fong, Donald Forand, Mary A. Fortner, Alice R. France, Leslye Friedberg, Sondra Frisch, Richard Fulkerson, Maureen Furniss, Diane Gabbard, Donald J. Gadow, Eric Gardner, Frieda Gardner, Gail Garloch, Darcey Garretson, Victoria Gaydosik, E. R. Gelber-Beechler, Scott Giantralley, Michael Patrick Gillespie, Paula Gillespie, Wallace Gober, Sara Gogol, Stuart Goodman, Joseph Gredler, Lucie Greenberg, Mildred Buza Gronek, Marilyn Hagans, Linda L. Hagge, Lee T. Hamilton, Carolyn Han, Phillip J. Hanse, Pat Hardré, Susan Harland, A. Leslie Harris, Carolyn G. Hartz, Theresia A. Hartz, Fredrik Hausmann, Michael Havens, William Hayes, Ursula K. Heise, Anne Helms, Tena Lea Helton, Peter C. Herman, Diane Price Herndl, Heidi Hobbs, William S. Hochman, Sharon E. Hockensmith, Andrew J. Hoffman, Joyce Hooker, Richard S. Hootman, Laura Hope-Aleman, David Hulm, Clarence Hundley, Patrick Hunter, Richard Ice, Mary Griffith Jackson, Ann S. Jagoe, Katherine James, Missy James, Ruth Jeffries, Owen Jenkins, Ruth Y. Jenkins, Iris Jennings, Linda Johnson, Richard M. Johnson, Janet Jubnke, E. C. Juckett, Catherine Kaikowska, George T. Karnezis, Richard Katula, Mary Jane Kearny, Joanne Keel, Patricia Kellogg-Dennis, N. Kesinger, Susan Kincaid, Jennifer Kirchoff, Joanne Kirkland, Judith Kirscht, Nancy Klug, John H. Knight, Paul D. Knoke, Frances Kritzer, George W. Kuntzman, Barbara Ladd, Jocelyn Ladner, M. Beardsley Land, Marlene J. Lang, Lisa Lebduska, Sara R. Lee, William Levine, Mary Levitt, Diana M. Liddle, Jack Longmate, Cynthia Lowenthal, Marjorie Lynn, Marcia MacLennan, Chantelle MacPhee, Kathryn McCormick, Nancy McGee, Patrick McGuire, Ray McKerrow, John McKinnis, Michael McKoski, Pamela J. McLagen, Suzanne McLaughlin, Patrick McMahon, Dennis McMillan, Donald McQuade, Christina M. McVay, D'Ann Madewell, Beth Madison, Susan Maloney, Dan M. Manolescu, Barbara A. Manrigue, Joyce Marks, Quentin E. Martin, Jim Matthews, Michael Matzinger, Charles May, Alan Merickel, Jean-Pierre Meterean, Ekra Miezan, Carolyn R. Miller, Lisa K. Miller, Amy Minervini, Logan D. Moon, Dennis D. Moore, Dan Morgan, Karen L. Morris, Curt Mortenson, Philip A. Mottola, Thomas Mullen, Charlotte A. Myers, Joan Naake, Michael B. Naas, Dana Nkana, Joseph Nassar, Byron Nelson, Elizabeth A. Nist, Jody Noerdlinger, Paralee F. Norman, Dr. Mary Jean Northcutt, Thomas O'Brien, James F. O'Neil, Mary O'Riordan, Arlene Okerland, Renee Olander, Elizabeth Oldfield, Amy Olsen, Richard D. Olson, Steven Olson, Lori Jo Oswald, Sushil K. Oswald, Roy Kenneth Pace II, Gary Pak, Linda J. Palumbo, Edna Parker, Jo Patterson, Laurine Paule, Leland S. Person, Betty Peters, Kelly S. Peterson, Nancy L. Peterson, Susan T. Peterson, Steve Phelan, Gail W. Pieper, Gloria Platzner, Rosanna Pronesti, Mildred Postar, Ralph David Powell, Jr., Teresa Marie Purvis, Nancy Raferty, Mark Razor, Barbara E. Rees, Karen L. Regal, Pat Regel, Charles Reinhart, Thomas C. Renzi, Janice M. Reynolds, Douglas F. Rice, G. A. Richardson, Beverly A.

Ricks, James M. Ritter, Katherine M. Rogers, Marilyn Mathias Root, Judith Klinger Rose, Cathy Rosenfeld, Robert A. Rubin, Norma L. Rudinsky, Lori Ruediger, Cheryl W. Ruggiero, Richard Ruppel, Victoria Anne Sager, Joseph L. Sanders, Marlissa Santos, Irene Schiller, Suzette Schlapkohl, Sybil Schlesinger, Richard Schneider, Eileen Schwartz, Esther L. Schwartz, Eugene Senff, Jeffrey Seyall, Ron Severson, Lucy Sheehey, William E. Sheidley, Sallye J. Sheppeard, Sally Bishop Shigley, John Shout, Craig L. Shurtleff, Dr. Barbara L. Siek, Thomas Simmons, Michael Simms, Jacqueline Simon, Richard Singletary, Roger L. Slakey, Thomas S. Sloane, Beth Slusser, Denzell Smith, Rebecca Smith, Margaret Smolik, Katherine Sotol, Donald L. Soucy, Minoo Southgate, Linda Spain, Richard Spilman, Sarah J. Stafford, Jim Stegman, Martha L. Stephens, Deborah Steward, Arlo Stoltenberg, Elissa L. Stuchlik, Judy Szaho, Andrew Tadie, Fernanda G. Tate-Owens, R. Terhorst, Marguerite B. Thompson, Arline R. Thorn, Mary Ann Trevathan, Sandia Tuttle, Whitney G. Vanderwerff, Andrea Van Vorhis, Jennie VerSteeg, Les Wade, David L. Wagner, Jeanne Walker, Joseph Walker, James Wallace, Linda D. Warwick, Carol Adams Watson, Roger D. Watson, Karen Webb, Raymond E. Whelan, Betty E. White, Julia Whitsitt, Toby Widdicombe, Mary Louise Willey, Heywood Williams, Matthew C. Wolfe, Alfred Wong, Bonnie B. Zitz, and Laura Zlogar.

We are also grateful to Kate Kiefer and Meg Morgan for their in-depth reviews.

We would like to thank those instructors who completed a questionnaire for the Sixth Edition: Kelly Alba, Terra Community College; Mark Edward Askren, Chaffey College; Michael Dinielli, Chaffey College; Marcia B. Dinneen, Bridgewater State College; Kevin T. Menton, California State Polytechnic University–Pomona; Shellie Michael, Volunteer State Community College; Steven R. Mohr, Terra State Community College; and Bonnie Spears, Chaffey College.

We appreciate the contributions that Gail Stygall of the University of Washington made to a previous edition of the instructor's manual, which have been retained in this edition. We also thank once again Fred Kemp of Texas Tech University, who drafted the section on responding online; Barbara Fister of Gustavus Adolphus College, who revised the discussion of information technologies; and Tim Barnett of Northeastern Illinois University, who enlarged and updated the sections on critical reading, evaluating electronic sources, note-taking, and summarizing, and for drafting the sample analysis of a Web site. All of their contributions have been retained in this edition.

We are grateful to those at Bedford/St. Martin's who have helped in numerous ways large and small: Joan Feinberg, Elizabeth Schaaf, Denise Wydra, Karen Henry, Steve Scipione, Sandy Schechter, Alicia Young, Naomi Kornhauser, Kendra LeFleur, Karen Stocz, Rebecca Merrill, Sue Brekka, Lisa Wehrle, and, most especially, John Sullivan.

Brief Contents

Contents

2. Reading and Listening Critically 31

Part One

Understanding Argument

CHAPTER 1

Understanding the Structure of Argument

THE NATURE OF ARGUMENT

Television news used to mean thirty minutes of local news followed by thirty minutes of national news in the early evening with a late-night local edition incorporating late-breaking news. A triumph like the first moon walk or a tragedy like the assassination of John F. Kennedy in 1963 or that of Martin Luther King Jr. in 1968 justified breaking into regularly scheduled programming, whatever the hour. An event as momentous as a royal wedding or the death of a president or former president, then as now, was the rare occasion for several days of televised coverage. Those were the days before the advent of twenty-four-hour news stations that today are a staple of American life. Now, the latest news is instantly as close as our remote controls.

News shows were originally designed to present, in brief, the facts of what was happening around the country and around the world. The need to broadcast day in and day out, however, has increasingly led to a need to fill time by talking about rather than presenting the news. Analysis of the news is crucial to understanding the events that shape our world, and hearing different perspectives can help enlighten the listening and reading public. Any subject, however, can become the subject of debate if at least two people have different opinions on it, and television networks seem never to be at a loss to find at least one advocate for any position. The early twenty-first century has found viewers increasingly questioning attempts by commentators to make a controversy out of everything, from the way a murder investigation was handled to the bad behavior of celebrities. They are sometimes left wondering what truly is worth arguing about.

Many controversial questions, some of them as old as human civilization itself, will not be settled nor will they vanish despite the energy we devote to settling them. Unresolved, they are submerged for a while and then reappear, sometimes in another form, sometimes virtually unchanged. Capital punishment is one such stubborn problem; abortion is another. Other issues of major concern today are different from the issues that writers focused on as recently as five or ten years ago. Today we are concerned about terrorism, stem-cell research, immigration, and the ethics of cloning, to name only a few. Whatever issues are of most immediate or most long-lasting concern, we value the argumentative process because it is indispensable to the preservation of a free society, even though that freedom may sometimes be abused. Clearly, if all of us agreed about everything, if harmony prevailed everywhere, the need for argument would disappear. But given what we know about the contentious nature of human beings and their conflicting interests, we should not be surprised to find ourselves drawn into the controversies that swirl around us daily.

Arguments are implicit dialogues. Thus the argumentative process is inherently dramatic; a good argument can create the kinds of tensions generated at sporting events. Who will win? What are the factors that enable a winner to emerge? One of the most popular and enduring situations on television is the courtroom debate, in which two lawyers confront each other before an audience of judge and jury that must render a heart-stopping verdict. Tensions are high because a life is in the balance. An occasional real court case will thus capture the attention of the nation, and in the real world, presidential debates have the power to make or break a candidate.

Of course, not all arguments end in clear victories for one side or another. Nor should they. In a democratic society of competing interests and values, a compromise between two or more extreme points of view may be the only viable solution to a vexing problem. Although formal debates under the auspices of a debating society, such as those that take place on many college campuses, usually end in winners and losers, real-life problems—both public and private—are often resolved through negotiation. Courtroom battles may result in compromise, and the law itself allows for exemptions and extenuating circumstances. Elsewhere in this book we speak of the importance of tradeoffs in social and political transactions, giving up one thing in return for another.

Keep in mind, however, that some compromises will not be morally defensible. In searching for a middle ground, the thoughtful arguer must determine that the consequences of a negotiated solution will contribute to the common good, not merely advance personal interests. (At the beginning of Chapter 4, you will find instructions for writing arguments in which you look for common ground.)

Consider how the writing of arguments that you will do in this course differs from simply reporting the facts about a subject. It is the difference between the articles that appear on the front page of the newspaper and those on the editorial page. The following piece from 2006 is a newspaper account of plans to test a new method of screening airline passengers. The author's purpose is not to take a stand but to provide information—information that could affect you in the near future.

X-ray Tests Both Security, Privacy

THOMAS FRANK

Scientists have struggled for four years to build what seemed impossible: an airport X-ray machine that can look through clothing to spot hidden weapons without producing explicit photos of a passenger's body.

The Transportation Security Administration (TSA) will start testing such a device next month in Phoenix. It is the first new passenger-screening machine deployed since mid-2004.

The technology has never been used for security screening. One privacy advocate, doubting TSA assurances, fears that the machine will produce graphic images of passengers that could end up on the Internet.

"People really need to understand that the TSA is putting in place technology that does in fact do a digital strip search and stores those images at least temporarily," said Marc Rotenberg, executive director of the Electronic Privacy Information Center.

5 "The TSA, however, says the images are cartoonlike sketches that show only outlines of each passenger and are never stored. "There's a privacy-security balance," spokeswoman Ellen Howe said. "We can see what we need to see without seeing what we don't need to see."

The technology, called backscatter X-ray, shoots low-intensity X-ray beams that penetrate clothing and bounce off a person's skin, or scatter backward. Sensors detect backscatter X-rays to create an image of the person's body and items being carried, such as watches, keys, and weapons.

Unlike traditional X-rays, which go through the body and involve more radiation, backscatter X-rays can't see inside a person.

A 2003 report by the National Council on Radiation Protection and Measurements, which Congress created to develop radiation guidelines, said someone would need 2,500 backscatter scans a year before reaching the limits of safe radiation exposure.

Frank Cerra, a physicist with the National Institute of Standards and Technology who co-wrote the report, said a backscatter scan gives off "very, very minimal" radiation. "It's like being out in the sun for 15 to 20 minutes."

10 The TSA has studied backscatter X-rays since shortly after the September 11 attacks because the technology has the potential to be better at finding weapons than metal detectors and screeners.

Thomas Frank is the aviation security correspondent for *USA Today*, where this article appeared on December 27, 2006.

"They're foolproof when it comes to finding metal guns and metal knives," said Clark Kent Ervin, the former Homeland Security Department inspector general who recommended backscatter after his investigations found screeners repeatedly missed hidden weapons.

"A big reason why our tests were so successful in getting guns and knives through is because there was a reluctance on screeners' parts to search people" if a metal detector sounded an alarm, Ervin said.

The technology is less foolproof at finding plastic explosives because of the modifications made to protect passenger privacy.

The backscatter machine to be tested in Phoenix is programmed to erase anatomical details. This "edge detection" technology looks for changes in density or molecular structure on the person and draws outlines around those areas.

A metal object, far more dense than human tissue, is highlighted by a 15
heavy black line. But body contours, if they register at all, appear as faint gray lines because "they don't have edges," said Daniel Strom, a scientist at Pacific Northwest National Laboratory. "It only shows anomalies, like metal and ceramics."

Robert Gould, a radiologist at the University of California, San Francisco who reviewed images from the backscatter machine TSA will test, said the machine also erases detail within highlighted areas. "They suppress all the information within the boundaries they detect."

The modifications could create problems in detecting some plastic explosives that have a density similar to human tissue, said Andrew Karam, a physicist and fellow at the Center for Advanced Defense Studies, a national-security think tank.

"I can smooth (plastic explosives) out like spackle so there really is not a sharp edge. That's something I think is going to be really hard to find," Karam said.

These backscatter X-rays "will find obvious stuff," Karam added.

"I don't know if it will find anything else." 20

The manufacturer, American Science and Engineering of suburban Boston, says its $100,000 backscatter machine finds many weapons missed by screeners and metal detectors.

The modifications made for the TSA "trade off detection for a level of privacy," Richard Mastronardi, a company vice president, told an aviation security conference in November. When the machine is programmed to maximize privacy protection, "you start to lose the ability to see" plastic explosives.

Karam said backscatter X-rays still have merit. "The object is not to prevent everything that can conceivably happen," he said. "The object is to make it difficult."

Although the purpose of Frank's article is to report the news, he brings in statements from others that make clear some of the conversation that is already going on regarding backscatter screening and some of the controversy it is already arousing. The piece presents the opinions of individuals who approach the controversy from different perspectives, yet it maintains the author's own subjectivity. You would expect Marc Rotenberg, executive director of the Electronic Privacy Information Center, to oppose the x-raying of airline passengers. You would expect those working for American Science and Engineering, the manufacturer of the x-ray machines, to defend their usefulness. And you would expect Frank, as a news reporter, to present the opposing views fairly.

Now consider the purpose of the following column written by Joe Sharkey on the same subject. What was Sharkey's purpose in writing? Is his purpose the same as Frank's? How does the tone of the two pieces differ?

Airport Screeners Could See X-rated X-rays

JOE SHARKEY

I am looking at a copy of an ad that ran in the back of comic books in the 1950s and early 1960s.

"X-Ray Specs! See Thru Clothing!" blares the copy, which is illustrated with a cartoon of a drooling geek wearing the amazing toy goggles and leering at a shapely woman.

Now, any kid with half a brain knew that X-Ray Specs were a novelty gag that didn't really work. But time marches on and technology makes the impossible possible. Stand by, air travelers, because the Homeland Security Department is preparing to install and test high-tech machines at airport checkpoints that will, as the comic-book ads promised, "See Thru Clothing!"

Get ready for electronic portals known as backscatters, expected to be tested at a handful of airports this year, that use X-ray imaging technology to allow a screener to scan a body. And yes, the body image is detailed. Let's not be coy here, ladies and gentlemen:

"Well, you'll see basically everything," said Bill Scannell, a privacy ad- 5
vocate and technology consultant. "It shows nipples. It shows the clear outline of genitals."

The Homeland Security Department's justification for the electronic strip searches has a certain logic. In field test after field test, it found that federal airport screeners using metal-detecting magnetometers did a miserable job identifying weapons concealed in carry-on bags or on the bodies of undercover agents.

Joe Sharkey is a columnist writing frequently about business travel for the *New York Times*.

In a clumsy response late last year, the department instituted intrusive pat-downs at checkpoints after two planes in Russia blew up from nonmetallic explosives that had apparently been smuggled into the aircraft by female Chechen terrorists. But it reduced the pat-downs after passengers erupted in outrage at the groping last December.

"The use of these more thorough examination procedures has been protested by passengers and interest groups, and have already been refined" by the Transportation Security Administration, Richard Skinner, the acting inspector general of the Homeland Security Department, told a Senate committee in January. Skinner said then that the TSA was ramping up tests of new technologies like backscatter imaging.

Last month, Michael Chertoff, the Homeland Security secretary, told a Senate subcommittee that "technology is really what we ultimately have to use in order to get to the next level" in security.

The technology is available, he said. "It's a question of the decision to de- 10
ploy it and to try to balance that with legitimate privacy concerns," he added. "We haven't put it out yet because people are still hand-wringing about it."

Steve Elson isn't exactly hand-wringing. Let's just say he is mighty skeptical. A former Federal Aviation Administration investigator, Elson led the agency's red team of undercover agents who poked around airports looking for—and finding—holes in security.

"Backscatting has been around for years," he said. "They started talking about this stuff back during the protests when they were grabbing women. Under the right circumstances, the technology has some efficacy and can work. That is, provided we're willing to pay the price in a further loss of personal privacy."

He isn't. "I have a beautiful 29-year-old daughter and a beautiful wife, and I don't want some screeners to be looking at them through their clothes, plain and simple," he said.

Like many security experts, Elson argues for a sensible balance between risk management and risk reduction. On numerous occasions since the 2001 terrorist attacks, he has led reporters on test runs at airports, showing how easy it is to penetrate security throughout the airport.

Thwarting body-scanning technology would be simple, he argues. Be- 15
cause of concerns about radiation, body scanners are designed not to penetrate the skin. All that's needed is someone heavily overweight to go through the system, he said. I won't quote him directly on the details; suffice it to say he posits that a weapon or explosives pack could be tucked into flabby body folds that won't be penetrated by the scanner.

Homeland Security has not identified the airports that will test backscatters. More than a dozen have been selected to test various new technologies.

One maker of backscatters is Rapiscan Security Products, a unit of OSI Systems. "Since the Russian plane tragedy, which is suspected due to suicide bombers, the interest has heightened for these needs, especially for the body scanner," Deepak Chopra, the chief executive of OSI Systems, recently told analysts.

Scannell, the privacy advocate, scorns that reasoning as alarmist nonsense. He does see one virtue, though, for some airport screeners if backscatting technology becomes the norm.

"They'll be paid to go to a peep show," he said. "They won't even need to bring any change."

Today, of course, the conversation about any controversial issue can go far beyond televised or printed news. If the latest news is as close as your remote control, it is also as close as your computer mouse or even your cell phone. The Internet provides everyone a voice on almost any subject.

Sharkey's piece, which appeared in the *New York Times* in May 2005, was the subject of hundreds of blog postings. The vast majority found the whole idea of being x-rayed at airports distasteful and a threat to privacy. Some writers said they would never fly again if the screening techniques were implemented. One of the few dissenting voices was that of Chris Kapper. Note that, unlike Frank, he clearly states his opinion about the new x-ray technique.

Freedom to Live Trumps All!

CHRIS KAPPER

I have read many different comments to this story.

The opinions against the technology seem to boil down to this:

1. It is offensive to be viewed naked.
2. Being viewed naked is an affront to personal freedom.
3. This is a slippery slope and once allowed here it will be allowed everywhere until there are virtually no personal freedoms left.

The opinions for the technology seem to boil down to this:

1. Who cares if one is viewed naked?
2. It is better to be seen naked and alive than be dead.
3. This will make the airplanes safer.
4. This is a less obtrusive way to search passengers.

Chris Kapper posted this response to Joe Sharkey's article, "Airport Screeners Could See X-rated X-rays," on CNET's TalkBack, on May 27, 2005.

I have to agree—for the most part—with the latter. Here is why:

1. In the demonstration I saw, the screeners could not see the people—all they could see were the images. Therefore, they never saw a person walk up, through, and then leave. The point is that if their own mother walked through, they would have no idea since you can't tell who it is.
2. Nobody else can see your image other than the security operator. That includes other passengers and employees of the airports.
3. This is much less obtrusive than removing shoes, clothing, and emptying out all of your pockets—in front of everyone.
4. The fundamental liberty is the right to life. One's right to live trumps others' rights.
5. It is not only the liberty of the passengers and crew that must be considered here. It is their lives as well as the lives of all the people on the ground as that airplane flies over. Additionally, it is the nation's and even the world's economy and peace that must be considered. Remember what 9/11 did to the economy and the peace in the world?
6. Air travel is not a required means of travel. You can use other public transportation. You can travel by car or even by boat. Air travel is a convenience—and a choice. When you buy your ticket, you agree to be bound by their rules and policies.
7. For the person who quoted Benjamin Franklin—"They who would give up an essential liberty for temporary security, deserve neither liberty or security." IMHO, this technology does not cause you to give up any ESSENTIAL liberty and there is nothing TEMPORARY about DEATH!

Most of the arguments in this book will deal with matters of public controversy, an area traditionally associated with the study of argument. As the word *public* suggests, these matters concern us as members of a community. In the arguments you will read in this book, human beings are engaged in explaining and defending their own actions and beliefs and opposing those of others. They do this for at least two reasons: to justify what they do and think both to themselves and to their opponents and, in the process, to solve problems and make decisions, especially those dependent on a consensus among conflicting views.

PRACTICE

1. Locate in Frank's article the one sentence that you believe best summarizes the thesis or main idea that he is trying to support. Do the same for Kapper's posting.

2. An author's tone reveals his attitude toward his subject. Describe the tone in Sharkey's piece. Give specific examples of words or phrases that contribute to that tone.
3. Locate online or in newspapers two articles on the same subject, one that is objective and one that is subjective. Be prepared to explain the difference.
4. As you read through articles that you and your classmates located for #3, what can you conclude about how the purpose in the objective articles is different from that in the subjective ones?

WHY STUDY ARGUMENT?

If you can listen to arguments daily courtesy of CNN or Fox News, and all you have to do to enter the dialogue is to open Internet Explorer or Firefox, why *study* argument? Since you've engaged in some form of the argumentative process all your life, is there anything to be learned that experience hasn't taught you? We think there is. If you've ever felt frustration in trying to decide what is wrong with an argument, either your own or someone else's, you might have wondered if there were rules to help in the analysis. If you've ever been dissatisfied with your attempt to prove a case, you might have wondered how good arguers, the ones who succeed in persuading people, construct their cases. Good arguers do, in fact, know and follow rules. Studying and practicing these rules can provide you with some of the same skills.

You will find yourself using these skills in a variety of situations, not only in arguing important public issues. You will use them, for example, in your academic career. Whatever your major field of study—the humanities, the social sciences, the physical sciences, business, education—you will be required to defend views about materials you have read and studied.

HUMANITIES Why have some of the greatest novels resisted translation into great films?

SOCIAL SCIENCE What is the evidence that upward social mobility continues to be a positive force in American life?

PHYSICAL SCIENCE What effect will global warming have on agriculture in North America?

BUSINESS Is a 401(k) the best way of investing for retirement?

EDUCATION Are standardized tests exerting too much control over the public school curriculum?

The conventions or rules for reporting results might differ from one field of study to another, but for the most part, the rules for defining terms, evaluating evidence, and arriving at conclusions cross disciplinary lines. In a variety of professions, you will encounter situations at work that will require analytical and argumentative skills. Almost everywhere—in the smallest businesses as well as the largest corporations—a worker who can articulate his or her views clearly and forcefully has an important advantage in gaining access to positions of greater interest and challenge.

You may not anticipate doing the kind of writing or speaking at your job that you will practice in your academic work. It is probably true that in some careers, writing constitutes a negligible part of a person's duties. But outside the office, the studio, the lab, and the salesroom, you will be called on to exhibit argumentative skills as a citizen, as a member of a community, and as a consumer of leisure. In these capacities, you can contribute to decision making if you are knowledgeable and prepared. By writing or speaking to the appropriate authorities, you can argue for a change in the grading policy at your school, against a change in automobile insurance rates, or for the reelection of a city council member.

A course in argumentation offers another invaluable dividend: It can help you to cope with the bewildering confusion of voices in the world around you. It can give you tools for distinguishing between what is true and what is false, what is valid and what is invalid, in the claims of politicians, promoters of causes, newscasters, advertisers, salespeople, teachers, parents and siblings, employers and employees, neighbors, friends, and lovers, any of whom may be engaged at some time in attempting to persuade you to accept a belief or adopt a course of action. It can even offer strategies for working through a personal dilemma. Most of us are painfully aware of opportunities we lost because we were uncertain of how to proceed, even in matters that affected us deeply.

So far we have treated argument as an essentially pragmatic activity that benefits the individual. But choosing argument over force or evasion has clear moral benefits for society as well. We can, in fact, defend the study of argumentation for the same reasons that we defend universal education despite its high cost and sometimes controversial results. In a democracy, widespread literacy ultimately benefits all members of a society, not only those who are the immediate beneficiaries of education, because only an informed citizenry can make responsible choices. Distinguished rhetorician Wayne C. Booth explains that "democracy depends on a citizenry that can reason for themselves, on men who know whether a case has been proved, or at least made probable."[1]

It is not too much to say that argument is a civilizing influence, the very basis of democratic order. In repressive regimes, coercion, which may express itself in a number of reprehensible forms—censorship, imprisonment, exile, torture, or execution—is a favored means of removing opposition to establishment "truth." In free societies, arguments and debate remain the preeminent means of arriving at consensus.

[1]Wayne C. Booth, "Boring from Within: The Art of the Freshman Essay," adapted from a speech delivered to the Illinois Council of College Teachers of English in May 1963.

Of course, rational discourse in a democracy can and does break down. Confrontations with police at abortion clinics, shouting and heckling at a meeting to prevent a speaker from being heard, student protests against university policies—such actions have become common in recent years. The demands of the demonstrators are often passionately and sincerely held, and the protestors sometimes succeed through force or intimidation in influencing policy changes. When this happens, however, we cannot be sure that the changes are justified. History and experience teach us that reason, to a far greater degree than other methods of persuasion, ultimately determines the rightness or wrongness of our actions.

THE TERMS OF ARGUMENT

A distinction is sometimes made between argument and persuasion. Argument, according to most authorities, gives primary importance to logical appeals. Persuasion introduces the element of ethical and emotional appeals. The difference is one of emphasis. In real-life arguments about social policy, the distinction is hard to measure. In this book, we use the term *argument* to represent forms of discourse that attempt to persuade readers or listeners to accept a claim, whether acceptance is based on logical or on emotional appeals or, as is usually the case, on both. The following is our brief definition of the term: An argument is a statement or statements offering support for a claim.

An argument is composed of at least three parts: the claim, the support, and the warrant.[2]

■ The Claim

The claim (also called a proposition) answers the question "What are you trying to prove?" It will generally appear as the thesis statement of your essay, although in some arguments, it may not be stated directly. There are three principal kinds of claim (discussed more fully in Chapter 6): claims of fact, of value, and of policy. *Claims of fact* assert that a condition has existed, exists, or will exist and are based on facts or data that the audience will accept as being objectively verifiable.

- The diagnosis of autism is now far more common than it was twenty years ago.

[2]Some of the terms and analyses used in this text are adapted from Stephen Toulmin's *The Uses of Argument* (Cambridge: Cambridge University Press, 1958).

- Fast foods are contributing significantly to today's epidemic of childhood obesity.
- Global warming will affect the coastlines of all continents.

All these claims must be supported by data. Although the last example is an inference or an educated guess about the future, a reader will probably find the prediction credible if the data seem authoritative.

Claims of value attempt to prove that some things are more or less desirable than others. They express approval or disapproval of standards of taste and morality. Advertisements and reviews of cultural events are one common source of value claims, but such claims emerge whenever people argue about what is good or bad, beautiful or ugly.

- Mel Gibson's *Apocalypto* is marred by its excessive violence.
- Abortion is wrong under any circumstances.
- The right to privacy is more important than the need to increase security at airports.

Claims of policy assert that specific policies should be instituted as solutions to problems. The expression *should, must,* or *ought to* usually appears in the statement.

- The electoral college should be replaced by popular vote as the means of electing a president.
- Attempts at making air travel more secure must not put in jeopardy the passengers' right to privacy.
- Backscatter x-raying ought to be implemented at every American airport as soon as possible as a means of detecting concealed weapons.

Policy claims call for analysis of both fact and value. (A full discussion of claims follows in Chapter 6.)

PRACTICE

1. Classify each of the following as a claim of fact, value, or policy.
   a. Solar power could supply 20 percent of the energy needs now satisfied by fossil and nuclear power.
   b. Violence on television produces violent behavior in children who watch more than four hours a day.
   c. Both intelligent design and evolutionary theory should be taught in the public schools.
   d. Some forms of cancer are caused by viruses.
   e. Dogs are smarter than cats.
   f. The money that our government spends on the space program would be better spent solving domestic problems like unemployment and homelessness.
   g. Wherever the number of illegal aliens increases, the crime rate also increases.

h. Movie sequels are generally inferior to their originals.
i. Tom Hanks is a more versatile actor than Tom Cruise.
j. Adopted children who are of a different race than their adoptive parents should be raised with an understanding of the culture of their biological parents.
k. Average yearly temperatures in North America are already being affected by global warming.
l. Human activity is the primary cause of global warming.

2. Classify Frank's claim in "X-ray Tests Both Security, Privacy" as a claim of fact, value, or policy. Do the same for Chris Kapper's in his posting "Freedom to Live Trumps All!"
3. Argue that Sharkey, in his "Airport Screeners Could See X-rated X-rays," is supporting a claim of fact or that he is supporting a claim of value.

The Support

Support consists of the materials used by the arguer to convince an audience that his or her claim is sound. These materials include evidence and motivational appeals. The *evidence* or data consist of facts, statistics, and testimony from experts. The *motivational appeals* are the ones that the arguer makes to the values and attitudes of the audience to win support for the claim. The word *motivational* points out that these appeals are the reasons that move an audience to accept a belief or adopt a course of action. (See chapter 7 for a detailed discussion of support.)

The Warrant

Certain assumptions underlie all the claims we make. In argument, the term *warrant* is used for such an assumption, a belief or principle that is taken for granted. It may be stated or unstated. If the arguer believes that the audience shares her assumption, she may believe it unnecessary to express it. But if she thinks that the audience is doubtful or hostile, she may decide to state the assumption to emphasize its importance or argue for its validity. The warrant, stated or not, allows the reader to make the same connection between the support and the claim that the author does.

This is how the warrant works. Before he posted on the blog about the proposed x-raying of airline passengers, Kapper had read earlier postings discussing the issue. He considered the arguments he had heard in favor of and against the x-ray technique and actually went so far as to summarize them in his posting. The conclusion he reached, which became the claim of his piece of writing, was that he agrees for the most part with those who argue in favor of the new screening technique. In outline form, a portion of his argument looks like this:

CLAIM: Backscatter screening should be implemented in America's airports.

SUPPORT: Backscatter screening will make planes safer.

WARRANT: Any screening technique that will make planes safer should be implemented.

The following example demonstrates how a different kind of warrant, based on values, can also lead an audience to accept a claim.

CLAIM: Backscatter screening should be implemented in America's airports.

SUPPORT: Being seen naked by a security screener is better than dying.

WARRANT: Being safe is worth a small loss of privacy.

Kapper's title shows how strongly he feels about this warrant: "Freedom to Live Trumps All!"

Let us suppose that the reader agrees with the supporting statement, that being seen naked by a security screener is better than dying. But to accept the claim, the reader must also agree with the principle expressed in the warrant, that being safe is worth a small loss of privacy. He or she can then agree that backscatter screening should be implemented. Notice that this warrant, like all warrants, certifies that the relationship between the support and the claim is sound.

One more important characteristic of the warrant deserves mention. In many cases, the warrant is a more general statement of belief than the

Writer's Guide: Learning the Key Terms

Claim — the proposition that the author is trying to prove. The claim may appear as the thesis statement of an essay but may be implied rather than stated directly.

- *Claims of fact* assert that a condition has existed, exists, or will exist and are based on facts or data that the audience will accept as being objectively verifiable.
- *Claims of value* attempt to prove that some things are more or less desirable than others; they express approval or disapproval of standards of taste and morality.
- *Claims of policy* assert that specific plans or courses of action should be instituted as solutions to problems.

Support — the materials used by the arguer to convince an audience that his or her claim is sound; those materials include evidence and motivational appeals.

Warrant — an inference or assumption; a belief or principle that is taken for granted in an argument.

claim. It can, therefore, support many claims, not only the one in a particular argument. For example, the warrant you have just read—being safe is worth a small loss of privacy—is a broad assumption or belief that we take for granted and that can underlie claims about many other practices in American society. (For more on warrants, see Chapter 8.)

PRACTICE

1. Report on an argument you have heard or read recently. Identify the parts of that argument—claim, support, warrant—as they are defined in this chapter. What were the strengths and weaknesses of the argument?
2. Choose one of the more controversial claims from the list on pages 13–14. Explain why it is controversial. Would it be difficult to support? Impossible? Are the warrants unacceptable to many people? If there has been a change in recent years in public acceptance of the claim, offer what you think may be an explanation for the change.

THE AUDIENCE

All arguments are composed with an audience in mind. We have already pointed out that an argument is an implicit dialogue or exchange. Often the writer of an argument about a public issue is responding to another writer or speaker who has made a claim that needs to be supported or opposed. Even when our audience is unknown, we write to persuade the unconvinced, to acquaint them with good reasons for changing their minds. In writing your own arguments, you should assume that there is a reader who may not agree with you. Throughout this book, we will continue to refer to ways of reaching such a reader.

Speakers are usually better informed than writers about their audience. Some writers, however, are familiar with the specific persons or groups who will read their arguments; advertising copywriters are a conspicuous example. They discover their audiences through sophisticated polling and marketing techniques and direct their messages to a well-targeted group of prospective buyers. Other professionals may be required to submit reports to persuade a specific and clearly defined audience of certain beliefs or courses of action: An engineer may be asked by an environmental interest group to defend his plans for the building of a sewage treatment plant; or a town planner may be called on to tell the town council why she believes that rent control may not work; or a sales manager may find it necessary to explain to his superior why a new product should be launched in the Midwest rather than the South.

In such cases, the writer asks some or all of the following questions about the audience:

- Why has the audience requested this report? What do they want to get out of it?
- How much do they already know about the subject?
- Are they divided or agreed on the subject?
- What is their emotional involvement with the issues?

Providing abundant evidence and making logical connections between the parts of an argument may not be enough to win agreement from an audience. In fact, success in convincing an audience is almost always inseparable from the writer's credibility or the audience's belief in the writer's trustworthiness. Aristotle, the Greek philosopher who wrote a treatise on argument that has influenced its study and practice for more than two thousand years, considered credibility—what he called *ethos*—the most important element in the arguer's ability to persuade the audience to accept his or her claim.

Aristotle named intelligence, character, and goodwill as the attributes that produce credibility. Today we might describe these qualities somewhat differently, but the criteria for judging a writer's credibility remain essentially the same. First, the writer must convince the audience that he is knowledgeable, that he is as well informed as possible about the subject. Second, he must persuade his audience that he is not only truthful in the presentation of his evidence but also morally upright and dependable. Third, he must show that, as an arguer with good intentions, he has considered the interests and needs of others as well as his own.

As an example in which the credibility of the arguer is at stake, consider a wealthy Sierra Club member who lives on ten acres of a magnificent oceanside estate and who appears before a community planning board to argue against future development of the area. The board, acting in the interests of all the citizens of the community, will ask themselves: Has the arguer proved that his information about environmental impact is complete and accurate? Has he demonstrated that he sincerely desires to preserve the wilderness, not merely his own privacy and space? And has he made clear that he has considered the needs and desires of those who might want to live in a housing development by the ocean? If the answers to all of these questions are yes, then the board will hear the arguer with respect, and the arguer will have begun to establish his credibility.

A reputation for intelligence, character, and goodwill is not often earned overnight. And it can be lost more quickly than it is gained. Once a writer or speaker has betrayed an audience's belief in her character or judgment, she may find it difficult to persuade an audience to accept subsequent claims, no matter how sound her data and reasoning are.

Political life is full of examples of lost and squandered credibility. After it was discovered that President Lyndon Johnson had deceived the American public about U.S. conduct in the Vietnam War, he could not regain his popularity. After President Gerald Ford pardoned former President Richard Nixon for his complicity in the cover up of the bugging and burglary of the Democratic National Committee headquarters at the Watergate office complex, Ford was no longer a serious candidate for reelection. After proof emerged that President Bill Clinton had lied to a grand jury and the public about his sexual relationship with a young White House intern, public approval of his political record remained high, but approval of his moral character declined and threatened to diminish his influence.

We can see the practical consequences when an audience realizes that an arguer has been guilty of a deception—misusing facts and authority, suppressing evidence, distorting statistics, violating the rules of logic. But suppose the arguer is successful in concealing his or her manipulation of the data and can persuade an uninformed audience to take the action or adopt the idea that he or she recommends. Even supposing that the argument promotes a "good" cause, is the arguer justified in using evasive or misleading tactics?

The answer is no. To encourage another person to make a decision on the basis of incomplete or dishonestly used data is profoundly unethical. It indicates lack of respect for the rights of others—their right to know at least as much as you do about the subject, to be allowed to judge and compare, to disagree with you if they challenge your interests or find holes in the logic of your argument. If the moral implications are still not clear, try to imagine yourself not as the perpetrator of the lie but as the victim.

There is also a danger in measuring success wholly by the degree to which audiences accept our arguments. Both as writers and readers, we must be able to respect the claim, or proposition, and what it tries to demonstrate. The English philosopher Stephen Toulmin has said, "To conclude that a proposition is true, it is not enough to know that this [person] or that finds it 'credible'; the proposition itself must be worthy of credence."[3]

No matter what the subject, there are certain basic steps that a writer can take to ensure that not only the proposition, or claim, but the whole argument is worthy of credence. You are not yet an expert in many of the subjects you will deal with in assignments, although you are knowledgeable about many other things, including your cultural and social activities. But there are several ways in which you can develop confidence by your discussion of topics derived from academic disciplines, such as political science, psychology, economics, sociology, and art, on which most assignments will be based. The following steps that every writer of argumentative texts should follow will be the basis for Chapters 5–10.

[3] *An Examination of the Place of Reason in Ethics* (Cambridge: Cambridge University Press, 1964), p. 71.

Defining Key Terms (Chapter 5)

Many of the controversial questions you will read or write about are primarily arguments of definition. Such terms as *abortion, pornography, racism, poverty, freedom of speech,* and *terrorism* must be defined before useful solutions to the problems they represent can be formulated. Even if the primary purpose of your essay is not definition, you can successfully communicate with an audience only if that audience understands how you are using key terms.

Choosing an Appropriate Claim (Chapter 6)

It must be clear to the individual or group that constitutes your audience what change in thought or what action you hope to achieve by presenting your case. If you are seeking a change in your reader's thinking on a subject, you will have a much greater chance of accomplishing your goal if you consider the audience's current thinking on the subject and are realistic about the extent to which you might hope to change that thinking. If there is something you want your audience to do, that action must be realistically within the power of that audience.

Choosing and Documenting Appropriate Sources (Chapter 7)

You must present evidence of careful research, demonstrating that you have been conscientious in finding the best authorities, giving credit, and attempting to arrive at the truth.

Analyzing Assumptions (Chapter 8)

You must consider the warrant or assumption on which your argument is based. A warrant need not be expressed if it is so widely accepted that you can assume any reasonable audience will not need proof of its validity. You must be prepared to defend any other warrant.

Analyzing Logical Errors (Chapter 9)

Understanding the ways in which inductive and deductive reasoning processes work can help you to determine the truth and validity of your arguments, as well as other arguments, and to identify and correct faulty reasoning.

Editing for Appropriate Language (Chapter 10)

Another important resource is the careful use of language, not only to define terms and express personal style but also to reflect clarity of thought, to avoid the clichés and outworn slogans that frequently substitute for fresh ideas, and to avoid word choices that would make your audience unwilling to consider your ideas.

Now let's turn to an example of argumentative writing and the analysis that follows it. Some of the terms introduced in this chapter appear in boldface in the analysis.

SAMPLE ANALYSIS

Will the Politics of Teen Sex Stop a Cancer Vaccine?

ADVOCATES FOR YOUTH

There's a Vaccine That Could Prevent Cervical Cancer?

After a decade of development, two drug companies—Merck and Glaxo-SmithKline—are close to marketing the first ever cancer vaccines that show 100 percent efficacy in combating the most dangerous strains of the human papilloma virus (HPV), the cause of almost all cervical cancers,[1] the second most common type of cancer among women worldwide, and the leading cause of cancer death among women in the developing world.[2]

Since genital HPV is a sexually transmitted disease (STD), to be effective, the vaccine must be administered to young women in their early teen years—*before* they initiate sex. Research and clinical trials continue to find the vaccine safe.

The policy question? With 10,000 American women contracting cervical cancer each year and 4,000 deaths from the disease annually, will *all* women, including young women, have access to a vaccine that could save their lives? The initial reaction of some religious conservatives to the HPV vaccine is disturbing because it appears to place the promotion of abstinence-only programs above the prevention of a killer disease. Yet, research and basic common sense state this is not an "either/or" issue. It's possible to promote abstinence, educate young people about contraception, and prevent cervical cancer without these objectives getting in the way of each other. It's not just the smart thing to do—it's the right thing to do.

Who Would Possibly Object?

Again, some religious conservatives object—religious conservatives who, in tandem with the Bush administration, have spent over $1.1 billion in federal and state taxpayers' dollars on programs that promote abstinence until marriage as the only acceptable behavior for Americans and the only way to prevent pregnancy, HIV, and other sexually transmitted diseases.

5 Groups that promote an abstinence-only-until-marriage approach to sex education intensely market the threat of HPV as a reason for promoting abstinence only. They claim a vaccine will promote promiscuity by lessening people's fears regarding HPV and cervical cancer.

"Our concern is that this vaccine will be marketed to a segment of the population that should be getting a message about abstinence," said Tony Perkins of the Family Research Council. He would not inoculate his own daughter, because she would be more inclined to have sex outside marriage. "It sends the wrong message." (Tony Perkins, President of the Family Research Council)[3]

> I personally object to vaccinating children against a disease that is 100 percent preventable with proper sexual behavior.
>
> —Leslie Unruh, Executive Director of the National Abstinence Clearinghouse[4]

Who Will Make the Decision?

The Advisory Committee on Immunization Practices (ACIP) will make the decision. Attached to the Centers for Disease Control and Prevention (CDC), ACIP sets the nation's list of recommended immunizations—setting the standard for doctors and insurers and for public funding of vaccinations. ACIP's ruling is not binding; but most states look to its recommendations to mandate which vaccines children must get before entering school.[3]

Will Ideology or Science Dictate the Decision?

Consider that the Bush administration has already appointed one ACIP member (Reginald Finger) from the ranks of the religious right. Until September 2005, Mr. Finger was the medical issues analyst at Focus on the Family,[3] an ultra-conservative religious organization founded by James Dobson.

10 The precedents set by this administration for medical decisions are also troubling. The FDA, in a highly criticized move, chose to placate religious conservatives by refusing non-prescription status for emergency contraception (EC), despite the fact that the FDA's own scientific advisory committee voted overwhelmingly to make EC available without a doctor's prescription.

This political decision prompted an editorial in the *New England Journal of Medicine* which stated:

> The recent actions of the FDA leadership have made a mockery of the process of evaluating scientific evidence, disillusioned many of the participating scientists both inside and outside the agency, squandered the public trust, and tarnished the agency's image. American women and the dedicated professionals at the FDA deserve better.[8]

The Myth That Prevention Causes Adolescent Promiscuity

Supporters of abstinence-only-until-marriage programs have long claimed that sex education, which includes information about condoms and birth control, encourages teens to have sex—a claim rebutted by scientific research:

> Current research indicates that encouraging abstinence and urging better use of contraception are compatible goals. Evidence shows that sexuality education that discusses contraception does not increase sexual activity, and programs that emphasize abstinence as the safest and best approach, while also teaching about contraceptives for sexually active youth, do not decrease contraceptive use.—American Academy of Pediatrics[9]

This myth was again promulgated by the FDA, which claimed that making EC available without prescription would fuel risky teen behavior, a claim that was also explicitly rejected by leading medical authorities:

> An increase in awareness and availability of emergency contraception to teens does not change reported rates of sexual activity or increase the frequency of unprotected intercourse among adolescents.—American Academy of Pediatrics[10]
>
> Data demonstrating that ready access to Plan B by adolescents as young as 15 did not lead to increased irresponsible sexual behavior were available in December 2003 and had been reviewed by the advisory committee. Moreover, the agency was conspicuously unable, then or later, to cite any data to support different safety or efficacy profiles in different age groups—a damning indictment of the basis for the disapproval.—*New England Journal of Medicine*[8]

Clearly, prevention does not cause risky sexual behavior. A vaccine to prevent cervical cancer will not cause promiscuity any more than an umbrella will cause rain or a seat belt will cause an accident.

Why Do Some Conservatives Seem to Need HPV?

In recent years, religious conservatives have become increasingly reliant 15
on HPV as a tool to attack condoms. They have denigrated condom use as "Russian roulette," relying on false claims that condoms fail to provide any protection for HPV.

Among their conservative allies in Congress, Senator Tom Coburn has in the past introduced legislation to require condom labeling, stressing the risk of HPV infection and warning that condoms offer "little or no protection" against the virus—a claim disputed by current research. Moreover, he has many conservative friends on the Hill who share his views on the efficacy, or lack thereof, of condoms:

> We need to yell it to the top of the rooftops that these condoms we're sending down to you don't protect you. . . . [You] have a false sense of security. So I think we're sending the wrong message when we use taxpayer dollars to give condoms out to these kids and we don't tell them, 'By the way, you'll probably be dead at age 24 by cervical cancer. But we're giving you condoms, so go do your thing.' To me, abstinence is the only way." —Representative Jo Ann Davis, R-Virginia[11]

What Will Happen?

The administration has shown significant deference to religious conservatives when it comes to issues involving sexual and reproductive health.

From stem-cell research to sex education, from a diminished emphasis on condoms to denying non-prescription status to EC, evidence-based prevention has taken a back seat to ideology and politics.

With respect to HPV and the cervical cancer vaccine, the religious conservative movement could persuade its base to avoid vaccination; it could work to prevent mass inoculation of young people by trying to block the vaccines' acceptance by regulators; or it could attack the vaccines' funding at federal and state levels.

Not all religious conservatives are on record opposing the HPV vaccine. 20
Some, such as Dr. Gene Rudd of the Christian Medical Association, have hailed the vaccine as an important medical breakthrough. Yet, even Dr. Rudd argues that the vaccine should not be mandatory. Nonetheless, if Dr. Rudd and others like him can convince their constituents that this vaccine is a positive development, public health will be the beneficiary.

Does "Saving Souls" Trump Saving Lives?

Clearly, there must be public consensus that no woman in this country should be denied the opportunity to avoid cervical cancer. Vaccinating young people, before they are sexually active, affords the best opportunity to use this medical breakthrough to do just that.

Cancer is a public health challenge that needs to be conquered; it is not an appropriate venue for political or ideological debate.

NOTE: About 67 percent of young people are sexually active by age 18[5]; roughly 90 percent of Americans are not virgins on their wedding nights[6]; and experts estimate that up to 70 percent of all sexually active adults worldwide have been exposed to HPV.[7]

REFERENCES

1. Walboomers JMM, Jacobs MV, Manos MM, Bosch FX, Kummer JA et al., Human papilloma virus is a necessary cause of invasive cervical cancer worldwide, *Journal of Pathology* 1999; 189:12–19.

2. National Cervical Cancer Coalition, *What Is the National Cervical Cancer Coalition (NCCC)?* http://www.nccc-online.org/; accessed 10/27/2005.
3. *Fortune Magazine*, October 17, 2005, Guyon J, Cancer and the culture wars: the coming storm over a cancer vaccine.
4. *AIDS Treatment Update*, October 24, 2005, Bernard EJ, An HPV vaccine, what it might really mean, Aidsmap; http://www.nam.org.uk/en/news/3429199D-5FE5-4795-B0E6-CD957617C160.asp; accessed 10/27/2005.
5. National Center for Health Statistics, Teenagers in the United States: sexual activity, contraceptive use, and childbearing, 2002. *Vital and Health Statistics* [Series 23, No. 24] December 25.
6. Michael RT, Gagnon JH, Laumann ED, Kolata G, *Sex in America: A Definitive Survey*, Boston: Little Brown, 1994.
7. Marr L, *Sexually Transmitted Diseases: A Physician Tells You What You Need to Know*, Baltimore, MD: Johns Hopkins University Press, 1998.
8. *New England Journal of Medicine*, editorial, September 22, 2005.
9. American Academy of Pediatrics (August 2005), Adolescent pregnancy: current trends and issues, *Pediatrics*.
10. American Academy of Pediatrics (October, 2005), Policy statement, emergency contraception, *Pediatrics*.
11. Representative Jo Ann Davis (R-VA), Subcommittee on Criminal Justice, Drug Policy and Human Resources of the House Government Reform Committee, *U.S. Representative Mark Souder (R-IN) Holds Hearing on Cervical Cancer and HPV*, March 11, 2004 [Committee Hearing].

■ Analysis

The author of the article, an anonymous writer for the organization Advocates of Youth, takes time in the first two paragraphs to make clear what the human papilloma virus is and why a vaccine against it must be administered while girls are young. To the extent that it is necessary, he is **defining** a key term. He also emphasizes the magnitude of this new development in cancer prevention when he cites statistics on how serious a threat to women HPV is. He then goes on in paragraph 3 to explain why the development of "the first ever cancer vaccines that show 100 percent efficacy in combating the most dangerous strains of the human papilloma virus (HPV), the cause of almost all cervical cancers" is even controversial. At the end of the third paragraph, he states his thesis, a **claim of value**: "It's possible to promote abstinence, educate young people about contraception, and prevent cervical cancer without these objectives getting in the way of each other. It's not just the smart thing to do—it's the right thing to do." The references in his opening paragraphs to promoting abstinence and educating young people look ahead to his further discussion of why he finds "disturbing" the objection to the vaccine expressed by some religious conservatives. He labels correctly as an either/or fallacy the tendency on the part of these conservatives to view the current situation as a choice between promoting abstinence-only programs and stopping a killer disease.

The headings in the essay help readers to follow the writer's argument from one main point to another. What religious conservatives fear is that with the threat of HPV gone, American youth will become more promiscuous. Like anyone trying to construct a strong argument, the writer shows an awareness of what his opponents' position is before attempting to undermine that position. He does so through the type of **support** he offers. He wants to establish that religious conservatives have backed abstinence-only programs, so he cites the $1.1 billion federal and state dollars that they "in tandem with the Bush administration" have spent on abstinence-only programs. To establish his opponents' position, he also quotes conservatives who do not support vaccination against a disease that is preventable through abstinence, establishing their conservative affiliations by providing their titles.

The author is guilty of his own either/or fallacy when he calls his fourth section "Will Ideology or Science Dictate the Decision?" In this instance, though, his support for his claim comes in the form of examples of how conservatives are affecting policy decisions. He attacks these conservatives indirectly when he quotes from the highly respected *New England Journal of Medicine*. He is still showing the flaws in his opponents' line of reasoning but also the political clout they have.

The author also supports his claim of value by offering scientific research in rebuttal of his opponents' claim of policy, which is that the HPV vaccine should not be given to our teenagers since infection is 100 percent preventable when young people abstain from sex. His quotations from the American Academy of Pediatrics and from the *New England Journal of Medicine* help dispel what he terms the "myth" that knowledge of contraceptives will lead teens into risky sexual behavior—or into sexual behavior of any kind. He also points out that those who, like Senator Tom Coburn and Representative Jo Ann Davis, argue that condoms do not protect against HPV do so in light of current research to the contrary. His argument here would have been stronger if he had cited supporting research.

The author concludes that religious conservatives clearly have political power in the areas of sexual and reproductive health. This is a power that they could use to support HPV vaccination. The piece ends with a section with the catchy title "Does 'Saving Souls' Trump Saving Lives?" The quotation marks around "Saving Souls" suggest that the writer questions whether it is the saving of souls that motivates religious conservatives or perhaps whether using the threat of the HPV virus as a means of scaring teenagers out of having sex is a legitimate means of trying to save their souls.

At the end the writer sums up his reservations about the politicization of health care: "From stem-cell research to sex education, from a diminished emphasis on condoms to denying non-prescription status to EC, evidence-based prevention has taken a back seat to ideology and politics." He then restates his claim of value: "Cancer is a public health challenge that needs to be conquered; it is not an appropriate venue for political or ideological debate."

What is the **warrant** underlying this argument? What assumption or assumptions are behind the author's argument? One could be worded in this form:

CLAIM: It is wrong to let politics or ideology stand in the way of administering the HPV vaccine.

SUPPORT: The HPV vaccine, if given early enough, will save lives.

WARRANT: It is wrong to let politics or ideology stand in the way of administering a medication that will save lives.

This warrant, like many, because it is a broad statement, could underlie a number of different arguments.

A few more points need to be made about this particular argument. Unlike others in this chapter, it is a documented essay. The notes at the end identify the sources from which the author drew his information. Often on the Internet and almost always in journalist writing, sources are referred to, but not cited in their entirety. In academic and scholarly writing, however, you should always completely identify your sources. Later chapters will provide more examples of documented essays and guidelines for documentation.

Keep in mind also the **audience** for which this essay was intended. It appeared originally on the Web site of Advocates for Youth. The organization sums up its mission in this way:

> Advocates for Youth is dedicated to creating programs and advocating for policies that help young people make informed and responsible decisions about their reproductive and sexual health. Advocates provides information, training, and strategic assistance to youth-serving organizations, policy makers, youth activists, and the media in the United States and the developing world.

The writer is addressing primarily those who already share his concern about the health of today's youth and about educating youth regarding their reproductive and sexual health. His is a voice of moderation compared to those who advocate abstinence as the only approach to sexuality. Even in his **language**, he wisely uses moderation, presenting himself as reasonable and knowledgeable yet not attacking those with whom he does not agree. His note at the end of the essay acknowledges a reality that he believes Americans must confront: the fact that most youth will not abstain from sex no matter what they are taught.

PRACTICE

Using the analysis of "Will the Politics of Teen Sex Stop a Cancer Vaccine?" as a model, apply to the following essay the terms of argument introduced in this chapter.

Why U.S. Health Care Costs Aren't Too High

CHARLES R. MORRIS

There is nearly a consensus that American health care is careening toward fiscal catastrophe. Reasonable estimates of unfunded health care liabilities are sky-high. But the belief that health care costs threaten to wreck the U.S. economy is misguided.

In the first place, procedure by procedure, those costs are quite probably falling. It is spending that is rising, which is not the same thing at all. The advent of minimally invasive techniques means that, for example, the cost of a gallbladder operation has dropped substantially, and the patient can usually return to work the next day instead of sitting at home for a week. But because many more people are now willing to undergo the surgery, total spending is up. It's the same story with all kinds of medical care, from hip replacement to the treatment of depression. In other industries, falling prices and added features have similarly led to big increases in spending—on PCs, cell phones, and video games, for example—but we call that a productivity triumph, not a "cost" problem.

Three-quarters of health care spending goes toward people who are very sick. Yes, interventions are sometimes overdone, but doctors don't know in advance which of their patients are going to die, and the great majority of very sick patients recover. Over the past thirty years, the death rate from heart attacks has plummeted, so millions of heart attack survivors are now going to work or playing with their grandchildren. And, of course, successful health care always breeds more spending: The people who used to die of heart attacks now live on to consume expensive medications, visit specialists, and contract cancer or Alzheimer's. Does that mean we should stop saving heart attack victims?

Besides, one person's spending is always someone else's revenue. Explain to GE Healthcare ($15 billion in revenues, 45,000 employees, sales in 100 countries) why rising health care spending is a bad thing. The profile of Medtronics—in the areas of growth, profitability, and R&D spending—closely tracks that of Intel ten years ago. Modern operating rooms boast millions of dollars' worth of equipment, and the vendors include global corporate giants and tiny start-ups.

Health care is now, by most measures, America's largest industry and 5
biggest private employer, as well as a major source of competitive advantage for the United States. Health care's growing share of GDP, moreover, is entirely in keeping with historical trends. A hundred and fifty years ago, agriculture accounted for about half of GDP; it accounts for only 3%

Charles R. Morris has written widely on topics such as Catholicism, IBM, and economics. This article appeared in the February 2007 *Harvard Business Review*.

now. Fifty years ago, a third of the workforce was in manufacturing, but only 10% is now, although real American manufacturing output is currently far higher. Simple economics is driving health care's expansion: As a society grows richer, the marginal value of one more toy inevitably pales in comparison with another year of life in which to enjoy all one's toys.

Without a truly radical adjustment in health care spending patterns, which there is no reason to expect, demographics alone will drive health care's share of GDP—now 16%—to as high as 25% to 30% over the next couple of decades. In purely economic terms, that would not be a bad thing. Indeed, in terms of trade balances and international competitiveness, it might be a positive development. And even at very modest levels of overall economic growth, people could still increase their spending on cosmetics, video games, and other fun things, although perhaps a tad more slowly than they do now. In short, at least for the foreseeable future, health care in the United States is an economic, a societal, and an affordable good.

To be sure, there are serious problems of waste in health care, just as there are in investment banking, the media, and most other industries. Better oversight may be the answer, but it will be the work of decades. In the meantime, the challenge is one of financing, not affordability. The current primary financing mechanisms—employer-based insurance and Medicare—are clearly breaking down. And privatization is an unrealistic solution: While it may, barely, be feasible to privatize old-age pensions (the savings shortfall is far smaller in pensions than it is in health care), privatizing both pensions and health care is a pipe dream.

Instead, in time-honored fashion, a succession of presidents and Congresses will respond to the challenge with a mix of cuts and patches. Spending will keep on rising, and it will continue to shift toward government accounts. Taxes will go up after a lag, and everyone will lie about it. Over time, some highly imperfect but tolerable new accommodation will emerge. Elegant it won't be. That's just the way we do things.

ASSIGNMENTS FOR UNDERSTANDING THE STRUCTURE OF ARGUMENT

READING AND DISCUSSION QUESTIONS

1. Consider at what point news stations cross the line between reporting the news and analyzing the news. Think of some examples from recent news stories that illustrate the argumentative nature of today's news coverage.
2. Do you believe that presidential debates are good examples of argumentation? Explain.

3. What are some of the controversial issues in the field of your major or a major that you are considering? Analyze one or more of them using the terms of argumentation introduced in this chapter.
4. When you write essays and reports for your classes, how do you establish your credibility? On the other hand, how do students lose their credibility with the instructors who read their work?

WRITING SUGGESTIONS

5. Write an essay in which you support your opinion about whether backscatter screening should be implemented at America's airports.
6. Write an essay in which you argue whether or not you believe that the HPV vaccination should be added to the list of vaccinations recommended by the Advisory Committee on Immunization Practices.

CHAPTER 2

Reading and Listening Critically

Most of us learn how to read, to listen to, to write—and, with the increased use of computer technology, to view—arguments by attending critically to the arguments of those who have already mastered the important elements as well as those who have not. As we acquire skill in analyzing arguments, we learn to uncover the clues that reveal meaning and to become sensitive to the kinds of claims and support, language and visuals that experienced writers use in persuading their audiences.

A full response to any argument means more than understanding the message. It also means evaluating, deciding whether the message is successful, and then determining *how* it succeeds or fails in persuading us. In making these judgments about the arguments of others, we learn how to deliver our own. We try to avoid what we perceive to be flaws in another's arguments, and we adapt the strategies that produce clear, honest, forceful arguments.

RESPONDING AS A CRITICAL READER

Critical reading is essential for mastery of most college subjects, but its importance for reading and writing about argument, where meaning is often complex and multilayered, cannot be overestimated. Reading arguments critically requires you to at least temporarily suspend notions of absolute "right" and "wrong" and to intellectually inhabit gray areas that do not allow for simple "yes" and "no" answers. Of course, even in these areas, significant decisions about such things as ethics, values, politics, and the law must be made, and in studying argument you shouldn't fall into the trap of simple relativism: the idea that all answers to a given problem are equally correct at all times. We must make decisions about arguments with the understanding that reasonable people can disagree on the validity of ideas. Read others' arguments carefully and consider how their ideas can contribute to or complicate your own. Also recognize that what appears to be a final solution will always be open to further negotiation as new participants, new historical circumstances, and new ideologies become involved in the debate.

The ability to read arguments critically is essential to advanced academic work—even in science and math—since it requires the debate of multifaceted issues rather than the memorization of facts. Just as important, learning to read arguments critically helps you develop the ability to *write* effective arguments, a process valued at the university, in the professional world, and in public life.

PREREADING STRATEGIES

Whether reading to comprehend or to evaluate any text, do the following:

1. Take prereading activities seriously. Clearly, the more information you have about an author and a subject, the easier and more productive your reading will be. However, you should learn to read in a way that allows you to discover not just meaning in the text itself but information about the author's point of view and background, the audience the author is writing for, and the author's motives and ideology. Such understanding comes from close analysis of texts but also from background reading on the author or the subject (a task made significantly easier by the Internet) and discussion with your classmates and instructors on the material.
2. Work hard to understand the kind of text you are reading. Was it published recently? Was it written for a specific or a general audience? Is it a textbook and therefore likely to cover the basic points of an issue but not to take a strong stance on anything? Does it come from a journal that publishes primarily conservative or liberal writers?
3. Imagine the initial context in which the author was writing, the problem the author was trying to deal with. What values and ideals are shared by the author and the audience most likely to agree with the argument? How might these values and ideals help make sense of the context?
4. Pay attention to the title, as it may state the purpose of the argument in specific terms.

PRACTICE

Apply the Prereading Strategies to this famous document from America's past.

The Declaration of Independence

THOMAS JEFFERSON

When in the course of human events, it becomes necessary for one people to dissolve the political bands which have connected them with another, and to assume among the Powers of the earth, the separate and equal station to which the Laws of Nature and Nature's God entitle them, a decent respect to the opinions of mankind requires that they should declare the causes which impel them to the separation.

We hold these truths to be self-evident, that all men are created equal, that they are endowed by their Creator with certain unalienable Rights, that among these are Life, Liberty and the pursuit of Happiness.

That to secure these rights, Governments are instituted among Men, deriving their just powers from the consent of the governed.

That whenever any Form of Government becomes destructive of these ends, it is the Right of the People to alter or to abolish it, and to institute a new Government laying its foundation on such principles and organizing its powers in such form, as to them shall seem most likely to effect their Safety and Happiness. Prudence, indeed, will dictate that Governments long established should not be changed for light and transient causes; and accordingly all experience hath shown that mankind are more disposed to suffer, while evils are sufferable, than to right themselves by abolishing the forms to which they are accustomed. But when a long train of abuses and usurpations pursuing invariably the same Object evinces a design to reduce them under absolute Despotism, it is their right, it is their duty, to throw off such government, and to provide new Guards for their future security.

Such has been the patient sufferance of these Colonies; and such is now the necessity which constrains them to alter their former Systems of Government. The history of the present King of Great Britain is a history of repeated injuries and usurpations, all having in direct object the establishment of an absolute Tyranny over these States. To prove this, let Facts be submitted to a candid world.

He has refused his Assent to Laws, the most wholesome and necessary for the public good.

He has forbidden his Governors to pass Laws of immediate and pressing importance, unless suspended in their operation till his Assent should be obtained; and when so suspended, he has utterly neglected to attend to them.

He has refused to pass other Laws for the accommodation of large districts of people, unless those people would relinquish the right of Representation in the Legislature, a right inestimable to them and formidable to tyrants only.

Thomas Jefferson (1743–1826) served as governor of Virginia, minister to France, secretary of state, vice president under John Adams, and president from 1801 to 1809.

He has called together legislative bodies at places unusual, uncomfortable, and distant from the depository of their Public Records, for the sole purpose of fatiguing them into compliance with his measures.

He has dissolved Representative Houses repeatedly, for opposing with manly firmness his invasions on the rights of the people.

He has refused for a long time, after such dissolutions, to cause others to be elected; whereby the Legislative Powers, incapable of Annihilation, have returned to the People at large for their exercise; the State remaining in the mean time exposed to all the danger of invasion from without, and convulsions within.

He has endeavored to prevent the population of these States; for that purpose obstructing the Laws of Naturalization of Foreigners; refusing to pass others to encourage their migration hither, and raising the conditions of new Appropriations of Lands.

He has obstructed the Administration of Justice, by refusing his Assent to Laws for establishing Judiciary Powers.

He has made Judges dependent on his Will alone, for the tenure of their offices, and the amount and payment of their salaries.

He has erected a multitude of New Offices, and sent hither swarms of Officers to harass our People, and eat out their substance.

He has kept among us, in time of peace, Standing Armies without the consent of our Legislature.

He has affected to render the Military independent of and superior to the Civil Power.

He has combined with others to subject us to jurisdictions foreign to our constitution, and unacknowledged by our laws; giving his Assent to their acts of pretended Legislation:

For quartering large bodies of armed troops among us:

For protecting them, by a mock Trial, from Punishment for any Murders which they should commit on the Inhabitants of these States:

For cutting off our Trade with all parts of the world:

For imposing Taxes on us without our Consent:

For depriving us in many cases, of the benefits of Trial by Jury:

For transporting us beyond Seas to be tried for pretended offenses:

For abolishing the free System of English Laws in a Neighbouring Province, establishing therein an Arbitrary government, and enlarging its boundaries so as to render it at once an example and fit instrument for introducing the same absolute rule into these Colonies:

For taking away our Charters, abolishing our most valuable Laws, and altering fundamentally the Forms of our Governments:

For suspending our own legislatures, and declaring themselves invested with Power to legislate for us in all cases whatsoever.

He has abdicated Government here, by declaring us out of his Protection and waging War against us.

He has plundered our seas, ravaged our Coasts, burnt our towns and destroyed the Lives of our people.

He is at this time transporting large Armies of foreign Mercenaries to compleat the works of death, desolation and tyranny, already begun with circumstances of Cruelty & perfidy scarcely paralleled in the most barbarous ages, and totally unworthy the Head of a civilized nation.

He has constrained our fellow Citizens taken Captive on the high Seas to bear Arms against their Country, to become the executioners of their friends and Brethren, or to fall themselves by their Hands.

He has excited domestic insurrections amongst us, and has endeavored to bring on the inhabitants of our frontiers, the merciless Indian Savages, whose known rule of warfare is an undistinguished destruction of all ages, sexes, and conditions.

In every stage of these Oppressions We Have Petitioned for Redress in the most humble terms. Our repeated petitions have been answered only by repeated injury. A Prince, whose character is thus marked by every act which may define a Tyrant, is unfit to be the ruler of a free People.

Not have We been wanting in attention to our British brethren. We have warned them from time to time of attempts by their legislature to extend an unwarrantable jurisdiction over us. We have reminded them of the circumstances of our emigration and settlement here. We have appealed to their native justice and magnanimity and we have conjured them by the ties of our common kindred to disavow these usurpations, which would inevitably interrupt our connections and correspondence. They too have been deaf to the voice of justice and of consanguinity. We must, therefore, acquiesce in the necessity, which denounces our Separation, and hold them, as we hold the rest of mankind, Enemies in War, in Peace Friends.

We, therefore, the Representatives of the United States of America, in General Congress, Assembled, appealing to the Supreme Judge of the world for the rectitude of our intentions, do, in the Name, and by Authority of the good People of these Colonies, solemnly publish and declare, That these United Colonies are, and of Right ought to be, Free and Independent States; that they are Absolved from all Allegiance to the British Crown, and that all political connection between them and the State of Great Britain, is and ought to be totally dissolved; and that as Free and Independent States, they have full power to levy War, conclude Peace, contract Alliances, establish Commerce, and to do all other Acts and Things which Independent States may of right do. And for the support of this Declaration, with a firm reliance on the protection of Divine Providence, we mutually pledge to each other our lives, our Fortunes and our sacred Honor.

COMPREHENDING ARGUMENTS

The first step in the critical reading process is comprehension—understanding what an author is trying to prove. Comprehending academic arguments can be difficult because they are often complex and often challenge accepted notions. Academic writing also sometimes assumes that readers already have a great deal of knowledge about a subject and therefore can require further research for comprehension.

Readers sometimes fail to comprehend a text they disagree with or that is new to them, especially in dealing with essays or books making controversial, value-laden arguments. Some research even shows that readers will sometimes remember only those parts of texts that match their points of view.[1] The study of argument does not require you to accept points of view you find morally or otherwise reprehensible, but to engage with these views, no matter how strange or repugnant they might seem, on your own terms.

To comprehend difficult texts you should understand that reading and writing are linked processes, and use writing to help your reading. This can mean writing comments in the margins of the book or essay itself or in a separate notebook; highlighting passages in the text that seem particularly important; or freewriting about the author's essential ideas after you finish reading. For complex arguments, write down the methods the author uses to make the argument: Did the text make use of historical evidence or rely on the voice of experts? Were emotional appeals made to try to convince readers, or did the text rely on scientific or logical forms of evidence? Did the author use analogies or comparisons to help readers understand the argument? Was some combination of these or other strategies used? Writing down the author's methods for argumentation can make even the most complex arguments understandable.

STRATEGIES FOR COMPREHENDING ARGUMENTS

1. Skim the article or book for the main idea and overall structure. At this stage, avoid concentrating on details.
   a. Make a skeleton outline of the text in your mind or on paper. From this outline and the text itself, consider the relationship between the beginning, middle, and end of the argument. How has the author divided these sections? Are there subheadings in the body of the text? If you are reading a book, how are the chapters broken up? What appears to be the logic of the author's organization?
   b. From your overview, what is the central claim or argument of the essay? What is the main argument against the author's central claim and how would the author respond to it?
2. Remember that the claim is usually in one of the first two or three paragraphs (if it is an essay) or in the first chapter (if it is a book). The beginning of an argument can have other purposes, however; it may describe the position that the author will oppose or provide background for the whole argument.
3. Pay attention to topic sentences. The topic sentence is usually but not always the first sentence of a paragraph. It is the general statement that controls the details and examples in the paragraph.

[1]See, for example, Patrick J. Slattery, "The Argumentative, Multiple-Source Paper: College Students Reading, Thinking, and Writing about Multiple Points of View," *Journal of Teaching Writing* 10, Fall/Winter 1991, pp. 181–99.

4. Don't overlook language signposts, especially transitional words and phrases that tell you whether the writer will change direction or offer support for a previous point — words and phrases like *but, however, nevertheless, yet, moreover, for example, at first glance, more important, the first reason,* and so on.
5. When it comes to vocabulary, you can either guess the meaning of an unfamiliar word from the context and go on or look it up immediately. The first method makes for more rapid reading and is sometimes recommended by teachers, but guessing can be risky. Keep a good dictionary handy. If a word you don't understand seems crucial to meaning, look it up before going on.
6. If you use a colored marker to highlight main points, use it sparingly. Marking passages in color is meant to direct you to the major ideas and reduce the necessity for rereading the whole passage when you review. Look over the marked passages after reading and do a five-minute freewrite to sum up the central parts of the argument.
7. Once you are done reading, think again about the original context the text was written in: Why did the author write it and for whom? Why might an editor have published it in a book or journal, and why did your instructor assign it for you to read?

SAMPLE ANNOTATED ESSAY

Sex And The Cinema

EDWARD JAY EPSTEIN

Background for the argument — contrast with early days

Examples of Top 25 movies with no sex

Claim

In the early days of Hollywood, nudity — or the illusion of it — was considered such an asset that director Cecil B. DeMille famously made bathing scenes an obligatory ingredient of his biblical epics. Nowadays, nudity is a decided liability when it comes to the commercial success of the movie. In 2004, none of the six major studios' top 25 grossing films, led by *Spider-Man 2, Shrek 2, Harry Potter and the Prisoner of Azkaban,* and *The Incredibles,* contained any sexually oriented nudity; only one had a restrictive R rating — Warner Bros.' *Troy* — and that was mainly due to the film's gory violence, not its sexual content. The absence

This essay appeared on August 15, 2005, in *Slate,* a daily online magazine affiliated with the *Washington Post.*

Claudette Colbert in *The Sign of the Cross* (1932), directed by Cecil B. DeMille

of sex—at least graphic sex—is key to the success of Hollywood's moneymaking movies. Directors may consider a sex scene artistically integral to their movie, but studios, which almost always have the right to exercise the final cut, also have to consider three factors.

Three factors to consider
I

First, there is the rating system. For a film to play in movie theaters belonging to the National Association of Theater Owners—which includes all the multiplexes in America—it first needs to obtain a rating from a board organized by the Motion Picture Association of America—the trade association of the six major studios. All the expenses for rating movies are paid to the MPAA by the studio out of a percentage deducted from box-office receipts. As it presently works, a movie that contains sexually oriented nudity gets either an NC-17 or an R rating, depending on how graphically sex is depicted. The NC-17 rating, which forbids theaters from admitting children under the age of 18, is the equivalent of a death sentence as far as the studios are concerned. In fact, since the

Topic sentence: NC-17 = box-office failure

financial disaster of Paul Verhoeven's NC-17 *Showgirls* in 1995, no studio has attempted a wide release of a NC-17 film. As one Paramount executive suggested, because of their sexually related nudity, movies such as Louis Malle's *Pretty Baby*, Bernardo Bertolucci's *Last Tango in Paris*, and Stanley Kubrick's *A Clockwork Orange* would not even be considered by a major studio today. So far this year there has been only one limited release of an NC-17 film by a studio: the documentary *Inside Deep Throat*, which yielded Universal less from the box-office—$330,000—than it cost to wrangle media stars and others to free screenings and dinners to promote it.

Old movies with sex that wouldn't be made today

If a movie contains less explicit nudity, it earns an R rating, which merely prohibits youth unaccompanied by an adult. Even though this option means that some number of multiplex employees—who might otherwise be selling popcorn—are required to check the identity documents of the teenage audience, theaters accept R rated films, especially when, as was the case with *Troy*, the R is for the sort of graphic violence that is also the principal attraction. But even if an R doesn't prevent studios from staging a wide opening of a movie at the multiplexes, it complicates the movie's all-important marketing drive. For one thing, if a film receives an R rating, many television stations and cable networks, particularly teenage-oriented ones, are not allowed to accept TV ads for the movies. In addition, an R rating—especially for sexual content—will preclude any of the fast-food chains, beverage companies, or toy manufacturers that act as the studios' merchandise tie-in partners from backing the movie with tens of millions of dollars in free advertising. As a result, it becomes much more expensive to alert and herd audiences to R rated films.

Topic sentence
–Many stations and networks can't show ads for R movies.
–Food and toy companies won't back R movies.

II

Second, there is the Wal-Mart consideration. In 2004, the six studios took in $20.9 billion from home-video sales, according to the studios' own internal numbers. Wal-Mart, including its Sam's Club stores, accounted for over one-quarter of those sales, which means that Wal-Mart wrote more than $5 billion in checks to the studios in 2004. Such enormous buying power comes dangerously close to constituting what the Justice Department calls a monopsony—control of a market by a single buyer—and it allows the giant retailer to effectively dictate the terms of trade. Internet mythology aside, Wal-Mart doesn't use its clout to advance any political agenda or social engineering objective, according to a studio executive involved in the process; it is "strictly business." Wal-Mart uses DVDs, especially the weekly released hits, to lure in customers who, while they pass through the store, may buy more profitable items, such as toys, clothing, or electronics.

New DVDs = more customers, who buy other products

5 Wal-Mart's main concern with the content of the DVDs is that they not offend important customers—especially mothers—by containing material that may be inappropriate for children. It guards against this risk with a "decency policy" that consigns DVDs containing sexually related nudity to "adult sections" of the store, which greatly reduces their sales. (Wal-Mart is less concerned with vulgar behavior and language.) These guidelines, in turn, put studios under tremendous pressure to sanitize their films of sexual content. The Wal-Mart buyer would merely have to order for their stores the "in-flight entertainment" version of DVDs, from which studios expunge nudity and other sexually explicit scenes for airline passengers (censorship that almost all directors quietly accept). In light of such leverage, studios have to weigh the Wal-Mart factor with great care.

Wal-Mart's "decency policy" forces studios to avoid sexual content

Topic sentence

Finally, movies with nudity are a problem for the studios' other main moneymaker: television. As became abundantly clear in the controversy surrounding Janet Jackson's wardrobe malfunction at Superbowl XXXVIII, broadcast television is a government-regulated enterprise. When the government grants a free license to a station to broadcast over the public airwaves, it does so under the condition that it conform to the rules enforced by the Federal Communications Commission. Among those rules is the standard of "public decency," which among other things specifically prohibits salacious nudity—which is why CBS had to pay a fine for Ms. Jackson's brief exposure. Because the FCC regulates broadcast television (though not cable television), television stations run similar

III Topic sentence

Movies on TV must meet standards of "public decency"

risks—and embarrassments—if they show movies that include even partial nudity. So, before a studio can license such a movie to a broadcast network, it first has to cut out all the nudity and other scenes that run afoul of the decency standard. Aside from the expense involved, it requires the hassle of obtaining the director's permission, which is contractually required by the Directors Guild of America. The same is true in studio sales to foreign television companies, which have their own government censorship. Since graphic sex in movies is a triple liability, the studios can be expected to increasingly find that the artistic gain that comes from including it does not compensate for the financial pain and greenlight fewer and fewer movies that present this problem. We may live in an anything-goes age, but if a studio wants to make money, it has to limit how much of "anything"—at least anything sexually explicit—it shows on the big screen. As one studio executive with an MBA lamented, "We may have to leave sex to the independents."

Conclusion restates claim

PRACTICE

1. Choose an editorial of at least two paragraphs from your school paper or another newspaper on a controversial subject that interests you. The title will probably reveal the subject. Annotate the editorial as you read, using the annotations on "Sex and the Cinema" as a model. Then read the article again. You should discover that annotating the article caused you to read more carefully, more critically, with greater comprehension and a more focused response.
2. Summarize the claim of the editorial in one sentence. Has the author proved his or her point?

EVALUATING ARGUMENTS

The second step in the critical reading of arguments involves evaluation—careful judgment of the extent to which the author has succeeded in making a point—which can be difficult because some readers who do not thoroughly engage with an author's point of view may immediately label an argument they disagree with as "wrong," and some readers believe they are incapable of evaluating the work of a published, "expert" author because they do not feel expert enough to make such judgments.

Evaluating arguments means moving beyond comprehending the context the author was writing within and starting to question it. One way to do this is to envision audiences the text was probably *not* written for, by considering, for example, whether an essay written for an academic audience takes into account the world outside the university. In addition, why is the problem significant to the author? For whom would it not be significant, and why?

When you evaluate an argument, imagine at least two kinds of audience for the text. Decide whose views would conflict most with the author's, and why. What ideology or values underlie the point of view most diametrically opposed to the author's argument? Then imagine yourself as a friend of the writer who simply wants him or her to succeed in clarifying and developing the argument. You could ask what additional methods the author should use to make the argument more effective or how the writer could more fully address opposing points of view. Are there any significant questions or issues the author has left unaddressed? How could he or she build on the strengths of the argument and downplay the weaknesses?

At this point, consider how you personally respond to the argument presented in the text, and your own response in light of the questions you've asked. Critically evaluating an argument means not simply reading a text and agreeing or disagreeing with it, but doing serious analytical work that addresses multiple viewpoints before deciding on the effectiveness of an argument.

STRATEGIES FOR EVALUATING ARGUMENTS

1. As you read the argument, don't be timid about asking questions of the text. No author is infallible, and some are not always clear. Disagree with the author if you feel confident of the support for your view, but first read the whole argument to see if your questions have been answered. If not, this may be a signal to read the article again. Be cautious about concluding that the author hasn't proved his or her point.
2. Reading an assigned work is usually a solitary activity, but what follows a reading should be shared. Talk about the material with classmates or others who have read it, especially those who have responded to the text differently than you did. Consider their points of view. You probably know that discussion of a book or a movie strengthens both your memory of details and your understanding of the whole. And defending or modifying your evaluation will mean going back to the text and finding clues that you may have overlooked. Not least, it can be fun to discuss even something you didn't enjoy.
3. Consider the strengths of the argument and examine the useful methods of argumentation, the points that are successfully made (and those which help the reader to better understand the argument), and what makes sense about the author's argument.

4. Consider the weaknesses of the argument and locate instances of faulty reasoning, unsupported statements, and the limitations of the author's assumptions about the world (the warrants that underlie the argument).
5. Consider how effective the title of the reading is and whether it accurately sums up a critical point of the essay. Come up with an alternative title that would suit the reading better, and be prepared to defend this alternative title.
6. Evaluate the organizational structure of the essay. The author should lead you from idea to idea in a logical progression, and each section should relate to the ones before and after it and to the central argument in significant ways. Determine whether the writer could have organized things more clearly, logically, or efficiently.
7. Look at how the author follows through on the main claim, or thesis, of the argument. The author should stick with this thesis and not waver throughout the text. If the thesis does waver, there could be a reason for the shift in the argument, or perhaps the author is being inconsistent. The conclusion should drive home the central argument.
8. Evaluate the vocabulary and style the author uses. Is it too simple or too complicated? The vocabulary and sentence structure the author uses could relate to the audience the author was initially writing for.

SAMPLE ANALYSIS

The Gettysburg Address

ABRAHAM LINCOLN

Four score and seven years ago our fathers brought forth on this continent, a new nation, conceived in Liberty, and dedicated to the proposition that all men are created equal.

Now we are engaged in a great civil war, testing whether that nation, or any nation so conceived and so dedicated, can long endure. We are met on a great battle-field of that war. We have come to dedicate a portion of that field, as a final resting place for those who here gave their lives that that nation might live. It is altogether fitting and proper that we should do this.

But, in a larger sense, we can not dedicate—we can not consecrate—we can not hallow—this ground. The brave men, living and dead, who struggled here, have consecrated it, far above our poor power to add or

Abraham Lincoln (1809–1865), the sixteenth president of the United States, delivered this speech at Gettysburg, Pennsylvania, on November 19, 1863.

detract. The world will little note, nor long remember what we say here, but it can never forget what they did here. It is for us the living, rather, to be dedicated here to the unfinished work which they who fought here have thus far so nobly advanced. It is rather for us to be here dedicated to the great task remaining before us—that from these honored dead we take increased devotion to that cause for which they gave the last full measure of devotion—that we here highly resolve that these dead shall not have died in vain—that this nation, under God, shall have a new birth of freedom—and that government of the people, by the people, for the people, shall not perish from the earth.

The following evaluation is by Charles Adams, whose stand on the Civil War is clear from the title of the book from which the excerpt is taken: *When in the Course of Human Events: Arguing the Case for Southern Secession* (2000). Lincoln made his famous short speech in 1863 as a memorial to the thousands who had died at Gettysburg, but in doing so, he was also making an argument. The text in quotation marks is from the address itself. The rest is Adams's evaluation of it. As you read, consider what argument Lincoln is making but also whether or not you agree with Adams's evaluation.

Lincoln's Logic

CHARLES ADAMS

> Lincoln has become one of our national deities and a realistic examination of him is thus no longer possible. —H. L. Mencken, 1931

At the Gettysburg Cemetery

Lincoln's mental processes and his logic have fascinated me ever since my university days. In a class in logic, we studied his Gettysburg Address. The analysis showed that this famous speech didn't fit the real world. It was good poetry, perhaps, but was it good thinking? It's chiseled in stone in the Lincoln Memorial in Washington, and it ranks in the minds of most

---

Charles Adams, a leading scholar on the history of taxation, is the author of *Fight, Flight, Fraud* (1982); *Those Dirty Rotten Taxes* (1998); and *For Good and Evil* (2nd Ed., 2001). His essay comes from *When in the Course of Human Events: Arguing the Case for Southern Secession* (2000).

Americans with the Declaration of Independence and the Constitution. This oration was given to dedicate the cemetery at Gettysburg, where tens of thousands of young men died in a battle that was probably the turning point of the war. The address is reminiscent of the funeral oration of Pericles of Athens in the fifth century B.C. But Pericles's oration seemed to fit the real world of his day and the virtues of Athenian democracy. Lincoln's address did not fit the world of his day. It reflected his logic, which was based on a number of errors and falsehoods. That it has survived with such reverence is one of the most bizarre aspects of the war.

"Four Score and Seven Years Ago"

By simple arithmetic that would be 1776, when the Revolutionary War started and the Declaration of Independence was signed. That declaration was written with "decent respect for the opinions of mankind," to explain the reasons for the separation of the thirteen colonies from Great Britain. It contained no endowment of governmental power and created no government. The government came later in 1781 with the Articles of Confederation. The articles stated that this confederation was established by "sovereign states," like many of the leagues of states throughout history. To be accurate, Lincoln should have said "four score and two years ago," or better still, "three score and fourteen years ago." Even the Northern newspapers winced. The *New York World* sharply criticized this historical folly. "*This* United States" was not created by the Declaration of Independence but "the result of the ratification of a compact known as the Constitution," a compact that said nothing about equality. Others accused Lincoln of "gross ignorance or willful misstatement." Yet today, that gross ignorance is chiseled in stone as if it were some great truth like scripture, instead of a willful misstatement.

"Our Fathers Brought Forth on This Continent, a New Nation"

The federal compact among the former thirteen colonies, the new "sovereign states," as expressed in the Articles of Confederation in 1781, was not a nation as that term was then and is normally used. That was recently explained by Carl N. Degler, professor of American history at Stanford University, in a memorial lecture given at Gettysburg College in 1990: "The Civil War, in short, was not a struggle to save a failed union, but to create a nation that until then had not come into being."

Thus Lincoln's "new nation" really came into being by force of arms in the war between the states. Lincoln, according to Professor Degler, had a lot in common with Germany's Otto von Bismarck, who built a united Germany in the nineteenth century and believed that "blood and iron" were the main force for national policy. When it came to blood, Lincoln surpassed them all. The slaughter of Confederate men only matched, on a proportionate basis, the losses incurred by the Russians and the Germans in World War II.

In Lincoln's first inaugural address he used the word "Union" twenty 5
times but "nation" not at all. But once the South seceded, the term began to disappear, and by the time of the Gettysburg Address, it was the American "nation" that was used, and the word "Union" had disappeared completely.

Thus the call from Northern peace Democrats—"the constitution as it is; the Union as it was"—seems to make sense, but as Lincoln took over control of the federal government, he soon wanted no part of it. Although he tried to trace the "new nation" back to 1776, he had to ignore history and the intention and words of the Founders, and create a new "gospel according to Lincoln" on the American commonwealth. Lincoln's new nation had no constitutional basis—no peaceful legal process. It was created by war, by "blood and iron," like Bismarck's Germany, and has survived to this day. In a sense, Lincoln did more to create America than did the Founding Fathers. It is Lincoln who is the father of our present country, not George Washington. Lincoln's Gettysburg reference to the Founders creating a new nation was not true. Just as Julius Caesar created an imperial order out of a republic, so Lincoln created a nation out of a compact among states, and both used their military forces to do so.

"Conceived in Liberty"

A leading man of letters in Britain during the American Revolution, Samuel Johnson, replied to the Americans' claims of tyranny in his book *Taxation Not Tyranny* (1775). He said, "How is it that we hear the loudest *yelps* for liberty among the drivers of negroes?"

The British are still chiding us for the absurdity of the Declaration of Independence. Some years ago, while I was living in a British colony, we Americans got together on the Fourth of July for a barbecue. One of my older English friends asked me what the celebration was all about. I took the bait and told him it was to celebrate the signing of the Declaration of Independence. He replied, "Wasn't that document kind of a farce? All that verbiage about equality of all men and liberty when over a million black people were in bondage for life, and their children and children's children?" Of course I had no answer, for the term "all men" meant all white men. And to make matters worse, it really meant "white guys," as white women weren't much better off. What is not known is that when Lincoln issued his Emancipation Proclamation, many of the early women's rights groups asked, How about us too? Thus the declaration that Lincoln refers to in his address, of four score and seven years ago, was *not* conceived in liberty *nor* was it dedicated to the proposition that all men were created equal. So much for logic and reality.

Lincoln's logic at Gettysburg, as elsewhere, reveals a trial lawyer with a tool of his craft—using the best logic he can muster to support his client's (the North's) case, however bad that case may be. It is also, of course, the craft of a politician, which may explain why so many politicians are lawyers.

"Today We Are Engaged in a Great Civil War"

Actually, it wasn't a civil war as that term was then, and is now, defined. 10
A civil war is a war that breaks out in a nation between opposing groups for control of the state, for example, in Russia in 1917 with the Red against the Whites or in China in the 1940s.

The War of Rebellion, as the war was called in the North, was really a war for Southern independence. The Southern states had withdrawn from the Union by democratic process—the same process they had followed to join the Union initially. The Northern federation went to war to prevent their secession from the Union just as Britain went to war in 1776 to prevent the colonies from seceding from the British nation. It was the fundamentals of the Revolutionary War, eighty-five years before. It was, if you get down to the nuts and bolts of it, a war of conquest by the North to destroy the Confederacy and to establish a new political leadership over the conquered territories. Illiterate slaves were given the vote, and the rest of the Southern society, the ruling groups, were not permitted to vote. The poor, illiterate blacks were then told by Northern occupation forces to vote as directed, and they did so, infuriating the conquered people and creating a zeal for white supremacy that is only in our time losing its grip on Southern society.

"Testing Whether That Nation . . . Can Long Endure"

That comment seems to presuppose that the South was out to conquer the Northern federation. That is as absurd as saying that the revolting colonies in 1776 were out to destroy the British nation. The thirteen colonies' withdrawal from the British Empire in 1776 was the same as the attempt of the Southern states to withdraw in 1861 from the 1789 federation. In reality, the 1789 federation was not in any danger. It would have endured with secession. Unlike Grant, Lee was not out to conquer the North. In reality, this logic was as absurd as the rest of Lincoln's funeral oration.

"A Final Resting Place for Those Who Here Gave Their Lives That That Nation Might Live"

Again, "that nation" was not in danger of dying—that was not Southern Confederate policy and Lincoln knew it. But again, he was only being a good lawyer, arguing his client's case as best he could, and with no rebuttal he was an easy winner.

"And That Government of the People, by the People and for the People Shall Not Perish from the Earth"

Why did Lincoln even suggest that secession by the Southern states would mean that democracy would perish from the earth—in America or elsewhere? That was perfect nonsense, and Lincoln knew it, but again, there was no one to rebut his argument.

15 Lincoln's repeated assertion that secession would amount to a failure of the American experiment with democracy and liberty "just is plain nonsense," wrote Professor Hummel in his refreshing book on the Civil War, *Emancipating Slaves, Enslaving Free Men*.[2] The London *Times* seems to have best understood what was going on in America with the Northern invasion to prevent secession: "If Northerners . . . had peaceably allowed the seceders to depart, the result might fairly have been quoted as illustrating the advantages of Democracy, but when Republicans put empire above liberty, and resorted to political oppression and war . . . . It was clear that nature at Washington was precisely the same as nature at St. Petersburg. . . . Democracy broke down . . . when it was upheld, like any other Empire, by force of arms."[3]

By 1860 democracy was strongly entrenched throughout Western civilization, and certainly in the American states. The democratic process had emerged decades before in Europe—in Britain, France, the Netherlands, Switzerland, and so on. The war in America for Southern independence was in no way a danger to the concept of government "of the people." Strange as it may seem, as it turned out, it was Lincoln who was out to destroy governments of the people in the eleven Southern states. The declaration's assertion that governments derive their "just powers from the consent of the governed" was not an acceptable idea in Lincoln's mind so far as the South was concerned. Like a good lawyer he ignored it.

What makes Lincoln's ending so outrageous is that he didn't believe in the self-determination of peoples, as British writers noted in 1861 and a hundred years later in 1961.

Ordinances of secession had been adopted in the Southern states, often with huge majorities. Their right to govern by consent was not acceptable to Lincoln's thinking—that would undermine his client's case. Yet it was Lincoln who ended up destroying the Union as it was and substituting an all-powerful national government in which the states were relegated to not much more than county status. There emerged the "imperial presidency" that is with us to this day, in which presidents can go to war, without congressional approval, spend money without congressional approval; in fact, they can rule by decree like the consuls of Rome. In other Western democracies, this is not so. Their chief executive must have the permission and approval of their legislature to do such things. Thus Lincoln did more to destroy the Union than preserve it. Is not this irony at its best?

[2]Jeffrey Hummel, *Emancipating Slaves, Enslaving Free Men* (Chicago: Open Court 1997), p. 352.

[3]*Times* editorial, September 13, 1862, p. 8, cited in *Emancipating Slaves*, p. 352.

PRACTICE

1. Return to "Sex and the Cinema" and reread it in light of the Strategies for Evaluating Arguments.
2. What is your evaluation of Adams's essay, "Lincoln's Logic"?

RESPONDING AS A WRITER

Notice the difference between the annotations a student made in response to the following essay and those another student made earlier in response to "Sex and the Cinema" (p. 37). In the earlier example, the student was making marginal notes primarily on the ideas presented in the essay. Here the annotations focus on how the essay is written. In other words, the student is looking at the piece from a writer's perspective.

The essay is a claim of value in which, as the title suggests, the author claims that competitive sports are destructive. In arguments about values, the author may or may not suggest a solution to the problem caused by the belief or behavior. If so, the solution will be implicit—that is, unexpressed or undeveloped—as is the case here, and the emphasis will remain on support for the claim.

Keep in mind that an essay of this length can never do justice to a complicated and highly debatable subject. It will probably lack sufficient evidence, as this one does, to answer all the questions and objections of readers who enjoy and approve of competitive games. What it can do is provoke thought and initiate an intelligent discussion.

SAMPLE ANNOTATED ESSAY

No-Win Situations

ALFIE KOHN

Intro: personal experience

I learned my first game at a birthday party. You remember it: X players scramble for X-minus-one chairs each time the music stops. In every round a child is eliminated until at the end only

This article by Alfie Kohn, author of *No Contest: The Case against Competition* (1986) and *The Homework Myth: Why Our Kids Get Too Much of a Bad Thing* (2006), appeared in *Women's Sports and Fitness Magazine* (July–August 1990).

one is left triumphantly seated while everyone else is standing on the sidelines, excluded from play, unhappy . . . losers.

This is how we learn to have a good time in America.

Competition

Warrant

Several years ago I wrote a book called *No Contest,* which, based on the findings of several hundred studies, argued that competition undermines self-esteem, poisons relationships, and holds us back from doing our best. I was mostly interested in the win/lose arrangement that defines our workplaces and classrooms, but I found myself nagged by the following question: If competition is so destructive and counterproductive during the week, why do we take for granted that it suddenly becomes benign and even desirable on the weekend?

Claim or thesis statement

This is a particularly unsettling line of inquiry for athletes or parents. Most of us, after all, assume that competitive sports teach all sorts of useful lessons and, indeed, that games by definition must produce a winner and a loser. But I've come to believe that recreation at its best does not require people to try to triumph over others. Quite to the contrary.

Support: expert opinion, alternatives to competitive games

5 Terry Orlick, a sports psychologist at the University of Ottawa, took a look at musical chairs and proposed that we keep the basic format of removing chairs but change the goal; the point becomes to fit everyone on a diminishing number of seats. At the end, a group of giggling children tries to figure out how to squish onto a single chair. Everybody plays to the end; everybody has a good time.

Orlick and others have devised or collected hundreds of such games for children and adults alike. The underlying theory is simple: All games involve achieving a goal despite the presence of an obstacle, but nowhere is it written that the obstacle has to be someone else. The idea can be for each person on the field to make a specified contribution to the goal, or for all the players to reach a certain score, or for everyone to work with her partners against a time limit.

Refuting the opposing view

Note the significance of an "opponent" becoming a "partner." The entire dynamic of the game shifts, and one's attitude toward the other players changes with it. Even the friendliest game of tennis can't help but be affected by the game's inherent structure, which demands that each person try to hit the ball where the other can't get to it. You may not be a malicious person, but to play tennis means that you try to make the other person fail.

No advantages in competition

I've become convinced that not a single one of the advantages attributed to sports actually requires competition. Running, climbing, biking, swimming, aerobics—all offer a fine workout without any need to try to outdo someone else. *1)* Some people point to the camaraderie that results from teamwork, but that's precisely the benefit of cooperative activity, whose very essence is that *everyone* on the field is working together for a common goal. By contrast, the distinguishing feature of team competition is that a given player works with and is encouraged to feel warmly toward only half of those present. Worse, a we-versus-they dynamic is set up, which George Orwell once called "war minus the shooting."

2) The dependence on sports to provide a sense of accomplishment or to test one's wits is similarly misplaced. One can aim instead at an objective standard (How far did I throw? How many miles did we cover?) or attempt to do better than last week. Such individual and group striving—like cooperative games—provides satisfaction and challenge without competition.

If large numbers of people insist that we can't 10
do without win/lose activities, the first question to ask is whether they've ever tasted the alternative. When Orlick taught a group of children noncompetitive games, two-thirds of the boys and all of the girls preferred them to the kind that require opponents. If our culture's idea of fun requires beating someone else, it may just be because we don't know any other way.

It may also be because we overlook the
3) psychological costs of competition. Most people lose in most competitive encounters, and it's obvious why that causes self-doubt. But even winning

doesn't build character. It just lets us gloat temporarily. Studies have shown that feelings of self-worth become dependent on external sources of evaluation as a result of competition. Your value is defined by what you've done and who you've beaten. The whole affair soon becomes a vicious circle: The more you compete, the more you *need* to compete to feel good about yourself. It's like drinking salt water when you're thirsty. This process is bad enough for us; it's a disaster for our children.

While this is going on, competition is having
4) an equally toxic effect on our relationships. By definition, not everyone can win a contest. That means that each child inevitably comes to regard others as obstacles to his or her own success. Competition leads children to envy winners, to dismiss losers (there's no nastier epithet in our language than "loser!"), and to be suspicious of just about everyone. Competition makes it difficult to regard others as potential friends or collaborators; even if you're not my rival today, you could be tomorrow.

This is not to say that competitors will always detest one another. But trying to outdo someone is not conducive to trust—indeed it would be irrational to trust a person who gains from your failure. At best, competition leads one to look at others through narrowed eyes; at worst, it invites outright aggression.

Changing the Structure of Sports

Conclusion

New idea that confirms his claim

But no matter how many bad feelings erupt during competition, we have a marvelous talent for blaming the individuals rather than focusing on the structure of the game itself, a structure that makes my success depend on your failure. Cheating may just represent the logical conclusion of this arrangement rather than an aberration. And sportsmanship is nothing more than an artificial way to try to limit the damage of competition. If we weren't set against each other on the court or the track, we wouldn't need to keep urging people to be good sports; they might well be working *with* each other in the first place.

As radical or surprising as it may sound, the 15
problem isn't just that we compete the wrong way or that we push winning on our children too early. The problem is competition itself. What we need to be teaching our daughters and sons is that it's possible to have a good time—a better time—without turning the playing field into a battlefield.

Analysis

The pattern of organization in this essay is primarily a *defense of the main idea*—that competitive sports are psychologically unhealthy. But because the author knows that competitive sports are hugely popular, not only in the United States but in many other parts of the world, he must also try to *refute the opposing view*—that competition is rewarding and enjoyable. In doing so, Kohn fails to make clear distinctions between competitive sports for children, who may find it difficult to accept defeat, and for adults, who understand the consequences of any competitive game and are psychologically equipped to deal with them. Readers may therefore share Kohn's misgivings about competition for children but doubt that his criteria apply equally to adults.

The *claim,* expressed as the *thesis statement* of the essay, appears at the end of paragraph 4: "recreation at its best does not require people to try to triumph over others. Quite to the contrary." The three-paragraph introduction recounts a relevant personal experience as well as the reasons that prompted Kohn to write his essay. Because we are all interested in stories, the recital of a personal experience is a popular device for introducing almost any subject.

The rest of the essay, until the last two paragraphs, is devoted to summarizing the benefits of cooperative play and the disadvantages of competitive sport. The emphasis is overwhelmingly on the disadvantages as stated in the third paragraph: "competition undermines self-esteem, poisons relationships, and holds us back from doing our best." This is the *warrant,* the assumption that underlies the claim. In fact, here Kohn is referring to a larger study that he wrote about competition in workplaces and classrooms. We must accept this broad generalization, which applies to many human activities, before we can agree that the claim about competition in sports is valid.

Kohn relies for support on examples from common experience and on the work of Terry Orlick, a sports psychologist. The examples from experience are ones that most of us will recognize. Here we are in a position to judge for ourselves, without the mediation of an expert, whether the influence of competition in sports is as hurtful as Kohn insists. Orlick's research suggests a solution—adaptations of familiar games that will provide enjoyment but avoid competition. On the other hand, the results from studies by one psychologist whose work we aren't able to verify and the mention of "studies" in paragraph 3 without further attribution are probably not enough to answer all the arguments in favor of competition. Critics may also ask if Kohn has offered support for one of his contentions—that competition "holds us back from doing our best" (para. 3). (Support for this may appear in one of Kohn's books.)

The last two paragraphs sum up his argument that "the problem is competition itself" (para. 15)—the structure of the game rather than the people who play. Notice that this summary does not merely repeat the main idea. Like many thoughtful summaries, it also offers a new idea about good sportsmanship that confirms his conclusion.

The language is clear and direct. Kohn's article, which appeared in a women's sports magazine, is meant for the educated general reader, not the expert. This is also the audience for whom most student papers are written. But the written essay need not be unduly formal. Kohn uses contractions and the personal pronouns *I* and *you* to establish a conversational context. One of the particular strengths of his style is the skillful use of transitional expressions, words like *this* and *also* and clauses like *This is not to say that* and *Note the significance of* to make connections between paragraphs and new ideas.

The tone is temperate despite the author's strong feelings about the subject. Other authors, supporting the same argument, have used language that borders on the abusive about coaches and trainers of children's games. But a less inflammatory voice is far more effective with an audience that may be neutral or antagonistic.

You will find it helpful to look back over the essay to see how the examples we've cited and others work to fulfill the writer's purpose.

Writer's Guide: Annotating a Text

One purpose of annotating a text is to comprehend it more fully. Another is to prepare to write about it.

1. If you use a highlighter as you read a text, use it sparingly. Highlighting too much of a text is not very useful when it comes time to review what you have marked. You might consider a more targeted approach to highlighting, focusing only on thesis statement and topic sentences in an essay, for example, or on conclusions in a report.
2. More useful than highlighting is making marginal notes, perhaps underlining the portion of the text that each note refers to. With underlining as with highlighting, however, increased quantity equals decreased usefulness. Some of the most useful marginal notes will be those that summarize key

ideas in your own words. Such paraphrases force you to understand the text well enough to reword its ideas, and reading the marginal notes is a quick way to review the text when you do not have time to reread all of it.

3. If you are making notes both on what a piece of writing says and how it says it, you may want to place marginal notes about content on one side of the text and those about rhetorical strategies on the other. Notations about how a piece is written can focus on structural devices such as topic sentences, transitional words or phrases, and the repetition of ideas or sentence structure but also on rhetorical concerns such as identifying the claim, support, and warrant; the tone; and the types of appeal.
4. As you annotate a text, you may also want to make note of questions you still have after having read the text. These questions may be the basis for class discussion.
5. You may also find it useful to note similarities that you see between the text you are reading and others you have read or between the text and your own experience.

PRACTICE

Using the annotations on Kohn's "No-Win Situations" as a model, respond to the following essay not primarily in terms of its ideas but in terms of the way it is written.

"Freak dancing": If Only It Stopped There

DESDA MOSS

With prom season approaching, some adults who haven't been to a school dance since the Hustle was the hot craze might need a lesson to prepare them for what's happening in gymnasiums across the nation.

It goes by many names and has been a growing trend in recent years. Some call it "freak dancing." Some call it grinding. Some call it booty dancing. Parents who see it for the first time generally call it, well, disgusting, and find it more than a little disturbing. (I won't explore the Freudian reasons why seeing kids in braces simulating sex is disturbing to grown-ups; check your local listings for *Dr. Phil.*) A friend of mine who recently attended a "sweet 16" birthday party observed partygoers engaging in moves that would make a lap dancer blush.

Desda Moss is a freelance writer in Virginia. This article appeared on April 7, 2005, on USA Today.com.

To be sure, dancing has always been risky business—from the forbidden passions of the Lambada to the hip-shaking roots of rock 'n' roll—every generation seems to have created a hormone-driven dance du jour. But with modesty and subtlety in short supply in our hypersexualized society, today's teens seem to be testing the limits of decency with unprecedented vigor. In some communities, schools have banned overtly suggestive dancing altogether.

As expected, that has set off a new round of intergenerational snipping, with parents and other authority figures being accused of overreacting and trouncing on the right of free expression. After all, some contend, it's only dancing. Others point out that what teens today are doing is no different from the slow dragging their middle-aged parents did in their day under the glow of blue lights in the basement.

5 I spent my teen years watching *Soul Train*, following every dance move and hoping to duplicate them after practicing for hours in my living room. Often, my dad would watch the show with me and offer comments. "Looks like maggots in a bucket," he'd say.

His own style was more one of restrained grace. His footwork was a study in cool, minimalist movement. It was only the look of pure bliss that revealed he was in the zone.

My late father didn't live to see the freak dancing trend hold. But should anyone be inclined to get their knickers in a twist over this latest form of teen rebellion, I would advise them to consider the findings of a new study in this month's edition of *Pediatrics*. It suggests we have bigger issues to deal with than mere simulated sex. It found that about one in five ninth-graders surveyed (we're talking 14-year-olds) reported they'd had oral sex. Almost a third said they'd like to try it within the next six months. Finally, this: 13 percent of the participants reported that they'd had intercourse.

Now that's something to freak about.

RESPONDING AS A CRITICAL LISTENER

Of course, not all public arguments are written. Oral arguments on radio and television now enjoy widespread popularity and influence. In fact, their proliferation means that we listen far more than we talk, read, or write. Today the art of listening has become an indispensable tool for learning about the world we live in. One informed critic predicts that the dissemination of information and opinions through the electronic media will "enable more and more Americans to participate directly in making the laws and policies by which they are governed."[4]

[4] Lawrence K. Grossman, *The Electronic Republic: Reshaping Democracy in the Information Age* (New York: Viking, 1995).

Because we are interested primarily in arguments about public issues—those that involve democratic decision making—we will not be concerned with the afternoon television talk shows that are largely devoted to personal problems. (Occasionally, however, *Oprah* introduces topics of broad social significance.) More relevant to the kinds of written arguments you will read and write about in this course are the television and radio shows that also examine social and political problems. The most intelligent and responsible programs usually consist of a panel of experts—politicians, journalists, scholars—led by a neutral moderator (or one who, at least, allows guests to express their views). Some of these programs are decades old; others are more recent—*Meet the Press, Face the Nation, Hardball with Chris Matthews, The McLaughlin Group, The NewsHour with Jim Lehrer*. An outstanding radio show, *Talk of the Nation* on National Public Radio, invites listeners, who are generally informed and articulate, to call in and ask questions of, or comment on remarks made by, experts on the topic of the day.

Several enormously popular radio talk shows are hosted by people with strong, sometimes extreme ideological positions. They may use offensive language and insult their listeners in a crude form of theater. Among the most influential shows are those of Don Imus and Howard Stern. In addition, elections and political crises bring speeches and debates on radio and television by representatives of a variety of views. Some are long and formal, written texts that are simply read aloud, but others are short and impromptu.

Whatever the merits or shortcomings of individual programs, significant general differences exist between arguments on radio and television and arguments in the print media. These differences include the degree of organization and development and the risk of personal attacks.

First (excluding for the moment the long, prepared speeches), contributions to a panel discussion must be delivered in fragments, usually no longer than a single paragraph, weakened by time constraints, interruptions, overlapping speech, memory gaps, and real or feigned displays of derision, impatience, and disbelief by critical panelists. Even on the best programs, the result is a lack of both coherence—or connections between ideas—and solid evidence that requires development. Too often we are treated to conclusions with little indication of how they were arrived at.

The following brief passage appeared in a newspaper review of "Resolved: The flat tax is better than the income tax," a debate on *Firing Line* by an impressive array of experts. It illustrates some of the difficulties that accompany programs attempting to capture the truth of a complicated issue on television or radio.

> "It is absolutely true," says a proponent. "It is factually untrue," counters an opponent. "It's factually correct," responds a proponent. "I did my math right," says a proponent. "You didn't do your math right," says an opponent. At one point in a discussion of interest income, one of the experts says, "Oh, excuse me, I think I got it backward."

No wonder the television critic called the exchange "disjointed and at times perplexing."[5]

In the sensational talk shows the participants rely on personal experience and vivid anecdotes, which may not be sufficiently typical to prove anything.

Second, listeners and viewers of all spoken arguments are in danger of evaluating them according to criteria that are largely absent from evaluation of written texts. It is true that writers may adopt a persona or a literary disguise, which the tone of the essay will reflect. But many read-

STRATEGIES FOR CRITICAL LISTENING

Listening is hearing with attention, a natural and immensely important human activity, which, unfortunately, many people don't do very well. The good news is that listening is a skill that can be learned and, unlike some other skills, practiced every day without big investments of money and effort.

Here are some of the characteristics of critical listening most appropriate to understanding and responding to arguments.

1. Above all, listening to arguments requires concentration. If you are distracted, you cannot go back as you do with the written word to clarify a point or recover a connection. Devices such as flow sheets and outlines can be useful aids to concentration. In following a debate, for example, judges and other listeners often use flow sheets — distant cousins of baseball scorecards — to record the major points on each side and their rebuttals. For roundtable discussions or debates you can make your own simple flow chart to fill out as you listen, with columns for claims, different kinds of support, and warrants. Leave spaces in the margin for your questions and comments about the soundness of the proof. An outline is more useful for longer presentations, such as lectures. As you listen, try to avoid being distracted by facts alone. Look for the overall pattern of the speech.
2. Listeners often concentrate on the wrong things in the spoken argument. We have already noted the distractions of appearance and delivery. Research shows that listeners are likely to give greater attention to the dramatic elements of speeches than to the logical ones. But you can enjoy the sound, the appearance, and the drama of a spoken argument without allowing these elements to overwhelm what is essential to the development of a claim.
3. Good listeners try not to allow their prejudices to prevent careful evaluation of the argument. This doesn't mean accepting everything or even most of what you hear. It means trying to avoid premature judgments about what is actually said. This precaution is especially relevant when the speakers and their views are well known and the listener has already formed an opinion about them, favorable or unfavorable.

[5]Walter Goodman, "The Joys of the Flat Tax, Excluding the Equations," *New York Times*, December 21, 1995, sec. C, p. 14.

ers will not be able to identify it or recognize their own response to it. Listeners and viewers, however, can hardly avoid being affected by characteristics that are clearly definable: a speaker's voice, delivery, bodily mannerisms, dress, and physical appearance. In addition, listeners may be adversely influenced by clumsy speech containing more slang, colloquialisms, and grammar and usage errors than written texts that have had the benefit of revision.

But if listeners allow consideration of physical attributes to influence their judgment of what the speaker is trying to prove, they are guilty of an ad hominem fallacy—that is, an evaluation of the speaker rather than the argument. This is true whether the evaluation is favorable or unfavorable. (See p. 341 for a discussion of this fallacy.)

Talk shows may indeed be disjointed and perplexing, but millions of us find them both instructive and entertaining. Over time we are exposed to an astonishing variety of opinions from every corner of American life, and we also acquire information from experts who might not otherwise be available to us. Then there is the appeal of hearing the voices, seeing the faces of people engaged in earnest, sometimes passionate, discourse—a short, unrehearsed drama in which we also play a part as active listeners in a far-flung audience.

ASSIGNMENTS FOR READING AND LISTENING CRITICALLY

READING AND DISCUSSION QUESTIONS

1. Consider the claim that Desda Moss is supporting in "'Freak Dancing': If Only It Stopped There." How valid do you consider that claim to be, and why?
2. Listen to a recording of Martin Luther King Jr.'s "I Have a Dream" and discuss how the language of the speech adds power to the ideas.
3. Watch (and *listen to*) one of the afternoon television talk shows like *Oprah* in which guests discuss a controversial social problem. (The *TV Guide*, daily newspapers, and online listings often list the subject. Past topics on *Oprah* include when parents abduct their children, when children kill children, and when surgery changes patients' lives.) Analyze the discussion, considering the major claims, the most important evidence, and the declared or hidden warrants. How much did the oral format contribute to success or failure of the arguments?
4. Watch one episode of either the *Daily Show with Jon Stewart* or the *Colbert Report* and discuss how the show, successfully or not, tries to use humor to make serious points about political and/or social issues.

WRITING SUGGESTIONS

5. Write an essay responding as a writer to "Sex and the Cinema." You may choose to support an evaluative claim that analyzes how effective the essay is or one that objectively analyzes how the essay is written.
6. Write an essay evaluating "'Freak Dancing': If Only It Stopped There."
7. Write a critical response to the Declaration of Independence.
8. Do you agree with Alfie Kohn in "No-Win Situations" that games and sports should not be so competitive? Write an essay explaining why or why not.
9. Choose an editorial from your school newspaper or a local newspaper and write an evaluation of it.
10. Listen to one of the television talk shows that feature experts on social and political issues. Choose a show such as the *O'Reilly Factor, Hannity and Colmes*, or *The McLaughlin Group*. Write a review, telling how much you learned about the subject(s) of discussion. Be specific about the features of the show that were either helpful or unhelpful to your understanding.
11. Given Charles Adams's criticism of Lincoln's "Gettysburg Address" what could you say in its defense? Explain in an essay why this short speech has become a classic when so many others have not.

CHAPTER 3

Reading Visual Texts Critically

RESPONDING TO A VISUAL ARGUMENT

> Man has been communicating by pictures longer than he has been using words. With the development of photography in this century we are using pictures as a means of communication to such an extent that in some areas they overshadow verbal language.[1]

Paul Wendt wrote these words long before the digital age. Now we can snap pictures with our cell phones and send them to the other side of the world. Most elementary school children know how to use *Google* or another search engine to find pictures of almost anything imaginable, and by middle school they know how to go to *YouTube* to see thousands of amateur videos or to submit their own.

Wendt was writing, however, about the persuasive power of pictures, or pictures as argument. The nation saw the power of the visual in the 2008 presidential campaign when questions for the candidates came for the first time in the form of video clips submitted via *YouTube*—and campaigns may never be the same. Questions were not merely read by a moderator or asked by a panel of journalists. They didn't come in the form of disembodied voices over a telephone line. They came from real people who were visible on the screen to the candidates and to the whole country. Two women looked straight into the camera and asked the candidates if they would let them get married to each other. A snowman asked about global warming and what it would mean to his son's future. A young man asked what they could do

[1]Paul Wendt, "The Language of Pictures," in S. I. Hayakawa, ed., *The Use and Misuse of Language* (Greenwich, Conn.: Fawcett, 1962), p. 175.

to protect his "baby" and held up an assault rifle. The visual images did not replace the verbal language, but complemented it. They were an integral part of the argument.

You've probably seen similarly powerful still images in photographic journalism: soldiers in battle, destruction by weather disasters, beautiful natural landscapes, inhumane living conditions, the great mushroom cloud of early atomic explosions. These photographs and thousands of others encapsulate arguments of fact, value, and policy. We often don't need to read their captions to understand what they tell us: *The tornado devastated the town. The Grand Canyon is our most stupendous national monument. We must not allow human beings to live like this.*

An exception would be a pair of pictures that gained wide circulation in the aftermath of Hurricane Katrina in 2005. They seemed innocuous enough when seen without commentary, except to show the extent of the flooding. One shows a young black man wading through the chest-deep floodwaters carrying a black garbage bag. Another shows a young white man also wading through chest-deep water, wearing a backpack and accompanied by a young white woman wearing a backpack and dragging a bag. The text accompanying the pictures, however, shows the bias of those who described the pictures. Next to the picture of the black youth are these words: "A young man walks through chest deep water after looting a grocery store in New Orleans on Tuesday, August 30, 2005." Notice the difference in the words accompanying the other picture: "Two residents wade through chest deep flood water after finding bread and soda from a local grocery store after Hurricane Katrina came through the area in New Orleans, Louisiana." The wording produced such a response that *Yahoo!* offered this statement:

> News photos are an especially popular section of Yahoo! News. In part, this is because we present thousands of news photos from some of the leading news services, including The Associated Press, Reuters, and Agence France Press. To make this volume of photos available in a timely manner, we present the photos and their captions as written, edited and distributed by the news services with no additional editing at Yahoo! News.
>
> In recent days, a number of readers of Yahoo! News have commented on differences in the language in two Hurricane Katrina-related photo captions (from two news services). Since the controversy began, the supplier of one of the photos has asked all its clients to remove the photo from their databases. Yahoo! News has complied with the AFP request. . . . Yahoo! News regrets that these photos and captions, viewed together, may have suggested a racial bias on our part. We remain committed to bringing our readers the full collection of photos as transmitted by our wire service partners.[2]

Other images provided additional glimpses into the aftermath of Katrina. The photograph of Milvertha Hendricks was striking enough that

[2]The Yahoo! News statement can be found at http://news.yahoo.com/page/photostatement.

"Looting" and "finding"

David Dante Troutt, Charles Ogletree, and Derrick Bell used a color version of it for the cover photo of their book, *After the Storm: Black Intellectuals Explore the Meaning of Hurricane Katrina.*

PRACTICE

1. Look closely at the photograph of a flag-draped woman taken following Hurricane Katrina. Who is pictured? What sort of expression does she have on her face? Then consider why the elderly woman might have a blanket that looks like an American flag draped over her. What do you know about the rescue of Katrina victims that might be relevant to how you "read" the picture as an argument? Under the circumstances, how might the flag blanket be seen as symbolic? What claim might you infer from the picture?
2. Now compare the picture to the next photo, "At the Time of the Louisville Flood," taken in 1937 by Margaret Bourke-White. Do you see any similarity in the message being conveyed by each? Explain.
3. Finally, look at the third picture and decide if you feel it conveys a similar or a very different message.

Edgar Hollingsworth, the seventy-four-year-old man shown being rescued in the third picture, snapped by Bruce Chambers of the *Orange County Register,* survived the hurricane but was found near death in his home fourteen days after the storm. He died four days later in the hospital.

The reactions this third picture has elicited provide an excellent illustration of varied responses to the same visual image. Not every viewer will "read" a picture in the same way. Not every viewer will see it as support for the same argument. These are some of the responses that the picture of Hollingsworth's rescue has produced:

- A typical headline accompanying the photo called the discovery of Hollingsworth a "miracle rescue." According to a report from Post-Gazette.com, "The rescue was a bright spot on a day in which the owners of a nursing home were charged in the deaths of dozens of patients killed by hurricane floodwaters, the death toll in Louisiana jumped to 423 and the New Orleans mayor warned that the city is broke."[3] And according to Keith Sharon of the *Orange County Register,* "The rescue pumped up the spirits of [California] Task Force 5, which has been mostly marking the locations of dead bodies for the last week."[4]
- *USA Today* termed the photo "iconic."[5] Marcia Prouse, director of photography at the *Orange County Register,* had a similar view: "This man's story needs to be told. He's an important symbol of the hurricane. . . . It's anybody's father or grandfather."[6]

[3] See http://www.post-gazette.com/pg/05257/570999.stm.
[4] See http://www.ocregister.com/blog/rescue/.
[5] See http://www.usatoday.com/news/nation/2005-11-10-hollingsworth-katrina_x.htm.
[6] See http://www.editorandpublisher.com/eandp/news/article_display.jsp?vnu_content_id=1001137369.

Eric Gay, "Milvertha Hendricks, 84, waiting in the rain outside the New Orleans Convention Center on September 1, 2005"

- Chambers's picture has become known through Internet chat as the *Katrina Pietá*. The *Pietá* alluded to is Michelangelo's famous sculpture of Mary holding the body of Christ after his crucifixion. The way that the National Guardsman is holding Hollingsworth is reminiscent

Margaret Bourke-White, "At the Time of the Louisville Flood" (1937)

Bruce Chambers, "Edgar Hollingsworth rescued from his home after Hurricane Katrina" (2005)

of Mary's pose, and the link to the loving mother of Jesus leads to a positive interpretation of the scene.

- For some, the sight of two white aid workers and one Hispanic one aiding a black man provides a sharp contrast to other images that stress the racial tension that grew out of Katrina's aftermath.
- Others were enraged by rules that could have kept the rescue team from entering Hollingsworth's home to rescue him. Keith Sharon wrote, "In the past few days, the Federal Emergency Management Agency has ordered searchers not to break into homes. They are supposed to look in through a window and knock on the door. If no one cries out for help, they are supposed to move on. If they see a body, they are supposed to log the address and move on." The rescue team went against orders in breaking down the door to reach Hollingsworth. Sharon added that earlier "they had been frustrated when FEMA delayed their deployment for four days, housing them in the Hyatt Regency in Dallas."[7] The Sharon quotes are referenced on DailyKOS.com, under the title "American Shame: The Edgar Hollingsworth Story."[8]

Just as readers bring to an argument their biases and their own personal store of experiences, so do viewers bring the same to a visual argument.

Photographs, of course, function everywhere as instruments of persuasion. Animal-rights groups show pictures of brutally mistreated dogs and cats; children's rights advocates publish pictures of sick and starving children in desolate refugee camps. On a very different scale, alluring photographs from advertisers—travel agencies, restaurants, sporting goods manufacturers, clothiers, jewelers, movie studios—promise to fulfill our dreams of pleasure.

But photographs are not the only visual images we respond to. We are also susceptible to other kinds of illustrations and to signs and symbols which over the years have acquired connotations, or suggestive significance. The flag or bald eagle, the shamrock, the crown, the cross, the hammer and sickle, and the swastika can all rouse strong feelings for or against the ideas they represent. These symbols may be defined as abbreviated claims of value. They summarize the moral, religious, and political principles by which groups of people live and often die. In commercial advertisements we recognize symbols that aren't likely to enlist our deepest loyalties but, nevertheless, have impact on our daily lives: the apple with a bite in it, the golden arches, the Prudential rock, the Nike swoosh, and a thousand others.

[7] Keith Sharon, "Survivor Rescued 16 Days after the Hurricane," *Orange County Register*, September 14, 2005.

[8] See www.dailykos.com/story/2005/9/14/12516/3649.

In fact, a closer look at commercial and political advertising, which is heavily dependent on visual argument and is something we are all familiar with, provides a useful introduction to this complex subject. We know that advertisements, with or without pictures, are short arguments, often lacking fully developed support, whose claims of policy urge us to take an action: Buy this product or service; vote for this candidate or issue. The claim may not be directly expressed, but it will be clearly implicit. In print, on television, or on the Internet, the visual representation of objects, carefully chosen to appeal to a particular audience, can be as important as, if not more important than, any verbal text.

PRACTICE

Analyze the argument being made by the advertisement on page 69. Consider these questions:

1. Why is the gun so much larger than the printed message below it?
2. What claim of policy is this ad making?
3. Would that claim be as successful if the note were excluded? Why, or why not?
4. Would additional facts about guns make the ad more effective?
5. What is the basis of the emotional appeal? Is there more than one?
6. Does the ad go too far in exploiting our emotions?

In a political advertisement we often see a picture of the candidate surrounded by a smiling family. The visual image is by now a cliché, suggesting traditional values—love and security, the importance of home and children. Even if we know little or nothing about his or her platform, we are expected to make a sympathetic connection with the candidate.

In a commercial advertisement the image may be a picture of a real or fictitious person to whom we will react favorably. Consider the picture on a jar of spaghetti sauce. As a famous designer remarked, "When you think about it, sauce is mostly sauce. It's the label that makes the difference."[9] And what, according to the designer, does the cheerful face of Paul Newman on jars of his spaghetti sauce suggest to the prospective buyer? "Paul Newman. Paul Newman. Paul Newman. Blue eyes. All the money goes to charity. It's humanitarian, funny, and sexy. Selling this is like falling off a log." Not a word about the quality of the sauce.

Even colleges, which are also selling a product, must think of appropriate images to attract their prospective customers—students. Today the fact that more women than men are enrolled in college has caused some schools to rethink their images. One college official explained:

[9]Tibor Kalman, "Message: Sweet-Talking Spaghetti Sauce," *New York Times Magazine*, December 13, 1998, p. 81.

West Monroe, LA.
Matilda Crabtree, 14.
Shot and killed by
father when she jumped
from closet and yelled
"Boo" to scare parents.
Last words: "I love
you, daddy."
A gun in the home is much more likely to
kill a family member than to kill an intruder.
CEASE FIRE
Think about your family before you think about getting a handgun.
Cease Fire, Inc. P.O. Box 33424, Washington, D.C. 20033-0424.

> We're having our recruiting literature redesigned, and we've been thinking about what's a feminine look and what's a masculine look. We have a picture of a library with a lot of stained glass, and people said that was kind of a feminine cover. Now we're using a picture of the quadrangle.[10]

In addition to the emblem itself, the designer pays careful attention to a number of other elements in the ad: colors, light and shadow, foreground and background, relative sizes of pictures and text, and placement of objects on the page or screen. Each of these contributes to the total effect, although we may be unaware of how the effect has been achieved. (In the ad that follows, you will be able to examine some of the psychological and aesthetic devices at work.)

When there is no verbal text, visual images are less subject to analysis and interpretation. For one thing, if we are familiar with the objects in the picture, we see the whole image at once, and it registers immediately. The verbal message is linear and takes far longer to be absorbed. Pictures, therefore, appear to need less translation. Advertisers and other arguers depend on this characteristic to provide quick and friendly acceptance of their claims, although the image may, in fact, be deceptive.

This expectation of easy understanding poses a danger with another visual ally of the arguer—the graph or chart. Graphics give us factual information at a glance. In addition to the relative ease with which they can be read, they are "at their best . . . instruments for reasoning about quantitative information. . . . Of all methods for analyzing and communicating statistical information, well-designed data graphics are usually the simplest and at the same time the most powerful."[11]

Nevertheless, they may mislead the quick reader. Graphics can lie. "The lies are told about the major issues of public policy—the government budget, medical care, prices, and fuel economy standards, for example. The lies are systematic and quite predictable, nearly always exaggerating the rate of recent change."[12]

Visual images, then, for all their apparent immediacy and directness, need to be read with at least the same attention we give to the verbal message if we are to understand the arguments they represent.

Consider these questions as you analyze images:

1. What does the arguer want me to do or believe? How important is the visual image in persuading me to comply?
2. Has the visual image been accompanied by sufficient text to answer questions I may have about the claim?

[10] *New York Times,* December 6, 1998, p. 38.

[11] Edward R. Tufte, *The Visual Display of Quantitative Information* (Cheshire, Conn.: Graphics Press, 1983), introduction.

[12] Tufte, *The Visual Display,* p. 76.

3. Are the visual elements more prominent than the text? If so, why?
4. Is the visual image representative of a large group, or is it an exception that cannot support the claim?
5. Does the arrangement of elements in the message tell me what the arguer considers most important? If so, what is the significance of this choice?
6. Can the validity of this chart or graph be verified?
7. Does the visual image lead me to entertain unrealistic expectations? (Can using this shampoo make hair look like that shining cascade on the television screen? Does the picture of the candidate for governor, shown answering questions in a classroom of eager, smiling youngsters, mean that he has a viable plan for educational reform?)

Sample Analysis of an Advertisement

We have pointed out that a commercial advertisement is a short argument that makes an obvious policy claim, which may or may not be explicit: *You should buy this product.* Depending on the medium—television, print, radio, or Internet—an ad may convey its message through language, picture, or sound.

Here is how one analyst of advertising sums up the goals of the advertiser: (1) attract attention, (2) arouse interest, (3) stimulate desire, (4) create conviction, and (5) get action.[13] Needless to say, not every ad successfully fulfills all these objectives. If you examine the ad reproduced on page 72, you can see how the advertiser brings language and visual image together in an attempt to support the claim.

The image in the ad appeals to our common knowledge as Americans. We have probably all heard the story of how George Washington, as a boy, chopped down a cherry tree. The clothes that the young boy in the ad is wearing—particularly the tricorner hat—along with the architecture, suggest a colonial setting. The hatchet hidden behind the boy's back combined with the exclamation "Oops!" calls to mind the specific story about Washington. Upon hearing the story, you may have envisioned a much smaller tree and less substantial damage, but it is critical to the ad's effect that in this rendering of the story of our first president's youth, the tree has fallen on someone's house, possibly the Washingtons'. The ad appears to have been reproduced on parchment, another detail that helps to place the incident historically, and each corner is subtly decorated with a cherry.

What has made the cherry tree story a classic for teaching morals is what the young Washington is said to have done after he chopped down the tree. All of us are familiar with the words "I can not tell a lie," Washington's response when questioned about what he had done. It was a fitting

[13] J. V. Lund, *Newspaper Advertising* (New York: Prentice-Hall, 1947), p. 83.

reply for a man who would later be chosen to lead the new nation. The largest text on the page—and the text most likely therefore to catch the attention of a reader casually flipping through *Newsweek*—is a play on this famous quote that changes *I* to *we*. The identification with Washington and his famous words is particularly critical for a company whose name may not be a household word. The designers of the ad, having captured the attention of the reader with the image and the quote, go on in the smaller text to build on the foundation they have established.

Like most ads, this one is a claim of policy asking the audience to buy a product. In this case the product is Encompass Insurance. One of the frustrations of dealing with an insurance company is that not every possible type of loss is covered by the standard policy. Unfortunately, the homeowner often does not find this out until the damage has already been done. The ad is designed to sell the company's *Elite* policy, which "covers many of life's unexpected perils," unlike most insurance companies, which "only cover things that are specifically listed in your policy." The text continues, "It covers pretty much everything that befalls your household, even if something like 'damage caused by child chopping down cherry tree' isn't specifically listed." Two examples of the sorts of damage that the company might cover are Worker's Compensation for an employee in your household and the recovery of lost computer data.

The support for the claim is not specific. The writer carefully avoided absolute statements, using instead such qualifiers as *many, pretty much,* and *most everything*. The last two are colloquial expressions that are designed to suggest that those who work for Encompass are simple folks with whom the average reader could identify. And if you want any more specifics about what the policy actually says—after all, the legal document that is an insurance policy can hardly use such qualifiers—you can call toll-free or visit the company's Web site.

The underlying warrant is that it is better to buy an insurance policy that covers you against damages that are not specifically listed on the policy than one that does not. A person in the market for insurance would certainly want to read the fine print and know the cost of the insurance compared to that offered by other companies before accepting the warrant and thus the claim.

The colloquial language and even the name of the policy—The Encompass Universal Security Policy—Elite—are designed to appeal to the reader's need to feel secure. The word choice also adds a subtle humor, from the cartoonlike "Oops!" to the final echo of the Pledge of Allegiance: "Liberty, Justice, and Really Good Insurance."

■ Sample Analysis of a Web Site

The Internet provides an important forum for individuals and organizations to make arguments. Through the Internet, anyone with access to a networked computer can potentially publish his or her ideas. While this ease of publication is exciting, it also means writers hoping to obtain reliable information from the Web need to read Web sites critically (see Prereading Strategies on page 32 for further insight into this issue).

With new genres being created daily, some researchers have noted five major types of Web pages:[14]

[14] See, for example, the Widener University Wolfgram Memorial Library Web site at http://www2.widener.edu/Wolfgram-Memorial-Library/webevaluation/webeval.htm.

1. *Advocacy Web Pages:* Advocacy pages are typically created by not-for-profit organizations wishing to influence public opinion, and the URL for the site is likely to contain the domain suffix *.org* (organization).
2. *Business/Marketing Web Pages:* The majority of businesses in the United States have a Web presence today, and most business pages are either advertising or provide online opportunities to purchase goods and services. The addresses for such sites typically contain the domain suffix *.com* (for commercial).
3. *News Web Pages:* News pages provide current information on local, national, and international events. The addresses for news sites also contain the abbreviation *.com,* reflecting the fact that the news industry is also a business.
4. *Informational Web Pages:* Informational pages provide data such as that found in dictionaries or atlases. The addresses for these sites sometimes include *.edu* (university), *.k12* (primary or secondary school), or *.gov* (government) because they are often sponsored by academic institutions or government agencies.
5. *Personal Web Pages:* Personal pages are created by individuals, and can be intimate, entertaining, informative, bizarre, or some combination of these things. While the addresses for personal sites can end in *.com, .edu, .k12, .org,* or *.gov,* the presence of a tilde (~) in the address suggests that the page represents an individual.

On page 75 is a copy of the home page for *The Hunger Site.* At first glance, the site appears to be a combination informational page (because it presents facts about world hunger) and business/marketing page (because it advertises a variety of products). It is in fact both of these things as well as a site for philanthropy (since advertisers' money pays for the food).

The significance of charitable giving to the site's mission is suggested by several things. Most directly, a viewer's eye is immediately drawn to the text at the top of the page that exclaims, "Click to Give FREE Food!" and to a gold icon reading "Click Here to Give—it's FREE." The icon appears in the upper right portion of the ad and draws the eye with its color and placement. It also presents an appealing prospect to readers: that they can be generous by supporting a significant cause and do so without spending money (the food is "free"). When you click on the icon, *The Hunger Site* donates 1.1 cups of food (or the financial equivalent) to the hungry. The large picture at the bottom of the opening screen of the site changes over time but through text and images emphasizes the need to fight hunger worldwide.

The emphasis on giving is furthered by the three links to the left of the gold icon: "1. You click daily. 2. Sponsors pay for cups of food. 3. Shop our store and give more." Two buttons below the icon and this list give the reader the chance to register, and in doing so to provide more food to the hungry, and to e-mail friends an electronic card with prewritten statis-

The Hunger Site Home Page

tics and other information provided by *The Hunger Site*. In this way, viewers become coauthors with the authors of the site in writing the card's text.

Down the left side of the home page are similar links: "Free Ways to Help," "Our Store Helps More," and "About This Site." Clicking on any of the list of items sold online through the site gives the reader more opportunities to provide food for others, opportunities linked to purchasing products. Buying a T-shirt, for instance, will mean an additional twenty-five cups of food provided by the merchant. Some of the less traditional "products" are items like shoes for children in another country or schooling for girls in a traditionally male-dominated region.

It is this connection that links *The Hunger Site* to business interests, interests highlighted by the *.com* in the site's URL. Though donations can be given without spending money, the site also links consumer needs and desires to philanthropy by providing visitors the opportunity to support the hungry by purchasing a wide variety of goods—from clothing to flowers to seasonal gifts and decorations. Consumer givers, then, can feel good that the money they are spending is contributing to a valuable cause. In this way, viewers feel inspired to shop more, meaning that *The Hunger Site* has the potential to bind together corporate interests, consumer interests, and international benevolence.

In many ways, then, *The Hunger Site* reads like a traditional advertisement. It appeals to customers because it represents an easy way to do something

The Hunger Site Thank You Page

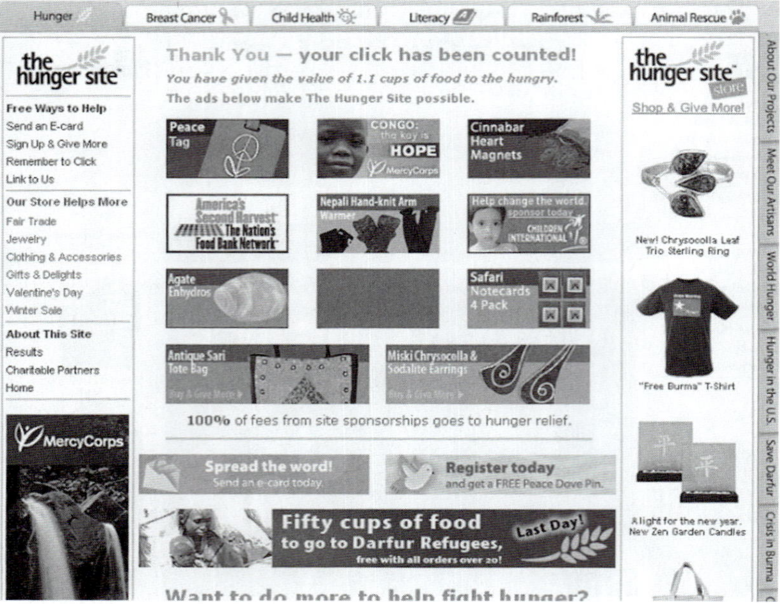

socially responsible. To develop customer loyalty, businesses and organizations strive for "brand recognition," and *The Hunger Site* is no exception. It uses a golden strand of wheat as its logo. Gold, symbolizing both wheat and true value, is the color of the icon that allows browsers to contribute food with a single click.

Distinguishing *The Hunger Site* from traditional print text is its embeddedness in a "web" of other pages. Through tabs down the right side of the page, *The Hunger Site* links directly to pages that provide additional information about the site as well as sales and charitable giving opportunities. Some pages are official parts of *The Hunger Site;* others such as *Save Darfur,* which receives donations from *The Hunger Site,* are separate sites.

One aim of a comprehensive Web site is to provide answers to questions about the site. Unlike a print advertisement, *The Hunger Site* has enough space to provide, for example, information about *The Hunger Site*'s projects and artisans. Readers interested in more information on *The Hunger Site* can do a general search of the Web to determine the legitimacy of the site.

Although it consists of multiple pages, *The Hunger Site* is also different from printed articles and books because it does not follow any traditional sense of order. Readers typically start on the site's home page, but from there they can go in multiple directions, each one equally logical. The authors of *The Hunger Site* have not determined a set path for readers to follow: Viewers can find information about world hunger, about hunger in the United States, about the amount of food given each day and each year, about ways of providing food to the hungry, and about bargains on a range of international products. The reader is in control of the direction to be taken in the text, and the possible directions are numerous and cater to multiple needs.

RESPONDING ONLINE

You have learned that writers need the responses of readers and other writers to improve their writing. Electronic networks now allow your writing to be distributed almost instantaneously to dozens or even thousands of readers with virtually no copying or mailing costs. Readers can respond to you just as quickly and cheaply. Even though there can be pitfalls and problems with communicating online, the overall ease of use encourages writers to seek, and readers to provide, editorial feedback.

■ Guidelines for Responding Online

You know that in face-to-face conversation the words themselves constitute only a part of your message. Much of what you say is communicated through your body language and tone of voice. Written words provide a much narrower channel of communication, which is why you must be more careful when you write to others than when you speak directly to them. Electronic writing, however, especially through e-mail, fosters a casualness and immediacy that often fools writers into assuming they are talking privately rather than writing publicly. Online you may find yourself writing quickly, carelessly, and intimately; without the help of your tone and body language, you may end up being seriously misunderstood. Words written hastily are often read much differently than intended; this is especially true when the writer attempts an ironic or sarcastic tone. For example, if a classmate walks up to you with a critical comment about one of your sentences and you respond by saying "I didn't realize you were so smart," the words, if unaccompanied by a placating smile and a pleasant, jocular tone, may come across as sarcastic or hostile. In e-writing, the same words appear without the mitigating body language and may be perceived as harsh, possibly insulting. You must keep this danger in mind as you respond online or risk alienating your reader.

Keep in mind, too, that e-mail may be read not only by your addressee but also by anyone with whom the addressee chooses to share your message. An intemperate or indiscreet message may be forwarded to other classmates or your instructor, or, depending on the limits of the system, to many other readers whom you do not know.

Experienced online communicators advocate a set of network etiquette guidelines. Here are some generally accepted rules:

- Keep your sentences short and uncomplicated.
- Separate blocks of text—which should be no more than four or five lines long—by blank lines. For those rare occasions when a comment requires more than ten or fifteen consecutive lines of text, use subheadings on separate lines to guide your reader.
- Refer specifically to the text to which you are responding. You may want to quote directly from it, cutting and pasting phrases or sentences from the document to help show exactly what you are responding to.
- Greet the person(s) to whom you are writing politely and by name.
- Be wary about attempting to be funny. Humor, as just explained, often requires a context, tone of voice, and body language to emphasize that it is not to be taken seriously. Writing witty comments that are sure to be taken humorously calls for skill and care, and e-mail messages usually are written too quickly for either.
- Avoid profanity or invective, and be wary of brusque or abrupt statements. Consider how you would feel if someone wrote to you that way.
- Avoid discussion of politics or religion unless that is the specific topic of your message.
- Do not ridicule public figures. Your reader may not share your opinions of, say, Senator Edward Kennedy or Stephen Colbert.
- Frame all comments in a helpful, not critical, tone. For instance, rather than beginning a critique with "I found a number of problems in your text," you may want to start out more like this: "You have some good ideas in this paper, and with a few changes I think it will do well."

ASSIGNMENTS FOR READING VISUAL TEXTS CRITICALLY

READING AND DISCUSSION QUESTIONS

1. Steven Johnson, author of *The Ghost Map*, writes, "It has become a cliché to say that we now live in a society where image is valued over substance, where our desires are continually stoked by the illusory fuel of marketing messages." Do you believe that we live in the society Johnson describes? Explain.

2. Locate an advertisement that you find interesting visually as well as verbally. Using as a model the analysis of the ad for Encompass Insurance (p. 72), what sorts of observations can you make about your ad?
3. Exchange ads with a classmate and discuss whether the two of you respond in the same way to each ad.
4. Research *The Hunger Site* and decide for yourself how effective it is in getting food to those in need.

WRITING SUGGESTIONS

5. Choose an advertisement taking into consideration both the visual and the verbal. Turn your obsevations into the thesis of an essay explaining the ad's argument.
6. Find a picture that you believe makes a political statement and write an analysis making clear what you believe that statement is.
7. Find two pictures that present either complementary or conflicting arguments. Write an essay explaining the arguments.
8. Write an essay explaining what visual images represent your school and why.
9. Virtually every charity these days has a Web site. Choose one of these sites to analyze, using as a model the analysis of *The Hunger Site*.
10. Analyze your school's Web site and explain in an essay the image or images of your school that the site presents. Do you believe that the site presents an accurate image of the school? In other words, is the argument that it makes about the school an appropriate one? Explain.

CHAPTER 4

Writing about Argument

Anytime the press cover a major speech, whether by the president, the chairman of the Federal Reserve, or the accused party in the most recent sex scandal, their next step is an analysis of every detail of the speaker's words and manner. People not only like to listen to arguments but they also like to argue about them. Political pundit Bill O'Reilly even has an analyst come in regularly to critique the body language of political and media headliners.

An understanding of the elements of argument provides you not only with the ability to write your own arguments but also with the vocabulary to write about those of others. When you write an essay about an argument that you have read, listened to, or seen, you have two major options. You may choose to make a factual, nonjudgmental statement about the argument, or you may choose to evaluate it.

WRITING THE CLAIM

If you examined the most recent McDonald's commercial and wrote an essay explaining what tactics were used to try to persuade consumers to eat at McDonalds's or to try McDonald's newest sandwich, you would be supporting a factual claim, or a claim of fact. On the other hand, if you evaluated the ad's effectiveness in attracting adult consumers, you would be supporting an evaluative claim, or a claim of value. It's the difference between *explaining* Geico's use of a talking gecko in its ads and *praising* that marketing decision. What this means, of course, is that what you write about a commercial or any other type of argument that you see or read will itself have a claim of fact or a claim of value as its thesis.

What about a claim of policy, the third type of claim introduced in Chapter 1? In writing about an argument, it would be rare to have a thesis that expressed what should or should not be done. Claims of policy are future oriented. They do not look back and express what should have been done in the past, but instead look forward to what should be done in the future. You might write an essay about what McDonald's should do in its future ads, but you would not really be writing about an existing argument, although you might use current ads as examples.

Think how claims of fact and claims of value might serve as thesis statements for essays *about* written arguments. In Chapter 2, Charles Adams's essay "Lincoln's Logic" is a criticism of Lincoln's Gettysburg Address and thus supports a claim of value:

> Lincoln's address did not fit the world of his day. It reflected his logic, which was based on a number of errors and falsehoods.

An objective analysis of the speech, based on a claim of fact, might explain the oration in the context of its time or Lincoln's use of poetic language.

In Chapter 2, you also read the Declaration of Independence. Consider how your thesis would look different if you were making a *statement* about the document than if you were making a *judgment*:

CLAIMS OF FACT: The Declaration of Independence bases its claim on two kinds of support: factual evidence and appeals to the values of its audience.

As a logical pattern of argument, the Declaration of Independence is largely deductive.

CLAIMS OF VALUE: Jefferson's clear, elegant, formal prose remains a masterpiece of English prose and persuades us that we are reading an important document.

The document's impact is lessened for modern readers because several significant terms are not defined.

In these examples based on the Gettysburg Address and the Declaration of Independence, we were looking at one document at a time and thus at a single argument. At times you will want to compare two (or more) arguments, synthesizing their ideas. Again, there are two basic types of thesis that you might choose to support, those that *objectively analyze* the points of comparison or contrast between the two and those that *evaluate* the two in relationship to each other. If you wrote claims about how the two pieces compare, they might look like these:

CLAIMS OF FACT: Where Jefferson based his argument primarily on logical appeal, Lincoln depended primarily on emotional appeal.

Because Lincoln's purpose was to dedicate a cemetery, he left implicit most of his references to the political situation that was on the minds of his listeners. Because Jefferson knew he was justifying rebellion for King George III but also for the future, he spelled out explicitly why the colonies were breaking with England.

CLAIMS OF VALUE: Lincoln's address is a period piece that recalls a dark chapter in American history, but Jefferson's Declaration has had a much greater impact as an inspiration for other reform movements worldwide.

Different as the two historical documents are, both the Gettysburg Address and the Declaration of Independence were effective in achieving their respective purposes.

PRACTICE

1. Read the following essay and then write two different thesis statements that you could support about it, one a claim of fact and the other a claim of value.

Let's Have No More Monkey Trials

CHARLES KRAUTHAMMER

The half-century campaign to eradicate any vestige of religion from public life has run its course. The backlash from a nation fed up with the A.C.L.U. kicking crèches out of municipal Christmas displays has created a new balance. State-supported universities may subsidize the activities of student religious groups. Monuments inscribed with the Ten Commandments are permitted on government grounds. The Federal Government is engaged in a major antipoverty initiative that gives money to churches. Religion is back out of the closet.

But nothing could do more to undermine this most salutary restoration than the new and gratuitous attempts to invade science, and most particularly evolution, with religion. Have we learned nothing? In Kansas, conservative school-board members are attempting to rewrite statewide standards for teaching evolution to make sure that creationism's modern stepchild, intelligent design, infiltrates the curriculum. Similar anti-Darwinian mandates are already in place in Ohio and are being fought over in 20 states. And then, as if to second the evangelical push for this tarted-up version of creationism, out of the blue appears a declaration from Christoph Cardinal

---

Charles Krauthammer, winner of the 1987 Pulitzer Prize for distinguished commentary, writes a nationally syndicated column for the *Washington Post* Writers Group. He also writes for *Time* magazine, the *Weekly Standard*, the *New Republic*, and the *National Interest*. This piece appeared in *Time* on August 1, 2005.

Schönborn of Vienna, a man very close to the Pope, asserting that the supposed acceptance of evolution by John Paul II is mistaken. In fact, he says, the Roman Catholic Church rejects "neo-Darwinism" with the declaration that an "unguided evolutionary process—one that falls outside the bounds of divine providence—simply cannot exist."

Cannot? On what scientific evidence? Evolution is one of the most powerful and elegant theories in all of human science and the bedrock of all modern biology. Schönborn's proclamation that it cannot exist unguided—that it is driven by an intelligent designer pushing and pulling and planning and shaping the process along the way—is a perfectly legitimate statement of faith. If he and the Evangelicals just stopped there and asked that intelligent design be included in a religion curriculum, I would support them. The scandal is to teach this as science—to pretend, as does Schönborn, that his statement of faith is a defense of science. "The Catholic Church," he says, "will again defend human reason" against "scientific theories that try to explain away the appearance of design as the result of 'chance and necessity,'" which "are not scientific at all." Well, if you believe that science is reason and that reason begins with recognizing the existence of an immanent providence, then this is science. But, of course, it is not. This is faith disguised as science. Science begins not with first principles but with observation and experimentation.

In this slippery slide from "reason" to science, Schönborn is a direct descendant of the early 17th century Dutch clergyman and astronomer David Fabricius, who could not accept Johannes Kepler's discovery of elliptical planetary orbits. Why? Because the circle is so pure and perfect that reason must reject anything less. "With your ellipse," Fabricius wrote Kepler, "you abolish the circularity and uniformity of the motions, which appears to me increasingly absurd the more profoundly I think about it." No matter that, using Tycho Brahe's most exhaustive astronomical observations in history, Kepler had empirically demonstrated that the planets orbit elliptically.

This conflict between faith and science had mercifully abated over the 5
past four centuries as each grew to permit the other its own independent sphere. What we are witnessing now is a frontier violation by the forces of religion. This new attack claims that because there are gaps in evolution, they therefore must be filled by a divine intelligent designer.

How many times do we have to rerun the Scopes "monkey trial"? There are gaps in science everywhere. Are we to fill them all with divinity? There were gaps in Newton's universe. They were ultimately filled by Einstein's revisions. There are gaps in Einstein's universe, great chasms between it and quantum theory. Perhaps they are filled by God. Perhaps not. But it is certainly not science to merely declare it so.

To teach faith as science is to undermine the very idea of science, which is the acquisition of new knowledge through hypothesis, experimentation, and evidence. To teach it as science is to encourage the supercilious caricature of America as a nation in the thrall of religious authority. To teach it as science is to discredit the welcome recent advances in permitting the public expression of religion. Faith can and should be proclaimed from every mountaintop and city square. But it has no place in science class. To impose it on the teaching of evolution is not just to invite ridicule but to earn it.

2. Share your possible thesis statements with your classmates and discuss how an essay with each might be organized.

PLANNING THE STRUCTURE

When your purpose in writing about an argument is to support a factual claim, you will most likely use a very simple and direct form of organization called defending the main idea. In all forms of organization, you need to defend your main idea, or claim, with support; in this case, the support will come from the argument or arguments you are writing about.

At times, your claim may set up the organization of your essay, as was the case with the first example about the Declaration of Independence:

> The Declaration of Independence bases its claim on two kinds of support: factual evidence and appeals to the values of its audience.

The body of an essay with this thesis would most likely have two main divisions, one about factual evidence, providing examples, and the other about appeals to values, also providing examples. The other thesis about the Declaration of Independence does not suggest such an obvious structure. An essay based on that thesis would need to explain how the Declaration is an example of deductive reasoning, most likely by first establishing what generalization the document is based on and then what specifics Jefferson uses to prove that the colonists' situation fits that generalization.

Remember that when you compare or contrast two arguments, there will be two basic patterns to choose from for structuring the essay. One, often called *point-by-point* comparison, discusses each point about Subject A and Subject B together before moving on to the second point, where again both subjects are discussed:

I. Introduction
II. Context
  A. Jefferson
  B. Lincoln
III. Implicitness/explicitness
  A. Jefferson
  B. Lincoln
IV. Language
  A. Jefferson
  B. Lincoln
V. Conclusion

The second, often called *parallel order* comparison, focuses in roughly half the essay on Subject A and then in the other half on Subject B. The points made in each half should be parallel and should be presented in the same order:

I. Introduction
II. Jefferson
   A. Context
   B. Implicitness/explicitness of references to politics
   C. Language
III. Lincoln
   A. Context
   B. Implicitness/explicitness of references to politics
   C. Language
IV. Conclusion

SAMPLE ESSAYS WITH ANALYSIS

The two essays below are an argument written by Alan Dershowitz shortly after the terrorist attacks of September 11, 2001, and an evaluation of it written by Seth Finkelstein approximately three months later. Notice what Finkelstein says about Dershowitz's article but also how each author organizes his essay.

Is There a Torturous Road to Justice?

ALAN M. DERSHOWITZ

The FBI's frustration over its inability to get material witnesses to talk has raised a disturbing question rarely debated in this country: When, if ever, is it justified to resort to unconventional techniques such as truth serum, moderate physical pressure, and outright torture?

The constitutional answer to this question may surprise people who are not familiar with the current U.S. Supreme Court interpretation of the 5th Amendment privilege against self-incrimination: Any interrogation technique, including the use of truth serum or even torture, is not prohibited. All that is prohibited is the introduction into evidence of the fruits of such techniques in a criminal trial against the person on whom the techniques were used. But the evidence could be used against that suspect

Alan M. Dershowitz is the Felix Frankfurter Professor of Law at Harvard Law School and a civil liberties attorney who defends the indigent as well as the famous. One of his many works of fiction and nonfiction is *The Case for Peace: How the Arab-Israeli Conflict Can Be Resolved* (2005). His article appeared in *Commentary* on November 8, 2001.

in a non-criminal case—such as a deportation hearing—or against someone else.

If a suspect is given "use immunity"—a judicial decree announcing in advance that nothing the defendant says (or its fruits) can be used against him in a criminal case—he can be compelled to answer all proper questions. The issue then becomes what sorts of pressures can constitutionally be used to implement that compulsion. We know that he can be imprisoned until he talks. But what if imprisonment is insufficient to compel him to do what he has a legal obligation to do? Can other techniques of compulsion be attempted?

Let's start with truth serum. What right would be violated if an immunized suspect who refused to comply with his legal obligation to answer questions truthfully were compelled to submit to an injection that made him do so?

Not his privilege against self-incrimination, since he has no such priv- 5
ilege now that he has been given immunity.

What about his right of bodily integrity? The involuntariness of the injection itself does not pose a constitutional barrier. No less a civil libertarian than Justice William J. Brennan rendered a decision that permitted an allegedly drunken driver to be involuntarily injected to remove blood for alcohol testing. Certainly there can be no constitutional distinction between an injection that removes a liquid and one that injects a liquid.

What about the nature of the substance injected? If it is relatively benign and creates no significant health risk, the only issue would be that it compels the recipient to do something he doesn't want to do. But he has a legal obligation to do precisely what the serum compels him to do: answer all questions truthfully.

What if the truth serum doesn't work? Could the judge issue a "torture warrant," authorizing the FBI to employ specified forms of non-lethal physical pressure to compel the immunized suspect to talk?

Here we run into another provision of the Constitution—the due process clause, which may include a general "shock the conscience" test. And torture in general certainly shocks the conscience of most civilized nations.

But what if it were limited to the rare "ticking bomb" case—the situ- 10
ation in which a captured terrorist who knows of an imminent large-scale threat refuses to disclose it?

Would torturing one guilty terrorist to prevent the deaths of a thousand innocent civilians shock the conscience of all decent people?

To prove that it would not, consider a situation in which a kidnapped child had been buried in a box with two hours of oxygen. The kidnapper refuses to disclose its location. Should we not consider torture in that situation?

All of that said, the argument for allowing torture as an approved technique, even in a narrowly specified range of cases, is very troubling.

We know from experience that law enforcement personnel who are given limited authority to torture will expand its use. The cases that have generated the current debate over torture illustrate this problem. And, concerning the arrests made following the September 11 attacks, there is no reason to believe that the detainees know about specific future terrorist targets. Yet there have been calls to torture these detainees.

I have no doubt that if an actual ticking bomb situation were to arise, 15
our law enforcement authorities would torture. The real debate is whether such torture should take place outside of our legal system or within it. The answer to this seems clear: If we are to have torture, it should be authorized by the law.

Judges should have to issue a "torture warrant" in each case. Thus we would not be winking an eye of quiet approval at torture while publicly condemning it.

Democracy requires accountability and transparency, especially when extraordinary steps are taken. Most important, it requires compliance with the rule of law. And such compliance is impossible when an extraordinary technique, such as torture, operates outside of the law.

Alan Dershowitz's Tortuous Torturous Argument

SETH FINKELSTEIN

It's torture. Literally. That is, whether or not the United States government should use torture as a method of interrogation for suspected terrorists is now a subject of debate.

Surprisingly, long-time civil-libertarian Alan Dershowitz has been writing unexpectedly in favor of the legal basis for torture. On November 8, 2001, in a commentary for *Los Angeles Times* "Is There a Torturous Road to Justice?" he discusses a proposal for a "torture warrant."

Much of the reaction to Alan Dershowitz's advocacy has blurred over a subtle point. Given that torture is such an incendiary subject, he's been accused of advocating torture itself ("Dershowitz: Make Torture an Option" reads a headline on cbsnews.com). However, a careful reading of his commentary makes it clear that he isn't putting forth an argument in favor of torture *per se*. Rather, he postulates it will occur (*"I have no doubt that if an actual ticking bomb situation were to arise, our law enforcement authorities would torture."*). His point is then almost tangential from that perspective, a professorial concern with the due process of torture! To wit:

Seth Finkelstein is a computer programmer, system administrator, and consultant programmer who has worked extensively doing anti-censorware research. He is the winner of an EFF Pioneer Award. This article was posted to the Ethical Spectacle Web site February 2002.

> *The real debate is whether such torture should take place outside of our legal system or within it. The answer to this seems clear: If we are to have torture, it should be authorized by the law.*

In this piece, I will not take up the arguments against torture. That's been done far better elsewhere, by other civil-libertarians such as Harvey Silverglate, or Amnesty International. Rather, I stand in awe of Dershowitz's focus on legal authorization of torture as the "*real debate.*" All the moral and practical questions are swept away by his assumption of inevitability. We are left only to consider how to deal with what, if any, judicial procedures should surround torture.

He goes on to assert: 5

> *Democracy requires accountability and transparency, especially when extraordinary steps are taken. Most important, it requires compliance with the rule of law. And such compliance is impossible when an extraordinary technique, such as torture, operates outside of the law.*

While this sounds stirring, on reflection, the meaning of the call for "accountability and transparency" is not at all clear to me. If torture is illegal, then by definition it's operating outside the law. So if a torture warrant is created, obviously torture *with warrant* would be within the law. But there seems to be a tail-wagging-the-dog situation here. Torture doesn't comply with the rule of law because it's against the law. If the law is changed so that torture is permitted (*with warrant*), then it's only become compliant with the rule of law because that rule has been changed to accept it.

What is the *purpose* of the torture warrant? Is it an anti-hypocrisy measure, to force us, as a society, to confront what we are doing? To have a public record of the event, that the defense attorney can use in a trial? To allow the torture to be supervised, with proper medical monitoring, to guard against it becoming life-threatening? To officially provide for doctors to treat the torturee during and after the ordeal?

Perhaps the idea is the simple belief that we can have legal torture, which is bad, but illegal torture would be worse. However, the obvious rebuttal is that we would end up having both legal and illegal torture, feeding off each other. Dershowitz even explicitly takes this into account ("*We know from experience that law enforcement personnel who are given limited authority to torture will expand its use.*").

So, in the face [of] this expansion of authority to torture, what is gained by making it "accountable"? The anti-hypocrisy basis seems to be Dershowitz's rationale, as he justified the above by saying:

> *Judges should have to issue a "torture warrant" in each case. Thus we would not be winking an eye of quiet approval at torture while publicly condemning it.*

Overall, Dershowitz's reasoning seems shockingly convoluted. We end 10
up resolving the conflict between torture and the rule of law by changing the rule of law to accommodate torture. Then an admitted following expansion

in torture (both from legal and illegal sources) is brushed aside with the argument that the legal torture would somehow possess accountability and transparency (accountable for what? transparent how?). Suppose Dershowitz is correct that there will be illegal torture under desperate circumstances, and without issuing a torture warrant, as a society we will be "winking an eye" to it. Is he really arguing that it's better to have more torture (due to the admitted effects of the tendency [to] "expand its use"), but at least some of the torture will then be *authorized* torture? That is, judicial process is regarded as so sacred that it's worth **torturing more people** in order to preserve it in the merest formal sense? That's both tortuous and torturous.

Analysis

The short article by Dershowitz has a very clear structure. In his first paragraph, he asks a question that sets up a list of three techniques that he believes could be used to get information from suspected terrorists: truth serum, moderate physical pressure, and outright torture. He leaves his mention of these techniques in the form of a question, questioning in turn each of the three techniques as he builds toward his claim, which comes at the end of the essay: "Most important, [democracy] requires compliance with the rule of law. And such compliance is impossible when an extraordinary technique, such as torture, operates outside of the law." He makes the surprising point that such forms of interrogation are not against the law, although it is against the law to use information so gained against the suspect in a criminal trial against him.

Dershowitz goes methodically through the three proposed techniques. In each case, he counters opposition based on the assumption that what he is proposing is illegal. He tries to achieve middle ground with skeptical readers when he writes, "All of that said, the argument for allowing torture as an approved technique, even in a narrowly specified range of cases, is very troubling." What troubles him more, ultimately, is that he feels sure that if law enforcement personnel were given limited authority to torture, they would not be bound by narrow guidelines, especially if faced with a "ticking bomb" situation. The only question for Dershowitz is whether the torture should take place within the law or outside of it. His specific proposal is that judges be given the right to issue "torture warrants" in specific cases.

Dershowitz's argument follows a common overall structure: He presents a problem and then possible solutions to it.

Finkelstein's piece is a response to and an evaluation of Dershowitz's article and an example of the type of writing discussed in this chapter. His is clearly a claim of value where Dershowitz's is a claim of policy. To describe Dershowitz's writing, Finkelstein uses such words as *convoluted* and, in the title, *tortuous*, which means full of twists and turns. (*Torturous* is the adjective form of *torture*.) For him, it's torture to think that "whether or not the

United States government should use torture as a method of interrogation for suspected terrorists is now a subject of debate." He mocks Dershowitz for being concerned with "the due process of torture" and for brushing aside all arguments against torture by assuming it will happen anyway, a logical fallacy called "begging the question" (see p. 343). He follows good form in quoting Dershowitz to make his points.

Much of the second half of Finkelstein's argument is devoted to questioning the purpose of making torture legal, even in a narrow range of circumstances approved by a judge. Finkelstein uses Dershowitz's own words to establish that illegal torture will go on even with the existence of legal torture and asks what the advantage is to having both illegal and legal torture.

USING SENTENCE FORMS TO CONSTRUCT AN ARGUMENT

When you present an argument, it may be important to clearly explain how a previous writer has approached a situation—and then explain how your view differs. There's no point repeating exactly what an author writes and then end by saying "and I agree with everything." Instead, academic writing means explaining current thinking on a topic and showing how it is different from what you believe. Sometimes the points of difference are large, sometimes small. But in writing for college, it is crucial that you explain your own understanding of a situation *and* express your own point of view.

It is easier to think about how you might summarize the argument of others and present your own if you have a model from which to work. This kind of model is called a sentence form, and it can help you to organize a presentation of another's views and your response to them.

Here is a basic sentence form for this kind of work.

PRESENTING ANOTHER'S VIEW AND RESPONDING TO IT

In his/her essay ________________, X writes that ________________.
However, I think that ________________.

Writing in college means taking part in an ongoing conversation. You need to be respectful of what others say and write, and you need to account for their positions accurately. You'll want to be sure to clearly summarize the author's presentation. We have more to say about summary shortly, but, briefly put, in writing arguments, you must show the author's point before you explain how your ideas differ. You'll need to be able to sum up in a neutral, fair way what the writer says. Then, when you respond, you can agree on some points, but you'll need to focus on the points of disagreement.

Where you agree with some of what a writer says, but not all of it, you must distinguish between the parts you think are correct and those parts that are not. A sentence form for that kind of response might look like this:

AGREEING IN PART

X argues that ______________. While I agree that ______________ and ______________ are valid points, I do not agree that ______________. Instead, I would argue that ______________.

At times you'll need to correct a distortion or misstatement of fact. Statistics, for instance, can be and often are manipulated to present the arguer's viewpoint in the best light. You may wish to propose an alternative interpretation or set the statistics in a different context, one more accurate and favorable to your own point of view. Of course, you'll want to be certain that you do not distort statistics. (For more on the importance of using statistics fairly, see the full discussion on pages 222–23.) Here's a sentence form for correcting factual information in an argument.

CORRECTING A FACTUAL MISTAKE

While X claims ______________, it is actually true that ______________.

More often, rather than correcting clear mistakes of fact, you'll need to refine the argument of a writer. You may find that much of the argument makes sense to you, but that the writer does not sufficiently anticipate important objections. In those cases, a sentence form such as the following can help you refine the argument to make a stronger conclusion.

REFINING ANOTHER'S ARGUMENT

While X claims ______________ and ______________, he/she fails to consider the important point ______________. Therefore, a more accurate conclusion is ______________.

At times you'll need to distinguish between the views of two different writers and then weigh in with your own assessment of the situation. When two authors write on the same topic, they will most likely share similar views on some of the points. They will, however, disagree on other points. Similarly, you may find that you agree with some of what each writer has to say, but disagree with some other parts. Your job is to identify the points of contrast between the two authors and then explain how your own position differs from one or both. In those cases, you may find the following sentence form helpful.

EXPLAINING CONTRASTING VIEWS AND ADDING YOUR POSITION

On the topic of ______________, X claims that ______________. In contrast, Y argues that ______________. However, I believe that ______________.

While these sentence forms seem rather simple—perhaps even simplistic—keep in mind that good writers use them all the time. Once you have tried them out a few times, you'll begin to use them automatically, perhaps without even realizing it. They are powerful tools for incorporating others' views into your own work and then helping you to make careful distinctions about various parts of arguments—a crucial skill in thinking and writing critically.

PROVIDING SUPPORT

In writing about any argument, you will need to understand the argument and to make it clear to your readers that you do. You cannot write a clear explanation or a fair evaluation if you do not have a clear understanding of your subject. You will need to look closely at the piece to recall what specific words or ideas led you to the thesis statement that you have chosen to support.

Your support for your thesis will come from the text or texts you are writing about in the form of summary, paraphrase, or quotations. The ability to summarize, paraphrase, and quote material from your source is necessary in writing about arguments, but it is also essential in writing your own arguments, especially those that require research.

■ Summarizing

A summary involves shortening the original passage as well as putting it into your own words. It gives the gist of the passage, including the important points, while leaving out details. What makes summarizing difficult is that it requires you to capture often long and complex texts in just a few lines or a short paragraph. To summarize well, you need to imagine yourself as the author of the piece you are summarizing and be true to the ideas the author is expressing, even when those ideas conflict with your point of view. You must then move smoothly from being a careful reader to being a writer who, in your own words, recreates another's thoughts.

We summarize for many reasons: to let our boss know the basics of what we have been doing or to tell a friend why she should or should not see a movie. In your classes you are often asked to summarize articles or books, and even when this is not an explicit part of an assignment, the ability to summarize is usually expected. That is, when you are instructed to analyze an essay or to compare and contrast two novels, central to this work is the ability to carefully comprehend and recreate authors' ideas. Summarizing is the cornerstone on which all other critical reading and writing tasks are built.

When you are asked to write a research paper, the ability to summarize effectively is especially critical, because some sources, though useful for your argument, will simply be too long to include in your text. It is up to you, then, to summarize those points and ideas that are most critical for your argument either because they support that argument or because they represent a counter point of view.

For instance, Charles Krauthammer's main idea in the first paragraph of his "Let's Have No More Monkey Trials" might be summarized in this way:

> According to Krauthammer (2005), after fifty years of attempts to separate religion from public life on the local, state, and federal levels, religion is making a comeback (p. 46).

The statement is not a direct quotation, so it would not be in quotation marks in an essay about the article. The example shows the American Psychological Association (APA) style of documentation used to acknowledge that the idea comes from an article by Krauthammer published in 2005. Returning to the original source makes it clear that the passage is far too long to quote in full in a short essay, but it is easily summarized without losing Krauthammer's idea. The summary illustrates APA style for documenting the use of a source that is named in the writer's sentence. In other examples in this chapter, you will see more illustrations of the use of both APA and Modern Language Association (MLA) styles of documentation, which are explained in more detail in the Writer's Guides in this chapter and in Chapter 11.

When summarizing long or difficult texts, try some of the following strategies to help you comprehend the essential points of the text.

1. Before you summarize, analyze the text using the strategies given in the section on "Responding as a Critical Reader" in Chapter 2 (p. 31). For example, you should always utilize prereading strategies by looking over the text as a whole before you read it carefully. Such work will often yield clues about the central idea of the text from the title, the subheadings, and the introduction. Also, use your pen once you begin to read the text so that you link the acts of reading and writing. Underline important ideas, ask questions in the margins about difficult or significant ideas, and highlight topic sentences. Take a few minutes after reading the text to jot down the essential ideas and any questions you have about the reading.
2. Reread the introduction and conclusion after you have read the essay once or twice. These two sections should complement each other and offer clues to the most significant issues of the text. An introduction or conclusion is often more than one paragraph; therefore, it is important that you read the first and last few paragraphs of an essay to understand what the author is trying to impress upon the reader. If you are summarizing a book, look especially at the preface, the first and last chapters, and any reviewers' comments. These sections will not tell you everything you need to know to summarize an entire book, but they will help you decide which points matter.
3. For a difficult essay, you may want to list all the subheadings (if they are used) or the topic sentence of each paragraph. These significant guideposts will map the piece as a whole: What do they tell

you about the central ideas and the main argument the author is making? After reviewing the subheads or topic sentences, can you reread the essay and engage more easily with its finer points? For a book, you can do the same thing with chapter headings to break down the essential ideas. Remember that when you summarize, you must put another's words into your own (and cite the original text as well), so do not simply let a list of the subheadings or chapter titles stand as your summary. They likely won't make sense when put together in paragraph form, but they will provide you with valuable ideas regarding the central points of the text.

4. Remember that summarizing requires attention to overall meanings and not to specific details. Therefore, avoid including many specific examples or concrete details from the text you are summarizing and try to let your reader know what these examples and details add up to. Some of the specificity and excitement of the original text will be lost, but when summarizing, the goal is to let the reader know the essential meaning of the original text in a clear, straightforward way. Of course, if you need to respond, as part of your argument, to specifics in the essay, you should do so, but you will most likely do so in the form of a paraphrase or a direct quotation.

There are two types of summaries, rhetorical and referential. The two share some characteristics. Both types should

- Be objective instead of expressing opinions.
- Identify the author and the work.
- Use present tense.
- Summarize the main points of the whole work or passage, not just part of it.

A *rhetorical* summary summarizes the text in terms of rhetorical choices the author made. An example:

> In "Let's Have No More Monkey Trials," Charles Krauthammer celebrates the end of the separation of religion from public life at the local, state, and federal levels but argues that the progress made will be undermined by those trying to replace the teaching of evolution with the teaching of intelligent design, a new form of creationism. He notes that Christoph Cardinal Schönborn of Vienna . . .

The other type of summary, a *referential* summary, focuses on ideas rather than on the author's actions and decisions.

> According to Charles Krauthammer in his article "Let's Have No More Monkey Trials," a fifty-year trend toward removing religion from public life is now being reversed. This positive movement, however, is threatened by those who are trying to replace the teaching of evolution with the teaching of intelligent design, a new form of creationism. Christoph Cardinal Schönborn of Vienna has asserted that . . .

Paraphrasing

Paraphrasing involves restating the content of an original source in your own words. It differs from summarizing in that a paraphrase is roughly the same length as the passage it paraphrases instead of a condensation of a longer passage. You will use paraphrasing when you want to capture the idea but there is nothing about the wording that makes repeating it necessary. You may also use it when the idea can be made clearer by rephrasing it or when the style is markedly different from your own. Here is an example drawn from a student paper presented in its entirely in Chapter 12:

> Randolph Warren, a victim of the thalidomide disaster himself and founder and executive director of the Thalidomide Victims Association of Canada, reports that it is estimated 10,000 to 12,000 deformed babies were born to mothers who took thalidomide. (40)

There is no single sentence on page 40 of the Warren article that both provides the estimate of number of affected babies and identifies Warren as one of them. Both the ideas were important, but neither of them was worded in such a unique way that a direct quote was needed. Therefore, a paraphrase was the logical choice. In this case, the writer correctly documents the paraphrase using Modern Language Association (MLA) style.

Quoting

You may want to quote passages or phrases from your sources if they express an idea in words more effective than your own. In reading a source, you may come across a statement that provides succinct, irrefutable evidence for an issue you wish to support. If the author of this statement is a professional in his or her field, someone with a great deal of authority on the subject, it would be appropriate to quote that author. A student research paper in Chapter 12 is Jessica Smith-Garcia's about women in combat. Suppose, during the course of Jessica's research for her paper, she found several sources that agree that women in the military who are denied combat experience are, as a result, essentially being denied a chance at promotion to the highest ranks. Others argue that such considerations should not be a deciding factor in assigning women to combat. To represent the latter of these two positions, Jessica chose to use a quotation from an authority in the field, using APA style:

> Elaine Donnelly, president of the Center for Military Readiness, says, "Equal opportunity is important, but the armed forces exist to defend the country. If there is a conflict between career opportunities and military necessity, the needs of the military must come first" (as qtd. in "Women in the Military," 2000).

It is especially important in argumentative writing to establish a source's authority on the subject under discussion. The most common way of doing this is to use that person's name and position of authority to introduce the quotation, as in the previous example. It is correct in both MLA and APA styles to provide the author's name in parentheses at the end of the quoted material, but that type of documentation precludes lending to the quote the weight of its having come from an authority. It is likely that those readers not in the military—and even some who are—will not know who Donnelly is just by seeing her name in parentheses. Your writing will always have more power if you establish the authority of each author from whose work you quote, paraphrase, or summarize. To establish authority, you may refer to the person's position, institutional affiliation, publications, or some other similar "claim to fame."

Another example, also using APA style:

> According to the late Ulysses S. Seal III (1982), founder of the Conservation Breeding Specialist Group and of a "computer dating service" for mateless animals, "None of these [zoo] budgets is allocated specifically for species preservation. Zoos have been established primarily as recreational institutions and are only secondarily programs in conservation, education, and research." (p. 74)

Notice that once the name of the author being cited has been mentioned in the writer's own text, it does not have to be repeated in the parentheses.

Writer's Guide: Incorporating Quotations into Your Text

1. The most effective way to lead into the first quotation from a source is to use the author's full name and his or her claim to authority — a few words identifying the person by title, institutional affiliation, or publications. Remember that for readers who are not specialists, the name of an author you are quoting may have little meaning, and relegating the last name to a parenthesis at the end of the quotation does not use that author's authority to strengthen your argument. Once you have used the full name, any future references may use only the last name of the author. If the author's name, full or last only, is used in your lead-in to the quote, you do not have to repeat it in the parentheses that complete the documentation. One additional advantage of mentioning the author or authors is that a reader can tell where your ideas leave off and those from your source begin.
2. There are three primary means of linking a supporting quotation to your own text. Remember that in each case, the full citation for the source will be listed alphabetically by the author's name in the list of works cited at the end of the paper, or by title if no author is given. The number in parentheses is the page of that source on which the quotation appears. The details of what appears in parentheses will be covered later in the discussion of APA (American Psychological Association) and MLA (Modern Language Association) documentation styles.

- You may choose to make a brief quotation a grammatical part of your own sentence. In that case, you do not separate the quotation from your sentence with a comma, unless there is another reason for the comma, and you do not capitalize the first word of the quotation, unless there is another reason for doing so. In this sort of situation, there may be times when you have to change the tense of a verb, in brackets, to make the quotation fit smoothly into your text or when you need to make other small changes, always in brackets.

  Examples:

  APA style

  James Rachels (1976), University Professor of Philosophy at the University of Alabama at Birmingham and author of several books on moral philosophy, explains that animals' right to liberty derives from "a more basic right not to have one's interests needlessly harmed" (p. 210).

  MLA style

  James Rachels, University Professor of Philosophy at the University of Alabama at Birmingham and author of several books on moral philosophy, explains that animals' right to liberty derives from "a more basic right not to have one's interests needlessly harmed" (210).

- You may use a traditional speech tag such as "he says" or "she writes." This is the most common way of introducing a quotation. Be sure to put a comma after the tag and to begin the quotation with a capital letter. At the end of the quotation, close the quotation, add the page number and any other necessary information in parentheses, and then add the period.

  Examples:

  APA style

  James Rachels (1976), University Professor of Philosophy at the University of Alabama at Birmingham and author of several books on moral philosophy, writes, "The right to liberty — the right to be free of external constraints on one's actions — may then be seen as derived from a more basic right not to have one's interests needlessly harmed" (p. 210).

  MLA style

  James Rachels, University Professor of Philosophy at the University of Alabama at Birmingham and author of several books on moral philosophy, writes, "The right to liberty — the right to be free of external constraints on one's actions — may then be seen as derived from a more basic right not to have one's interests needlessly harmed" (210).

Students are sometimes at a loss as to what sorts of verbs to use in these tag statements. Try using different terms from this list or others like them. Remember that in writing about a printed or electronic text, it is customary to write in present tense unless there is a compelling reason to use past tense.

argues
asks
asserts
concludes
continues
counters

declares	questions
explains	replies
implores	responds
insists	states
proclaims	suggests

- You may vary the way you introduce quotations by at times using a colon to separate the quotation from a *complete sentence* that introduces it.

  Examples:

  APA style

  For example, the Zurich Zoo's Dr. Heini Hediger (1985) protests that it is absurd to attribute human qualities to animals at all, but he nevertheless resorts to a human analogy: "Wild animals in the zoo rather resemble estate owners. Far from desiring to escape and regain their freedom, they are only bent on defending the space they inhabit and keeping it safe from invasion" (p. 9).

  MLA style

  The late Ulysses S. Seal III, founder of the Conservation Breeding Specialist Group and of a "computer dating service" for mateless animals, acknowledges the subordinate position species preservation plays in budgeting decisions: "Zoos have been established primarily as recreational institutions and are only secondarily developing programs in conservation, education, and research" (74).

3. Long quotations are handled differently from shorter ones. In APA style, a quotation of more than forty words, and in MLA style, a quotation of more than four lines, is set off as a block quotation. That means that the writer must doublespace before and after the quotation — as well as double-spacing the quotation itself — and indent the whole quotation ten spaces from the left margin. The passage is not placed in quotation marks because the placement on the page indicates that it is a quotation. With block quotations, the parentheses used to provide documentation at the end of the passage are placed after, rather than before, the period. Block quotations should be used sparingly.
4. Avoid "floating" quotations. That is, do not jump from a sentence of your own text into a quotation with no connection between the two. Introduce every direct quotation.
5. Avoid back-to-back quotations. There should always be some of your own ideas to justify including a quotation, so some of your own text should always intervene between quoted passages.

PRACTICE

Write a summary of Alan Dershowitz's "Is There a Torturous Road to Justice?" using either the rhetorical method, which explains what the author is doing in the piece, or using the referential method, which focuses instead on the ideas.

Be sure to remain objective. Include at least one direct quotation in your summary. Identify the author and the title in your first sentence and provide in parentheses the page number for the quotation(s).

DOCUMENTING YOUR SOURCES

Chapter 12 will provide additional information about documenting sources, but you should start now documenting your use of others' work, even when the only sources you use are essays from this textbook. The single most important thing to remember is why you need to inform your reader about your use of sources. Once it is clear from your writing that an idea or some language came from a source and thus is not your own original thought or language, full documentation provides the reader with a means of identifying and, if necessary, locating your source. If you do not indicate your source, your reader will naturally assume that the ideas and the language are yours. It is careless to forget to give credit to your sources. It is dishonest to intentionally take credit for what is not your own intellectual property.

The following Writer's Guide provides the general guidelines for documenting your use of sources.

Writer's Guide: Documenting Use of Summary, Paraphrase, and Quotation

1. One of the most common mistakes that student writers make is to think that material needs to be documented only if they use another author's words. In fact, you must give credit for any *ideas* you get from others, not only for wording you get from them.
2. You must identify the author and the location of ideas that you summarize. A *summary* is the condensing of a longer passage into a shorter one, using your own words. You will use summary often in your academic writing when you want to report briefly on an idea covered at greater length in your source.
3. You must identify the author and the location of ideas that you paraphrase. A *paraphrase* is a rewording of another author's idea into your own words. A paraphrased passage is roughly the same length as the original.
4. You must identify the author and the location of language that you quote. A *quotation* is the copying of the exact wording of your source and is placed in quotation marks. Remember that *exact* means just that. You cannot change anything inside quotation marks, with these exceptions: (a) If there is a portion of the quotation that is not relevant to the point that you are making and *that can be omitted without distorting the author's meaning,*

you may indicate an omission of a portion of the quotation with an ellipsis (. . .). If there is a sentence break within the portion you are omitting, add a fourth period to the ellipsis to so indicate. (b) If you need to make a very slight change in the quote to make the quote fit grammatically into your own text or to avoid confusion and if the change does not distort the author's meaning, you may make that slight change and place the changed portion in square brackets ([ ]). This method is used primarily to change the tense of a quoted passage to match that of your text or to identify a person identified in the quotation only by a pronoun.

5. Both the MLA and the APA systems make use of in-text or parenthetical documentation. That means that while a complete bibliographical listing for each work summarized, paraphrased, or quoted in your text is included in a Works Cited or References list at the end of your paper, each is also identified exactly at the point in the text where you use the source. If you are using the MLA system of documentation, the system most commonly used in the humanities, immediately following the sentence in which you use material from a source, you need to add in parentheses the author's name and the page number on which the material you are using appeared in the original source. However, since the credibility of your sources is critical in argumentative writing, it is even better to name the source in your own sentence and to identify the position or experience that makes that person a reliable source for the subject being discussed. In that case, you do not need to repeat the author's name in the parentheses. In fact, any time the author's name is clear from the context, you do not need to repeat it in the parentheses.

   Acceptable: The mall has been called "a common experience for the majority of American youth" (Kowinski 3).

   Better: According to William Severini Kowinski, author of *The Malling of America*, "The mall is a common experience for the majority of American youth" (3).

   In the APA system, the system most commonly use in the social sciences, in-text or parenthetical documentation is handled a bit differently because the citation includes the year of publication. The most basic forms are these:

   The mall has been called "a common experience for the majority of American youth" (Kowinski, 1985, p. 3).

   Kowinski (1985) writes, "The mall is a common experience for the majority of American youth (p. 3).

6. Remember that these examples show only the most basic forms for documenting your sources. Some works will have more than one author. Sometimes you will be using more than one work by the same author. Usually Web sites do not have page numbers. Long quotations need to be handled differently from short ones. For all questions about documenting your use of sources not covered here, see Chapter 12.

   Note: If you are writing about an essay in this book, you have a slightly more complicated situation than if you were looking at the essay in its original place of publication. Unless your instructor indicates otherwise, use the page numbers on which the essay appears in this textbook when summarizing, paraphrasing, or quoting from it instead of going back to the page numbers of the original. Also, unless your instructor indicates otherwise, use this model for listing in your Works Cited page an essay reprinted here:

Kowinski, William Severini. "Kids in the Mall: Growing Up Controlled." New York: Morrow, 1985. Rpt. in *Elements of Argument: A Text and Reader.* Annette T. Rottenberg and Donna Haisty Winchell. 9th ed. Boston: Bedford/St. Martin's, 2009. 171–176.

AVOIDING PLAGIARISM

Plagiarism is the use of someone else's words or ideas without adequate acknowledgment—that is, presenting such words or ideas as your own. Putting something into your own words is not in itself a defense against plagiarism; the source of the ideas must be identified as well. Giving credit to the sources you use serves three important purposes: (1) it reflects your own honesty and seriousness as a researcher; (2) it enables the reader to find the source of the reference and read further, sometimes to verify that the source has been correctly used; and (3) it adds the authority of experts to your argument. Plagiarism is nothing less than cheating, and it is an offense that deserves serious punishment. You can avoid accidentally slipping into plagiarism if you are careful in researching and writing your papers.

Taking care to document sources is an obvious way to avoid plagiarism. You should also be careful in taking notes and, when writing your paper, indicating where your ideas end and someone else's begin. When taking notes, make sure either to quote word for word or to paraphrase—one or the other, not both. If you quote, enclose any language that you borrow from other sources in quotation marks. That way, when you look back at your notes days or weeks later, you won't mistakenly assume that the language is your own. If you know that you aren't going to use a particular writer's exact words, then take the time to summarize that person's ideas right away. That will save you time and trouble later.

When using someone else's ideas in your paper, always let the reader know where that person's ideas begin and end. Here is an example from a student paper that uses APA style:

> When zoo animals do mate successfully, the offspring is often weakened by inbreeding. According to geneticists, this is because a population of 150 breeder animals is necessary in order to "assure the more or less permanent survival of a species in captivity." (Ehrlich & Ehrlich, 1981, p. 211).

The phrase "according to geneticists" indicates that the material to follow comes from another source, cited parenthetically at the end of the borrowed material. If the student had not included the phrase "according to geneticists," it might look as if she only borrowed the passage in quotation marks, and not the information that precedes that passage.

READINGS FOR ANALYSIS

Should We Fight Terror with Torture?

ALAN M. DERSHOWITZ

The great American justice Oliver Wendell Holmes Jr. once remarked that "it is revolting to have no better reason for a rule of law than that it was laid down in the time of Henry IV. It is still more revolting if the grounds upon which it was laid down have vanished long since, and the rule simply persists from blind imitation of the past." The rules of law regulating how civilized societies protect their citizens from aggression were not laid down as far back as the time of Henry IV. They were enacted, in significant part, following the two awful wars of the 20th century in which massive numbers of civilians were targeted for death and murdered in cold blood. The human-rights revolution of the mid-20th century was largely a reaction to the human wrongs of the Holocaust.

The period between the end of the Second World War and now has seen more profound changes in the nature of warfare than occurred from the time of Henry IV to the beginning of the First World War. Weapons of mass destruction in the hands of suicide terrorists with no fear of death and no home address have rendered useless the deterrent threat of massive retaliation. This threat has been the staple of military policy since the days of the Bible. Because suicide terrorists cannot be deterred, they must be pre-empted and prevented from carrying out their threats against civilians before they occur. This change in tactics requires significant changes in the laws of war—laws that have long been premised on the deterrent model.

Consider, for example, the United Nations Charter, drafted in the aftermath of Germany's aggressive war between 1939 and 1945. Article 51 confirms "the inherent right of individual or collective [to] self-defense if an armed attack occurs against a member." The use of the word "occurs" would seem to require a nation, seeking to act in compliance with the charter, to wait until it is actually attacked before it responds in self-defense. But what

For information on Alan M. Dershowitz, see the footnote on p. 85.

should a democratic nation do if it becomes aware of an imminent threat of attack by a group of suicide terrorists in a distant part of the world? Surely it should not simply wait until an "armed attack occurs" and then engage in retaliatory self-defense. First, there is often no known entity to attack, since the suicide terrorists have died and the leaders who sent them have gone into hiding among civilians and may well be preparing renewed terrorist attacks. Second, there is no good reason for a democracy to have to absorb a first blow against its civilian population, especially if that blow can be catastrophic. Third, there is little possibility that potentially catastrophic first blows can be deterred by the threat of retaliation against a phantom enemy who welcomes martyrdom.

Despite these new realities, the old UN charter has not been changed, though it is currently in the process of being "redefined." A "High Level Panel on Threats, Challenge, and Change" has recommended that despite the "restrictive" language of Article 51, a nation should be free to take proportional military action against an "imminent" attack if no other means are available. But it also proposed that if a threat, though catastrophic and highly likely, is not imminent, a nation may not resort to preventive self-help. Instead it must seek the approval of the Security Council. In other words, pre-emptive self-defense against imminent threat is consistent with Article 51, but preventive self-defense against more distant, though equally certain, threats requires approval by the Security Council. While this distinction makes sense in theory, it fails to recognize that the Security Council is a highly politicized body, with veto-power in the hands of nations that have long supported terrorism, at least on a selective basis. No nation, facing a highly likely catastrophic threat—even if it is not imminent—will rely on the whim of other nations with agendas different from its own. As the former U.S. Secretary of State Dean Acheson once, aptly, put it, "The survival of states is not a matter of law." States will do what they deem necessary, not only to ensure their own survival, but also to protect the lives of their citizens from catastrophic threats.

5 Consider, for example, the developing Iranian nuclear threat. The Iranian leadership has threatened to attack Israel and American targets. If Iran gets close to having a deliverable nuclear weapon, and if one of its target nations has the capacity to destroy its nuclear program the way Israel destroyed the Iraqi reactor back in 1981—with one air-strike and a single casualty—it should have the legal right to do so. This would be especially so if the Security Council refused to do anything to stop Iran because of self-serving Russian or Chinese vetoes. We are not yet at that decision point, and it is unlikely that the Iranian nuclear threat can be ended by surgical air strikes, but international law should authorize preventive self-defense if the threat is cataclysmic and relatively certain, even if not imminent, and if it can be abated with few civilian casualities.

In any event, the UN report "sees no need to amend Article 51" since it can be reinterpreted to permit states to take pre-emptive action against imminent threat, but not to take preventive action against longer-term threats. Even the recommended reinterpretation does not have the force of law. It is merely the opinion of a high-level panel which has received no formal approval by the United Nations. It would be far better to change Article 51 [yet] there is an apparent allergy to changing old laws, whether they go back to Henry IV or to the post–World War II period, [to] reflect the new realities.

The laws of pre-emptive and preventive self-defense are but one example of the legal sclerosis from which we are suffering in the war against terrorism. The human-rights rules that were enacted to protect civilians are now being turned on their heads by self-proclaimed human-rights groups. Instead of being a shield for innocent civilians, they are being used as a sword by terrorists against civilians. Terrorists deliberately hide among civilians, most often civilians who support them. In order to prevent the terrorists from carrying out their threats, democratic nations must often take actions that endanger some civilians. For example, when coalition forces targeted Abu Musab al-Zarqawi and his "spiritual adviser," Abu Abdul-Rahman, they inadvertently killed several civilians, including a child. This was not the first time that targeting terrorists has resulted in collateral casualities. When the U.S. targeted Abu Ali, known as Qaed Salim Sinan al-Harethi, in Yemen in 2002, they also killed five other people, at least some of whom were probably al-Qa'ida members or supporters. Israel, as well, has caused the deaths of civilians in its efforts to pre-empt terrorist attacks by targeting "ticking bomb" terrorists as well as terrorist commanders who were the equivalents of Zarqawi and Rahman.

Human-rights organizations often fail to distinguish between civilian deaths accidentally caused by democracies despite their best efforts to avoid them, and civilian deaths deliberately caused by terrorists who seek to maximize civilian casualties by constructing anti-personnel bombs, designed to kill as many innocent people as possible, and by specifically targeting crowded buses and other soft targets. These human-rights organizations blink at the reality that terrorists seek not only to maximize civilian deaths among their enemies, but also seek to maximize civilian deaths caused by their enemies, even if the victims are their own supporters. As one European diplomat told the *New York Times*, the terrorists understand the "harsh arithmetic of pain." Enemy "casualties play in their favor" and casualties inflicted on their own people by the enemy "play in their favor."

By condemning all targeted killing of terrorists, human-rights groups actually increase the risks to civilians. The law should permit the targeting of individuals who are actively engaged in terrorist planning and actions, so long as it is highly likely that the target is an actual terrorist, that the number of likely civilian deaths is proportional to the likely civilian deaths that would have been caused by the targeted terrorists, and that there is no other alternative—such as arrest—that is feasible under the circumstances. The law should also cast the blame for unintended civilian deaths caused by democracies on the terrorists who deliberately hide among civilians using them as "shields." The domestic law of most democratic nations does precisely that. If a bank robber takes a teller hostage and uses him as a shield against the police, and if the police, in an effort to shoot the robber who is firing from behind his shield, kills the shield, it is the robber who is guilty of murder, even though it was the policeman who fired the fatal shot. The same should be the case in international law.

Next, consider the problem of what to do with captured "prisoners" 10
who are believed to be terrorists. This vague category of detainees is comprised of several different sub-groups. There are those who were captured in the course of military action in a foreign country. The United States and its allies captured Taliban "soldiers" and those fighting alongside them in Afghanistan. A few wore ersatz uniforms; most did not. Some were just in the wrong place at the wrong time. Then there were admitted members of al-Qa'ida, ranging from Khalid Sheikh Mohammed, the alleged number two or three man in the organization, to Zacarias Moussaoui, a terrorist wannabe who may or may not have been the "20th" September 11 hijacker. Some of the detainees are believed to have valuable real-time information that could save lives. Others are simply terrorist pawns willing to do whatever they are told, even if it entails suicide. Inevitably, some, probably, are completely innocent and not dangerous.

The problem is that the current laws regulating the detention of combatants are near useless when it comes to this motley array of detainees. These detainees simply do not fit into the old, anachronistic categories. Most are not classic prisoners of war. They were not part of a uniformed army under the command of a nation. But neither do they fit into the classic definition of "unlawful combatants." They are not spies or saboteurs, as those terms have been understood in the context of conventional warfare. Nor are many of them simple "criminals," subject to ordinary trials under the domestic law of crimes. They comprise a new category—or set of categories—unto themselves. They cannot be held as POWs until the end of the war, because this is a war that will never end. They cannot simply be released, because many of them would quickly volunteer to engage in suicide terrorist missions against their former captors, as some already have done. Most cannot be tried as criminals, because their actions took place outside the jurisdiction of the detaining nation. Those who have valuable, real-time information will be interrogated, and—short of the absolute law against "torture"—there are few, if any, rules governing the nature of permissible interrogation when the object is not to elicit "incrimination confessions" for purposes of criminal prosecution, but rather to obtain "preventive intelligence" for the purpose of pre-empting future terrorist attacks.

Should the same rules that govern the interrogation of ordinary criminal suspects be applicable? Or should more latitude be afforded to interrogators in the preventive context? Should sleep deprivation be authorized? Loud music? Alternating heat and cold? Uncomfortable and/or painful seating? What about truth serum? False threats? We know that the United States has used "water boarding"—a technique that produces a near-drowning experience but no physical after-effects—on Khalid Sheikh Mohammed, a high-ranking al-Qa'ida detainee. Is that categorized as torture? I certainly think so, but the United States government apparently does not. We need rules even for such unpleasant practices.

There is today a vast "black hole" in the law. It is this hole that accounts for Guantanamo, extraordinary renditions and other phantom places and actions about which we know nothing. As a lifelong civil libertarian, I strongly oppose such gaps in the law. The rule of law requires that all governmental action be subject to legal constraints. The refusal to change old laws that do not fit new situations is bad for human rights and dangerous to democratic accountability.

Nor does it help the situation when Amnesty International and other human-rights groups exaggerate the problems and cast all the blame on democracies that are seeking—sometimes by questionable means—to keep their citizens safe from terrorists. Anne Fitzgerald of Amnesty recently compared the alleged terrorists being detained by the U.S. and its allies to the "disappeared" in Argentina during the Junta. The comparison is obscene. The disappeared in Argentina were mostly political opponents of the Junta, many of whom were tortured to death and dropped into the ocean from aircraft. Credible sources estimate that as many as 30,000 people may have been killed. Pregnant women had their babies ripped from their wombs so they could be adopted by childless friends of the Junta. There is no evidence of anything even close to this being done by the United States today in its sometimes excessive efforts to prevent terrorism. The problems are bad enough without the need to exaggerate them for political and ideological purposes.

Human-rights groups undercut the real interests of human rights when 15
they exaggerate the faults of democracies and minimize the faults of terrorists. Most democracies seek to operate within the rule of laws, and laws must realistically reflect the desirable balance between the legitimate needs of security and the equally legitimate claims of human rights. Striking this balance is a daunting task, and it is in the nature of such balances that few are ever satisfied that it has been properly struck. It is far easier to stick with the comfortable old ways, even if it produces hypocrisy and gaping holes in the law.

Laws must change with the times. They must adapt to new challenges. That has been the genius of the common law. Ironically, it is generally the left that seeks change in the laws, while the right is satisfied with Henry IV. Today it is many on the left who resist any changes in the law of war or human rights. They deny the reality that the war against terrorism is any way different from conventional wars of the past, or that the old laws must be adapted to the new threats. The result is often an unreasonable debate of extremes: the hard left insists that the old laws should not be tampered with in the least; the hard right insists that the old laws are entirely inapplicable to the new threats, and that democratic governments should be entirely free to do whatever it takes to combat terrorism, without regard to anachronistic laws. Both extremes are dangerous. What is needed is a new set of laws, based on the principles of the old laws of war and human rights—the protection of civilians—but adapted to the new threats against civilian victims of terrorism.

The President of the supreme court of Israel, Aharon Barak, in deciding that torture could not be justified even for purposes of securing information that might prevent terrorism, wrote the following lines: "[It] is the destiny of democracy that not all means are acceptable to it, and not all practices employed by its enemies are open before it. Although a democracy must often fight with one hand tied behind its back, it nonetheless has the upper hand. Preserving the Rule of Law and recognition of an individual's liberty constitutes an important component in its understanding of security. At the end of the day, they [add to] its strength. . . ."

But, while it may well be necessary for democracies to fight terrorists with one hand tied behind their backs, it is neither necessary nor desirable for a democracy to fight with two hands tied behind its back, especially when the ropes that bind the second hand are anachronistic laws that can be changed without compromising legitimate human rights. The laws must be changed to permit democracies to fight fairly and effectively against those who threaten its citizens. To paraphrase Robert Jackson, who served as the United States chief prosecutor at Nuremberg—the law must not be "a suicide pact."

READING AND DISCUSSION QUESTIONS

1. Why does Dershowitz believe that the deterrent model of war is no longer a realistic model to use? What, specifically, in Article 51 of the United Nations Charter is it that he sees as no longer realistic?
2. Why does he believe even the "redefinition" of Article 51 is not enough?
3. Dershowitz quotes a European diplomat who uses the term "harsh arithmetic of pain." What does that term mean, applied to terrorism?
4. What is Dershowitz's view of civilian casualties?
5. Why are prisoners of war in the war on terrorism different from other prisoners before them?
6. What is Dershowitz's claim in the essay? Where is it most clearly stated?
7. What title could the essay be given that is more relevant to what the essay actually says?

WRITING SUGGESTIONS

8. In his much briefer article earlier in the chapter, Dershowitz argues in favor of very special techniques for eliciting information from suspected terrorists. Write an argument supporting whether or not that claim is more convincing once it is placed in the context of this more fully developed piece.
9. Write an essay explaining two or more of the techniques that Dershowitz uses in supporting his argument.
10. Write an essay evaluating how successful Dershowitz is in defending his claim.

Parents Need Help: Restricting Access to Video Games

BARBARA DAFOE WHITEHEAD

A century ago, Jane Addams and other progressive reformers in Chicago responded to the dangers of the industrial age by creating laws and institutions that would protect children from the unwholesome lures of the city streets. Her work is rightly honored. A similar, and equally important, struggle is being waged in Illinois today. On the surface, it's about the sale of video games to kids. It's also a debate about a deeper question: To what degree does the responsibility for teaching good values to children fall solely on parents? Should some of that responsibility be shared by the state?

Those who make and sell video games say parents alone should bear the responsibility. On the other side is Illinois Governor Rod Blagojevich. He's trying to outlaw the sale of excessively violent or sexually explicit video games to children under eighteen. In his effort to restrict such sales he's making the argument that raising children is a shared responsibility: "Parenting is hard work and the state has a compelling interest in helping parents raise their children to be upstanding men and women."

The governor firmly believes that parents have the primary responsibility for teaching their children right from wrong. He believes just as firmly that parents should not have their efforts subverted by the avalanche of "amusements" that tell kids it is fun to blow people up. "Too many of the video games marketed to our children teach them all of the wrong lessons and all of the wrong values," Blagojevich writes in a "letter to Illinois parents" posted on the state's informational Web site (www.safegamesIllinois.com). "These games use violence, rage, and sexual aggression as play. That is not acceptable. When kids play, they should play like children, not like gangland assassins."

The governor's reference to gangland assassins is not an overstatement. One video game, the top-selling, industry-award-winning Grand Theft Auto: San Andreas, features gang warfare and the killing of prostitutes. Another, released on the forty-first anniversary of the Kennedy assassination, gets players to step into the shoes of Lee Harvey Oswald and to aim at the president's head as his motorcade rolls by. "Content descriptors" for video games also suggest how lurid the violence can be. These games include depictions of "blood and gore (mutilation of body parts)," "intense violence (human injury or death)," and "sexual violence (depictions of rape and other sexual acts)."

Barbara Dafoe Whitehead is codirector of the National Marriage Project at Rutgers University and the author of *The Divorce Culture: Rethinking Our Commitments to Marriage and Family* (1998) and *Why There Are No Good Men Left: The Romantic Plight of the New Single Woman* (2003). The column appeared in *Commonweal* on January 28, 2005.

5 No sooner had Blagojevich unveiled his proposal than he faced powerful organized opposition from the entertainment industry. The Illinois Retail Merchants Association, the National Association of Theater Owners, the Entertainment Software Rating Board, and the Motion Picture Association of America took strong exception to the legislation. Imposing a curb on the free market is not the way to protect kids, these critics argued. Instead, parents should screen what their kids are buying and playing. As one lobbyist put it: "Retailers can't be held accountable for lack of oversight by parents."

This is a distortion of the governor's position, and of the problem. No one denies that parents have the primary responsibility for monitoring their kids. Blagojevich points out, though, that the sophisticated technology of video games makes that very hard to do. Consequently, it's up to the state to step in on the side of parents and children to help them cope.

The industry argument would be plausible if it were still 1955. Back then, it was easier for parents to exercise strict oversight. The big, boxy home entertainment technologies of that era—radio, television, and record players—produced images and sounds that parents could see and hear. They came with OFF buttons for parents to push and plugs for parents to pull. All that has changed. The new entertainment technologies include a dizzying and ever-multiplying array of small, portable, individual, kid-friendly devices that defy close parental supervision. It was easy for parents to check on a half-hour TV show. It's much harder to review a video game. The games feature successive levels of difficulty; players must qualify at a lower level before earning the right to move to a higher level. So it takes time and practice before acquiring the skill to progress to the highest level of the game—which may also be its highest level of violence. To ensure that a video game isn't excessively violent, a parent would have to be looking over a child's shoulder until the highest level of play was finally revealed. This could take days.

Moreover, it isn't as if parents and the video-game industry meet each other on a level playing field. This is a multibillion-dollar industry that spends all its time and money devising ever more ingenious ways to market to kids over the heads of their parents and to deliberately undermine the ability of parents to regulate what their children are seeing. And in a tactic called "age compression," the marketers target their appeals to ever-younger kids. Like the youth sex revolution, the youth marketing revolution has migrated down the age scale. Even four-year-olds know what is cool.

To be sure, the industry's Entertainment Software Rating Board has voluntarily established its own ratings system. The trouble is: It isn't enforced. A study by the Federal Trade Commission found that early teens were able to buy games rated M (Mature 17+) 69 percent of the time.

10 It is telling that the makers and sellers of video games have responded so quickly and vigorously to Governor Blagojevich's very modest proposal. Clearly the corporate sector finds it in its interest to prompt kids to engage in fantasy rape, beheadings, and mass murder. And why should we expect otherwise? Its interest is the bottom line. Violence sells. But isn't it in the compelling interest of the community to curb such violent play?

READING AND DISCUSSION QUESTIONS

1. Do you believe that video games are getting too violent and sexually explicit?
2. Is Whitehead right that the rating system for video games is not enforced? What might be done to make it work?
3. What is your position as to who should bear the responsibility of keeping violent and sexually explicit video games away from children? Or is there a need to keep them away?
4. Why are our children and teens attracted to games that are so violent?
5. How do you respond to Whitehead's statement that the video-game industry "spends all its time and money devising ever more ingenious ways to market to kids over the heads of their parents and to deliberately undermine the ability of parents to regulate what their children are seeing"?
6. To what extent are the choices children and teens make when it comes to video games in keeping with choices they make in choosing movies and television shows? Is there a difference in the level of control parents and the businesses involved have?

WRITING SUGGESTIONS

7. Write an essay explaining how Whitehead's bias is revealed not only in her statements about the governor and the video-game industry but also in the language she uses in discussing them.
8. How convincing is Whitehead in arguing that, as her title says, parents need help?
9. What warrants, or underlying assumptions, are behind Whitehead's argument?

Warfare: An Invention — Not a Biological Necessity

MARGARET MEAD

Is war a biological necessity, a sociological inevitability, or just a bad invention? Those who argue for the first view endow man with such pugnacious instincts that some outlet in aggressive behaviour is necessary if man is to reach full human stature. It was this point of view which lay behind William

---

Margaret Mead (1901–1978), the first American anthropologist to study childhood, adolescence, and gender, focused her work on culture rather than biology or race as the primary focus in determining variations in human behavior and personality. Her findings are detailed in hundreds of articles and numerous bestselling books, such as *Coming of Age in Samoa* (1928), *Growing Up in New Guinea* (1930), and *Sex and Temperament* (1935). This article, in which Mead argues that warfare is a cultural invention and not a biological necessity, was published in *Asia* in 1940.

James's famous essay, "The Moral Equivalent of War," in which he tried to retain the warlike virtues and channel them in new directions. A similar point of view has lain behind the Soviet Union's attempt to make competition between groups rather than between individuals. A basic, competitive, aggressive, warring human nature is assumed, and those who wish to outlaw war or outlaw competitiveness merely try to find new and less socially destructive ways in which these biologically given aspects of man's nature can find expression. Then there are those who take the second view: warfare is the inevitable concomitant of the development of the state, the struggle for land and natural resources, of class societies springing not from the nature of man, but, from the nature of history. War is nevertheless inevitable unless we change our social system and outlaw classes, the struggle for power, and possessions; and in the event of our success warfare would disappear, as a symptom vanishes when the disease is cured.

One may hold a sort of compromise position between these two extremes; one may claim that all aggression springs from the frustration of man's biologically determined drives and that, since all forms of culture are frustrating, it is certain each new generation will be aggressive and the aggression will find its natural and inevitable expression in race war, class war, nationalistic war, and so on.

All three of these positions are very popular today among those who think seriously about the problems of war and its possible prevention, but I wish to urge another point of view, less defeatist, perhaps, than the first and third and more accurate than the second: that is, that warfare, by which I mean recognized conflict between two groups as groups, in which each group puts an army (even if the army is only fifteen pygmies) into the field to fight and kill, if possible, some of the members of the army of the other group—that warfare of this sort is an invention like any other of the inventions in terms of which we order our lives, such as writing, marriage, cooking our food instead of eating it raw, trial by jury, or burial of the dead, and so on. Some of this list anyone will grant are inventions: trial by jury is confined to very limited portions of the globe; we know that there are tribes that do not bury their dead but instead expose or cremate them; and we know that only part of the human race has had the knowledge of writing as its cultural inheritance. But, whenever a way of doing things is found universally, such as the use of fire or the practice of some form of marriage, we tend to think at once that it is not an invention at all but an attribute of humanity itself. And yet even such universals as marriage and the use of fire are inventions like the rest, very basic ones, inventions which were, perhaps, necessary if human history was to take the turn that it has taken, but nevertheless inventions. At some point in his social development man was undoubtedly without the institution of marriage or the knowledge of the use of fire.

The case for warfare is much clearer because there are peoples even today who have no warfare. Of these the Eskimos are perhaps the most conspicuous examples, but the Lepchas of Sikkim described by Geoffrey Gorer in

Himalayan Village are as good. Neither of these peoples understands war, not even defensive warfare. The idea of warfare is lacking, and this idea is as essential to really carrying on war as an alphabet or a syllabary is to writing. But, whereas the Lepchas are a gentle, unquarrelsome people, and the advocates of other points of view might argue that they are not full human beings or that they had never been frustrated and so had no aggression to expand in warfare, the Eskimo case gives no such possibility of interpretation. The Eskimos are not a mild and meek people; many of them are turbulent and troublesome. Fights, theft of wives, murder, cannibalism, occur among them—all outbursts of passionate men goaded by desire or intolerable circumstance. Here are men faced with hunger, men faced with loss of their wives, men faced with the threat of extermination by other men, and here are orphan children, growing up miserably with no one to care for them, mocked and neglected by those about them. The personality necessary for war, the circumstances necessary to goad men to desperation are present, but there is no war. When a travelling Eskimo entered a settlement, he might have to fight the strongest man in the settlement to establish his position among them, but this was a test of strength and bravery, not war. The idea of warfare, of one group organizing against another group to maim and wound and kill them was absent. And, without that idea, passions might rage but there was no war.

But, it may be argued, is not this because the Eskimos have such a low 5
and undeveloped form of social organization? They own no land, they move from place to place, camping, it is true, season after season on the same site, but this is not something to fight for as the modern nations of the world fight for land and raw materials. They have no permanent possessions that can be looted, no towns that can be burned. They have no social classes to produce stress and strains within the society which might force it to go to war outside. Does not the absence of war among the Eskimos, while disproving the biological necessity of war, just go to confirm the point that it is the state of development of the society which accounts for war and nothing else?

We find the answer among the pygmy peoples of the Andaman Islands in the Bay of Bengal. The Andamans also represent an exceedingly low level of society; they are a hunting and food-gathering people; they live in tiny hordes without any class stratification; their houses are simpler than the snow houses of the Eskimo. But they knew about warfare. The army might contain only fifteen determined pygmies marching in a straight line, but it was the real thing none the less. Tiny army met tiny army in open battle, blows were exchanged, casualties suffered, and the state of warfare could only be concluded by a peacemaking ceremony.

Similarly, among the Australian aborigines, who built no permanent dwellings but wandered from water hole to water hole over their almost desert country, warfare—and rules of "international law"—were highly developed. The student of social evolution will seek in vain for his obvious causes of war, struggle for lands, struggle for power of one group over another, expansion of population, need to divert the minds of a populace restive under tyranny, or even the ambition of a successful leader to enhance his own prestige. All are absent, but warfare as a practice remained, and men engaged in it and killed one another in the course of a war because killing is what is done in wars.

From instances like these it becomes apparent that an inquiry into the causes of war misses the fundamental point as completely as does an insistence upon the biological necessity of war. If a people have an idea of going to war and the idea that war is the way in which certain situations, defined within their society, are to be handled, they will sometimes go to war. If they are a mild and unaggressive people, like the Pueblo Indians, they may limit themselves to defensive warfare, but they will be forced to think in terms of war because there are peoples near them who have warfare as a pattern, and offensive, raiding, pillaging warfare at that. When the pattern of warfare is known, people like the Pueblo Indians will defend themselves, taking advantage of their natural defenses, the mesa village site, and people like the Lepchas, having no natural defenses and no idea of warfare, will merely submit to the invader. But the essential point remains the same. There is a way of behaving which is known to a given people and labeled as an appropriate form of behavior; a bold and warlike people like the Sioux or the Maori may label warfare as desirable as well as possible, a mild people like the Pueblo Indians may label warfare as undesirable, but to the minds of both peoples the possibility of warfare is present. Their thoughts, their hopes, their plans are oriented about this idea—that warfare may be selected as the way to meet some situation.

So simple peoples and civilized peoples, mild peoples and violent, assertive peoples, will all go to war if they have the invention, just as those peoples who have the custom of dueling will have duels and peoples who have the pattern of vendetta will indulge in vendetta. And, conversely, peoples who do not know of dueling will not fight duels, even though their wives are seduced and their daughters ravished; they may on occasion commit murder but they will not fight duels. Cultures which lack the idea of the vendetta will not meet every quarrel in this way. A people can use only the forms it has. So the Balinese have their special way of dealing with a quarrel between two individuals: if the two feel that the causes of quarrel are heavy, they may go and register their quarrel in the temple before the gods, and, making offerings, they may swear never to have anything to do with each other again. . . . But in other societies, although individuals might feel as full of animosity and as unwilling to have any further contact as do the Balinese, they cannot register their quarrel with the gods and go on quietly about their business because registering quarrels with the gods is not an invention of which they know.

Yet, if it be granted that warfare is, after all, an invention, it may never- 10
theless be an invention that lends itself to certain types of personality, to the exigent needs of autocrats, to the expansionist desires of crowded peoples, to the desire for plunder and rape and loot which is engendered by a dull

and frustrating life. What, then, can we say of this congruence between warfare and its uses? If it is a form which fits so well, is not this congruence the essential point? But even here the primitive material causes us to wonder, because there are tribes who go to war merely for glory, having no quarrel with the enemy, suffering from no tyrant within their boundaries, anxious neither for land nor loot nor women, but merely anxious to win prestige which within that tribe has been declared obtainable only by war and without which no young man can hope to win his sweetheart's smile of approval. But if, as was the case with the Bush Negroes of Dutch Guiana, it is artistic ability which is necessary to win a girl's approval, the same young man would have to be carving rather than going out on a war party.

In many parts of the world, war is a game in which the individual can win counters—counters which bring him prestige in the eyes of his own sex or of the opposite sex; he plays for these counters as he might, in our society, strive for a tennis championship. Warfare is a frame for such prestige-seeking merely because it calls for the display of certain skills and certain virtues; all of these skills—riding straight, shooting straight, dodging the missiles of the enemy and sending one's own straight to the mark—can be equally well exercised in some other framework and, equally, the virtues endurance, bravery, loyalty, steadfastness—can be displayed in other contexts. The tie-up between proving oneself a man and proving this by a success in organized killing is due to a definition which many societies have made of manliness. And often, even in those societies which counted success in warfare a proof of human worth, strange turns were given to the idea, as when the plains Indians gave their highest awards to the man who touched a live enemy rather than to the man who brought in a scalp—from a dead enemy—because the latter was less risky. Warfare is just an invention known to the majority of human societies by which they permit their young men either to accumulate prestige or avenge their honor or acquire loot or wives or slaves or sago lands or cattle or appease the blood lust of their gods or the restless souls of the recently dead. It is just an invention, older and more widespread than the jury system, but none the less an invention.

But, once we have said this, have we said anything at all? Despite a few stances, dear to the instances of controversialist, of the loss of the useful arts, once an invention is made which proves congruent with human needs or social forms, it tends to persist. Grant that war is an invention, that it is not a biological necessity nor the outcome of certain special types of social forms, still once the invention is made, what are we to do about it? The Indian who had been subsisting on the buffalo for generations because with his primitive weapons he could slaughter only a limited number of buffalo did not return to his primitive weapons when he saw that the white man's more efficient weapons were exterminating the buffalo. A desire for the white man's cloth may mortgage the South Sea Islander to the white man's plantation, but he does not return to making bark cloth, which would have left him free. Once an invention is known and accepted, men do not easily relinquish it. The skilled workers may smash the first steam looms which they feel are to be their undoing, but they accept them in the end, and no movement which has insisted upon the mere abandonment of usable inventions has ever had much success. Warfare is here, as part of our thought; the deeds of warriors are immortalized in the words of our poets, the toys of our children are modeled upon the weapons of the soldier, the frame of reference within which our statesmen and our diplomats work always contains war. If we know that it is not inevitable, that it is due to historical accident that warfare is one of the ways in which we think of behaving, are we given any hope by that? What hope is there of persuading nations to abandon war, nations so thoroughly imbued with the idea that to resort to war is, if not actually desirable and noble, at least inevitable whenever certain defined circumstances arise?

In answer to this question I think we might turn to the history of other social inventions, and inventions which must once have seemed as finally entrenched as warfare. Take the methods of trial which preceded the jury system: ordeal and trial by combat. Unfair, capricious, alien as they are to our feeling today, they were once the only methods open to individuals accused of some offense. The invention of trial by jury gradually replaced these methods until only witches, and finally not even witches, had to resort to the ordeal. And for a long time the jury system seemed the best and finest method of settling legal disputes, but today new inventions, trial before judges only or before commissions, are replacing the jury system. In each case the old method was replaced by a new social invention. The ordeal did not go out because people thought it unjust or wrong; it went out because a method more congruent with the institutions and feelings of the period was invented. And, if we despair over the way in which war seems such an ingrained habit of most of the human race, we can take comfort from the fact that a poor invention will usually give place to a better invention.

For this, two conditions, at least, are necessary. The people must recognize the defects of the old invention, and someone must make a new one. Propaganda against warfare, documentation of its terrible cost in human suffering and social waste, these prepare the ground by teaching people to feel that warfare is a defective social institution. There is further needed a belief that social invention is possible and the invention of new methods which will render warfare as out of date as the tractor is making the plough, or the motor car the horse and buggy. A form of behavior becomes out of date only when something else takes its place, and, in order to invent forms of behavior which will make war obsolete, it is a first requirement to believe that an invention is possible.

READING AND DISCUSSION QUESTIONS

1. What theories does Mead refute before explaining her own?
2. To what other inventions does Mead compare war?
3. What conclusions does she draw from her observations about Eskimos?

4. She ponders if it does any good to recognize war as an invention. How does she answer her own question?
5. What solution to the problem of warfare does Mead propose? Do you find any flaws in her proposal? Explain your agreement or disagreement with the plausibility of her solution.
6. In an article entitled "Where Have All the Young Men Gone? The Perfect Substitute for War," the author, Paul Auster, marvels at the significance of a gathering in 1998 of more than a million people to celebrate France's victory in the World Cup of soccer. "The vast majority of Europeans," he writes, "have found a way to hate one another without hacking one another to pieces."[1] Do you agree that sports are an outlet for hostility that once would have found an outlet in battle? Explain.

WRITING SUGGESTIONS

7. Mead uses a common organizational strategy—refuting the opposing view. In this essay she refutes several theories about the origins of warfare. Summarize these theories. Where does she state her own thesis?
8. Mead supports her argument with examples and analogies. Are they all equally convincing? To what extent does the success of her essay depend on her use of examples?

DEBATE: How Serious Is the Problem of Online Predators?

MySpace and Sex Offenders: What's the Problem?

BOB SULLIVAN

In October, Wired News reporter Kevin Poulsen ran a simple experiment that produced some disturbing results. He wrote a computer program that matched databases of registered sex offenders with MySpace profiles and found hundreds of matches.

On Poulsen's list: A thrice-convicted sex offender who had recently finished a nine-year jail term for sexually abusing two young boys. It turned out he was using MySpace to approach and proposition young boys. The offender was soon arrested again.

[1] *New York Times Magazine,* April 4, 1999, p. 144.

Bob Sullivan covers Internet scams and consumer fraud for MSNBC.com and has received numerous awards for that work. In 2004 he published *Your Evil Twin: Behind the Identity Theft Epidemic.* He posted this essay to his blog on May 29, 2007.

Two months after Poulsen's story was published, MySpace announced it had hired an outside company, Sentinel Tech Holding Corp., to compare registered sex offenders rolls with MySpace profiles and root out sex criminals from the site. Until earlier this month, though, it appeared little progress had been made.

Then, a public spat erupted between a group of state attorneys general and MySpace, with the AGs demanding to know how many offenders the review had uncovered. After about a week of public jousting, MySpace said it had removed 7,000 profiles that might have belonged to registered sex offenders.

5 The controversy has raised questions about MySpace's diligence in trying to keep predators off its service and its ability to work with some law enforcement officials.

That so many registered offenders were attracted to MySpace, largely a haunt for young Web users, is disturbing to Connecticut Attorney General Richard Blumenthal.

"It is a very, very frightening number when you consider they . . . are using their real names," he said. "One would think a convicted sex offender would use an alias. This number is just the most visible tip of the predatory problem on MySpace and other social networking sites."

Why did this rather public controversy over sex offender MySpace pages erupt this month? Curiously, it began when MySpace—often criticized for inaction on child safety issues—took a strong action against registered sex offenders.

Sentinel Starts

The initial spark flew on May 2, when MySpace unceremoniously turned on the product developed by Sentinel and began removing profiles from the site.

10 Within days, the group of attorney general offices already eyeing MySpace policies found out about the deletions and became concerned that evidence of crimes might be destroyed.

"We were rather concerned that we were hearing back channel information about profiles being removed and deleted without us receiving that information," said Nils Frederiksen, a spokesman for Pennsylvania Attorney General Tom Corbett. "We need to know which Pennsylvania residents have been identified because of possible terms and conditions of their release that may have been violated."

Some probation agreements prevent sex offenders from using computers at all; others prevent them from any contact with minors. The offenders' MySpace profiles may have included clear evidence that such provisions were being violated, Frederiksen said.

"Along the way we were hearing that this was a work in progress, that it wasn't ready," he said. "Then in the spring we found out they'd already deleted profiles. That was what motivated the public call to action."

On May 15, eight attorneys general sent a letter to MySpace demanding more information about registered offenders on the site. The next day, MySpace refused to provide the data, saying it could only do so if compelled by a court order. Several states began seeking court orders to obtain the data, but five days later MySpace announced that an agreement had been reached to share the information.

A Misunderstanding

To MySpace officials, it was all a misunderstanding. The new system was still 15
being tested when the suspect profiles began being removed, so the company believed there was no need, at that point, to notify attorneys general who were already working with the company, said one MySpace official, who agreed to discuss the matter on condition he not be identified.

And the profile removal process was designed to preserve any evidence law enforcement might subsequently need, the company said.

"In addition to immediately removing registered sex offenders from MySpace, our plans have always been to provide the information collected by Sentinel . . . to law enforcement, including the attorneys general," Mike Angus, executive vice president and general counsel for Fox Interactive Media, which owns MySpace, said in a statement.

But the spat likely signals more than concern about deletion of evidence. There is obvious sentiment among law enforcement agencies that MySpace was acting too slowly to remove known sex offenders from the site.

"We were disappointed it's taken a year to get to this point," Frederiksen said. His office had approached MySpace about the sex offender issue even before the Wired story was published. "We would like to see things move forward in a faster pace."

No National Sex Offender Registry

But company officials say government sex offender registries are to blame 20
for the hold-up.

Because most registries are maintained by state offices and there is no national database, Sentinel had to build a tool that collected information on 600,000 offenders from more than 50 sources, the company said. Because the data couldn't be downloaded from registry Web sites, collecting the data was a complicated project. Building the tool took about 6 months, the official said.

Still, some officials in the various attorney general offices suggested MySpace had another motivation for moving slowly and deleting profiles without informing public officials: quietly removing the offender profiles without drawing attention to the number of convicted sex criminals who lurk on the site.

"In fairness to MySpace, it did take the step of hiring Sentinel . . . but they are ambivalent about releasing the results," Blumenthal said. "Perhaps they feel it may reflect badly on this site and other sites."

In his October story, Poulsen concluded that matching sex offender registries to MySpace profiles was hardly the most effective tool for improving the site's safety. After all, would-be predators could easily foil such filters by registering with fake names and other information. Blumenthal and other attorneys general are pushing for additional measures, such as mandatory age verification to keep kids off the site altogether.

25 But the presence of 7,000 registered offenders on the site—and the time span required to remove them—raises inevitable questions about MySpace's ability to keep its neighborhood safe.

"The measures taken by MySpace have been baby steps when giant strides are needed," Blumenthal said.

MySpace Not Responsible for Predators

KEVIN ALEXANDER

There is no way to stop a determined predator. There is no way to stop a determined victim.

On June 19, a 14-year-old girl and her mother filed a lawsuit against MySpace. The suit claims that MySpace's lack of age verification allowed a 19-year-old man, Pete Solis, to lie about his age and contact the girl. Solis convinced the 14-year-old to meet him outside of cyberspace, where he took her to dinner and a movie and then allegedly raped her.

The family's lawyer, Adam Loewy, said the family is seeking $30 million worth of damages, citing MySpace's security features as "utterly ineffective." He also dropped this bombshell: "MySpace is more concerned with making money than protecting children online." Get out of town, Mr. Loewy. MySpace is a business, and one that has never advertised itself as an online baby-sitting service. Making money is its reason for existence.

If the rape allegations are true, then this is a tragedy. Nearly all actions taken by predators are tragedies, but this lawsuit is frivolous, and potentially damaging to the nature of the Internet.

5 This kind of thing happens cyclically. Video games, music, and television have all been blamed for the actions of a few naive or demented people. Corporations and organizations are demonized, lawsuits are filed, most are thrown out, and the parents of the offender or victim sneak off the radar. That's what is happening here. Any police officer will tell you that nearly all youth crimes happen because some moron forgot to be a parent.

Kevin Alexander was a student at Texas A&M when he wrote this for the independent student newspaper the *Battalion* in June 2006.

This girl's mother failed here several times. She didn't convince her daughter of the dangers of cyberspace; she didn't monitor her Internet usage well enough, she let her 14-year-old daughter physically meet a 19-year-old man, and she's now sending the wrong message by deflecting the responsibility onto a Web site that has no control over sociopaths.

The girl, as traumatic as her experience was, should be held responsible, too. At 14 years of age, she's capable of calculating risk and other higher brain functions. She ignored the danger of dealing with someone she didn't know. She gave away personal information and she consented to physically meet Solis. She could've prevented being a victim, but she was determined to ignore all the apparent risks, and she paid for it.

There are more than 80 million users on MySpace. So far, only three cases of molestation have hit the courts. They are anomalies, and they are impossible to extinguish completely. Teenage socialization is oftentimes chaotic, and predators are unbalanced equations.

Fortunately, MySpace has foreseen this, and has attempted to protect itself. When creating an account, users must sign a waiver that states, "MySpace.com is not responsible for the conduct, whether online or offline, of any user of the MySpace Services." The 14-year-old signed this agreement, and thus signed away her protection under naiveté. This should be enough to get the suit thrown out, but it's big trouble for the Internet if it isn't.

The Internet is a gigantic medium for everything. If this lawsuit goes 10
through, then any Web site that deals with any sort of exchange, be it monetary, information, or services, is at risk for lawsuit. If someone does something stupid while on the Internet, then that person can sue the Net. There are tons of predators out there, and there are tons of waiting victims. It's unknown as of now which ones are more dangerous.

DISCUSSION QUESTIONS

1. To what extent are those who are responsible for MySpace to be applauded for their attempts to make their site safer? What do you believe has been wrong with their attempts?
2. Do you believe that deleting profiles of sex offenders is the best way to solve the problem of online predators? Why, or why not?
3. What is your opinion of the state's use of MySpace profiles to catch predators violating their parole?
4. Are you convinced that there really is danger in using MySpace? Explain.
5. What is Sullivan's thesis?
6. In Alexander's article, how culpable do you believe the teenaged girl is in what happened to her? Do you think that many girls her age actually meet men they have communicated with online?
7. How much responsibility do you believe her mother has to bear for what happened?
8. Respond to this statement by Adam Loewy, the lawyer: "'MySpace is more concerned with making money than protecting children online.'"

9. How would you state Alexander's thesis?
10. Research what happened to the lawsuit filed by the girl's family.
11. Explain which you believe to be a stronger argument—Sullivan's or Alexander's—and why.

ASSIGNMENTS FOR WRITING ABOUT ARGUMENT

READING AND DISCUSSION QUESTIONS

1. Choose an editorial from your campus or local newspaper and evaluate it. How successful an argument does it make?
2. In his essay, "Should We Fight Terror with Torture?," Alan Dershowitz argues for new rules of war. In her essay, "War: An Invention—Not a Biological Necessity," Margaret Mead argues for a new perception of why human beings go to war. How are Mead's ideas from 1940 relevant to Dershowitz's from 2001?
3. Evaluate the argument that Charles Krauthammer makes in his essay, "Let's Have No More Monkey Trials."
4. Barbara Dafoe Whitehead argues that parents need help from the state in controlling their children's leisure activities. Charles Krauthammer argues that parents should not interfere with the way the state says that science should be taught in public schools. Who provides a more convincing argument?

WRITING SUGGESTIONS

5. Choose an editorial from your campus or local newspaper and write an objective analysis of it. Your thesis statement will be a claim of fact.
6. Locate two editorials or two articles that take different stands on the same controversial issue. Write an analysis in which you objectively compare the two as examples of argumentation.
7. Locate two editorials or two articles that take different stands on the same controversial issue. Write an essay in which you argue which of the two is a more effective argument and why.
8. Explain in an essay which of the two essays about MySpace presents a stronger argument, Kevin Alexander's or Bob Sullivan's.

CHAPTER 5

Defining Key Terms

THE PURPOSES OF DEFINITION

Before we examine the other elements of argument, we need to consider definition, a component you may have to deal with early in writing an essay. Definition may be used in two ways: to clarify the meanings of vague or ambiguous terms or as a method of development for the whole essay. In some arguments your claims will contain words that need explanation before you can proceed with any discussion. But you may also want to devote an entire essay to the elaboration of a broad concept or experience that cannot be adequately defined in a shorter space.

The Roman statesman Cicero said, "Every rational discussion of anything whatsoever should begin with a definition in order to make clear what is the subject of dispute." Arguments often revolve around definitions of crucial terms. For example, how does one define *democracy*? Does a democracy guarantee freedom of the press, freedom of worship, freedom of assembly, and freedom of movement? In the United States, we would argue that such freedoms are essential to any definition of *democracy*. But countries in which these freedoms are nonexistent also represent themselves as democracies or governments of the people. In the words of Senator Daniel P. Moynihan, "For years now the most brutal totalitarian regimes have called themselves 'people's' or 'democratic' republics." Rulers in such governments are aware that defining their regimes as democratic may win the approval of people who would otherwise condemn them. In his formidable attack on totalitarianism in *1984*, George Orwell coined the slogans "War Is Peace" and "Slavery Is Freedom," phrases that represent the corrupt use of definition to distort reality.

But even where there is no intention to deceive, the snares of definition are difficult to avoid. How do you define *abortion*? Is it "termination of pregnancy"? Or is it "murder of an unborn child"? During a celebrated trial in 1975 of a physician who performed an abortion and was accused of manslaughter, the prosecution often used the word *baby* to refer to the fetus, but the defense referred to "the products of conception." These definitions of *fetus* reflected the differing judgments of those on opposite sides. Not only do judgments create definitions; definitions influence judgments. In the abortion trial, the definitions of *fetus* used by both sides were meant to promote either approval or disapproval of the doctor's action.

Definitions can indeed change the nature of an event or a "fact." How many farms are there in the state of New York? The answer to the question depends on the definition of *farm*. In 1979 the *New York Times* reported:

> Because of a change in the official definition of the word "farm," New York lost 20 percent of its farms on January 1, with numbers dropping from 56,000 to 45,000. . . .
>
> Before the change, a farm was defined as "any place from which $250 or more of agricultural products is sold" yearly or "any place of 10 acres or more from which $50 or more of agricultural products is sold" yearly. Now a farm is "any place from which $1,000 or more of agricultural products is sold" in a year.[1]

A change in the definition of *poverty* can have similar results. An article in the *New York Times*, whose headline reads, "A Revised Definition of Poverty May Raise Number of U.S. Poor," makes this clear:

> The official definition of *poverty* used by the Federal Government for three decades is based simply on cash income before taxes. But in a report to be issued on Wednesday, a panel of experts convened by the [National] Academy of Sciences three years ago at the behest of Congress says the Government should move toward a concept of poverty based on disposable income, the amount left after a family pays taxes and essential expenses.[2]

The differences are wholly a matter of definition. But such differences can have serious consequences for those being defined, most of all in the disposition of billions of federal dollars in aid of various kinds. In 1992 the Census Bureau classified 14.5 percent of Americans as poor. Under the new guidelines, at least 15 or 16 percent would be poor, and, under some measures recommended by a government panel, 18 percent would be so defined.

In fact, local and federal courts almost every day redefine traditional concepts that can have a direct impact on our everyday lives. The definition of *family*, for example, has undergone significant changes that acknowledge the existence of new relationships. In January 1990 the New Jersey

[1] *New York Times*, March 4, 1979, sec. 1, p. 40.
[2] *New York Times*, April 10, 1995, sec. A, p. 1.

Supreme Court ruled that a family may be defined as "one or more persons occupying a dwelling unit as a single nonprofit housekeeping unit, who are living together as a stable and permanent living unit, being a traditional family unit or the *functional equivalent* thereof" (italics for emphasis added). This meant that ten Glassboro State College students, unrelated by blood, could continue to occupy a single-family house despite the objection of the borough of Glassboro.[3] Even the legal definition of *maternity* has shifted. Who is the mother—the woman who contributes the egg or the woman (the surrogate) who bears the child? Several states, acknowledging the changes brought by medical technology, now recognize a difference between the birth mother and the legal mother.

DEFINING THE TERMS IN YOUR ARGUMENT

In some of your arguments you will introduce terms that require definition. We've pointed out that a definition of *poverty* is crucial to any debate on the existence of poverty in the United States. The same may be true in a debate about the legality of euthanasia, or mercy killing. Are the arguers referring to passive euthanasia (the withdrawal of life-support systems) or to active euthanasia (the direct administration of drugs to hasten death)?

It is not uncommon, in fact, for arguments about controversial questions to turn into arguments about the definition of terms. If, for example, you wanted to argue in favor of the regulation of religious cults, you would first have to define *cult*. In so doing, you might discover that it is not easy to distinguish clearly between conventional religions and cults. Then you would have to define *regulation*, spelling out the legal restrictions you favored so as to make them apply only to cults, not to established religions. An argument on the subject might end almost before it began if writer and reader could not agree on definitions of these terms. While clear definitions do not guarantee agreement, they do ensure that all parties understand the nature of the argument.

Defining Vague and Ambiguous Terms

You will need to define other terms in addition to those in your claim. If you use words and phrases that have two or more meanings, they may appear vague and ambiguous to your reader. In arguments of value and policy abstract terms such as *freedom*, *justice*, *patriotism*, and *equality* require clarification. Despite their abstract nature, however, they are among the most important in the language because they represent the ideals that shape our laws. When conflicts arise, the courts must define these terms to establish the legality of certain practices. Is the Ku Klux Klan permitted to make dis-

[3] *New York Times*, February 1, 1990, sec. B, p. 5.

paraging public statements about ethnic and racial groups? That depends on the court's definition of *free speech*. Can execution for some crimes be considered cruel and unusual punishment? That, too, depends on the court's definition of *cruel and unusual punishment*. In addition, such terms as *happiness, mental health, success*, and *creativity* often defy precise definition because they reflect the differing values within a society or a culture.

The definition of *success*, for example, varies not only among social groups but also among individuals within the group. One scientist has postulated five signs by which to measure success: wealth (including health), security (confidence in retaining the wealth), reputation, performance, and contentment.[4] Consider whether all of these are necessary to your own definition of *success*. If not, which may be omitted? Do you think others should be added? Notice that one of the signs—reputation—is defined by the community; another—contentment—can be measured only by the individual. The assessment of performance probably owes something to both the group and the individual.

Christopher Atkins, an actor, gave an interviewer an example of an externalized definition of success—that is, a definition based on the standards imposed by other people:

> Success to me is judged through the eyes of others. I mean, if you're walking around saying, "I own a green Porsche," you might meet somebody who says, "Hey, that's no big deal. I own a green Porsche and a house." So all of a sudden, you don't feel so successful. Really, it's in the eyes of others.[5]

So difficult is the formulation of a universally accepted measure for success that some scholars regard the concept as meaningless. Nevertheless, we continue to use the word as if it represented a definable concept because the idea of success, however defined, is important for the identity and development of the individual and the group. It is clear, however, that when crossing subcultural boundaries, even within a small group, we need to be aware of differences in the use of the word. If contentment—that is, the satisfaction of achieving a small personal goal—is enough, then a person making a minimal salary but doing work that he or she loves may be a success. But you should not expect all your readers to agree that these criteria are enough to define *success*.

In arguing about aesthetic matters, whose vocabulary is almost always abstract, the criteria for judgment must be revealed, either directly or indirectly, and then the abstract terms that represent the criteria must be defined. If you want to say that a film is distinguished by great acting, have you made clear what you mean by *great*? That we do not always understand or agree on the definition of *great* is apparent, say, on the morning after the Oscar winners have been announced.

[4] Gwynn Nettler, *Social Concerns* (New York: McGraw-Hill, 1976), pp. 196–97.
[5] *New York Times*, August 6, 1982, sec. 3, p. 8.

Even subjects that you feel sure you can identify may offer surprising insights when you rethink them for an extended definition. One critic, defining *rock music,* argued that the distinguishing characteristic of rock music was noise—not beat, not harmonies, not lyrics, not vocal style, but noise, "nasty, discordant, irritating noise—or, to its practitioners, unfettered, liberating, expressive noise."[6] In producing this definition, the author had to give a number of examples to prove that he was justified in rejecting the most familiar criteria.

Consider the definition of *race,* around which so much of American history has revolved, often with tragic consequences. Until recently, the only categories listed in the census were white, black, Asian-Pacific, and Native American, "with the Hispanic population straddling them all." But rapidly increasing intermarriage and ethnic identity caused a number of political and ethnic groups to demand changes in the classifications of the Census Bureau. Some Arab Americans, for example, prefer to be counted as "Middle Eastern" rather than white. Children of black-white unions are defined as black 60 percent of the time, while children of Asian-white unions are described as Asian 42 percent of the time. Research is now being conducted to discover how people feel about the terms being used to define them. As one anthropologist pointed out, "Socially and politically assigned attributes have a lot to do with access to economic resources."[7]

PRACTICE

1. Use one or more cases to illustrate how, in a court of law, guilt or innocence can hinge on a matter of definition.
2. Choose two terms that are sometimes confused and define them to make their differences clear. Some examples are *active euthanasia* and *passive euthanasia, psychologist* and *psychiatrist, manslaughter* and *murder, envy* and *jealousy, sympathy* and *pity,* and *liberal* and *radical.*
3. Many recent controversial movements and causes are identified by terms that have come to mean different things to different people. Define the following terms, considering any positive or negative connotations of each. Also consider whether there is a term with a similar meaning that has more positive or more negative connotations.
   a. abortion
   b. war on terror
   c. affirmative action
   d. assisted suicide
   e. the Patriot Act
   f. undocumented workers

[6]Jon Pareles, "Noise Evokes Modern Chaos for a Band," *New York Times,* March 9, 1986, sec. H, p. 26.

[7]*Wall Street Journal,* September 9, 1995, sec. B, p. 1.

METHODS FOR DEFINING TERMS

Reading a dictionary definition is the simplest and most obvious way to learn the basic definition of a term. An unabridged dictionary is the best source because it usually gives examples of the way a word can be used in a sentence; that is, it furnishes the proper context.

In many cases, the dictionary definition alone is not sufficient. It may be too broad or too narrow for your purpose. Suppose, in an argument about pornography, you wanted to define the word *obscene*. *Webster's New International Dictionary* (third edition, unabridged) gives the definition of *obscene* as "offensive to taste; foul; loathsome; disgusting." But these synonyms do not tell you what qualities make an object or an event or an action "foul," "loathsome," and "disgusting." In 1973 the Supreme Court, attempting to narrow the definition of *obscenity*, ruled that obscenity was to be determined by the community in accordance with local standards. One person's obscenity, as numerous cases have demonstrated, may be another person's art. The celebrated trials in the early twentieth century about the distribution of novels regarded as pornographic—D. H. Lawrence's *Lady Chatterley's Lover* and James Joyce's *Ulysses*—emphasized the problems of defining obscenity.

Another dictionary definition may strike you as too narrow. *Patriotism*, for example, is defined in one dictionary as "love and loyal or zealous support of one's country, especially in all matters involving other countries." Some readers may want to include an unwillingness to support government policies they consider wrong.

These limitations are the reason that opening an essay with a dictionary definition is often not a very effective strategy, although it is a strategy often used by beginning writers. In order to initiate the effective discussion of a key term, you should be able to define it in your own words.

■ Stipulation

In stipulating the meaning of a term, the writer asks the reader to accept a definition that may be different from the conventional one. He or she does this to limit or control the argument. Someone has said, "Part of the task of keeping definitions in our civilization clear and pure is to keep a firm democratic rein on those with the power, or craving the power, to stipulate meaning." Perhaps this writer was thinking of a term like *national security*, which can be defined by a nation's leaders in such a way as to sanction persecution of citizens and reckless military adventures. Likewise, a term such as *liberation* can be appropriated by terrorist groups whose activities often lead to oppression rather than liberation.

Religion is usually defined as a belief in a supernatural power to be obeyed and worshiped. But in an article entitled "Civil Religion in America," a sociologist offers a different meaning:

> While some have argued that Christianity is the national faith, and others that church and synagogue celebrate only the generalized religion of "the American way of life," few have realized that there actually exists alongside of and rather clearly differentiated from the churches an elaborate and well-institutionalized civil religion in America. This article argues not only that there is such a thing, but also that this religion . . . has its own seriousness and integrity and requires the same care in understanding that any other religion does.[8]

When the author adds, "This religion—there seems no other word for it—was neither sectarian nor in any specific sense Christian," he emphasizes that he is distinguishing his definition of religion from definitions that associate religion and church.

Even the word *violence,* which the dictionary defines as "physical force used so as to injure or damage" and whose meaning seems so clear and uncompromising, can be manipulated to produce a definition different from the one normally understood by most people. Some pacifists refer to conditions in which "people are deprived of choices in a systematic way" as "institutionalized quiet violence." Even where no physical force is employed, this lack of choice in schools, in the workplace, in the black ghettos is defined as violence.[9]

In *Through the Looking-Glass* Alice asked Humpty Dumpty "whether you can make words mean so many different things."

> "When *I* use a word," Humpty Dumpty said scornfully, "it means just what I choose it to mean—neither more nor less."[10]

A writer, however, is not free to invent definitions that no one will recognize or that create rather than solve problems between writer and reader.

■ Negation

To avoid confusion it is sometimes helpful to tell the reader what a term is *not.* In discussing euthanasia, a writer might say, "By euthanasia I do not mean active intervention to hasten the death of the patient."

A negative definition may be more extensive, depending on the complexity of the term and the writer's ingenuity. The critic of rock music quoted earlier in this chapter arrived at his definition of *noise* by rejecting attributes that seemed misleading. The former Communist party member Whittaker Chambers, in a foreword to a book on the spy trial of Alger Hiss, defined *communism* this way:

[8]Robert N. Bellah, "Civil Religion in America," *Daedalus*, Winter 1967, p. 1.

[9]Newton Garver, "What Violence Is," in James Rachels, ed., *Moral Choices* (New York: Harper and Row, 1971), pp. 248–49.

[10]Lewis Carroll, *Alice in Wonderland and Through the Looking-Glass* (New York: Grosset and Dunlap, 1948), p. 238.

> First, let me try to say what Communism is not. It is not simply a vicious plot hatched by wicked men in a subcellar. It is not just the writings of Marx and Lenin, dialectical materialism, the Politburo, the labor theory of value, the theory of the general strike, the Red Army secret police, labor camps, underground conspiracy, the dictatorship of the proletariat, the technique of the coup d'état. It is not even those chanting, bannered millions that stream periodically, like disorganized armies, through the heart of the world's capitals: Moscow, New York, Tokyo, Paris, Rome. These are expressions, but they are not what Communism is about.[11]

This, of course, is only part of the definition. Any writer beginning a definition in the negative must go on to define what the term *is*.

Examples

One of the most effective ways of defining terms in an argument is to use examples. Both real and hypothetical examples can bring life to abstract and ambiguous terms. The writer in the following passage defines *preferred categories* (classes of people who are meant to benefit from affirmative action policies) by invoking specific cases:

> The absence of definitions points up one of the problems with preferred categories. . . . These preferred categories take no account of family wealth or educational advantages. A black whose father is a judge or physician deserves preferential treatment over any nonminority applicant. The latter might have fought his way out of the grinding poverty of Appalachia, or might be the first member of an Italian American or a Polish American family to complete high school. But no matter.[12]

Insanity is a word that has been used and misused to describe a variety of conditions. Even psychiatrists are in dispute about its meaning. In the following anecdote, examples narrow and refine the definition.

> Dr. Zilboorg says that present-day psychiatry does not possess any satisfactory definition of mental illness or neurosis. To illustrate, he told a story: A psychiatrist was recently asked for a definition of a "well-adjusted person" (not even slightly peculiar). The definition: "A person who feels in harmony with himself and who is not in conflict with his environment." It sounded fine, but up popped a heckler. "Would you then consider an anti-Nazi working in the underground against Hitler a maladjusted person?" "Well," the psychiatrist hemmed, "I withdraw the latter part of my definition." Dr. Zilboorg withdrew the first half for him. Many persons in perfect harmony with themselves, he pointed out, are in "distinctly pathological states."[13]

[11]*Witness* (New York: Random House, 1952), p. 8.
[12]Anthony Lombardo, "Quotas Work Both Ways," *U.S. Catholic*, February 1974, p. 39.
[13]Quoted in *The Art of Making Sense*, p. 48.

Extended Definition

When we speak of an extended definition, we usually refer not only to length but also to the variety of methods for developing the definition. Let's take the word *materialism*. A dictionary entry offers the following sentence fragments as definitions: "1. the doctrine that comfort, pleasure, and wealth are the only or highest goals or values. 2. the tendency to be more concerned with material than the spiritual goals or values." But the term *materialism* has acquired so many additional meanings, especially emotional ones, that an extended definition serves a useful purpose in clarifying the many different ideas surrounding our understanding of the term.

Below is a much longer definition of *materialism*, which appears at the beginning of an essay entitled "People and Things: Reflections on Materialism."[14]

> There are two contemporary usages of the term *materialism*, and it is important to distinguish between them. On the one hand we can talk about *instrumental materialism*, or the use of material objects to make life longer, safer, more enjoyable. By instrumental, we mean that objects act as essential means for discovering and furthering personal values and goals of life, so that the objects are instruments used to realize and further those goals. There is little negative connotation attached to this meaning of the word, since one would think that it is perfectly sensible to use things for such purposes. While it is true that the United States is the epitome of materialism in this sense, it is also true that most people in every society aspire to reach our level of instrumental materialism.
>
> On the other hand the term has a more negative connotation, which might be conveyed by the phrase *terminal materialism*. This is the sense critics use when they apply the term to Americans. What they mean is that we not only use our material resources as instruments to make life more manageable, but that we reduce our ultimate goals to the possession of things. They believe that we don't just use our cars to get from place to place, but that we consider the ownership of expensive cars one of the central values in life. Terminal materialism means that the object is valued only because it indicates an end in itself, a possession. In instrumental materialism there is a sense of directionality, in which a person's goals may be furthered through the interactions with the object. A book, for example, can reveal new possibilities or widen a person's view of the world, or an old photograph can be cherished because it embodies a relationship. But in terminal materialism, there is no sense of reciprocal interaction in the relation between the object and the end. The end is valued as final, not as itself a means to further ends. And quite often it is only the status label or image associated with the object that is valued, rather than the actual object.

In the essay from which this passage is taken, the authors distinguish between two kinds of materialism and provide an extended explanation, using contrast and examples as methods of development. They are aware

[14]Mihaly Csikszentmihalyi and Eugene Rochberg-Halton, "People and Things: Reflections on Materialism," *University of Chicago Magazine*, Spring 1978, pp. 7–8.

that the common perception of materialism—the love of things for their own sake—is a negative one. But this view, according to the authors, doesn't fully account for the attitudes of many Americans toward the things they own. There is, in fact, another more positive meaning that the authors call *instrumental materialism*. You will recognize that the authors are *stipulating* a meaning with which their readers might not be familiar. In their essay they distinguish between *terminal materialism*, in which "the object is valued only because it indicates an end in itself," and *instrumental materialism*, "the use of material objects to make life longer, safer, more enjoyable." Since *instrumental materialism* is the less familiar definition, the essay provides a great number of examples that show how people of three different generations value photographs, furniture, musical instruments, plants, and other objects for their memories and personal associations rather than as proof of the owners' ability to acquire the objects or win the approval of others.

THE DEFINITION ESSAY

The argumentative essay can take the form of an extended definition. An example of such an essay is the one from which we've just quoted, as well as the essays at the end of this chapter. The definition essay is appropriate when the idea under consideration is so controversial or so heavy with historical connotations that even a paragraph or two cannot make clear exactly what the arguer wants his or her readers to understand. For example, if you were preparing a definition of *patriotism*, you would probably use a number of methods to develop your definition: personal narrative, examples, stipulation, comparison and contrast, and cause-and-effect analysis.

Writer's Guide: Writing a Definition Essay

The following important steps should be taken when you write an essay of definition.

1. Choose a term that needs definition because it is controversial or ambiguous, or because you want to offer a personal definition that differs from the accepted interpretation. Explain why an extended definition is necessary. Or choose an experience that lends itself to treatment in an extended definition. One student defined *culture shock* as she had experienced it while studying abroad in Hawaii among students of a different ethnic background.
2. Decide on the thesis — the point of view you wish to develop about the term you are defining. If you want to define *heroism*, for example, you may choose to develop the idea that this quality depends on motivation and awareness of danger rather than on the specific act performed by the hero.

3. Distinguish wherever possible between the term you are defining and other terms with which it might be confused. If you are defining *love,* can you make a clear distinction between the different kinds of emotional attachments contained in the word?
4. Try to think of several methods of developing the definition — using examples, comparison and contrast, analogy, cause-and-effect analysis. However, you may discover that one method alone — say, use of examples — will suffice to narrow and refine your definition.
5. Arrange your supporting material in an order that gives emphasis to the most important ideas.

SAMPLE ANNOTATED ESSAY

The Definition of Terrorism

BRIAN WHITAKER

Decide for yourself whether to believe this, but according to a new report there were only 16 cases of international terrorism in the Middle East last year.

That is the lowest number for any region in the world apart from North America (where there were none at all). Europe had 30 cases—almost twice as many as the Middle East—and Latin America came top with 193.

Statistics on terrorism from before 9/11

The figures come from the U.S. state department's annual review of global terrorism, which has just been published on the internet. Worldwide, the report says confidently, "there were 423 international terrorist attacks in 2000, an increase of 8% from the 392 attacks recorded during 1999."

No doubt a lot of painstaking effort went into counting them, but the statistics are fundamentally meaningless because, as the report points

This article was published May 7, 2001, in *Guardian Unlimited*, the daily online version of the British newspaper the *Guardian*. Whitaker is an editor on Comment Is Free, the *Guardian*'s Web expansion.

Problems with attempts to define terrorism

out, "no one definition of terrorism has gained universal acceptance."

5 That is an understatement. While most people agree that terrorism exists, few can agree on what it is. A recent book discussing attempts by the UN and other international bodies to define terrorism runs to three volumes and 1,866 pages without reaching any firm conclusion.

U.S. State Department's definition

Using the definition preferred by the state department, terrorism is: "Premeditated, politically motivated violence perpetrated against noncombatant* targets by subnational groups or clandestine agents, usually intended to influence an audience." (The asterisk is important, as we shall see later.)

Definition of "international" terrorism

"International" terrorism—the subject of the American report—is defined as "terrorism involving citizens or the territory of more than one country."

Main point of agreement is motivation

The key point about terrorism, on which almost everyone agrees, is that it's politically motivated. This is what distinguishes it from, say, murder or football hooliganism. But this also causes a problem for those who compile statistics because the motive is not always clear—especially if no one has claimed responsibility.

Example of incidents with no known motivation

So the American report states—correctly—that there were no confirmed terrorist incidents in Saudi Arabia last year. There were, nevertheless, three unexplained bombings and one shooting incident, all directed against foreigners.

Another part of the definition

10 Another essential ingredient (you might think) is that terrorism is calculated to terrorize the public or a particular section of it. The American definition does not mention spreading terror at all, because that would exclude attacks against property. It is, after all, impossible to frighten an inanimate object.

Among last year's attacks, 152 were directed against a pipeline in Colombia which is owned by multinational oil companies. Such attacks are of concern to the United States and so a definition is required which allows them to be counted.

Questions about which examples meet the criteria

For those who accept that terrorism is about terrorizing people, other questions arise. Does it include threats, as well as actual violence? A few years ago, for example, the Islamic Army in Yemen warned foreigners to leave the country if they valued their lives but did not actually carry out its threat.

More recently, a group of Israeli peace activists were arrested for driving around in a loudspeaker van, announcing a curfew of the kind that is imposed on Palestinians. Terrifying for any Israelis who believed it, but was it terrorism?

Another characteristic

Another characteristic of terrorism, according to some people, is that targets must be random—the intention being to make everyone fear they might be the next victim. Some of the Hamas suicide bombings appear to follow this principle but when attacks are aimed at predictable targets (such as the military) they are less likely to terrorize the public at large.

What terrorism is not

Definitions usually try to distinguish between 15
terrorism and warfare. In general this means that attacks on soldiers are warfare and those against civilians are terrorism, but the dividing lines quickly become blurred.

Examples

The state department regards attacks against "noncombatant* targets" as terrorism. But follow the asterisk to the small print and you find that "noncombatants" includes both civilians and military personnel who are unarmed or off duty at the time. Several examples are given, such as the 1986 disco bombing in Berlin, which killed two servicemen.

The most lethal bombing in the Middle East last year was the suicide attack on USS *Cole* in Aden harbor which killed 17 American sailors and injured 39 more.

Unanswered questions

As the ship was armed and its crew on duty at the time, why is this classified as terrorism? Look again at the small print, which adds: "We also consider as acts of terrorism attacks on military installations or on armed military personnel when a state of military hostilities does not exist at the site, such as bombings against U.S. bases."

A similar question arises with Palestinian attacks on quasi-military targets such as Israeli settlements. Many settlers are armed (with weapons supplied by the army) and the settlements themselves—though they contain civilians—might be considered military targets because they are there to consolidate a military occupation.

If, under the state department rules, Palestinian 20
mortar attacks on settlements count as terrorism, it would be reasonable to expect Israeli rocket attacks on Palestinian communities to be treated in the same way—but they are not. In the American definition, terrorism can never be inflicted by a state.

Limitations of American definition

Israeli treatment of the Palestinians is classified as a human rights issue (for which the Israelis get a rap over the knuckles) in a separate state department report.

Denying that states can commit terrorism is generally useful, because it gets the U.S. and its allies off the hook in a variety of situations. The disadvantage is that it might also get hostile states off the hook—which is why there has to be a list of states that are said to "sponsor" terrorism while not actually committing it themselves.

The term's original meaning

Interestingly, the American definition of terrorism is a reversal of the word's original meaning, given in the Oxford English Dictionary as "government by intimidation." Today it usually refers to intimidation of governments.

Its history

The first recorded use of "terrorism" and "terrorist" was in 1795, relating to the Reign of Terror instituted by the French government. Of course, the Jacobins, who led the government at the time, were also revolutionaries and gradually "terrorism" came to be applied to violent revolutionary activity in general. But the use of "terrorist" in an anti-government sense is not recorded until 1866 (referring to Ireland) and 1883 (referring to Russia).

The difficulty of making laws against terrorism

In the absence of an agreed meaning, making 25
laws against terrorism is especially difficult. The latest British anti-terrorism law gets round the problem by listing 21 international terrorist organizations by name. Membership of these is illegal in the UK.

There are six Islamic groups, four anti-Israel groups, eight separatist groups, and three opposition groups. The list includes Hizbullah, which though armed, is a legal political party in Lebanon, with elected members of parliament.

Among the separatist groups, the Kurdistan Workers Party—active in Turkey—is banned, but not the KDP or PUK, which are Kurdish organizations active in Iraq. Among opposition groups, the Iranian People's Mujahedeen is banned, but not its Iraqi equivalent, the INC, which happens to be financed by the United States.

Issuing such a list does at least highlight the anomalies and inconsistencies behind anti-terrorism laws. It also points toward a simpler—and perhaps more honest—definition: terrorism is violence committed by those we disapprove of.

This author's stipulated definition

Analysis

In the United States, terrorism has received unprecedented attention since the tragic events of September 11, 2001. You may have been surprised to learn that Whitaker's essay was written in May of that year, before planes crashing into the World Trade Center, the Pentagon, and a field in Pennsylvania forever gave the term new meaning for Americans. Just as the problem of terrorism has not yet been solved, however, the problem of defining terrorism remains unsolved as well. It is still true that "no one definition of terrorism has gained universal acceptance."

The essay starts on an unusual note: "Decide for yourself whether to believe this," referring to the low number of cases of international terrorism reported in the Middle East for 2000. That statement suggests that readers should approach the numbers with skepticism. Although the specific numbers cited in the essay are at first attributed only to "a new report," Whitaker goes on to indicate that his statistical support comes from the U.S. State Department. He acknowledges that "a lot of painstaking effort" went into counting the instances of terrorism, but goes on to declare the numbers "fundamentally meaningless" because of the lack of an agreed-upon definition of the term.

In paragraphs 6 and 7, Whitaker provides the State Department's definitions of terrorism and international terrorism. He then goes on to use a combination of types of support to back up his claim, as is common in writing an extended definition. In paragraphs 8, 10, and 14, he introduces three characteristics of terrorism—that it is politically motivated, that it "is calculated to terrorize the public or a particular section of it," and that its targets must be random. Throughout the body of the essay, he includes examples to illustrate his key points. In paragraph 15, Whitaker employs another technique used often in extended definition: He tells what terrorism is not.

The last third of the essay deals in part with unanswered questions and the limitations of the State Department's definition, illustrating the complications involved in defining terrorism and in passing laws against it.

Only at the end does Whitaker stipulate his own definition of terrorism. He is not providing a technical definition or one that he believes will gain universal acceptance. What he offers is his honest assessment of what Americans really perceive terrorism to be: "violence committed by those we disapprove of."

READINGS FOR ANALYSIS

Race by the Numbers

ORLANDO PATTERSON

In recent weeks, reporting and commentary that misinterpret early census results have been persistently misinforming the nation about its ethnic and racial composition. The misinformation is dangerous, since it fuels fears of decline and displacement among some whites, anxieties that are not only divisive but groundless. The Center for Immigration Studies, for example, a think tank in Washington, recently warned that by the middle of the century non-Hispanic whites will cease to be a majority and that "each group in the new minority-majority country has longstanding grievances against whites."

Many articles have echoed the view that whites are fast becoming a minority in many areas of the country, largely because of the growth of the Hispanic population. The *New York Times* reported that seventy-one of the top 100 cities had lost white residents and made clear only in the third paragraph of the article that it is really "non-Hispanic whites" who are now a minority in these cities. Similarly, the *Miami Herald* reported that 20 cities and unincorporated communities in Miami-Dade county "went from majority to minority white, non-Hispanic." Left without commentary was the fact that the total white population—including Hispanic whites—of Miami, for example, is actually a shade under 70 percent.

These articles and too many others have failed to take account of the fact that nearly half of the Hispanic population is white in every social sense of this term; 48 percent of so-called Hispanics classified themselves as solely white, giving only one race to the census taker. Although all reports routinely note that "Hispanics can be of any race," they almost always go on to neglect this critical fact, treating Hispanics as if they were, in fact, a sociological race comparable to "whites" and "blacks."

Orlando Patterson is a professor of sociology at Harvard and the author of *Rituals of Blood* (1998), the second volume of a trilogy on race relations, as well as *Slavery and Social Death: A Comparative Study* (2007). This article appeared in the *New York Times* on May 8, 2001.

In any case, the suggestion that the white population of America is fast on the way to becoming a minority is a gross distortion. Even if we view only the non-Hispanic white population, whites remain a robust 69.1 percent of the total population of the nation. If we include Hispanic whites, as we should, whites constitute 75.14 percent of the total population, down by only 5 percent from the 1990 census. And this does not take account of the 6.8 million people who identified in the census with "two or more races," 80 percent of whom listed white as one of these races.

5 Even with the most liberal of assumptions, there is no possibility that whites will become a minority in this nation in this century. The most recent census projections indicate that whites will constitute 74.8 percent of the total population in 2050, and that non-Hispanic whites will still be 52.8 percent of the total. And when we make certain realistic sociological assumptions about which groups the future progeny of Hispanic whites, mixed couples, and descendants of people now acknowledging two or more races are likely to identify with, there is every reason to believe that the non-Hispanic white population will remain a substantial majority—and possibly even grow as a portion of the population.

Recent studies indicate that second-generation Hispanic whites are intermarrying and assimilating mainstream language and cultural patterns at a faster rate than second-generation European migrants of the late nineteenth and early twentieth centuries.

The misleading reports of white proportional decline are likely not only to sustain the racist fears of white supremacist groups but also to affect the views of ordinary white, nonextremist Americans. A false assumption that whites are becoming a minority in the nation their ancestors conquered and developed may be adding to the deep resentment of poor or struggling whites toward affirmative action and other policies aimed at righting the wrongs of discrimination.

How do we account for this persistent pattern of misinformation? Apart from the intellectually lazy journalistic tendency to overemphasize race, two influences are playing into the discussion.

One is the policy of the Census Bureau itself. Though on the one hand, the census has taken the progressive step of allowing citizens to classify themselves in as many racial ways as they wish, breaking up the traditional notion of races as immutable categories, on the other hand it is up to its age-old mischief of making and unmaking racial groups. As it makes a new social category out of the sociologically meaningless collection of peoples from Latin America and Spain, it is quietly abetting the process of demoting and removing white Hispanics from the "true" white race—native-born non-Hispanic whites.

10 There is a long history of such reclassification by federal agencies. In the early decades of the twentieth century, the Irish, Italians, and Jews were

classified as separate races by the federal immigration office, and the practice was discontinued only after long and vehement protests from Jewish leaders. In 1930 Mexicans were classified as a separate race by the Census Bureau—which reclassified them as white in 1940, after protests. Between then and the 1960s, people from Latin America were routinely classified as whites; then, when vast numbers of poor immigrants began coming from Latin America, the Hispanic category emerged.

The first stage of racial classification, now nearly successfully completed for Hispanics, is naming and nailing them all together while disingenuously admitting that they can be "of any race." Next, the repeated naming and sociological classification of different groups under a single category inevitably leads to the gradual perception and reconstruction of the group as another race. Much the same process of racialization is taking place with that other enormous sociological nongroup, Asian Americans.

The other influence on perceptions of who is "white" originates among the so-called Hispanics. For political and economic reasons, including the benefits of affirmative action programs, the leadership of many Hispanic groups pursues a liberal, coalition-based agenda with African Americans and presses hard for a separate, unified Latino classification. This strategy is highly influential even though nearly half of Hispanics consider themselves white.

For African Americans, the nation's major disadvantaged minority, these tendencies are problematic, although African American leaders are too shortsighted to notice. Latino coalition strategies, by vastly increasing the number of people entitled to affirmative action, have been a major factor in the loss of political support for it. And any fear of a "white" group that it might lose status tends to reinforce stigmatization of those Americans who will never be "white."

In this volatile transitional situation, where the best and worst are equally possible in our racial relations and attitudes, the very worst thing that journalists, analysts and commentators can do is to misinform the white majority that it is losing its majority status—something that recent surveys indicate it is already all too inclined to believe. We should stop obsessing on race in interpreting the census results. But if we must compulsively racialize the data, let's at least keep the facts straight and the interpretations honest.

READING AND DISCUSSION QUESTIONS

1. Where does Patterson state his claim?
2. What subtitles can you provide for the different parts of his argument? The topic sentences in several paragraphs offer clues to the organization.
3. According to Patterson, how is the matter of definition relevant to statistics about race?

4. Patterson's claim is strongly supported by statistics, history, and political analysis. Do you think these different kinds of support are equally persuasive? Which one is most susceptible to challenge? Why?
5. What is Patterson's objection to the definitions of *Hispanic* and *non-Hispanic* that are published by the Census Bureau and other agencies?

WRITING SUGGESTIONS

6. Narrate an experience you have had in which you felt you were either aided or hindered by the fact that you were defined as a member of a specific group. It could be a group such as those defined by gender, race, religious affiliation, or membership on a team or in a club.
7. Would adoption at the state level of a policy prohibiting classifying people by race, color, ethnicity, or national origin be beneficial or pernicious for the individual and for society? In other words, what is good or bad about classifying people?
8. Find a subject in which definition is critical to how statistics are interpreted and which can be argued successfully in a 750- to 1,000-word paper. Your essay should provide proof for a claim. (Patterson uses numbers to prove that whites need not fear that their numbers are declining.) Other subjects that depend on statistical support can be found throughout this book.

Family a Symbol of Love and Life, but Not Politics

ERIC ZORN

Family is one of our loveliest words. It speaks of a warm, enveloping, comforting, inspiring connection—a love relationship, a commitment, a safe harbor, a common enterprise.

Sometimes, sure, it's a messy and maddening entanglement. But even when it's imperfect, family is the foundation of identity and the cornerstone of success.

To many people—people of all faiths, orientations, and political beliefs—"family" is the word that expresses that which they hold most dear.

Not money. Not possessions. Not fame. Not career. Not country. Not friendship. Not romance. Not even freedom.

Eric Zorn is a columnist for the *Chicago Tribune*, where this essay was first published on May 23, 2004, and coauthor of *Murder of Innocence* (1990).

Family. 5

So it's time we took it back.

Sorry, Family PAC and Illinois Family Institute.

You, too, Focus on the Family, Family Research Council, Family Foundation, Pro-Family Network, American Family Association, and Culture and Family Institute.

Set that word down and back away slowly. It belongs to all of us.

You and other conservative organizations have monopolized it for 10
too long, turned it into shorthand for a social and political outlook that excludes rather than includes, and hectors those who don't, can't, or won't conform to your notions of morality.

"Family values" has come to mean the promotion of abstinence-only sex education, religion in the public sphere, education vouchers, traditional gender roles, and censorship. It's come to mean opposition to abortion rights and, particularly these days, resistance to the extension of full civil rights to gays and lesbians.

In covering the landmark beginning of legal gay marriages in Massachusetts last week, virtually every news organization featured the fulminations of officials from the Massachusetts Family Institute ("The piece of paper that says 'marriage' has been redefined and devalued!"), while Peter LaBarbera, executive director of the Illinois Family Institute ("A man marrying another man is a far cry from Rosa Parks!"), has become the go-to guy for local journalists seeking quotes from opponents of gay marriage.

The irony is that gay weddings mark an endorsement of family—of the power of that formal and lasting bond.

When two people get married, they are saying to society, "Yes! We believe in the fundamental importance of this institution in building and maintaining family ties. We want to join it and affirm that belief to the world."

And when a culture expands its definition of marriage to include the 15
expressions of lifelong commitment between two people of the same sex, it strengthens families by advancing the acceptance and tolerance of gay people.

Not every parent is as accepting of his gay child as Chicago Alderman Richard Mell, whose personal and political support for his daughter, who is a lesbian, has become a local legend. But the more our society loses its judgmental attitude about who loves whom and what sorts of unions are most normal, the closer we get to the day when extended families no longer are ripped apart by homosexuality.

I could argue that strengthening families is why we need to provide quality day care for working parents, why we need to work hard to maintain strict government neutrality in matters of faith, and why we should offer nonideological sex education to children and reproductive choice to women.

I could make the case that it reflects good family values to shift more of the tax burden to the rich, to support stem cell medical research and universal health care, to devote our energies to boosting public education, and to protect our natural environment against industrial polluters.

I could, but I won't.

"Family" is too important to too many of us to drag its name through 20
the muck of our bitter sociopolitical debates, let alone to yield it to one side or the other in the culture wars.

No one owns it. The left doesn't own peace and compassion, the right doesn't own the flag or the family.

The word "family" resonates profoundly in all of us—married, single, gay, straight, adopted, "biological," living alone or in crowded households bursting with the exuberant chaos of children. To have family, to be family with others, is to be fully human.

Mom always taught me to share. So, shall we?

READING AND DISCUSSION QUESTIONS

1. Where does Zorn most directly define the word *family*?
2. What does he mean when he says that we need to take family back? From whom?
3. How has the definition of the word *family* been politicized?
4. How do gay marriages expand the definition of family, according to Zorn?
5. What strategy is Zorn using when he tells his readers what he could argue, but won't?
6. What claim is Zorn supporting in the essay?

WRITING SUGGESTIONS

7. Even if you do not support same-sex marriage, do you believe that the definition of marriage is changing? Explain.
8. Explain whether or not you agree with this statement by Zorn: "And when a culture expands its definition of marriage to include the expressions of lifelong commitment between two people of the same sex, it strengthens families by advancing the acceptance and tolerance of gay people."

Don't Torture English to Soft-Pedal Abuse

GEOFFREY NUNBERG

"Torture is torture is torture," Secretary of State Colin Powell said this week in an interview on *Fox News Sunday* with Chris Wallace.

That depends on what papers you read. The media in France, Italy, and Germany have been routinely using the word "torture" in the headings of their stories on the abuses in the Abu Ghraib prison.[1] And so have the British papers, not just the left-wing *Guardian* ("Torture at Abu Ghraib") but the right-wing *Express* ("Outrage at U.S. Torture of Prisoners") and Rupert Murdoch's *Times* ("Inside Baghdad's Torture Jail").

But the American press has been more circumspect, sticking with vaguer terms such as "abuse" and "mistreatment." In that, they may have been taking a cue from Defense Secretary Donald Rumsfeld. Asked about torture in the prison, he said, "What has been charged so far is abuse, which is different from torture. I'm not going to address the 'torture' word."

Some on the right have depicted the abuses even more mildly than that. In an opinion piece in the Los Angeles *Times*, Midge Decter called the treatment of detainees a "nasty hazing." Rush Limbaugh said it was "no different than what happens at the Skull and Bones initiation." On a San Francisco radio station, shock jocks were describing the prison as "Abu Grab-Ass" and talking about the treatment in a ribald way that made it sound like *Animal House III—Bluto Bonks Baghdad.*

Some American media have avoided "the 'torture' word" because 5
they want to play down the abuse of prisoners. Others are nervous about provoking attacks from the moral equivalence police: "Are you suggesting we're as bad as they are?"

But to a lot of Americans, *torture* and *torturer* don't seem quite the right words for the scenes in those photos. Torture may be familiar in the modern world, but it's also remote; we only see it up close in the movies. *Torture* suggests an aestheticized ritual. It doesn't seem odd that the torture scenes in *Battle of Algiers* should have a Bach chorale in the background.

[1] In April 2004, news broke in *The New Yorker* and on *60 Minutes* that presented in a particularly bad light a handful of American soldiers on duty at the Abu Ghraib prison in Iraq. In photos on the Internet, which were shown repeatedly on televised news and in print around the world, the young men and women were shown standing by smiling while forcing Iraqi detainees at the prison to strike a series of humiliating poses. Some of the American soldiers are now in prison themselves as a result of their actions.

Geoffrey Nunberg is a consulting professor in Stanford University's Department of Linguistics, the author of the books *Going Nucular* (2004) and *Talking Right* (2007), and a featured radio commentator. This essay was adapted from a piece he did on NPR's *Fresh Air*, which appeared in *Newsday* in May 2004.

In the movies, the torturer's cruelty is ironically counterpoised by a cosmopolitan and often effete manner—Laurence Olivier in *Marathon Man*, Gert Frobe in *Goldfinger*, or the Mohammed Khan character in *Lives of a Bengal Lancer* telling Gary Cooper, "We have ways of making men talk."

There are no middle-class middle-American torturers in our gallery, much less torturers with the pudding faces of those GIs who could have been working at McDonald's a year ago. And the humiliations they were inflicting didn't seem to have much in common with the rituals of pain and submission that *torture* brings to mind. The GIs went down another road, even if it fell off just as sharply.

That's what creates the sense of incongruity we feel when we see those photos. Those may have been far from Delta House high jinks, but you wouldn't know it from the clowning poses the GIs were striking.

True, "hazing" is a shamefully dishonest name for this. Leaving aside 10
the severity of the abuses, the prisoners weren't in a position to resign from the club, nor were they about to be given membership pins when pledge week was over. You may as well say that the Los Angeles police were hazing Rodney King.

But what went on in Abu Ghraib has at least this in common with hazing: It's the sort of thing that any adolescent with a normal libido might be capable of—or worse, if the circumstances permit. As the Stanford psychologist Phil Zimbardo showed in a famous experiment more than thirty years ago, it doesn't take a lot to transform a group of well-mannered college students into sadistic prison guards, provided someone in authority seems to be giving them the nod.

Granted, what the Americans did in Abu Ghraib isn't remotely comparable to what went on there during Saddam Hussein's regime.

But it was torture, not just by the definitions of the Geneva Conventions, but by any ordinary standards of decency. Torture is torture is torture, as Secretary Powell put it—it isn't a place to be drawing fine semantic distinctions.

And it would be a good thing to acknowledge that "torture" is not quite as exotic an activity as the movies make it out to be. Looking at the unsettlingly familiar faces of the American soldiers in the Abu Ghraib photos, you realize that what can be most disturbing isn't the brutality that is inhuman so much as the brutality that is all too.

READING AND DISCUSSION QUESTIONS

1. Nunberg argues that the media control, to a certain extent at least, how the public perceive events. Besides the treatment of prisoners at Abu Ghraib prison in Iraq, how have the media exerted control over public perceptions?
2. What is Nunberg referring to when he makes this statement: "Others are nervous about provoking attacks from the moral equivalence police: 'Are you suggesting we're as bad as they are?'"

3. What is it that creates the sense of incongruity in the pictures from Abu Ghraib to which Nunberg refers?
4. In what sense was what went on at Abu Ghraib similar to hazing, although Nunberg calls hazing "a shamefully dishonest name for this"?
5. Explain what you believe Nunberg means by his last sentence.

WRITING SUGGESTIONS

6. Choose an event other than the Abu Ghraib scandal that was widely publicized and explain to what extent you believe the media controlled public perceptions of the event.
7. Write an essay in which you explain how governments sometimes hide the full truth behind euphemisms and other careful word choices. You may want to compare your ideas about language use with those expressed by George Orwell in his classic 1946 essay "Politics and the English Language."

DEBATE: Is the definition of marriage changing?

Gay Marriage Shows Why We Need to Separate Church and State

HOWARD MOODY

If members of the church that I served for more than three decades were told I would be writing an article in defense of marriage, they wouldn't believe it. My reputation was that when people came to me for counsel about getting married, I tried to talk them out of it. More about that later.

We are now in the midst of a national debate on the nature of marriage, and it promises to be as emotional and polemical as the issues of abortion and homosexuality have been over the past century. What all these debates have in common is that they involved both the laws of the state and the theology of the church. The purpose of this writing is to suggest that the gay-marriage debate is less about the legitimacy of the loving relationship of a same-sex couple than about the relationship of church and state and how they define marriage.

In Western civilization, the faith and beliefs of Christendom played a major role in shaping the laws regarding social relations and moral behavior. Having been nurtured in the Christian faith from childhood and having served a lifetime as an ordained Baptist minister, I feel obligated

Reverend Howard Moody is minister emeritus of Judson Memorial Church in New York City. This article was published in July 2004 in the *Nation*.

first to address the religious controversy concerning the nature of marriage. If we look at the history of religious institutions regarding marriage we will find not much unanimity but amazing diversity—it is really a mixed bag. Those who base their position on "tradition" or "what the Bible says" will find anything but clarity. It depends on which "tradition" in what age reading from whose holy scriptures.

In the early tradition of the Jewish people, there were multiple wives and not all of them equal. Remember the story of Abraham's wives, Sara and Hagar. Sara couldn't get pregnant, so Hagar presented Abraham with a son. When Sara got angry with Hagar, she forced Abraham to send Hagar and her son Ishmael into the wilderness. In case Christians feel superior about their "tradition" of marriage, I would remind them that their scriptural basis is not as clear about marriage as we might hope. We have Saint Paul's conflicting and condescending words about the institution: "It's better not to marry." Karl Barth called this passage the Magna Carta of the single person. (Maybe we should have taken Saint Paul's advice more seriously. It might have prevented an earlier generation of parents from harassing, cajoling, and prodding our young until they were married.) In certain religious branches, the church doesn't recognize the licensed legality of marriage but requires that persons meet certain religious qualifications before the marriage is recognized by the church. For members of the Roman Catholic Church, a "legal divorce" and the right to remarry may not be recognized unless the first marriage has been declared null and void by a decree of the church. It is clear that there is no single religious view of marriage and that history has witnessed some monumental changes in the way "husband and wife" are seen in the relationship of marriage.

In my faith-based understanding, if freedom of choice means any- 5
thing to individuals (male or female), it means they have several options. They can be single and celibate without being thought of as strange or psychologically unbalanced. They can be single and sexually active without being labeled loose or immoral. Women can be single with child without being thought of as unfit or inadequate. If these choices had been real options, the divorce rate may never have reached nearly 50 percent.

The other, equally significant choice for people to make is that of lifetime commitment to each other and to seal that desire in the vows of a wedding ceremony. That understanding of marriage came out of my community of faith. In my years of ministry I ran a tight ship in regard to the performance of weddings. It wasn't because I didn't believe in marriage (I've been married for sixty years and have two wonderful offspring) but rather my unease about the way marriage was used to force people to marry so they wouldn't be "living in sin."

The failure of the institution can be seen in divorce statistics. I wanted people to know how challenging the promise of those vows was and not to feel this was something they had to do. My first question in premarital counseling was, "Why do you want to get married and spoil a beautiful friendship?" That question often elicited a thoughtful and emotional answer. Though I was miserly in the number of weddings I performed, I always made exceptions when there were couples who had difficulty finding clergy who would officiate. Their difficulty was because they weren't of the same religion, or they had made marital mistakes, or what they couldn't believe. Most of them were "ecclesiastical outlaws," barred from certain sacraments in the church of their choice.

The church I served had a number of gay and lesbian couples who had been together for many years, but none of them had asked for public weddings or blessings on their relationship. (There was one commitment ceremony for a gay couple at the end of my tenure.) It was as though they didn't need a piece of paper or a ritual to symbolize their lifelong commitment. They knew if they wanted a religious ceremony, their ministers would officiate and our religious community would joyfully witness.

It was my hope that since the institution of marriage had been used to exclude and demean members of the homosexual community, our church, which was open and affirming, would create with gays and lesbians a new kind of ceremony. It would be an occasion that symbolized, between two people of the same gender, a covenant of intimacy of two people to journey together, breaking new ground in human relationships—an alternative to marriage as we have known it.

10 However, I can understand why homosexuals want "to be married" in the old-fashioned "heterosexual way." After all, most gays and lesbians were born of married parents, raised in a family of siblings; many were nourished in churches and synagogues, taught about a living God before Whom all Her creatures were equally loved. Why wouldn't they conceive their loving relationships in terms of marriage and family and desire that they be confirmed and understood as such? It follows that if these gays and lesbians see their relationship as faith-based, they would want a religious ceremony that seals their intentions to become lifelong partners, lovers and friends, that they would want to be "married."

Even though most religious denominations deny this ceremony to homosexual couples, more and more clergy are, silently and publicly, officiating at religious rituals in which gays and lesbians declare their vows before God and a faith community. One Catholic priest who defied his church's ban said: "We can bless a dog, we can bless a boat, but we can't say a prayer over two people who love each other. You don't have to call it marriage, you can call it a deep and abiding friendship, but you can bless it."

We have the right to engage in "religious disobedience" to the regulations of the judicatory that granted us the privilege to officiate at wedding ceremonies, and suffer the consequences. However, when it comes to civil law, it is my contention that the church and its clergy are on much shakier ground in defying the law.

In order to fully understand the conflict that has arisen in this debate over the nature of marriage, it is important to understand the difference between the religious definition of marriage and the state's secular and civil definition. The government's interest is in a legal definition of marriage—a social and voluntary contract between a man and woman in order to protect money, property, and children. Marriage is a civil union without benefit of clergy or religious definition. The state is not interested in why two people are "tying the knot," whether it's to gain money, secure a dynasty, or raise children. It may be hard for those of us who have a religious or romantic view of marriage to realize that loveless marriages are not that rare. Before the Pill, pregnancy was a frequent motive for getting married. The state doesn't care what the commitment of two people is, whether it's for life or as long as both of you love, whether it's sexually monogamous or an open marriage. There is nothing spiritual, mystical, or romantic about the state's license to marry—it's a legal contract.

Thus, George W. Bush is right when he says that "marriage is a sacred institution" when speaking as a Christian, as a member of his Methodist church. But as president of the United States and leader of all Americans, believers and unbelievers, he is wrong. What will surface in this debate as litigation and court decisions multiply is the history of the conflict between the church and the state in defining the nature of marriage. That history will become significant as we move toward a decision on who may be married.

15 After Christianity became the state religion of the Roman empire in A.D. 325, the church maintained absolute control over the regulation of marriage for some 1,000 years. Beginning in the sixteenth century, English kings (especially Henry VIII, who found the inability to get rid of a wife extremely oppressive) and other monarchs in Europe began to wrest control from the church over marital regulations. Ever since, kings, presidents, and rulers of all kinds have seen how important the control of marriage is to the regulation of social order. In this nation, the government has always been in charge of marriage.

That is why it was not a San Francisco mayor licensing same-sex couples that really threatened the president's religious understanding of marriage but rather the Supreme Judicial Court of Massachusetts, declaring marriage between same-sex couples a constitutional right, that demanded a call for constitutional amendment. I didn't understand how important that was until I read an op-ed piece in the *Boston Globe* by Peter Gomes, professor of Christian morals and the minister of Memorial Church at Harvard University, that reminds us of a seminal piece of our history:

> The Dutch made civil marriage the law of the land in 1590, and the first marriage in New England, that of Edward Winslow to the widow Susannah White, was performed on May 12, 1621, in Plymouth by Governor William Bradford, in exercise of his office as magistrate.

> There would be no clergyman in Plymouth until the arrival of the Reverend Ralph Smith in 1629, but even then marriage would continue to be a civil affair, as these first Puritans opposed the English custom of clerical marriage as unscriptural. Not until 1692, when Plymouth Colony was merged into that of Massachusetts Bay, were the clergy authorized by the new province to solemnize marriages. To this day in the Commonwealth the clergy, including those of the archdiocese, solemnize marriage legally as agents of the Commonwealth and by its civil authority. Chapter 207 of the General Laws of Massachusetts tells us who may perform such ceremonies.

Now even though it is the civil authority of the state that defines the rights and responsibilities of marriage and therefore who can be married, the state is no more infallible than the church in its judgments. It wasn't until the mid-twentieth century that the Supreme Court declared anti-miscegenation laws unconstitutional. Even after that decision, many mainline churches, where I started my ministry, unofficially discouraged interracial marriages, and many of my colleagues were forbidden to perform such weddings.

The civil law view of marriage has as much historical diversity as the church's own experience because, in part, the church continued to influence the civil law. Although it was the Bible that made "the husband the head of his wife," it was common law that "turned the married pair legally into one person—the husband," as Nancy Cott documents in her book *Public Vows: A History of Marriage and the Nation* (an indispensable resource for anyone seeking to understand the changing nature of marriage in the nation's history). She suggests that "the legal doctrine of marital unity was called coverture . . . [which] meant that the wife could not use legal avenues such as suits or contracts, own assets, or execute legal documents without her husband's collaboration." This view of the wife would not hold water in any court in the land today.

As a matter of fact, even in the religious understanding of President Bush and his followers, allowing same-sex couples the right to marry seems a logical conclusion. If marriage is "the most fundamental institution of civilization" and a major contributor to the social order in our society, why would anyone want to shut out homosexuals from the "glorious attributes" of this "sacred institution"? Obviously, the only reason one can discern is that the opponents believe that gay and lesbian people are not worthy of the benefits and spiritual blessings of "marriage."

At the heart of the controversy raging over same-sex marriage is the 20
religious and constitutional principle of the separation of church and state. All of us can probably agree that there was never a solid wall of separation, riddled as it is with breaches. The evidence of that is seen in the ambiguity of tax-free religious institutions, "in God we trust" printed on our money and "under God" in the Pledge of Allegiance to our country.

All of us clergy, who are granted permission by the state to officiate at legal marriage ceremonies, have already compromised the "solid wall" by signing the license issued by the state. I would like to believe that my authority to perform religious ceremonies does not come from the state but derives from the vows of ordination and my commitment to God. I refuse to repeat the words, "by the authority invested in me by the State of New York, I pronounce you husband and wife," but by signing the license, I've become the state's "handmaiden."

It seems fitting therefore that we religious folk should now seek to sharpen the difference between ecclesiastical law and civil law as we beseech the state to clarify who can be married by civil law. Further evidence that the issue of church and state is part of the gay-marriage controversy is that two Unitarian ministers have been arrested for solemnizing unions between same-sex couples when no state licenses were involved. Ecclesiastical law may punish those clergy who disobey marital regulations, but the state has no right to invade church practices and criminalize clergy under civil law. There should have been a noisy outcry from all churches, synagogues, and mosques at the government's outrageous contravention of the sacred principle of the "free exercise of religion."

I come from a long line of Protestants who believe in a "free church in a free state." In the issue before this nation, the civil law is the determinant of the regulation of marriage, regardless of our religious views, and the Supreme Court will finally decide what the principle of equality means in our Constitution in the third century of our life together as a people. It is likely that the Commonwealth of Massachusetts will probably lead the nation on this matter, as the State of New York led to the Supreme Court decision to allow women reproductive freedom.

So what is marriage? It depends on whom you ask, in what era, in what culture. Like all words or institutions, human definitions, whether religious or secular, change with time and history. When our beloved Constitution was written, blacks, Native Americans, and, to some extent, women were quasi-human beings with no rights or privileges, but today they are recognized as persons with full citizenship rights. The definition of marriage has been changing over the centuries in this nation, and it will change yet again as homosexuals are seen as ordinary human beings.

In time, and I believe that time is now, we Americans will see that all the fears foisted on us by religious zealots were not real. Heterosexual marriage will still flourish with its statistical failures. The only difference will be that some homosexual couples will join them and probably account for about the same number of failed relationships. And we will discover that it did not matter whether the couples were joined in a religious ceremony or a secular and civil occasion for the statement of their intentions.

Will It Be Marriage or Civil Union?

JO ANN CITRON

This fall, while the right was still staggering from the U.S. Supreme Court's decision in *Lawrence v. Texas*, Massachusetts dealt conservatives another body blow when its highest court legalized same-sex marriage. In a 4–3 ruling authored by Chief Justice Margaret Marshall, the Supreme Judicial Court (SJC) held that denying marriage to homosexuals violates the Massachusetts Declaration of Rights, the state constitution. To remedy the violation, the court changed the common-law definition of civil marriage to eliminate its opposite-sex requirement and to compel the issuance of marriage licenses to qualified persons of the same sex. Civil marriage in Massachusetts now means "the voluntary union of two persons as spouses, to the exclusion of all others." The legislature, which was directed to "take such action as it may deem appropriate in light of this opinion," has been running for cover ever since.[1]

A friend recently asked me how important the Massachusetts decision is in the struggle to achieve marriage equality in the United States. I was struck, first of all, by the terms of the question because "marriage equality" is not the same as "marriage." The issue all along has been whether gays will get marriage or some equivalent formality that will make them equal to their heterosexual counterparts. There are those who say that civil union is marriage equality. It's what Vermont said and what many Massachusetts legislators are saying in their desperate search for an escape route from the SJC ruling. It's also what William Eskridge claimed in his 2002 book, *Equality Practice: Civil Union and the Future of Gay Rights*, where he argues that, while there is no principled basis for withholding marriage from gays and lesbians, the gay community should bow to the political will of the majority and move slowly, accepting the equality of civil union now and pressing for marriage later when it becomes more palatable to the majority. Eskridge views *Baker v. State*, the Vermont civil union decision, as the equivalent of *Brown v. Board of Education*, the 1954 landmark civil rights decision that opened the way to racial integration in this country. Marriage activist Evan Wolfson, on the other hand, views *Baker* as the gay rights version of *Plessy v. Ferguson*, the railway carriage case that authorized "separate but equal" status for disfavored minorities.

[1] *Goodridge v. Department of Public Health.*

Jo Ann Citron practices alternate family and civil rights law with the firm Altman & Citron and is a member of the Women's Studies Department at Wellesley College. The article was published in the *Gay and Lesbian Review Worldwide* in March–April 2004.

This essay is being written during the 180-day waiting period following the issuance of the decision, a period of either genuine confusion or deliberate obfuscation, depending on the degree of cynicism with which you view the political process. It might be useful at this point to summarize what the court said and how the legislature has responded. The court began by reminding everyone that the Massachusetts marriage statute is a licensing law. Because marriage has always been understood to mean the union of a man and a woman, the statute cannot be construed to authorize issuing a license to two people of the same sex. But to bar gay couples from all the benefits, protections, and obligations that accompany marriage violates the Massachusetts constitution, which means that the current marriage licensing law is unconstitutional. The remedy the court fashioned was to change the common law definition of civil marriage to eliminate its opposite-sex requirement, thereby removing the bar that excludes gay couples from obtaining marriage licenses.

Rather than declare that cities and towns must immediately begin to issue marriage licenses to gays, which would have created chaos, the court granted the legislature 180 days to revise state statutes so as to bring them into line with its ruling and to clean up a complicated domestic relations regulatory scheme that refers to husbands and wives. The court reminded the legislature that it retains "broad discretion to regulate marriage." This means that the Legislature can continue to impose certain restrictions upon persons who wish to marry. The legislature may refuse to authorize granting a marriage license to persons under a certain age, or to siblings, or to a parent and child. It may require a blood test or a birth certificate, or that applicants turn around three times and face north, or anything else that would be constitutional. But, as I read the decision, the legislature may not refuse to grant a license to otherwise qualified gay couples.

5 The SJC was perfectly clear in stating that the remedy for the constitutional violation was the reformulation of the definition of civil marriage. Yet many legislators, together with the current attorney general, want to take a different view of the matter. They have seized upon the "protections, benefits, and obligations" language in the opinion in the hope that, by providing the benefits that marriage yields in our society, they can avoid providing marriage itself. The legislature has asked the SJC to render an advisory opinion about a civil union bill, and the SJC has invited interested parties to submit briefs. Meanwhile, the Massachusetts constitutional convention is scheduled to meet on February 11, 2004, to vote on a Defense of Marriage Act or DOMA that, in its present form, would not only prevent gay marriage but would also outlaw domestic partner benefits. If the legislature passes the DOMA in a second convention, the measure would appear on the ballot in November of 2006 and voters could, by a simple majority, amend the state constitution to make gay marriage, civil union, and domestic partnerships illegal. The political reality is that such a DOMA will probably not garner the necessary votes

either in the legislature or among voters; however, a simple DOMA limiting itself to marriage is more likely to succeed, especially in the face of the SJC decision, which presents the right with what it would call a "clear and present danger." This means that gay marriage could become legal in Massachusetts on May 18, 2004, via the SJC decision and illegal in Massachusetts on November 14, 2006, via a voter referendum. No one knows what will happen to gay couples who marry in the interim. Let the courts sort through that one!

Massachusetts has a good track record when it comes to gay families: It permits second-parent adoption; it allows two women to appear as "parent" on a child's birth certificate; it protects the relationship between a child and her nonbiological parent. At the very least, *Goodridge* is going to yield "marriage equality" in some form of civil union. The problem, of course, is that there is no such thing as "marriage equality" for anyone who files federal income tax returns, bequeaths an estate, or travels outside of Massachusetts. When it comes to federal benefits or the tax-free transfer of marital property or the ability to have another state recognize your Massachusetts relationship, marriage is the only status that will do. This is why some are downplaying the SJC decision, pointing out that even if people are able to marry in Massachusetts, their status will not be recognized by the federal government or by any other state with a DOMA. In that respect, marriage is indeed no different from civil union. In fact, it might even be worse for a while. We're beginning to see judges in some states accept the validity of a Vermont civil union. Even in states with a DOMA, it will be possible to find a judge who would give full faith and credit to a civil union because most DOMA laws have nothing to say about civil unions. Not so with marriage. For the time being, a Massachusetts marriage will be even less portable than a Vermont civil union.

But let there be no mistake: Whatever happens in Massachusetts is absolutely critical to how the gay marriage question will be answered in the rest of the United States. What happens here is even more important than what happened in Vermont. Here's why. The next marriage case with a reasonable likelihood of success is working its way through the courts in New Jersey, a state with a history of progressive court decisions. New Jersey will be looking very carefully at the way Vermont and Massachusetts have addressed the marriage question. If the Massachusetts SJC ratifies its decision and mandates the issuance of marriage licenses, New Jersey will look at its predecessor states and see two alternative models, marriage and civil union. New Jersey will choose one or the other. But the SJC could fail to confirm its marriage decision and approve instead some form of civil union. Coupled with the Vermont ruling, this will create a critical mass in favor of civil union, an outcome that will make it far more likely that New Jersey will opt for civil union over marriage. After that, the rest of the states will almost certainly fall into line with civil unions, and that will spell the end of gay marriage, probably forever.

Ironically, it may also mean the end of marriage in its present form, the one that the right is working so hard to preserve. Conservatives Andrew Sullivan and David Brooks have argued that the best way to protect marriage would be to open it to anyone who wants to vow fidelity and is willing to forego an easy exit from a supposedly permanent relationship. Marriage is, after all, a conservative institution, and persons who enter it with the blessing of the state may not leave it without the state's permission. Already, as a result of the marriage cases and their surrounding discourse, the very term "marriage" is being qualified. We now speak of "civil marriage" to distinguish it from the religious ceremonies that are but one of its aspects. Insofar as material benefits are concerned, marriage is a civil institution. Those material benefits can attach just as easily to any civil institution the state cares to identify. This is, after all, the point of wanting to offer gays something called "union" rather than something called "marriage." Nothing but prejudice prevents state and federal governments from offering to partners in a civil union the identical benefits, protections, and obligations that the state now offers to spouses.

William Eskridge is wrong in thinking that civil union is a step on the path towards marriage. Civil union and marriage are not sequential; they are alternatives to one another. There is no reason to think that the country will permit civil union now and confer marriage later. In fact, the reality is likely to be quite the reverse. Because of equal protection considerations, the civil union alternative will have to be available to straights as well as gays. And if my analysis is correct, it will become more widely available to everyone in the coming years. At the moment, there is little incentive for marriage-eligible couples to elect a civil union. But this will change.

It is not difficult to imagine a tacit compromise in which the right is 10
allowed to maintain its stranglehold on marriage in exchange for allowing the material benefits now associated with it to break free and accompany civil union. This is another reason why the Massachusetts decision in favor of marriage is strategically important. As long as even a single state has legalized marriage, civil union becomes more attractive to the right. And the gay community can leverage those few gay marriage licenses into a demand that marriage benefits attach to civil unions.

In my view, this would be a good outcome. I say this as someone who views marriage as a regressive institution that has never been good to women, that insidiously creates insiders and outsiders, and, most importantly, that violates the separation of church and state at the heart of our form of government. The state should not be in the business of attaching material benefits to a religious institution. The right to social security death benefits, the right to favorable tax treatment, the right to take your formalized relationship with you when you travel, should be detached from marriage altogether and should be awarded according to some other equitable system. To the extent that this becomes so, there will eventually be no material difference between the old form of marriage and the new form of civil unions. Traditional marriage will endure as a religious institution. Already there are hundreds of clergy willing to perform marriage ceremonies for gay congregants and thousands of gay couples who have participated in these ceremonies whose benefits are wholly spiritual. Over time, civil union and civil marriage will ultimately come to mean much the same thing. Whether the SJC ratifies its original position or abandons it, *Goodridge* brings us closer to a consensus around civil union. It is time for the gay community to turn its attention to winning for civil union all the rights, benefits, protections, and obligations of marriage. That is the truly revolutionary project.

DISCUSSION QUESTIONS

1. Why is definition a critical element in Moody's argument? Why is it a critical element in Citron's? Do the two of them agree on a definition of marriage?
2. What is Moody's attitude toward same-sex marriage? Why, in his opinion, do more serious problems arise when it comes to the laws of the state than the theology of the church?
3. Why does Moody believe that President Bush was wrong in saying, as president, that "marriage is a sacred institution"? Were you surprised by Moody's explanation of the history of marriage in the United States?
4. When Citron published her essay, the nation was awaiting Massachusetts's decision on the legality of same-sex marriages. What was her biggest fear about the future of the legal standing of same-sex relationships?
5. Analyze Citron's analogy between decisions regarding same-sex unions and two Supreme Court decisions regarding racial integration, *Plessy v. Ferguson* and *Brown v. Board of Education.*
6. What is the author's claim in each of the two essays?

ASSIGNMENTS FOR UNDERSTANDING DEFINITION

READING AND DISCUSSION QUESTIONS

1. Contrast the claims made by Jo Ann Citron in "Will It Be Marriage or Civil Union?" and Howard Moody in "Gay Marriage Shows Why We Need to Separate Church and State."
2. Contrast Citron's claim with that supported by Eric Zorn in "Family a Symbol of Love and Life, but Not Politics."
3. Use Orlando Patterson's "Race by the Numbers" as a starting point to discuss to what extent you believe you either are or are not defined by your racial identity.

WRITING ASSIGNMENTS

4. Using Geoffrey Nunberg's "Don't Torture English to Soft-Pedal Abuse" as a model, choose a term and explain in an essay of 500 words how its meaning has been manipulated for political purposes.
5. Explain in a brief essay to what extent you found Orlando Patterson's argument convincing and why.
6. Write about an important or widely used term whose meaning has changed since you first learned it. Such terms often come from the slang of particular groups: drug users, rock music fans, musicians, athletes, computer programmers, or software developers.
7. Define the differences between necessities, comforts, and luxuries. Consider how they have changed over time.

CHAPTER 6

Defending Claims

Claims, or propositions, represent answers to the question "What are you trying to prove?" Although they are the conclusions of your arguments, they often appear as thesis statements. Claims can be classified as *claims of fact, claims of value,* and *claims of policy.*

CLAIMS OF FACT

Claims of fact assert that a condition has existed, exists, or will exist and that their support consists of factual information—information such as statistics, examples, and testimony that most responsible observers assume can be verified.

Many facts are not matters for argument: Our own senses can confirm them, and other observers will agree about them. We can agree that a certain number of students were in the classroom at a particular time, that lions make a louder sound than kittens, and that apples are sweeter than potatoes.

We can also agree about information that most of us can rarely confirm for ourselves—information in reference books, such as atlases, almanacs, and telephone directories; data from scientific resources about the physical world; and happenings reported in the media. We can agree on the reliability of such information because we trust the observers who report it.

However, the factual map is constantly being redrawn by new data in such fields as history and science that cause us to reevaluate our conclusions. For example, the discovery of the Dead Sea Scrolls in 1947 revealed that some books of the Bible—Isaiah, for one—were far older than we had thought. Recent research has proven that cervical cancer is caused by a virus and that a vaccination given early enough can possibly prevent it.

In your conversations with other students you probably generate claims of fact every day, some of which can be verified without much effort, others of which are more difficult to substantiate.

CLAIM: Most of the students in this class come from towns within fifty miles of Boston.

To prove this the arguer would need only to ask the students in the class where they come from.

CLAIM: More students entering this fall had AP credit for one or more courses than in any past year.

To prove this claim, the arguer would have to have access to entering students' records from the time Advanced Placement was first accepted to the present.

CLAIM: The Red Sox will win the pennant this year.

This claim is different from the others because it is an opinion about what will happen in the future. But it can be verified (in the future) and is therefore classified as a claim of fact.

More complex factual claims about political and scientific matters remain controversial because proof on which all or most observers will agree is difficult or impossible to obtain.

CLAIM: Bilingual programs are less effective than English-only programs in preparing students for higher education.

CLAIM: The only life in the universe exists on this planet.

Not all claims are so neatly stated or make such unambiguous assertions. Because we recognize that there are exceptions to most generalizations, we often qualify our claims with words such as *generally, usually, probably,* and *as a rule.* It would not be true to state flatly, for example, "College graduates earn more than high school graduates." This statement is generally true, but we know that some high school graduates who are electricians or city bus drivers or sanitation workers earn more than college graduates who are schoolteachers or nurses or social workers. In making such a claim, therefore, the writer should qualify it with a word that limits the claim.

To support a claim of fact, the writer needs to produce sufficient and appropriate data—that is, examples, statistics, and testimony from reliable sources. Provided this requirement is met, the task of establishing a factual claim would seem to be relatively straightforward. But as you have probably already discovered in ordinary conversation, finding convincing support for factual claims can pose a number of problems. Whenever you try to establish a claim of fact, you will need to ask at least three questions about the material you plan to use: *What are sufficient and appropriate data? Who are the reliable authorities?* and *Have I made clear whether my statements are facts or inferences?*

Sufficient and Appropriate Data

The amount and kind of data for a particular argument depend on the importance and complexity of the subject. The more controversial the subject, the more facts and testimony you will need to supply. Consider the claim "The murder rate in New York City has decreased steadily over the last ten years." If you want to prove the truth of this claim, obviously you will have to provide a larger quantity of data than for a claim that says, "The number of students at Trenton High School increased 10 percent between 2005–2006 and 2006–2007." In examining your facts and opinions, an alert reader will want to know if they are accurate, current, and typical of other facts and opinions that you have not mentioned.

In arguments about more controversial issues, the reader will also look for testimony from more than one authority, although there may be cases where only one or two experts who have achieved a unique breakthrough in their field will be sufficient. These cases would probably occur most frequently in the physical sciences. The Nobel Prize winners James Watson and Francis Crick, who first discovered the structure of the DNA molecule, are an example of such experts. However, in the case of the so-called Hitler diaries that surfaced in 1983, at least a dozen experts—journalists, historians, bibliographers who could verify the age of the paper and the ink—were needed to establish that they were forgeries.

Reliable Authorities

Not all those who pronounce themselves experts are trustworthy. Your own experience has probably taught you that you cannot always believe the reports of an event by a single witness. The witness may be poorly trained to make accurate observations—about the size of a crowd, the speed of a vehicle, his distance from an object. Or his own physical conditions—illness, intoxication, disability—may prevent him from seeing or hearing or smelling accurately. The circumstances under which he observes the event—darkness, confusion, noise—may also impair his observation. In addition, the witness may be biased for or against the outcome of the event, as in a hotly contested baseball game, where the observer sees the play that he wants to see. You will find the problems associated with the biases of witnesses to be relevant to your work as a reader and writer of argumentative essays.

You will undoubtedly want to quote authors in some of your arguments. In most cases you will not be familiar with the authors. But there are guidelines for determining their reliability: the rank or title of the experts, the acceptance of their publications by other experts, their association with reputable universities, research centers, or think tanks. For example, for a paper on euthanasia, you might decide to quote from an article by Paul R. McHugh, the Henry Phipps Professor of Psychiatry at the Johns Hopkins University School of Medicine and psychiatrist in chief at the Johns Hopkins Hospital in Baltimore. For a paper on crime by youth groups, you might want to use material supplied by Elizabeth Glazer, chief of Crime Control Strategies in the U.S. Attorney's office for the Southern District of New York, where she previously served as chief of both the Organized Crime Unit and Violent Gang Unit. Most readers of your arguments would agree that these authors have impressive credentials in their fields.

What if several respectable sources are in conflict? What if the experts disagree? After a preliminary investigation of a controversial subject, you may decide that you have sufficient material to support your claim. But if you read further, you may discover that other material presented by equally qualified experts contradicts your original claim. In such circumstances you will find it impossible to make a definitive claim. (On pp. 213–27 in the treatment of support of a claim by evidence, you will find a more elaborate discussion of this vexing problem.)

Facts or Inferences

We have defined a fact as a statement that can be verified. An inference is "a statement about the unknown on the basis of the known."[1] The difference between facts and inferences is important to you as the writer of an argument because an inference is an *interpretation,* or an opinion reached after informed evaluation of evidence.

You have probably come across a statement such as the following in a newspaper or magazine: "Excessive television viewing has caused the steady decline in the reading ability of children and teenagers." Presented this way, the statement is clearly intended to be read as a factual claim that has been or can be proved. But it is an inference. The facts, which can be and have been verified, are (1) the reading ability of children and teenagers has declined and (2) the average child views television for six or more hours a day. (Whether this amount of time is "excessive" is also an opinion.) The cause-and-effect relation between the two facts is an interpretation of the investigator, who has examined both the reading scores and the amount of time spent in front of the television set and *inferred* that one is the cause of

[1] S. I. Hayakawa, *Language in Thought and Action* (New York: Harcourt, Brace, Jovanovich, 1978), p. 35.

the other. The causes of the decline in reading scores are probably more complex than the original statement indicates. Since we can seldom or never create laboratory conditions for testing the influence of television separate from other influences in the family and the community, any statement about the connection between reading scores and television viewing can only be a guess.

By definition, no inference can ever do more than suggest probabilities. Of course, some inferences are much more reliable than others and afford a high degree of probability. Almost all claims in science are based on inferences, interpretations of data on which most scientists agree. Paleontologists find a few ancient bones from which they make inferences about an animal that might have been alive millions of years ago. We can never be absolutely certain that the reconstruction of the dinosaur in the museum is an exact copy of the animal it is supposed to represent, but the probability is fairly high because no other interpretation works so well to explain all the observable data—the existence of the bones in a particular place, their age, their relation to other fossils, and their resemblance to the bones of existing animals with which the paleontologist is familiar.

Inferences are profoundly important, and most arguments could not proceed very far without them. But an inference is not a fact. The writer of an argument must make it clear when he or she offers an inference, an interpretation, or an opinion that it is not a fact.

Writer's Guide: Defending a Claim of Fact

Here are some guidelines that should help you to defend a factual claim. (We'll say more about support of factual claims in Chapter 7.)

1. Be sure that the claim — what you are trying to prove — is clearly stated, preferably at the beginning of your paper.
2. Define terms that may be controversial or ambiguous. For example, in trying to prove that "radicals" had captured the student government, you would have to define "radicals," distinguishing them from "liberals" or members of other ideological groups, so that your readers would understand exactly what you meant.
3. As far as possible, make sure that your evidence — facts and opinions, or interpretations of the facts — fulfills the appropriate criteria. The data should be sufficient, accurate, recent, typical; the authorities should be reliable.
4. Make clear when conclusions about the data are inferences or interpretations, not facts. For example, you should not write, "The series of lectures

titled Modern Architecture, sponsored by our fraternity, was poorly attended because the students at this college aren't interested in discussions of art." What proof could you offer that this *was* the reason and that your statement was a *fact*? Perhaps there were other reasons that you hadn't considered.

5. Emphasize your most important evidence by placing it at the beginning or the end of your paper (the most emphatic positions in an essay) and devoting more space to it.

SAMPLE ANNOTATED ESSAY: CLAIM OF FACT

A Reassuring Scorecard for Affirmative Action

MICHAEL M. WEINSTEIN

Introduction: a) Review of the attack on affirmative action

Affirmative action—preferential treatment toward women and minority applicants as practiced by employers, university admissions officers, and government contractors—remains under attack thirty-two years after President Johnson ordered federal contractors to seek female and minority employees. Two states have voted to wipe out the use of race- and gender-based preferences by state agencies. Parents have challenged the race-based admissions policies of public schools. Even Joseph Lieberman, the [2000] Democratic candidate for vice president, once opposed policies "based on group preference instead of individual merit."

b) Specific criticism

Some of affirmative action's critics contend that preferential hiring and admissions are always wrong in principle no matter how attractive the consequences. But other critics focus on affirmative action's alleged failings. According to this argument, the policy creates divisive workplaces, breeds cynicism and corruption, and hurts many of the individuals it is supposed to help. That debate should turn on the facts. Instead it has been fueled almost entirely by anecdotes—until now.

Michael M. Weinstein, Ph.D., is director of programs for the Robin Hood Foundation. He was on the editorial board of the *New York Times* when he wrote this October 17, 2000, article.

Refutation: authoritative source of new data

In the most recent issue of the *Journal of Economic Literature,* a publication of the American Economic Association, two respected economists provide an eighty-five page review of over two hundred serious scientific studies of affirmative action. Harry Holzer of Georgetown University and David Neumark of Michigan State University ferret out every statistic from the studies to measure the effects of affirmative action. Harsh critics of affirmative action will not find much comfort.

Claim: general benefits for women and minorities under affirmative action

Support: a) Data about employment, education, business

The authors concede the evidence is sometimes murky. Yet they find that affirmative action produces tangible benefits for women, for minority entrepreneurs, students, and workers, and for the overall economy. Employers adopting the policy increase the relative number of women and minority employees by an average of between 10 and 15 percent. Affirmative action has helped boost the percentage of blacks attending college by a factor of three and the percentage of blacks enrolled in medical school by a factor of four since the early 1960s. Between 1982 and 1991 the number of federal contracts going to black-owned businesses rose by 125 percent, even though the total number of federal contracts rose by less than 25 percent during the period.

To no one's surprise, the two economists rivet 5
on economic performance. Here, the survey is interesting for what it does *not* find. There is, the authors say, little credible evidence that affirmative action appointees perform badly or diminish the overall performance of the economy.

b) Data about credentials

Women hired under affirmative action, they say, largely match their male counterparts in credentials and performance. Blacks and Hispanics hired under affirmative action generally lag behind on credentials, such as education, but usually perform about as well as nonminority employees.

c) Data about worker performance

In a separate study, Mr. Holzer and Mr. Neumark interviewed thousands of supervisors and showed that they ranked most affirmative action hires roughly the same as ordinary hires. The authors find that companies undertaking affirmative action use extensive recruitment and training to bring workers who fall a notch below average on credentials up to the performance level of other workers.

d) Data about student performance

Critics have often pointed to the wide gap between SAT scores of black and white students admitted to selective universities as proof that they are lowering standards for minority students and putting them in settings they cannot handle. But the use of a test gap as a measure of reverse discrimination is misleading. Much of the gap would exist even if admissions were race-blind. Colleges pull applicants from a population that includes many more high-scoring whites than blacks.

A discrimination-free procedure would start by tapping the pool, largely white, of high scorers and then turn to the pool of lower-scoring whites and blacks. The average test scores for whites admitted to the college would thus exceed that of the blacks admitted.

To be sure, some selective universities add to 10
the test gap by giving preference to minority applicants. But, the data shows, black students at elite colleges graduate at greater rates than blacks at less demanding colleges, disproving claims that affirmative action disserves minority students.

e) Data about social benefits

The Holzer-Neumark survey shows that affirmative action in admissions has produced significant social benefits. For example, black doctors choose more often than their white medical school classmates to serve indigent or minority patients in inner cities and rural areas.

Conclusion: Contrary to criticism, evidence justifies affirmative action.

Though favorable, these findings hardly end the debate on affirmative action. The critics who refuse to accept government-sanctioned racial or gender preferences no matter what the benefit will continue to object. Affirmative action can be misused, as when whites running a company create a fiction of black ownership to qualify for credits in seeking government contracts. But the evidence marshaled by the authors largely vindicates affirmative action and should provide the ammunition for rebutting those critics who refuse to take facts into account.

Analysis

This article offers evidence that affirmative action provides benefits to women and minorities. A claim of fact often responds to some widely held belief that the author considers to be wrong—in this case, the failure of affirmative action. We need to ask three questions about a claim of fact: Are the data sufficient and appropriate? Are the authorities reliable? Are the distinctions between facts and inferences clear? Within its brief compass, this argument comes close to satisfying these criteria. In addition, its organization is straightforward, with a clearly defined introduction, body, and conclusion.

The first three paragraphs constitute the introduction. First, the author reviews some of the claims of the opposition. At the end of the second paragraph, he makes clear his own emphasis: "That debate should turn on the facts." He then cites his source for the facts—a report in a respected professional journal by two university economists, who have examined the data on affirmative action in over two hundred serious scientific studies. This information reassures the reader that the first two criteria for judging a claim of fact will be met.

The body of the essay contains support for the claim, first in a short summary, then in substantial detail. Much of the data is statistical, a specific form of information that most readers find convincing and relatively easy to assimilate. (Of course, readers must regard the source as trustworthy.) The author has offered some interpretations—in paragraph 8, for example—to clarify what he considers a misunderstanding. Notice also the use of "To be sure," an expression that usually indicates that the writer recognizes an exception to his view. But the argument stands firmly on the facts. The ending is one often used by debaters—a modest challenge to the opposing side.

PRACTICE

As you read the following essay, answer these questions:

1. What is Samuelson's claim?
2. Has Samuelson defined key terms? Are there terms that need to be defined that are not?
3. What type of evidence does he offer? Is the evidence sufficient, accurate, recent, and typical? Are the authorities reliable?
4. Are any inferences presented as inferences rather than as facts?
5. What might Samuelson's rationale have been for organizing the essay as he did?

Picking Sides for the News

ROBERT J. SAMUELSON

We in the news business think we're impartial seekers of truth, but most Americans think otherwise. They view us as sloppy, biased, and self-serving. In 1985, 56 percent of the public felt news organizations usually got their facts straight, says the Pew Research Center. By 2002 that was 35 percent. In 1985 the public thought the media "moral" by 54 to 13 percent; by 2003 opinion was split 40 to 38 percent. Americans think the "media make news rather than just report it," says Pew's Andrew Kohut. The obsession with "scandal in high places" is seen as building audiences rather than advancing the public interest.

Still, the latest Pew survey confirms—with lots of numbers—something disturbing that we all sense: people are increasingly picking their media on the basis of partisanship. If you're Republican and conservative, you listen to talk radio and watch the Fox News Channel. If you're liberal and Democratic, you listen to National Public Radio and watch "NewsHour with Jim Lehrer." It's like picking restaurants: Chinese for some, Italian for others. And everyone can punch up partisan blogs—the fast food of the news business. What's disturbing is that, like restaurants, the news media may increasingly cater to their customers' (partisan) tastes. News slowly becomes more selective and slanted.

Rush Limbaugh has 14.5 million weekly listeners. By Pew, 77 percent are conservative, 16 percent moderate, and 7 percent liberal. Or take Fox's 1.3 million prime-time viewers: 52 percent are conservative, 30 percent moderate, and 13 percent liberal. By contrast, 36 percent of Americans are conservative, 38 percent moderate, and 18 percent liberal. The liberals' media favorites are slightly less lopsided. "NewsHour's" audience is 22 percent conservative, 44 percent moderate, and 27 percent liberal. NPR's audience is 31 percent conservative, 33 percent moderate, and 30 percent liberal. Of course, many news outlets still have broad audiences. Daily newspapers are collectively close to national averages; so is CNN.

But the partisan drift may grow because distrust is spreading. In 1988 Pew found that 58 percent of the public thought there was "no bias" in election coverage. Now that's 38 percent: 22 percent find a Democratic bias, 17 percent a Republican. Almost all major media have suffered confidence declines. Among Republicans, only 12 percent say they believe "all or most" of Newsweek; for Democrats the figure is twice that, 26 percent. In 1985 the overall figure was higher (31 percent), with little partisan gap. Newsweek's numbers typify mainstream media. Only 14 percent of Republicans believe "all or most" of the *New York Times*, versus 31 percent of Democrats.

What's going on? Why should we care? 5

Robert J. Samuelson, a contributing editor of *Newsweek*, has written a column for the *Washington Post* since 1977. This article appeared in *Newsweek* on June 28, 2004.

Up to a point, conservative talk radio and Fox represent a desirable backlash against the perceived "liberal bias" of network news and mainstream media. I've worked in the mainstream press for 35 years. Editors and reporters reflexively deny a liberal bias, even though many ordinary people find it and mainstream newsrooms are politically skewed. Here are the latest Pew figures: 7 percent of national reporters and editors are conservative (a fifth the national rate), and 34 percent are liberal (almost twice the national rate). Most reporters I know believe fiercely in being fair and objective. Still, the debate over "what's news and significant?" is warped. Talk radio and Fox add other views.

But the sorting of audiences by politics also poses dangers—for the media and the country. We journalists think we define news, and from day to day, we do. Over the longer run, that's less true. All news organizations must satisfy their audiences. If they don't, they go out of business. "Media bias is product differentiation," says James T. Hamilton of Duke, whose book "All the News That's Fit to Sell" shows how economic forces powerfully shape news judgments. If liberals and conservatives migrate to rival media camps, both camps may ultimately submit to the same narrow logic: like-minded editors and reporters increasingly feed like-minded customers stories that reinforce their world view.

Economic interests and editorial biases will converge. The New York Times is now a national paper; 49 percent of its daily circulation is outside the New York area, up from 38 percent five years ago. There's home delivery in 275 markets, up from 171 five years ago. But if the Times sells largely to upscale readers (average household income is $90,381, almost twice the national average) with vaguely liberal views, it risks becoming hostage to their sensibilities. No less does Fox risk becoming hostage to its base.

The worthy, if unattainable, ideals of fairness and objectivity will silently erode. Many forces push that way: new technologies (cable, the Internet); the blending of news and entertainment; the breakdown between "hard news" and interpretation; intense competition; changing news habits of the young. The damage will not just be to good journalism. Tom Rosenstiel of the Project for Excellence in Journalism notes that respected national media develop common facts and language that helps hold society together and solve common problems. It will be a sad day when we trust only the media that voice our views.

CLAIMS OF VALUE

Unlike claims of fact, which attempt to prove that something is true and which can be validated by reference to the data, claims of value make a judgment. They express approval or disapproval. They attempt to prove that some action, belief, or condition is right or wrong, good or bad, beautiful or ugly, worthwhile or undesirable.

CLAIM: Democracy is superior to any other form of government.

CLAIM: Killing animals for sport is wrong.

CLAIM: The Sam Rayburn Building in Washington is an aesthetic failure.

Some claims of value are simply expressions of tastes, likes and dislikes, or preferences and prejudices. The Latin proverb *"De gustibus non est disputandum"* states that we cannot dispute about tastes. Suppose you express a preference for chocolate over vanilla. If your listener should ask why you prefer this flavor, you cannot refer to an outside authority or produce data or appeal to her moral sense to convince her that your preference is justified.

Many claims of value, however, can be defended or attacked on the basis of standards that measure the worth of an action, a belief, or an object. As far as possible, our personal likes and dislikes should be supported by reference to these standards. Value judgments occur in any area of human experience, but whatever the area, the analysis will be the same. We ask the arguer who is defending a claim of value: *What are the standards or criteria for deciding that this action, this belief, or this object is good or bad, beautiful or ugly, desirable or undesirable? Does the thing you are defending fulfill these criteria?*

There are two general areas in which people often disagree about matters of value: aesthetics and morality. They are also the areas that offer the greatest challenge to the writer. What follows is a discussion of some of the elements of analysis that you should consider in defending a claim of value in these areas.

Aesthetics is the study of beauty and the fine arts. Controversies over works of art — the aesthetic value of books, paintings, sculpture, architecture, dance, drama, and movies — rage fiercely among experts and laypeople alike. They may disagree on the standards for judging or, even if they agree about standards, may disagree about how successfully the art object under discussion has met these standards.

Consider a discussion about popular music. Hearing someone praise the singing of Manu Chao, a hugely popular European singer now playing to American crowds, you might ask why he is highly regarded. You expect Chao's fans to say more than "I like him" or "He's great." You expect them to give reasons to support their claims. They might show you a short review from a respected newspaper that says, "Mr. Chao's gift is simplicity. His music owes a considerable amount to Bob Marley . . . but Mr. Chao has a nasal, regular-guy voice, and instead of the Wailers' brooding, bass-heavy undertow, Mr. Chao's band delivers a lighter bounce. His tunes have the singing directness of nursery rhymes."[2] Chao's fans accept these criteria for judging a singer's appeal.

[2]Jon Pareles, *New York Times*, July 10, 2001, p. B1.

You may not agree that simplicity, directness, and a regular-guy voice are the most important qualities in a popular singer. But the establishment of standards itself offers material for a discussion or an argument. You may argue about the relevance of the criteria, or you may agree with the criteria but argue about the success of the singer in meeting them. Perhaps you prefer complexity to simplicity. Or even if you choose simplicity, you may not think that Chao has exhibited this quality to good effect.

It is probably not surprising then, that, despite wide differences in taste, professional critics more often than not agree on criteria and whether an art object has met the criteria. For example, almost all movie critics agree that *Citizen Kane* and *Gone with the Wind* are superior films. They also agree that *Plan 9 from Outer Space,* a horror film, is terrible.

Value claims about morality express judgments about the rightness or wrongness of conduct or belief. Here disagreements are as wide and deep as in the arts. The first two examples on page 168 reveal how controversial such claims can be. Although you and your reader may share many values—among them a belief in democracy, a respect for learning, and a desire for peace—you may also disagree, even profoundly, about other values. The subject of divorce, for example, despite its prevalence in our society, can produce a conflict between people who have differing moral standards. Some people may insist on adherence to absolute standards, arguing that the values they hold are based on immutable religious precepts derived from God and biblical scripture. Since marriage is sacred, divorce is always wrong, they say, whether or not the conditions of society change. Other people may argue that values are relative, based on the changing needs of societies in different places and at different times. Since marriage is an institution created by human beings at a particular time in history to serve particular social needs, they may say, it can also be dissolved when other social needs arise. The same conflicts between moral values might occur in discussions of abortion or suicide.

As a writer you cannot always know what system of values your reader holds. Yet it might be possible to find a rule on which almost all readers agree. One such rule was expressed by the eighteenth-century German philosopher Immanuel Kant: "Man and, in general, every rational being exists as an end in itself and not merely as a means to be arbitrarily used by this or that will." Kant's prescription urges us not to subject any creature to a condition that it has not freely chosen. In other words, we cannot use other creatures, as in slavery, for our own purposes. (Some philosophers would extend this rule to the treatment of animals by human beings.) This standard of judgment has, in fact, been invoked in recent years against medical experimentation on human beings in prisons and hospitals without their consent and against the sterilization of poor or mentally retarded women without their consent.

Nevertheless, even where people agree about standards for measuring behavior, a majority preference is not enough to confer moral value. If in a certain neighborhood a majority of heterosexual men decide to harass a

Writer's Guide: Defending a Claim of Value

The following suggestions are a preliminary guide to the defense of a value claim. (We discuss support for value claims further in Chapter 7.)

1. Try to make clear that the values or principles you are defending are important and relatively more significant than other values. Keep in mind that you and your readers may differ about their relative importance. For example, although your readers may agree with you that brilliant photography is important in a film, they may think that a well-written script is even more crucial to its success. And although they may agree that freedom of the press is a mainstay of democracy, they may regard the right to privacy as even more fundamental.
2. Suggest that adherence to the values you are defending will bring about good results in some specific situation or bad results if respect for the values is ignored. You might argue, for example, that a belief in freedom of the press will make citizens better informed and the country stronger while a failure to protect this freedom will strengthen the forces of authoritarianism.
3. Since value terms are abstract, use examples and illustrations to clarify meanings and make distinctions. Comparisons and contrasts are especially helpful. If you use the term *heroism,* can you provide examples to differentiate between *heroism* and *foolhardiness* or *exhibitionism*?
4. Use testimony of others to prove that knowledgeable or highly regarded people share your values.

few gay men and lesbians, that consensus does not make their action right. In formulating value claims, you should be prepared to ask and answer questions about the way in which your value claims and those of others have been arrived at. Lionel Ruby, an American philosopher, sums it up in these words: "The law of rationality tells us that we ought to justify our beliefs by evidence and reasons, instead of asserting them dogmatically."[3]

Of course, you will not always be able to persuade those with whom you argue that your values are superior to theirs and that they should therefore change their attitudes. Nor, on the other hand, would you want to compromise your values or pretend that they were different to win an argument. What you can and should do, however, as Lionel Ruby advises, is give *good reasons* that you think one thing is better than another. If as a child you asked why it was wrong to take your brother's toys, you might have been told by an exasperated parent, "Because I say so." Some adults still give such answers in defending their judgments, but such answers are not arguments and do nothing to win the agreement of others.

[3] *The Art of Making Sense* (New York: Lippincott, 1968), p. 271.

SAMPLE ANNOTATED ESSAY: CLAIM OF VALUE

Kids in the Mall: Growing Up Controlled

WILLIAM SEVERINI KOWINSKI

> Butch heaved himself up and loomed over the group. "Like it was different for me," he piped. "My folks used to drop me off at the shopping mall every morning and leave me all day. It was like a big free baby-sitter, you know? One night they never came back for me. Maybe they moved away. Maybe there's some kind of a Bureau of Missing Parents I could check with."
>
> —Richard Peck, *Secrets of the Shopping Mall,* a novel for teenagers

Introduction: interesting personal anecdote

From his sister at Swarthmore, I'd heard about a kid in Florida whose mother picked him up after school every day, drove him straight to the mall, and left him there until it closed—all at his insistence. I'd heard about a boy in Washington who, when his family moved from one suburb to another, pedaled his bicycle five miles every day to get back to his old mall, where he once belonged.

Additional examples of mall experience

These stories aren't unusual. The mall is a common experience for the majority of American youth; they have probably been going there all their lives. Some ran within their first large open space, saw their first fountain, bought their first toy, and read their first book in a mall. They may have smoked their first cigarette or first joint, or turned them down, had their first kiss or lost their virginity in the mall parking lot. Teenagers in America now spend more time in the mall than anywhere else but home and school. Mostly it is their choice, but some of that mall time is put in as the result of two-paycheck and single-parent

---

William Severini Kowinski is a freelance writer who has been the book review editor and managing arts editor of the *Boston Phoenix.* This excerpt is from his book *The Malling of America: An Inside Look at the Great Consumer Paradise* (1985, revised 2002).

households, and the lack of other viable alternatives. But are these kids being harmed by the mall?

Reasons for the author's interest

I wondered first of all what difference it makes for adolescents to experience so many important moments in the mall. They are, after all, at play in the fields of its little world and they learn its ways; they adapt to it and make it adapt to them. It's here that these kids get their street sense, only it's mall sense. They are learning the ways of a large-scale, artificial environment; its subtleties and flexibilities, its particular pleasures and resonances, and the attitudes it fosters.

Expert opinion

The presence of so many teenagers for so much time was not something mall developers planned on. In fact, it came as a big surprise. But kids became a fact of mall life very easily, and the International Council of Shopping Centers found it necessary to commission a study, which they published along with a guide to mall managers on how to handle the teenage incursion.

5 The study found that "teenagers in suburban centers are bored and come to the shopping centers mainly as a place to go. Teenagers in suburban centers spent more time fighting, drinking, littering and walking than did their urban counterparts, but presented fewer overall problems." The report observed that "adolescents congregated in groups of two to four and predominantly at locations selected by them rather than management." This probably had something to do with the decision to install game arcades, which allow management to channel these restless adolescents into naturally contained areas away from major traffic points of adult shoppers.

Why the malls encourage adolescent presence

The guide concluded that mall management should tolerate and even encourage the teenage presence because, in the words of the report, "The vast majority support the same set of values as does shopping center management." *The same set of values* means simply that mall kids are already preprogrammed to be consumers and that the mall can put the finishing touches to them as hard-core, lifelong shoppers just like everybody else. That, after all, is what the mall is about. So it shouldn't be surprising that in spending a lot of

Disadvantages:
a) Exposure to high-consumption society

time there, adolescents find little that challenges the assumption that the goal of life is to make money and buy products, or that just about everything else in life is to be used to serve those ends.

Growing up in a high-consumption society already adds inestimable pressure to kids' lives. Clothes consciousness has invaded the grade schools, and popularity is linked with having the best, newest clothes in the currently acceptable styles. Even what they read has been affected. "Miss [Nancy] Drew wasn't obsessed with her wardrobe," noted the *Wall Street Journal*. "But today the mystery in teen fiction for girls is what outfit the heroine will wear next." Shopping has become a survival skill and there is certainly no better place to learn it than the mall, where its importance is powerfully reinforced and certainly never questioned.

b) Social pressures to buy

The mall as a university of suburban materialism, where Valley Girls and Boys from coast to coast are educated in consumption, has its other lessons in this era of change in family life and sexual mores and their economic and social ramifications. The plethora of products in the mall, plus the pressure on teens to buy them, may contribute to the phenomenon that psychologist David Elkind calls "the hurried child": kids who are exposed to too much of the adult world too quickly and must respond with a sophistication that belies their still-tender emotional development. Certainly the adult products marketed for children—form-fitting designer jeans, sexy tops for preteen girls—add to the social pressure to look like an adult, along with the home-grown need to understand adult finances (why mothers must work) and adult emotions (when parents divorce).

c) Mall as babysitter

Kids spend so much time at the mall partly because their parents allow it and even encourage it. The mall is safe, doesn't seem to harbor any unsavory activities, and there is adult supervision; it is, after all, a controlled environment. So the temptation, especially for working parents, is to let the mall be their baby-sitter. At least the kids aren't watching TV. But the mall's role as a surrogate mother may be more extensive and more profound.

d) Mall as substitute for home

10 Karen Lansky, a writer living in Los Angeles, has looked into the subject, and she told me some of her conclusions about the effects on its teenaged denizens of the mall's controlled and controlling environment. "Structure is the dominant idea, since true 'mall rats' lack just that in their home lives," she said, "and adolescents about to make the big leap into growing up crave more structure than our modern society cares to acknowledge." Karen pointed out some of the elements malls supply that kids used to get from their families, like warmth (Strawberry Shortcake dolls and similar cute and cuddly merchandise), old-fashioned mothering ("We do it all for you," the fast-food slogan), and even home cooking (the "homemade" treats at the food court).

e) Encouragement of passivity

The problem in all this, as Karen Lansky sees it, is that while families nurture children by encouraging growth through the assumption of responsibility and then by letting them rest in the bosom of the family from the rigors of growing up, the mall as a structural mother encourages passivity and consumption, as long as the kid doesn't make trouble. Therefore all they learn about becoming adults is how to act and how to consume.

f) Undemanding jobs

Example

Kids are in the mall not only in the passive role of shoppers—they also work there, especially as fast-food outlets infiltrate the mall's enclosure. There they learn how to hold a job and take responsibility, but still within the same value context. When *CBS Reports* went to Oak Park Mall in suburban Kansas City, Kansas, to tape part of their hour-long consideration of malls, "After the Dream Comes True," they interviewed a teenaged girl who worked in a fast-food outlet there. In a sequence that didn't make the final program, she described the major goal of her present life, which was to perfect the curl on top of the ice-cream cones that were her store's specialty. If she could do that, she would be moved from the lowly soft-drink dispenser to the more prestigious ice-cream division, the curl on top of the status ladder at her restaurant. These are the achievements that are important at the mall.

Other benefits of such jobs may also be overrated, according to Laurence D. Steinberg of the

Details

University of California at Irvine's social ecology department, who did a study on teenage employment. Their jobs, he found, are generally simple, mindlessly repetitive, and boring. They don't really learn anything, and the jobs don't lead anywhere. Teenagers also work primarily with other teenagers; even their supervisors are often just a little older than they are. "Kids need to spend time with adults," Steinberg told me. "Although they get benefits from peer relationships, without parents and other adults it's one-side socialization. They hang out with each other, have age-segregated jobs, and watch TV."

Advantages: a) Time with other adolescents

Perhaps much of this is not so terrible or even so terribly different. Now that they have so much more to contend with in their lives, adolescents probably need more time to spend with other adolescents without adult impositions, just to sort things out. Though it is more concentrated in the mall (and therefore perhaps a clearer target), the value system there is really the dominant one of the whole society. Attitudes about curiosity, initiative, self-expression, empathy, and disinterested learning aren't necessarily made in the mall; they are mirrored there, perhaps a bit more intensely—as through a glass brightly.

b) Educational opportunities

Besides, the mall is not without its educational 15
opportunities. There are bookstores, where there is at least a short shelf of classics at great prices, and other books from which it is possible to learn more than how to do sit-ups. There are tools, from hammers to VCRs, and products, from clothes to records, that can help the young find and express themselves. There are older people with stories, and places to be alone or to talk one-on-one with a kindred spirit. And there is always the passing show.

Conclusion and claim of value: mall as a controlled environment that teaches a few valuable lessons

The mall itself may very well be an education about the future. I was struck with the realization, as early as my first forays into Greengate, that the mall is only one of a number of enclosed and controlled environments that are part of the lives of today's young. The mall is just an extension, say, of those large suburban schools—only there's Karmelkorn instead of chem lab, the ice rink instead of the gym: It's high school without the impertinence of classes.

Growing up, moving from home to school to the mall—from enclosure to enclosure, transported in cars—is a curiously continuous process, without much in the way of contrast or contact with unenclosed reality. Places must tend to blur into one another. But whatever differences and dangers there are in this, the skills these adolescents are learning may turn out to be useful in their later lives. For we seem to be moving inexorably into an age of preplanned and regulated environments, and this is the world they will inherit.

Still, it might be better if they had more of a choice. One teenaged girl confessed to *CBS Reports* that she sometimes felt she was missing something by hanging out at the mall so much. "But I'm here," she said, "and this is what I have."

Analysis

Kowinski has chosen to evaluate one aspect of an extraordinarily successful economic and cultural phenomenon—the commercial mall. He asks whether the influence of the mall on adolescents is good or bad. The answer seems to be a little of both. The good values may be described as exposure to a variety of experiences, a protective structure for adolescents who often live in unstable environments, and immersion in a world that may well serve as an introduction to adulthood. But the bad values, which Kowinski thinks are more influential (as the title suggests), are those of the shoppers' paradise, a society that believes in acquisition and consumption of goods as ultimate goals, and too much control over the choices available to adolescents. The tone of the judgment, however, is moderate and reflects a balanced, even scholarly, attitude. More than other arguments, the treatment of values requires such a voice, one that respects differences of opinion among readers. But serious doesn't mean heavy. His style is formal but highly readable, brightened by interesting examples and precise details. The opening paragraph is a strikingly effective lead.

Some of his observations are personal, but others are derived from studies by professional researchers, from *CBS Reports* to a well-known writer on childhood. These studies give weight and authority to his conclusions. Here and there we detect an appealing sympathy for adolescents who spend time in their controlled mall environments.

Like any thoughtful social commentator, Kowinski casts a wide net. He sees the mall not only as a hangout for teens but as a good deal more, an institution that offers insights into family life and work, the changing urban culture, the nature of contemporary entertainment, even glimpses of a somewhat forbidding future.

PRACTICE

As you read the following essay, answer these questions:

1. What is Ebert's claim?
2. What criteria does Ebert seem to use in judging the film? What values seem to underlie his review?
3. What type of support does he offer to convince his readers that his value judgment is valid? Is the evidence sufficient?
4. Do you find Ebert's argument convincing? Why or why not?

Crash

ROGER EBERT

"Crash" tells interlocking stories of whites, blacks, Latinos, Koreans, Iranians, cops and criminals, the rich and the poor, the powerful and powerless, all defined in one way or another by racism. All are victims of it, and all are guilty of it. Sometimes, yes, they rise above it, although it is never that simple. Their negative impulses may be instinctive, their positive impulses may be dangerous, and who knows what the other person is thinking?

The result is a movie of intense fascination; we understand quickly enough who the characters are and what their lives are like, but we have no idea how they will behave, because so much depends on accident. Most movies enact rituals; we know the form and watch for variations. "Crash" is a movie with free will, and anything can happen. Because we care about the characters, the movie is uncanny in its ability to rope us in and get us involved.

"Crash" was directed by Paul Haggis, whose screenplay for "Million Dollar Baby" led to Academy Awards. It connects stories based on coincidence, serendipity, and luck, as the lives of the characters crash against one another like pinballs. The movie presumes that most people feel prejudice and resentment against members of other groups, and observes the consequences of those feelings.

Roger Ebert has been the film critic of the *Chicago Sun-Times* since 1967 and is the author of more than fifteen books about film. He appeared for years on a televised show about movies, first with the late Gene Siskel and then with Richard Roeper. He won the Pulitzer Prize for criticism in 1975, and his reviews are now syndicated in more than two hundred newspapers in the United States, Canada, England, Japan, and Greece.

One thing that happens, again and again, is that peoples' assumptions prevent them from seeing the actual person standing before them. An Iranian (Shaun Toub) is thought to be an Arab, although Iranians are Persian. Both the Iranian and the white wife of the district attorney (Sandra Bullock) believe a Mexican-American locksmith (Michael Pena) is a gang member and a crook, but he is a family man.

A black cop (Don Cheadle) is having an affair with his Latina partner 5
(Jennifer Esposito), but never gets it straight which country she's from. A cop (Matt Dillon) thinks a light-skinned black woman (Thandie Newton) is white. When a white producer tells a black TV director (Terrence Dashon Howard) that a black character "doesn't sound black enough," it never occurs to him that the director doesn't "sound black," either. For that matter, neither do two young black men (Larenz Tate and Ludacris), who dress and act like college students, but have a surprise for us.

You see how it goes. Along the way, these people say exactly what they are thinking, without the filters of political correctness. The district attorney's wife is so frightened by a street encounter that she has the locks changed, then assumes the locksmith will be back with his "homies" to attack them. The white cop can't get medical care for his dying father, and accuses a black woman at his HMO with taking advantage of preferential racial treatment. The Iranian can't understand what the locksmith is trying to tell him, freaks out, and buys a gun to protect himself. The gun dealer and the Iranian get into a shouting match.

I make this sound almost like episodic TV, but Haggis writes with such directness and such a good ear for everyday speech that the characters seem real and plausible after only a few words. His cast is uniformly strong; the actors sidestep cliches and make their characters particular.

For me, the strongest performance is by Matt Dillon, as the racist cop in anguish over his father. He makes an unnecessary traffic stop when he thinks he sees the black TV director and his light-skinned wife doing something they really shouldn't be doing at the same time they're driving. True enough, but he wouldn't have stopped a black couple or a white couple. He humiliates the woman with an invasive body search, while her husband is forced to stand by powerless, because the cops have the guns—Dillon, and also an unseasoned rookie (Ryan Phillippe), who hates what he's seeing but has to back up his partner.

That traffic stop shows Dillon's cop as vile and hateful. But later we see him trying to care for his sick father, and we understand why he explodes at the HMO worker (whose race is only an excuse for his anger). He victimizes others by exercising his power, and is impotent when it comes to helping his father. Then the plot turns ironically on itself, and both of the cops find themselves, in very different ways, saving the lives of the very same TV director and his wife. Is this just manipulative storytelling? It didn't feel that way to me, because it serves a deeper purpose than mere irony: Haggis is telling parables, in which the characters learn the lessons they have earned by their behavior.

10 Other cross-cutting Los Angeles stories come to mind, especially Lawrence Kasdan's more optimistic "Grand Canyon" and Robert Altman's more humanistic "Short Cuts." But "Crash" finds a way of its own. It shows the way we all leap to conclusions based on race—yes, all of us, of all races, and however fair-minded we may try to be—and we pay a price for that. If there is hope in the story, it comes because as the characters crash into one another, they learn things, mostly about themselves. Almost all of them are still alive at the end, and are better people because of what has happened to them. Not happier, not calmer, not even wiser, but better. Then there are those few who kill or get killed; racism has tragedy built in.

Not many films have the possibility of making their audiences better people. I don't expect "Crash" to work any miracles, but I believe anyone seeing it is likely to be moved to have a little more sympathy for people not like themselves. The movie contains hurt, coldness, and cruelty, but is it without hope? Not at all. Stand back and consider. All of these people, superficially so different, share the city and learn that they share similar fears and hopes. Until several hundred years ago, most people everywhere on earth never saw anybody who didn't look like them. They were not racist because, as far as they knew, there was only one race. You may have to look hard to see it, but "Crash" is a film about progress.

CLAIMS OF POLICY

Claims of policy argue that certain conditions should exist. As the name suggests, they advocate adoption of policies or courses of action because problems have arisen that call for solution. Almost always *should* or *ought to* or *must* is expressed or implied in the claim.

CLAIM: Voluntary prayer should be permitted in public schools.

CLAIM: A dress code should be introduced for all public high schools.

CLAIM: A law should permit sixteen-year-olds and parents to "divorce" each other in cases of extreme incompatibility.

CLAIM: Mandatory jail terms should be imposed for drunk driving violations.

In defending such claims of policy you may find that you must first convince your audience that a problem exists. This will require that, as part of your longer argument, you make a factual claim, offering data to prove that present conditions are unsatisfactory. You may also find it necessary to refer to the values that support your claim. Then you will be ready to introduce your policy, to persuade your audience that the solution you propose will solve the problem.

Writer's Guide: Defending a Claim of Policy

The following steps will help you organize arguments for a claim of policy.

1. Make your proposal clear. The terms in the proposal should be precisely defined.
2. If necessary, establish that there is a need for a change. When changes have been resisted, present reasons that explain this resistance. (It is often wrongly assumed that people cling to cultural practices long after their significance and necessity have eroded. But rational human beings observe practices that serve a purpose. The fact that you and I may see no value or purpose in the activities of another is irrelevant.)
3. Consider the opposing arguments. You may want to state the opposing arguments in a brief paragraph before answering them in the body of your argument.
4. Devote the major part of your essay to proving that your proposal is an answer to the opposing arguments and enumerating its distinct benefits for your readers.
5. Support your proposal with solid data, but don't neglect the moral considerations and the commonsense reasons, which may be even more persuasive.

We will examine a policy claim in which all these parts are at work. The claim can be stated as follows: "The time required for an undergraduate degree should be extended to five years." Immediate agreement with this policy among student readers would certainly not be universal. Some students would not recognize a problem. They would say, "The college curriculum we have now is fine. There's no need for a change. Besides, we don't want to spend more time in school." First, then, the arguer would have to persuade a skeptical audience that there is a problem—that four years of college are no longer enough because the stock of knowledge in almost all fields of study continues to increase. The arguer would provide data to show that students today have many more choices in history, literature, and science than students had in those fields a generation ago. She would also emphasize the value of greater knowledge and more schooling compared to the value of other goods the audience cherishes, such as earlier independence. Finally, the arguer would offer a plan for implementing her policy. Her plan would have to consider initial psychological resistance, revision of the curriculum, costs of more instruction, and costs of lost production in the workforce. Most important, she would point out the benefits for both individuals and society if this policy were adopted.

In this example, we assumed that the reader would disagree that a problem existed. In many cases, however, the reader may agree that there is a problem but disagree with the arguer about the way to solve it. Most of us, no doubt, agree that we want to reduce or eliminate the following problems: misbehavior and vandalism in schools, drunk driving, crime on the streets, child abuse, pornography, pollution. But how should we go about solving those problems? What public policy will give us well-behaved, diligent students who never destroy school property? Safe streets where no one is ever robbed or assaulted? Loving homes where no child is ever mistreated? Some members of society would choose to introduce rules or laws that punish infractions so severely that wrongdoers would be unwilling or unable to repeat their offenses. Other members of society would prefer policies that attempt to rehabilitate or reeducate offenders through training, therapy, counseling, and new opportunities.

SAMPLE ANNOTATED ESSAY: CLAIM OF POLICY

College Life versus My Moral Code

ELISHA DOV HACK

Many people envy my status as a freshman at Yale College. My classmates and I made it through some fierce competition, and we are excited to have been accepted to one of the best academic and extracurricular programs in American higher education. I have an older brother who attended Yale, and I've heard from him what life at Yale is like.

Background that reveals his respect for Yale and his connection to it through his brother

He spent all his college years living at home because our parents are New Haven residents, and Yale's rules then did not require him to live in the dorms. But Yale's new regulations demand that I spend my freshman and sophomore years living in the college dormitories.

How residency rules have changed

I, two other freshmen, and two sophomores have refused to do this because life in the dorms, even on the floors Yale calls "single sex," is contrary

Establishes the problem

Elisha Dov Hack was a member of the Yale College freshman class of 1997. This article appeared on September 9, 1997, in the *New York Times*. The case brought by Hack and four other Jewish students remained in court until all but Hack had graduated. Hack went on to marry before his 2003 graduation in engineering sciences.

to the fundamental principles we have been taught as long as we can remember—the principles of Judaism lived according to the Torah and 3,000-year-old rabbinic teachings. Unless Yale waives its residence requirement, we may have no choice but to sue the university to protect our religious way of life.

Examples of affronts to his religious beliefs

Bingham Hall, on the Yale quadrangle known as the Old Campus, is one of the dorms for incoming students. When I entered it two weeks ago during an orientation tour, I literally saw the handwriting on the wall. A sign titled "Safe Sex" told me where to pick up condoms on campus. Another sign touted 100 ways to make love without having sex, like "take a nap together" and "take a steamy shower together."

Another example of accepted dorm standards

5 That, I am told, is real life in the dorms. The "freshperson" issue of the *Yale Daily News* sent to entering students contained a "Yale lexicon" defining *sexile* as "banishment from your dorm room because your roommate is having more fun than you." If you live in the dorms, you're expected to be part of the crowd, to accept these standards as the framework for your life.

Challenges whether Yale should make it difficult for students to maintain their morals outside of class

Can we stand up to classmates whose sexual morality differs from ours? We've had years of rigorous religious teaching, and we've watched and learned from our parents. We can hold our own in the intellectual debate that flows naturally from exchanges during and after class. But I'm upset and hurt by this requirement that I live in the dorms. Why is Yale—an institution that professes to be so tolerant and open-minded—making it particularly hard for students like us to maintain our moral standards through difficult college years?

Tries to achieve middle ground by acknowledging that morality has changed but argues that exceptions to the policy are already made

We are not trying to impose our moral standards on our classmates or on Yale. Our parents tell us that things were very different in college dormitories in their day and that in most colleges in the 1950s students who allowed guests of the opposite sex into their dorm rooms were subject to expulsion. We acknowledge that today's morality is not that of the 50s. We are asking only that Yale give us the same permission to live off campus that it gives any lower classman who is married or at least twenty-one years old.

Yale is proud of the fact that it has no "parietal rules" and that sexual morality is a student's own business. Maybe this is what Dean Richard H. Brodhead meant when he said that "Yale's residential colleges carry . . . a moral meaning." That moral meaning is, basically, "Anything goes." This morality is Yale's own residential religion, which it is proselytizing by force of its regulations.

Attacks the opposition by defining immorality as Yale's religion

We cannot, in good conscience, live in a place where women are permitted to stay overnight in men's rooms, and where visiting men can traipse through the common halls on the women's floors—in various stages of undress—in the middle of the night. The dormitories on Yale's Old Campus have floors designated by gender, but there is easy access through open stairwells from one floor to the next.

Floors designated by gender are not the solution

The source of conflict

The moral message Yale's residences convey today 10
is not one that our religion accepts. Nor is it a moral environment in which the five of us can spend our nights, or a moral surrounding that we can call home.

Yale sent me a glossy brochure when it welcomed me as an entering student. It said, "Yale retains a deep respect for its early history and for the continuity that its history provides—a continuity based on constant reflection and reappraisal." Yale ought to reflect on and reappraise a policy that compels us to compromise our religious principles.

Uses Yale's own advertising against it

CLAIM OF POLICY: A university that espouses a willingness to reflect and reappraise should not compel Hack and the other Jewish students to compromise their principles.

Analysis

Notice that Hack's article originally appeared in the *New York Times*. Most would agree that it is unusual to see a piece written by a college freshman in such a prestigious publication, but the fact that he was accepted at Yale immediately establishes him as a member of an academically elite group, as Hack points out in his second sentence. He meets the possible objection that he does not yet know enough about what life at Yale is like by pointing out that his older brother went there. The crucial difference is that the university's rules have been changed in the interim. Where his older brother lived at home, Hack is required by university policy to live on campus his first two years. Therein lies the problem.

Hack most directly states his objection to Yale's residency requirement in his third paragraph—that life in the dorms "is contrary to the fundamental principles [he and four other Jewish students] have been taught as long as [they] can remember—"the principles of Judaism lived according to the Torah and 3,000-year-old rabbinic teachings." He also captures the intensity of his feelings on the subject by stating that he and the four other students who are in the same position "may have no choice but to sue the university to protect [their] religious way of life."

Hack supports his assertion that life in a Yale dormitory would pose a threat to his moral standards by citing examples of posters on dorm walls that advise safe sex and newspaper articles that joke about premarital sex. Hack feels that his religious training has prepared him to defend his moral principles, but he asks why an institution considered so tolerant cannot also be tolerant of those who want to maintain their conservative practices and beliefs: "Why is Yale—an institution that professes to be so tolerant and open-minded—making it particularly hard for students like us to maintain our moral standards through difficult college years?"

Hack heads off a possible objection to his argument by explaining that he and the other Jewish students are not trying to impose their moral standards on others. They simply don't want to have others' standards imposed on them. Some would argue that an assignment to a dorm that has floors designated by gender should be accommodation enough, but even those have open stairwells between floors. If exceptions are made for students who are married or who are twenty-one, why can an exception not be made for those who object to dorm life for religious reasons?

A characteristic of good arguers is that they know well their opponents' position. Hack acknowledges that he even knows well the language Yale uses in "selling" itself to new students. He quotes the brochure that Yale sent him: "Yale retains a deep respect for its early history and for the continuity that its history provides—a continuity based on constant reflection and reappraisal." His request and claim is that Yale should reappraise a position that compels him to compromise his religious principles.

What happened to the lawsuit to which Hack refers? It was tied up in court until 2001, when all of the students involved except Hack had graduated. The students lost the legal battle at all levels, primarily because their case depended on their proving that having to live in a residence hall constituted discrimination based on religion. The university successfully argued that the residence requirement was not discriminatory. Hack graduated from Yale in 2003. All five students chose to live in apartments during their first two years while paying full housing fees for dorm rooms they never occupied.

READINGS FOR ANALYSIS

Supersize Your Child?

RICHARD HAYES

In the late 1950s, soon after Watson and Crick had discovered DNA's structure, scientists began predicting that someday we'd be able to genetically engineer our children. We'd design them to be healthy, smart, and attractive, with life spans of 200 years, photographic memories, enhanced lung capacity for athletic endurance, and more. Our children would pass these modifications to their own children and add new ones as well. Humanity would take control of its own evolution and kick it into overdrive.

Few people took these speculations very seriously. Could this sort of genetic engineering really be done? Even if it could, would anyone really want to do it? If they did, wouldn't society step in and set limits? In any event, wouldn't it be decades before we'd have to worry about this?

Now it's 2004, and those decades have passed. The era of genetically modified humans is close upon us. Almost every day we read of new breakthroughs: cloning, artificial chromosomes and now high-tech sex selection. Scientists create genetically modified animals on an assembly-line basis. Biotech entrepreneurs discuss the potential market for genetically modified children at investors' conferences. For the most part, society has not stepped in and set limits.

Last year *Science* magazine reported that a variant of the human 5-HTT gene reduces the risk of depression following stressful experiences. Depression can be a devastating condition. Would it be wrong if a couple planning to start a family used in vitro fertilization procedures to have the 5-HTT gene variant inserted into the embryos of their prospective children? Taken as an isolated instance, many people would be hard-pressed to say that it was.

In 1993, University of California at San Francisco biochemist Dr. 5
Cynthia Kenyon discovered a variant of the DAF-2 gene that doubles the two-week life span of nematode worms. The university filed for patents based on knowledge of the metabolic pathway regulated by the human version of the DAF-2 gene. In 1999, Kenyon and others founded Elixir Pharmaceuticals, a biotech firm. In early 2003, Elixir licensed the university's patent rights to Kenyon's discoveries and secured $17 million in private financing. In an earlier interview with *ABC News*, Kenyon said she saw no reason humans might not be able to achieve 200-year life spans.

Richard Hayes is the executive director of the Center for Genetics and Society, a California-based nonprofit organization working for the responsible governance of genetic technologies. This piece was published on the TomPaine.com Web site in February 2004.

"Post-human" Nature

Last June at Yale University, the World Transhumanist Association held its first national conference. The Transhumanists have chapters in more than 20 countries and advocate the breeding of "genetically enriched" forms of "post-human" beings. Other advocates of the new techno-eugenics, such as Princeton University professor Lee Silver, predict that by the end of this century, "All aspects of the economy, the media, the entertainment industry, and the knowledge industry [will be] controlled by members of the GenRich class . . . Naturals [will] work as low-paid service providers or as laborers . . .".

What happens then? Here's Dr. Richard Lynn, emeritus professor at the University of Ulster, who, like Silver, supports human genetic modification: "What is called for here is not genocide, the killing off of the population of incompetent cultures. But we do need to think realistically in terms of the 'phasing out' of such peoples. . . . Evolutionary progress means the extinction of the less competent."

Notice that I've gone, in just four steps, from reducing susceptibility to depression, to extending the human life span, to the creation of a genetic elite, to proposals that genetically inferior people be "phased out."

When first presented with this scenario, people typically respond in one of two ways. Some say, "It's impossible." Others say, "It's inevitable." Notice what these otherwise diametrically different responses have in common: both counsel passivity. If the "post-human future" is impossible, there's no need to try to prevent it. If it's inevitable, such efforts would be in vain.

10 Will it actually be possible to genetically engineer our children? Most scientists who have studied this question conclude that although the techniques need to be refined, there's no reason to believe it can't be done. Meanwhile, research on stem cells, cloning, artificial chromosomes and more continues to refine those techniques.

Many people believe that to suggest that manipulating genes can affect behavioral and cognitive traits in humans is to indulge discredited ideologies of "genetic determinism." It's true that the crude sociobiology of the 1970s has been discredited, as have simplistic notions that there exist "I.Q. genes" or "gay genes" that determine one's intelligence or sexual orientation. But to say that genes have no influence over traits is equally simplistic. Some genes have minimal influence, others have greater influence. Some have influence in the presence of certain environmental factors but no influence otherwise. Few genes determine anything; most confer propensities.

Deepening Inequality

Suppose scientists found a gene giving male children a 15 percent greater chance of growing one inch taller than they would have grown without that gene, all else equal. If fertility clinics offered to engineer embryos to include this gene, would there be customers? Yes. Couples would say, "In this competitive world, I want to do anything I can that might give my child an edge."

Once we allow children to be designed through embryo modification, where would we stop? If it's acceptable to modify one gene, why not two? If two, why not 20? Or 200? There are some 30,000 genes in the human genome. Each contributes, in smaller or larger proportions, to some propensity. Where would we stop? On what grounds?

Some suggest we allow embryo modification for certified medical conditions and prohibit it for cosmetic or enhancement purposes. It's unlikely that this would succeed. Prozac, Viagra, and Botox were all developed for medical purposes but in the blink of an eye became hugely profitable cosmetic and enhancement consumer products.

Will the use of genetic engineering to redesign our children exacer- 15
bate inequality? Amazingly, the neo-eugenic advocates don't deny that it will. As good libertarians, they celebrate free markets and social Darwinism, and counsel us to accept a rising tide of genetically enhanced inequality as the inevitable result of human ingenuity and desire.

But couldn't this be prevented? Wouldn't society step in? Several years ago, a team of health policy academics examined a range of proposals, including systems of national health insurance making eugenic engineering available to all, or preferentially to the poor, or by lottery. Despite their best efforts, they couldn't identify any realistic set of policies that would prevent the new eugenic technologies, once allowed at all, from generating unprecedented inequality.

And consider the international implications. What happens when some country announces an aggressive program of eugenic engineering explicitly intended to create a new, superior, omni-competent breed of human? What does the rest of the world do then?

We need to take a deep breath and realize what is going on here. The birth of the first genetically modified child would be a watershed moment in human history. It would set off a chain of events that would feed back upon themselves in ways impossible to control.

Unnatural Selection

Everything we experience, everything we know, everything we do is experienced, known and done by a species—homo sapiens—which evolved through natural selection over hundreds of thousands of years. We differ as individuals, but we are a single human species with a shared biology so fundamental to what we are that we are not even conscious of it, or of the manifold ways it unites us. What happens if we begin changing that fundamental shared biology?

Three hundred years ago the scientific and political leaders of that era 20
took as a self-evident fact the division of humanity into "superior" and "inferior" types, designed by Providence respectively as masters and slaves.

Human beings were bred, bought and sold, like cattle or dogs. After three hundred years of struggle and bloodshed we are on the verge—barely—of putting this awful legacy behind us.

Or maybe not. If left uncontrolled, the new human genetic technologies could set us on a trajectory leading to a new Dark Age in which people are once again regarded as little better than cattle or dogs. Here is "bioethicist" Gregory Pence, who has testified in support of human cloning before the U.S. Congress and elsewhere:

> [M]any people love their retrievers and their sunny dispositions around children and adults. Could people be chosen in the same way? Would it be so terrible to allow parents to at least aim for a certain type, in the same way that great breeders . . . try to match a breed of dog to the needs of a family?

The common initial responses to the prospect of the new techno-eugenics—"It's impossible," and "It's inevitable"—are incorrect and unhelpful. The response we need to affirm is at once more realistic and more challenging: The techno-eugenic future certainly is possible, and is certainly not inevitable.

Road to Regulation

In 1997, the Council of Europe negotiated an important international agreement, the Convention on Biomedicine and Human Rights. Thus far, it has been signed by more than two-thirds of the council's 45 member countries. The convention draws the lines on human genetic modification in just the right ways. It allows medical research, including stem cell research, to continue, and does not restrict abortion rights, but it bans genetic modifications that would open the door to high-tech eugenic engineering. Many countries in Asia, Africa, and Latin America have likewise begun to address these issues through legislation.

These efforts are encouraging, but we have a long way to go before such policies are implemented, as they must be, worldwide. In some countries, notably the United States, the politics of the new genetic technologies have become polarized to the point of gridlock. The religious right insists on total bans on nearly all human embryo research, while bio-research interests and the biotech industry insist on nearly total freedom from any meaningful social oversight and accountability.

In other countries, and at the international level, the challenge of a new 25
high-tech, free market eugenics, while worrisome, can seem remote in comparison with the real existing challenges of warfare, hunger, and disease.

What is to be done? More than anything, we need to realize the unprecedented nature of the challenges that the new human genetic technologies present. We need to distinguish benign applications of these technologies from pernicious ones, and support the former while opposing the latter. Concerned organizations and individuals need to engage these challenges and make their voices heard worldwide. National and international leaders in politics, the sciences and the arts need to declare that humanity is not going to let itself be split asunder by human genetic technology. The United Nations and other international bodies need to give these issues the highest attention. The hour is late. There is no greater challenge before us.

READING AND DISCUSSION QUESTIONS

1. Hayes alerts us that he is using the organization of his essay to help make his point. Explain where and how he does that. How does he appeal to his readers' need to feel secure? Why might his readers feel their sense of security being threatened?
2. Is Hayes supporting a claim of fact, value, or policy? Where does he state that claim most directly?
3. What types of support does Hayes offer to back up his opinion? How convincing do you find his support to be?
4. Can you identify the warrant underlying Hayes's argument? In order to accept his claim, what assumption of his must you agree with? Does he state his warrant explicitly anywhere in the essay?

WRITING SUGGESTIONS

5. Write an essay in which you either support or argue against Hayes's claim.
6. Write an essay in which you explain your own position on who should set limits on genetic engineering.
7. Choose an invention or scientific development that people once said was impossible and explain how those skeptics were proved wrong.
8. Choose an invention or scientific development and explain how it is now used, for good or ill, for purposes it was never intended to serve.

"Saw" Good at Tying Things in Knots

WESLEY MORRIS

All anybody should want from a horror movie is the steady tightening in the pit of your stomach. While the new sado-masochistic gross-out flick "Saw" often resembles the ghastliest editions yet of "Fear Factor" and "Survivor" and features some of the grodiest direction this side of "Project Greenlight," it does manage at times to knead your tummy like dough, using real suspense for a rolling pin.

Wesley Morris is currently a film critic at the *Boston Globe* and formerly wrote film reviews and essays for the *San Francisco Examiner* and the *San Francisco Sun-Chronicle*. This review appeared on October 24, 2004, in the *Boston Globe*.

Most of it is generated from wondering whether the movie will deliver on the promise of one of its posters, which shows a foot severed from its leg. It's the kind of terror that really has nothing to do with the plot, which, by the time it's been fully carried out, is as twisted as your stomach.

A doctor (Cary Elwes) and a bratty young photographer (Leigh Whannell, the movie's writer) wake up on either side of the sort of big, grimy bathroom you see only in bad horror movies and good music videos. Each man's leg is chained to a pipe, and neither has any idea how he got there or what that male body is doing lying dead between them in its undies. There's a gun in one hand, a tape recorder in the other, and a pool of blood around the head.

After beginning the dopey dialogue (mostly from Elwes, who brings a dinner-theater zest to his predicament), both men discover personal notes that indicate what they have to do: One has to kill the other to survive. And while you wait for Joe Rogan or Jeff Probst to supervise the mayhem, the two men start following the series of clues, which have been left on cassette tapes and elsewhere by a sicko watching on a surveillance camera. The contestants (what else are they?) turn up a pair of hacksaws and immediately start using them in vain on their chains. Silly rabbits, hacksaws are for ankles.

5 By this point, the movie has likely won your dread. So rather than commence with the cutting, "Saw" takes a break, in order for the doctor to treat the photographer to the hunch he has about who might be behind this stunt. It's in these flashbacks that screenwriter Whannell and director James Wan are exposed as being under the dubious influence of every movie in the modern psychopath-movie liquor cabinet—and "The Usual Suspects," too.

Someone has been rounding up people who've been "wasting their lives" and subjecting them to horrific tortures to prove how much they want to live. While the victims demonstrate this, the editing and photography go predictably nuts, running around them and deliriously speeding up their futile escapes. One man tried to crawl through a nest of barbed wire to freedom. Another was slathered in a flammable jelly and asked to crawl across a floor strewn with glass to decipher a code that would free him. He had to do this holding a candle. (He failed.) The sole "winner" was a woman who had to fish a key from a living man's stomach or her head would explode. Frankly, that looks comparatively easy.

Two detectives on the case—Ken Leung and a never nuttier Danny Glover—fingered the good doctor as the culprit. He was innocent of those crimes but guilty of a lesser one that makes a decent alibi. But the movie persists in dredging up more implausible mysteries and domestic drama, namely through some terribly handled scenes between the doctor and his soon-to-be-jeopardized family.

Eventually, it grows frustrating to watch the movie's puzzle assemble itself—even once it does, there are pieces still missing. Why, for instance, does Glover's freaky character love news clippings as much as the average serial killer? And are we really to believe the major curveball in the final scene?

Not really. But as long as "Saw" stays in that big, nasty bathroom, all we need to believe is the knot in our stomachs.

READING AND DISCUSSION QUESTIONS

1. Morris establishes immediately "[a]ll anybody should want from a horror movie." What is it that all viewers should want?
2. The reference in the first paragraph to the way the movie makes a viewer's stomach feel may not seem significant at first glance, but how does Morris follow through on this idea of a "gut-level" response to horror?
3. How does Morris manage to praise the movie in the first paragraph in spite of referring to it as a "sado-masochistics gross-out flick" with "grody" direction?
4. What other weakness does Morris see in the film?
5. What is Morris's ultimate judgment regarding the film? On what criteria does he base that judgment?
6. How effective is the support that Morris offers for his assessment?

WRITING SUGGESTIONS

7. Write an essay in which you explain your own criteria for evaluating horror films. Or choose another genre (romantic comedy, drama, or mockumentry, for example) and write evaluating criteria for it.
8. If you have seen *Saw*, write an essay explaining whether or not you agree with Morris's assessment of the film.
9. Write your own review of a recent movie, being sure to establish the criteria for evaluation on which you base your review. See Ebert's review of *Crash* earlier in this chapter for another example of a movie review.

Letter from Birmingham Jail

MARTIN LUTHER KING JR.

A Call for Unity: A Letter from Eight White Clergymen

April 12, 1963

We the undersigned clergymen are among those who, in January, issued “An Appeal for Law and Order and Common Sense,” in dealing with racial problems in Alabama. We expressed understanding that honest convictions in racial matters could properly be pursued in the courts, but urged that decisions of those courts should in the meantime be peacefully obeyed.

Since that time there had been some evidence of increased forebearance and a willingness to face facts. Responsible citizens have undertaken to work on various problems which cause racial friction and unrest. In Birmingham, recent public events have given indication that we all have opportunity for a new constructive and realistic approach to racial problems.

However, we are now confronted by a series of demonstrations by some of our Negro citizens, directed and led in part by outsiders. We recognize the natural impatience of people who feel that their hopes are slow in being realized. But we are convinced that these demonstrations are unwise and untimely.

We agree rather with certain local Negro leadership which has called for honest and open negotiation of racial issues in our area. And we believe this kind of facing of issues can best be accomplished by citizens of our own metropolitan area, white and Negro, meeting with their knowledge and experience of the local situation. All of us need to face that responsibility and find proper channels for its accomplishment.

Just as we formerly pointed out that “hatred and violence have no 5
sanction in our religious and political traditions,” we also point out that such actions as incite to hatred and violence, however technically peaceful those actions may be, have not contributed to the resolution of our local problems. We do not believe that these days of new hope are days when extreme measures are justified in Birmingham.

Martin Luther King Jr. (1929–1968) was a clergyman, author, distinguished civil rights leader, and winner of the Nobel Prize for peace in 1964 for his contributions to racial harmony and his advocacy of nonviolent response to aggression. He was assassinated in 1968. In “Letter from Birmingham Jail,” he appears as a historian and philosopher. He wrote the letter from a jail cell on April 16, 1963, after his arrest for participation in a demonstration for civil rights for African Americans. The letter was a reply to eight Alabama clergymen who, in the first letter reprinted here, had condemned demonstrations in the streets. King's essay is from *A Testament of Hope* (1986).

We commend the community as a whole, and the local news media and law enforcement officials in particular, on the calm manner in which these demonstrations have been handled. We urge the public to continue to show restraint should the demonstrations continue, and the law enforcement officials to remain calm and continue to protect our city from violence.

We further strongly urge our own Negro community to withdraw support from these demonstrations, and to unite locally in working peacefully for a better Birmingham. When rights are consistently denied, a cause should be pressed in the courts and in negotiations among local leaders, and not in the streets. We appeal to both our white and Negro citizenry to observe the principles of law and order and common sense.

(Signed)
C.C.J. Carpenter, D.D., L.L.D., Bishop of Alabama; Joseph A. Durick, D.D., Auxiliary Bishop, Diocese of Mobile-Birmingham; Rabbi Milton L. Grafman, Temple Emanu-El, Birmingham, Alabama; Bishop Paul Hardin, Bishop of the Alabama–West Florida Conference of the Methodist Church; Bishop Nolan B. Harmon, Bishop of the North Alabama Conference of the Methodist Church; George M. Murray, D.D., L.L.D., Bishop Coadjutor, Episcopal Diocese of Alabama; Edward V. Ramage, Moderator, Synod of the Alabama Presbyterian Church in the United States; Earl Stallings, Pastor, First Baptist Church, Birmingham.

King's Reply from Birmingham Jail

My dear Fellow Clergymen,

While confined here in the Birmingham city jail, I came across your recent statement calling our present activities "unwise and untimely." Seldom, if ever, do I pause to answer criticism of my work and ideas. If I sought to answer all of the criticisms that cross my desk, my secretaries would be engaged in little else in the course of the day, and I would have no time for constructive work. But since I feel that you are men of genuine good will and your criticisms are sincerely set forth, I would like to answer your statement in what I hope will be patient and reasonable terms.

I think I should give the reason for my being in Birmingham, since you have been influenced by the argument of "outsiders coming in." I have the honor of serving as president of the Southern Christian Leadership Conference, an organization operating in every southern state, with headquarters in Atlanta, Georgia. We have some eighty-five affiliate organizations all across the South—one being the Alabama Christian Movement for Human Rights. Whenever necessary and possible we share staff, educational, and financial resources with our affiliates. Several months ago our local affiliate here in Birmingham invited us to be on call to engage in a nonviolent direct-action program if such were deemed necessary. We readily consented and when the hour came we lived up to our promises. So I am here, along with several members of my staff, because we were invited here. I am here because I have basic organizational ties here.

Beyond this, I am in Birmingham because injustice is here. Just as the eighth-century prophets left their little villages and carried their "thus saith the Lord" far beyond the boundaries of their hometowns; and just as the Apostle Paul left his little village of Tarsus and carried the gospel of Jesus Christ to practically every hamlet and city of the Graeco-Roman world, I too am compelled to carry the gospel of freedom beyond my particular hometown. Like Paul, I must constantly respond to the Macedonian call for aid.

Moreover, I am cognizant of the interrelatedness of all communities and states. I cannot sit idly by in Atlanta and not be concerned about what happens in Birmingham. Injustice anywhere is a threat to justice everywhere. We are caught in an inescapable network of mutuality, tied in a single garment of destiny. Whatever affects one directly affects all indirectly. Never again can we afford to live with the narrow, provincial "outside agitator" idea. Anyone who lives in the United States can never be considered an outsider anywhere in this country.

You deplore the demonstrations that are presently taking place in 5
Birmingham. But I am sorry that your statement did not express a similar concern for the conditions that brought the demonstrations into being. I am sure that each of you would want to go beyond the superficial social analyst who looks merely at effects, and does not grapple with underlying causes. I would not hesitate to say that it is unfortunate that so-called demonstrations are taking place in Birmingham at this time, but I would say in more emphatic terms that it is even more unfortunate that the white power structure of this city left the Negro community with no other alternative.

In any nonviolent campaign there are four basic steps: (1) collection of the facts to determine whether injustices are alive, (2) negotiation, (3) self-purification, and (4) direct action. We have gone through all of these steps in Birmingham. There can be no gainsaying of the fact that racial injustice engulfs this community.

Birmingham is probably the most thoroughly segregated city in the United States. Its ugly record of police brutality is known in every section of this country. Its unjust treatment of Negroes in the courts is a notorious reality. There have been more unsolved bombings of Negro homes and churches in Birmingham than any city in this nation. These are the hard, brutal, and unbelievable facts. On the basis of these conditions Negro leaders sought to negotiate with the city fathers. But the political leaders consistently refused to engage in good faith negotiation.

Then came the opportunity last September to talk with some of the leaders of the economic community. In these negotiating sessions certain promises were made by the merchants—such as the promise to remove the humiliating racial signs from the stores. On the basis of these promises Reverend Shuttlesworth and the leaders of the Alabama Christian Movement for Human Rights agreed to call a moratorium on any type of demonstrations. As the weeks and months unfolded we realized that we were the victims of a broken promise. The signs remained. Like so many experiences of the past we were confronted with blasted hopes, and the dark shadow of a deep disappointment settled upon us. So we had no alternative except that of preparing for direct action, whereby we would present our very bodies as a means of laying our case before the conscience of the local and national community. We were not unmindful of the difficulties involved. So we decided to go through a process of self-purification. We started having workshops on nonviolence and repeatedly asking ourselves the questions, "Are you able to accept blows without retaliating?" "Are you able to endure the ordeals of jail?" We decided to set our direct-action program around the Easter season, realizing that with the exception of Christmas, this was the largest shopping period of the year. Knowing that a strong economic withdrawal program would be the by-product of direct action, we felt that this was the best time to bring pressure on the merchants for the needed changes. Then it occurred to us that the March election was ahead and so we speedily decided to postpone action until after election day. When we discovered that Mr. Connor was in the run-off, we decided again to postpone action so that the demonstrations could not be used to cloud the issues. At this time we agreed to begin our nonviolent witness the day after the run-off.

This reveals that we did not move irresponsibly into direct actions. We too wanted to see Mr. Connor defeated; so we went through postponement after postponement to aid in this community need. After this we felt that direct action could be delayed no longer.

You may well ask, "Why direct action? Why sit-ins, marches, etc.? 10
Isn't negotiation a better path?" You are exactly right in your call for negotiation. Indeed, this is the purpose of direct action. Nonviolent direct action seeks to create such a crisis and establish such creative tension that a community that has constantly refused to negotiate is forced to confront the issue. It seeks so to dramatize the issue that it can no longer be ignored. I just referred to the creation of tension as a part of the work of the nonviolent resister. This may sound rather shocking. But I must confess that I am not afraid of the word tension. I have earnestly worked and preached against violent tension, but there is a type of constructive nonviolent tension that is necessary for growth. Just as Socrates felt that it was necessary to create a tension in the mind so that individuals could rise from the bondage of myths and half-truths to the unfettered realm of creative analysis and objective appraisal, we must see the need of having nonviolent gadflies to create the kind of tension in society that will help men to rise from the dark depths of prejudice and racism to the majestic heights of understanding and brotherhood. So the purpose of the direct

action is to create a situation so crisis-packed that it will inevitably open the door to negotiation. We, therefore, concur with you in your call for negotiation. Too long has our beloved Southland been bogged down in the tragic attempt to live in monologue rather than dialogue.

One of the basic points in your statement is that our acts are untimely. Some have asked, "Why didn't you give the new administration time to act?" The only answer that I can give to this inquiry is that the new administration must be prodded about as much as the outgoing one before it acts. We will be sadly mistaken if we feel that the election of Mr. Boutwell will bring the millennium to Birmingham. While Mr. Boutwell is much more articulate and gentle than Mr. Connor, they are both segregationists, dedicated to the task of maintaining the status quo. The hope I see in Mr. Boutwell is that he will be reasonable enough to see the futility of massive resistance to desegregation. But he will not see this without pressure from the devotees of civil rights. My friends, I must say to you that we have not made a single gain in civil rights without determined legal and nonviolent pressure. History is the long and tragic story of the fact that privileged groups seldom give up their privileges voluntarily. Individuals may see the moral light and voluntarily give up their unjust posture; but as Reinhold Niebuhr has reminded us, groups are more immoral than individuals.

We know through painful experience that freedom is never voluntarily given by the oppressor; it must be demanded by the oppressed. Frankly, I have never yet engaged in a direct-action movement that was "well-timed," according to the timetable of those who have not suffered unduly from the disease of segregation. For years now I have heard the words "Wait!" It rings in the ear of every Negro with a piercing familiarity. This "Wait" has almost always meant "Never." It has been a tranquilizing thalidomide, relieving the emotional stress for a moment, only to give birth to an ill-formed infant of frustration. We must come to see with the distinguished jurist of yesterday that "justice too long delayed is justice denied." We have waited for more than 340 years for our constitutional and God-given rights. The nations of Asia and Africa are moving with jetlike speed toward the goal of political independence, and we still creep at horse and buggy pace toward the gaining of a cup of coffee at a lunch counter. I guess it is easy for those who have never felt the stinging darts of segregation to say, "Wait." But when you have seen vicious mobs lynch your mothers and fathers at will and drown your sisters and brothers at whim; when you see hate-filled policemen curse, kick, brutalize, and even kill your black brothers and sisters with impunity; when you see the vast majority of your 20 million Negro brothers smothering in an airtight cage of poverty in the midst of an affluent society; when you suddenly find your tongue twisted and your speech stammering as you seek to explain to your six-year-old daughter why she can't go to the public amusement park that has just been advertised on television, and see tears welling up in her little eyes when she is told that Funtown is closed to colored children, and see the depressing clouds of inferiority begin to form in her little mental sky, and see her begin to distort her little personality by unconsciously developing a bitterness toward white people; when you have to concoct an answer for a five-year-old son asking in agonizing pathos: "Daddy, why do white people treat colored people so mean?"; when you take a cross-country drive and find it necessary to sleep night after night in the uncomfortable corners of your automobile because no motel will accept you; when you are humiliated day in and day out by nagging signs reading "white" and "colored"; when your first name becomes "nigger" and your middle name becomes "boy" (however old you are) and your last name becomes "John," and when your wife and mother are never given the respected title "Mrs."; when you are harried by day and haunted by night by the fact that you are a Negro, living constantly at tiptoe stance never quite knowing what to expect next, and plagued with inner fears and outer resentments; when you are forever fighting a degenerating sense of "nobodiness"; then you will understand why we find it difficult to wait. There comes a time when the cup of endurance runs over, and men are no longer willing to be plunged into an abyss of injustice where they experience the blackness of corroding despair. I hope, sirs, you can understand our legitimate and unavoidable impatience.

You express a great deal of anxiety over our willingness to break laws. This is certainly a legitimate concern. Since we so diligently urge people to obey the Supreme Court's decision of 1954 outlawing segregation in the public schools, it is rather strange and paradoxical to find us consciously breaking laws. One may well ask, "How can you advocate breaking some laws and obeying others?" The answer is found in the fact that there are two types of laws: There are *just* and there are *unjust* laws. I would agree with Saint Augustine that "An unjust law is no law at all."

Now what is the difference between the two? How does one determine when a law is just or unjust? A just law is a man-made code that squares with the moral law or the law of God. An unjust law is a code that is out of harmony with the moral law. To put it in the terms of Saint Thomas Aquinas, an unjust law is a human law that is not rooted in eternal and natural law. Any law that uplifts human personality is just. Any law that degrades human personality is unjust. All segregation statutes are unjust because segregation distorts the soul and damages the personality. It gives the segregator a false sense of superiority, and the segregated a false sense of inferiority. To use the words of Martin Buber, the great Jewish philosopher, segregation substitutes an "I-it" relationship for the "I-thou" relationship, and ends up relegating persons to the status of things. So segregation is not only politically, economically, and sociologically unsound, but it is morally wrong and sinful. Paul Tillich has said that sin is separation. Isn't segregation an existential expression of man's tragic separation, an expression of his awful estrangement, his terrible sinfulness? So I can urge men to disobey segregation ordinances because they are morally wrong.

15 Let us turn to a more concrete example of just and unjust laws. An unjust law is a code that a majority inflicts on a minority that is not binding on itself. This is difference made legal. On the other hand, a just law is a code that a majority compels a minority to follow that it is willing to follow itself. This is sameness made legal.

Let me give another explanation. An unjust law is a code inflicted upon a minority which that minority had no part in enacting or creating because they did not have the unhampered right to vote. Who can say that the legislature of Alabama which set up the segregation laws was democratically elected? Throughout the state of Alabama all types of conniving methods are used to prevent Negroes from becoming registered voters, and there are some counties without a single Negro registered to vote despite the fact that the Negro constitutes a majority of the population. Can any law set up in such a state be considered democratically structured?

These are just a few examples of unjust and just laws. There are some instances when a law is just on its face and unjust in its application. For instance, I was arrested Friday on a charge of parading without a permit. Now there is nothing wrong with an ordinance which requires a permit for a parade, but when the ordinance is used to preserve segregation and to deny citizens the First Amendment privilege of peaceful assembly and peaceful protest, then it becomes unjust.

I hope you can see the distinction I am trying to point out. In no sense do I advocate evading or defying the law as the rabid segregationist would do. This would lead to anarchy. One who breaks an unjust law must do it *openly, lovingly* (not hatefully as the white mothers did in New Orleans when they were seen on television screaming, "nigger, nigger, nigger"), and with a willingness to accept the penalty. I submit that an individual who breaks a law that conscience tells him is unjust, and willingly accepts the penalty by staying in jail to arouse the conscience of the community over its injustice, is in reality expressing the very highest respect for law.

Of course, there is nothing new about this kind of civil disobedience. It was seen sublimely in the refusal of Shadrach, Meshach, and Abednego to obey the laws of Nebuchadnezzar because a higher moral law was involved. It was practiced superbly by the early Christians who were willing to face hungry lions and the excruciating pain of chopping blocks, before submitting to certain unjust laws of the Roman Empire. To a degree academic freedom is a reality today because Socrates practiced civil disobedience.

20 We can never forget that everything Hitler did in Germany was "legal" and everything the Hungarian freedom fighters did in Hungary was "illegal." It was "illegal" to aid and comfort a Jew in Hitler's Germany. But I am sure that if I had lived in Germany during that time I would have aided and comforted my Jewish brothers even though it was illegal. If I lived in a Communist country today where certain principles dear to the

Christian faith are suppressed, I believe I would openly advocate disobeying these antireligious laws. I must make two honest confessions to you, my Christian and Jewish brothers. First, I must confess that over the last few years I have been gravely disappointed with the white moderate. I have almost reached the regrettable conclusion that the Negro's great stumbling block in the stride toward freedom is not the White Citizen's Councilor or the Ku Klux Klanner, but the white moderate who is more devoted to "order" than to justice; who prefers a negative peace which is the absence of tension to a positive peace which is the presence of justice; who constantly says, "I agree with you in the goal you seek, but I can't agree with your methods of direct action"; who paternalistically feels that he can set the timetable for another man's freedom; who lives by the myth of time and who constantly advises the Negro to wait until a "more convenient season." Shallow understanding from people of good will is more frustrating than absolute misunderstanding from people of ill will. Lukewarm acceptance is much more bewildering than outright rejection.

I had hoped that the white moderate would understand that law and order exist for the purpose of establishing justice, and that when they fail to do this they become dangerously structured dams that block the flow of social progress. I had hoped that the white moderate would understand that the present tension of the South is merely a necessary phase of the transition from an obnoxious negative peace, where the Negro passively accepted his unjust plight, to a substance-filled positive peace, where all men will respect the dignity and worth of human personality. Actually, we who engage in nonviolent direct action are not the creators of tension. We merely bring to the surface the hidden tension that is already alive. We bring it out in the open where it can be seen and dealt with. Like a boil that can never be cured as long as it is covered up but must be opened with all its pus-flowing ugliness to the natural medicines of air and light, injustice must likewise be exposed, with all of the tension its exposing creates, to the light of human conscience and the air of national opinion before it can be cured.

In your statement you asserted that our actions, even though peaceful, must be condemned because they precipitate violence. But can this assertion be logically made? Isn't this like condemning the robbed man because his possession of money precipitated the evil act of robbery? Isn't this like condemning Socrates because his unswerving commitment to truth and his philosophical delvings precipitated the misguided popular mind to make him drink the hemlock? Isn't this like condemning Jesus because His unique God-consciousness and never-ceasing devotion to His will precipitated the evil act of crucifixion? We must come to see, as federal courts have consistently affirmed, that it is immoral to urge an individual to withdraw his efforts to gain his basic constitutional rights because the quest precipitates violence. Society must protect the robbed and punish the robber.

I had also hoped that the white moderate would reject the myth of time. I received a letter this morning from a white brother in Texas which said: "All Christians know that the colored people will receive equal rights eventually, but it is possible that you are in too great of a religious hurry. It has taken Christianity almost two thousand years to accomplish what it has. The teachings of Christ take time to come to earth." All that is said here grows out of a tragic misconception of time. It is the strangely irrational notion that there is something in the very flow of time that will inevitably cure all ills. Actually time is neutral. It can be used either destructively or constructively. I am coming to feel that the people of ill will have used time much more effectively than the people of good will. We will have to repent in this generation not merely for the vitriolic words and actions of the bad people, but for the appalling silence of the good people. We must come to see that human progress never rolls in on wheels of inevitability. It comes through the tireless efforts and persistent work of men willing to be co-workers with God, and without this hard work time itself becomes an ally of the forces of social stagnation. We must use time creatively, and forever realize that the time is always ripe to do right. Now is the time to make real the promise of democracy, and transform our pending national elegy into a creative psalm of brotherhood. Now is the time to lift our national policy from the quicksand of racial injustice to the solid rock of human dignity.

You spoke of our activity in Birmingham as extreme. At first I was rather disappointed that fellow clergymen would see my nonviolent efforts as those of the extremist. I started thinking about the fact that I stand in the middle of two opposing forces in the Negro community. One is a force of complacency made up of Negroes who, as a result of long years of oppression, have been so completely drained of self-respect and a sense of "somebodiness" that they have adjusted to segregation, and of a few Negroes in the middle class who, because of a degree of academic and economic security, and because at points they profit by segregation, have unconsciously become insensitive to the problems of the masses. The other force is one of bitterness and hatred, and comes perilously close to advocating violence. It is expressed in the various black nationalist groups that are springing up over the nation, the largest and best known being Elijah Muhammad's Muslim movement. This movement is nourished by the contemporary frustration over the continued existence of racial discrimination. It is made up of people who have lost faith in America, who have absolutely repudiated Christianity, and who have concluded that the white man is an incurable "devil." I have tried to stand between these two forces, saying that we need not follow the "do-nothingism" of the complacent or the hatred and despair of the black nationalist. There is the more excellent way of love and nonviolent protest. I'm grateful to God that, through the Negro church, the dimension of nonviolence entered our struggle. If this philosophy had not emerged, I am convinced that by now many streets of the South would be flowing with floods of blood. And I am further convinced that if our white brothers dismiss us as "rabble-rousers" and "outside agitators" those of us who are working through the channels of nonviolent direct action and refuse to support our nonviolent efforts, millions of Negroes, out of frustration and despair, will seek solace and security in black nationalist ideologies, a development that will lead inevitably to a frightening racial nightmare.

25 Oppressed people cannot remain oppressed forever. The urge for freedom will eventually come. This is what happened to the American Negro. Something within has reminded him of his birthright of freedom; something without has reminded him that he can gain it. Consciously and unconsciously, he has been swept in by what the Germans call the *Zeitgeist*, and with his black brothers of Africa, and his brown and yellow brothers of Asia, South America, and the Caribbean, he is moving with a sense of cosmic urgency toward the promised land of racial justice. Recognizing this vital urge that has engulfed the Negro community, one should readily understand public demonstrations. The Negro has many pent-up resentments and latent frustrations. He has to get them out. So let him march sometime; let him have his prayer pilgrimages to the city hall; understand why he must have sit-ins and freedom rides. If his repressed emotions do not come out in these nonviolent ways, they will come out in ominous expressions of violence. This is not a threat; it is a fact of history. So I have not said to my people "get rid of your discontent." But I have tried to say that this normal and healthy discontent can be channelized through the creative outlet of nonviolent direct action. Now this approach is being dismissed as extremist. I must admit that I was initially disappointed in being so categorized.

But as I continued to think about the matter I gradually gained a bit of satisfaction from being considered an extremist. Was not Jesus an extremist in love—"Love your enemies, bless them that curse you, pray for them that despitefully use you." Was not Amos an extremist for justice—"Let justice roll down like waters and righteousness like a mighty stream." Was not Paul an extremist for the gospel of Jesus Christ—"I bear in my body the marks of the Lord Jesus." Was not Martin Luther an extremist—"Here I stand; I can do none other so help me God." Was not John Bunyan an extremist—"I will stay in jail to the end of my days before I make a butchery of my conscience." Was not Abraham Lincoln an extremist—"This nation cannot survive half slave and half free." Was not Thomas Jefferson an extremist—"We hold these truths to be self-evident, that all men are created equal." So the question is not whether we will be extremist but what kind of extremist will we be. Will we be extremists for hate or will we be extremists for love? Will we be extremists for the preservation of injustice—or will we be extremists for the cause of justice? In that dramatic scene on Calvary's hill, three men were crucified. We must not forget that all three were crucified for the same crime—the crime of extremism. Two were extremists for immorality, and thusly fell below their environment. The other, Jesus Christ, was an extremist for love, truth, and goodness, and thereby rose above his environment. So, after all, maybe the South, the nation, and the world are in dire need of creative extremists.

I had hoped that the white moderate would see this. Maybe I was too optimistic. Maybe I expected too much. I guess I should have realized that few members of a race that has oppressed another race can understand or appreciate the deep groans and passionate yearnings of those that have been oppressed and still fewer have the vision to see that injustice must be rooted out by strong, persistent, and determined action. I am thankful, however, that some of our white brothers have grasped the meaning of this social revolution and committed themselves to it. They are still all too small in quantity, but they are big in quality. Some like Ralph McGill, Lillian Smith, Harry Golden, and James Dabbs have written about our struggle in eloquent, prophetic, and understanding terms. Others have marched with us down nameless streets of the South. They have languished in filthy roach-infested jails, suffering the abuse and brutality of angry policemen who see them as "dirty nigger-lovers." They, unlike so many of their moderate brothers and sisters, have recognized the urgency of the moment and sensed the need for powerful "action" antidotes to combat the disease of segregation.

Let me rush on to mention my other disappointment. I have been so greatly disappointed with the white church and its leadership. Of course, there are some notable exceptions. I am not unmindful of the fact that each of you has taken some significant stands on this issue. I commend you, Reverend Stallings, for your Christian stance on this past Sunday, in welcoming Negroes to your worship service on a nonsegregated basis. I commend the Catholic leaders of this state for integrating Springhill College several years ago.

But despite these notable exceptions I must honestly reiterate that I have been disappointed with the church. I do not say that as one of the negative critics who can always find something wrong with the church. I say it as a minister of the gospel, who loves the church; who was nurtured in its bosom; who has been sustained by its spiritual blessings, and who will remain true to it as long as the cord of life shall lengthen.

30 I had the strange feeling when I was suddenly catapulted into the leadership of the bus protest in Montgomery several years ago that we would have the support of the white church. I felt that the white ministers, priests, and rabbis of the South would be some of our strongest allies. Instead, some have been outright opponents, refusing to understand the freedom movement and misrepresenting its leaders; all too many others have been more cautious than courageous and have remained silent behind the anesthetizing security of the stained-glass windows.

In spite of my shattered dreams of the past, I came to Birmingham with the hope that the white religious leadership of this community would see the justice of our cause, and with deep moral concern, serve as the channel through which our just grievances would get to the power structure. I had hoped that each of you would understand. But again I have been disappointed. I have heard numerous religious leaders of the South call upon their worshipers to comply with a desegregation decision because it is the *law,* but I have longed to hear white ministers say, "Follow this decree because integration is morally *right* and the Negro is your brother." In the midst of blatant injustices inflicted upon the Negro, I have watched white churches stand on the sideline and merely mouth pious irrelevancies and sanctimonious trivialities. In the midst of a mighty struggle to rid our nation of racial and economic injustice, I have heard so many ministers say, "Those are social issues with which the gospel has no real concern," and I have watched so many churches commit themselves to a completely otherworldly religion which made a strange distinction between body and soul, the sacred and the secular.

So here we are moving toward the exit of the twentieth century with a religious community largely adjusted to the status quo, standing as a taillight behind other community agencies rather than a headlight leading men to higher levels of justice.

I have traveled the length and breadth of Alabama, Mississippi, and all the other southern states. On sweltering summer days and crisp autumn mornings I have looked at her beautiful churches with their lofty spires pointing heavenward. I have beheld the impressive outlay of her massive religious education buildings. Over and over again I have found myself asking: "What kind of people worship here? Who is their God? Where were their voices when the lips of Governor Barnett dripped with words of interposition and nullification? Where were they when Governor Wallace gave the clarion call for defiance and hatred? Where were their voices of support when tired, bruised, and weary Negro men and women decided to rise from the dark dungeons of complacency to the bright hills of creative protest?"

Yes, these questions are still in my mind. In deep disappointment, I have wept over the laxity of the church. But be assured that my tears have been tears of love. There can be no deep disappointment where there is not deep love. Yes, I love the church; I love her sacred walls. How could I do otherwise? I am in the rather unique position of being the son, the grandson, and the great-grandson of preachers. Yes, I see the church as the body of Christ. But, oh! How we have blemished and scarred that body through social neglect and fear of being nonconformists.

There was a time when the church was very powerful. It was during 35
that period when the early Christians rejoiced when they were deemed worthy to suffer for what they believed. In those days the church was not merely a thermometer that recorded the ideas and principles of popular opinion; it was a thermostat that transformed the mores of society. Wherever the early Christians entered a town the power structure got disturbed

and immediately sought to convict them for being "disturbers of the peace" and "outside agitators." But they went on with the conviction that they were "a colony of heaven," and had to obey God rather than man. They were small in number but big in commitment. They were too God-intoxicated to be "astronomically intimidated." They brought an end to such ancient evils as infanticide and gladiatorial contest.

Things are different now. The contemporary church is often a weak, ineffectual voice with an uncertain sound. It is so often the archsupporter of the status quo. Far from being disturbed by the presence of the church, the power structure of the average community is consoled by the church's silent and often vocal sanction of things as they are.

But the judgment of God is upon the church as never before. If the church of today does not recapture the sacrificial spirit of the early church, it will lose its authentic ring, forfeit the loyalty of millions, and be dismissed as an irrelevant social club with no meaning for the twentieth century. I am meeting young people every day whose disappointment with the church has risen to outright disgust.

Maybe again, I have been too optimistic. Is organized religion too inextricably bound to the status quo to save our nation and the world? Maybe I must turn my faith to the inner spiritual church, the church within the church, as the true *ecclesia* and the hope of the world. But again I am thankful to God that some noble souls from the ranks of organized religion have broken loose from the paralyzing chains of conformity and joined us as active partners in the struggle for freedom. They have left their secure congregations and walked the streets of Albany, Georgia, with us. They have gone through the highways of the South on tortuous rides for freedom. Yes, they have gone to jail with us. Some have been kicked out of their churches, and lost support of their bishops and fellow ministers. But they have gone with the faith that right defeated is stronger than evil triumphant. These men have been the leaven in the lump of the race. Their witness has been the spiritual salt that has preserved the true meaning of the gospel in these troubled times. They have carved a tunnel of hope through the dark mountain of disappointment.

I hope the church as a whole will meet the challenge of this decisive hour. But even if the church does not come to the aid of justice, I have no despair about the future. I have no fear about the outcome of our struggle in Birmingham, even if our motives are presently misunderstood. We will reach the goal of freedom in Birmingham and all over the nation, because the goal of America is freedom. Abused and scorned though we may be, our destiny is tied up with the destiny of America. Before the Pilgrims landed at Plymouth we were here. Before the pen of Jefferson etched across the pages of history the majestic words of the Declaration of Independence, we were here. For more than two centuries our foreparents labored in this country without wages; they made cotton king; and they built the homes of their masters in the midst of brutal injustice and shameful humiliation—and yet out of a bottomless vitality they continued to thrive and develop. If the inexpressible cruelties of slavery could not stop us, the opposition we now face will surely fail. We will win our freedom because the sacred heritage of our nation and the eternal will of God are embodied in our echoing demands.

I must close now. But before closing I am impelled to mention one 40
other point in your statement that troubled me profoundly. You warmly commended the Birmingham police force for keeping "order" and "preventing violence." I don't believe you would have so warmly commended the police force if you had seen its angry violent dogs literally biting six unarmed, nonviolent Negroes. I don't believe you would so quickly commend the policemen if you would observe their ugly and inhuman treatment of Negroes here in the city jail; if you would watch them push and curse old Negro women and young Negro girls; if you would see them slap and kick old Negro men and young boys; if you will observe them, as they did on two occasions, refuse to give us food because we wanted to sing our grace together. I'm sorry that I can't join you in your praise for the police department.

It is true that they have been rather disciplined in their public handling of the demonstrators. In this sense they have been rather publicly "nonviolent." But for what purpose? To preserve the evil system of segregation. Over the last few years I have consistently preached that nonviolence demands that the means we use must be as pure as the ends we seek. So I have tried to make it clear that it is wrong to use immoral means to attain moral ends. But now I must affirm that it is just as wrong, or even more so, to use moral means to preserve immoral ends. Maybe Mr. Connor and his policemen have been rather publicly nonviolent, as Chief Pritchett was in Albany, Georgia, but they have used the moral means of nonviolence to maintain the immoral end of flagrant racial injustice. T. S. Eliot has said that there is no greater treason than to do the right deed for the wrong reason.

I wish you had commended the Negro sit-inners and demonstrators of Birmingham for their sublime courage, their willingness to suffer, and their amazing discipline in the midst of the most inhuman provocation. One day the South will recognize its real heroes. They will be the James Merediths, courageously and with a majestic sense of purpose facing jeering and hostile mobs and the agonizing loneliness that characterizes the life of the pioneer. They will be old, oppressed, battered Negro women, symbolized in a seventy-two-year-old woman of Montgomery, Alabama, who rose up with a sense of dignity and with her people decided not to ride the segregated buses, and responded to one who inquired about her tiredness with ungrammatical profundity: "My feet is tired, but my soul is rested." They will be the young high school and college students, young ministers of the gospel, and a host of their elders courageously and nonviolently sitting-in at lunch counters and willingly going to jail for conscience's sake. One day the South will know that when these disinherited children of God sat down at lunch counters they were in reality standing up for the best in the American dream and the most sacred values in our Judeo-Christian heritage, and thusly, carrying our whole nation back to those great wells of democracy which were dug deep by the Founding Fathers in the formulation of the Constitution and the Declaration of Independence.

Never before have I written a letter this long (or should I say a book?). I'm afraid that it is much too long to take your precious time. I can assure you that it would have been much shorter if I had been writing from a comfortable desk, but what else is there to do when you are alone for days in the dull monotony of a narrow jail cell other than write long letters, think strange thoughts, and pray long prayers?

If I have said anything in this letter that is an overstatement of the truth and is indicative of an unreasonable impatience, I beg you to forgive me. If I have said anything in this letter that is an understatement of the truth and is indicative of my having a patience that makes me patient with anything less than brotherhood, I beg God to forgive me.

I hope this letter finds you strong in the faith. I also hope that cir- 45
cumstances will soon make it possible for me to meet each of you, not as an integrationist or a civil rights leader, but as a fellow clergyman and a Christian brother. Let us all hope that the dark clouds of racial prejudice will soon pass away and the deep fog of misunderstanding will be lifted from our fear-drenched communities and in some not too distant tomorrow the radiant stars of love and brotherhood will shine over our great nation with all of their scintillating beauty.

Yours for the cause of Peace and Brotherhood,
Martin Luther King Jr.

READING AND DISCUSSION QUESTIONS

1. What are some of the steps that King and his sympathizers took to try to avoid direct action in Birmingham? Why was Birmingham a logical target for the action, when it came?
2. Explain King's distinction between just and unjust laws. Are there dangers in attempting to make such a distinction?
3. What are some of the most vivid examples of the sort of discrimination that King and his followers hoped to end?
4. Why does King say that the white moderate is a greater threat to African American progress than the outspoken racist? Is his explanation convincing?
5. What other group does King express disappointment with?
6. What claim is King supporting in the letter?
7. King uses figurative language in the letter. Find some particularly vivid passages and evaluate their effectiveness in the context of the letter.

WRITING SUGGESTIONS

8. Write a one-paragraph summary of the letter.
9. Can you think of a law against which defiance would be justified? Explain why the law is unjust and why refusal to obey it would be morally defensible.
10. Write an essay in which you summarize and evaluate King's criticism of the political and religious establishments of his day.

DEBATE: Under what circumstances should the government have the right to seize personal property?

One Year later, Power to Seize Property Ripe for Abuse

USA TODAY

Remember Susette Kelo? The New London, Connecticut, nurse lost a landmark legal fight to save her pink cottage from being seized by city officials, who wanted to hand it over to developers. Just over a year ago, the U.S. Supreme Court ruled against her. It held 5–4 that local governments could condemn private property, not just for a public purpose such as a road or school, but also to give to developers if a locality's economic future is at issue.

As it turned out, that wasn't the end of the story. The house won't be bulldozed after all. Last month, officials agreed to move it to another location so that her land can round out a waterfront development site—a compromise Kelo suggested years ago to little avail.

Meanwhile, the ruling has ignited a nationwide fight between developers rushing to seize a fresh opportunity and an unlikely political coalition that sees the decision as an assault on America's "home-as-castle" mind-set.

Emboldened by the ruling, local governments have threatened or condemned 5,783 properties for private projects in the past year, according to the Institute for Justice, the libertarian law firm that defended Kelo. That's up from an annual average of 2,056 such threats and takings from 1998 to 2002, the Institute said.

This unsigned piece expresses *USA Today*'s editorial stance on eminent domain. It and the opposing view by Donald J. Borut appeared in the July 10, 2006, issue of that newspaper.

Of 117 projects the Institute studied over the past year, most involved 5
taking lower-income homes, apartments and mobile home parks to construct upscale condominiums or retail development, driving the working poor from their homes.

But the Kelo case also has inspired a political backlash unusual in the annals of Supreme Court rulings. It has united conservative defenders of property rights and liberals who say the seizures amount to corporate welfare at the expense of the powerless.

They've scored significant victories:

- Twenty-five states have enacted laws to curb eminent domain seizures—something the Supreme Court invited them to do in making its ruling.
- The U.S. House of Representatives voted 376–38 last year to bar federal economic development funds to state and local agencies that use eminent domain for private commercial development. A similar bill is stalled in the Senate.
- On June 23, one year after the Kelo decision, President Bush issued an executive order that federal agencies can seize private property only for public projects.

Those actions should help ensure that the growing movement to prevent unjustified seizures of private property will gain momentum. In the words of dissenting Justice Sandra Day O'Connor, "the government now has the license to transfer property from those with fewer resources to those with more" as long as there is some purported economic benefit. And that is wrong.

Supporters of seizures such as the one in New London argue that abuses are rare and that condemnation is needed to revitalize abandoned or blighted areas and encourage the growth of jobs. But the truth is that under the court's ruling almost no one's property is safe unless states impose limits.

Seizures of one person's property to benefit another should be rare and 10
a last resort. The halfway happy ending to Susette Kelo's ordeal should encourage political leaders to do more to stop bulldozers from plowing through the American dream.

Vital Tool of Last Resort

DONALD J. BORUT

In all the noise that surrounded the decision by the Supreme Court one year ago to continue to allow cities to use eminent domain when considering the economic future of their communities, something vital was left out: the facts.

Without eminent domain to clear title on abandoned and vacant properties—the primary use of eminent domain in this country—rundown buildings and empty lots would attract trash, rodents and trouble. Blighted structures would sit abandoned. If owners didn't want to sell or were holding out for more money, the cities and their taxpayers could do nothing to get rid of them.

Despite what some might claim, this is how eminent domain has been and continues to be used in this country: to revitalize older parts of Philadelphia; to transform an area in Indianapolis once referred to as "Dodge City" into a beautiful, mixed-income neighborhood; to save a historic church in Fitzgerald, Georgia.

Let's take a closer look at the facts:

5 Since the Supreme Court's *Kelo* ruling, 43 state legislatures reviewed eminent domain laws and made changes to meet the needs of their communities. In a few cases, after numerous public hearings, legislators determined that no change was needed.

According to a survey by the National League of Cities, 76% of municipalities had not used eminent domain in the past three years in connection with an economic development project. But where it was invoked, eminent domain was used only as a last resort after all other options were explored.

Of the 5,700-plus properties claimed by the Institute for Justice to involve eminent domain in the past year, many were part of 117 multiphased and publicly scrutinized economic development projects begun well before the *Kelo* decision to eradicate blight—a practice even dissenting Justice Sandra Day O'Connor found appropriate.

Ensuring that owners receive appropriate compensation for their properties is equally important. In cases such as Norwood, Ohio, which was cited by the Institute as an abuse, the majority of owners willingly received twice the assessed fair market value; the "hold-outs" three times their value.

The prudent use of eminent domain has brought hope and opportunity—through good jobs and better housing—to thousands of Americans. That story deserves to be told.

Donald J. Borut is the executive director of the National League of Cities, the nation's oldest and largest national organization representing municipal governments. Before assuming that position in 1990, he was deputy executive director of the International City Management Association, an organization of professional administrators in local governments.

DISCUSSION QUESTIONS

1. Why was the *Kelo* case considered a landmark decision? What have been some of the effects of the ruling, according to the editorial?
2. What claim are the *USA Today* editors supporting? What types of support do these unnamed editors offer for their claim?
3. According to Borut, what is the primary use of eminent domain in this country? What facts does Borut offer in defending his position? Is there any overlap between his facts and those offered in the editorial?
4. What is Borut's claim?
5. Where, if anywhere, do the two arguments share common ground?
6. Which of the two arguments do you find more convincing? Is your opinion influenced by any experience you or someone you know has had with eminent domain? By previous reading or discussion of the subject? Explain.

ASSIGNMENTS FOR DEFENDING CLAIMS

READING AND DISCUSSION QUESTIONS

1. Locate a movie review online or in hard copy that has a clear claim and is based on clear evaluative criteria. Choose a review that is an essay, not just a single paragraph. Bring it to class and share it with your class or group. By looking at a range of different reviews, come to some conclusions about the sort of criteria used in making judgment calls about movies and what sort of claims provide good thesis statements for reviews. What are some other characteristics that all or most good movie reviews share?
2. Consider one or more of your school's policies that you would like to see changed. In your opinion, what exactly is wrong with the policy as it currently exists? What exactly would you recommend be done to improve the situation?
3. Samuelson argues that different news sources slant their news toward different audiences. Do you agree with his argument? Why, or why not? What examples can you provide in support of your opinion?

WRITING ASSIGNMENTS

4. Write an essay explaining whether you believe that the editors of *USA Today* or Borut has the stronger argument regarding eminent domain, and why.
5. Choose a controversial issue in the field in which you are majoring or one in which you might major. Practice differentiating among the three types of claims by writing a claim of fact, a claim of value, and a claim of policy on that issue.
6. Choose one of the three claims you wrote for assignment five above and write an essay supporting it.

CHAPTER 7

Providing Support

TYPES OF SUPPORT: EVIDENCE AND APPEALS TO NEEDS AND VALUES

All the claims you make—whether of fact, of value, or of policy—must be supported. Sometimes you will use your own experience as support for a claim. At other times you may conduct interviews, field research, lab experiments, or surveys to obtain support for your position. For the majority of your assignments, you will most likely turn primarily to print and electronic sources.

Support for a claim represents the answer to the question "What have you got to go on?"[1] There are two basic kinds of support in an argument: evidence and appeals to needs and values.

Evidence, as one dictionary defines it, is "something that tends to prove; ground for belief." When you provide evidence, you use facts, including statistics, and opinions, or interpretations of facts—both your own and those of experts. In the following conversation, the first speaker offers facts and the opinion of an expert to convince the second speaker that robots are exceptional machines.

"You know, robots do a lot more than work on assembly lines in factories."
"Like what?"

[1]Stephen Toulmin, *The Uses of Argument* (Cambridge: Cambridge University Press, 1958), p. 98.

"They shear sheep, pick citrus fruit, and even assist in neurosurgery. And by the end of the century, every house will have a robot slave."

"No kidding. Who says so?"

"An engineer who's the head of the world's largest manufacturer of industrial robots."

A writer often appeals to readers' needs (that is, requirements for physical and psychological survival and well-being) and values (or standards for right and wrong, good and bad). In the following conversation, the first speaker makes an appeal to the universal need for self-esteem and to the principle of helping others, a value the second speaker probably shares.

"I think you ought to come help us at the nursing home. We need an extra hand."

"I'd like to, but I really don't have the time."

"You could give us an hour a week, couldn't you? Think how good you'd feel about helping out, and the residents would be so grateful. Some of them are very lonely."

Although they use the same kinds of support, conversations are less rigorous than arguments addressed to larger audiences in academic or public situations. In the debates on public policy that appear in the media and in the courts, the quality of support can be crucial in settling urgent matters. The following summary of a well-known court case demonstrates the critical use of both evidence and value appeals in the support of opposing claims.

On March 30, 1981, President Ronald Reagan and three other men were shot by John W. Hinckley Jr., a young drifter from a wealthy Colorado family. Hinckley was arrested at the scene of the shooting. In his trial the factual evidence was presented first: Dozens of reliable witnesses had seen the shooting at close range. Hinckley's diaries, letters, and poems revealed that he had planned the shooting to impress actress Jodie Foster. Opinions, consisting of testimony by experts, were introduced by both the defense and the prosecution. This evidence was contradictory. Defense attorneys produced several psychiatrists who defined Hinckley as insane. If this interpretation of his conduct convinced the jury, then Hinckley would be confined to a mental hospital rather than a prison. The prosecution introduced psychiatrists who interpreted Hinckley's motives and actions as those of a man who knew what he was doing and knew it was wrong. They claimed he was *not* insane by legal definition. The fact that experts can make differing conclusions about the meaning of the same information indicates that interpretations are less reliable than other kinds of support.

Finally, the defense made an appeal to the moral values of the jury. Under the law, criminals judged to be insane are not to be punished as harshly as criminals judged to be sane. The laws assume that criminals who cannot be held responsible for their actions are entitled to more compassionate treatment, confinement to a mental hospital rather than prison. The jury accepted the interpretive evidence supporting the claim of the defense, and Hinckley was pronounced not guilty by reason of insanity. Clearly the moral concern for the rights of the insane proved to be decisive.

In your arguments you will advance your claims, not unlike a lawyer, with these same kinds of support. But before you begin, you should ask two questions: Which kind of support should I use in convincing an audience to accept my claim? and How do I decide that each item of support is valid and worthy of acceptance? This chapter presents the different types of evidence and appeals you can use to support your claim and examines the criteria by which you can evaluate the soundness of that support.

EVIDENCE

Factual Evidence

In Chapter 6, we defined facts as statements possessing a high degree of public acceptance. In theory, facts can be verified by experience alone. Eating too much will make us sick; we can get from Hopkinton to Boston in a half hour by car; in the Northern Hemisphere it is colder in December than in July. The experience of any individual is limited in both time and space, so we must accept as fact thousands of assertions about the world that we ourselves can never verify. Thus we accept the report that human beings landed on the moon in 1969 because we trust those who can verify it. (Country people in Morocco, however, received the news with disbelief because they had no reason to trust the reporters of the event. They insisted on trusting their senses instead. One man said, "I can see the moon very clearly. If a man were walking around up there, wouldn't I be able to see him?")

Factual evidence appears most frequently as examples and statistics, which are a numerical form of examples.

Examples

Examples are the most familiar kind of factual evidence. In addition to providing support for the truth of a generalization, examples can enliven otherwise dense or monotonous prose.

In the following paragraph the writer supports the claim in the topic sentence by offering a series of specific examples.

> Americans expect the next century to bring some striking political and social changes, but people are discerning. Two-thirds believe gay marriages

probably will be legal and over half think that fathers will spend as much time and energy with their kids as mothers. Half of the public also predicts that Social Security will probably die; that view is particularly prevalent among younger Americans. But a majority doubts that cigarette smoking will be illegal or that all racial and gender discrimination will disappear.[2]

Hypothetical examples, which create imaginary situations for the audience and encourage them to visualize what might happen under certain circumstances, can also be effective. The following paragraph illustrates the use of hypothetical examples. (The author is describing megaschools, high schools with more than two thousand students.)

> And in schools that big there is inevitably a critical mass of kids who are neither jocks nor artists nor even nerds, kids who are nothing at all, nonentities in their own lives. . . . The creditable ballplayer who might have made the team in a smaller school is edged out by better athletes. The artist who might have had work hung in a smaller school is supplanted by abler talents. And the disaffected and depressed boy who might have found a niche, or a friend, or a teacher who noticed, falls between the cracks. Sometimes he quietly drops out. Sometimes he quietly passes through. And sometimes he comes to school with a gun.[3]

All claims about vague or abstract terms would be boring or unintelligible without examples to illuminate them. For example, if you claim that a movie contains "unusual sound effects," you will certainly have to describe some of the effects to convince the reader that your generalization can be trusted.

Statistics

Statistics express information in numbers. In the following example statistics have been used to express raw data in numerical form.

> Surveys have shown that almost half of all male high school seniors— and nearly 20 percent of all ninth grade boys—can be called "problem drinkers." . . . Over 5,000 teenagers are killed yearly in auto accidents due to drunken driving.[4]

These grim numbers probably have meaning for you, partly because you already know that alcoholism exists even among young teenagers and partly because your own experience enables you to evaluate the numbers. But if you are unfamiliar with the subject, such numbers may be difficult or impossible to understand. Statistics, therefore, are more effective in

[2] Elizabeth Crowley, "Putting Faith in Technology for Year 3000," *Wall Street Journal*, September 15, 2000, sec. A, p. 10.

[3] Anna Quindlen, "The Problem of the Megaschool," *Newsweek*, March 26, 2001, p. 68.

[4] "The Kinds of Drugs Kids Are Getting Into" (Spring House, Pa.: McNeil Pharmaceutical, n.d.).

comparisons that indicate whether a quantity is relatively large or small and sometimes even whether a reader should interpret the result as gratifying or disappointing. For example, if a novice gambler were told that for every dollar wagered in a state lottery, 50 percent goes back to the players as prizes, would the gambler be able to conclude that the percentage is high or low? Would he be able to choose between playing the state lottery and playing a casino game? Unless he had more information, probably not. But if he were informed that in casino games, the return to the players is over 90 percent and in slot machines and racetracks the return is around 80 percent, the comparison would enable him to evaluate the meaning of the 50 percent return in the state lottery and even to make a decision about where to gamble his money.[5]

Comparative statistics are also useful for measurements over time. For instance, the following statistics show what comparisons based on BMI or body mass index reveal about how Miss America contestants have changed over the years.

> Miss America contestants have become increasing thinner over the past 75 years. In the 1920s, contestants had BMIs in the normal range of 20–25. Since then, pageant winners' body weights have decreased steadily to a level about 12 percent below levels from the mid-1900s. Since 1970, nearly all of the winners have had BMIs below the healthy range, with some as low as 16.9, a BMI that would meet part of the diagnostic criteria for anorexia nervosa.[6]

Diagrams, tables, charts, and graphs can make clear the relations among many sets of numbers. Such charts and diagrams allow readers to grasp the information more easily than if it were presented in paragraph form.

The graphs that constitute Figures 1 and 2 on pages 216 and 217 summarize the information produced by polls about cancer care and cancer costs. The pie charts on page 218 (Figures 3 and 4) clarify coverage of Africa by two popular newsmagazines.

■ Opinions: Interpretations of the Facts

We have seen how opinions of experts influenced the verdict in the trial of John Hinckley. Facts alone were not enough to substantiate the claim that Hinckley was guilty of attempted assassination. Both the defense and the prosecution relied on experts—psychiatrists—to interpret the facts. Opinions or interpretations about the facts are the inferences discussed in Chapter 6. They are an indispensable source of support for your claims.

[5] Curt Suphee, "Lotto Baloney," *Harper's,* July 1983, p. 201.

[6] S. Rubenstein and B. Caballero, "Is Miss America an Undernourished Role Model?" *JAMA* (2000), p. 1569. Qtd. in Jillian Croll, "Body Image and Adolescents," *Guidelines for Adolescent Nutrition Services*, J. Stang and M. Story, eds. (2005). June 9, 2007. http://www.epi.umn.edu/let/pubs/adol_book.shtm.

FIGURE 1
Ratings of Health-Care System for Cancer Care

How would you rate the health-care system in America today when it comes to providing cancer care?

Comparison question asked of general public: How would you rate the health-care system in America today?

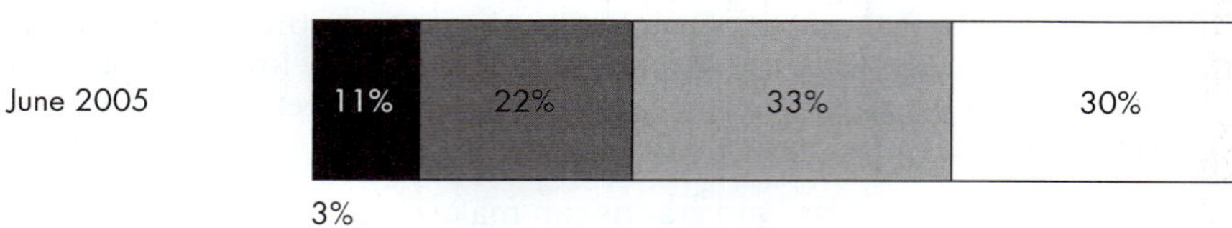

Note: Don't know and refused responses not shown.
Source: USA Today/Kaiser Family Foundation/Harvard School of Public Health, *National Survey of Households Affected by Cancer* (conducted Aug. 1–Sept. 14, 2006); Employee Benefit Research Institute, *Health Confidence Survey* (conducted June 30–Aug. 6, 2005).

Suppose a nightclub for teenagers has opened in your town. That is a fact. What is the significance of it? Is the club's existence good or bad? What consequences will it have for the community? Some parents oppose the idea of a nightclub, fearing that it may allow teenagers to escape from parental control and engage in dangerous activities. Other parents approve of a club, hoping that it will serve as a substitute for unsupervised congregation in the streets. The importance of these interpretations is that they, not the fact itself, help people decide what actions they should take. If the community accepts the interpretation that the club is a source of delinquency, they may decide to revoke the owner's license and close it. As one writer puts it, "The interpretation of data becomes a struggle over power."

Opinions or interpretations of facts generally take four forms: (1) They may suggest the cause for a condition or a causal connection between two sets of data; (2) they may offer predictions about the future; (3) they may suggest solutions to a problem; (4) they may refer to the opinion of experts.

FIGURE 2
Financial Burden of Cancer Care by Insurance Status, Income, and Age

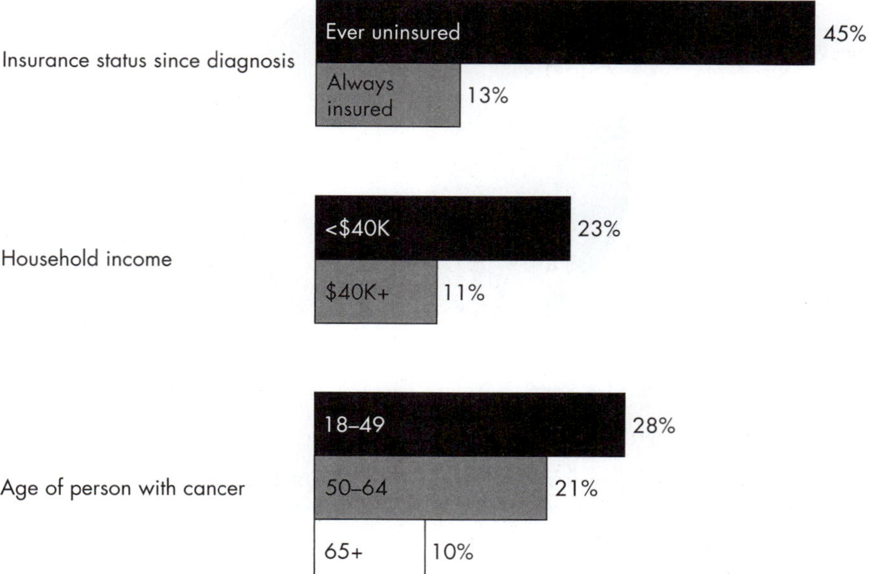

Source: USA Today/Kaiser Family Foundation/Harvard School of Public Health, *National Survey of Households Affected by Cancer* (conducted Aug. 1–Sept. 14, 2006).

Causal Connection

Anorexia nervosa is a serious, sometimes fatal, disease characterized by self-starvation. It is found largely among young women. Physicians, psychologists, and social scientists have speculated about the causes, which remain unclear. A leading researcher in the field, Hilde Bruch, believes that food refusal expresses a desire to postpone sexual development. Another authority, Joan Blumberg, believes that one cause may be biological, a nervous dysfunction of the hypothalamus. Still others infer that the causes are cultural, a response to the admiration of the thin female body.[7]

Predictions about the Future

In the fall and winter of 1989 to 1990 extraordinary events shook Eastern Europe, toppling Communist regimes and raising more popular forms of

[7] Phyllis Rose, "Hunger Artists," *Harper's*, July 1988, p. 82.

FIGURE 3
Percentages of Five Story Topics about Africa in *Newsweek*, August 1989 to August 1991

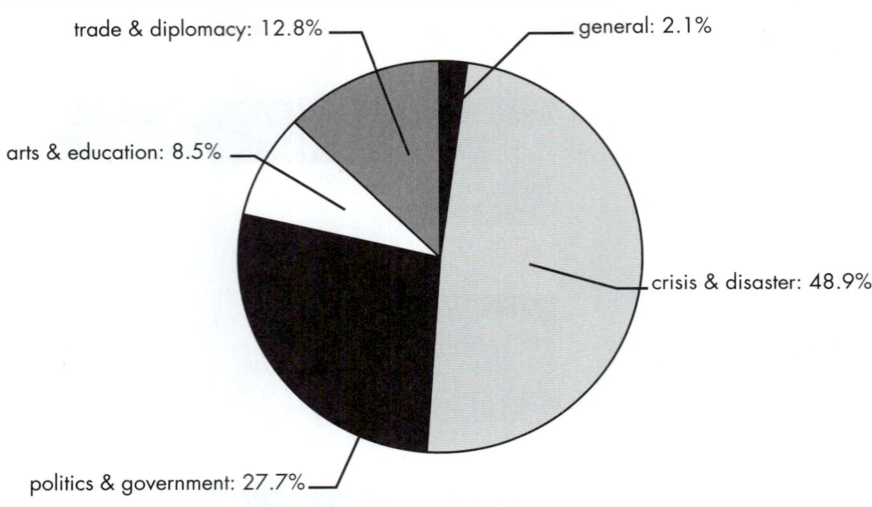

FIGURE 4
Percentages of Five Story Topics about Africa in *Time*, August 1989 to August 1991

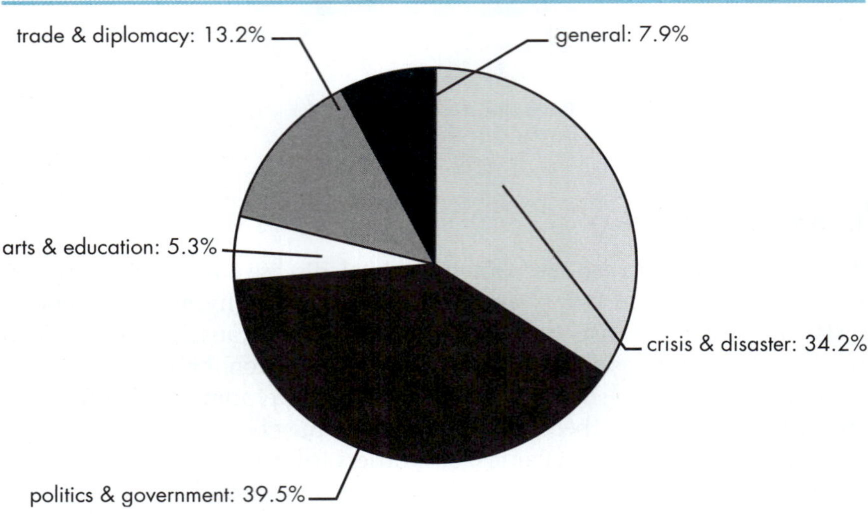

Source: Jerry Domatob, "Coverage of Africa in American Popular Magazines," *Issue: A Journal of Opinion*, 22 (Winter-Spring 1994): 25.

government. Politicians and scholars offered predictions about future changes in the region. One expert, Zbigniew Brzezinski, former national security adviser under President Carter, concluded that the changes for the Soviet Union might be destructive.

> It would be a mistake to see the recent decisions as marking a breakthrough for democracy. Much more likely is a prolonged period of democratizing chaos. One will see the rise in the Soviet Union of increasingly irreconcilable conflicts between varying national political and social aspirations, all united by a shared hatred for the existing Communist nomenklatura. One is also likely to see a flashback of a nationalist type among the Great Russians, fearful of the prospective breakup of the existing Great Russian Empire.[8]

Solutions to Problems

How shall we solve the problems caused by young people in our cities "who commit crimes and create the staggering statistics in teenage pregnancies and the high abortion rate"? The minister emeritus of the Abyssinian Baptist Church in New York City proposes establishment of a national youth academy with fifty campuses on inactive military bases. "It is a 'parenting' institution. . . . It is not a penal institution, not a prep school, not a Job Corps Center, not a Civilian Conservation Camp, but it borrows from them." Although such an institution has not been tried before, the author of the proposal thinks that it would represent an effort "to provide for the academic, moral, and social development of young people, to cause them to become responsible and productive citizens."[9]

Expert Opinion

For many of the subjects you discuss and write about, you will find it necessary to accept and use the opinions of experts. Based on their reading of the facts, experts express opinions on a variety of controversial subjects: whether capital punishment is a deterrent to crime; whether legalization of marijuana will lead to an increase in its use; whether children, if left untaught, will grow up honest and cooperative; whether sex education courses will result in less sexual activity and fewer illegitimate births. The interpretations of the data are often profoundly important because they influence social policy and affect our lives directly and indirectly.

For the problems mentioned above, the opinions of people recognized as authorities are more reliable than those of people who have neither thought about nor done research on the subject. But opinions may also be offered by student writers in areas in which they are knowledgeable. If you were asked, for example, to defend or refute the statement that work has advantages for teenagers, you could call on your own experience and that of your friends to support your claim. You can also draw on your experience to write convincingly about your special interests.

[8] *New York Times,* February 9, 1990, sec. A, p. 13.

[9] Samuel D. Proctor, "To the Rescue: A National Youth Academy," *New York Times,* September 16, 1989, sec. A, p. 27.

One opinion, however, is not as good as another. The value of any opinion depends on the quality of the evidence and the trustworthiness of the person offering it.

PRACTICE

1. Choose either Figure 1, "Ratings of Health-Care System for Cancer Care" (p. 216), or Figure 2, "Financial Burden of Cancer Care by Insurance Status, Income, and Age" (p. 217). Consider the facts presented in the graph you chose. What is one conclusion you can draw based on those facts? Summarize that conclusion in one sentence and make it the topic sentence for a paragraph. Then use facts from the graph as specific support to complete the paragraph.
2. Do the same with Figure 3 and Figure 4 (p. 218), the pie charts about Africa, but this time consider both charts.
3. Write two possible topic sentences supporting conclusions you were able to draw from the information in Figure 1, one a statement of fact and the other a statement of opinion. Do the same with Figure 2.

EVALUATION OF EVIDENCE

Before you begin to write, you must determine whether the facts and opinions you have chosen to support your claim are sound. Can they convince your readers? A distinction between the evaluation of facts and the evaluation of opinions is somewhat artificial because many facts are verified by expert opinion, but for our analysis we discuss them separately.

■ Evaluation of Factual Evidence

As you evaluate factual evidence, you should keep in mind the following questions:

1. Is the evidence up to date? The importance of up-to-date information depends on the subject. If you are defending the claim that suicide is immoral, you will not need to examine new data. For many of the subjects you write about, recent research and scholarship will be important, even decisive, in proving the soundness of your data. "New" does not always mean "best," but in fields where research is ongoing—education, psychology, technology, medicine, and all the natural and physical sciences—you should be sensitive to the dates of the research.

In writing a paper a few years ago warning about the health hazards of air pollution, you would have used data referring only to outdoor pollution produced by automobile and factory emissions. But writing about air pollution today, you would have to take into account new data about indoor pollution, which has become a serious problem as a result of attempts to conserve energy. Because research studies in indoor pollution are continually being updated, recent evidence will probably be more accurate than past research.

2. Is the evidence sufficient? The amount of evidence you need depends on the complexity of the subject and the length of your paper. Given the relative brevity of most of your assignments, you will need to be selective. For the claim that indoor pollution is a serious problem, one example would obviously not be enough. For a 750- to 1,000-word paper, three or four examples would probably be sufficient. The choice of examples should reflect different aspects of the problem: in this case, different sources of indoor pollution—gas stoves, fireplaces, kerosene heaters, insulation—and the consequences for health.

Indoor pollution is a fairly limited subject for which the evidence is clear. But more complex problems require more evidence. A common fault in argument is generalization based on insufficient evidence. In a 1,000-word paper you could not adequately treat the causes of conflict in the Middle East; you could not develop workable proposals for health-care reform; you could not predict the development of education in the next century. In choosing a subject for a brief paper, determine whether you can produce sufficient evidence to convince a reader who may not agree with you. If not, the subject may be too large for a brief paper.

3. Is the evidence relevant? All the evidence should, of course, contribute to the development of your argument. Sometimes the arguer loses sight of the subject and introduces examples that are wide of the claim. In defending a national health-care plan, one student offered examples of the success of health maintenance organizations, but such organizations, although subsidized by the federal government, were not the structure favored by sponsors of a national health-care plan. The examples were interesting but irrelevant.

Also keep in mind that not all readers will agree on what is relevant. Is the unsavory private life of a politician relevant to his or her performance in office? If you want to prove that a politician is unfit to serve because of his or her private activities, you may first have to convince some members of the audience that private activities are relevant to public service.

4. Are the examples representative? This question emphasizes your responsibility to choose examples that are typical of all the examples you do not use. Suppose you offered Vermont's experience to support your claim that same-sex marriage should be legal. Is the experience of Vermont typical of what is happening or may happen in other states? Or is Vermont, a small, mostly rural New England state, different enough from other states to make the example unrepresentative?

5. Are the examples consistent with the experience of the audience? The members of your audience use their own experiences to judge the soundness of your evidence. If your examples are unfamiliar or extreme, they will probably reject your conclusion. Consider the following excerpt from Jacob Neusner's hypothetical commencement speech, which is meant to represent a faculty member's response to student apathy.

> For years we have created an altogether forgiving world, in which whatever slight effort you gave was all that was demanded. When you did not keep appointments, we made new ones. When your work came in beyond the deadline, we pretended not to care.
>
> Worse still, when you were boring, we acted as if you were saying something important. When you were garrulous and talked to hear yourself talk, we listened as if it mattered. When you tossed on our desks writing upon which you had not labored, we read it and even responded, as though you earned a response. When you were dull, we pretended you were smart. When you were predictable, unimaginative, and routine, we listened as if to new and wonderful things. When you demanded free lunch we served it.

If most members of the audience find that such a description doesn't reflect their own attitudes or those of their friends, they will probably question the validity of the claim.

Evaluation of Statistics

The questions you must ask about examples also apply to statistics. Are they recent? Are they sufficient? Are they relevant? Are they typical? Are they consistent with the experience of the audience? But there are additional questions directed specifically to evaluation of statistics.

1. Do the statistics come from trustworthy sources? Perhaps you have read newspaper accounts of very old people, some reported to be as old as 135, living in the Caucasus or the Andes, nourished by yogurt and hard work. But these statistics are hearsay; no birth records or other official documents exist to verify them. Now two anthropologists have concluded that the numbers were part of a rural mythology and that the ages of the people were actually within the normal range for human populations elsewhere.[10]

Hearsay statistics should be treated with the same skepticism accorded to gossip or rumor. Sampling a population to gather statistical information is a sophisticated science; you should ask whether the reporter of the statistics is qualified and likely to be free of bias. Among the generally reliable sources are polling organizations such as Gallup, Roper, and Louis Harris and agencies of the U.S. government such as the Census Bureau and the Bureau of Labor Statistics. Other qualified sources are well-known research foundations, university centers, and insurance com-

[10] Richard B. Mazess and Sylvia H. Forman, "Longevity and Age Exaggeration in Vilcabamba, Ecuador," *Journal of Gerontology* (1979), pp. 94–98.

panies that prepare actuarial tables. Statistics from underdeveloped countries are less reliable for obvious reasons: lack of funds, lack of trained statisticians, lack of communication and transportation facilities to carry out accurate censuses.

2. Are the terms clearly defined? In an example in Chapter 5, the reference to poverty (p. 123) made clear that any statistics would be meaningless unless we knew exactly how *poverty* was defined by the user. *Unemployment* is another term for which statistics will be difficult to read if the definition varies from one user to another. For example, are seasonal workers employed or unemployed during the off-season? Are part-time workers employed? (In Russia they are unemployed.) Are workers on government projects employed? (During the 1930s they were considered employed by the Germans and unemployed by the Americans.) The more abstract or controversial the term, the greater the necessity for clear definition.

3. Are the comparisons between comparable things? Folk wisdom warns us that we cannot compare apples and oranges. Population statistics for the world's largest city, for example, should indicate the units being compared. Greater London is defined in one way, greater New York in another, and greater Tokyo in still another. The population numbers will mean little unless you can be sure that the same geographical units are being compared.

4. Has any significant information been omitted? *The Plain Truth,* a magazine published by the World-Wide Church of God, advertises itself as follows:

> *The Plain Truth* has now topped 5,000,000 copies per issue. It is now the fastest-growing magazine in the world and one of the widest circulated mass-circulation magazines on earth. Our circulation is now greater than *Newsweek.* New subscribers are coming in at the rate of around 40,000 per week.

What the magazine neglects to mention is that it is *free.* There is no subscription fee, and the magazine is widely distributed in drugstores, supermarkets, and airports. *Newsweek* is sold on newsstands and by subscription. The comparison therefore omits significant information.

Evaluation of Opinions

When you evaluate the reliability of opinions in subjects with which you are not familiar, you will be dealing almost exclusively with opinions of experts. Most of the following questions are directed to an evaluation of authoritative sources. But you can also ask these questions of students or of others with opinions based on their own experience and research. Keep them in mind when doing research on the Web.

1. Is the source of the opinion qualified to give an opinion on the subject? The discussion on credibility in Chapter 1 (pp. 17–21) pointed out that certain achievements by the interpreter of the data—publications, acceptance by colleagues—can tell us something about his or her competence. Although these standards are by no means foolproof (people of outstanding reputations have been known to falsify their data), nevertheless they offer assurance that the source is generally trustworthy. The answers to questions you must ask are not hard to find: Is the source qualified by education? Is the source associated with a reputable institution—a university or a research organization? Is the source credited with having made contributions to the field—books, articles, research studies? Suppose that in writing a paper on organ transplants you came across an article by Peter Medawar. He is identified as follows:

> Sir Peter Medawar, British zoologist, winner of the 1960 Nobel Prize in Physiology or Medicine, for proving that the rejection by the body of foreign organs can be overcome; president of the Royal Society; head of the National Institute for Medical Research in London; a world leader in immunology.

These credentials would suggest to almost any reader that Medawar was a reliable source for information about organ transplants.

If the source is not so clearly identified, you should treat the data with caution. Such advice is especially relevant when you are dealing with popular works about such subjects as miracle diets, formulas for instant wealth, and sightings of monsters and UFOs. Do not use such data until you can verify them from other, more authoritative sources.

In addition, you should question the identity of any source listed as "spokesperson" or "reliable source" or "an unidentified authority." The mass media are especially fond of this type of attribution. Sometimes the sources are people in public life who plant stories anonymously or off the record for purposes they prefer to keep hidden.

Even when the identification is clear and genuine, you should ask if the credentials are relevant to the field in which the authority claims expertise. So specialized are areas of scientific study today that scientists in one field may not be competent to make judgments in another. William Shockley is a distinguished engineer, a Nobel Prize winner for his contribution to the invention of the electronic transistor. But when he made the claim, based on his own research, that blacks are genetically inferior to whites, geneticists accused Shockley of venturing into a field where he was unqualified to make judgments. Similarly, advertisers invite stars from the entertainment world to express opinions about products with which they are probably less familiar than members of their audience. All citizens have the right to express their views, but this does not mean that all views are equally credible or worthy of attention.

2. Is the source biased for or against his or her interpretation? Even authorities who satisfy the criteria for expertise may be guilty of bias. Bias arises as a result of economic reward, religious affiliation, political loyalty, and other interests. The expert may not be aware of the bias; even an expert can fall into the trap of ignoring evidence that contradicts his or her own intellectual preferences. A British psychologist has said:

> The search for meaning in data is bound to involve all of us in distortion to greater or lesser degree. . . . Transgression consists not so much in a clear break with professional ethics, as in an unusually high-handed, extreme or self-deceptive attempt to promote one particular view of reality at the expense of all others.[11]

Before accepting the interpretation of an expert, you should ask: Is there some reason why I should suspect the motives of this particular source?

Consider, for example, an advertisement claiming that sweetened breakfast cereals are nutritious. The advertisement, placed by the manufacturer of the cereal, provides impeccable references from scientific sources to support its claims. But since you are aware of the economic interest of the company in promoting sales, you may wonder if they have reproduced only facts that favor their claims. Are there other facts that might prove the opposite? As a careful researcher you would certainly want to look further for data about the advantages and disadvantages of sugar in our diets.

It is harder to determine bias in the research done by scientists and university members even when the research is funded by companies interested in a favorable review of their products. If you discover that a respected biologist who advocates the use of sugar in baby food receives a consultant's fee from a sugar company, should you conclude that the research is slanted and that the scientist has ignored contrary evidence? Not necessarily. The truth may be that the scientist arrived at conclusions about the use of sugar legitimately through experiments that no other scientist would question. But it would probably occur to you that a critical reader might ask about the connection between the results of the research and the payment by a company that profits from the research. In this case you would be wise to read further to find confirmation or rejection of the claim by other scientists.

The most difficult evaluations concern ideological bias. Early in our lives we learn to discount the special interest that makes a small child brag, "My mother (or father) is the greatest!" Later we become aware that the claims of people who are avowed Democrats or Republicans or supply-side economists or Yankee fans or zealous San Franciscans or joggers must be

[11] Liam Hudson, *The Cult of the Fact* (New York: Harper and Row, 1972), p. 125.

examined somewhat more carefully than those of people who have no special commitment to a cause or a place or an activity. This is not to say that all partisan claims lack support. They may, in fact, be based on the best available support. But whenever special interest is apparent, there is always the danger that an argument will reflect this bias.

3. Has the source bolstered the claim with sufficient and appropriate evidence? An author might claim, "Statistics show that watching violence on television leads to violent behavior in children." But if the author gave no further information—neither statistics nor proof that a cause-effect relation exists between televised violence and violence in children, the critical reader would ask, "What are the numbers? Who compiled them?"

Even those who are reputed to be experts in the subjects they discuss must do more than simply allege that a claim is valid or that the data exist. They must provide facts to support their interpretations.

When Experts Disagree

Authoritative sources can disagree. Such disagreement is probably most common in the social sciences. They are called the "soft" sciences precisely because a consensus about conclusions in these areas is more difficult to arrive at than in the natural and physical sciences. Consider the controversy over what determines the best interests of the child where both biological and foster parents are engaged in trying to secure custody. Experts are deeply divided on this issue. Dr. Daniel J. Cohen, a child psychologist and director of the Yale Child Study Center, argues that the psychological needs of the child should take precedence. If the child has a stable and loving relationship with foster parents, that is where he should stay. But Bruce Bozer and Bernadine Dohrn of the Children and Family Justice Center at Northwestern University Law School insist that "such a solution may be overly simplistic." The child may suffer in later life when he learns that he has been prevented from returning to biological parents "who fought to get him back."[12]

But even in the natural and physical sciences, where the results of observation and experiment are more conclusive, we encounter heated differences of opinion. A popular argument concerns the extinction of the dinosaurs. Was it the effect of an asteroid striking the earth? Or widespread volcanic activity? Or a cooling of the planet? All these theories have their champions among the experts.

Environmental concerns also produce lively disagreements. Scientists have lined up on both sides of a debate about the importance of protecting the tropical rain forest as a source of biological, especially mammalian, diversity. Dr. Edward O. Wilson, a Harvard biologist, whose books

[12]*New York Times,* September 4, 1994, sec. E, p. 3.

have made us familiar with the term *biodiversity,* says, "The great majority of organisms appears to reach maximum diversity in the rain forest. There is no question that the rain forests are the world's headquarters of diversity." But in the journal *Science* another biologist, Dr. Michael Mares, a professor of zoology at the University of Oklahoma, argues that "if one could choose only a single South American habitat in which to preserve the greatest mammalian diversity, it would be the dry lands. . . . The dry lands are very likely far more highly threatened than the largely inaccessible rain forests."[13] A debate of more immediate relevance concerns possible dangers in genetically modified foods, as distinguished from foods modified by traditional breeding practices. Dr. Louis Pribyl, a U.S. Food and Drug Administration microbiologist, has accused the agency of claiming "that there are no unintended effects that raise the FDA's level of concern. But . . . there are no data to back up this contention." On the other hand, Dr. James Marjanski, the FDA's biotechnology coordinator, maintains that "as long as developers of these foods follow agency guidelines, genetically engineered foods are as safe as any on the market."[14]

How can you choose between authorities who disagree? If you have applied the tests discussed so far and discovered that one source is less qualified by training and experience or makes claims with little support or appears to be biased in favor of one interpretation, you will have no difficulty in rejecting that person's opinion. If conflicting sources prove to be equally reliable in all respects, then continue reading other authorities to determine whether a greater number of experts support one opinion rather than another. Although numbers alone, even of experts, don't guarantee the truth, nonexperts have little choice but to accept the authority of the greater number until evidence to the contrary is forthcoming. Finally, if you are unable to decide between competing sources of evidence, you may conclude that the argument must remain unsettled. Such an admission is not a failure; after all, such questions are considered controversial because even the experts cannot agree, and such questions are often the most interesting to consider and argue about.

APPEALS TO NEEDS AND VALUES

Good factual evidence is usually enough to convince an audience that your factual claim is sound. Using examples, statistics, and expert opinion, you can prove, for example, that women do not earn as much as men for the same work. But even good evidence may not be enough to convince your audience that unequal pay is wrong or that something should

[13]*New York Times,* April 7, 1992, sec. C, p. 4.
[14]*New York Times,* December 1, 1999, sec. A, p. 15.

be done about it. In making value and policy claims, an appeal to the needs and values of your audience is absolutely essential to the success of your argument. If you want to persuade the audience to change their minds or adopt a course of action—in this case, to demand legalization of equal pay for equal work—you will have to show that assent to your claim will bring about what they want and care deeply about.

As a writer, you cannot always know who your audience is; it's impossible, for example, to predict exactly who will read a letter you write to a newspaper. Even in the classroom, you have only partial knowledge of your readers. You may not always know or be able to infer what the goals and principles of your audience are. You may not know how they feel about big government, the draft, private school education, feminism, environmental protection, homosexuality, religion, or any of the other subjects you might write about. If the audience concludes that the things you care about are very different from what they care about, if they cannot identify with your goals and principles, they may treat your argument with indifference, even hostility, and finally reject it. But you can hope that decent and reasonable people will share many of the needs and values that underlie your claims.

Appeals to Needs

The most familiar classification of needs was developed by the psychologist Abraham H. Maslow in 1954.[15] These needs, said Maslow, motivate human thought and action. In satisfying our needs, we attain both long- and short-term goals. Because Maslow believed that some needs are more important than others, he arranged them in hierarchical order from the most urgent biological needs to the psychological needs that are related to our roles as members of a society.

PHYSIOLOGICAL NEEDS Basic bodily requirements: food and drink; health; sex

SAFETY NEEDS Security; freedom from harm; order and stability

BELONGINGNESS AND LOVE NEEDS Love within a family and among friends; roots within a group or a community

ESTEEM NEEDS Material success; achievement; power, status, and recognition by others

SELF-ACTUALIZATION NEEDS Fulfillment in realizing one's potential

For most of your arguments you won't have to address the audience's basic physiological needs for nourishment or shelter. The desire for health, however, now receives extraordinary attention. Appeals to buy

[15] *Motivation and Personality* (New York: Harper and Row, 1954), pp. 80–92.

health foods, vitamin supplements, drugs, exercise and diet courses, and health books are all around us. Many of the claims are supported by little or no evidence, but readers are so eager to satisfy the need for good health that they often overlook the lack of facts or authoritative opinion. The desire for physical well-being, however, is not so simple as it seems; it is strongly related to our need for self-esteem and love.

Appeals to our needs to feel safe from harm, to be assured of order and stability in our lives are also common. Insurance companies, politicians who promise to rid our streets of crime, and companies that offer security services all appeal to this profound and nearly universal need. (We say "nearly" because some people are apparently attracted to risk and danger.) At this writing those who monitor terrorist activity are attempting both to arouse fear for our safety and to suggest ways of reducing the dangers that make us fearful.

The last three needs in Maslow's hierarchy are the ones you will find most challenging to appeal to in your arguments. It is clear that these needs arise out of human relationships and participation in society. Advertisers make much use of appeals to these needs.

BELONGINGNESS AND LOVE NEEDS

"Whether you are young or old, the need for companionship is universal." (ad for dating service)

"Share the Fun of High School with Your Little Girl!" (ad for a Barbie Doll)

ESTEEM NEEDS

"Enrich your home with the distinction of an Oxford library."

"Apply your expertise to more challenges and more opportunities. Here are outstanding opportunities for challenge, achievement, and growth." (Perkin-Elmer Co.)

SELF-ACTUALIZATION NEEDS

"Be all that you can be." (former U.S. Army slogan)

"Are you demanding enough? Somewhere beyond the cortex is a small voice whose mere whisper can silence an army of arguments. It goes by many names: integrity, excellence, standards. And it stands alone in final judgment as to whether we have demanded enough of ourselves and, by that example, have inspired the best in those around us." (*New York Times*)

Of course, it is not only advertisers who use these appeals. We hear them from family and friends, from teachers, from employers, from editorials and letters to the editor, from people in public life.

Appeals to Values

Needs give rise to values. If we feel the need to belong to a group, we learn to value commitment, sacrifice, and sharing. And we then respond to arguments that promise to protect our values. It is hardly surprising that values, the principles by which we judge what is good or bad, beautiful or ugly, worthwhile or undesirable, should exercise a profound influence on our behavior. Virtually all claims, even those that seem to be purely factual, contain expressed or unexpressed judgments. When Michael M. Weinstein in Chapter 6 (pp. 162–64) quotes evidence that affirmative action does not promote unqualified candidates, he does so not because he is doing research for academic reasons but because he hopes to persuade people that affirmative action is good social policy.

For our study of argument, we will speak of groups or systems of values because any single value is usually related to others. People and institutions are often defined by such systems of values. We can distinguish, for example, between those who think of themselves as traditional and those who think of themselves as modern by listing their differing values. One writer contrasts such values in this way:

> Among the values of traditionalism are merit, accomplishment, competition, and success; self-restraint, self-discipline, and the postponement of gratification; the stability of the family; and a belief in certain moral universals. The modernist ethos scorns the pursuit of success; is egalitarian and redistributionist in emphasis; tolerates or encourages sensual gratification; values self-expression as against self-restraint; accepts alternative or deviant forms of the family; and emphasizes ethical relativism.[16]

Systems of values are neither so rigid nor so distinct from one another as this list suggests. Some people who are traditional in their advocacy of competition and success may also accept the modernist values of self-expression and alternative family structures. Values, like needs, are arranged in a hierarchy; that is, some are clearly more important than others to the people who hold them. Moreover, the arrangement may shift over time or as a result of new experiences. In 1962, for example, two speech teachers prepared a list of what they called "Relatively Unchanging Values Shared by Most Americans."[17] Included were "puritan and pioneer standards of morality" and "perennial optimism about the future." More than forty-five years later, an appeal to these values might fall on a number of deaf ears.

You should also be aware of not only changes over time but also different or competing value systems that reflect a multitude of subcultures

[16]Joseph Adelson, "What Happened to the Schools," *Commentary,* March 1981, p. 37.

[17]Edward Steele and W. Charles Redding, "The American Value System: Premises for Persuasion," *Western Speech,* 26 (Spring 1962), pp. 83–91.

in the United States. Differences in age, sex, race, ethnic background, social environment, religion, even in the personalities and characters of its members define the groups we belong to. Such terms as *honor, loyalty, justice, patriotism, duty, responsibility, equality, freedom,* and *courage* will be interpreted very differently by different groups.

All of us belong to more than one group, and the values of the several groups may be in conflict. If one group to which you belong—say, peers of your own age and class—is generally uninterested in and even scornful of religion, you may nevertheless hold to the values of your family and continue to place a high value on religious belief.

How can a knowledge of your readers' values enable you to make a more effective appeal? Suppose you want to argue in favor of a sex education program in the middle school you attended. The program you support would not only give students information about contraception and venereal disease but also teach them about the pleasures of sex, the importance of small families, and alternatives to heterosexuality. If the readers of your argument are your classmates or your peers, you can be fairly sure that their agreement will be easier to obtain than that of their parents, especially if their parents think of themselves as conservative. Your peers are more likely to value experimentation, tolerance of alternative sexual practices, freedom, and novelty. Their parents are more likely to value restraint, conformity to conventional sexual practices, obedience to family rules, and foresight in planning for the future.

Knowing that your peers share your values and your goals will mean that you need not spell out the values supporting your claim; they are understood by your readers. Convincing their parents, however, who think that freedom, tolerance, and experimentation have been abused by their children, will be a far more challenging task. In one written piece you have little chance of changing their values, a result that might be achieved only over a longer period of time. So you might first attempt to reduce their hostility by suggesting that, even if a community-wide program were adopted, students would need parental permission to enroll. This might convince some parents that you share their values regarding parental authority and primacy of the family. Second, you might look for other values to which the parents subscribe and to which you can make an appeal. Do they prize maturity, self-reliance, responsibility in their children? If so, you could attempt to prove, with authoritative evidence, that the sex education program would promote these qualities in students who took the course.

But familiarity with the value systems of prospective readers may also lead you to conclude that winning assent to your argument will be impossible. It would probably be fruitless to attempt to persuade a group of lifelong pacifists to endorse the use of nuclear weapons. The beliefs, attitudes, and habits that support their value systems are too fundamental to yield to one or two attempts at persuasion.

EVALUATION OF APPEALS TO NEEDS AND VALUES

If your argument is based on an appeal to the needs and values of your audience, the following questions will help you evaluate the soundness of your appeal.

1. Have the values been clearly defined? If you are appealing to the patriotism of your readers, can you be sure that they agree with your definition? Does patriotism mean "Our country, right or wrong!" or does it mean dissent, even violent dissent, if you think your country is wrong? Because value terms are abstractions, you must make their meaning explicit by placing them in context and providing examples.

2. Are the needs and values to which you appeal prominent in the reader's hierarchy at the time you are writing? An affluent community, fearful of further erosion of quiet and open countryside, might resist an appeal to allow establishment of a high-technology firm, even though the firm would bring increased prosperity to the area.

3. Is the evidence in your argument clearly related to the needs and values to which you appeal? Remember that the reader must see some connection between your evidence and his or her goals. Suppose you were writing an argument to persuade a group of people to vote in an upcoming election. You could provide evidence to prove that only 20 percent of the town voted in the last election. But this evidence would not motivate your audience to vote unless you could provide other evidence to show that their needs were not being served by such a low turnout.

Writer's Guide: Using Effective Support

1. In deciding how much support you need for your claim, it is always a good idea to assume that you are addressing an audience that may be at least slightly hostile to that claim. Those who already agree with you do not need convincing.
2. Keep a mental, if not a written, list of the different types of support you use in an essay. Few essays will use all of the different types of support, but being aware of all the possibilities will prevent you from forgetting to draw on one or more types of support that may advance your argument.
3. In that checklist of types of support, don't forget that there are two main categories: evidence and appeals to needs and values. Appeals to needs and values will generally need the reinforcement that comes from more objective forms of evidence, but the two in combination can often provide the strongest case for your claim. Aristotle explained that in an ideal world, arguers could depend on logic alone, but we live in a world that is far from ideal.

4. Use the following questions about the evaluation of evidence as a checklist to analyze the support you use in your argumentative essays:

Factual evidence:

- Is the evidence up to date?
- Is the evidence sufficient?
- Is the evidence relevant?
- Are the examples representative?
- Are the examples consistent with the experience of the audience?

Statistics:

- Do the statistics come from trustworthy sources?
- Are the terms clearly defined?
- Are the comparisons between comparable things?
- Has any significant information been omitted?

Opinion:

- Is the source of the opinion qualified to give an opinion on the subject?
- Is the source biased for or against his or her interpretation?
- Has the source bolstered the claim with sufficient and appropriate evidence?

5. Also check your essays against the list of questions regarding appeals to needs and values:

- Have the values been clearly defined?
- Are the needs and values to which you appeal prominent in the reader's hierarchy at the time you are writing?
- Is the evidence in your argument clearly related to the needs and values to which you appeal?

PRACTICE

1. Locate two advertisements from magazines or newspapers that appeal to needs or values or both. Be prepared to explain what needs and/or values the ads appeal to.
2. Share your ads with your classmates so that everyone can get an idea of the range of how ads appeal to needs and values.
3. Choose one of the ads your class compiled and write a paragraph analyzing its appeal to needs and/or values.
4. Write an essay in which you compare two ads for the same product or same type of product in terms of the types of appeal that they use.

SAMPLE ANNOTATED ESSAY

Single-Sex Education Benefits Men Too

CLAUDIUS E. WATTS III

Introduction: background of the problem

Last week Virginia Military Institute, an all-male state college, got the good news from a federal judge that it can continue its single-sex program if it opens a leadership program at Mary Baldwin College, a nearby private women's school. But it is likely that the government will appeal the decision. Meanwhile, the Citadel, another such institution in Charleston, S.C., remains under attack. Unwittingly, so are some fundamental beliefs prevalent in our society: namely, the value of single-sex education, the need for diversity in education, and the freedom of choice in associating with, and not associating with, whomever one chooses.

The values that the author will defend

When Shannon Faulkner received a preliminary injunction to attend day classes with the Citadel's Corps of Cadets, she was depicted as a nineteen-year-old woman fighting for her constitutional rights, while the Citadel was painted as an outdated and chauvinistic Southern school that had to be dragged into the twentieth century.

Claim of policy: to preserve single-sex education for men

But the Citadel is not fighting to keep women out of the Corps of Cadets because there is a grandiose level of nineteenth-century machismo to protect. Rather, we at the Citadel are trying to preserve an educational environment that molds young men into grown men of good character, honor, and integrity. It is part of a single-sex educational system that has proven itself successful throughout history.

Support: expert opinion, appeal to values

The benefits of single-sex education for men are clear: Says Harvard sociologist David Riesman, not only is single-sex education an optimal means of character development, but it also removes the dis-

---

Lieutenant General Claudius E. Watts III, retired from the U.S. Air Force, is a former president of the Citadel in South Carolina. This selection is from the May 3, 1995, edition of the *Wall Street Journal*.

tractions of the "mating-dating" game so prevalent in society and enables institutions to focus students on values and academics.

In short, the value of separate education is, 5
simply, the fact it is separate.

Support: statistics

In October 1992, a federal appeals court ruled that "single-sex education is pedagogically justifiable." Indeed, a cursory glance at some notable statistics bears that out. For instance, the Citadel has the highest retention rate for minority students of any public college in South Carolina: 67 percent of black students graduate in four years, which is more than 2½ times the national average. Additionally, the Citadel's four-year graduation rate for all students is 70 percent, which compares with 48 percent nationally for all other public institutions and 67 percent nationally for private institutions. Moreover, many of the students come from modest backgrounds. Clearly, the Citadel is not the bastion of male privilege that the U.S. Justice Department, in briefs filed by that agency, would have us all believe.

Support: facts, statistics

While the Justice Department continues to reject the court's ruling affirming the values of single-sex education, others continue to argue that because the federal military academies are coeducational, so should the Citadel be. However, it is not the Citadel's primary mission to train officers for the U.S. armed forces. We currently commission approximately 30 percent of our graduates, but only 18 percent actually pursue military careers. At the Citadel, the military model is a means to an end, not the end itself.

Support: facts, statistics

Support: causal connection

Today there are eighty-four women's colleges scattered throughout the United States, including two that are public. These colleges defend their programs as necessary to help women overcome intangible barriers in male-dominated professions. This argument has merit; women's colleges produce only 4.5 percent of all female college graduates but have produced one-fourth of all women board members of Fortune 500 companies and one-half of the women in Congress. However, the educational benefits of men's colleges are equally clear; and to allow women alone to benefit from single-sex education seems to perpetuate the very stereotypes that women—including Ms. Faulkner—are trying to correct.

Warrant: men should enjoy the same freedom of choice

If young women want and need to study and learn in single-sex schools, why is it automatically wrong for young men to want and need the same? Where is the fairness in this assumption?

Support: causal connection

10 "At what point does the insistence that one individual not be deprived of choice spill over into depriving countless individuals of choice?" asks Emory University's Elizabeth Fox Genovese in an article by Jeffrey Rosen published in the February 14 *New Republic*.

Support: appeal to values

Yet so it is at the Citadel. While one student maintains that she is protecting her freedom to associate, we mustn't forget that the Citadel's cadets also have a freedom—the freedom not to associate. While we have read about one female student's rights, what hasn't been addressed are the rights of the 1,900 cadets who chose the Citadel—and the accompanying discipline and drill—because it offered them the single-sex educational experience they wanted. Why do one student's rights supersede all theirs?

Support: predictions about the future

One might be easily tempted to argue on the grounds that Ms. Faulkner is a taxpayer and the Citadel is a tax-supported institution. But if the taxpayer argument holds, the next step is to forbid all public support for institutions that enroll students of only one sex. A draconian measure such as this would surely mean the end of private—as well as public—single-gender colleges.

Backing for warrant: tax-supported education should be equal for men and women

Most private colleges—Columbia and Converse, the two all-female schools in South Carolina, included—could not survive without federal financial aid, tax exemptions, and state tax support in the form of tuition grants. In fact, nearly 900 of Columbia and Converse's female students receive state-funded tuition grants, a student population that is almost half the size of the Corps of Cadets. In essence, South Carolina's two private women's colleges may stand or fall with the Citadel.

Carried to its logical conclusion, then, the effort to coeducate the Citadel might mean the end of all single-sex education—for women as well as men, in private as well as public schools.

■ Analysis: Support

In 1993 Shannon Faulkner, a woman, was rejected for admission to the Citadel, an all-male state-supported military academy in South Carolina. In 1995, after a long court battle, she was admitted but resigned after a week of physical and emotional stress. The Court was asked to decide if an education equal to that of the Citadel could be provided for women at a nearby school.

Claudius Watts III tackles a subject that is no longer controversial in regard to women's colleges: the virtues of single-sex education. But in this essay he argues that colleges for men only deserve the same right as women's colleges to exclude the opposite sex.

The author has taken care in the limited space available to cover all the arguments that had emerged in the case of Shannon Faulkner. At the end of the opening paragraph he lays out the three ideas he will develop—the value of single-sex education, the need for diversity in education, and freedom of choice. In paragraphs 3 through 6 he supports his case for the benefits of separate education by first quoting a prominent sociologist and then offering statistics to prove that the male Citadel population is both diverse and successful. In paragraph 7 he refutes a popular analogy—that since the service academies, like West Point and the Naval Academy, admit women, so should the Citadel. The goals of the Citadel, he says, are broader than those of the service academies. But he does more. In paragraph 8 he provides data that women's colleges produce successful graduates. This reinforces his claim that separate education has advantages over coed schooling. Perhaps it also helps to make friends of opponents who might otherwise be hostile to arguments favoring male privileges.

Notice the transition in paragraph 10. This leads the author to the defense of his last point, the far more elusive concept of freedom of choice and the rights of individuals, ideas whose validity cannot be measured in numbers. He introduces this part of his argument by quoting the words of a supporter of single-sex education, a woman professor at Emory University. He makes a strong appeal to the reader's sense of fairness and belief in the rights of the majority, represented here by the male students at the Citadel. There is also an obvious appeal to fear, an implied threat of the danger to women's colleges, in the next-to-last sentence of the essay. Finally, he invokes logic. If single-sex education cannot be defended for males, neither can it be defended for females. He assumes that against logic there can be no real defense.

Some leading advocates for women's rights have, in fact, agreed with General Watts's arguments for that reason. But those who supported both Shannon Faulkner's admission to the Citadel and the sanctity of women's colleges will claim that women, as a disadvantaged group, deserve special consideration, while men do not. (One writer even insisted that the Citadel *needed* women as a civilizing influence.) General Watts's argument, however, went some distance toward reopening the dialogue.

SAMPLE ANALYSIS

At times, assignments may ask you to analyze or evaluate the evidence and appeals to needs and values offered in support of a claim. At other times, you will have to discover your own support for use in an argument that you are writing. After the following essay about sport utility vehicles and its reading and discussion questions, you will first find an example of an essay of the type you might write if you were asked to evaluate an author's use of support. It is followed by a student essay that illustrates effective use of support.

The True Costs of SUVs

HAL R. VARIAN

Traffic fatalities in the United States fell steadily from 54,600 in 1972 to 34,900 in 1992. But then they started to rise again, and by 2002 there were 38,300 traffic deaths a year.

Our performance compared with other countries has also deteriorated. America's ranking has fallen from first to ninth over the last thirty years, with Australia, Britain, and Canada all having better records.

A big part of the difference between the United States and other countries seems to be the prevalence of sport utility vehicles and pickups on American highways. Sales of light trucks—SUVs, pickups, and minivans—were about a fifth of total automobile sales thirty years ago. Now they account for more than half.

But aren't large vehicles supposed to be safer than small cars? Yes, they are safer for their occupants in collisions, but their design makes them all the more dangerous for anyone they hit.

Michelle White, an economist at the University of California, San 5
Diego, estimates that for each fatality that light-truck drivers avoid for themselves and their passengers, they cause four fatalities involving car occupants, pedestrians, bicyclists, and motorcyclists. "Safety gains for those driving light trucks," Ms. White said, "come at an extremely high cost to others."

Being larger than ordinary vehicles, SUVs and light trucks cause more damage to upper bodies and heads in collisions. Furthermore, their bumpers

---

A professor in the School of Information Management and Systems at the University of California at Berkeley, Hal R. Varian has written economics textbooks as well as columns for the *New York Times*. This piece appeared in the *Times* as the "Economic Scene" article on December 18, 2003.

do not always align with automobile bumpers, and their body structure is stiffer, transferring more force to other vehicles during impact.

A few weeks ago, the auto industry announced a voluntary plan to deal with some of these design problems. They intend to make side-impact airbags standard to help protect heads and upper bodies better in collisions, and they intend to standardize bumper heights.

These will no doubt be helpful improvements, but do they go far enough?

Recently Ms. White examined the econometrics of traffic accidents in an attempt to measure the benefits and costs of changing the number of light trucks on the road. . . .

10 Ms. White notes that changing average vehicle size could, in principle, increase or decrease the cost of accidents.

Suppose the cost of a small vehicle–large vehicle collision is $50, the cost of a small vehicle–small vehicle collision is $45, and the cost of a large vehicle–large vehicle collision is $40.

If all vehicles are small, and there are 10 accidents a year, the total cost of the accidents is $450. But if 10 percent of the small vehicles are replaced by large ones, the average cost of collisions becomes $458.50, since more collisions will be between large and small vehicles. On the other hand, if

The results of an accident in New York involving a sport utility vehicle and a smaller car. Traffic fatalities are on the rise, apparently linked to the increase of SUVs.

G. Paul Burnett/*New York Times*

60 percent of the vehicles on the road are large, the average cost of a collision is only $456, since more collisions are between large vehicles.

Think about a safety-conscious soccer mom choosing a vehicle. If there are mostly small cars in her town, she can reduce the risk to her and her family in the event of a collision by buying an SUV.

The unfortunate side effect is that the large SUV would cause significant damage to smaller cars if she was involved in an accident.

The laudable private incentive to choose a safe vehicle could, per- 15
versely, reduce overall safety.

In addition, Ms. White finds that people involved in single-vehicle crashes are more likely to be killed or seriously injured if they are in SUVs or light trucks rather than cars. This may be a result of the increased likelihood of rollovers.

On the other hand, suppose everybody in town drives an SUV. Then the soccer mom will definitely want to purchase one for herself, since it would both increase her family's safety and reduce the overall costs of collisions.

In this case, private incentives and social incentives are aligned.

The dynamics involved is the same as that of an arms race: If other families buy bigger vehicles, then you will want to as well, if only in self-defense.

To see where we are in this arms race, Ms. White examined crash data 20
maintained by the National Highway Safety Administration. . . .

Using this data, Ms. White was able to estimate how the probability of fatalities or serious injury varied with the types of vehicles involved in collisions.

For example, in a two-car accident, the probability of a fatality in the car is 38 percent less than in a car–light truck accident. However, in car–light truck accidents, the probability of fatalities in the light truck is 55 percent less than it would be in a truck–truck accident.

If a light truck hits a pedestrian or a cyclist, the probability of fatalities is about 82 percent greater than if a car is involved.

Ms. White then asked what the impact would be of replacing a million light trucks with cars. She considered two models for driver behavior. In the first, she assumed that the former drivers of light trucks would have the same number of accidents as they did when driving trucks. In the second, she assumed that the former drivers of light trucks would have the same accident probabilities as other car drivers.

Using conventional methods for value-of-life calculations, she finds 25
that each light-truck owner who switches to a car saves about $447 in total expected costs of accidents.

Ms. White examines various policies that might persuade drivers to adopt such changes, including changes in liability rules, traffic rules, and insurance rules.

Unfortunately, each of these policies has its problems, so there are no easy solutions.

One interesting way to reduce the arms race problem would be to link automobile liability insurance to gasoline taxes. This means drivers whose cars use more gasoline and those who drive a lot would pay more for their insurance—not unreasonable, since, on average, they impose more costs in accidents.

Aaron Edlin, a professor of economics and law at the University of California, Berkeley, has argued that such "pay at the pump" insurance premiums would have many other benefits (www.bepress.com/aaronedlin/contribution5/). So this type of payment scheme is worth considering for a variety of reasons.

READING AND DISCUSSION QUESTIONS

1. For the purposes of his article, how is Varian defining *light truck*?
2. What relationship does he see between light trucks and the number of traffic fatalities?
3. What type of support does Varian use in the three opening paragraphs? Does he use that type of support anywhere else in the essay?
4. What other types of support does Varian make use of in his essay? What types of support do you find most effective in making his argument? What types do you find least effective?
5. What claim is Varian supporting in the essay?
6. How does Varian document his sources? How does he try to establish that his sources are reliable?

The True Confusion about SUV Costs

BETHANY ROYCE

Hal R. Varian entitled his December 18, 2003, *New York Times* piece on sport utility vehicles "The True Costs of SUVs." A more accurate title might have been "The Confusing Costs of SUVs." While Varian turns to the right type of support for his subject—statistics—his use of that support is more confusing than enlightening.

Varian made a wise choice in appealing to his readers' need to feel safe and secure. His statistics are most appealing when he points out that for twenty years the number of traffic fatalities in our country went down and that parents can feel secure knowing that they can make their children safer by buying light trucks (SUVs, pickups, or minivans) instead of cars. In each

Bethany Royce teaches business courses and introductory economics at a two-year college in Florida and writes a consumer advice column for a local newspaper.

case, however, there is a negative side. The number of fatalities started rising again between 1992 and 2002, in part because of the increase in the number of sales of light trucks during that time. And Varian tells us that in making their families safer by buying light trucks, they are increasing the risk of doing more harm to others should they be involved in accidents.

For the rest of his support, Varian draws primarily on research done by Michelle White, whom he identifies only as "an economist at the University of California, San Diego" (238). She may have done excellent work, but the way that Varian explains it is confusing and unconvincing. White tries to predict how the cost of accidents would change depending on the size of the vehicles involved. Instead of using realistic cost estimates, however, she arbitrarily assigns the cost of $50 to a small vehicle–large vehicle collision, the cost of $45 to a small vehicle–small vehicle collision, and the cost of $40 to a large vehicle–large vehicle collision. Varian summarizes what this hypothetical scenario reveals:

> If all vehicles are small, and there are 10 accidents a year, the total cost of the accidents is $450. But if 10 percent of the small vehicles are replaced by large ones, the average cost of collisions becomes $458.50, since more collisions will be between large and small vehicles. On the other hand, if 60 percent of the vehicles on the road are large, the average cost of a collision is only $456, since more collisions are between large vehicles. (239–40)

Average Americans are left wondering what all of this means to them. The hypothetical situation cannot be easily applied to any individual driver and certainly not to any specific accident. How should a reader evaluate the information in attempting to make the decision regarding what size vehicle to buy? The driver who just paid $3000 in car repairs is going to find any of the numbers Varian cites attractive.

There are a lot of "ifs" in Varian's argument. If you live in a town with lots of SUVs, it is safer to drive one yourself. If you live in a town where there are few SUVs, you should drive a car so that you would not be as likely to hurt someone else in a wreck. If you have a single-vehicle accident in an SUV, you are more likely to be killed. If you hit a pedestrian while driving one, you are more likely to kill that person.

There are also few clear conclusions to be drawn from the support 5
that Varian offers. After Ms. White examines "various policies that might persuade drivers to adopt such changes, including changes in liability rules, traffic rules, and insurance rates," the unfortunate conclusion is that "each of these policies has its problems, so there are no easy solutions" (240). The only solution that Varian advances as "worth considering" is one by a colleague of his at the University of California, Berkeley, that would link a vehicle owner's liability insurance to gas taxes (241). Overall the article succeeds more in revealing the complexities involved in the increased use of SUVs than in clarifying any of those complexities.

STUDENT ESSAY

Safer? Tastier? More Nutritious? The Dubious Merits of Organic Foods

KRISTEN WEINACKER

Organic foods are attractive to some consumers because of the principles behind them and the farming techniques used to produce them. There is a special respect for organic farmers who strive to maintain the ecological balance and harmony that exist among living things. As these farmers work in partnership with nature, some consumers too feel a certain attachment to the earth (Wolf 1–2). They feel happier knowing that these foods are produced without chemical fertilizers, pesticides, and additives to extend their shelf life (Pickerell; Agricultural Extension Service 5). They feel that they have returned to nature by eating organic foods that are advertised as being healthy for maintaining a vigorous lifestyle. Unfortunately, research has not provided statistical evidence that organic foods are more nutritious than conventionally grown ones.

The debate over the nutritional benefits has raged for decades. Defenders of the nutritional value of organic foods have employed excellent marketing and sales strategies. First, they freely share the philosophy behind their farming and follow up with detailed descriptions of their management techniques. Second, organic farmers skillfully appeal to our common sense. It seems reasonable to believe that organic foods are more nutritious since they are grown without chemical fertilizers and pesticides. Third, since the soil in which these crops are grown is so rich and healthy, it seems plausible that these crops have absorbed and developed better nutrients. As Lynda Brown asserts in her book *Living Organic*, "Organic farmers believe that growing crops organically provides the best possible way to produce healthy food" (26). Brown provides beautifully illustrated and enlarged microscopic photographs to show the more developed structure of organic foods compared to conventional products to convince the consumer to believe that organic foods are more nutritious (27). Fourth, many consumers view the higher price tags on organic foods and assume that they must be more nutritious. Generalizations permeate the whole world of organic foods. These marketing strategies persuade the consumer that organic foods are healthier than conventional foods without providing any factual comparisons.

At the time she wrote this essay, Kristen Weinacker was an undergraduate at Clemson University.

In their book *Is Our Food Safe?* Warren Leon and Caroline Smith Dewaal compare organic and conventionally produced foods. They strongly suggest that consumers buy organic foods to help the environment (68). They believe that organic foods are healthier than conventional ones. However, statistics supporting this belief are not provided. The authors even warn consumers that they need to read product labels because some organic foods may be as unhealthy as conventional ones (68–69). An interesting poll involving 1,041 adults was conducted by ABC News asking, “Why do people buy organic?” Analyst Daniel Merkle concluded that 45% of the American public *believes* that organic products are more nutritious than conventionally grown ones. Also, 57% of the population maintains that organic farming is beneficial for the environment. According to the pollsters, the primary reason why people bought organic foods is the belief that they are healthier because they have less pesticide residue. However, there has never been any link established between the nutritional value of organic foods and the residue found on them. Clever marketing strategies have made the need for concrete data really not of prime importance for the consumer to join the bandwagon promoting organic foods.

This pervasive belief among the American public that organic foods are probably healthier than conventionally grown foods was reiterated in my telephone interview with Mr. Joseph Williamson, an agricultural county extension agent working with Clemson University. When asked if organically grown foods are more nutritious than those grown conventionally, he replied that they probably were for two reasons. First, organic crops tend to grow more slowly. Therefore, the nutrients have more time to build up in the plants. Second, organic plants are usually grown locally. The fruits and vegetables are allowed to stay on the plants for a longer period of time. They ripen more than those picked green and transported across miles. He contends that these conditions promote a better nutrient buildup. Unfortunately, the extension agent acknowledges that statistical evidence is not available to support the claim that organic products are more nutritious.

An article entitled “Effects of Agricultural Methods in Nutritional 5
Quality: A Comparison of Organic with Conventional Crops” reports on conclusions drawn by Dr. Virginia Worthington, a certified nutrition specialist. Worthington examines why it is so difficult to ascertain if organic foods are more nutritious. First, “the difference in terms of health effects is not large enough to be readily apparent.” There is no concrete evidence that people are healthier eating organic foods or, conversely, that people become more ill eating conventionally grown produce. Second, Dr. Worthington notes that variables such as sunlight, temperature, and amount of rain are so inconsistent that the nutrients in crops vary yearly. Third, she points out that the nutrient value of products can be changed by the way products are stored and shipped. After reviewing at least thirty

studies dealing with the question if organic foods are more nutritious than conventionally grown ones, Dr. Worthington concludes that there is too little data available to substantiate the claim of higher nutritional value in organic foods. She also believes that it is an impossible task to make a direct connection between organic foods and the health of those people who consume them.

After being asked for thirty years about organic foods by her readers and associates, Joan Dye Gussow, writer for *Eating Well* magazine, firmly concludes that there is "little hard proof that organically grown produce is reliably more nutritious." Reviewing seventy years' worth of studies on the subject, Gussow has no doubt that organic foods should be healthier because of the way they are produced and cultivated. Gussow brings up an interesting point about chemical and pesticide residue. She believes that the fact that organic foods have been found to have fewer residues does not make them automatically more nutritious and healthier for the consumer. As scientific technologies advance, Gussow predicts that research will someday discover statistical data that will prove that organic foods have a higher nutritional value compared to conventionally grown ones.

In order to provide the public with more information about the nature of organic foods, the well-known and highly regarded magazine *Consumer Reports* decided to take a closer look at organic foods in their January 1998 magazine, in an article entitled "Organic Foods: Safer? Tastier? More nutritious?" By conducting comparison tests, their researchers discovered that organic foods have less pesticide residue, and that their flavors are just about the same as conventionally grown foods. These scientists came to the conclusion that the "variability within a given crop is greater than the variability between one cropping system and another." *Consumer Reports* contacted Professor Willie Lockeretz from the Tufts University School of Nutrition Science and Policy. He told researchers that "the growing system you use probably does affect nutrition. . . . But it does it in ways so complex you might be studying the problem forever." Keeping in mind these comments made by Dr. Lockeretz, *Consumer Reports* believes it would be an impossible task to compare the nutritional values of organic and conventional foods. Therefore, researchers at *Consumer Reports* decided not to carry out that part of their comparison testing.

Although statistical evidence is not available at this time to support the claim that organic foods are more nutritious than conventionally grown ones, there is a very strong feeling shared by a majority of the general public that they are. We are called back to nature as we observe the love that organic farmers have for the soil and their desire to work in partnership with nature. We are easily lured to the attractive displays of organic foods in the grocery stores. However, we must keep in mind the successful marketing techniques that have been used to convince us that organic foods are more nutritious than conventionally grown ones. Although common sense tells us that organic foods should be more nutritious, research has not provided us with any statistical data to prove this claim.

Works Cited

Agricultural Extension Service. *Organic Vegetable Gardening*. The University of Tennessee. PB 1391.

Brown, Lynda. *Organic Living*. New York: Dorling Kindersley Publishing, Inc., 2000.

Gussow, Joan Dye. "Is Organic Food More Nutritious?" *Eating Well* (May/June 1997). 27 March 2003. <http://www.prnac.net/rodmap-nutrition.html>.

"Effect of Agricultural Methods on Nutritional Quality: A Comparison of Organic with Conventional Crops." *Alternative Therapies* 4 (1998): 58–69. 18 Feb. 2003. <http://www.purefood.org/healthier101101.cfm>.

Leon, Warren, and Caroline Smith DeWaal. *Is Our Food Safe?* New York: Three Rivers Press, 2002.

Merkle, Daniel. "Why Do People Buy Organic?" ABCNews.com. 3 Feb. 2000. 27 March 2003.

"Organic Foods: Safer? Tastier? More Nutritious?" *Consumer Reports*. Jan. 1998. 24 Feb. 2003. <http://www.consumerreports.org/main/detailsv2.jsp?content%3%ecnt_id+18959&f>.

Pickrell, John. "Federal Government Launches Organic Standards." *Science News* 162.17 (Nov. 2002). <http://www.sciencenews.org/20021102/food.asp._17_March 2003>.

Williamson, Joseph. Telephone interview. 28 Feb. 2003.

Wolf, Ray, ed. *Organic Farming: Yesterday's and Tomorrow's Agriculture*. Philadelphia: Rodale Press, 1977.

READINGS FOR ANALYSIS

Connecting the Dots . . . to Terrorism

BERNARD GOLDBERG

Most of the time television is nothing more than a diversion—proof, as the old quip goes, that we would rather do anything than talk to each other. We'd also rather watch a bad sitcom than read a good book. Bad sitcoms get millions of viewers; good books get thousands. In an "entertainment culture," even the news is entertainment. Certainly too much local news has been pure fluff for some time now, with their Ken and Barbie anchors who have nothing intelligent to say but look great

---

Bernard Goldberg was a reporter and producer for CBS for more than thirty years. He has won seven Emmy awards and was once rated by *TV Guide* as one of the ten most interesting people on television. This chapter is from his 2002 book *Bias: A CBS Insider Exposes How the Media Distort the News*, written after he left the network.

while they're saying it. And because network news is losing viewers every year, executives and producers are trying to figure out ways to hold on to the ones they still have. They think cosmetics will work, so they change the anchor desk or they change the graphics. They get the anchor to stand instead of sit. They feature more "news you can use." They put Chandra Levy[18] on all over the place, hoping they can concoct a ratings cocktail by mixing one part missing intern with ten parts sex scandal.

And then something genuinely big and really important happens that shakes us to our core, and all those producers who couldn't get enough of Chandra are through with her. Only in the fickle world of television news can someone who has disappeared without a trace disappear a second time.

And it's when that history-making story comes along that Americans—no matter what their politics, religion, age, race, or sex—turn to television, not just for information, but also for comfort and for peace of mind. It doesn't happen often, but when it does, television becomes a lot more than just a diversion.

It happened when John Kennedy was assassinated. We all turned to Walter Cronkite and Huntley and Brinkley, not just for facts, but also for reassurance—that despite the terrible tragedy, America was going to be okay.

5 It happened when *Challenger* blew up. And it happened again on September 11, 2001, when a band of religious lunatics declared war on the United States of America to punish us for not wanting to dwell in the fourteenth century, where they currently reside, and, of course, to show the world that their intense hatred of Israel—*and of Israel's friends*—knows no bounds. On September 11, they not only killed as many innocent Americans as they could in the most dramatic way they knew how, but, as the *Wall Street Journal* put it, they also "wiped out any remaining illusions that America is safe from mass organized violence."

On that day we all turned to television. We turned to Dan Rather and Peter Jennings and Tom Brokaw and the others. And they did a fine job, as they often do when covering tragedy. They showed empathy. They were fair and accurate, and the information they passed along to us wasn't filtered through the usual liberal political and social sensibilities. They gave us the news on that day the way they should give us the news *all the time*, whether the story is about race or feminism or taxes or gay rights or anything else. *For a change, they gave it to us straight.*

On the night of September 11, 2001, Peter Jennings made a point about how, in times of danger and tragedy, television serves the function that campfires used to serve in the old days when Americans migrated westward in covered wagons. Back then, they would sit around the campfire and get the news from other travelers about what they should look

[18] *Chandra Levy*: A government intern whose disappearance was widely covered in the press in 2001. —EDS.

out for down the road. "Some people pulled the wagons around," Peter said, "and discussed what was going on and tried to understand it." But the campfire was more than just a meeting place where families could pick up important information. The campfire also provided a sense of community, a sense that *we're all in this together*. That's what television was on September 11.

As I listened to Peter tell that story, I thought about another American tragedy that shocked us six years earlier, when Timothy McVeigh—another true believer who cared nothing about killing innocent Americans—blew up the federal building in Oklahoma City. I thought about how it took some of the media elites only a few days before they started to play one of their favorite games—connect the dots. What they found back then—or more accurately, what they convinced themselves they found—was a line stretching from Oklahoma City to the Republican Party to conservatives in general and finally to Rush Limbaugh.

Dan Rather said, "Even after Oklahoma City, you can turn on your radio in any city and still dial up hate talk: extremist, racist, and violent from the hosts and those who call in."

Time senior writer Richard Lacayo put it this way: "In a nation that 10
has entertained and appalled itself for years with hot talk on radio and the campaign trail, the inflamed rhetoric of the '90s is suddenly an unindicted coconspirator in the blast."

Nina Easton wrote in the *Los Angeles Times*, "The Oklahoma City attack on federal workers and their children also alters the once-easy dynamic between charismatic talk show host and adoring audience. Hosts who routinely espouse the same antigovernment themes as the militia movement now must walk a fine line between inspiring their audience—and inciting the most radical among them."

On *Face the Nation*, Bob Schieffer asked this question: "Mr. Panetta, there's been a lot of antigovernment rhetoric, it comes over talk radio, it comes from various quarters. Do you think that that somehow has led these people to commit this act, do they feed on that kind of rhetoric, and what impact do you think it had?"

Carl Rowan, the late columnist, was quoted in a *Washington Post* story saying that, "Unless Gingrich and Dole[19] and the Republicans say 'Am I inflaming a bunch of nuts?' you know we're going to have some more events. I am absolutely certain the harsher rhetoric of the Gingriches and the Doles . . . creates a climate of violence in America."

And David Broder had this to say in the *Washington Post*: "The bombing shows how dangerous it really is to inflame twisted minds with statements that suggest political opponents are enemies. For two years, Rush

[19] *Gingrich and Dole*: Newt Gingrich (b. 1943) was Speaker of the House of Representatives from 1995 to 1999. Robert Dole (b. 1923) was a Senate majority leader and served in the Senate from 1968 to 1996. —EDS.

Limbaugh described this nation as 'America held hostage' to the policies of the liberal Democrats, as if the duly elected president and Congress were equivalent to the regime in Tehran. I think there will be less tolerance and fewer cheers for that kind of rhetoric."

The message was clear: Conservative talk radio and conservative politicians created an antigovernment atmosphere in America that spawned Timothy McVeigh and therefore were at least partially to blame for his terrorism. It's true, of course, that the atmosphere in which we live contributes to everything that happens in our culture. Calling people "kikes" or "niggers" makes it easier to see them as less than human and to treat them as something less than human. But to point fingers at talk radio for somehow encouraging Timothy McVeigh strikes me as a stretch at best; more likely it's just another opportunity for liberal journalists to blame conservatives for one more evil. And if this kind of connecting the dots is fair game, then should we also accuse Americans who spoke out loudly and forcefully against the war in Vietnam—including many journalists—of contributing to the 1972 bombing of the Pentagon and to other sometimes deadly terrorism, perpetuated by fanatics on the Left? According to the media elites' rulebook, when liberals rant it's called free speech; when conservatives rant it's called incitement to terrorism.

As I watched the coverage of the attacks on the Pentagon and the World Trade Center, I wondered why I hadn't seen more stories on television news, long before these zealots flew their hijacked planes into American buildings, about the culture of anti-American hate that permeates so much of the Middle East—stories that might help explain how little Arab children can grow up to become fanatical suicide bombers.

If the media found it so important to discuss the malignant atmosphere created by "hot" conservative talk radio, then why didn't they find it important to delve into this malignant atmosphere that seems to have bred such maniacal killers? Why would journalists, so interested in connecting the dots when they thought they led to Rush Limbaugh, be so uninterested in connecting the dots when there might actually be dots to connect—*from hateful, widely held popular attitudes in much of the Arab world straight to the cockpits of those hijacked jetliners?*

One of the networks put an American Muslim woman on the news who said that no one blamed Christianity when McVeigh killed all those people. Why blame Islam now? The reporter interviewing this woman let her have her say, never bothering to point out that Timothy McVeigh didn't kill all those people in the name of Christianity. Suicide airplane hijackers, on the other hand, are people who actually believe their murderous acts will earn them a one-way ticket to Paradise.

Was what happened on September 11 a subversion of Islam, as pundits and journalists on network and cable TV told us over and over again? Or was it the result of an *honest* reading of the Koran? It's true, of course, that if taken too literally by uncritical minds, just about any holy book can lead to bad things. Still, why are there no Christian suicide bombers, or Jewish suicide bombers, or Hindu suicide bombers, or Buddhist suicide bombers, but no apparent shortage of Muslim suicide bombers? If Islam is "a religion of peace" as so many people from President Bush on down were telling us (and, for what it's worth, I'm prepared to believe that it is), then what exactly is it in the Koran that so appeals to these Islamic fanatics? Don't look for that answer on the network news. A *Lexis-Nexis* search going back to 1991 linking the words "Koran" and "terrorist" produced absolutely nothing that told us what the Koran actually says which *might* encourage a Muslim, no matter how misguided, to commit acts of terrorism.

20 I understand that even to ask questions about a possible connection between Islam and violence is to tread into politically incorrect terrain. But it seems to me that the media need to go there anyway. And any network that can put thousands of stories on the air about sex and murder should be able to give us a few on the atmosphere that breeds religious zealotry. It might have helped us see what was coming on September 11.

In fact, I learned much more about the atmosphere that breeds suicide bombers from one short article in *Commentary* magazine than I have from watching twenty years of network television news. In its September 2001 issue (which came out before the attack on America), there was an article by Fiamma Nirenstein, an Italian journalist based in Israel, entitled "How Suicide Bombers Are Made." In it, she tells about a "river of hatred" that runs through not just the most radical of Arab nations but also much of what we like to think of as the "moderate" Arab world.

She tells us about a series of articles that ran in the leading government-sponsored newspaper in Egypt, *Al Ahram*, about how Jews supposedly use the blood of Christians to make matzah for Passover.

She tells us about a hit song in Cairo, Damascus, and the West Bank with the catchy title "I Hate Israel."

Why didn't I know this? A computer check soon answered my question. On television, only CNN reported the "I Hate Israel" story. On radio, NPR did a piece. So did the *Christian Science Monitor* and the *Chicago Tribune*. The *Los Angeles Times* ran a short wire service story that said "'I Hate Israel' . . . made an overnight singing sensation of a working-class crooner."

25 Can you imagine if the big hit song in Israel was "I Hate Palestine" or "I Hate Arabs"? The *New York Times* would have put the story on page one and then run an editorial just to make sure we all got the message—that the song is indecent and contributes to an atmosphere of hate. And since the *Times* sets the agenda for the networks, Dan Rather, Tom Brokaw, and Peter Jennings would have all fallen into line and run big stories on their evening newscasts, too, saying the exact same thing. A week later, Mike Wallace would have landed in Tel Aviv looking absolutely mortified that those Jews would do such a thing.

And that's part of the problem. Despite the liberalism of the media, there is a subtle form of racism at work here. As Fiamma Nirenstein writes, "The Arabs, it is implicitly suggested, are a backward people, not to be held to civilized standards of the West." Of the Israelis, however, the American media expect much more. That is why a song called "I Hate Israel" becomes a big hit, and yet is not a news story. And it is why a series of stories in a government-sponsored newspaper—in a supposedly moderate country—about Jews killing Christians for their blood holds almost no interest for American journalists.

It's true that not long after the twin towers of the World Trade Center came tumbling down, the networks showed us pictures of Palestinians in East Jerusalem honking their horns, firing their guns into the air, and generally having a good old time celebrating the death of so many Americans in New York and Washington. They cheered "God is great" while they handed out candy, which is a tradition in the Arab world when something good happens.

It's not that there's been a total news blackout of anti-American hate in the Middle East—*Nightline* has done some good, intelligent work in this area—it's just that we need more than pictures of happy Palestinians reveling in the death of thousands of Americans. And we need more than what has become a staple of Middle East television news coverage: young children throwing stones at Israeli soldiers—the perfect made-for-television David and Goliath story. What we need are stories that connect the dots, not just back to Afghanistan and its backward and repressive Taliban government, but also between the fanatics in New York and Washington and a cultural environment in the Arab world where even "moderates" hand out candy to celebrate the massacre of Americans.

But here the media—apparently feeling squeamish about stories that put the "underdogs" in a bad light—keep us virtually in the dark. And it's not just little tidbits like "I Hate Israel" and articles about Jews taking Christian blood that I—and almost all Americans—knew nothing about. Here's a quick rundown of what goes on in much of the Middle East as reported by Ms. Nirenstein in *Commentary*—news that is virtually ignored on the big American TV networks:

> In Egypt and Jordan, news sources have repeatedly warned that Israel has distributed drug-laced chewing gum and candy, intended (it is said) to kill children and make women sexually corrupt. . . .
>
> [Palestinian television] recently asserted that, far from being extermination camps, Chelmo, Dachau, and Auschwitz were in fact mere "places of disinfection."
>
> On April 13—observed in Israel as Holocaust Remembrance Day—the official Palestinian newspaper *Al-Hayat al-Jadida* featured a column . . . entitled "The Fable of the Holocaust."

> A columnist in Egypt's government-sponsored Al-Akhbar thus expressed his "thanks to Hitler, of blessed memory, who on behalf of the Palestinians took revenge in advance on the most vile criminals on the face of the earth. Still, we do have a complaint against [Hitler], for his revenge on them was not enough."

In addition to these examples, Ms. Nirenstein cites a textbook for Syr- 30
ian tenth graders which teaches them that "the logic of justice obligates the application of the single verdict [on the Jews] from which there is no escape: namely, that their criminal intentions be turned against them and that they be exterminated." And she notes that in June 2001, two weeks after the fatal collapse of a Jewish wedding hall in Jerusalem, Palestinian television broadcast a sermon by a Muslim imam praying that "this oppressive Knesset [Israel's parliament] will [similarly] collapse over the heads of the Jews."

I did not know any of that because it's simply not the kind of news that we normally get from the Middle East—certainly not from network evening newscasts or from *Dateline, 20/20,* or *48 Hours,* three news magazine programs that are usually too busy peddling the trivial and sensational to bother with more significant stories. And besides, that kind of news makes liberal journalists uneasy. After all, these are the same people who bend over backwards to find "moral equivalence" between Palestinian terrorists who blow up discos in Tel Aviv filled with teenagers, on the one hand, and Israeli commandos who *preemptively* kill terrorist ringleaders *before* they send their suicide bombers into Israel on a mission to kill Jews, on the other.

On September 11, right after the networks showed us the pictures of Palestinians celebrating American deaths, they also showed us Yasser Arafat expressing his condolences and giving blood for the American victims. This, in its way, represented a kind of moral equivalence: while some Palestinians celebrate, the news anchors were suggesting, their leader does not; he is somber and, we're led to believe, absolutely shocked. But we could have done with a little less moral equivalence on the part of the press and a little more tough journalism. Someone should have asked the leader of the Palestinian people if he understood that the cultures that he and other "moderate" Arab leaders preside over "carefully nurture and inculcate resentments and hatreds against America and the non-Arab world," as a *Wall Street Journal* editorial put it. And if that's asking too much of a field reporter covering a seemingly shaken and distraught Arafat in the wake of September 11, then an anchor back in New York should have wondered out loud about that very connection.

But to have asked such a question might have been viewed as anti-Arab (and therefore pro-Israeli), and reporters and anchors would rather be stoned by an angry mob in Ramallah than be seen in that light. So we didn't learn that day if Chairman Arafat quite understood his role in the celebration he so deplored. Nor did we get an explanation on the news about why there were not thousands of other Arabs in the streets—on the West Bank or in Jerusalem or in the "moderate" Arab countries—expressing their *condolences*. Was it because they are afraid to show support for American victims of terrorism? Or was it because they, like the Palestinians we saw with great big smiles, didn't feel that bad about what happened?

If the networks can give us months and months of Chandra and JonBenet and Lorena Bobbitt and Joey Buttafuoco,[20] then they can give us more than they do about the river of hatred that breeds suicide bombers.

But this is where journalists—given their liberal tendency to em- 35
pathize with, and sometimes even root for, the "underdog"—run into a big problem: if they start to connect those ideological and religious dots, they may not like what they find.

American journalists who covered the civil rights struggle recognized the pathology of racism and rightly made no allowance for it. They understood that in order for evil to flourish in places throughout the South, all it took was a few fundamentally bad people—while everybody else sat around making believe it wasn't happening, either because they were afraid or because they just didn't want to get involved.

The Middle East, of course, is a place with a long and troubled history. But it should be obvious that a place that turns "I Hate Israel" into a hit, that runs stories in its most important newspaper about Jews killing Christians for their blood, that faults Hitler *only because he did not kill more Jews*, and that celebrates the murder of thousands of innocent Americans is a place populated by many nasty people. Perhaps it has many good people, too, who just don't want to get involved. The point is, a story about all of this is at least as important as a story about Anne Heche and her sex life, even if sex does better in the ratings than disturbing news about raw, ignorant hatred in the world of Islam.

None of this is an argument that the media are intentionally pro-Arab. Rather, like the U.S. State Department, they are pro "moral equivalence." If they connect the dots with stories on the news about hit songs called "I Hate Israel" and all the rest, the Arab world will accuse the "Jewish-controlled" American media of being sympathetic to "Israeli oppression." If journalists—who were so willing to connect the dots when there was a belief that they led to Rush Limbaugh—connected *these* dots, they might find that there are a lot fewer moderates in those moderate places than they keep telling us about.

[20] JonBenet and Lorena Bobbitt and Joey Buttafucco: JonBenet Ramsey was a six-year-old beauty pageant contestant found murdered in the basement of her home in Boulder, Colorado, the day after Christmas 1996, whose case has never been solved. Lorena Bobbit cut off her husband's penis in 1993 allegedly because of long-term abuse. Joey Buttafuoco's under-aged lover, Amy Fisher, shot his wife in the face in 1992.

So they look the other way, which, as Ms. Nirenstein tells us, is not that easy. One has to turn "a determinedly blind eye to this river of hatred . . . [and] to be persuaded that, after all, 'everybody' in the Middle East really wants the same thing."

Obviously, there are legitimate issues about which there are differing 40
viewpoints in the Middle East: Should Israel blow up the houses that belong to the families of terrorists? Should Israel allow the construction of new settlements on the West Bank? These are two that come quickly to mind.

But moral equivalence and the quest for evenhanded journalism should not stop the media from telling us more—much more in my view—about the kind of backwardness and hatred that is alive and well, *not just in places like Kabul and Baghdad,* but in "moderate" cities and villages all over the Arab world. Even if it means going against their liberal sensibilities and reporting that sometimes even the underdog can be evil.

READING AND DISCUSSION QUESTIONS

1. How does Goldberg support his claim that television draws Americans together in times of crisis?
2. How does he believe the news is different during times of crisis from how it usually is?
3. Explain the title that Goldberg chose for this piece. What does he claim the "media elites" have "connected the dots" to find?
4. What does Goldberg believe the news media are *not* telling Americans? What sort of support does he offer for that part of his argument?
5. What type or types of support that Goldberg uses do you find most effective? Why?

WRITING SUGGESTIONS

6. Analyze the types of support that Goldberg makes use of in his essay.
7. Evaluate the effectiveness of the major types of support that he uses in his essay.
8. Attack or defend the claim that Goldberg is advancing in his essay.
9. What is your personal opinion of the media coverage of the tragedies of September 11?
10. Do you believe that your education has exposed you to recent history as well as the more distant past? Explain.

A New Look, an Old Battle

ANNA QUINDLEN

Public personification has always been the struggle on both sides of the abortion battle lines. That is why the people outside clinics on Saturday mornings carry signs with photographs of infants rather than of zygotes, why they wear lapel pins fashioned in the image of tiny feet and shout, "Don't kill your baby," rather than, more accurately, "Don't destroy your embryo." Those who support the legal right to an abortion have always been somewhat at a loss in the face of all this. From time to time women have come forward to speak about their decision to have an abortion, but when they are prominent, it seems a bit like grandstanding, and when they are not, it seems a terrible invasion of privacy when privacy is the point in the first place. Easier to marshal the act of presumptive ventriloquism practiced by the opponents, pretending to speak for those unborn unknown to them by circumstance or story.

But the battle of personification will assume a different and more sympathetic visage in the years to come. Perhaps the change in the weather was best illustrated when conservative Sen. Strom Thurmond invoked his own daughter to explain a position opposed by the anti-abortion forces. The senator's daughter has diabetes. The actor Michael J. Fox has Parkinson's disease. Christopher Reeve is in a wheelchair because of a spinal-cord injury, Ronald Reagan locked in his own devolving mind by Alzheimer's. In the faces of the publicly and personally beloved lies enormous danger for the life-begins-at-conception lobby.

The catalytic issue is research on stem cells. These are versatile building blocks that may be coaxed into becoming any other cell type; they could therefore hold the key to endless mysteries of human biology, as well as someday help provide a cure for ailments as diverse as diabetes, Parkinson's, spinal-cord degeneration, and Alzheimer's. By some estimates, more than 100 million Americans have diseases that scientists suspect could be affected by research on stem cells. Scientists hope that the astonishing potential of this research will persuade the federal government to help fund it and allow the National Institutes of Health to help oversee it. This is not political, researchers insist. It is about science, not abortion.

And they are correct. Stem-cell research is typically done by using frozen embryos left over from in vitro fertilization. If these embryos were placed in the womb, they might eventually implant, become a fetus, then a child. Unused, they are the earliest undifferentiated collection of cells

---

Anna Quindlen is a Pulitzer Prize–winning journalist and best-selling novelist. This piece appeared in the April 9, 2001, issue of *Newsweek* magazine.

made by the joining of the egg and sperm, no larger than the period at the end of this sentence. One of the oft-used slogans of the anti-abortion movement is "abortion stops a beating heart." There is no heart in this preimplantation embryo, but there are stem cells that, in the hands of scientists, might lead to extraordinary work affecting everything from cancer to heart disease.

All of which leaves the anti-abortion movement trying desperately to 5
hold its hard line, and failing. Judie Brown of the American Life League can refer to these embryos as "the tiniest person," and the National Right to Life organization can publish papers that refer to stem-cell research as the "destruction of life." But ordinary people with family members losing their mobility or their grasp on reality will be able to be more thoughtful and reasonable about the issues involved.

The anti-abortion activists know this, because they have already seen the defections. Some senators have abandoned them to support fetal-tissue research, less promising than stem-cell work but still with significant potential for treating various ailments. Elected officials who had voted against abortion rights found themselves able to support procedures that used tissue from aborted fetuses; perhaps they were men who had fathers with heart disease, who had mothers with arthritis and whose hearts resonated with the possibilities for alleviating pain and prolonging life. Senator Thurmond was one, Senator McCain another. Former senator Connie Mack of Florida recently sent a letter to the president, who must decide the future role of the federal government in this area, describing himself "as a conservative pro-life now former member" of Congress, and adding that there "were those of us identified as such who supported embryonic stem-cell research."

When a recent test of fetal tissue in patients with Parkinson's had disastrous side effects, the National Right to Life Web site ran an almost gloating report: "horrific," "rips to shreds," "media cheerleaders," "defy description." The tone is a reflection of fear. It's the fear that the use of fetal tissue to produce cures for debilitating ailments might somehow launder the process of terminating a pregnancy, a positive result from what many people still see as a negative act. And it's the fear that thinking—really thinking—about the use of the earliest embryo for life-saving research might bring a certain long-overdue relativism to discussions of abortion across the board.

The majority of Americans have always been able to apply that relativism to these issues. They are more likely to accept early abortions than later ones. They are more tolerant of a single abortion under exigent circumstances than multiple abortions. Some who disapprove of abortion in theory have discovered that they can accept it in fact if a daughter or a girlfriend is pregnant.

And some who believe that life begins at conception may look into the vacant eyes of an adored parent with Alzheimer's or picture a paralyzed child walking again, and take a closer look at what an embryo really is, at what stem-cell research really does, and then consider the true cost of a cure. That is what Senator Thurmond obviously did when he looked at his daughter and broke ranks with the true believers. It may be an oversimplification to say that real live loved ones trump the imagined unborn, that a cluster of undifferentiated cells due to be discarded anyway is a small price to pay for the health and welfare of millions. Or perhaps it is only a simple commonsensical truth.

READING AND DISCUSSION QUESTIONS

1. Understanding Quindlen's argument requires an understanding of the terms she uses. In her introductory paragraph, she refers to "public personification," "grandstanding," and "presumptive ventriloquism." Explain these terms in the context of her argument.
2. Why are anti-abortion activists opposed to the use of stem-cell research? How does Quindlen defend her own position?
3. What does Quindlen mean when she says that stem-cell research "might bring a certain long-overdue relativism to discussions of abortion" (para. 7)? (The meaning of *relativism* is the key.)
4. Although this essay clearly suggests a policy, it is primarily a claim of value: Stem-cell research is vital because it will contribute to the life and health of our loved ones. Point out places in the essay where Quindlen makes an emotional appeal to our compassion.

WRITING SUGGESTIONS

5. The debate about stem-cell research in the Congress, the media, and the medical and scientific professions, expanded after a speech by President Bush on August 9, 2001, in which he agreed to permit limited research on stem cells. Look up some of the news stories, editorials, and letters to the editors that followed his speech, and summarize the opposition to the president's proposal.
6. Quindlen explores the possible influence of stem-cell research on increased acceptance of abortion. Write an essay that argues for or against the right of a woman to an abortion. If you have reservations, make clear what circumstances would govern your judgment.

Marriage-Plus

THEODORA OOMS

The public has been concerned about "family breakdown" for a long time, but it was not until the passage of welfare reform in 1996 that the federal government decided to get into the business of promoting marriage. Although it was little noticed at the time, three of the four purposes of the welfare legislation refer directly or indirectly to marriage and family formation. The law exhorts states to promote "job preparation, work and marriage," to "prevent and reduce the incidence of out-of-wedlock pregnancies," and to "encourage the formation and maintenance of two-parent families."

The Bush administration, as it contemplates this year's extension of welfare legislation, plans to make marriage even more central. The administration's reauthorization proposal, announced February 27, includes $300 million for demonstration grants to focus on promoting healthy marriages and reducing out-of-wedlock births.[21] Meanwhile, Oklahoma Governor Frank Keating has launched a $10 million, multisector marriage initiative, and other smaller-scale government-sponsored initiatives have been enacted in Arizona, Florida, Louisiana, Michigan, and Utah. The federal government is primarily concerned with reducing out-of-wedlock births, which it views as a principal cause of welfare dependency and a host of other social problems. By contrast, state marriage initiatives are most concerned about the effects of high divorce rates and father absence on children.[22]

This new emphasis on marriage as a panacea for social problems is troubling to many liberals. For one thing, it risks being dismissive of children who happen to find themselves in single-parent families. It also can be seen as disparaging single mothers and ignoring the fact that many women have left abusive marriages for good reasons.

That said, it's hard to dismiss an overwhelming consensus of social-science research findings that children tend to be better off, financially and emotionally, when their parents are married to each other. Around 50 percent of all first marriages are expected to end in divorce, and 60 percent of all divorces involve children. One-third of all births are out of

[21]See *Working Toward Independence: The President's Plan to Strengthen Welfare Reform*, February 2002. http://www.whitehouse.gov/news/releases/2002/02/welfare-reform-announcement-book.pdf.

[22]Theodora Ooms, "The Role of the Federal Government in Strengthening Marriage," in *Virginia Journal of Social Policy and the Law*, Fall 2002. To be posted on www.clasp.org.

Theodora Ooms is a senior policy analyst at the Center for Law and Social Policy. Her article is an annotated version of one that originally appeared in a special issue of *The American Prospect* on "The Politics of the American Family," April 8, 2002.

wedlock, nearly 40 percent of children do not live with their biological fathers, and too many nonresident fathers neither support nor see their children on a regular basis.

Children living with single mothers are five times as likely to be poor 5
as those in two-parent families. Growing up in a single-parent family also roughly doubles the risk that a child will drop out of school, have difficulty finding a job, or become a teen parent. About half of these effects appear to be attributable to the reduced income available to single parents, but the other half is due to non-economic factors.[23] It's not just the presence of two adults in the home that helps children, as some argue. Children living with cohabiting partners and in stepfamilies generally do less well than those living with both married biological parents.[24]

Marriage also brings benefits to husbands and wives. Married adults are more productive on the job, earn more, save more, have better physical and mental health, and live longer, according to an extensive review of research, conducted by scholar Linda Waite. Although Waite admits that these findings partly reflect the selection of better-adjusted people into marriage, she finds that when people marry, they act in more health promoting and productive ways.[25]

Conservatives are prone to exaggerate these research findings and underplay the importance of economics. If married people are more likely (other things being equal) to produce thriving children, other things are not, in fact, equal. It's not just the case that single mothers find themselves poor because they are unmarried; they find themselves unmarried because they are poor. Successful marriages are more difficult when husbands and wives are poorly educated, lack access to jobs that pay decently, and cannot afford decent child care. Economic hardship and other problems associated with poverty can wreak havoc on couples' relationships.

The controversy mostly isn't about research, however, but about values.[26] Most people regard decisions to marry, divorce, and bear children

[23]Sara McLanahan and Julien Teitler, "The Consequences of Father Absence," in *Parenting and Child Development in "Non-Traditional" Families*, ed. Michael E. Lamb (Mahwah, NJ: Lawrence Erlbaum, 1998). Also see Sara McLanahan and Gary Sanderfur, *Growing Up with a Single Parent: What Hurts, What Helps* (Cambridge, MA: Harvard UP, 1994).

[24]See McLanahan and Teitler; Susan L. Brown, "Child Well-Being in Cohabiting Unions" and Wendy D. Manning, "The Implications of Cohabitation for Children's Well-Being," in *Just Living Together: Implications of Cohabitation for Children, Families and Social Policy*, eds. Alan Booth and Ann C. Crouter (Mahwah, NJ: Lawrence Erlbaum, 2002).

[25]Linda J. Waite and Maggie Gallagher, *The Case for Marriage: Why Married People Are Happier, Healthier and Better Off Financially* (New York: Doubleday, 2000).

[26]Theodora Ooms, *Toward More Perfect Unions: Putting Marriage on the Public Agenda* (Washington, DC: Family Impact Seminar, 1998). Available from tooms@clasp.org.

as intensely private. Any policy proposals that hint at coercing people to marry, reinforcing Victorian conceptions of gender roles, or limiting the right to end bad marriages are viewed as counter to American values of individual autonomy and privacy. Some worry about the existence of hidden agendas that threaten to put women back into the kitchen, ignore domestic violence, and eliminate public assistance for low-income families. Others fear that holding out marriage as the ideal blames single parents, many of whom do a terrific job under difficult circumstances. Use of the term "illegitimate" is especially offensive because it stigmatizes children (and, in fact, is legally inaccurate, as children born outside of marriage now have virtually the same legal rights as those born within marriage).[27] And some worry that the pro-marriage agenda discriminates against ethnic and sexual minorities and their children, particularly gays and lesbians.

There are also more pragmatic concerns. Skeptics of the pro-marriage agenda observe that the decline in marriage is worldwide, a result of overwhelming social and economic forces that cannot be reversed. In their view, attempts to change family formation behavior are largely futile; we should instead just accept and help support the increasing diversity of family forms. For others, the concern is less about the value of promoting marriage and more about whether government, rather than individuals, communities, or faith institutions, should lead the charge.

Finally, marriage per se is too simplistic a solution to the complex 10
problems of the poor. Marrying a low-income, unmarried mother to her child's father will not magically raise the family out of poverty when the parents often have no skills, no jobs, terrible housing, and may be struggling with depression, substance abuse, or domestic violence. Advocates also worry that funds spent on untested marriage-promotion activities will be taken away from programs that provide desperately needed services for single parents, such as child care.

In response to some of these concerns—as well as research showing that serious parental conflict harms children—some marriage advocates respond that marriage per se should not be the goal but rather voluntary, "healthy" marriages.[28] They also agree that protections should be built into programs to guard against domestic violence. But this only raises doubts about how "healthy" will be defined, and by whom, and whether we even know how to help people create better relationships.

There also are some plainly foolish ideas in the marriage movement. West Virginia currently gives married families an extra $100 a month in welfare payments as a "marriage incentive." Robert Rector of the Heritage

[27] Ruth-Arlene W. Howe, "Legal Rights and Obligations: An Uneven Evolution," in *Young Unwed Fathers: Changing Roles and Emerging Policies*, eds. Robert I. Lerman and Theodora Ooms (Philadelphia: Temple UP, 1993), pp. 141–69.

[28] See, for example, Robin Toner, "Welfare Chief Is Hoping to Promote Marriage," *New York Times*, February 19, 2002, sec. A, p. 1.

Foundation has proposed giving a $4,000 government bounty to welfare recipients who marry before they have a child and stay married for two years.[29] Charles Murray wants to end public assistance altogether and has proposed eliminating all aid to *unmarried* mothers under 21 in one state to test the idea. This proposal is especially egregious and surely would harm children of single mothers.[30]

Progressives and others thus are placed in a quandary. They don't want to oppose marriage—which most Americans still value highly—but are skeptical of many pro-marriage initiatives. Given that healthy marriage is plainly good for children, however, one can envision a reasonable agenda—one that would gain broad support—that we might call marriage-plus. This approach puts the well-being of children first by helping more of them grow up in married, healthy, two-parent families. However, for many children, the reality is that marriage is not a feasible or even a desirable option for their parents. Thus, a secondary goal is to help these parents—whether unmarried, separated, divorced, or remarried—cooperate better in raising their children. These are not alternative strategies. Children need us to do both.

A marriage-plus agenda does not promote marriage just for marriage's sake. It acknowledges that married and unmarried parents, mothers and fathers, may need both economic resources and non-economic supports to increase the likelihood of stable, healthy marriages and better co-parenting relationships. In addition, a marriage-plus agenda focuses more on the front end—making marriage better to be in—rather than the back end—making marriage more difficult to get out of.

Here are some elements of this agenda. 15

Strengthen "fragile families" at the birth of a child. For many poor families, relationship-education programs may be helpful but not enough. A new national study finds that at the time of their child's birth, one-half of unmarried parents (so-called "fragile families") are living together, and another third are romantically attached but not cohabiting.[31] The majorities of these parents are committed to each other and to their child and have high hopes of eventual marriage and a future together—although these hopes too often are not realized. We should reach out to young parents to help them achieve their desire to remain together as a family. A

[29] Robert Rector, *A Plan to Reduce Illegitimacy*, memorandum handed out at a meeting on Capitol Hill in early 2001.

[30] Charles Murray, "Family Formation," in *The New World of Welfare*, eds. Rebecca M. Blank and Ron Haskins (Washington, DC: Brookings Institution Press, 2001), pp. 137–68.

[31] Sara McLanahan et al., *The Fragile Families and Child Wellbeing Study Baseline Report*, August 2001, http://crcw.princeton.edu/fragilefamilies/nationalreport.pdf; and Sara McLanahan, Irwin Garfinkel, and Ronald B. Mincy, "Fragile Families, Welfare Reform, and Marriage," *Welfare Reform and Beyond Policy Brief*, No. 10, November 2001. http://www.brookings.edu/dybdocroot/wrb/publications/pb/pb10.htm. For additional papers from the Fragile Families study, see http://crcw.princeton.edu/fragilefamilies/index.htm.

helpful package of services to offer these young families might include a combination of "soft" services—relationship-skills and marriage-education workshops, financial-management classes, and peer-support groups—and "hard" services, such as job training and placement, housing, medical coverage, and substance-abuse treatment, if necessary. At present, all we do is get the father to admit paternity and hound him for child support.

Reduce economic stress by reducing poverty. Poverty and unemployment can stress couples' relationships to their breaking point. Results of a welfare-to-work demonstration program in Minnesota suggest that enhancing the income of the working poor can indirectly promote marriage. The Minnesota Family Investment Program (MFIP), which subsidized the earnings of employed welfare families, found that marriage rates increased for both single-parent long-term recipients and two-parent families. Married two-parent families were significantly more likely to remain married. MFIP also reduced the reported incidence of domestic abuse.[32]

Provide better-paying jobs and job assistance for the poor. The inability of low-skilled, unemployed men to provide income to their families is a major reason for their failure to marry the mothers of their children. Better employment opportunities help low-income fathers, and men in general, to become responsible fathers and, perhaps, more attractive and economically stable marriage partners.[33] There is also growing support for making changes in the child-support system to ensure that more support paid by fathers goes to the children (rather than being used to recoup government program costs).[34]

Invest more in proven programs that reduce out-of-wedlock childbearing. Teen pregnancy and birth rates have fallen by over 20 percent since the early 1990s, and there is now strong evidence that a number of prevention programs are effective. A related strategy is enforcement of child support. States that have tough, effective child support systems have been found to have lower nonmarital birth rates, presumably because men are beginning to understand there are serious costs associated with fathering a child.[35]

[32]Virginia Knox, Cynthia Miller, and Lisa A. Gennetian, *Reforming Welfare and Rewarding Work: A Summary of the Final Report on the Minnesota Family Investment Program* (New York: Manpower Demonstration Research Corporation, September, 2000).

[33]See Chapter 4, "The Fading Inner-City Family," in William Julius Wilson, *When Work Disappears: The World of the New Urban Poor* (New York: Alfred A. Knopf, 1996), pp. 87–110; Kathy Edin, "Few Good Men: Why Poor Mothers Don't Marry or Remarry," *The American Prospect*, January 3, 2000.

[34]See Vicki Turetsky, Testimony Given to the Social Security and Family Policy Subcommittee of the U.S. Senate Finance Committee, October 11, 2001, and Vick Turetsky, *What If All the Money Came Home?* (Washington, DC: Center for Law and Social Policy, June, 2000). Both available online at www.clasp.org.

[35]Robert D. Plotnick, Inhoe Ku, Irwin Garfinkel, and Sara S. McLanahan, *The Impact of Child Support Enforcement Policy on Nonmarital Childbearing*. Paper presented at the Association for Public Policy Analysis and Management, Year 2000 Research Conference in Seattle, WA.

Institute workplace policies to reduce work/family conflict and stress on couples. Stress in the workplace spills over into the home. Persistent overtime, frequent travel, and inflexible leave policies place great strain on couples at all income levels. Employers are increasingly demanding nonstandard work schedules. A recent study found that married couples with children who work night and rotating shifts are at higher risk of separation and divorce.[36] The absence of affordable and reliable child care forces many parents who would prefer a normal workday to working split shifts solely to make sure that a parent is home with the children. 20

Reduce tax penalties and other disincentives to marriage. There has always been strong support for reducing marriage tax penalties for many two-earner families. This is a complicated task because the majority of married couples, in fact, receive tax bonuses rather than penalties.[37] A positive step was taken in 2001 to reduce significantly the marriage penalty affecting low-income working families in the Earned Income Tax Credit program. While there is uncertainty about the extent to which these tax-related marriage penalties affect marital behavior, there is broad general agreement that government has a responsibility to "first do no harm" when it comes to marriage.

Similarly, there is near unanimous agreement that government should not make it harder for eligible two-parent families to receive welfare benefits and assistance. In the past, the old welfare program, Aid to Families with Dependent Children, was much criticized for offering incentives to break up families. At least 33 states already have removed the stricter eligibility rules placed on two-parent families,[38] and the president's welfare reauthorization proposal encourages the other states to do the same. In addition, it proposes to end the higher work participation rate for two-parent families, a federal rule that has been criticized widely by the states. Another needed reform would forgive accumulated child-support debt owed by noncustodial fathers if they marry the mothers of their children. (Currently, such debt is owed to the state if the mothers and children are receiving welfare benefits.)[39]

Educate those who want *to marry and stay married about how to have healthy relationships and good marriages.* A vast industry is devoted to helping couples plan a successful wedding day—wedding planners, 500-page

[36] Harriet B. Presser, "Nonstandard Work Schedules and Marital Instability," *Journal of Marriage and the Family* (February 2000).

[37] Congressional Budget Office, *For Better or For Worse: Marriage and the Federal Income Tax* (Washington, DC: Congress of the United States, Congressional Budget Office, June 1997).

[38] Gene Falk and Jill Tauber, *Welfare Reform: TANF Provisions Related to Marriage and Two-Parent Families* (Washington, DC: Congressional Research Service, Library of Congress, October 30, 2001).

[39] Paul Roberts, *An Ounce of Prevention and a Pound of Cure: Developing State Policy on the Payment of Child Support Arrears by Low Income Parents.* (Washington, DC: Center for Law and Social Policy, May 2001). Available online at www.clasp.org.

bridal guides, specialty caterers, the list goes on. But where do young people go to learn about how to sustain good, lifelong marriages? In fact, we now know a lot about what makes contemporary marriages work. With the transformation of gender roles, there now are fewer fixed rules for couples to follow, meaning they have to negotiate daily about who does what and when. In the absence of the legal and social constraints that used to keep marriages together, there's now a premium on developing effective relationship skills. Building on three decades of research, there are a small but rapidly growing number of programs (both religious and secular) that help people from high school through adulthood understand the benefits of marriage for children and for themselves, develop realistic expectations for healthy relationships, understand the meaning of commitment, and learn the skills and attitudes needed to make marriage succeed.[40] Other programs help married couples survive the inevitable ups and downs that occur in most marriages, and remarried couples with the additional challenges of step-parenting. Oklahoma, Utah, and Michigan have begun using government funds to make these relationship- and marriage-education programs accessible to low-income couples. The Greater Grand Rapids Community Marriage Policy initiative is urging area businesses to include marriage education as an Employee Assistance Program benefit, arguing that it's more cost-effective to prevent marital distress than incur the costs of counseling and lost productivity involved when employees' marriages break up.[41]

A marriage-plus agenda that includes activities such as these is not just the responsibility of government. Some of the strategies proposed here are being implemented by private and religious groups, some by governments, and some by partnerships between these sectors. The approach adopted in Oklahoma, Greater Grand Rapids, and Chattanooga, for example, mobilizes the resources of many sectors of the community—government, education, legal, faith, business, and media—in a comprehensive effort to create a more marriage-supportive culture and to provide new services to promote, support, and strengthen couples and marriage and reduce out-of-wedlock childbearing and divorce. This "saturation model" seems particularly promising because it takes into account the many factors that influence individuals' decisions to marry, to divorce, or to remain unmarried. We should proceed cautiously, trying out and evaluating new ideas before applying them widely.

[40] See Scott Stanley, "Making a Case for Premarital Education," in *Family Relations* (July 2001). Also see *Directory of Couples and Marriage Education Programs* at www.smartmarriages.com.

[41] Personal communication with Mark Eastburg, Ph.D., director of Pine Rest Family Institute, Grand Rapids, Michigan. See Web site for the Greater Grand Rapids Community Marriage Initiative, www.ggrcmarriagepolicy.org.

25 Ironically, in the midst of this furor about government's role in marriage, it's worth noting that the federal government recently has begun to shirk a basic responsibility: counting the numbers of marriages and divorces in the United States. Since budget cuts in 1995, the government has been unable to report on marriage and divorce rates in the states or for the nation as a whole.[42] And, for the first time in the history of the Census, Americans were not asked to give their marital status in the 2000 survey. What kind of pro-marriage message from the government is that?

If liberals and conservatives are serious about strengthening families for the sake of helping children, liberals ought to acknowledge that noncoercive and egalitarian approaches to bolstering marriage are sound policy. Conservatives, meanwhile, should admit that much of what it takes to make marriage work for the benefit of spouses and children is not just moral but economic.

READING AND DISCUSSION QUESTIONS

1. What does Ooms mean when she says in the first paragraph that in 1996 "the federal government decided to get into the business of promoting marriage"?
2. How does Ooms support her belief that children are better off in a two-parent home?
3. What type of support does she use in the sixth paragraph to argue that "[m]arriage also brings benefits to husbands and wives"?
4. What are some of the problems that arise when government gets involved in promoting marriage?
5. What claim is Ooms supporting? How effective is she in supporting that claim? Are some types of support that she uses more effective than others, in your opinion?

WRITING SUGGESTIONS

6. Write an essay in which you oppose or support Ooms's marriage-plus plan.
7. Analyze the primary types of support that Ooms uses. If you wish, you may go a step further and evaluate the effectiveness of her support.

[42] Stephanie Ventura, "Vital Statistics from the National Center for Health Statistics," in *Data Needs for Measuring Family and Fertility Change after Welfare Reform*, ed. Douglas Besharov (College Park, MD: Maryland School of Public Affairs, Welfare Reform Academy).

DEBATE: Is assuming the role of citizen journalist worth the risk?

Praise for Student's Footage of Virginia Tech Mass Killing

LILY YULIANTI

On a CNN Larry King Live special report of the student massacre at Virginia Tech that saw 33 people killed King praised Jamal Albarghouti, the Palestinian graduate student who took the eyewitness footage of the immediate aftermath on his cellphone.

At roughly 10 a.m. Albarghouti was at the Blacksburg, VA, campus to meet with his graduate adviser. He sensed that something terrible had just happened on campus, explaining, "Everyone [was] running and screaming. The situation was so frightening. I ran to a safe place and then decided to record the situation using my cellphone."

He then sent his video to CNN's I-Report, a citizen-reporter video blog site, which repeatedly used it to accompany its other reporting of the incident. This has been without doubt the worst mass shooting tragedy in U.S. history, and Albarghouti was the one to capture the incident for the world.

His footage, some of it shaky, set the scene inside the campus: an empty road outside a nearby building being approached by three police officers, then sounds of gunshots registering almost simultaneously, the last sounding like a bomb blast.

In the CNN interview with Larry King, Albarghouti explained how the 5
scene reminded him of his homeland of Palestine. King and another CNN news anchor tried to get at why Albarghouti decided not to dash for safety with other students and staffers, but chose to stand fast and record the incident. "Weren't you scared? What sort of cellphone did you use? Did you think you were really safe at that time?"

His response was to demonstrate the value of a citizen reporter in providing an on-the-spot report of a history-making, traumatic event, in having the gadget at the ready to take the footage, and in having the presence of mind and the passion to play his historical role. He was not the only eyewitness, but also stood his ground as a resourceful citizen reporter, taking the initiative to record the scene.

Lily Yulianti is a journalist and writer from Indonesia who works in Tokyo as an Indonesian language specialist and broadcaster for Radio Tokyo. As a citizen journalist herself, she posted this article on Korea's massive online outlet for citizen journalists, Ohmynews, on April 17, 2007.

We can understand how CNN's professional journalists and a famous TV personality like Larry King could be so taken with Albarghouti's "journalism skill." Tempted to discount the capability of ordinary citizens in their chosen field of journalism, there are many well-trained professional journalists, proud of their skill and experience, who become intrigued whenever an unsung citizen reporter performs such a heroic act of historical reportage.

Apart from the unevenness of the footage he provided, Albarghouti showed that being confident in the use of his cellphone and uploading the resulting footage could be taken as matters of course. Above all, he provided King a clear and firm account of the situation, exactly in the manner of a professional TV journalist making a live report. What added special depth and human interest to this live report was his being reminded of the grievous situation in his own country when hearing the gun shots on campus. "I am quite familiar with the sound of gunshots, because they remind me of the situation in the West Bank and Gaza. But when I saw it was happening here, in a peaceful place like this, it was hard to believe."

Such was the personal background of a citizen-reporter that made Larry King say later, "What an irony . . .".

Again, Albarghouti and his cellphone video have shown the power of 10
the ordinary citizen to capture a news event. Granted that the efforts of ordinary people as citizen journalists are a matter for debate, the traditional media still make a reflexively negative comparison between citizen journalism and that provided by their professionals. Interestingly, when presented with a citizen who sent an exclusive report to the mainstream media, as Albarghouti did to CNN's I-Report, they insist on wondering, in grudging amazement, "What made you record the event? How did you record it?"

Of course, the mainstream media should first of all be thankful, because there is a live video record from the site. The role of Albarghouti was not only that of eyewitness but also of a citizen reporter who in fact provided a high-quality report for CNN.

In raising questions like these, professionals in the media show a tendency to overlook the existence of many ordinary citizens out there who embrace the idea of participatory journalism, people who have shifted from being passive media consumers to active citizen reporters, believing they can create a better society if they get involved in conveying the news. They make videos, they write on various issues, and they raise their voices. As for the mainstream media, they have begun to open their doors to citizen reporters, seeing that their well-trained professionals cannot always respond quickly enough to reach the location of an epochal event.

Disaster Photos: Newsworthy or Irresponsible?

MARK MEMMOTT WITH ALAN LEVIN AND GREG LIVADAS

Photos taken by survivors of the London bombings[43] and Tuesday's plane crash in Toronto are prompting concerns by safety investigators and journalism scholars.

At issue: Whether as camera phones and digital cameras multiply, so do the odds that victims will put themselves and others at risk by pausing to snap pictures.

Questions are also being raised about whether the media may be encouraging risky behavior by broadcasting the images.

On the other side of the debate, such photos may aid investigators.

5 Within a few hours of the London attacks [on] July 7, photos taken by survivors with camera phones were ricocheting around the world on the Internet and on television.

Four photos taken Tuesday by Air France Flight 358 passenger Eddie Ho were broadcast later on several outlets, including ABC's *Good Morning America*, CNN, and NBC's *Today*. One was snapped inside the jet moments after it skidded to a halt in Toronto. It shows passengers heading to an exit. The others were taken outside the jet and show passengers fleeing the crippled fuselage.

All 309 people aboard survived.

Ho, 19, a South African attending college in Canada, said Thursday in a telephone interview with USA TODAY that his digital camera was in his pocket during the flight. He is an "airline enthusiast" who often takes pictures while flying. Ho sold the photos to two syndicates, which are now reselling them to the media.

Ho said he doesn't think he delayed his exit or anyone else's. "I was running and taking pictures," he said. "I just kept pressing the button." He said he would not have tried to retrieve his camera if it had been in a bag.

10 Still, a top accident investigation official in the USA strongly advises passengers not to do such things.

[43] On two different dates in July 2005, London's bus and subway system was the target of a synchronized cluster of bombs. On July 7, fifty-two people were killed and 770 injured. On July 21, four devices were planted on three subways and one bus, as in the previous incident, but this time all failed to go off.

Mark Memmott has worked for *USA Today* since 1984 as a reporter and editor, and he has been a blogger for *USA Today* since they launched its On Deadline blog in January 2006. He specializes in the media's coverage of politics and campaign advertising and Internet efforts. This article was published on August 4, 2005. Alan Levin is a reporter for *USA Today* and Greg Livadas is a reporter for the *Rochester Democrat and Chronicle* in New York.

Mark Rosenker, acting chairman of the National Transportation Safety Board, said, "Your business is to get off the airplane. Your business is to help anybody who needs help." Taking photos is "irresponsible," he said.

Helen Muir, aerospace psychology professor at Cranfield University in Great Britain, said in most crashes "you only have two minutes from the first spark to conditions not being survivable in the cabin." Pausing even for a second "is just what we don't want people to do." But, Muir said, the pictures could be "very valuable to accident investigators." They contain clues to the jet's condition after the crash.

More such photos are inevitable. There are digital cameras in about half of U.S. households and camera phones in about 40%, the market research firm IDC estimates. About 92 million camera phones have been sold in the USA, IDC says.

Kelly McBride, who lectures about media ethics at the Poynter Institute for professional journalists, said the media have a responsibility "to refuse to publish photos taken (by amateurs) when someone was obviously risking his life or the lives of others."

McBride said journalists must "talk to the person about the circum- 15
stances under which he took the photos and share that information with the public."

Ben Sherwood, executive producer at *Good Morning America,* said there was no reason to think Ho had caused any problems at the scene. "From what we could tell" from the photos, Sherwood said, "one was taken (in the jet) during what appeared to be an orderly evacuation. The others were taken from outside, looking back."

Sherwood said *Good Morning America* "welcomes contributions from people who find themselves in the middle of news stories [but] would never encourage anyone to take an unnecessary risk."

Jonathan Klein, president of CNN/US, said his network "urges folks, on the air, not to take foolish risks." He doubts many survivors are thinking about the media when they pull out their cameras.

"They're taking (pictures) in order to satisfy that primordial urge to record one's history," Klein said.

Mark Glaser, a columnist at the USC Annenberg School of Journalism's 20
Online Journalism Review, said, "Over time, people will recognize when it's the right time to use your camera in an emergency."

Unfortunately, he said, "it may take someone dying" because they stopped to take a picture before that "cultural norm" is reached.

DISCUSSION QUESTIONS

1. What, if any, events can you recall that had better or more complete coverage because of the presence of citizen journalists?
2. The South Korean online newspaper to which Yulianti submitted her article, Ohmynews, draws 80 percent of its content from reporters who are

not professional journalists. What sort of assumptions would you make about the quality of the reporting you would find in it?

3. What did Larry King mean when he said that Albarghouti's situation was ironic?
4. What is your opinion about what Albarghouti did during the massacre at Virginia Tech?
5. What is your opinion about what Ho did during the evacuation of Air France Flight 358?
6. In general, do you believe that Yulianti or Memmott builds a more compelling case?

ASSIGNMENTS FOR PROVIDING SUPPORT

READING AND DISCUSSION QUESTIONS

1. Consider what types of evidence you find most convincing in an argument. Is the best type of evidence dependent on the topic and the context? Explain.
2. Look for examples in the media of the misuse of evidence. Explain why the evidence is misleading.
3. Use examples to explain which news shows depend on factual evidence and which depend largely on opinion. Do both have a useful role to play in our society? Explain.
4. Consider what Claudius E. Watts's warrant is in "Single-Sex Education Benefits Men Too." Could the same warrant be used in other contexts to justify discrimination? Explain.
5. In the aftermath of the massacre at Virginia Tech, at least one state tried to pass a law allowing registered owners to carry their weapons on school and college campuses. What needs of the people were those who proposed the law appealing to? How could the opponents have used similar types of appeal to argue their case?
6. Consider presidential debates you have seen or other televised coverage of candidates during the months leading up to an election. What are some specific examples of how the candidates try to appeal to the voters' needs and values?
7. Bernard Goldberg argues in his essay, "Connecting the Dots . . . to Terrorism," that the average American citizen is usually ignorant of much of the reality of what goes on in the Arab world. When Americans take a stand on issues such as U.S. involvement in Iraq, to what extent do you believe they are basing that stand on solid supporting evidence?

WRITING ASSIGNMENTS

8. Using Bethany Royce's "The True Confusion about SUV Costs" as a model, write an essay evaluating the use of support in one of the Readings for Analysis.

9. Write an essay explaining the types of support used in one of the Readings for Analysis or comparing the use of support in two of them.
10. Write an essay explaining which of the two authors in the debate over citizen journalists you believe presents a more convincing argument, Lily Yulianti or Mark Memmott.
11. Analyze different television commercials for the same product or similar products. Write an essay supporting a conclusion you are able to draw about the types of appeal used in the commercials.
12. Write a letter about a problem on your campus to the person who is in a position to correct the problem. Provide convincing evidence that a problem exists and, in suggesting a solution to the problem, keep in mind the needs and values of your audience as well as those of others on campus.

CHAPTER 8

Analyzing Warrants

WHAT ARE WARRANTS?

We now come to the third element in the structure of the argument—the warrant. Claim and support, the other major elements we have discussed, are more familiar in ordinary discourse, but there is nothing mysterious or unusual about the warrant. All our claims, both formal and informal, are grounded in warrants or assumptions that the audience must share with us if our claims are to prove to be acceptable.

The following exercise provides a good starting point for this chapter. Do the assigned task by yourself or in a small group.

PRACTICE

A series of environmental catastrophic events has virtually wiped out human life on Earth. The only known survivors in your vicinity are the eleven listed below. There are resources to sustain only seven. Choose seven of the following people to survive. List them in the order in which you would choose them and be prepared to explain the reasons for your selection: that is, why you chose these particular persons and why you placed them in this certain order.

- Dr. D.—thirty-seven, Ph.D. in history, college professor, in good health (jogs daily), hobby is botany, enjoys politics, married with one child (Bobby).
- Mrs. D.—thirty-eight, rather obese, diabetic, M.A. in psychology, counselor in a mental health clinic, married to Dr. D., has one child.
- Bobby D.—ten, mentally retarded with IQ of 70, healthy and strong for his age.

- Mrs. G.—twenty-three, ninth-grade education, cocktail waitress, worked as a prostitute, married at age sixteen, divorced at age eighteen, one son (Joseph).
- Joseph G.—three months old, healthy.
- Mary E.—eighteen, trade school education, wears glasses, artistic.
- Mr. N.—twenty-five, starting last year of medical school, music as a hobby, physical fitness buff.
- Mrs. C.—twenty-eight, daughter of a minister, college graduate, electronics engineer, single now after a brief marriage, member of Zero Population Growth.
- Mr. B.—fifty-one, B.S. in mechanics, married with four children, enjoys outdoors, much experience in construction, quite handy.
- Father Frans—thirty-seven, Catholic priest, active in civil rights, former college athlete, farming background, often criticized for liberal views.
- Dr. L.—sixty-six, doctor in general practice, two heart attacks in the past five years, loves literature and quotes extensively.

There may have been a great deal of disagreement over which survivors to select. If so, the reason for that disagreement was that in making their choices, different members of your group or of your class as a whole were operating under different assumptions or basing their decisions on different warrants. Some of you may have chosen not to let Mrs. G. survive because she seemed to have nothing particularly vital to offer to the survival of the group as a whole. Others of you may have felt that she should be allowed to survive along with her child, the infant in the group. Some of you, whether you acknowledge it or not, may have opposed letting Mrs. G. survive because she was once a prostitute. Think about the warrant that would underlie the claim that Mrs. G. should not be one of the seven allowed to survive. What assumption—what generalized principle—would a person who made that claim be accepting about women who were once prostitutes? What assumption would underlie the claim that she should be allowed to survive? What assumption would underlie the claim that Bobby D. should be allowed to live (or die)?

Obviously this is an exercise with no right answer. What it can teach us, however, is to consider the assumptions on which our beliefs are based. There are reasons you might have chosen certain individuals to survive that could be stated as general principles: Those who are in the best physical condition should be allowed to survive. Those with the most useful skills should be allowed to survive. Those who are mentally deficient should not be allowed to survive. Those who are most likely to reproduce should be allowed to survive.

Fortunately, this is merely an intellectual exercise. Whenever you take a stand in a real-life situation, though, you do so on the basis of certain general principles that guide your choices. Those general principles that you feel most strongly about exist as part of your intellectual and moral being because of what you have experienced in your life thus far. They have been shaped by your observations, your personal experience, and your participation in a culture. But because these observations, experiences, and cultural associations will vary, the audience may not always agree with the warrants or assumptions of the writer.

What does this have to do with argumentation? Any time you support an argumentative claim, you have to analyze the assumptions behind the argument and consider whether the members of your audience share the same assumptions. Some warrants are so widely accepted that you do not need to state them or to offer any proof of their validity. If you argue that every new dorm on campus should have a sprinkler system, you probably do not even need to state your warrant. If you did, it would be something like this: Measures that would increase the likelihood that dorm residents would survive a fire should be implemented in all dorms.

What about claims that are more controversial? Why is it so difficult for those who oppose abortion, for example, to communicate with those who favor it and vice versa? Anyone who believes that abortion is the murder of an unborn child is basing that argument on the warrant that a fetus is a child from conception. Many on the other side of the debate do not accept that warrant and thus do not accept the claim. Obviously disagreements on such emotionally charged issues are very difficult to resolve because the underlying warrants are based on firmly held beliefs that are difficult to change. It is always better to be aware of your opponent's warrants, however, than to simply dismiss them as irrelevant.

The British philosopher Stephen Toulmin, who developed the concept of warrants, dismissed more traditional forms of logical reasoning in favor of a more audience-based, courtroom-derived approach to argumentation. He refers to warrants as "general, hypothetical statements, which can act as bridges" and "entitle one to draw conclusions or make claims."[1] The word *bridges* to denote the action of the warrant is crucial. One dictionary defines warrant as a "guarantee or justification." We use the word *warrant* to emphasize that in an argument it guarantees a connecting link—a bridge—between the claim and the support. This means that even if a reader agrees that the support is sound, the support cannot prove the validity of the claim unless the reader also agrees with the underlying warrant. Recall the sample argument outlined in Chapter 1 (p. 15):

CLAIM: Backscatter screening should be implemented in America's airports.

SUPPORT: Backscatter screening will make planes safer.

WARRANT: Any screening technique that will make planes safer should be implemented.

[1]Stephen Toulmin, *The Uses of Argument* (Cambridge: Cambridge University Press, 1958), p. 98.

Notice that the reader must agree with the assumption that safety is worth undergoing any screening technique, even one that some would consider an invasion of privacy. Simply providing evidence that a certain technique will make planes safer is not enough to convince all readers that backscatter screening should be implemented in America's airports.

The following dialogue offers another example of the relationship between the warrant and the other elements of the argument.

"I don't think that Larry can do the job. He's pretty dumb."
"Really? I thought he was smart. What makes you say he's dumb?"
"Did you know that he's illiterate—can't read above third-grade level? In my book that makes him dumb."

If we put this into outline form, the warrant or assumption in the argument becomes clear.

CLAIM: Larry is pretty dumb.

EVIDENCE: He can't read above third-grade level.

WARRANT: Anybody who can't read above third-grade level must be dumb.

We can also represent the argument in diagram form, which shows the warrant as a bridge between the claim and the support.

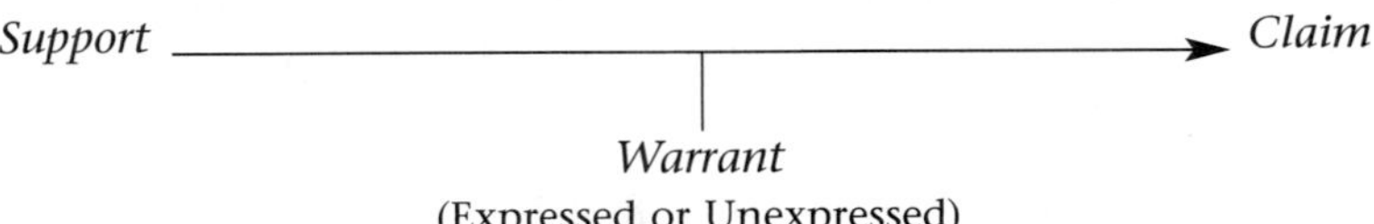

The argument above can then be written like this:

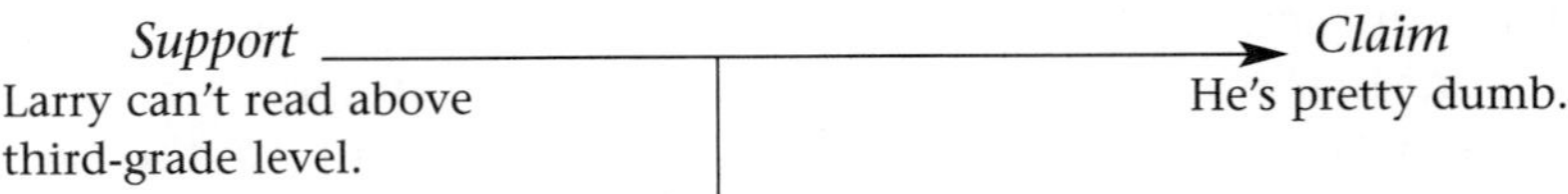

Is this warrant valid? We cannot answer this question until we consider the *backing*. Every warrant or assumption rests on something else that gives it authority; this is what we call backing. Backing or authority for the warrant in this example would consist of research data that prove a relationship between stupidity and low reading ability. This particular warrant, we would discover, lacks backing because we know that the failure to learn to read well may be due to a number of things unrelated to intelligence. So if the warrant is unprovable, the claim—that Larry is dumb—is also unprovable, even if the evidence is true. In this case, then, the evidence does not guarantee the soundness of the claim.

Now consider this example of a somewhat more complicated warrant: The beautiful and unspoiled Eastern Shore of Maryland is being discovered by thousands of tourists, vacationers, and developers who will, according to the residents, change the landscape and the way of life, which is now based largely on fishing and farming. In a few years the Eastern Shore may become a noisy, crowded string of resorts. Mrs. Walkup, the Kent County commissioner, says,

> Catering to the wealthy puts property back on the tax rolls, but it's going to make the Eastern Shore look like the rest of the country. Everything that made our way of life so special is being eroded. We are a fragile area. The Eastern Shore is still special, but it is feeling pressure from all directions. Lots of people don't seem to appreciate the fact that God made us to need a little peace and quiet now and then.[2]

In simplified form the argument of those opposed to development would be outlined this way:

CLAIM: Development will bring undesirable changes to the present way of life on the Eastern Shore, a life of farming and fishing, peace and quiet.

SUPPORT: Developers will build express highways, condominiums, casinos, and nightclubs.

WARRANT: A pastoral life of fishing and farming is superior to the way of life brought by expensive, fast-paced modern development.

Notice that the warrant is a broad generalization that can apply to a number of different situations, while the claim is about a specific place and time. It should be added that in other arguments the warrant may not be stated in such general terms. However, even in arguments in which the warrant makes a more specific reference to the claim, the reader can infer an extension of the warrant to other similar arguments. In the backscatter screening example outlined on page 274, the warrant mentions a specific screening technique. But it is clear that such warrants can be generalized to apply to other arguments in which we accept a claim based on an appeal to our very human need to feel secure.

To be convinced of the validity of Mrs. Walkup's claim, you must first find that the support is true, that the developers plan to introduce drastic changes that will destroy the pastoral life of the Eastern Shore. You may, however, believe that the support is not entirely sound, that the development will be much more modest than residents fear, and that the Eastern Shore will not be seriously altered. Next, you may want to see more justification for the warrant. Is pastoral life superior to the life that will result

[2]Michael Wright, "The Changing Chesapeake," *New York Times Magazine*, July 10, 1983, p. 27.

from large-scale development? Perhaps you have always thought that a life of fishing and farming means poverty and limited opportunities for the majority of the residents. Although the superiority of a way of life is largely a matter of taste and therefore difficult to prove, Mrs. Walkup may need to produce backing for her belief that the present way of life is more desirable than one based on developing the area for new residents and summer visitors. If you find either the support or the warrant unconvincing, you cannot accept the claim.

Remember that a claim is often modified by one or more qualifiers, which limit the claim. Mrs. Walkup might have said, "Development will *probably* destroy *some aspects of* the present way of life on the Eastern Shore." Warrants can also be modified or limited by *reservations*, which remind the reader that there are conditions under which the warrants will not be relevant. Mrs. Walkup might have added, "unless increased prosperity and exposure to the outside world brought by development improve some aspects of our lives."

A diagram of Mrs. Walkup's argument shows the additional elements:

Support ⟶ *Claim*

The developers will build highways, condos, casinos, nightclubs.

Development will bring undesirable changes to life on the Eastern Shore.

Warrant

A way of life devoted to farming and fishing is superior to a way of life brought by development.

Qualifier

Development will *most likely* bring undesirable changes.

Backing

We have experienced crowds, traffic, noise, rich strangers, and high-rises, and they destroy peace and quiet.

Reservation

But increased development might improve some aspects of our lives.

Claim and support (or lack of support) are relatively easy to uncover in most arguments. One thing that makes the warrant different is that it is often unexpressed and therefore unexamined by both writer and reader because they take it for granted. In the argument about Larry's intelligence, the warrant was stated. But in the argument about development on the Eastern Shore, Mrs. Walkup did not state her warrant directly, although her meaning is perfectly clear. She probably felt that it was not necessary to be more explicit because her readers would understand and supply the warrant.

We can make the discovery of warrants even clearer by examining another argument, in this case a policy claim. We've looked at a factual claim (that Larry is dumb) and a value claim (that Eastern Shore development is undesirable). Now we examine a policy claim that rests on one expressed and one unexpressed warrant. Policy claims are usually more complicated than other claims because the statement of policy is preceded by an array of facts and values. In addition, such claims may represent chains of reasoning in which one argument is dependent on another. These complicated arguments may be difficult or impossible to summarize in a simple diagram, but careful reading, asking the same kinds of questions that the author may have asked about his claim, can help you to find the warrant or chain of warrants that must be accepted before evidence and claim can be linked.

In a familiar argument that appeared a few years ago,[3] the author argues for a radical reform in college sports—the elimination of subprofessional intermural team sports, as practiced above all in football and basketball. The claim is clear, and evidence for the professional character of college sports not hard to find: the large salaries paid to coaches, the generous perquisites offered to players, the recruitment policies that ignore academic standing, the virtually full-time commitment of the players, the lucrative television contracts. But can this evidence support the author's claim that such sports do not belong on college campuses? Advocates of these sports may ask, Why not? In the conclusion of the article the author states one warrant or assumption underlying his claim.

> Even if the money to pay college athletes could be found, though, a larger question must be answered—namely, why should a system of professional athletics be affiliated with universities at all? For the truth is that the requirements of athletics and academics operate at cross purposes, and the attempt to play both games at once serves only to reduce the level of performance of each.

In other words, the author assumes that the goals of an academic education on the one hand and the goals of big-time college sports on the other hand are incompatible. In the article he develops the ways in which each enterprise harms the other.

But the argument clearly rests on another warrant that is not expressed because the author takes for granted that his readers will supply it: The academic goals of the university are primary and should take precedence over all other collegiate activities. This is an argument based on an authority warrant, the authority of those who define the goals of the university—scholars, public officials, university administrators, and others. (Types of warrants are discussed in the following section.)

This warrant makes clear that the evidence of the professional nature of college sports cited above supports the claim that they should be elim-

[3]D. G. Myers, "Why College Sports?" *Commentary*, December 1990, pp. 49–51.

inated. If quasiprofessional college sports are harmful to the primary educational function of the college or university, then they must go. In the author's words, "The two are separate enterprises, to be judged by separate criteria. . . . For college sports, the university is not an educational institution at all; it is merely a locus, a means of coordinating the different aspects of the sporting enterprise."

This argument may be summarized in outline form as follows:

CLAIM:	Intermural college team sports should be abolished.
SUPPORT:	College sports have become subprofessional.
WARRANT:	The goals of an academic education and big-time college sports are incompatible.
BACKING FOR THE WARRANT:	Academic education is the primary goal of the college and must take precedence over athletic activity.

PRACTICE

Read the following argument by Robert A. Sirico. Then summarize the argument in a paragraph. Next, explain what the claim is, what types of support are used, and what the warrant is. Is the warrant one that you agree with? Explain.

An Unjust Sacrifice

ROBERT A. SIRICO

An appeals court in London has made a Solomonic ruling, deciding that eight-week-old twins joined at the pelvis must be separated. In effect, one twin, known as Mary, is to be sacrificed to save the other, known as Jodie, in an operation the babies' parents oppose.

The judges invoked a utilitarian rationale, justified on the basis of medical testimony. The specialists agreed that there is an 80 to 90 percent chance that the strong and alert Jodie could not survive more than a few months if she continued to support the weak heart and lungs of Mary, whose brain is underdeveloped.

This is a heartbreaking case, and the decision of the court was not arrived at lightly. But even the best of intentions, on the part of the state or the parents, is no substitute for sound moral reasoning. Utilitarian considerations like Mary's quality of life are not the issue. Nor should doctors' expert testimony, which is subject to error, be considered decisive.

Here, as in the case of abortion, one simple principle applies: There is no justification for deliberately destroying innocent life. In this case, the court has turned its back on a tenet that the West has stood by: Life, no matter how limited, should be protected.

Robert A. Sirico, a Roman Catholic priest, is president of the Acton Institute for the Study of Religion and Liberty in Grand Rapids, Michigan. This article appeared in the September 28, 2000, *New York Times*.

While this case is so far unique, there are guidelines that must be followed. No human being, for instance, can be coerced into donating an organ—even if the individual donating the organ is unlikely to be harmed and the individual receiving the organ could be saved. In principle, no person should ever be forced to volunteer his own body to save another's life, even if that individual is a newborn baby. 5

To understand the gravity of the court's error, consider the parents' point of view. They are from Gozo, an island in Malta. After being told of their daughters' condition, while the twins were in utero, they went to Manchester, England, seeking out the best possible medical care. Yet, after the birth on August 8, the parents were told that they needed to separate the twins, which would be fatal for Mary.

They protested, telling the court: "We cannot begin to accept or contemplate that one of our children should die to enable the other one to survive. That is not God's will. Everyone has a right to life, so why should we kill one of our daughters to enable the other one to survive?"

And yet, a court in a country in which they sought refuge has overruled their wishes. This is a clear evil: coercion against the parents and coercion against their child, justified in the name of a speculative medical calculus.

The parents' phrase "God's will" is easily caricatured, as if they believed divine revelation were guiding them to ignore science. In fact, they believe in the merit of science, or they would not have gone to Britain for help in the first place.

But utilitarian rationality has overtaken their case. The lawyer appointed by the court to represent Jodie insisted that Mary's was "a futile life." That is a dangerous statement—sending us down a slippery slope where lives can be measured for their supposed value and discarded if deemed not useful enough. 10

Some might argue that in thinking about the twins, we should apply the philosophical principle known as "double effect," which, in some circumstances, permits the loss of a life when it is an unintended consequence of saving another. But in this case, ending Mary's life would be a deliberate decision, not an unintended effect.

Can we ever take one life in favor of another? No, not even in this case, however fateful the consequences.

Arguers will often neglect to state their warrants for one of two reasons: First, like Mrs. Walkup, they may believe that the warrant is obvious and need not be expressed; second, they may want to conceal the warrant in the hope that the reader will overlook its weakness.

What kinds of warrants are so obvious that they need not be expressed? Here are a few that will probably sound familiar:

Mothers love their children.

The more expensive the product, the more satisfactory it will be.

A good harvest will result in lower prices for produce.

First come, first served.

These statements seem to embody beliefs that most of us would share and that might be unnecessary to make explicit in an argument. The last statement, for example, is taken as axiomatic, an article of faith that we seldom question in ordinary circumstances. Suppose you hear someone make the claim, "I deserve to get the last ticket to the concert." If you ask why he is entitled to a ticket that you also would like to have, he may answer in support of his claim, "Because I was here first." No doubt you accept his claim without further argument because you understand and agree with the warrant that is not expressed: "If you arrive first, you deserve to be served before those who come later." Your acceptance of the warrant probably also takes into account the unexpressed backing that is based on a belief in justice: "It is only fair that those who sacrifice time and comfort to be first in line should be rewarded for their trouble."

In this case it may not be necessary to expose the warrant and examine it. Indeed, as Stephen Toulmin tells us, "If we demanded the credentials of all warrants at sight and never let one pass unchallenged, argument could scarcely begin."[4]

But even those warrants that seem to express universal truths invite analysis if we can think of claims for which these warrants might not, after all, be relevant. "First in line," for example, may justify the claim of a person who wants a concert ticket, but it cannot in itself justify the claim of someone who wants a vital medication that is in short supply. Moreover, offering a rebuttal to a long-held but unexamined warrant can often produce an interesting and original argument. If someone exclaims, "All this buying of gifts! I think people have forgotten that Christmas celebrates the birth of Christ," she need not express the assumption—that the buying of gifts violates what ought to be a religious celebration. It goes unstated by the speaker because it has been uttered so often that she knows the hearer will supply it. But one writer, in an essay titled "God's Gift: A Commercial Christmas," argued that, contrary to popular belief, the purchase of gifts, which means the expenditure of time, money, and thought on others rather than oneself, is not a violation but an affirmation of the Christmas spirit.[5]

The second reason for refusal to state the warrant lies in the arguer's intention to disarm or deceive the reader, although the arguer may not be aware of this. For instance, failure to state the warrant is common in advertising and politics, where the desire to sell a product or an idea may outweigh the responsibility to argue explicitly. The following advertisement is famous not only for what it says but for what it does not say:

> In 1918 Leona Currie scandalized a New Jersey beach with a bathing suit cut above her knees. And to irk the establishment even more, she smoked a cigarette. Leona Currie was promptly arrested.
>
> Oh, how Leona would smile if she could see you today.

[4] *The Uses of Argument* (Cambridge: Cambridge University Press, 1958), p. 106.
[5] Robert A. Sirico, *Wall Street Journal*, December 21, 1993, sec. A, p. 12.

> You've come a long way, baby. *Virginia Slims.* The taste for today's woman.

What is the unstated warrant? The manufacturer of Virginia Slims hopes we will agree that being permitted to smoke cigarettes is a significant sign of female liberation. But many readers would insist that proving "You've come a long way, baby" requires more evidence than women's freedom to smoke (or wear short bathing suits). The shaky warrant weakens the claim.

Politicians, too, conceal warrants that may not survive close scrutiny. In the 1983 mayoral election in Chicago, one candidate revealed that his opponent had undergone psychiatric treatment. He did not have to state the warrant supporting his claim. He knew that many in his audience would assume that anyone who had undergone psychiatric treatment was unfit to hold public office. This same assumption contributed to the withdrawal of a vice-presidential candidate from the 1972 campaign.

TYPES OF WARRANTS

Arguments may be classified according to the types of warrants offered as proof. Because warrants represent the reasoning process by which we establish the relationship between support and claim, analysis of the major types of warrants enables us to see the whole argument as a sum of its parts.

Warrants may be organized into three categories: "*authoritative, substantive,* and *motivational.*"[6] The *authoritative warrant* is based on the credibility or trustworthiness of the source. If we assume that the source of the data is authoritative, then we find that the support justifies the claim. A *substantive warrant* is based on beliefs about reliability of factual evidence. In the example on page 275 the speaker assumes, although mistakenly, that the relationship between low reading level and stupidity is a verifiable datum, one that can be proved by objective research. A *motivational warrant,* on the other hand, is based on the needs and values of the audience. For example, the warrant about backscatter screening reflects a concern for safety, a value that would cause a reader who held it to agree that more rigid screening techniques are a good idea.

Each type of warrant requires a different set of questions for testing its soundness. The following list of questions will help you to decide whether a particular warrant is valid and can justify a particular claim.

1. *Authoritative* (based on the credibility of the sources)

   Is the authority sufficiently respected to make a credible claim?

   Do other equally reputable authorities agree with the authority cited?

   Are there equally reputable authorities who disagree?

[6] D. Ehninger and W. Brockriede, *Decision by Debate* (New York: Dodd, Mead, 1953).

2. *Substantive* (based on beliefs about the reliability of factual evidence)

   Are sufficient examples given to convince us that a general statement is justified? That is, are the examples given representative of the whole community?

   If you have argued that one event or condition can bring about another (a cause-and-effect argument), does the cause given seem to account entirely for the effect? Are other possible causes equally important as explanations for the effect?

   If you have used comparisons, are the similarities between the two situations greater than the differences?

   If you have used analogies, does the analogy explain or merely describe? Are there sufficient similarities between the two elements to make the analogy appropriate?

3. *Motivational* (based on the values of the arguer and the audience)

   Are the values ones that the audience will regard as important?

   Are the values relevant to the claim?

SAMPLE ANNOTATED ESSAY

The Case for Torture

MICHAEL LEVIN

Introduction: statement of opposing view

It is generally assumed that torture is impermissible, a throwback to a more brutal age. Enlightened societies reject it outright, and regimes suspected of using it risk the wrath of the United States.

Claim of policy: rebuttal of opposing view

I believe this attitude is unwise. There are situations in which torture is not merely permissible but morally mandatory. Moreover, these situations are moving from the realm of imagination to fact.

Support: hypothetical example to test the reader's belief

Suppose a terrorist has hidden an atomic bomb on Manhattan Island which will detonate at noon on July 4 unless . . . (here follow the usual demands for money and release of his friends from jail). Suppose, further, that he is caught at 10 A.M. of the fateful day, but—preferring death to failure—won't

Michael Levin is a professor of philosophy at the City University of New York. This essay is reprinted from the June 7, 1982, issue of *Newsweek*.

disclose where the bomb is. What do we do? If we follow due process—wait for his lawyer, arraign him—millions of people will die. If the only way to save those lives is to subject the terrorist to the most excruciating possible pain, what grounds can there be for not doing so? I suggest there are none. In any case, I ask you to face the question with an open mind.

Torturing the terrorist is unconstitutional? Probably. But millions of lives surely outweigh constitutionality. Torture is barbaric? Mass murder is far more barbaric. Indeed, letting millions of innocents die in deference to one who flaunts his guilt is moral cowardice, an unwillingness to dirty one's hands. If *you* caught the terrorist, could you sleep nights knowing that millions died because you couldn't bring yourself to apply the electrodes?

Support: hypothetical example

5 Once you concede that torture is justified in extreme cases, you have admitted that the decision to use torture is a matter of balancing innocent lives against the means needed to save them. You must now face more realistic cases involving more modest numbers. Someone plants a bomb on a jumbo jet. He alone can disarm it, and his demands cannot be met (or if they can, we refuse to set a precedent by yielding to his threats). Surely we can, we must, do anything to the extortionist to save the passengers. How can we tell 300, or 100, or 10 people who never asked to be put in danger, "I'm sorry, you'll have to die in agony, we just couldn't bring ourselves to . . ."

Support: informal poll

Here are the results of an informal poll about a third, hypothetical, case. Suppose a terrorist group kidnapped a newborn baby from a hospital. I asked four mothers if they would approve of torturing kidnappers if that were necessary to get their own newborns back. All said yes, the most "liberal" adding that she would administer it herself.

Defense of the claim
a) Not punishment but protection of the innocent

I am not advocating torture as punishment. Punishment is addressed to deeds irrevocably past. Rather, I am advocating torture as an acceptable measure for preventing future evils. So understood, it is far less objectionable than many extant punishments. Opponents of the death penalty, for example, are forever insisting that executing a murderer will not bring back his victim (as if the purpose of capital punishment were supposed to be resurrection, not deterrence or retribution). But torture, in the cases described, is intended not to bring anyone back but to keep innocents from being dispatched. The most powerful argument against using torture as a punishment or to secure confessions is that such practices disregard the rights of the individual. Well, if the individual is all that important—and he is—it is correspondingly important to protect the rights of individuals threatened by terrorists. If life is so valuable that it must never be taken, the lives of the innocents must be saved even at the price of hurting the one who endangers them.

Hypothetical examples:
b) Analogies with World War II

Better precedents for torture are assassination and preemptive attack. No Allied leader would have flinched at assassinating Hitler, had that been possible. (The Allies did assassinate Heydrich.) Americans would be angered to learn that Roosevelt could have had Hitler killed in 1943—thereby shortening the war and saving millions of lives—but refused on moral grounds. Similarly, if nation A learns that nation B is about to launch an unprovoked attack, A has a right to save itself by destroying B's military capability first. In the same way, if the police can by torture save those who would otherwise die at the hands of kidnappers or terrorists, they must.

c) Denial that terrorists have rights

There is an important difference between terrorists and their victims that should mute talk of the terrorists' "rights." The terrorist's victims are at risk unintentionally, not having asked to be endangered. But the terrorist knowingly initiated his actions. Unlike his victims, he volunteered for the risks of his deed. By threatening to kill for profit or idealism, he renounces civilized standards, and he can have no complaint if civilization tries to thwart him by whatever means necessary.

Just as torture is justified only to save lives (not 10
extort confessions or recantations), it is justifiably administered only to those *known* to hold innocent lives in their hands. Ah, but how can the authorities ever be sure they have the right malefactor? Isn't there a danger of error and abuse? Won't We turn into Them?

d) Easy identification of terrorists

Questions like these are disingenuous in a world in which terrorists proclaim themselves and perform for television. The name of their game is public recognition. After all, you can't very well intimidate a government into releasing your freedom fighters unless you announce that it is your group that has seized its embassy. "Clear guilt" is difficult to define, but when 40 million people see a group of masked gunmen seize an airplane on the evening news, there is not much question about who the perpetrators are. There will be hard cases where the situation is murkier. Nonetheless, a line demarcating the legitimate use of torture can be drawn. Torture only the obviously guilty, and only for the sake of saving innocents, and the line between Us and Them will remain clear.

Conclusion warrant: "Paralysis in the face of evil is the greater danger."

There is little danger that the Western democracies will lose their way if they choose to inflict pain as one way of preserving order. Paralysis in the face of evil is the greater danger. Some day soon a terrorist will threaten tens of thousands of lives, and torture will be the only way to save them. We had better start thinking about this.

Analysis

Levin's controversial essay attacks a popular assumption that most people have never thought to question — that torture is impermissible under any circumstances. Levin argues that in extreme cases torture is morally justified to bring about a greater good than the rights of the individual who is tortured.

Against the initial resistance that most readers may feel, Levin makes a strong case. Its strength lies in the backing he provides for the warrant that torture is sometimes necessary. This backing consists in the use of two effective argumentative strategies. One is the anticipation of objections. Unprecedented? No. Unconstitutional? No. Barbaric? No. Second, and more important, are the hypothetical examples that compel readers to rethink their positions and possibly arrive at agreement with the author. Levin chooses extreme examples — kidnapping of a newborn child, planting a bomb on a jumbo jet, detonating an atomic bomb in Manhattan — that draw a line between clear and murky cases and make agreement easier. And he bolsters his moral position by insisting that torture is not to be used as punishment or revenge but only to save innocent lives.

To support such an unpopular assumption the writer must convey the impression that he is a reasonable man, and this Levin attempts to do by a searching definition of terms, the careful organization and development of his argument, including references to the opinions of other people, and the expression of compassion for innocent lives.

Another strength of the article is its readability—the use of contractions, informal questions, conversational locutions. This easy, familiar style is disarming; the reader doesn't feel threatened by heavy admonitions from a writer who affects a superior, moral attitude.

Writer's Guide: Recognizing Warrants

1. Locate in your essay the one sentence that best states your claim, or if there is no single sentence that does so, try to express your claim in a single sentence.
2. If you have not already done so, think about for what audience you are writing. How is that audience likely to respond to your claim? The most important question to ask about your audience regarding warrants is this one: What assumption or assumptions must my audience make to be able to accept my claim? The answer to that question will be the warrant or warrants on which your essay is based.
3. The support you offer will make it easier for your audience to accept your claim. Remember that the warrant is the link between claim and support. It may help to use the formula used in this chapter to think systematically through your argument. Ask yourself what the claim is, what support you are offering, and what warrant connects the two. Do that for each major supporting statement that you make.
4. You may not need to state your warrant directly if it is a universally accepted truth that most reasonable readers would agree with it. You should be able to do so, however, in order to check your own logic.
5. If you are asking the members of your audience to accept a warrant that they are not likely to accept, you must offer backing for that warrant or consider restating your claim in a way that does not ask them to agree to an assumption that they will not be willing to agree with.

READINGS FOR ANALYSIS

We're All Celebrities in Post-Privacy Age

ERIC AUCHARD

Move over, Paris Hilton. We all have celebrity issues in an age when anyone can create an online profile, post confessional videos on YouTube, or make snarky online comments about other people.

The latest generation of Web sites—which attract tens of millions of users daily to share words, photos, and videos about themselves and their friends—make a virtue of openness at the expense of traditional notions of privacy.

"My grandparents would have had a different attitude about privacy," says Jeff Jarvis, a former critic for *TV Guide* turned top blogger and columnist for the *Guardian* in London.

"There is a different calculus now," he says.

5 Sites like Facebook, Photobucket, and Flickr are enjoying surging popularity for allowing people to control their online identities in ways that make the danger of revealing too much information a constant worry—and all part of the game.

"Within the Web realm there is no private self," argues David Weinberger, author of a newly published book, "Everything Is Miscellaneous: The Power of the New Digital Disorder."

"The closest you can mean is that you are with a small group behind some password-protected mechanism," he says.

The danger of such exposure is that it could affect careers when students seek jobs in the real world or private citizens seek public office.

George W. Bush and Bill Clinton might never have been elected president had sites like Google Inc.'s YouTube or News Corp.'s MySpace, the world's biggest online meeting places, existed to record the events of their younger years.

10 But while policy makers ponder how to bolster online anonymity, social network users are more concerned about deciding what to reveal about themselves next.

Control, Community Trump Privacy

Most users of the new self-publishing tools report finding a stronger sense of community among friends, family, and random Web site visitors who share their interests.

Eric Auchard has worked for Reuters news service since 1992. In 1993 he switched to technology writing and now coordinates the technology news covered by 200 reporters and editors worldwide, working himself as both a reporter and an editor for Reuters. This article appeared online on June 21, 2007.

Facebook, a site started by a Harvard University undergraduate as a way for students to get to know one another, has exploded in popularity among professional users in Britain and the United States since the site took steps to open up to people of all ages over the past year. It now claims 25 million active users, who like the control Facebook gives them over who they let into their network of online acquaintances.

"What Facebook does is it allows me to control my identity and my society—my group of friends," Jarvis says. "You can call it privacy or you can call it publicness. I am controlling both sides of that equation, together—that's the secret."

Highlighting his own change of thinking on the subject of privacy, Jarvis revealed last year in a blog post, entitled "My cheatin' heart," that he was suffering from a medical condition that slowed work on his widely read media criticism blog, BuzzMachine (http://www.buzzmachine.com/). Supportive comments, and advice about potential treatments, poured in.

15 "Revealing a little bit of yourself is the only way to make connections to other people and that is how the Internet works," Jarvis says. "I couldn't have gotten that benefit unless I revealed the condition."

Caterina Fake, co-founder of popular photo sharing site Flickr, said recently that the defining moment for her start-up was when it decided all photos on the site would be public. Previously, photo sites had assumed users' photos should be private, unless deliberately published for public consumption.

Mena Trott, who, with her husband, Ben, developed Movable Type, a software system for publishing blogs, says "control" is a better word than "privacy" for defining oneself in different situations on the Web.

"We think blogging is sharing the stuff you care about with the people you care about," Trott says. "It comes down to control. They may or may not use it. But people want control."

Trott's company, Six Apart, makes publishing tools used by everyone from Hollywood gossip reporters to moms who seek to document their everyday lives, in private or semi-public mode.

20 "The Internet is often accused of leading to uncivil behavior," Jarvis says. "Identity will lead to civility because we are being watched. It's like living in a small town again."

READING AND DISCUSSION QUESTIONS

1. What experience, if any, have you had with the sort of sites to which Auchard refers: for example, Facebook, Photobucket, and Flickr?
2. What are the pros and cons of posting to such social networking sites?
3. The heading halfway through the article reads, "Control, Community Trump Privacy." Explain what Auchard means by that.
4. What is Auchard's claim?
5. What types of support does he use?
6. What is his warrant?
7. Explain whether or not you accept his warrant.

WRITING SUGGESTIONS

8. Attack or defend this statement made by Auchard: "The danger of such exposure [on the Web] is that it could affect careers when students seek jobs in the real world or private citizens seek public office."
9. Write an essay in which you explain whether or not you believe that it is possible to achieve, on the Web, a balance between publicness and privacy.
10. What are the dangers of exposing personal information on the Internet?
11. Explain why you believe that sites like Facebook and MySpace are so popular.

DISCUSSION QUESTIONS

1. What is the significance of the name of the product?
2. What assumptions underlie the remaining text in the ad?
3. How do the visual elements reinforce the text?
4. Can you think of other ads that make use of celebrities? What are some of the warrants that underlie the use of celebrities to sell products?

Do We Need the Census Race Question?

NATHAN GLAZER

A FEW years ago, when I was asked to comment on the controversy over how best to handle the demand of so-called multiracial advocacy groups for a "multiracial" category in the census, I made a brash and wildly unrealistic proposal.[1] Before describing my proposal, however, I should explain what concerned me about the existing questions on race, Hispanicity, and ancestry in the census. These questions had evolved by the 1980 and 1990 censuses in a way that was to my mind false to American racial and ethnic reality and incapable of getting coherent responses, to the degree that that is possible and that is normally expected in a census.

The census short form is the piece of official government paper that is probably seen by more Americans than any other, surpassing in the extent of its distribution the income tax forms. It is a message to the American people, and like any message it educates them to some reality: This is what the government needs, this what it wants, this is what it thinks is important. The census tells the American people that the government thinks the most important thing about them is to get them classified by race and ethnicity—ethnicity, that is, only if it qualifies as something called "Hispanic"; otherwise, the government is not interested. The census asks Americans first for the kinds of information that almost any form does, whether for a credit card or a driver's license—name, sex, age, family status—but then it turns out the main thing the government is interested in is their "race," described in the greatest detail, down to distinctions between Samoan and Guamanian and, if the respondent is Hispanic, between Argentinean, Colombian, Dominican, Nicaraguan, and even Spanish.

The government, in this message sent to all of us, apparently considers these matters more important than how educated we are, or whether we are citizens, or whether we are foreign born, or whether we voted in the last election. Scholars and researchers who follow the matter closely know why these questions are there, so prominently, so fully detailed. Do the American people in general know? If they do not—and it is hardly likely they are fully briefed on the legislation and regulations and politics and the pressures that have made the census form, with respect to race and Hispanicity, what it is today—what are they to conclude?

Nathan Glazer is a professor emeritus at the Graduate School of Education at Harvard University and past professor of sociology at the University of California at Berkeley. He is a former assistant editor for *Commentary* magazine and is a contributing editor of the *New Republic*. His books include *Beyond the Melting Pot* (with Daniel Patrick Moynihan; 1970), *We Are All Multiculturalists Now* (1997), and *The Lonely Crowd* (with David Riesman; rev. ed. 2001). He has served on presidential task forces on education and urban policy and on National Academy of Science committees on urban policy and minority issues.

The census is supposed to give us a portrait of America. Is this what America looks like? Is the matter of race so important that it deserves this prominence and degree of detail?

5 A further problem is evident: that these questions are trying to impose on identities in flux—not all, of course, but many—a categorization scheme that will inevitably confuse many people. It is a scheme in which many cannot place themselves, and one that requires all sorts of manipulations by the census professionals to put the results into a form in which it can be presented to Congress, the press, and the American people. There is bound to be a substantial degree of error in these final figures, which are never rounded to indicate their uncertainty nor presented with any indication of their degree of error—in contrast with public opinion polls. Yet asking about race and ethnicity has many similarities to public opinion polls about attitudes, compared with questions about age, or amount of schooling, or a number of other topics on which respondents are pretty clear.

Finally, there is simply the irrationality of the categories. Why does Hispanicity include people from Argentina and Spain but not those from Brazil or Portugal? Are there really all those races in Asia, where each country seems to consist of a single and different race, compared with simply "white" for all of Europe and the Middle East? Why, indeed, do people of Spanish origin rate special treatment, as against people from Italy, Poland, or Greece?

All this is familiar. And so I made my proposal. I confess that underlying my proposal was an ideological or political position—just as ideological and political positions underlie the present census arrangements. My position was that it is necessary and desirable to recognize and encourage the ongoing assimilation of the many strands that make the American people into a common culture. It is, I realize, a delicate task to draw a line between "recognize"—which is what the census should do—and "encourage," which it should not see as part of its task. Any form of recognition or nonrecognition is also, however, a form of encouragement or dissuasion. One encourages what one recognizes and dissuades what one does not. My proposal also responded to my interest as a social scientist in recording the progress of this change, which has been continuous in American history, affecting all groups in different degree but tragically leaving aside, for most of our history, one major group.

So then, my brash and unrealistic proposal: I proposed reducing the mishmash of race, Hispanicity, and ancestry to basically two questions. One question would determine whether a person considered himself or herself black or African American. That would remain the only race for which the census requested information. A second question or group of questions would ask in which country the respondent was born and in which country his or her parents were born and could be extended to ask where that person's grandparents were born. These questions on the country of birth of parents and grandparents would be filled in by respondents rather than presented in a multiple-choice format with predetermined options.

Why the interest in only one race? The census has counted blacks, slave and free, since the first enumeration of 1790. History alone and the virtues of continuity would make a claim that that determination be continued. There are, of course, far more potent reasons. This is the group that has suffered from prejudice, discrimination, and a lower-caste status since the origins of the Republic. In law, all this is now overcome and does not exist, but African Americans, we know, despite their presence in large numbers from our origins as a group of British colonies on the Atlantic shore, are less integrated in American society than any other large group. They are more segregated residentially. The rate of intermarriage with others outside the group, even if rapidly increasing, is still the lowest for any large group. They have a clear sense of their identity. One can depend on a high degree of reliability in the answers they give to the race question, as census research has shown.

The second question or group of questions replaces the "ancestry" 10
question because of the rapid rate of assimilation of all groups except blacks or African Americans. The limitation of these questions to the parental generation, and possibly the grandparental, is first a response to the reality that by the third generation and certainly by the fourth, the mix of ethnicities is extensive; second, it serves as an indication that the census and the government are not interested in group characteristics in the third generation and beyond.[2] With intermarriage rates in new nonblack immigrant groups of 30 percent or thereabouts, we assume that by the third generation assimilation has progressed to the point at which identity is mixed and fluctuating and its ethnic character has become largely symbolic. We leave the question of what that identity consists of to the excellent sociologists, such as Richard Alba and Mary Waters, who have studied the nature of ethnic identification in these later generations. The census thereby gets out of the business of trying to affix an ancestry to each American.

If one thinks that each of the peoples of Asia forms a distinct race, this question will be able to encompass all the immigrants from that country and their children. There are not many yet in the third generation. By the time there is a substantial third generation of the post-1960s wave of immigrants, many will be of mixed ancestry, and the question of their identity will be left to them. Intermarriage statistics suggest the same for Hispanics, the great majority of whom are now immigrants and the children of immigrants. The only distinct group for which the census will try to get statistics on all those identified with it is the black or African American, for historical reasons we all know but also because black or African American identity does not fade after a few generations in this country but maintains itself in a varying but full form generation after generation.

I realize that problems remain regarding American Indians, Alaska Natives, Hawaiians, and part-Hawaiians. All these groups have a legal status, and there are means for determining who does and does not belong to each of these groups. I can see the virtue of specific questions beyond those I have suggested for Hawaii and Alaska, but I do not think 280 million

Americans have to be troubled to determine the numbers of these very small groups.

Questions on birthplace and parental birthplace as posed today, as against the same questions during the last great wave of immigration, have one virtue: during that earlier wave, immigrants came from Europe, where many ethnic groups could be found within the boundaries of great multi-ethnic empires, and thus birthplace said little about ethnicity. In addition, the boundaries of eastern Europe have been radically recast three times in a century, and European immigrants and their children could be properly confused as to the country of their birth. What was the birthplace of a person born in Bukowina? If the census asks, "what country were you born in?" there are at least four reasonable candidates. Most of today's immigrants, in contrast, come from countries whose boundaries have been stable for a century or more, and their birthplaces and those of their parents permit us to make reasonable judgments as to their ethnic group.

This, I argued, was all that was needed in place of the present questions on race, Hispanicity, and ancestry. These two questions would provide less detailed data but more accurate data. They would also be more responsive to what America was like, and what it was becoming.

I knew the proposal was politically naive, but I was not aware of how 15
powerful and steady were the forces that created the present unsatisfactory situation until I went further into the history of the creation of the present categories (Skerry 2000; Nobles 2000; Anderson and Fienberg 1999; Bryant and Dunn 1995; Mitroff, Mason, and Barabba 1983). This research underlines the somewhat utopian character of my proposals today.

The experts seem to agree that when it comes to the census, the political outweighs the scientific, and this is a reality we have to live with. The word "political" can, of course, refer to many things, from the more to the less noble. What we have today in the census is political in all these senses. Some of it is, in part, the result of major civil rights legislation, which, to my mind, falls on the noble side. That legislation had to be interpreted by the courts and by the administrative agencies, however, under the pressure of ethnic groups. As we follow this process further into the details that shaped the form of the census questions, the element of nobility in the political process declines. I am not sure the legislation itself, which was concerned with the right to vote, required what the census has done in its effort to respond to the demand for small-area data on Hispanics and Asian Americans. One could make a case that questions on birthplace and parental birthplace alone and the language question could give us the data to satisfy the legislation. But it would not give us the data in a form that satisfies proponents of distinct group interests and activists.

There are also the less noble political interventions. The census questions, whatever we think of their incongruity and irrationality, are the direct result of powerful pressures from the ethnic groups concerned, from

Congress, and from the Executive Office of the President. These are political, alas, not only in the sense that political actors are involved but also in the narrower and less respectable sense that they are often motivated by narrow partisan political considerations.

Thus, Peter Skerry informs us, the unfortunate "ancestry" question was "criticized by social scientists for being vague and uninformative" in comparison with the question on birthplace of respondent's parents that it replaced. The Census Bureau also opposed it. "So why did the ancestry question end up on the questionnaire?" Skerry asks. "According to former deputy census director Louis Kincannon, who was working at the Statistical Policy Division of OMB when the decision was made, 'the ethnic desk' in the [Carter] White House insisted that the ancestry question go on the census. . . . It is evident that in the period leading up to the 1980 Presidential campaign, politics overrode the objections of both the OMB and the Census Bureau" (Skerry 2000, 37).

Democrats are understandably more responsive than Republicans to ethnic-group pressures, but Skerry tells us that Republican administrations have been no help, either. Concerning the origins of the Hispanic question, he notes that:

> the finalized questionnaires for the 1970 census were already at the printers when a Mexican American member of the U.S. Interagency Committee on Mexican American Affairs demanded that a specific Hispanic-origin question be included. . . . Over the opposition of Census Bureau officials, who argued against inclusion of an untested question so late in the process, Nixon ordered the secretary of commerce and the census director to add the question. . . . So it was hastily added to the long form. As former bureau official Conrad Taeuber recalls, "The order came down that we were to ask a direct question, have the people identify themselves as Hispanic." (Skerry 2000, 37–38)

The pressures initially come from the ethnic groups involved or their 20
leaders. Although there is only an uncertain relation between the numbers and the benefits that members of a group might get from one affirmative action program or another, undoubtedly the notion that one will in some way benefit from being counted as a distinct group plays a role in these pressures. At one time, Asian Indians were divided as to whether they should be "Caucasian" or yet another Asian race. Melissa Nobles reports on the discussion in the 1970s of the Federal Interagency Committee on Education on devising racial and ethnic categories for various federal programs. "The committee debated whether persons from India should be categorized under the 'Asian and Pacific Islander' category or under the 'White/Caucasian' category. . . . In the trial directive, they were classified as Caucasian, but they were reclassified as Asian in the final version (most likely in response to Asian Indian lobbying to ensure racial minority status)" (Nobles 2000, 79).

At the time, many in the Asian Indian community, taking into account their relatively high educational and economic position in the United States, rejected the idea that they should be eligible for benefits. Alas, the possibility of getting preferences for Indians under affirmative action programs for government contracts outweighed other considerations, and Indians—or at least some leadership groups—decided it was best to join the Chinese, Japanese, Koreans, and the rest as an "Asian race." I recall a report in an Indian newspaper that President Ronald Reagan's Small Business Administration (SBA) director had announced to an Indian conference that the SBA had decided to include South Asians among the groups that were considered qualified for preference in bidding for government contracts—this despite the fact that President Reagan was publicly an opponent of affirmative action programs. No doubt the administration hoped to garner a few Indian contributions or votes.

Congressional intervention can go into a level of detail that boggles the mind. Congress intervened in the wording of the 1990 race question when the Census Bureau shortened it to include only seven categories. Representative Robert Matsui introduced legislation "in which the formatting of the . . . race question was spelled out, even to the point of stipulating that 'Taiwanese' be one of the subgroups." Both houses passed it. "It was only President Reagan's pocket veto that blocked this extraordinary degree of congressional involvement in what is ordinarily considered the technical side of questionnaire design" (Skerry 2000, 41).

Social scientists deal with levels of irrationality—irrationality, that is, from the point of view of social science—that cannot be much affected by reasoned argument. Stanley Lieberson describes what happened when he attended a conference preparatory to the 1990 census. "I naively suggested that there was no reason to have a Hispanic question separate from the ethnic ancestry question since the former—as far as I could tell—could be classified as a subpart of the latter. Several participants from prominent Hispanic organizations were furious with such a proposal. They were furious, by the way, not at me (just a naive academic), rather it was in the form of a warning to census personnel of the consequences that would follow were this proposal to be taken seriously" (Lieberson 1993, 30).

So, what else is new? Undoubtedly the degree of political intervention, however we understand the term "political," is now at a peak, and to propose changes in the race, Hispanicity, and ancestry questions is probably an exercise in futility. (I wonder whether Reynolds Farley's excellent suggestion that the three questions be combined into one—"What is this person's primary identity?"—followed by the five "official" group designations, with write-ins permitted under each, has ever gotten any public discussion.)

25 In the longer view, we know that politics has always played a significant role in the census. Melissa Nobles tells us the fascinating history of the use of "mulatto" in the census—a term that was included in censuses from 1850 until 1920 (Nobles 2000). It was originally introduced to sup-

port slaveholders' arguments that freedom and intermixture was bad for blacks. The abolition of slavery did not end the use of the category—it could still be used, its proponents believed, to argue that races were best off separated and that intermixture produced an inferior human being. In 1888, a member of Congress from Alabama, having decided that it was necessary to go into more detail on this thesis, introduced legislation—which passed both houses and became law—directing the census to "take such steps as may be necessary to ascertain . . . the birth rate and death rate among pure whites, and among negroes, Chinamen, Indians, and half-breeds or hybrids of any description . . . as well as of mulattoes, quadroons, and octoroons" (quoted in Nobles 2000, 56). Indeed, so directed, the census did have categories for quadroons and octoroons in the 1890 census—however useless may have been the results.

The mulattoes, quadroons, and octoroons are gone. What are the long-term prospects for that astonishing list of races in the census and that equally astonishing list of "Hispanics"? Will the lists get longer in the future, or shorter, and what factors might affect their future?

This is an interesting exercise in forecasting and prediction. It is possible that the pressures that derive from affirmative action and the hope for benefits from it, for example, will decline as affirmative action itself is restricted. It has already been banned, by public referendum, judicial action, or administrative action, in the public colleges and universities of four states. One effect of this ban has been an increase in the number of students giving no racial or ethnic identity to university authorities. There has been a substantial increase in the number of such students at the University of California at Berkeley. Why identify oneself if there is no longer a benefit in doing so? Is there an incipient revolt one can detect against the degree of racial and ethnic categorization that has been institutionalized, a revolt that will reduce further the reliability of these questions?

Much of the institutionalization of these categories in the census can be traced to the Voting Rights Act, and the ill-advised extension of this act in 1975 to "language minorities," persons of Spanish heritage, American Indians, and Asian Americans. I do not know what evidence there was, even in 1975, that these groups were prevented from voting because of lack of knowledge of English. This act requires hundreds of jurisdictions to produce voting materials in various languages—itself an irritation in various parts of the country. I wonder whether there is any evidence this has increased voting among members of these groups. (I would guess there is not.) These provisions require the census to tabulate and distribute census small-area data on the groups protected in the Voting Rights Act very rapidly after a census has been taken.

There is an inherent contradiction between the assumptions of this act and the requirement that one know English to be naturalized as a citizen. When a large number of Jewish immigrants spoke Yiddish and read only Yiddish-language newspapers, they had no trouble voting in substantial numbers equivalent to their English-speaking neighbors—even electing Socialist legislators. Are matters very different for current immigrants speaking foreign languages? Will these provisions survive, even to the census of 2010? Note that whenever a measure to declare English the "official language" gets on the ballot, as it has in a number of states, it passes. This suggests a popular hostility to these Voting Rights Act provisions. How long would they survive if submitted to a popular vote? The original point of the act was to overcome barriers to voting by blacks in the South, which were indeed great, were enforced by white officials, and had little to do with knowledge of English. The bilingual voting assistance provisions come up for renewal in 2007. Is it possible that some bold member of Congress will suggest that they are no longer needed?

All this suggests that the present distribution of political forces is not 30
eternal, and the time may come when the questions now used for race and Hispanicity will seem as outlandish as the 1890 attempt to count quadroons and octoroons. The powerful assimilatory forces in American life are at work—working more slowly, it is true, for blacks than for other groups but still working to an end that will change how the census asks about race, Hispanicity, and ancestry. I hope that change comes about not because of some xenophobic revolt against this excessive census involvement in racial and ethnic categorization but because the members of the groups so marked out themselves no longer see any reason for the U.S. government to inquire officially into an ever murkier and indeterminate racial and ethnic identity.

Notes

1. My proposal is most easily found in Hartman 1997. It originally appeared in *Poverty and Race*, the newsletter of the Poverty and Race Research Action Council.

2. On the mix of ethnicities, see the impressive demonstration in Perlmann 2000. It is also evident in the analysis of responses to the ancestry question presented in Lieberson and Waters 1998.

References

Anderson, Margo J., & Fienberg, Stephen E. (1999). *Who Counts? The Politics of Census-Taking in Contemporary America*. New York: Russell Sage Foundation.

Bryant, Barbara Everitt, & Dunn, William. (1995). *Moving Power and Money: The Politics of Census Taking*. Ithaca: New Strategist Publications.

Hartman, Chester. (Ed.) (1997). *Double Exposure: Poverty and Race in America*. Armonk: M. E. Sharpe.

Lieberson, Stanley. (1993). "The Enumeration of Ethnic and Racial Groups in the Census: Some Devilish Principles." In *Challenges of Measuring an Ethnic World*. Proceedings of the Joint Canada-United States Conference on the Measurement of Ethnicity. Washington: U.S. Department of Commerce, U.S. Bureau of the Census.

Lieberson, Stanley, & Waters, Mary. (1988). *From Many Strands*. New York: Russell Sage Foundation.

Mitroff, Ian I., Mason, Richard O., & Barabba, Vincent P. (1983). *The 1980 Census: Policymaking Amid Turbulence*. Lexington: Lexington Books.
Nobles, Melissa. (2000). *Shades of Citizenship*. Stanford: Stanford University Press.
Perlmann, Joel. (2000). "Demographic Outcomes of Ethnic Intermarriage in American History: Italian-Americans Through Four Generations." Working Paper 312. Annandale-on-Hudson: Jerome Levy Economics Institute.
Skerry, Peter. (2000). *Counting on the Census: Race, Group Identity, and the Evasion of Politics*. Washington: Brookings Institution.

READING AND DISCUSSION QUESTIONS

1. Glazer is discussing a change in the census form that he suggested "a few years ago." (The article was published in 2002.) What was his proposal?
2. Why does he believe his proposal offers an improvement over the current census form's questions about race and ethnicity?
3. What warrant or warrants underlie his argument?
4. Does his proposal seem to be reasonable? Does it seem to be an improvement on the current form?
5. This article by Glazer appeared on the Web before it was published in print form in a collection of essays. In the online article, Glazer had no documentation. He did have a note, however, that explained that a version with documentation was forthcoming in print. Is there less need for documentation when a piece of writing appears in electronic form? Why add documentation only when the piece moves into print?

WRITING SUGGESTIONS

6. Write an essay in which you either agree or disagree with Glazer's proposed change.
7. Glazer argues that ethnic and racial lines become blurred quickly after a short time in America. Do you believe that is a positive or a negative result of immigration to America?
8. Why do so many forms that we fill out ask for our race or national origin? Are there some situations in which race and national origin are relevant and others in which they are not? Explain. (Can you think of situations in which it is unlawful to ask such a question?)

Civil Disobedience

HENRY DAVID THOREAU

I heartily accept the motto,—"That government is best which governs least"; and I should like to see it acted up to more rapidly and systematically. Carried out, it finally amounts to this, which also I believe,—"That government is best which governs not at all"; and when men are prepared for it, that will be the kind of government which they will have. Government is at best but an expedient; but most governments are usually, and all governments are sometimes, inexpedient. The objections which have been brought against a standing army, and they are many and weighty, and deserve to prevail, may also at last be brought against a standing government. The standing army is only an arm of the standing government. The government itself, which is only the mode which the people have chosen to execute their will, is equally liable to be abused and perverted before the people can act through it. Witness the present Mexican war, the work of comparatively a few individuals using the standing government as their tool; for, in the outset, the people would not have consented to this measure.

This American government,—what is it but a tradition, though a recent one, endeavoring to transmit itself unimpaired to posterity, but each instant losing some of its integrity? It has not the vitality and force of a single living man; for a single man can bend it to his will. It is a sort of wooden gun to the people themselves. But it is not the less necessary for this; for the people must have some complicated machinery or other, and hear its din, to satisfy that idea of government which they have. Governments show thus how successfully men can be imposed on, even impose on themselves, for their own advantage. It is excellent, we must all allow. Yet this government never of itself furthered any enterprise, but by the alacrity with which it got out of its way. *It* does not keep the country free. *It* does not settle the West. *It* does not educate. The character inherent in the American people has done all that has been accomplished; and it would have done somewhat more, if the government had not sometimes got in its way. For government is an expedient by which men would fain succeed in letting one another alone; and, as has been said, when it is most expedient, the governed are most let alone by it. Trade and commerce, if they were not made of India-rubber, would never manage to bounce over the

---

Henry David Thoreau (1817–1862), philosopher and writer, is best known for *Walden*, an account of his solitary retreat to Walden Pond, near Concord, Massachusetts. Here he remained for more than two years in an effort to "live deliberately, to front only the essential facts of life." "Civil Disobedience" was first given as a lecture in 1848 and published in 1849. It was widely read and influenced both Mahatma Gandhi in the passive-resistance campaign he led against the British in India and Martin Luther King Jr. in the U.S. civil rights movement.

obstacles which legislators are continually putting in their way; and, if one were to judge these men wholly by the effects of their actions, and not partly by their intentions, they would deserve to be classed and punished with those mischievous persons who put obstructions on the railroads.

But, to speak practically and as a citizen, unlike those who call themselves no-government men, I ask for, not at once no government, but *at once* a better government. Let every man make known what kind of government would command his respect, and that will be one step toward obtaining it.

After all, the practical reason why, when the power is once in the hands of the people, a majority are permitted, and for a long period continue, to rule, is not because they are most likely to be in the right, nor because this seems fairest to the minority, but because they are physically the strongest. But a government in which the majority rule in all cases cannot be based on justice, even as far as men understand it. Can there not be a government in which majorities do not virtually decide right and wrong, but conscience?—in which majorities decide only those questions to which the rule of expediency is applicable? Must the citizen ever for a moment, or in the least degree, resign his conscience to the legislator? Why has every man a conscience, then? I think that we should be men first, and subjects afterward. It is not desirable to cultivate a respect for the law, so much as for the right. The only obligation which I have a right to assume, is to do at any time what I think right. It is truly enough said, that a corporation has no conscience; but a corporation of conscientious men is a corporation *with* a conscience. Law never made men a whit more just; and, by means of their respect for it, even the well-disposed are daily made the agents of injustice. A common and natural result of an undue respect for law is, that you may see a file of soldiers, colonel, captain, corporal, privates, powder-monkeys, and all, marching in admirable order over hill and dale to the wars, against their wills, aye, against their common sense and consciences, which makes it very steep marching indeed, and produces a palpitation of the heart. They have no doubt that it is a damnable business in which they are concerned; they are all peaceably inclined. Now, what are they? Men at all? or small moveable forts and magazines, at the service of some unscrupulous man in power? Visit the Navy-Yard, and behold a marine, such a man as an American government can make, or such as it can make a man with its black arts,—a mere shadow and reminiscence of humanity, a man laid out alive and standing, and already, as one may say, buried under arms with funeral accompaniments, though it may be, —

Not a drum was heard, nor a funeral note,
As his corse to the rampart we hurried;
Not a soldier discharged his farewell shot
O'er the grave where our hero we buried.

5 The mass of men serve the state thus, not as men mainly, but as machines, with their bodies. They are the standing army, and the militia, jailers, constables, posse comitatus, &c. In most cases there is no free exercise whatever of the judgment or of the moral sense; but they put themselves on a level with wood and earth and stones; and wooden men can perhaps be manufactured that will serve the purpose as well. Such command no more respect than men of straw, or a lump of dirt. They have the same sort of worth only as horses and dogs. Yet such as these even are commonly esteemed good citizens. Others,—as most legislators, politicians, lawyers, ministers, and office-holders,—serve the State chiefly with their heads; and, as they rarely make any moral distinctions, they are as likely to serve the Devil, without *intending* it, as God. A very few, as heroes, patriots, martyrs, reformers in the great sense, and *men*, serve the state with their consciences also, and so necessarily resist it for the most part, and they are commonly treated as enemies by it. A wise man will only be useful as a man, and will not submit to be "clay," and "stop a hole to keep the wind away," but leave that office to his dust at least:—

> I am too high-born to be propertied,
> To be a secondary at control,
> Or useful serving-man and instrument
> To any sovereign state throughout the world.

He who gives himself entirely to his fellow-men appears to them useless and selfish; but he who gives himself partially to them is pronounced a benefactor and philanthropist.

How does it become a man to behave toward this American government today? I answer that he cannot without disgrace be associated with it. I cannot for an instant recognize that political organization as *my* government which is the *slave's* government also.

All men recognize the right of revolution; that is, the right to refuse allegiance to, and to resist, the government, when its tyranny or its inefficiency are great and unendurable. But almost all say that such is not the case now. But such was the case, they think, in the Revolution of '75. If one were to tell me that this was a bad government because it taxed certain foreign commodities brought to its ports, it is most probable that I should not make an ado about it, for I can do without them. All machines have their friction; and possibly this does enough good to counterbalance the evil. At any rate, it is a great evil to make a stir about it. But when the friction comes to have its machine, and oppression and robbery are organized, I say, let us not have such a machine any longer. In other words, when a sixth of the population of a nation which has undertaken to be the refuge of liberty are slaves, and a whole country is unjustly overrun and conquered by a foreign army, and subjected to military law, I think that it is not too soon for honest men to rebel and revolutionize. What makes this duty the more urgent is the fact, that the country so overrun is not our own, but ours is the invading army.

Paley, a common authority with many on moral questions, in his chapter on the "Duty of Submission to Civil Government," resolves all civil obligation into expediency; and he proceeds to say, "that so long as the interest of the whole society requires it, that is, so long as the established government cannot be resisted or changed without public inconveniency, it is the will of God that the established government be obeyed, and no longer. . . . This principle being admitted, the justice of every particular case of resistance is reduced to a computation of the quantity of the danger and grievance on the one side, and of the probability and expense of redressing it on the other." Of this, he says, every man shall judge for himself. But Paley appears never to have contemplated those cases to which the rule of expediency does not apply, in which a people, as well as an individual, must do justice, cost what it may. If I have unjustly wrested a plank from a drowning man, I must restore it to him though I drown myself. This, according to Paley, would be inconvenient. But he that would save his life, in such a case, shall lose it. This people must cease to hold slaves, and to make war on Mexico, though it cost them their existence as a people.

In their practice, nations agree with Paley; but does any one think 10
that Massachusetts does exactly what is right at the present crisis?

> A drab of state, a cloth-'o-silver slut,
> To have her train borne up, and her soul trail in the dirt.

Practically speaking, the opponents to a reform in Massachusetts are not a hundred thousand politicians at the South, but a hundred thousand merchants and farmers here, who are more interested in commerce and agriculture than they are in humanity, and are not prepared to do justice to the slave and to Mexico, *cost what it may*. I quarrel not with far-off foes, but with those who, near at home, cooperate with, and do the bidding of, those far away, and without whom the latter would be harmless. We are accustomed to say, that the mass of men are unprepared; but improvement is slow, because the few are not materially wiser or better than the many. It is not so important that many should be as good as you, as that there be some absolute goodness somewhere; for that will leaven the whole lump. There are thousands who are *in opinion* opposed to slavery and to the war, who yet in effect do nothing to put an end to them; who, esteeming themselves children of Washington and Franklin, sit down with their hands in their pockets, and say that they know not what to do, and do nothing; who even postpone the question of freedom to the question of free-trade, and quietly read the prices-current along with the latest advice from Mexico, after dinner, and, it may be, fall asleep over them both. What is the price-current of an honest man and patriot today? They hesitate, and they regret, and sometimes they petition; but they do nothing in earnest and with effect. They will wait, well disposed, for others to remedy the evil, that they may no longer have it to regret. At most, they give only a cheap vote, and a feeble countenance and God-speed, to the right, as it goes by them. There are nine hundred and ninety-nine patrons of virtue to one virtuous man; but it is easier to deal with the real possessor of a thing than with the temporary guardian of it.

All voting is a sort of gaming, like checkers or backgammon, with a slight moral tinge to it, a playing with right and wrong, with moral questions; and betting naturally accompanies it. The character of the voters is not staked. I cast my vote, perchance, as I think right; but I am not vitally concerned that that right should prevail. I am willing to leave it to the majority. Its obligation, therefore, never exceeds that of expediency. Even voting *for the right* is *doing* nothing for it. It is only expressing to men feebly your desire that it should prevail. A wise man will not leave the right to the mercy of chance, nor wish it to prevail through the power of the majority. There is but little virtue in the action of masses of men. When the majority shall at length vote for the abolition of slavery, it will be because they are indifferent to slavery, or because there is but little slavery left to be abolished by their vote. *They* will then be the only slaves. Only *his* vote can hasten the abolition of slavery who asserts his own freedom by his vote.

I hear of a convention to be held at Baltimore, or elsewhere, for the selection of a candidate for the presidency, made up chiefly of editors, and men who are politicians by profession; but I think, what is it to any independent, intelligent, and respectable man what decision they may come to? Shall we not have the advantage of his wisdom and honesty, nevertheless? Can we not count upon some independent votes? Are there not many individuals in the country who do not attend conventions? But no: I find that the respectable man, so called, has immediately drifted from his position, and despairs of his country, when his country has more reason to despair of him. He forthwith adopts one of the candidates thus selected as the only *available* one, thus providing that he is himself *available* for any purposes of the demagogue. His vote is of no more worth than that of any unprincipled foreigner or hireling native, who may have been bought. O for a man who is *a man*, and, as my neighbor says, has a bone in his back which you cannot pass your hand through! Our statistics are at fault: The population has been returned too large. How many *men* are there to a square thousand miles in this country? Hardly one. Does not America offer any inducement for men to settle here? The American has dwindled into an Odd Fellow,—one who may be known by the development of his organ of gregariousness, and a manifest lack of intellect and cheerful self-reliance; whose first and chief concern, on coming into the world, is to see that the Almshouses are in good repair; and, before yet he has lawfully donned the virile garb, to collect a fund for the support of the widows and orphans that may be; who, in short, ventures to live only by the aid of the Mutual Insurance company, which has promised to bury him decently.

It is not a man's duty, as a matter of course, to devote himself to the eradication of any, even the most enormous wrong; he may still properly have other concerns to engage him; but it is his duty, at least, to wash his hands of it, and, if he gives it no thought longer, not to give it practically his support. If I devote myself to other pursuits and contemplations, I must first see, at least, that I do not pursue them sitting upon another man's shoulders. I must get off him first, that he may pursue his contemplations too. See what gross inconsistency is tolerated. I have heard some of my townsmen say, "I should like to have them order me out to help put down an insurrection of the slaves, or to march to Mexico;—see if I would go"; and yet these very men have each, directly by their allegiance, and so indirectly, at least, by their money, furnished a substitute. The soldier is applauded who refuses to serve in an unjust war by those who do not refuse to sustain the unjust government which makes the war; is applauded by those whose own act and authority he disregards and sets at nought; as if the State were penitent to that degree that it hired one to scourge it while it sinned, but not to that degree that it left off sinning for a moment. Thus, under the name of Order and Civil Government, we are all made at last to pay homage to and support our own meanness. After the first blush of sin, comes its indifference; and from immoral it becomes, as it were, *un*moral, and not quite unnecessary to that life which we have made.

The broadest and most prevalent error requires the most disinterested virtue to sustain it. The slight reproach to which the virtue of patriotism is commonly liable, the noble are most likely to incur. Those who, while they disapprove of the character and measures of a government, yield to it their allegiance and support, are undoubtedly its most conscientious supporters, and so frequently the most serious obstacles to reform. Some are petitioning the State to dissolve the Union, to disregard the requisitions of the President. Why do they not dissolve it themselves,—the union between themselves and the State,—and refuse to pay their quota into its treasury? Do not they stand in the same relation to the State, that the State does to the Union? And have not the same reasons prevented the State from resisting the Union which have prevented them from resisting the State?

How can a man be satisfied to entertain an opinion merely, and enjoy 15
it? Is there any enjoyment in it, if his opinion is that he is aggrieved? If you are cheated out of a single dollar by your neighbor, you do not rest satisfied with knowing that you are cheated, or with saying that you are cheated, or even with petitioning him to pay you your due; but you take effectual steps at once to obtain the full amount, and see that you are never cheated again. Action from principle, the perception and the performance of right, changes

things and relations; it is essentially revolutionary, and does not consist wholly with anything which was. It not only divides states and churches, it divides families; ay, it divides the *individual*, separating the diabolical in him from the divine.

Unjust laws exist: Shall we be content to obey them, or shall we endeavor to amend them, and obey them until we have succeeded, or shall we transgress them at once? Men generally, under such a government as this, think that they ought to wait until they have persuaded the majority to alter them. They think that, if they should resist, the remedy would be worse than the evil. But it is the fault of the government itself that the remedy *is* worse than the evil. *It* makes it worse. Why is it not more apt to anticipate and provide for reform? Why does it not cherish its wise minority? Why does it cry and resist before it is hurt? Why does it not encourage its citizens to be on the alert to point out its faults, and *do* better than it would have them? Why does it always crucify Christ, and excommunicate Copernicus and Luther, and pronounce Washington and Franklin rebels?

One would think, that a deliberate and practical denial of its authority was the only offence never contemplated by government; else, why has it not assigned its definite, its suitable and proportionate penalty? If a man who has no property refuses but once to earn nine shillings for the State, he is put in prison for a period unlimited by any law that I know, and determined only by the discretion of those who placed him there; but if he should steal ninety times nine shillings from the State, he is soon permitted to go at large again.

If the injustice is part of the necessary friction of the machine of government, let it go, let it go: Perchance it will wear smooth,—certainly the machine will wear out. If the injustice has a spring, or a pulley, or a rope, or a crank, exclusively for itself, then perhaps you may consider whether the remedy will not be worse than the evil; but if it is of such a nature that it requires you to be the agent of injustice to another, then, I say, break the law. Let your life be a counter friction to stop the machine. What I have to do is to see, at any rate, that I do not lend myself to the wrong which I condemn.

As for adopting the ways which the State has provided for remedying the evil, I know not of such ways. They take too much time, and a man's life will be gone. I have other affairs to attend to. I came into this world, not chiefly to make this a good place to live in, but to live in it, be it good or bad. A man has not everything to do, but something; and because he cannot do *everything*, it is not necessary that he should do *something* wrong. It is not my business to be petitioning the Governor or the Legislature any more than it is theirs to petition me; and, if they should not hear my petition, what should I do then? But in this case the State has provided no way: Its very Constitution is the evil. This may seem to be harsh and stubborn and unconciliatory; but it is to treat with the utmost kindness and consideration the only spirit that can appreciate or deserves it. So is all change for the better, like birth and death, which convulse the body.

20 I do not hesitate to say, that those who call themselves Abolitionists should at once effectually withdraw their support, both in person and property, from the government of Massachusetts, and not wait till they constitute a majority of one, before they suffer the right to prevail through them. I think that it is enough if they have God on their side, without waiting for that other one. Moreover, any man more right than his neighbors, constitutes a majority of one already.

I meet this American government, or its representative, the State government, directly, and face to face, once a year—no more—in the person of its tax-gatherer; this is the only mode in which a man situated as I am necessarily meets it; and it then says distinctly, Recognize me; and the simplest, the most effectual, and, in the present posture of affairs, the indispensablest mode of treating with it on this head, of expressing your little satisfaction with and love for it, is to deny it then. My civil neighbor, the tax-gatherer, is the very man I have to deal with,—for it is, after all, with men and not with parchment that I quarrel,—and he has voluntarily chosen to be an agent of the government. How shall he ever know well what he is and does as an officer of the government, or as a man, until he is obliged to consider whether he shall treat me, his neighbor, for whom he has respect, as a neighbor and well-disposed man, or as a maniac and disturber of the peace, and see if he can get over this obstruction to his neighborliness without a ruder and more impetuous thought or speech corresponding with his action? I know this well, that if one thousand, if one hundred, if ten men whom I could name,—if ten *honest* men only,—aye, if *one* HONEST man, in this State of Massachusetts, *ceasing to hold slaves*, were actually to withdraw from this copartnership, and be locked up in the county jail therefor, it would be the abolition of slavery in America. For it matters not how small the beginning may seem to be: What is once well done is done forever. But we love better to talk about it: That we say is our mission. Reform keeps many scores of newspapers in its service, but not one man. If my esteemed neighbor, the State's ambassador, who will devote his days to the settlement of the question of human rights in the Council Chamber, instead of being threatened with the prisons of Carolina, were to sit down the prisoner of Massachusetts, that State which is so anxious to foist the sin of slavery upon her sister,—though at present she can discover only an act of inhospitality to be the ground of a quarrel with her,—the Legislature would not wholly waive the subject the following winter.

Under a government which imprisons any unjustly, the true place for a just man is also a prison. The proper place today, the only place which Massachusetts has provided for her freer and less desponding spirits, is in her prisons, to be put out and locked out of the State by her own act, as they have already put themselves out by their principles. It is there that the fugitive slave, and the Mexican prisoner on parole, and the Indian come to plead the wrongs of his race, should find them; on that separate, but more free and honorable ground, where the State places those who are not *with* her, but *against* her,—the only house in a slave State in which a free man can abide with honor. If any think that their influence would be lost there, and their voices no longer afflict the ear of the State, that they would not be as an enemy within its walls, they do not know by how much truth is stronger than error, nor how much more eloquently and effectively he can combat injustice who has experienced a little in his own person. Cast your whole vote, not a strip of paper merely, but your whole influence. A minority is powerless while it conforms to the majority; it is not even a minority then; but it is irresistible when it clogs by its whole weight. If the alternative is to keep all just men in prison, or give up war and slavery, the State will not hesitate which to choose. If a thousand men were not to pay their tax-bills this year, that would not be a violent and bloody measure, as it would be to pay them, and enable the State to commit violence and shed innocent blood. This is, in fact, the definition of a peaceable revolution, if any such is possible. If the tax-gatherer, or any other public officer, asks me, as one has done, "But what shall I do?" my answer is, "If you really wish to do any thing, resign your office." When the subject has refused allegiance, and the officer has resigned his office, then the revolution is accomplished. But even suppose blood should flow. Is there not a sort of blood shed when the conscience is wounded? Through this wound a man's real manhood and immortality flow out, and he bleeds to an everlasting death. I see this blood flowing now.

I have contemplated the imprisonment of the offender, rather than the seizure of his goods,—though both will serve the same purpose,—because they who assert the purest right, and consequently are most dangerous to a corrupt State, commonly have not spent much time in accumulating property. To such the State renders comparatively small service, and a slight tax is wont to appear exorbitant, particularly if they are obliged to earn it by special labor with their hands. If there were one who lived wholly without the use of money, the State itself would hesitate to demand it of him. But the rich man,—not to make any invidious comparison,—is always sold to the institution which makes him rich. Absolutely speaking, the more money, the less virtue; for money comes between a man and his objects, and obtains them for him; and it was certainly no great virtue to obtain it. It puts to rest many questions which he would otherwise be taxed to answer; while the only new question which it puts is the hard but superfluous one, how to spend it. Thus his moral ground is taken from under his feet. The opportunities of living are diminished in proportion as what are called the "means" are increased. The best thing a man can do for his culture when he is rich is to endeavor to carry out those schemes which he entertained when he was poor. Christ answered the Herodians according to their condition. "Show me the tribute-money," said he;—and one took a penny out of his pocket;—if you use money which has the image of Cæsar on it, and which he has made current and valuable, that is, *if you are men of the State,* and gladly enjoy the advantages of Cæsar's government, then pay him back some of his own when he demands it; "Render therefore to Cæsar that which is Cæsar's, and to God those things which are God's,"—leaving them no wiser than before as to which was which; for they did not wish to know.

When I converse with the freest of my neighbors, I perceive that, whatever they may say about the magnitude and seriousness of the question, and their regard for the public tranquility, the long and the short of the matter is, that they cannot spare the protection of the existing government, and they dread the consequences to their property and families of disobedience to it. For my own part, I should not like to think that I ever rely on the protection of the State. But, if I deny the authority of the State when it presents its tax-bill, it will soon take and waste all my property, and so harass me and my children without end. This is hard. This makes it impossible for a man to live honestly, and at the same time comfortably, in outward respects. It will not be worth the while to accumulate property; that would be sure to go again. You must hire or squat somewhere, and raise but a small crop, and eat that soon. You must live within yourself, and depend upon yourself always tucked up and ready for a start, and not have many affairs. A man may grow rich in Turkey even, if he will be in all respects a good subject of the Turkish government. Confucius said: "If a state is governed by the principles of reason, poverty and misery are subjects of shame; if a state is not governed by the principles of reason, riches and honors are the subjects of shame." No: Until I want the protection of Massachusetts to be extended to me in some distant southern port, where my liberty is endangered, or until I am bent solely on building up an estate at home by peaceful enterprise, I can afford to refuse allegiance to Massachusetts, and her right to my property and life. It costs me less in every sense to incur the penalty of disobedience to the State, than it would to obey. I should feel as if I were worth less in that case.

Some years ago, the State met me in behalf of the Church, and com- 25
manded me to pay a certain sum toward the support of a clergyman whose preaching my father attended, but never I myself. "Pay," it said, "or be locked up in the jail." I declined to pay. But, unfortunately, another man saw fit to pay it. I did not see why the schoolmaster should be taxed to support the priest, and not the priest the schoolmaster; for I was not the State's schoolmaster, but I supported myself by voluntary subscription. I did not see why the lyceum should not present its tax-bill, and have the State to back its demand, as well as the Church. However, at the request of the selectmen, I condescended to make some such statement as this in writing:—"Know all men by these presents, that I, Henry

Thoreau, do not wish to be regarded as a member of any incorporated society which I have not joined." This I gave to the town clerk; and he has it. The State, having thus learned that I did not wish to be regarded as a member of that church, has never made a like demand on me since; though it said that it must adhere to its original presumption that time. If I had known how to name them, I should then have signed off in detail from all the societies which I never signed on to; but I did not know where to find a complete list.

I have paid no poll-tax for six years. I was put into a jail once on this account, for one night; and, as I stood considering the walls of solid stone, two or three feet thick, the door of wood and iron, a foot thick, and the iron grating which strained the light, I could not help being struck with the foolishness of that institution which treated me as if I were mere flesh and blood and bones, to be locked up. I wondered that it should have concluded at length that this was the best use it could put me to, and had never thought to avail itself of my services in some way. I saw that, if there was a wall of stone between me and my townsmen, there was a still more difficult one to climb or break through, before they could get to be as free as I was. I did not for a moment feel confined, and the walls seemed a great waste of stone and mortar. I felt as if I alone of all my townsmen had paid my tax. They plainly did not know how to treat me, but behaved like persons who are underbred. In every threat and in every compliment there was a blunder; for they thought that my chief desire was to stand the other side of that stone wall. I could not but smile to see how industriously they locked the door on my meditations, which followed them out again without let or hindrance, and *they* were really all that was dangerous. As they could not reach me, they had resolved to punish my body; just as boys, if they cannot come at some person against whom they have a spite, will abuse his dog. I saw that the State was half-witted, and it was timid as a lone woman with her silver spoons, and that it did not know its friends from its foes, and I lost all my remaining respect for it, and pitied it.

Thus the State never intentionally confronts a man's sense, intellectual or moral, but only his body, his senses. It is not armed with superior wit or honesty, but with superior physical strength. I was not born to be forced. I will breathe after my own fashion. Let us see who is the strongest. What force has a multitude? They only can force me who obey a higher law than I. They force me to become like themselves. I do not hear of *men* being *forced* to live this way or that by masses of men. What sort of life were that to live? When I meet a government which says to me, "Your money or your life," why should I be in haste to give it my money? It may be in a great strait, and not know what to do: I cannot help that. It must help itself; do as I do. It is not worth the while to snivel about it. I am not responsible for the successful working of the machinery of society. I am not the son of the engineer. I perceive that, when an acorn and a chestnut fall side by side, the one does not remain inert to make way for the other, but both obey their own laws, and spring and grow and flourish as best they can, till one, perchance, overshadows and destroys the other. If a plant cannot live according to its nature, it dies; and so a man.

The night in prison was novel and interesting enough. The prisoners in their shirt-sleeves were enjoying a chat and the evening air in the doorway, when I entered. But the jailer said, "Come, boys, it is time to lock up"; and so they dispersed, and I heard the sound of their steps returning into the hollow apartments. My roommate was introduced to me by the jailer, as "a first-rate fellow and a clever man." When the door was locked, he showed me where to hang my hat, and how he managed matters there. The rooms were white-washed once a month; and this one, at least, was the whitest, most simply furnished, and probably the neatest apartment in the town. He naturally wanted to know where I came from, and what brought me there; and, when I had told him, I asked him in my turn how he came there, presuming him to be an honest man, of course; and, as the world goes, I believe he was. "Why," said he, "they accuse me of burning a barn; but I never did it." As near as I could discover, he had probably gone to bed in a barn when drunk, and smoked his pipe there; and so a barn was burnt. He had the reputation of being a clever man, had been there some three months waiting for his trial to come on, and would have to wait as much longer; but he was quite domesticated and contented, since he got his board for nothing, and thought that he was well-treated.

He occupied one window, and I the other; and I saw, that if one stayed there long, his principal business would be to look out the window. I had soon read all the tracts that were left there, and examined where former prisoners had broken out, and where a grate had been sawed off, and heard the history of the various occupants of that room; for I found that even here there was a history and a gossip which never circulated beyond the walls of the jail. Probably this is the only house in the town where verses are composed, which are afterward printed in a circular form, but not published. I was shown quite a long list of verses which were composed by some young men who had been detected in an attempt to escape, who avenged themselves by singing them.

I pumped my fellow-prisoner as dry as I could, for fear I should never 30
see him again; but at length he showed me which was my bed, and left me to blow out the lamp.

It was like travelling into a far country, such as I had never expected to behold, to lie there for one night. It seemed to me that I never had heard the town-clock strike before, nor the evening sounds of the village; for we slept with the windows open, which were inside the grating. It was to see my native village in the light of the Middle Ages, and our Concord was turned into a Rhine stream, and visions of knights and castles passed before me. They were the voices of old burghers that I heard in the streets. I was an involuntary spectator and auditor of whatever was done and said in the kitchen of the adjacent village-inn,—a wholly new and rare experience to me. It was a closer view of my native town. I was fairly inside of it. I never had seen its institutions before. This is one of its peculiar institutions; for it is a shire town. I began to comprehend what its inhabitants were about.

In the morning, our breakfasts were put through the hole in the door, in small oblong-square tin pans, made to fit, and holding a pint of chocolate, with brown bread, and an iron spoon. When they called for the vessels again, I was green enough to return what bread I had left; but my comrade seized it, and said that I should lay that up for lunch or dinner. Soon after, he was let out to work at haying in a neighboring field, whither he went every day, and would not be back till noon; so he bade me good-day, saying that he doubted if he should see me again.

When I came out of prison,—for some one interfered, and paid that tax,—I did not perceive that great changes had taken place on the common, such as he observed who went in a youth, and emerged a tottering and gray-headed man; and yet a change had to my eyes come over the scene,—the town, and State, and country,—greater than any that mere time could effect. I saw yet more distinctly the State in which I lived. I saw to what extent the people among whom I lived could be trusted as good neighbors and friends; that their friendship was for summer weather only; that they did not greatly propose to do right; that they were a distinct race from me by their prejudices and superstitions, as the Chinamen and Malays are; that, in their sacrifices to humanity, they ran no risks, not even to their property; that, after all, they were not so noble but they treated the thief as he had treated them, and hoped, by a certain outward observance and a few prayers, and by walking in a particular straight though useless path from time to time, to save their souls. This may be to judge my neighbors harshly; for I believe that many of them are not aware that they have such an institution as the jail in their village.

It was formerly the custom in our village, when a poor debtor came out of jail, for his acquaintances to salute him, looking through their fingers, which were crossed to represent the grating of a jail window, "How do ye do?" My neighbors did not thus salute me, but first looked at me, and then at one another, as if I had returned from a long journey. I was put into jail as I was going to the shoemaker's to get a shoe which was mended. When I was let out the next morning, I proceeded to finish my errand, and having put on my mended shoe, joined a huckleberry party, who were impatient to put themselves under my conduct; and in half an hour,—for the horse was soon tackled,—was in the midst of a huckleberry field, on one of our highest hills, two miles off, and then the State was nowhere to be seen.

This is the whole story of "My Prisons." 35

I have never declined paying the highway tax, because I am as desirous of being a good neighbor as I am of being a bad subject; and, as for supporting schools, I am doing my part to educate my fellow-countrymen now. It is for no particular item in the tax-bill that I refuse to pay it. I simply wish to refuse allegiance to the State, to withdraw and stand aloof from it effectually. I do not care to trace the course of my dollar, if I could, till it buys a man, or a musket to shoot one with, — the dollar is innocent, — but I am concerned to trace the effects of my allegiance. In fact, I quietly declare war with the State, after my fashion, though I will still make what use and get what advantage of her I can, as is usual in such cases.

If others pay the tax which is demanded of me, from a sympathy with the State, they do but what they have already done in their own case, or rather they abet injustice to a greater extent than the State requires. If they pay the tax from a mistaken interest in the individual taxed, to save his property or prevent his going to jail, it is because they have not considered wisely how far they let their private feelings interfere with the public good.

This, then, is my position at present. But one cannot be too much on his guard in such a case, lest his action be biased by obstinacy, or an undue regard for the opinions of men. Let him see that he does only what belongs to himself and to the hour.

I think sometimes, Why, this people mean well; they are only ignorant; they would do better if they knew how: why give your neighbors this pain to treat you as they are inclined to? But I think again, this is no reason why I should do as they do, or permit others to suffer much greater pain of a different kind. Again, I sometimes say to myself, When many millions of men, without heat, without ill will, without personal feelings of any kind, demand of you a few shillings only, without the possibility, such is their constitution, of retracing or altering their present demand, and without the possibility, on your side, of appeal to any other millions, why expose yourself to this overwhelming brute force? You do not resist cold and hunger, the winds and the waves, thus obstinately; you quietly submit to a thousand similar necessities. You do not put your head into the fire. But just in proportion as I regard this as not wholly a brute force, partly a human force, and consider that I have relations to those millions as to so many millions of men, and not of mere brute or inanimate things, I see that appeal is possible, first and instantaneously, from them to the Maker of them, and, secondly, from them to themselves. But, if I put my head deliberately into the fire, there is no appeal to fire or to the Maker of fire, and I have only myself to blame. If I could convince myself that I have any right to be satisfied with men as they are, and to treat them according, and not according, in some respects, to my requisitions and expectations of what they and I ought to be, then, like a good Mussulman and fatalist, I should endeavor to be satisfied with things as they are, and say it is the will of God. And, above all, there is this difference between resisting this and a purely brute or natural force, that I can resist this with some effect; but I cannot expect, like Orpheus, to change the nature of the rocks and trees and beasts.

I do not wish to quarrel with any man or nation. I do not wish to split 40
hairs, to make fine distinctions, or set myself up as better than my neighbors. I seek rather, I may say, even an excuse for conforming to the laws of the land. I am but too ready to conform to them. Indeed, I have reason to suspect myself on this head; and each year, as the tax-gatherer comes round, I find myself disposed to review the acts and position of the general and State governments, and the spirit of the people, to discover a pretext for conformity.

> We must affect our country as our parents;
> And if at any time we alienate
> Our love or industry from doing it honor,
> We must respect effects and teach the soul
> Matter of conscience and religion,
> And not desire of rule or benefit.

I believe that the State will soon be able to take all my work of this sort out of my hands, and then I shall be no better a patriot than my fellow-countrymen. Seen from a lower point of view, the Constitution, with all its faults, is very good; the law and the courts are very respectable; even this State and this American government are, in many respects, very admirable and rare things, to be thankful for, such as a great many have described them; but seen from a point of view a little higher, they are what I have described them; seen from a higher still, and the highest, who shall say what they are, or that they are worth looking at or thinking of at all?

However, the government does not concern me much, and I shall bestow the fewest possible thoughts on it. It is not many moments that I live under a government, even in this world. If a man is thought-free, fancy-free, imagination-free, that which *is not* never for a long time appearing *to be* to him, unwise rulers or reformers cannot fatally interrupt him.

I know that most men think differently from myself; but those whose lives are by profession devoted to the study of these or kindred subjects, content me as little as any. Statesmen and legislators, standing so completely within the institution, never distinctly and nakedly behold it. They speak of moving society, but have no resting-place without it. They may be men of a certain experience and discrimination, and have no doubt invented ingenious and even useful systems, for which we sincerely thank them; but all their wit and usefulness lie within certain not very wide limits. They are wont to forget that the world is not governed by policy and expediency. Webster never goes behind government, and so cannot speak with authority about it. His words are wisdom to those legislators who contemplate no essential reform in the existing government; but for thinkers, and those who legislate for all time, he never once glances at the subject. I know of those whose serene and wise speculations on this theme would soon reveal the limits of his mind's range and hospitality. Yet, compared with the cheap professions of most reformers, and the still cheaper wisdom and eloquence of politicians in general, his are almost the only sensible and valuable words, and we thank Heaven for him. Comparatively, he is always strong, original, and, above all, practical. Still his quality is not wisdom, but prudence. The lawyer's truth is not Truth, but consistency, or a consistent expediency. Truth is always in harmony with herself, and is not concerned chiefly to reveal the justice that may consist with wrong-doing. He well deserves to be called, as he has been called, the Defender of the Constitution. There are really no blows to be given by him but defensive ones. He is not a leader, but a follower. His leaders are the men of '87. "I have never made an effort," he says, "and never propose to make an effort; I have never countenanced an effort, and never mean to countenance an effort, to disturb the arrangement as originally made, by which the various States came into the Union." Still thinking of the sanction which the Constitution gives to slavery, he says, "Because it was a part of the original compact,—let it stand." Notwithstanding his special acuteness and ability, he is unable to take a fact out of its merely political relations, and behold it as it lies absolutely to be disposed of by the intellect,—what, for instance, it behooves a man to do here in America today with regard to slavery, but ventures, or is driven, to make some such desperate answer as the following, while professing to speak absolutely, and as a private man,—from which what new and singular code of social duties might be inferred? "The manner," says he, "in which the governments of those States where slavery exists are to regulate it, is for their own consideration, under their responsibility to their constituents, to the general laws of propriety, humanity, and justice, and to God. Associations formed elsewhere, springing from a feeling of humanity, or any other cause, have nothing whatever to do with it. They have never received any encouragement from me, and they never will."[1]

They who know of no purer sources of truth, who have traced up its stream no higher, stand, and wisely stand, by the Bible and the Constitution, and drink at it there with reverence and humility; but they who behold where it comes trickling into this lake or that pool, gird up their loins once more, and continue their pilgrimage toward its fountainhead.

No man with a genius for legislation has appeared in America. They are rare in the history of the world. There are orators, politicians, and eloquent men, by the thousand; but the speaker has not yet opened his

[1] These extracts have been inserted since the Lecture was read.

mouth to speak, who is capable of settling the much-vexed questions of the day. We love eloquence for its own sake, and not for any truth which it may utter, or any heroism it may inspire. Our legislators have not yet learned the comparative value of free-trade and of freedom, of union, and of rectitude, to a nation. They have no genius or talent for comparatively humble questions of taxation and finance, commerce and manufactures and agriculture. If we were left solely to the wordy wit of legislators in Congress for our guidance, uncorrected by the seasonable experience and the effectual complaints of the people, America would not long retain her rank among the nations. For eighteen hundred years, though perchance I have no right to say it, the New Testament has been written; yet where is the legislator who has wisdom and practical talent enough to avail himself of the light which it sheds on the science of legislation?

The authority of government, even such as I am willing to submit 45
to,—for I will cheerfully obey those who know and can do better than I, and in many things even those who neither know nor can do so well,—is still an impure one: To be strictly just, it must have the sanction and consent of the governed. It can have no pure right over my person and property but what I concede to it. The progress from an absolute to a limited monarchy, from a limited monarchy to a democracy, is a progress toward a true respect for the individual. Even the Chinese philosopher was wise enough to regard the individual as the basis of the empire. Is a democracy, such as we know it, the last improvement possible in government? Is it not possible to take a step further towards recognizing and organizing the rights of man? There will never be a really free and enlightened State, until the State comes to recognize the individual as a higher and independent power, from which all its own power and authority are derived, and treats him accordingly. I please myself with imagining a State at last which can afford to be just to all men, and to treat the individual with respect as a neighbor; which even would not think it inconsistent with its own repose, if a few were to live aloof from it, not meddling with it, nor embraced by it, who fulfilled all the duties of neighbors and fellowmen. A State which bore this kind of fruit, and suffered it to drop off as fast as it ripened, would prepare the way for a still more perfect and glorious State, which also I have imagined, but not yet anywhere seen.

DISCUSSION QUESTIONS

1. Summarize briefly Thoreau's reasons for arguing that civil disobedience is sometimes a *duty*.
2. Thoreau, like Martin Luther King Jr. in "Letter from Birmingham Jail" (p. 192), speaks of "unjust laws" (para. 16). Do they agree on the positions that citizens should take in response to these laws? Are Thoreau and King guided by the same principles?

3. What examples of government policy and action does Thoreau use to prove that civil disobedience is a duty? Explain why they are—or are not—effective.
4. Why do you think Thoreau provides such a detailed account of one day in prison? (Notice that King does not give a description of his confinement.) What observation about the community struck Thoreau when he emerged from jail?
5. What warrant or warrants must readers accept in order to accept Thoreau's argument?

WRITING SUGGESTIONS

6. Argue that civil disobedience to a school policy or action is justified. (Examples might include failure to establish an ethnic studies department, refusal to allow ROTC on campus, refusal to suspend a professor accused of sexual harassment.) Be specific about the injustice of the policy or action and the values that underlie the resistance.
7. Under what circumstances might civil disobedience prove to be dangerous and immoral? Can you think of cases of disobedience when *conscience*, as Thoreau uses the term, did not appear to be the guiding principle? Try to identify what you think is the true motivation for the resistance.

DEBATE: Are you responsible for your own weight?

Absolutely. Government Has No Business Interfering with What You Eat

RADLEY BALKO

Nutrition activists are agitating for a panoply of initiatives that would bring the government between you and your waistline. President Bush earmarked $125 million in his budget for the encouragement of healthy lifestyles. State legislatures and school boards have begun banning snacks and soda from school campuses and vending machines. Several state legislators and Oakland, California, Mayor Jerry Brown, among others, have called for a "fat tax" on high-calorie foods. Congress is considering menu-labeling legislation that would force chain restaurants to list fat, sodium and calories for each item.

Radley Balko is a senior editor for *Reason* magazine, a former policy analyst with the Cato Institute, and a columnist for FoxNews.com. This article first appeared in *Time* on June 7, 2004.

That is precisely the wrong way to fight obesity. Instead of intervening in the array of food options available to Americans, our government ought to be working to foster a personal sense of responsibility for our health and well-being.

We're doing just the opposite. For decades, America's health-care system has been migrating toward nationalized medicine. We have a law that requires some Americans to pay for other Americans' medicine, and several states bar health insurers from charging lower premiums to people who stay fit. That removes the financial incentive for making healthy decisions. Worse, socialized health care makes us troublingly tolerant of government trespasses on our personal freedom. If my neighbor's heart attack shows up on my tax bill, I'm more likely to support state regulation of what he eats—restrictions on what grocery stores can put on their shelves, for example, or what McDonald's can put between its sesame-seed buns.

The best way to combat the public-health threat of obesity is to remove obesity from the realm of "public health." It's difficult to think of a matter more private and less public than what we choose to put in our bodies. Give Americans moral, financial and personal responsibility for their own health, and obesity is no longer a public matter but a private one—with all the costs, concerns, and worries of being overweight borne only by those people who are actually overweight.

Let each of us take full responsibility for our diet and lifestyle. We're 5
likely to make better decisions when someone else isn't paying for the consequences.

Not If Blaming the Victim Is Just an Excuse to Let Industry Off the Hook

KELLY BROWNELL AND MARION NESTLE

The food industry, like any other, must grow to stay in business. One way it does so is by promoting unhealthy foods, particularly to children. Each year kids see more than 10,000 food ads on TV alone, almost all for items like soft drinks, fast foods and sugared cereals. In the same year that the government spent $2 million on its main nutrition-education program, McDonald's spent $500 million on its We Love to See You Smile campaign. It can be no surprise that teenagers consume nearly twice as much soda as milk (the reverse was true twenty years ago) and that 25 percent of all vegetables eaten in the United States are french fries.

To counter criticism, the food industry and pro-business groups use a public relations script focused on personal responsibility. The script has three elements: (1) if people are overweight, it is their own fault; (2) industry responds to consumer demand but does not create it; and (3) insisting that industry change—say, by not marketing to children or requiring restaurants to reveal calories—is an attack on freedom.

Why quarrel with the personal-responsibility argument?

First, it's wrong. The prevalence of obesity increases year after year. Were people less responsible in 2002 than in 2001? Obesity is a global problem. Is irresponsibility an epidemic around the world?

Second, it ignores biology. Humans are hardwired, as a survival strat- 5
egy, to like foods high in sugar, fat, and calories.

Third, the argument is not helpful. Imploring people to eat better and exercise more has been the default approach to obesity for years. That is a failed experiment.

Fourth, personal responsibility is a trap. The argument is startlingly similar to the tobacco industry's efforts to stave off legislative and regulatory

---

Kelly D. Brownell is professor and chair of psychology at Yale University and also serves as professor of epidemiology and public health and as director of the Yale Center for Eating and Weight Disorders. He has written numerous books, and one of his articles, "Understanding and Preventing Relapse," published in the *American Psychologist*, is one of the most frequently cited articles in the field of psychology.

Marion Nestle is Paulette Goddard Professor in the Department of Nutrition, Food Studies, and Public Health at New York University. Her degrees include a Ph.D. in molecular biology and an M.P.H. in public health nutrition, both from the University of California, at Berkeley. She is the author of *Food Politics: How the Food Industry Influences Nutrition and Health* (2002), *Safe Food: Bacteria, Biotechnology, and Bioterrorism* (2003), and *What to Eat* (2007).

interventions. The nation tolerated personal-responsibility arguments from Big Tobacco for decades, with disastrous results.

Governments collude with industry when they shift attention from conditions promoting poor diets to the individuals who consume them. Government should be doing everything it can to create conditions that lead to healthy eating, support parents in raising healthy children, and make decisions in the interests of public health rather than private profit.

DISCUSSION QUESTIONS

1. In his first paragraph, Balko mentions some specific initiatives that would involve some governmental control over Americans' eating habits. Which of them, if any, do you support?
2. What does Balko favor instead of such initiatives?
3. According to Balko, what mistakes have Americans made in the way they have tried to fight obesity?
4. Why do Brownell and Nestle believe that the government must bear some of the blame for obesity?
5. What does the food industry offer in its defense?
6. How did the practice of making health the personal responsibility of the consumer work when it came to smoking?
7. Whose argument do you find more convincing, and why?

ASSIGNMENTS FOR ANALYZING WARRANTS

READING AND DISCUSSION QUESTIONS

1. Should students be given a direct voice in the hiring of faculty members? On what warrants about education do you base your answer?
2. Discuss the validity of the warrant in this statement from the *Watch Tower* (a publication of the Jehovah's Witnesses) about genital herpes: "The sexually loose are indeed 'receiving in themselves the full recompense, which was due for their error' (Romans 1:27)."
3. Read the following passage about suicide by the Greek philosopher Aristotle (adapted from his *Ethics*). Then defend or attack his argument, being careful to make clear both Aristotle's and your own warrants.

   > Just as a murderer does not have the right to take a mother from her family or a child from her parents and simultaneously to deny society the use of a productive citizen, so the suicide, even though he or she freely chooses to be his or her own victim, does not possess the right to thus diminish the welfare of so many others.

4. In view of the increasing interest in health in general, and nutrition and exercise in particular, do you think that universities and colleges should impose physical education requirements? If so, what form should they take? If not, why not? What warrant underlies your position?
5. What are some of the assumptions underlying the preference for natural foods and medicines? Can *natural* be clearly defined? Is this preference part of a broader philosophy? Try to evaluate the validity of the assumption.
6. The author of the following passage, Katherine Butler Hathaway, became a hunchback as a result of a childhood illness. Here she writes about the relationship between love and beauty from the point of view of someone who is deformed. Discuss the warrants on which the author bases her conclusions.

   I could secretly pretend that I had a lover . . . but I could never risk showing that I thought such a thing was possible for me . . . with any man. Because of my repeated encounters with the mirror and my irrepressible tendency to forget what I had seen, I had begun to force myself to believe and to remember, and especially to remember, that I would never be chosen for what I imagined to be the supreme and most intimate of all experience. I thought of sexual love as an honor that was too great and too beautiful for the body in which I was doomed to live.

WRITING ASSIGNMENTS

7. In "An Unjust Sacrifice," Robert A. Sirico presents a case in which he finds no justification for letting one Siamese twin die in order to save the other. His belief in the sanctity of human life appears to be absolute, even when it will most likely lead to the death of both twins. Write an essay in which you give examples of how your value system underlies your political views.
8. Write an essay explaining why you think either Radley Balko or Kelly Brownell and Marion Nestle make a better argument.
9. Both state and federal governments have been embroiled in controversies concerning the rights of citizens to engage in harmful practices. In Massachusetts, for example, a mandatory seat-belt law was repealed by voters who considered the law an infringement of their freedom. (It was later reinstated.) Write an essay in which you explain what principles you believe should guide government regulation of dangerous practices.
10. Henry David Thoreau writes, "Unjust laws exist: Shall we be content to obey them, or shall we endeavor to amend them, and obey them until we have succeeded, or shall we transgress them at once?" Write an essay in which you explain under what circumstances you would feel compelled to break the law, or why you feel that you would never do so.

CHAPTER 9

Avoiding Flawed Logic

Throughout the book we have pointed out the weaknesses that cause arguments to break down. In the vast majority of cases these weaknesses represent breakdowns in logic or the reasoning process. We call such weaknesses *fallacies*, a term derived from Latin. Sometimes these false or erroneous arguments are deliberate; in fact, the Latin word *fallere* means "to deceive." But more often these arguments are either carelessly or unintentionally constructed. Thoughtful readers learn to recognize them; thoughtful writers learn to avoid them.

The reasoning process was first given formal expression by Aristotle, the Greek philosopher, almost 2,500 years ago. In his famous treatises, he described the way we try to discover the truth—observing the world, selecting impressions, making inferences, generalizing. In this process Aristotle identified two forms of reasoning: *induction* and *deduction*. Both forms, he realized, are subject to error. Our observations may be incorrect or insufficient, and our conclusions may be faulty because they have violated the rules governing the relationship between statements. The terms we've introduced may be unfamiliar, but the processes of reasoning, as well as the fallacies that violate these processes, are not. Induction and deduction are not reserved only for formal arguments about important problems; they also represent our everyday thinking about the most ordinary matters. As for the fallacies, they, too, unfortunately, may crop up anywhere, whenever we are careless in our use of the reasoning process.

In this chapter we examine some of the most common fallacies. First, however, a closer look at induction and deduction will make clear what happens when fallacies occur.

INDUCTION

Induction is the form of reasoning in which we come to conclusions about the whole on the basis of observations of particular instances. If you notice that prices on the four items you bought in the campus bookstore are higher than similar items in the bookstore in town, you may come to the conclusion that the campus store is a more expensive place to shop. If you also noticed that all three of the instructors you saw on the first day of school were wearing faded jeans and running shoes, you might say that your teachers are generally informal in their dress. In both cases you have made an *inductive leap*, reasoning from what you have learned about a few examples to what you think is true of a whole class of things.

How safe are you in coming to these conclusions? As we've noticed in discussing data and generalization warrants, the reliability of your conclusion depends on the quantity and quality of your observations. Were four items out of the thousands available in the campus store a sufficiently large sample? Would you come to the same conclusion if you chose fifty items? Might another selection have produced a different conclusion? As for the casually dressed instructors, perhaps further investigation would disclose that the teachers wearing jeans were all teaching assistants and that associate and full professors usually wore business clothes. Or the difference might lie in the academic discipline; anthropology teachers might turn out to dress less formally than business school teachers.

In these two situations, you could come closer to verifying your conclusions by further observation and experience—that is, by pricing more items at both stores over a longer period of time and by coming into contact with a greater number of teachers during a whole semester. Even without pricing every item in both stores or encountering every instructor on campus, you would be more confident of your generalization as the quality and quantity of your samples increased.

In some cases you can observe all the instances in a particular situation. For example, by acquiring information about the religious beliefs of all the residents of the dormitory, you can arrive at an accurate assessment of the number of Buddhists. But since our ability to make definitive observations about everything is limited, we must also make an inductive leap about categories of things that we ourselves can never encounter in their entirety. For some generalizations, as we have learned about evidence, we rely on the testimony of reliable witnesses who report that they have experienced or observed many more instances of the phenomenon. A television documentary may give us information about unwed teenage mothers in a city neighborhood; four girls are interviewed and followed for several days by the reporter. Are these girls typical of thousands of others? A sociologist on the program assures us that, in fact, they are. She herself has consulted with hundreds of other young mothers and can vouch for the fact that a conclusion about them, based on our observation of the four, will be sound. Obviously, though, our conclusion can only be probable, not certain. The sociologist's sample is large, but she can account only for hundreds, not thousands, and there may be unexamined cases that will seriously weaken our conclusions.

In other cases, we may rely on a principle known in science as "the uniformity of nature." We assume that certain conclusions about oak trees in the temperate zone of North America, for example, will also be true for oak trees growing elsewhere under similar climatic conditions. We also use this principle in attempting to explain the causes of behavior in human beings. If we discover that institutionalization of some children from infancy results in severe emotional retardation, we think it safe to conclude that under the same circumstances all children would suffer the same consequences. As in the previous example, we are aware that certainty about every case of institutionalization is impossible. With rare exceptions, the process of induction can offer only probability, not certain truth.

SAMPLE ESSAY: AN INDUCTIVE ARGUMENT

True or False: Schools Fail Immigrants

RICHARD ROTHSTEIN

A common indictment of public schools is that they no longer offer upward mobility to most immigrants. It is said that in the first half of the twentieth century, children learned English, went to college, and joined the middle class but that many of today's immigrants are more likely to drop out, take dead-end jobs, or end up in prison.

Many true accounts reinforce these beliefs. But less noticed are equally valid anecdotes pointing to an opposite claim.

Policy by anecdote is flawed because too often we notice only what confirms our preconceptions. California's recent experience with Mexican immigrants provides ample material for stories about school failure. But on a day to celebrate the American promise, we might also turn to anecdotes of another kind.

Recent college commencements across California featured many immigrants from impoverished families whose first language was Spanish, who came through much-maligned bilingual education programs, learned English, and now head for graduate schools or professions.

Richard Rothstein is a research associate of the Economic Policy Institute, a senior correspondent of the *American Prospect*, and the former national education columnist of the *New York Times*, where this article appeared on July 4, 2001. He is the author of *The Way We Were: Myths and Realities of America's Student Achievement* (1997), *All Else Equal: Are Public and Private Schools Different?* (2003), and *The Charter School Dust-up* (2005).

At California State University at Fresno, for example, about 700 of 4,000 5
graduates this spring were Latino, typically the first in their families to attend college. Top-ranked were Pedro Nava and Maria Rocio Magaña, Mexican-born children of farm laborers and cannery workers.

Mr. Nava did not settle in the United States until the third grade. Before that, he lived in migrant labor camps during harvests and in Mexico the rest of the year. His California schooling was in Spanish until the fifth grade, when he was moved to English instruction. Now, with a college degree, he has enrolled in management and teacher training courses.

Ms. Magaña did not place into English classes until the second half of the eleventh grade. Now fluent in both academic and conversational English, she will soon begin a Ph.D. program in anthropology at the University of Chicago.

Their achievements are not unique. Both credit success to their mothers' emphasis on education. Both mothers enrolled in English and high school equivalency courses at the local community college.

Across California, these two-year institutions play an especially important role for immigrants.

Lourdes Andrade just finished her junior year at Brown University, 10
having transferred there after getting associate of arts degrees in history and liberal arts at Oxnard Community College, about forty miles northwest of Los Angeles.

Ms. Andrade arrived here at the age of four and all through elementary school worked with her mother making beds and cleaning bathrooms in hotels. Ms. Andrade, too, attributes her success to her mother's strong academic pressure and also to mentoring she received in a federally financed program to give extra academic support to migrant children.

The program's director, Lorenzo Moraza, also grew up speaking only Spanish. Now a school principal, Mr. Moraza estimates that about 30 percent of the immigrant children he has worked with acquired public school records that led them to college. Those who receive bachelor's degrees are many fewer, but Mr. Moraza says he thinks most drop out of college for economic reasons, not academic ones.

At the Fresno campus, nearly two-thirds of the immigrants and children of immigrants who enter as freshmen eventually graduate. The university operates special support services to help them do so.

You cannot spend time in California without noticing an extensive middle class of Latino schoolteachers, doctors, lawyers, and small-business people. Not all are recent immigrants, but many are. Some attended Catholic schools, but most are products of the public system. Many had bilingual education in the 1970s, 80s, and 90s. California has now banned such instruction, assuming it failed.

There are plenty of anecdotes to support a claim that schools fail im- 15
migrant children or an equally persuasive claim that schools serve them well. Getting better statistics should be a priority. Government numbers do not distinguish between students who are immigrants (or whose parents immigrated) from Hispanics with American roots for several generations.

To help interpret California's experience, the best federal data tell only that in 1996, there were 100,000 college students nationwide who were American citizens born in Mexico. This is less than 1 percent of all college students. But uncounted are even larger numbers of those born here to recent migrants.

Even a balanced collection of anecdotes that include successes as well as failures cannot determine whether California schools are less effective than we should expect, and whether wholesale change is needed to move more immigrants to the middle class. But the answer is certainly more complex than the stereotypes of systematic failure that pervade most accounts.

Analysis

An inductive argument proceeds by examining particulars and arriving at a generalization that represents a probable truth. The author of this article arrives at the truth he will defend—that public schools have been more successful than is often acknowledged in moving many immigrants into the middle class—by offering statistical data and a number of stories about immigrants from poor families who have entered graduate school or one of the professions.

Rothstein begins, as many arguers do, with a brief summary of the popular position with which he disagrees. At the end of the third paragraph, he announces that he will provide examples that point to a different conclusion.

The reader should ask three questions of an inductive argument: Is the evidence sufficient? Is it representative? Is it up-to-date? The evidence that Rothstein assembles consists of a series of anecdotes and statistical data about the performance of immigrant students. The success stories of five real persons are impressive, despite limitations imposed by the brevity of the essay, in part because they offer vivid examples of struggle that appeal to our emotions and bring to life an issue with which some of us may not be familiar. But five stories are hardly enough to prove a case; perhaps they are not representative. Rothstein, therefore, adds other data about the rate at which immigrant students graduate and the growing number of Latino professionals and businesspeople.

Although the essay was published in 2001, his numbers are drawn from the 1990s and are thus a bit dated. A look at more recent data would reveal whether his conclusions remain valid.

The reader has some reason to believe that the facts are accurate. At the time this article was published, Rothstein wrote a regular column for a prestigious daily newspaper whose readers would have been quick to find errors in arguments of which they were critical. At the same time, he does not claim that his argument is beyond debate, since the data are incomplete. Even the title suggests that the issue is still unsettled. Modesty in the arguer is always welcome and disposes the reader to view the argument more favorably.

PRACTICE

Read Goldberg's essay "Connecting the Dots . . . to Terrorism" (p. 246). Explain how Goldberg uses inductive reasoning in the essay while not structuring the whole essay around it. What larger purpose does he have in the essay, and how does inductive reasoning help him achieve that purpose?

DEDUCTION

While induction attempts to arrive at the truth, deduction guarantees sound relationships between statements. If each of a series of statements, called *premises,* is true, deductive logic tells us that the conclusion must also be true. Unlike the conclusions from induction, which are only probable, the conclusions from deduction are certain. The simplest deductive argument consists of two premises and a conclusion. In outline such an argument looks like this:

MAJOR PREMISE:	All students with 3.5 averages and above for three years are invited to become members of Kappa Gamma Pi, the honor society.
MINOR PREMISE:	George has had a 3.8 average for over three years.
CONCLUSION:	Therefore, he will be invited to join Kappa Gamma Pi.

This deductive conclusion is *valid,* or logically consistent, because it follows necessarily from the premises. No other conclusion is possible. Validity, however, refers only to the form of the argument. The argument itself may not be satisfactory if the premises are not true—if Kappa Gamma Pi has imposed other conditions or if George has only a 3.4 average. The difference between truth and validity is important because it alerts us to the necessity for examining the truth of the premises before we decide that the conclusion is sound.

One way of discovering how the deductive process works is to look at the methods used by Sherlock Holmes, that most famous of literary detectives, in solving his mysteries. His reasoning process follows a familiar pattern. Through the inductive process—that is, observing the particulars of the world—he came to certain conclusions about those particulars. Then he applied deductive reasoning to come to a conclusion about a particular person or event.

On one occasion Holmes observed that a man sitting opposite him on a train had chalk dust on his fingers. From this observation Holmes deduced that the man was a schoolteacher. If his thinking were outlined, it would take the form of the syllogism, the classic form of deductive reasoning:

MAJOR PREMISE:	All men with chalk dust on their fingers are schoolteachers.
MINOR PREMISE:	This man has chalk dust on his fingers.
CONCLUSION:	Therefore, this man is a schoolteacher.

One dictionary defines *syllogism* as "a formula of argument consisting of three propositions." The first proposition is called the major premise and offers a generalization about a large group or class. This generalization has been arrived at through inductive reasoning or observation of particulars. The second proposition is called the minor premise, and it makes a statement about a member of that group or class. The third proposition is the conclusion, which links the other two propositions, in much the same way that the warrant links the support and the claim.

If we look back at the syllogism that summarizes Holmes's thinking, we see how it represents the deductive process. The major premise, the first statement, is an inductive generalization, a statement arrived at after observation of a number of men with chalk on their fingers. The minor premise, the second statement, assigns a particular member, the man on the train, to the general class of those who have dust on their fingers.

But although the argument may be logical, it is faulty. The deductive argument is only as strong as its premises. As Lionel Ruby pointed out, Sherlock Holmes was often wrong.[1] Holmes once deduced from the size of a large hat found in the street that the owner was intelligent. He obviously believed that a large head meant a large brain and that a large brain indicated intelligence. Had he lived one hundred years later, new information about the relationship of brain size to intelligence would have enabled him to come to a different and better conclusion.

In this case, we might first object to the major premise, the generalization that all men with chalk dust on their fingers are schoolteachers. Is it true? Perhaps all the men with dusty fingers whom Holmes had so far observed had turned out to be schoolteachers, but was his sample sufficiently large to allow him to conclude that all dust-fingered men, even those with whom he might never have contact, were teachers? Were there no other vocations or situations that might require the use of chalk? In Holmes's day draftsmen or carpenters or tailors might have had fingers just as white as those of schoolteachers. In other words, Holmes may have ascertained that all schoolteachers have chalk dust on their fingers, but he had not determined that *only* schoolteachers could be thus identified. Sometimes it is helpful to draw circles representing the various groups in their relation to the whole.

If a large circle (see the figure below) represents all those who have chalk dust on their fingers, we see that several different groups may be contained

[1] *The Art of Making Sense* (Philadelphia: Lippincott, 1954), ch. 17.

in this universe. To be safe, Holmes should have deduced that the man on the train *might* have been a schoolteacher; he was not safe in deducing more than that. Obviously, if the inductive generalization or major premise is false, the conclusion of the particular argument is also false or invalid.

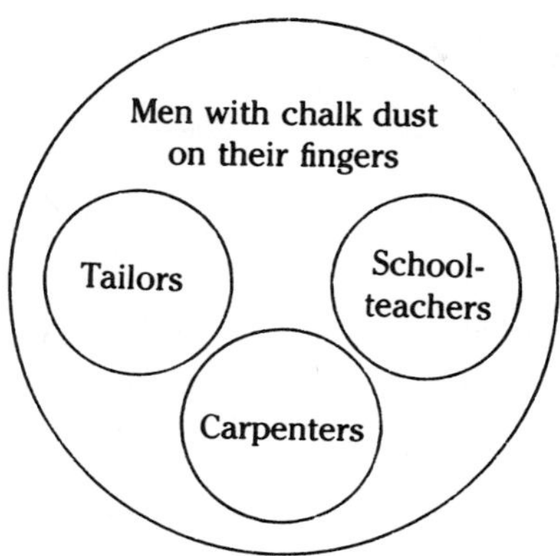

The deductive argument may also go wrong elsewhere. What if the minor premise is untrue? Could Holmes have mistaken the source of the white powder on the man's fingers? Suppose it was not chalk dust but flour or confectioner's sugar or talcum or heroin? Any of these possibilities would weaken or invalidate his conclusion.

Another example, closer to the kinds of arguments you will examine, reveals the flaw in the deductive process.

MAJOR PREMISE: All Communists oppose organized religion.

MINOR PREMISE: Robert Roe opposes organized religion.

CONCLUSION: Therefore, Robert Roe is a Communist.

The common name for this fallacy is "guilt by association." The fact that two things share an attribute does not mean that they are the same thing. The following diagram makes clear that Robert Roe and Communists do not necessarily share all attributes. Remembering that Holmes may have misinterpreted the signs of chalk on the traveler's fingers, we may also want to question whether Robert Roe's opposition to organized religion has been misinterpreted.

An example from history shows us how such an argument may be used. In a campaign speech during the summer of 1952, Senator Joseph McCarthy, who had made a reputation as a tireless enemy of communism, said, "I do not tell you that Schlesinger, Stevenson's number one

man, number one braintrust, I don't tell you he's a Communist. I have no information on that point. But I do know that if he were a Communist he would also ridicule religion as Schlesinger has done."[2] This is an argument based on a sign warrant. Clearly the sign referred to by Senator McCarthy, ridicule of religion, would not be sufficient to characterize someone as a Communist.

Some deductive arguments give trouble because one of the premises, usually the major premise, is omitted. As in the warrants we examined in Chapter 8, a failure to evaluate the truth of the unexpressed premise may lead to an invalid conclusion. When only two parts of the syllogism appear, we call the resulting form an *enthymeme.* Suppose we overhear the following snatch of conversation:

> *"Did you hear about Jean's father? He had a heart attack last week."*
> *"That's too bad. But I'm not surprised. I know he always refused to go for his annual physical checkups."*

The second speaker has used an unexpressed major premise, the cause-and-effect warrant "If you have annual physical checkups, you can avoid heart attacks." He does not express it because he assumes that it is unnecessary to do so. The first speaker recognizes the unspoken warrant and may agree with it. Or the first speaker may produce evidence from reputable sources that such a generalization is by no means universally true, in which case the conclusion of the second speaker is suspect.

A knowledge of the deductive process can help guide you toward an evaluation of the soundness of your reasoning in an argument you are constructing. The syllogism is often clearer than an outline in establishing the relations between the different parts of an argument.

[2]Joseph R. McCarthy, "The Red-Tinted Washington Crowd," speech delivered to a Republican campaign meeting at Appleton, Wisconsin, November 3, 1952.

Suppose you wanted to argue that your former high school should introduce a dress code. You might begin by asking these questions: What would be the purpose of such a regulation? How would a dress code fulfill that purpose? What reasons could you provide to support your claim? Then you might set down part of your argument like this:

> Dressing in different styles makes students more aware of social differences among themselves.
>
> The students in this school dress in many different styles.
>
> Therefore, they are more aware of differences in social status among the student body.

As you diagram this first part of the argument, you should ask two sets of questions:

1. Is the major premise true? Do differences in dress cause awareness of differences in social status? Has my experience confirmed this?
2. Is the minor premise true? Has my observation confirmed this?

The conclusion, of course, represents something that you don't have to observe. You can deduce with certainty that it is true if both the major and minor premises are true.

So far the testing of your argument has been relatively easy because you have been concerned with the testing of observation and experience. Now you must examine something that does not appear in the syllogism. You have determined certain facts about perceptions of social status, but you have not arrived at the policy you want to recommend: that a dress code should be mandated. Notice that the dress code argument is based on acceptance of a moral value.

> Reducing awareness of social differences is a desirable goal for the school.
>
> A uniform dress code would help to achieve that goal.
>
> Therefore, students should be required to dress uniformly.

The major premise in this syllogism is clearly different from the previous one. While the premise in the previous syllogism can be tested by examining sufficient examples to determine probability, this statement, about the desirability of the goal, is a value judgment and cannot be proved by counting examples. Whether equality of social status is a desirable goal depends on an appeal to other, more basic values.

Setting down your own or someone else's argument in this form will not necessarily give you the answers to questions about how to support your claim, but it should clearly indicate what your claims are and, above all, what logical connections exist between your statements.

SAMPLE ANNOTATED ESSAY: A DEDUCTIVE ARGUMENT

It's All about Him

DAVID VON DREHLE

The author establishes his knowledge of mass murders, his "claim to authority."

My reporter's odyssey has taken me from the chill dawn outside the Florida prison in which serial killer Ted Bundy met his end, to the charred façade of a Bronx nightclub where Julio Gonzalez incinerated 87 people, to a muddy Colorado hillside overlooking the Columbine High School library, in which Eric Harris and Dylan Klebold wrought their mayhem. Along the way, I've come to believe that we're looking for why in all the wrong places.

His thesis statement (and major premise): mass murderers are narcissists

I've lost interest in the cracks, chips, holes, and broken places in the lives of men like Cho Seung-Hui, the mass murderer of Virginia Tech. The pain, grievances, and self-pity of mass killers are only symptoms of the real explanation. Those who do these things share one common trait. They are raging narcissists. "I died—like Jesus Christ," Cho said in a video sent to NBC.

The traits of the narcissist

Psychologists from South Africa to Chicago have begun to recognize that extreme self-centeredness is the forest in these stories, and all the other things—guns, games, lyrics, pornography—are just trees. To list the traits of the narcissist is enough to prove the point: grandiosity, numbness to the needs and pain of others, emotional isolation, resentment, and envy.

Major premise applied to Ted Bundy

In interviews with Ted Bundy taped a quarter-century ago, journalists Stephen Michaud and Hugh Aynesworth captured the essence of homicidal narcissism. Through hour after tedious hour, a man who killed 30 or more young women and girls preened for his audience. He spoke of himself as an actor, of life as a series of roles, and of other people as props and scenery. His desires were simple: "control" and

---

David von Drehle is a senior writer at the *Washington Post*, where he has also been national political writer, magazine staff writer, New York bureau chief, and assistant managing editor. His most recent book is *Triangle: The Fire That Changed America* (2003). This article appeared in *Time* on April 30, 2007.

"mastery." He took whatever he wanted, from shoplifted tube socks to human lives, because nothing mattered beyond his desires. Bundy said he was always surprised that anyone noticed his victims had vanished. "I mean, there are so many people," he explained. The only death he regretted was his own.

5 Criminologists distinguish between serial killers like Bundy, whose crimes occur one at a time and who try hard to avoid capture, and mass killers like Cho. But the central role of narcissism plainly connects them. Only a narcissist could decide that his alienation should be underlined in the blood of strangers. The flamboyant nature of these crimes is like a neon sign pointing to the truth. Charles Whitman playing God in his Texas clock tower, James Huberty spraying lead in a California restaurant, Harris and Klebold in their theatrical trench coats—they're all stars in the cinema of their self-absorbed minds.

Other examples of narcissistic mass murderers

Freud explained narcissism as a failure to grow up. All infants are narcissists, he pointed out, but as we grow, we ought to learn that other people have lives independent of our own. It's not their job to please us, applaud for us, or even notice us—let alone die because we're unhappy.

Freud said narcissists never grow up. They put their happiness over others' lives.

A generation ago, the social critic Christopher Lasch diagnosed narcissism as the signal disorder of contemporary American culture. The cult of celebrity, the marketing of instant gratification, skepticism toward moral codes, and the politics of victimhood were signs of a society regressing toward the infant stage. You don't have to buy Freud's explanation or Lasch's indictment, however, to see an immediate danger in the way we examine the lives of mass killers. Earnestly and honestly, detectives and journalists dig up apparent clues and weave them into a sort of explanation. In the days after Columbine, for example, Harris and Klebold emerged as alienated misfits in the jock culture of their suburban high school. We learned about their morbid taste in music and their violent video games. Largely missing, though, was the proper frame around the picture: the extreme narcissism that licensed these boys, in their minds, to murder their teachers and classmates.

Investigators have failed to recognize narcissism as the real motivation in mass murder cases.

Major premise applied to Cho

Something similar is now going on with Cho, whose florid writings and videos were an almanac of gripes. "I'm so lonely," he moped to a teacher, failing to mention that he often refused to answer even when people said hello. Of course he was lonely.

Outside the context of narcissism, the murderers' actions can seem too logical.

In Holocaust studies, there is a school of thought that says to explain is to forgive. I won't go that far. But we must stop explaining killers on their terms. Minus the clear context of narcissism, the biographical details of these men can begin to look like a plausible chain of cause and effect—especially to other narcissists. And they don't need any more encouragement.

The author reiterates that the killer's problem is not lack of attention but how the killer sees himself.

There's a telling moment in Michael Moore's 10
film *Bowling for Columbine*, in which singer Marilyn Manson dismisses the idea that listening to his lyrics contributed to the disintegration of Harris and Klebold. What the Columbine killers needed, Manson suggests, was for someone to listen to them. This is the narcissist's view of narcissism: everything would be fine if only he received more attention. The real problem can be found in the killer's mirror.

■ Analysis

Von Drehle wrote "It's All about Him" shortly after the 2007 massacre at Virginia Tech. Although we cannot know exactly how he arrived at the thesis, we can reasonably assume he went through something of an inductive process on the way to writing this deductive essay. Perhaps he read and watched enough about Cho, the shooter at Virginia Tech, to start to hypothesize about Cho's motivation. His earlier observations of other mass murderers led him to notice similarities among them. Once he arrived at a theory about what they had in common, he had the major premise for a deductive argument that he could test out on other mass murderers. He was able to construct an argument that could be summarized in syllogistic form:

MAJOR PREMISE:	Mass murderers are narcissistic.
MINOR PREMISE:	Cho was a mass murderer.
CONCLUSION:	Cho was narcissistic.

In his essay he presents his major premise early and then applies it to other U.S. mass murderers: Ted Bundy, Charles Whitman, James Huberty, Eric Harris, and Dylan Klebold.

Remember that there is a difference between a syllogism being valid or logically consistent and its conclusion being true. If von Drehle's major and minor premises are true, the conclusion, of necessity, must be true. That Cho was a mass murderer is an indisputable fact; thus the minor premise is true. But what of the major premise? If you applied the deduction that mass murderers are narcissistic to mass murderers not mentioned by von Drehle, would the conclusion be the same in each case? In other words, is it true that mass murderers are narcissistic?

Because it would be virtually impossible to apply von Drehle's deduction to all mass murderers, he would have built a more convincing case had he restricted his thesis statement with a word like *most* or *many*. That, however, would have invalidated the deductive logic that tells us that a syllogism's conclusion must be true. As it is, the examples he offers are not enough to convince all readers that his theory of narcissism is valid. Still, he offers a unique look at the motivation of mass murderers and one that makes it impossible for anyone else to be blamed for the crimes that these men and boys have committed. Behind his argument are his many years of journalistic experience and his opening revelation that he has been on the scene during the aftermath of many of the crimes to which he refers.

PRACTICE

Reread the Declaration of Independence (p. 33). Explain why it is an example of deductive reasoning.

A NOTE ON THE SYLLOGISM AND THE TOULMIN MODEL

In examining the classical deductive syllogism, you may have noticed the resemblance of its three-part outline to the three-part structure of claim, support, and warrant that we have used throughout the text to illustrate the elements of argument. We mentioned that the syllogism was articulated over two thousand years ago by the Greek philosopher Aristotle. By contrast, the claim-support-warrant structure is based on the model of argument proposed by the modern British philosopher Stephen Toulmin.

Now, there is every reason to think that all models of argument will share some similarities. Nevertheless, the differences between the formal syllogism and the informal Toulmin model suggest that the latter is a more effective instrument for writers who want to know which questions to ask, both before they begin and during the process of developing their arguments.

The syllogism is useful for laying out the basic elements of an argument, as we have seen in several examples. It lends itself more readily to simple arguments. The following syllogism summarizes a familiar argument.

MAJOR PREMISE:	Advertising of things harmful to our health should be legally banned.
MINOR PREMISE:	Cigarettes are harmful to our health.
CONCLUSION:	Therefore, advertising of cigarettes should be legally banned.

Cast in the form of a Toulmin outline, the argument looks like this:

CLAIM:	Advertising of cigarettes should be legally banned.
SUPPORT (EVIDENCE):	Cigarettes are harmful to our health.
WARRANT:	Advertising of things harmful to our health should be legally banned.

Or in diagram form:

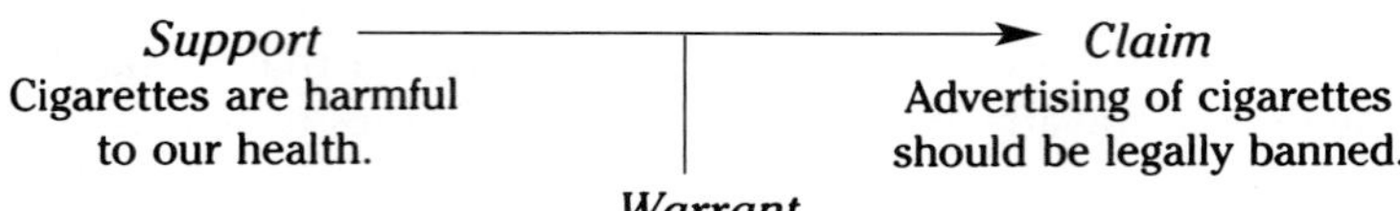

In both the syllogism and the Toulmin model the principal elements of the argument are expressed in three statements. You can see that the claim in the Toulmin model is the conclusion in the syllogism—that is, the proposition that you are trying to prove. The evidence (support) in the Toulmin model corresponds to the minor premise in the syllogism. And the warrant in the Toulmin model resembles the major premise of the syllogism.

But the differences are significant. One difference is the use of language. The syllogism represents an argument "in which the validity of the assumption underlying the inference 'leap' is uncontested."[3] That is, the words "major premise" seem to suggest that the assumption has been proved. They do not emphasize that an analysis of the premise—"Advertising of things harmful to our health should be legally banned"—is necessary before we can decide that the conclusion is acceptable. Of course, a

[3]Wayne E. Brockenreide and Douglas Ehninger, "Toulmin on Argument: An Interpretation and Application," *Contemporary Theories of Rhetoric: Selected Readings,* ed. Richard L. Johannesen (New York: Harper and Row, 1971), p. 245. This comparative analysis is indebted to Brockenreide and Ehninger's influential article.

careful arguer will try to establish the truth and validity of all parts of the syllogism, but the terms in which the syllogism is framed do not encourage him or her to examine the real relationship among the three elements. Sometimes the enthymeme (see p. 330), which uses only two elements in the argument and suppresses the third, makes analyzing the relationship even more difficult.

In the Toulmin model, the use of the term *warrant* indicates that the validity of the proposition must be established to *guarantee* the claim or make the crossing from support to claim. It makes clear that the arguer must ask *why* such advertising must be banned.

Nor is the term *minor premise* as useful to the arguer as "support." The word *support* instructs the arguer that he or she must take steps to provide the claim with factual evidence or an appeal to values.

A second difference is that while the syllogism is essentially static, with all three parts logically locked into place, the Toulmin model suggests that an argument is a *movement* from support to claim by way of the warrant, which acts as a bridge. Toulmin introduced the concept of warrant by asking "How do you get there?" (His first two questions, introducing the claim and support, were, "What are you trying to prove?" and "What have you got to go on?")

Lastly, recall that in addition to the three basic elements, the Toulmin model offers supplementary elements of argument. The *qualifier,* in the form of words like "probably" or "more likely," shows that the claim is not absolute. The *backing* offers support for the validity of the warrant. The *reservation* suggests that the validity of the warrant may be limited. These additional elements, which refine and expand the argument itself, reflect the real flexibility and complexity of the argumentative process.

COMMON FALLACIES

In this necessarily brief review it would be impossible to discuss all the fallacies listed by logicians, but we can examine the ones most likely to be found in the arguments you will read and write. Fallacies are difficult to classify, first, because there are literally dozens of systems for classifying, and second, because under any system there is always a good deal of overlap. Our discussion of the reasoning process, however, tells us where faulty reasoning occurs.

Inductive fallacies, as we know, result from the wrong use of evidence: That is, the arguer leaps to a conclusion on the basis of an insufficient sample, ignoring evidence that might have altered his or her conclusion. Deductive fallacies, on the other hand, result from a failure to follow the logic of a series of statements. Here the arguer neglects to make a clear connection between the parts of his or her argument. One of the commonest strategies is the introduction of an irrelevant issue, one that has little or no direct bearing on the development of the claim and serves only to distract the reader.

It's helpful to remember that, even if you cannot name the particular fallacy, you can learn to recognize it and not only refute it in the arguments of others but avoid it in your own as well.

1. Hasty Generalization

In Chapter 7 (see pp. 211–71) we discussed the dangers in drawing conclusions on the basis of insufficient evidence. Many of our prejudices are a result of hasty generalization. A prejudice is literally a judgment made before the facts are in. On the basis of experience with two or three members of an ethnic group, for example, we may form the prejudice that all members of the group share the characteristics that we have attributed to the two or three in our experience.

Superstitions are also based in part on hasty generalization. As a result of a very small number of experiences with black cats, broken mirrors, Friday the thirteenth, or spilled salt, some people will assume a cause-and-effect relation between these signs and misfortunes. *Superstition* has been defined as "a notion maintained despite evidence to the contrary." The evidence would certainly show that, contrary to the superstitious belief, in a lifetime hundreds of such "unlucky" signs are not followed by unfortunate events. To generalize about a connection is therefore unjustified.

2. Faulty Use of Authority

The use of authority—the attempt to bolster claims by citing the opinions of experts—was discussed in Chapter 7. Experts are a valuable source of information on subjects we have no personal experience with or specialized knowledge about. Properly identified, they can provide essential support. The faulty use of authority occurs when individuals are presented as authorities in fields in which they are not. An actor who plays a doctor on television may be hired to advertise the latest sleep medicine but actually has no more expertise with medications than the average consumer. The role that he plays may make him appear to be an authority but does not make him one. No matter how impressive credentials sound, they are largely meaningless unless they establish relevant authority. Both writers and readers need to be especially aware of the testimony of authorities who may disagree with those cited. In circumstances where experts disagree, you are encouraged to undertake a careful evaluation and comparison of credentials.

3. Post Hoc or Doubtful Cause

The entire Latin term for this fallacy is *post hoc, ergo propter hoc,* meaning, "After this, therefore because of this." The arguer infers that because one event follows another event, the first event must be the cause of the second. But proximity of events or conditions does not guarantee a causal relation. The rooster crows every morning at 5:00 and, seeing the sun rise immediately after, decides that his crowing has caused the sun to rise. A month after A-bomb tests are concluded, tornadoes damage the area where the tests were held, and residents decide that the tests caused the tornadoes. After the school principal suspends daily prayers in the classroom, acts of vandalism increase, and some parents are convinced that failure to conduct prayer is responsible for the rise in vandalism. In each of these cases, the fact that one event follows another does not prove a causal connection. The two events may be coincidental, or the first event may be only one, and an insignificant one, of many causes that have produced the second event. The reader or writer of causal arguments must determine whether another more plausible explanation exists and whether several causes have combined to produce the effect. Perhaps the suspension of prayer was only one of a number of related causes: a decline in disciplinary action, a relaxation of academic standards, a change in school administration, and changes in family structure in the school community.

In a previous section we saw that superstitions are the result not only of hasty generalization but also of the willingness to find a cause-and-effect connection in the juxtaposition of two events. A belief in astrological signs also derives from erroneous inferences about cause and effect. Only a very few of the millions of people who consult the astrology charts every day in newspapers and magazines have submitted the predictions to statistical analysis. A curious reader might try this strategy: Save the columns, usually at the beginning or end of the year, in which astrologers and clairvoyants make predictions for events in the coming year, allegedly based on their reading of the stars and other signs. At the end of the year evaluate the percentage of predictions that were fulfilled. The number will be very small. But even if some of the predictions prove true, there may be other less fanciful explanations for their accuracy.

In defending simple explanations against complex ones, philosophers and scientists often refer to a maxim called *Occam's razor,* a principle formulated by the medieval philosopher and theologian William of Occam. A modern science writer says this principle "urges a preference for the simplest hypothesis that does all we want it to do."[4] Bertrand Russell, the twentieth-century British philosopher, explained it this way:

> It is vain to do with more what can be done with fewer. That is to say, if everything in some science can be interpreted without assuming this or that hypothetical entity, there is no ground for assuming it. I have myself found this a most fruitful principle in logical analysis.[5]

In other words, choose the simpler, more credible explanation wherever possible.

[4]Martin Gardner, *The Whys of a Philosophical Scrivener* (New York: Quill, 1983), p. 174.
[5]*Dictionary of Mind, Matter and Morals* (New York: Philosophical Library, 1952), p. 166.

We all share the belief that scientific experimentation and research can answer questions about a wide range of natural and social phenomena: evolutionary development, hurricanes, disease, crime, poverty. It is true that repeated experiments in controlled situations can establish what seem to be solid relations suggesting cause and effect. But even scientists prefer to talk not about cause but about an extremely high probability that under controlled conditions one event will follow another.

In the social sciences cause-and-effect relations are especially susceptible to challenge. Human experiences can seldom be subjected to laboratory conditions. In addition, the complexity of the social environment makes it difficult, even impossible, to extract one cause from among the many that influence human behavior.

4. False Analogy

Many analogies are merely descriptive and offer no proof of the connection between the two things being compared. In recent years a debate has emerged between weight-loss professionals about the wisdom of urging overweight people to lose weight for health reasons. Susan Wooley, director of the eating disorders clinic at the University of Cincinnati and a professor of psychiatry, offered the following analogy in defense of her view that dieting is dangerous.

> We know that overweight people have a higher mortality rate than thin people. We also know that black people have a higher mortality rate than white people. Do we subject black people to torturous treatments to bleach their skin? Of course not. We have enough sense to know skin-bleaching will not eliminate sickle-cell anemia. So why do we have blind faith that weight loss will cure the diseases associated with obesity?"[6]

But it is clear that the false analogy between black skin and excessive weight does not work. Bleaching one's skin does not eliminate sickle-cell anemia, but there is an abundance of proof that excess weight influences mortality.

Historians are fond of using analogical arguments to demonstrate that particular circumstances prevailing in the past are being reproduced in the present. They therefore feel safe in predicting that the present course of history will follow that of the past. British historian Arnold Toynbee argues by analogy that humans' tenure on earth may be limited.

> On the evidence of the past history of life on this planet, even the extinction of the human race is not entirely unlikely. After all, the reign of man on the Earth, if we are right in thinking that man established his present ascendancy in the middle paleolithic age, is so far only about 100,000 years old, and what is that compared to the 500 million or 900 million years during which life has been in existence on the sur-

[6] *New York Times,* April 12, 1992, sec. C, p. 43.

> face of this planet? In the past, other forms of life have enjoyed reigns which have lasted for almost inconceivably longer periods—and which yet at last have come to an end.[7]

Toynbee finds similarities between the limited reigns of other animal species and the possible disappearance of the human race. For this analogy, however, we need to ask whether the conditions of the past, so far as we know them, at all resemble the conditions under which human existence on earth might be terminated. Is the fact that human beings are also members of the animal kingdom sufficient support for this comparison?

5. Ad Hominem

The Latin term *ad hominem* means "against the man" and refers to an attack on the person rather than on the argument or the issue. The assumption in such a fallacy is that if the speaker proves to be unacceptable in some way, his or her statements must also be judged unacceptable. Attacking the author of the statement is a strategy of diversion that prevents the reader from giving attention where it is due—to the issue under discussion.

You might hear someone complain, "What can the priest tell us about marriage? He's never been married himself." This ad hominem accusation ignores the validity of the advice the priest might offer. In the same way an overweight patient might reject the advice on diet by an overweight physician. In politics it is not uncommon for antagonists to attack each other for personal characteristics that may not be relevant to the tasks they will be elected to perform. They may be accused of infidelity to their partners, homosexuality, atheism, or a flamboyant social life. Even if certain accusations should be proved true, voters should not ignore the substance of what politicians do and say in their public offices.

This confusion of private life with professional record also exists in literature and the other arts. According to their biographers, the American writers Thomas Wolfe, Robert Frost, and William Saroyan—to name only a few—and numbers of film stars, including Charlie Chaplin, Joan Crawford, and Bing Crosby, made life miserable for those closest to them. Having read about their unpleasant personal characteristics, some people find it hard to separate the artist from his or her creation, although the personality and character of the artist are often irrelevant to the content of the work.

Ad hominem accusations against the person do *not* constitute a fallacy if the characteristics under attack are relevant to the argument. If the politician is irresponsible and dishonest in the conduct of his or her personal life, we may be justified in thinking that the person will also behave irresponsibly and dishonestly in public office.

[7] *Civilization on Trial* (New York: Oxford University Press, 1948), pp. 162–63.

6. False Dilemma

As the name tells us, the false dilemma, sometimes called the *black-white fallacy,* poses an either-or situation. The arguer suggests that only two alternatives exist, although there may be other explanations of or solutions to the problem under discussion. The false dilemma reflects the simplification of a complex problem. Sometimes it is offered out of ignorance or laziness, sometimes to divert attention from the real explanation or solution that the arguer rejects for doubtful reasons.

You may encounter the either-or situation in dilemmas about personal choices. "At the University of Georgia," says one writer, "the measure of a man was football. You either played it or worshiped those who did, and there was no middle ground."[8] Clearly this dilemma—playing football or worshiping those who do—ignores other measures of manhood.

Politics and government offer a wealth of examples. In an interview with the *New York Times* in 1975, the Shah of Iran was asked why he could not introduce into his authoritarian regime greater freedom for his subjects. His reply was, "What's wrong with authority? Is anarchy better?" Apparently he considered that only two paths were open to him—authoritarianism or anarchy. Of course, democracy was also an option, which, perhaps fatally, he declined to consider.

7. Slippery Slope

If an arguer predicts that taking a first step will lead inevitably to a second, usually undesirable step, he or she must provide evidence that this will happen. Otherwise, the arguer is guilty of a slippery slope fallacy.

Asked by an inquiring photographer on the street how he felt about censorship of a pornographic magazine, a man replied, "I don't think any publication should be banned. It's a slippery slope when you start making decisions on what people should be permitted to read. . . . It's a dangerous precedent." Perhaps. But if questioned further, the man should have offered evidence that a ban on some things leads inevitably to a ban on everything.

Predictions based on the danger inherent in taking the first step are commonplace:

> Legalization of abortion will lead to murder of the old and the physically and mentally handicapped.
>
> The Connecticut law allowing sixteen-year-olds and their parents to divorce each other will mean the death of the family.
>
> If we ban handguns, we will end up banning rifles and other hunting weapons.

[8]Phil Gailey, "A Nonsports Fan," *New York Times Magazine,* December 18, 1983, sec. 6, p. 96.

Distinguishing between probable and improbable predictions—that is, recognizing the slippery-slope fallacy—poses special problems because only future developments can verify or refute predictions. For example, in 1941 the imposition of military conscription aroused some opponents to predict that the draft was a precursor of fascism in this country. Only after the war, when 10 million draftees were demobilized, did it become clear that the draft had been an insufficient sign for a prediction of fascism. In this case the slippery-slope prediction of fascism might have been avoided if closer attention had been paid to other influences pointing to the strength of democracy.

More recently, the debate about cloning has raised fears of creation of genetic copies of adults. The *New York Times* reported that

> Many lawmakers today warned that if therapeutic cloning went forward, scientists would step onto a slippery slope that would inevitably lead to cloning people.[9]

Most scientists, however, reject this possibility for the foreseeable future.

Slippery slope predictions are simplistic. They ignore not only the dissimilarities between first and last steps but also the complexity of the developments in any long chain of events.

8. Begging the Question

If the writer makes a statement that assumes that the very question being argued has already been proved, the writer is guilty of begging the question. In a letter to the editor of a college newspaper protesting the failure of the majority of students to meet the writing requirement because they had failed an exemption test, the writer said, "Not exempting all students who honestly qualify for exemption is an insult." But whether the students are honestly qualified is precisely the question that the exemption test was supposed to resolve. The writer has not proved that the students who failed the writing test were qualified for exemption. She has only made an assertion *as if* she had already proved it.

Circular reasoning is an extreme example of begging the question: "Women should not be permitted to join men's clubs because the clubs are for men only." The question to be resolved first, of course, is whether clubs for men only should continue to exist.

9. Straw Man

The straw-man fallacy consists of an attack on a view similar to but not the same as the one your opponent holds. It is a familiar diversionary tactic. The name probably derives from an old game in which a straw man was

[9]August 1, 2001, sec. A, p. 11.

set up to divert attention from the real target that a contestant was supposed to knock down.

One of the outstanding examples of the straw-man fallacy occurred in the famous Checkers speech of Senator Richard Nixon. In 1952 during his vice-presidential campaign, Nixon was accused of having appropriated $18,000 in campaign funds for his personal use. At one point in the radio and television speech in which he defended his reputation, he said:

> One other thing I probably should tell you, because if I don't they will probably be saying this about me, too. We did get something, a gift, after the election.
>
> A man down in Texas heard Pat on the radio mention the fact that our two youngsters would like to have a dog, and, believe it or not, the day before we left on this campaign trip we got a message from Union Station in Baltimore saying they had a package for us. We went down to get it. You know what it was?
>
> It was a little cocker spaniel dog, in a crate that he had sent all the way from Texas, black and white, spotted, and our little girl, Tricia, the six-year-old, named it Checkers.
>
> And, you know, the kids, like all kids, loved the dog, and I just want to say this, right now, that regardless of what they say about it, we are going to keep it.[10]

Of course, Nixon knew that the issue was the alleged misappropriation of funds, not the ownership of the dog, which no one had asked him to return.

10. Two Wrongs Make a Right

The two-wrongs-make-a-right fallacy is another example of the way in which attention may be diverted from the question at issue.

After President Jimmy Carter in March 1977 attacked the human rights record of the Soviet Union, Russian officials responded:

> As for the present state of human rights in the United States, it is characterized by the following facts: millions of unemployed, racial discrimination, social inequality of women, infringement of citizens' personal freedom, the growth of crime, and so on.[11]

The Russians made no attempt to deny the failure of *their* human rights record; instead they attacked by pointing out that the Americans are not blameless either.

[10] Radio and television address of Senator Nixon from Los Angeles on September 23, 1952.

[11] *New York Times,* March 3, 1977, p. 1.

11. Non Sequitur

The Latin term *non sequitur,* which means "it does not follow," is another fallacy of irrelevance. An advertisement for a book, *Worlds in Collision,* whose theories about the origin of the earth and evolutionary development have been challenged by almost all reputable scientists, states:

> Once rejected as "preposterous"! Critics called it an outrage! It aroused incredible antagonism in scientific and literary circles. Yet half a million copies were sold and for twenty-seven years it remained an outstanding bestseller.

We know, of course, that the popularity of a book does not bestow scientific respectability. The number of sales, therefore, is irrelevant to proof of the book's theoretical soundness—a non sequitur.

Other examples sometimes appear in the comments of political candidates. Donald Trump, the wealthy real-estate developer, in considering a run for president of the United States in 2000, told an interviewer:

> My entire life, I've watched politicians bragging about how poor they are, how they came from nothing, how poor their parents and grandparents were. And I said to myself, if they can stay so poor for so many generations, maybe this isn't the kind of person we want to be electing to higher office. How smart can they be? They're morons. . . . Do you want someone who gets to be president and that's literally the highest paying job he's ever had?[12]

As a brief glance at U.S. history shows, it does not follow that men of small success in the world of commerce are unfit to make sound decisions about matters of state.

12. Ad Populum

Arguers guilty of the *ad populum* fallacy make an appeal to the prejudices of the people (*populum* in Latin). They assume that their claim can be adequately defended without further support if they emphasize a belief or attitude that the audience shares with them. One common form of ad populum is an appeal to patriotism, which may allow arguers to omit evidence that the audience needs for proper evaluation of the claim. In the following advertisement the makers of Zippo lighters made such an appeal in urging readers to buy their product.

> It's a grand old lighter. Zippo—the grand old lighter that's made right here in the good old U.S.A.
>
> We truly make an all-American product. The raw materials used in making a Zippo lighter are all right from this great land of ours.
>
> Zippo windproof lighters are proud to be Americans.

[12] *New York Times,* November 28, 1999, p. 11.

13. Appeal to Tradition

In making an appeal to tradition, the arguer assumes that what has existed for a long time and has therefore become a tradition should continue to exist *because* it is a tradition. If the arguer avoids telling his or her reader *why* the tradition should be preserved, he or she may be accused of failing to meet the real issue.

The following statement appeared in a letter defending the membership policy of the Century Club, an all-male club established in New York City in 1847 that was under pressure to admit women. The writer was a Presbyterian minister who opposed the admission of women.

> I am totally opposed to a proposal which would radically change the nature of the Century. . . . A club creates an ethos of its own over the years, and I would deeply deplore a step that would inevitably create an entirely different kind of place.
>
> A club like the Century should surely be unaffected by fashionable whims. . . .[13]

14. Faulty Emotional Appeals

In some discussions of fallacies, appeals to the emotions of the audience are treated as illegitimate or "counterfeit proofs." All such appeals, however, are *not* illegitimate. As we saw in Chapter 7 on support, appeals to the values and emotions of an audience are an appropriate form of persuasion. You can recognize fallacious emotional appeals if (1) they are irrelevant to the argument or draw attention from the issues being argued or (2) they appear to conceal another purpose. Here we treat two of the most popular appeals—to pity and to fear.

Appeals to pity, compassion, and natural willingness to help the unfortunate are particularly hard to resist. The requests for aid by most charitable organizations—for hungry children, victims of disaster, stray animals—offer examples of legitimate appeals. But these appeals to our sympathetic feelings should not divert us from considering other issues in a particular case. It would be wrong, for example, to allow a multiple murderer to escape punishment because he or she had experienced a wretched childhood. Likewise, if you are asked to contribute to a charitable cause, you should try to learn how many unfortunate people or animals are being helped and what percentage of the contribution will be allocated to maintaining the organization and its officers. In some cases the financial records are closed to public review, and only a small share of the contribution will reach the alleged beneficiaries.

Appeals to fear are likely to be even more effective. But they must be based on evidence that fear is an appropriate response to the issues and that

[13] David H. C. Read, letter to the *New York Times*, January 13, 1983, p. 14.

it can move an audience toward a solution to the problem. (Fear can also have the adverse effect of preventing people from taking a necessary action.) Insurance companies, for example, make appeals to our fears of destitution for ourselves and our families as a result of injury, unemployment, sickness, and death. These appeals are justified if the possibilities of such destitution are real and if the insurance will provide relief. It would also be legitimate to arouse fear of the consequences of drunk driving, provided, again, that the descriptions were accurate. On the other hand, it would be wrong to induce fear that fluoridation of public water supplies causes cancer without presenting sound evidence of the probability.

An emotional response by itself is not always the soundest basis for making decisions. Your own experience has probably taught you that in the grip of a strong emotion like love or hate or anger you often overlook good reasons for making different and better choices. Like you, your readers want to be given the opportunity to consider all the available kinds of support for an argument.

PRACTICE

Decide whether the reasoning in the following examples is faulty. Explain your answers.

1. The presiding judge of a revolutionary tribunal, being asked why people are being executed without trial, replies, "Why should we put them on trial when we know that they're guilty?"

Writer's Guide: Avoiding Logical Fallacies

1. If you are making use of induction, that is, drawing a conclusion based on a number of individual examples, do you have enough examples with variety to justify the conclusion? In other words, will your readers be able to make the inductive leap from examples to the conclusion you are asking them to make?
2. If you are making use of deduction, is your conclusion a logical one based on the premises underlying it? To be sure, write out your argument in the form of a syllogism. Also avoid wording your thesis in absolute terms like *all, every, everyone, everybody,* and *always.*
3. It is relatively easy—and sometimes humorous—to notice other writers' logical fallacies. It is harder to notice your own. Use the list of fallacies in this chapter as a checklist as you read the draft of each of your essays with a critical eye, looking for any breakdown in logic. It may be useful to read your essay aloud to someone because if that listener cannot follow your logic, you may need to clarify your points.

2. The government has the right to require the wearing of helmets while operating or riding on a motorcycle because of the high rate of head injuries incurred in motorcycle accidents.
3. Children who watch game shows rather than situation comedies receive higher grades in school. So it must be true that game shows are more educational than situation comedies.
4. The meteorologist predicted the wrong amount of rain for May. Obviously the meteorologist is unreliable.
5. Women ought to be permitted to serve in combat. Why should men be the only ones to face death and danger?
6. If Cher uses Equal, it must taste better than Sweet 'n Low.
7. People will gamble anyway, so why not legalize gambling in this state?
8. Because so much money was spent on public education in the last decade while educational achievement declined, more money to improve education can't be the answer to reversing the decline.
9. He's a columnist for a campus newspaper, so he must be a pretty good writer.
10. We tend to exaggerate the need for Standard English. You don't need much Standard English for most jobs in this country.
11. It's discriminatory to mandate that police officers must conform to a certain height and weight.
12. A doctor can consult books to make a diagnosis, so a medical student should be able to consult books when being tested.
13. Because this soft drink contains so many chemicals, it must be unsafe.
14. Core requirements should be eliminated. After all, students are paying for their education, so they should be able to earn a diploma by choosing the courses they want.
15. We should encourage a return to arranged marriages in this country since marriages based on romantic love haven't been very successful.
16. I know three redheads who have terrible tempers, and since Annabel has red hair, I'll bet she has a terrible temper, too.
17. Supreme Court Justice Byron White was an all-American football player while in college, so how can you say that athletes are dumb?
18. Benjamin H. Sasway, a student at Humboldt State University in California, was indicted for failure to register for possible conscription. Barry Lynn, president of Draft Action, an antidraft group, said, "It is disgraceful that this administration is embarking on an effort to fill the prisons with men of conscience and moral commitment."
19. James A. Harris, former president of the National Education Association: "Twenty-three percent of schoolchildren are failing to graduate and another large segment graduates as functional illiterates. If 23 percent of anything else failed—23 percent of automobiles didn't run, 23 percent of the buildings fell down, 23 percent of stuffed ham spoiled—we'd look at the producer."

20. A professor at Rutgers University: "The arrest rate for women is rising three times as fast as that of men. Women, inflamed by the doctrines of feminism, are pursuing criminal careers with the same zeal as business and the professions."
21. Physical education should be required because physical activity is healthful.
22. George Meany, former president of the AFL-CIO, in 1968: "To these people who constantly say you have got to listen to these younger people, they have got something to say, I just don't buy that at all. They smoke more pot than we do and if the younger generation are the hundred thousand kids that lay around a field up in Woodstock, New York, I am not going to trust the destiny of the country to that group."
23. That candidate was poor as a child, so he will certainly be sympathetic to the poor if he's elected.
24. When the federal government sent troops into Little Rock, Arkansas, to enforce integration of the public school system, the governor of Arkansas attacked the action, saying that it was as brutal an act of intervention as Russia's sending troops into Hungary to squelch the Hungarians' rebellion. In both cases, the governor said, the rights of a freedom-loving, independent people were being violated.
25. Governor Jones was elected two years ago. Since that time constant examples of corruption and subversion have been unearthed. It is time to get rid of the man responsible for this kind of corrupt government.
26. Are we going to vote a pay increase for our teachers, or are we going to allow our schools to deteriorate into substandard custodial institutions?
27. You see, the priests were right. After we threw those virgins into the volcano, it quit erupting.
28. The people of Rome lost their vitality and desire for freedom when their emperors decided that the way to keep them happy was to provide them with bread and circuses. What can we expect of our own country now that the government gives people free food and there is a constant round of entertainment provided by television?
29. From Mark Clifton, "The Dread Tomato Affliction" (proving that eating tomatoes is dangerous and even deadly): "Ninety-two point four percent of juvenile delinquents have eaten tomatoes. Fifty-seven point one percent of the adult criminals in penitentiaries throughout the United States have eaten tomatoes. Eighty-four percent of all people killed in automobile accidents during the year have eaten tomatoes."
30. From Galileo, *Dialogues Concerning Two New Sciences*: "But can you doubt that air has weight when you have the clear testimony of Aristotle affirming that all elements have weight, including air, and excepting only fire?"
31. Robert Brustein, artistic director of the American Repertory Theatre, commenting on a threat by Congress in 1989 to withhold funding from an offensive art show: "Once we allow lawmakers to become art critics, we take the first step into the world of Ayatollah Khomeini, whose murderous review of *The Satanic Verses* still chills the heart of everyone committed to

free expression." (The Ayatollah Khomeini called for the death of the author, Salman Rushdie, because Rushdie had allegedly committed blasphemy against Islam in his novel.)

READINGS FOR ANALYSIS

Show Biz Encourages Looser Teen Sex Habits

SHERYL McCARTHY

As the high school prom season winds down, we are learning more than we ever wanted to know about the social and sexual mores of today's teenagers.

Such as how they're avoiding "dating," opting instead to attend the prom with groups of friends. Everybody has a blast without suffering the angst of waiting for some guy to ask you to be his date, or worrying that the girl you ask will reject you.

This seems a lot healthier than it was when I went to my high school prom. I was lucky enough to have a great date and a wonderful prom night. But I've heard countless women complain thirty years later about missing their prom because nobody invited them. Going as a group takes the power to decide who gets to go out of the boys' hands, and takes the pressure of having to find a date off everybody.

Some of the other recent trends aren't so hot. A newspaper reporter who attended several local proms this year was shocked by the highly sexualized dancing that went on. When I was in school, the occasional guy put you in a back-breaking full-body lock that lasted the duration of a song. But now, virtually all the males and females engage in "freaking" and "backing up"—which amounts to simulating sex on the dance floor.

And there's the growing phenomenon of "hooking up." Having steady 5
boyfriends or girlfriends has been replaced by kids who travel in packs, breaking away to have casual sexual encounters with friends or mere acquaintances. These encounters range from kissing to petting, masturbating each other to oral sex—all without emotional strings. And they say they like it that way.

I find this retreat from intimacy rather depressing. My classmates weren't into sex, by and large. But there was something nice about the boyfriend-

---

Sheryl McCarthy is on the faculty of the Graduate School of Journalism of Columbia University. She has been a reporter for the *Boston Globe*, the *Baltimore Evening Sun*, and the New York *Daily News* and a national correspondent for ABC News. She is now a columnist for *Newsday*, where this article appeared on June 24, 2004.

girlfriend thing. In endless phone calls or Sunday night sofa-sitting, we achieved a certain emotional intimacy, along with our sexual gropings. The guys may have been thinking mostly about sex, but there was at least an idealized notion of what it meant to be a couple.

The current teenage social scene strikes me as rather aimless. Those who work with teenagers attribute the surge in dirty dancing to the music videos in which young musical stars like Britney Spears, Christina Aguilera, and Beyonce Knowles provocatively shake their scantily-clad booties, and legions of gorgeous females swarming over ordinary-looking men seem to define what relations between males and females are supposed to be.

Tamar Rothenberg, editor of *New Youth Connections*, a newspaper put out by New York City high school students, says she worries about the message the videos give to teenagers trying to figure out what they're supposed to be doing in relationships.

"Hooking up" apparently results from teenagers wanting to avoid being tied down in relationships that can cause pain and disappointment. Teenage girls may also be rebelling against the old sexual double standard and wanting to have the same freedom as boys. But the girls are often on the giving end of the casual sex, and teens often don't realize that they can catch diseases from oral sex.

The moguls of MTV and BET and the video producers and the titans of 10
hip-hop deserve a lot of the blame for this, and deserve to be booed off any stage where they are hypocritical enough to lament the high rate of teen pregnancy and the social fallout from irresponsible male sexual behavior.

But so do the spineless politicians and educators and the squeamish parents who are far more obsessed with keeping teenagers chaste than with helping them to have responsible relationships.

That's why I applaud groups like Planned Parenthood and *New Youth Connections* that treat teenagers like the semi-adults they are, and try to be helpful instead of self-righteous.

"I'm cool with kids having sex if they're being careful," says Rothenberg. "But they have to understand the possible emotional consequences and the health consequences."

Yeah, it was nice having prom dates who made no sexual demands, and having boyfriends instead of sexual hookups. But times have changed, and, to be helpful to teens living in a more sexualized world, the adults have to change too.

READING AND DISCUSSION QUESTIONS

1. Did McCarthy choose to use an inductive or a deductive approach to her subject?
2. Do you find the conclusions that McCarthy has drawn about today's teens convincing? Are they discredited by your own observations of teens?
3. Do you believe that there are any logical fallacies in McCarthy's argument? If so, what type of fallacies are they?

WRITING SUGGESTIONS

4. Examine how teen dating and/or sex habits are characterized on at least one current television show.
5. How do you respond to McCarthy's indictment of teens' sexual mores?

Food for Thought (and for Credit)

JENNIFER GROSSMAN

Want to combat the epidemic of obesity? Bring back home economics. Before you choke on your 300-calorie, trans-fat-laden Krispy Kreme, consider: Teaching basic nutrition and food preparation is a far less radical remedy than gastric bypass surgery or fast-food lawsuits. And probably far more effective. Obesity tends to invite such drastic solutions because it is so frustratingly difficult to treat. This intractability, coupled with the sad fact that obese children commonly grow up to be obese adults, argues for a preventative approach. As the new school year begins, we need to equip kids with the skills and practical knowledge to take control of their dietary destinies.

Despite its bad rep as Wife Ed 101, home economics has progressive roots. At the turn of the century it "helped transform domesticity into a vehicle to expand women's political power," according to Sarah Stage in *Rethinking Home Economics: Women and the History of a Profession*. In time, focus shifted from social reform to the practical priorities of sanitation and electrification, and then again to an emphasis on homemaking after World War II—giving ammunition to later critics like Betty Friedan who charged home ec with having helped foster the "feminine mystique."

Banished by feminists, Becky Home-ecky was left to wander backwater school districts. For a while it seemed that mandating male participation might salvage the discipline while satisfying political correctness. By the late 1970s one-third of male high school graduates had some home-ec training, whereas they comprised a mere 3.5 percent of home-ec students in 1962. Since then, "home economics has moved from the mainstream to the margins of American high school," according to the United States De-

Jennifer Grossman is director of the Dole Nutrition Institute, which distributes health information to the public through lectures and publications. Formerly, she was director of Education Policy at the Cato Institute and a speechwriter for President George H. W. Bush. She appears frequently as a commentator on shows such as *Larry King Live*, the *O'Reilly Factor*, the *Today Show*, and *Politically Incorrect*. She has written editorials for the *New York Times*, where this column appeared on September 2, 2003; the *Wall Street Journal*; the *Los Angeles Times*; the *New York Post*; the *Weekly Standard*; the *National Review*; and the *Women's Quarterly*.

partment of Education, with even female participation—near universal in the 1950s—plummeting by 67 percent.

What has happened since? Ronald McDonald and Colonel Sanders stepped in as the new mascots of American food culture, while the number of meals consumed outside the home has doubled—from a quarter in 1970 to nearly half today. As a result, market economics has increasingly determined ingredients, nutrient content, and portion size. Agricultural surpluses and technological breakthroughs supplied the cheap sweeteners and hydrogenated oils necessary for food to survive indefinitely on store shelves or under fast-food heat lamps.

Unsurprisingly, the caloric density of such foods soared relative to those 5
consumed at home. Good value no longer meant taste, presentation, and proper nutrition—but merely more-for-less. Thus, the serving of McDonald's French fries that contained 200 calories in 1960 contains 610 today. The lure of large was not limited to fast-food, inflating everything from snack foods to cereal boxes.

But the hunger for home economics didn't die with its academic exile. Martha Stewart made millions filling the void, vexing home-ec haters like Erica Jong for having "earned her freedom by glorifying the slavery of home." Home and Garden TV, the Food Network, and countless publications thrive on topics once taught by home ec.

All of which begs the question: If the free market has done such a good job of picking up the slack, why bring home ec back? Because much of the D.I.Y. (do-it-yourself) culture is divorced from the exigencies of everyday life. It's more like home rec: catering to pampered chefs with maids to clean up the kitchen.

The new home economics should be both pragmatic and egalitarian. Traditional topics—food and nutrition, family studies, home management—should be retooled for the twenty-first century. Children should be able to decipher headlines about the dangers of dioxin or the benefits of antioxidants. Subjects like home finance might include domestic problem-solving: How would you spend $100 to feed a family of four, including a diabetic, a nursing mother, and infant, for one week?

While this kind of training might most benefit those low-income minority children at highest risk of obesity, all children will be better equipped to make smart choices in the face of the more than $33 billion that food companies spend annually to promote their products. And consumer education is just part of the larger purpose: to teach kids to think, make, fix, and generally fend for themselves.

Some detractors will doubtless smell a plot to turn women back into 10
stitching, stirring Stepford Wives. Others will argue that schools should focus on the basics. But what could be more basic than life, food, home and hearth? A generation has grown up since we swept home ec into the dust heap of history and hung up our brooms. It's time to reevaluate the domestic discipline, and recapture lost skills.

READING AND DISCUSSION QUESTIONS

1. How would the students at the high school you attended have responded to a course such as the one Grossman describes?
2. Do you think that offering such a course would be a good idea? Why, or why not?
3. How convincing is Grossman's argument that there is a need for consumer education? How convincing is her argument that it should be offered in school?
4. Do you find any logical fallacies in her argument? If so, what type of fallacies are they?

WRITING SUGGESTIONS

5. Write a claim of policy essay arguing that the sort of course Grossman describes should be required of high school students.
6. Write an essay refuting what Grossman suggests.
7. Write an essay in which you argue that the majority of teenagers are responsible consumers or that they are not.

A Modest Proposal

JONATHAN SWIFT

It is a melancholy object to those who walk through this great town[1] or travel in the country, when they see the streets, the roads, and cabin doors, crowded with beggars of the female sex, followed by three, four, or six children, all in rags and importuning every passenger for an alms. These mothers, instead of being able to work for their honest livelihood, are forced to employ all their time in strolling to beg sustenance for their helpless infants, who, as they grow up, either turn thieves for want of work, or leave their

[1] Dublin. — EDS. [All notes are the editors'.]

This essay is acknowledged by almost all critics to be the most powerful example of irony in the English language. (*Irony* means saying one thing but meaning another.) In 1729 Jonathan Swift (1667–1745), prolific satirist and dean of St. Patrick's Cathedral in Dublin, was moved to write in protest against the terrible poverty in which the Irish were living under British rule. Notice that the essay is organized according to one of the patterns outlined in Part Two of this book (see Presenting the Stock Issues, Chapter 12, p. 481). First, Swift establishes the need for a change, then he offers his proposal, and finally, he lists its advantages.

dear native country to fight for the Pretender in Spain, or sell themselves to the Barbados.[2]

I think it is agreed by all parties that this prodigious number of children in the arms, or on the backs, or at the heels of their mothers, and frequently of their fathers, is in the present deplorable state of the kingdom a very great additional grievance; and therefore whoever could find out a fair, cheap, and easy method of making these children sound, useful members of the commonwealth would deserve so well of the public as to have his statue set up for a preserver of the nation.

But my intention is very far from being confined to provide only for the children of professed beggars; it is of a much greater extent, and shall take in the whole number of infants at a certain age who are born of parents in effect as little able to support them as those who demand our charity in the streets.

As to my own part, having turned my thoughts for many years upon this important subject, and maturely weighed the several schemes of other projectors,[3] I have always found them grossly mistaken in their computation. It is true, a child just dropped from its dam may be supported by her milk for a solar year, with little other nourishment; at most not above the value of two shillings, which the mother may certainly get, or the value in scraps, by her lawful occupation of begging; and it is exactly at one year that I propose to provide for them in such a manner as instead of being a charge upon their parents or the parish, or wanting food and raiment for the rest of their lives, they shall on the contrary contribute to the feeding, and partly to the clothing, of many thousands.

There is likewise another great advantage in my scheme, that it will 5
prevent those voluntary abortions, and that horrid practice of women murdering their bastard children, alas, too frequent among us, sacrificing the poor innocent babes, I doubt, more to avoid the expense than the shame, which would move tears and pity in the most savage and inhuman breast.

The number of souls in this kingdom being usually reckoned one million and a half, of these I calculate there may be about two hundred thousand couples whose wives are breeders; from which number I subtract thirty thousand couples who are able to maintain their own children, although I apprehend there cannot be so many under the present distress of the kingdom; but this being granted, there will remain an hundred and seventy thousand breeders. I again subtract fifty thousand for those women who miscarry, or whose children die by accident or disease within the year. There

[2]The Pretender was James Stuart, who was exiled to Spain. Many Irish men had joined an army attempting to return him to the English throne in 1715. Others had become indentured servants, agreeing to work for a set number of years in Barbados or other British colonies in exchange for their transportation out of Ireland.

[3]Planners.

only remain an hundred and twenty thousand children of poor parents annually born. The question therefore is, how this number shall be reared and provided for, which, as I have already said, under the present situation of affairs, is utterly impossible by all the methods hitherto proposed. For we can neither employ them in handicraft or agriculture; we neither build houses (I mean in the country) nor cultivate land. They can very seldom pick up a livelihood by stealing till they arrive at six years old, except where they are of towardly parts;[4] although I confess they learn the rudiments much earlier, during which time they can however be looked upon only as probationers, as I have been informed by a principal gentleman in the county of Cavan, who protested to me that he never knew above one or two instances under the age of six, even in a part of the kingdom so renowned for the quickest proficiency in that art.

I am assured by our merchants that a boy or a girl before twelve years old is no salable commodity; and even when they come to this age they will not yield above three pounds, or three pounds and a half a crown at most on the Exchange; which cannot turn to account either to the parents or the kingdom, the charge of nutriment and rags having been at least four times that value.

I shall now therefore humbly propose my own thoughts, which I hope will not be liable to the least objection.

I have been assured by a very knowing American of my acquaintance in London, that a young healthy child well nursed is at a year old a most delicious, nourishing, and wholesome food, whether stewed, roasted, baked, or boiled; and I make no doubt that it will equally serve in a fricassee or a ragout.[5]

I do therefore humbly offer it to public consideration that of the hun- 10
dred and twenty thousand children, already computed, twenty thousand may be reserved for breed, whereof only one fourth part to be males, which is more than we allow to sheep, black cattle, or swine; and my reason is that these children are seldom the fruits of marriage, a circumstance not much regarded by our savages, therefore one male will be sufficient to serve four females. That the remaining hundred thousand may at a year old be offered in sale to the persons of quality and fortune through the kingdom, always advising the mother to let them suck plentifully in the last month, so as to render them plump and fat for a good table. A child will make two dishes at an entertainment for friends; and when the family dines alone, the fore or hind quarter will make a reasonable dish, and seasoned with a little pepper or salt will be very good boiled on the fourth day, especially in winter.

I have reckoned upon a medium that a child just born will weigh twelve pounds, and in a solar year if tolerably nursed increaseth to twenty-eight pounds.

[4]Innate talents.
[5]Stew.

I grant this food will be somewhat dear, and therefore very proper for landlords, who, as they have already devoured most of the parents, seem to have the best title to the children.

Infant's flesh will be in season throughout the year, but more plentiful in March, and a little before and after. For we are told by a grave author, an eminent French physician,[6] that fish being a prolific diet, there are more children born in Roman Catholic countries about nine months after Lent than at any other season; therefore, reckoning a year after Lent, the markets will be more glutted than usual, because the number of popish infants is at least three to one in this kingdom; and therefore it will have one other collateral advantage, by lessening the number of Papists among us.

I have already computed the charge of nursing a beggar's child (in which list I reckon all cottagers, laborers, and four-fifths of the farmers) to be about two shillings per annum, rags included; and I believe no gentleman would repine to give ten shillings for the carcass of a good fat child, which, as I have said, will make four dishes of excellent nutritive meat, when he hath only some particular friend or his own family to dine with him. Thus the squire will learn to be a good landlord, and grow popular among the tenants; the mother will have eight shillings net profit, and be fit for work till she produces another child.

15 Those who are more thrifty (as I must confess the times require) may flay the carcass; the skin of which artificially[7] dressed will make admirable gloves for ladies, and summer boots for fine gentlemen.

As to our city of Dublin, shambles[8] may be appointed for this purpose in the most convenient parts of it, and butchers we may be assured will not be wanting; although I rather recommend buying the children alive, and dressing them hot from the knife as we do roasting pigs.

A very worthy person, a true lover of his country, and whose virtues I highly esteem, was lately pleased in discoursing on this matter to offer a refinement upon my scheme. He said that many gentlemen of his kingdom, having of late destroyed their deer, he conceived that the want of venison might be well supplied by the bodies of young lads and maidens, not exceeding fourteen years of age nor under twelve, so great a number of both sexes in every county being now ready to starve for want of work and service; and these to be disposed of by their parents, if alive, or otherwise by their nearest relations. But with due deference to so excellent a friend and so deserving a patriot, I cannot be altogether in his sentiments; for as to the males, my American acquaintance assured me from frequent experience that their flesh was generally tough and lean, like that of our schoolboys, by continual exercise, and their taste disagreeable; and to fatten them would

[6] A reference to Swift's favorite French writer, François Rabelais (1494?–1553), who was actually a broad satirist known for his coarse humor.

[7] With art or craft.

[8] Butcher shops or slaughterhouses.

not answer the charge. Then as to the females, it would, I think with humble submission, be a loss to the public, because they soon would become breeders themselves; and besides, it is not improbable that some scrupulous people might be apt to censure such a practice (although indeed very unjustly) as a little bordering upon cruelty; which, I confess, hath always been with me the strongest objection against any project, how well soever intended.

But in order to justify my friend, he confessed that this expedient was put into his head by the famous Psalmanazar,[9] a native of the island Formosa, who came from thence to London above twenty years ago, and in conversation told my friend that in his country when any young person happened to be put to death, the executioner sold the carcass to persons of quality as a prime dainty; and that in his time the body of a plump girl of fifteen, who was crucified for an attempt to poison the emperor, was sold to his Imperial Majesty's prime minister of state, and other great mandarins of the court, in joints from the gibbet, at four hundred crowns. Neither indeed can I deny that if the same use were made of several plump young girls in this town, who without one single groat to their fortunes cannot stir abroad without a chair, and appear at the playhouse and assemblies in foreign fineries which they never will pay for, the kingdom would not be the worse.

Some persons of a desponding spirit are in great concern about that vast number of poor people who are aged, diseased, or maimed, and I have been desired to employ my thoughts what course may be taken to ease the nation of so grievous an encumbrance. But I am not in the least pain upon that matter, because it is very well known that they are every day dying and rotting by cold and famine, and filth and vermin, as fast as can be reasonably expected. And as to the younger laborers, they are now in almost as hopeful a condition. They cannot get work, and consequently pine away for want of nourishment to a degree that if any time they are accidentally hired to common labor, they have not strength to perform it; and thus the country and themselves are happily delivered from the evils to come.

I have too long digressed, and therefore shall return to my subject. I 20
think the advantages by the proposal which I have made are obvious and many, as well as of the highest importance.

For first, as I have already observed, it would greatly lessen the number of Papists, with whom we are yearly overrun, being the principal breeders of the nation as well as our most dangerous enemies; and who stay at home on purpose to deliver the kingdom to the Pretender, hoping to take their advantage by the absence of so many good Protestants, who have chosen rather to leave their country than to stay at home and pay tithes against their conscience to an Episcopal curate.

[9] Georges Psalmanazar was a Frenchman who pretended to be Japanese and wrote an entirely imaginary *Description of the Isle Formosa.* He had become well known in gullible London society.

Secondly, the poorer tenants will have something valuable of their own, which by law may be made liable to distress,[10] and help to pay their landlord's rent, their corn and cattle being already seized and money a thing unknown.

Thirdly, whereas the maintenance of an hundred thousand children, from two years old and upwards, cannot be computed at less than ten shillings a piece per annum, the nation's stock will be thereby increased fifty thousand pounds per annum, besides the profit of a new dish introduced to the tables of all gentlemen of fortune in the kingdom who have any refinement in taste. And the money will circulate among ourselves, the goods being entirely of our own growth and manufacture.

Fourthly, the constant breeders, besides the gain of eight shillings sterling per annum by the sale of their children, will be rid of the charge of maintaining them after the first year.

Fifthly, this food would likewise bring great custom to taverns, where 25
the vintners will certainly be so prudent as to procure the best receipts for dressing it to perfection, and consequently have their houses frequented by all the fine gentlemen, who justly value themselves upon their knowledge in good eating; and a skillful cook, who understands how to oblige his guests, will contrive to make it as expensive as they please.

Sixthly, this would be a great inducement to marriage, which all wise nations have either encouraged by rewards or enforced by laws and penalties. It would increase the care and tenderness of mothers toward their children, when they were sure of a settlement for life to the poor babes, provided in some sort by the public, to their annual profit instead of expense. We should see an honest emulation among the married women, which of them could bring the fattest child to the market. Men would become as fond of their wives during the time of their pregnancy as they are now of their mares in foal, their cows in calf, or sows when they are ready to farrow; nor offer to beat or kick them (as is too frequent a practice) for fear of a miscarriage.

Many other advantages might be enumerated. For instance, the addition of some thousand carcasses in our exportation of barreled beef, the propagation of swine's flesh, and improvements in the art of making good bacon, so much wanted among us by the great destruction of pigs, too frequent at our tables, which are no way comparable in taste or magnificence to a well-grown, fat, yearling child, which roasted whole will make a considerable figure at a lord mayor's feast or any other public entertainment. But this and many others I omit, being studious of brevity.

Supposing that one thousand families in this city would be constant customers for infants' flesh, besides others who might have it at merry meetings, particularly weddings and christenings, I compute that Dublin would take off annually about twenty thousand carcasses, and the rest of

[10]Subject to possession by lenders.

the kingdom (where probably they will be sold somewhat cheaper) the remaining eighty thousand.

I can think of no one objection that will possibly be raised against this proposal, unless it should be urged that the number of people will be thereby much lessened in the kingdom. This I freely own, and it was indeed one principal design in offering it to the world. I desire the reader will observe, that I calculate my remedy for this one individual kingdom of Ireland and for no other that ever was, is, or I think ever can be upon earth. Therefore let no man talk to me of other expedients: of taxing our absentees at five shillings a pound: of using neither clothes nor household furniture except what is of our own growth and manufacture: of utterly rejecting the materials and instruments that promote foreign luxury: of curing the expensiveness of pride, vanity, idleness, and gaming in our women: of introducing a vein of parsimony, prudence, and temperance: of learning to love our country, in the want of which we differ even from Laplanders and the inhabitants of Topinamboo:[11] of quitting our animosities and factions, nor acting any longer like the Jews, who were murdering one another at the very moment their city was taken:[12] of being a little cautious not to sell our country and conscience for nothing: of teaching landlords to have at least one degree of mercy toward their tenants: lastly, of putting a spirit of honesty, industry, and skill into our shopkeepers; who, if a resolution could now be taken to buy only our native goods, would immediately unite to cheat and exact upon us in the price, the measure, and the goodness, nor could ever yet be brought to make one fair proposal of just dealing, though often and earnestly invited to it.

Therefore I repeat, let no man talk to me of these and the like expedi- 30
ents, till he hath at least some glimpse of hope that there will ever be some hearty and sincere attempt to put them in practice.

But as to myself, having been wearied out for many years with offering vain, idle, visionary thoughts, and at length utterly despairing of success, I fortunately fell upon this proposal, which, as it is wholly new, so it hath something solid and real, of no expense and little trouble, full in our own power, and whereby we can incur no danger in disobliging England. For this kind of commodity will not bear exportation, the flesh being of too tender a consistence to admit a long continuance in salt, although perhaps I could name a country which would be glad to eat up our whole nation without it.

After all, I am not so violently bent upon my own opinion as to reject any offer proposed by wise men, which shall be found equally innocent, cheap, easy, and effectual. But before something of that kind shall be advanced in contradiction to my scheme, and offering a better, I desire the author or authors will be pleased maturely to consider two points.

[11] District of Brazil.

[12] During the Roman siege of Jerusalem (A.D. 70), prominent Jews were charged with collaborating with the enemy and put to death.

First, as things now stand, how they will be able to find food and raiment for an hundred thousand useless mouths and backs. And secondly, there being a round million of creatures in human figure throughout this kingdom, whose sole subsistence put into a common stock would leave them in debt two millions of pounds sterling, adding those who are beggars by profession to the bulk of farmers, cottagers, and laborers, with their wives and children who are beggars in effect; I desire those politicians who dislike my overture, and may perhaps be so bold to attempt an answer, that they will first ask the parents of these mortals whether they would not at this day think it a great happiness to have been sold for food at a year old in this manner I prescribe, and thereby have avoided such a perpetual scene of misfortunes as they have since gone through by the oppression of landlords, the impossibility of paying rent without money or trade, the want of common sustenance, with neither house nor clothes to cover them from the inclemencies of the weather, and the most inevitable prospect of entailing the like of greater miseries upon their breed forever.

I profess, in the sincerity of my heart, that I have not the least personal interest in endeavoring to promote this necessary work, having no other motive than the public good of my country, by advancing our trade, providing for infants, relieving the poor, and giving some pleasure to the rich. I have no children by which I can propose to get a single penny; the youngest being nine years old, and my wife past childbearing.

DISCUSSION QUESTIONS

1. What implicit assumption about the treatment of the Irish underlies Swift's proposal? Do expressions such as "just dropped from its dam" (para. 4) and "whose wives are breeders" (para. 6) give the reader a clue?
2. In this essay Swift assumes a persona; that is, for the purposes of the proposal he makes, he pretends to be a different person. Describe the characteristics of that person. Point out the places in the essay that reveal them.
3. In several places, however, Swift reveals himself as the outraged witness of English cruelty and indifference. Note the language that seems to reflect his own feelings.
4. Throughout the essay Swift recites lists of facts, many of them in the form of statistics. How do these facts contribute to the persuasiveness of his argument? How do they affect the reader?
5. What social practices and attitudes of both the Irish and the English does Swift condemn?
6. Does Swift offer any solutions for the problems he attacks? How do you know?
7. When this essay first appeared in 1729, some readers took it seriously and accused Swift of monstrous cruelty. Can you think of reasons that these readers failed to recognize the ironic intent?
8. What logical fallacies do you find in the essay?

WRITING SUGGESTIONS

9. Try an ironical essay of your own. Choose a subject that clearly lends itself to such treatment. As Swift did, use logic and restraint in your language.
10. Choose a problem for which you think you have a solution. Defend your solution by using the stock issues as your pattern of organization.

DEBATE: Should the federal government fund embryonic stem-cell research?

Use the Body's "Repair Kit": We Must Pursue Research on Embryonic Stem Cells

CHRISTOPHER REEVE

With the life expectancy of average Americans heading as high as 75 to 80 years, it is our responsibility to do everything possible to protect the quality of life of the present and future generations. A critical factor will be what we do with human embryonic stem cells. These cells have the potential to cure diseases and conditions ranging from Parkinson's and multiple sclerosis to diabetes and heart disease, Alzheimer's, Lou Gehrig's disease, even spinal-cord injuries like my own. They have been called the body's self-repair kit.

Their extraordinary potential is a recent discovery. And much basic research needs to be done before they can be sent to the front lines in the battle against disease. But no obstacle should stand in the way of responsible investigation of their possibilities. To that end, the work should be funded and supervised by the federal government through the National Institutes of Health. That will avoid abuses by for-profit corporations, avoid secrecy and destructive competition between laboratories, and ensure the widest possible dissemination of scientific breakthroughs. Human trials

Christopher Reeve was a well-established actor when in 1995 he was paralyzed from the shoulders down in a riding accident. From that time until his death in 2004, he served as an outspoken and respected advocate for the sort of stem-cell research he believed would eventually help him and others like him. Through his personal example and his books *Still Me* (1999) and *Nothing Is Impossible: Reflections on a New Life* (2002), he offered hope and inspiration to the disabled and others. This article is from the May 1, 2000, edition of *Time*.

should be conducted either on the NIH campus or in carefully monitored clinical facilities.

Fortunately, stem cells are readily available and easily harvested. In fertility clinics, women are given a choice of what to do with unused fertilized embryos: they can be discarded, donated to research, or frozen for future use. Under NIH supervision, scientists should be allowed to take cells only from women who freely consent to their use for research. This process would not be open ended; within one to two years a sufficient number could be gathered and made available to investigators. For those reasons, the ban on federally funded human embryonic stem-cell research should be lifted as quickly as possible.

But why has the use of discarded embryos for research suddenly become such an issue? Is it more ethical for a woman to donate unused embryos that will never become human beings, or to let them be tossed away as so much garbage when they could help save thousands of lives?

Treatment with stem cells has already begun. They have been taken 5
from umbilical cords and become healthy red cells used as a potential cure for sickle-cell anemia. Stem-cell therapy is also being used against certain types of cancer. But those are cells that have significantly differentiated; that is, they are no longer pluripotent, or capable of transforming into other cell types. For the true biological miracles that researchers have only begun to foresee, medical science must turn to undifferentiated stem cells. We need to clear the path for them as rapidly as possible.

Controversy over the treatment of certain diseases is nothing new in this country: witness the overwhelming opposition to government funding of AIDS research in the early '80s. For years the issue was a political football—until a massive grass-roots effort forced legislators to respond. Today, the NIH is authorized to spend approximately $1.8 billion annually on new protocols, and the virus is largely under control in the United States.

While we prolong the stem-cell debate, millions continue to suffer. It is time to harness the power of government and go forward.

The Misleading Debate on Stem-Cell Research

MONA CHAREN

Addressing the Democratic National Convention, Ron Reagan told the delegates that in the debate over funding research on embryonic stem cells, we face a choice between "the future and the past; between reason and ignorance; between true compassion and mere ideology." Not satisfied with that contrast, he elaborated that "a few of these folks (who oppose funding this research) are just grinding a political axe, and they should be ashamed of themselves."

It is Reagan who ought to be ashamed. As the mother of a ten-year-old with juvenile diabetes, I yearn more than most for breakthroughs in scientific research. My son takes between four and six shots of insulin daily and must test his blood sugar by pricking his finger the same number of times. This disease affects every major organ system in the body and places him in the high-risk category for more problems than I care to name. When he settles down to sleep at night, I can never be entirely sure that he won't slip into a coma from a sudden low blood sugar. How happily I would take the disease upon myself if I could only spare him! So please don't lecture me about grinding a political axe.

But like millions of others, I am troubled by the idea of embryonic stem-cell research. It crosses a moral line that this society should be loath to cross—even for the best of motives. Taking the stem cells from human embryos kills them. Before turning to the arguments of the pro-research side, permit a word about the pro-life position. Too many pro-life activists, it seems to me, have argued this case on the wrong grounds. My inbox is full of missives about the scientific misfires that stem-cell research has led to, as well as breathless announcements that adult stem cells actually hold more promise.

This is neither an honest nor a productive line of argument. The reason pro-lifers oppose embryonic stem-cell research is because they hold life sacred at all stages of development. They ought not to deny this or dress it up in a lab coat to give it greater palatability. The moral case is an honorable one. Leave it at that.

5 Proponents of embryonic stem-cell research point out that some of the embryos currently sitting in freezers in fertility clinics around the world are going to be washed down the drain anyway—which surely kills them, and

---

Mona Charen is a syndicated columnist whose column appears in over two hundred newspapers nationwide and a political analyst who for six years was a regular on CNN's *Capital Gang* and *Capital Gang Sunday*. From 1984 to 1986, she worked at the White House as a speechwriter for Nancy Reagan and in the Public Affairs Office. This article appeared on townhall.com in August 2004.

without any benefit to mankind. This is true. There are several answers to this. The first is that a society that truly honored each human life would take a different approach. Fertility clinics and the couples who use them would understand the moral obligation not to create more embryos than they can reasonably expect to transfer to the mother's uterus. In cases where this was impossible, the embryos could be placed for adoption with other infertile couples (this is already a widespread practice).

Once you begin to pull apart a human embryo and use its parts, you have thoroughly dehumanized it. You have justified taking one life to (speculatively) save another. Despite the rosy future painted by Ron Reagan and others, those of us who follow the field with avid interest have been disappointed by avenues of research that have failed, thus far, to pan out. Still, opponents of stem-cell research should not argue that the research is going to be fruitless. No one knows. The problem is that this kind of research is morally problematic. Germany, Italy, Portugal, Luxembourg, and Austria ban it. (The United States does not. We simply withhold federal funding.)

There is something else, as well. While the idea of growing spare parts—say, spinal nerves for a paraplegic—in a Petri dish seems wonderful, it may not be possible to do so from embryonic stem cells. As the *Wall Street Journal* reported on August 12 [2004], scientists have been frustrated by their inability to get stem cells to grow into endoderm (the cells that make up the liver, stomach, and pancreas), whereas they can coax them to become heart and nerve tissue.

"Scientists speculate," the *Journal* explained, "that might be because the embryo early on needs blood and nerve tissue to grow, while endoderm-based organs aren't needed until later." If we can use the stem cells of normal human embryos for research, by what logic would we shrink from allowing an embryo to reach a later stage of development in order to study better how endoderm forms?

These are treacherous moral waters we're setting sail in, and those who hesitate ought not to be scorned as ignorant, uncompassionate, or blinkered.

DISCUSSION QUESTIONS

1. Do both of these authors use evidence and appeal to needs and values? Explain. How is your reading of each piece affected by the author's personal circumstances?
2. What is the effect of Reeve's choosing to call stem cells "the body's self-repair kit"? Give other examples of how his word choice either helps or hurts his argument.
3. Is the language that Reeve uses in discussing the embryos different from that used by Charen? How and why?
4. In what other ways does Charen's choice of words affect her argument?
5. Where does each author most directly state the claim of his or her piece?

ASSIGNMENTS FOR AVOIDING FLAWED LOGIC

READING AND DISCUSSION QUESTIONS

1. Read through the draft of an essay that you are writing, looking for and correcting any logical fallacies that you find.
2. Compare the argument made to Congress by President Roosevelt on the day after the attack on Pearl Harbor in 1941 and the one made by President Bush after the attacks on the World Trade Center and the Pentagon in 2001.

WRITING ASSIGNMENTS

3. Write an essay explaining the logical fallacies in one of the essays from the Readings for Analysis portion of this chapter.
4. Explain in an essay whether you find Christopher Reeve's or Mona Charen's argument on stem-cell research more convincing, and why.
5. Find the printed text of a major political speech such as a State of the Union Address, a major political convention speech, or an inaugural address and analyze its logic. Does it use an inductive approach, a deductive approach, a combination? What types of support are used? Do you detect any logical fallacies? Write an essay about the speech that supports either a claim of fact or a claim of value.

CHAPTER 10

Choosing Fair and Precise Language

THE POWER OF WORDS

Words play such a critical role in argument that they deserve special treatment. An important part of successful writers' equipment is a large and active vocabulary, but no single chapter in a book can give this to you; only reading and study can widen your range of word choices. Even in a brief chapter, however, we can point out how words influence the feelings and attitudes of an audience, both favorably and unfavorably.

One kind of language responsible for shaping attitudes and feelings is *emotive language,* language that expresses and arouses emotions. Understanding it and using it effectively are indispensable to the arguer who wants to move an audience to accept a point of view or undertake an action.

In one of the most memorable speeches in the history of America, President Franklin Delano Roosevelt asked the country both to accept a point of view and to prepare to take action. In his brief speech to Congress he captured some of the grief and the feeling of outrage Americans were experiencing. Except for the most famous phrase in the speech, in which he declares December 7, 1941, a "date which will live in infamy," most of the first portion of the speech establishes the facts. A turning point in the speech comes when he shifts from facts to implications. The speech then builds to its emotional climax in the next-to-last paragraph before he concludes with a declaration of war.

Address to Congress, December 8, 1941

FRANKLIN DELANO ROOSEVELT

Yesterday, December 7, 1941—a date which will live in infamy—the United States of America was suddenly and deliberately attacked by naval and air forces of the Empire of Japan.

The United States was at peace with that nation, and, at the solicitation of Japan, was still in conversation with its government and its Emperor looking toward the maintenance of peace in the Pacific.

Indeed, one hour after Japanese air squadrons had commenced bombing in the American island of Oahu, the Japanese Ambassador to the United States and his colleague delivered to our Secretary of State a formal reply to a recent American message. And, while this reply stated that it seemed useless to continue the existing diplomatic negotiations, it contained no threat or hint of war or of armed attack.

It will be recorded that the distance of Hawaii from Japan makes it obvious that the attack was deliberately planned many days or even weeks ago. During the intervening time the Japanese Government has deliberately sought to deceive the United States by false statements and expressions of hope for continued peace.

5 The attack yesterday on the Hawaiian Islands has caused severe damage to American naval and military forces. I regret to tell you that very many American lives have been lost. In addition, American ships have been reported torpedoed on the high seas between San Francisco and Honolulu.

Yesterday the Japanese Government also launched an attack against Malaya. Last night Japanese forces attacked Hong Kong. Last night Japanese forces attacked Guam. Last night Japanese forces attacked the Philippine Islands. Last night the Japanese attacked Wake Island. And this morning the Japanese attacked Midway Island.

Japan has therefore undertaken a surprise offensive extending throughout the Pacific area. The facts of yesterday and today speak for themselves. The people of the United States have already formed their opinions and well understand the implications to the very life and safety of our nation.

As Commander-in-Chief of the Army and Navy I have directed that all measures be taken for our defense, that always will our whole nation remember the character of the onslaught against us.

No matter how long it may take us to overcome this premeditated invasion, the American people, in their righteous might, will win through to absolute victory.

10 I believe that I interpret the will of the Congress and of the people when I assert that we will not only defend ourselves to the uttermost but will make it very certain that this form of treachery shall never again endanger us.

Hostilities exist. There is no blinking at the fact that our people, our territory, and our interests are in grave danger.

With confidence in our armed forces, with the unbounding determination of our people, we will gain the inevitable triumph, so help us God.

I ask that the Congress declare that since the unprovoked and dastardly attack by Japan on Sunday, December 7, 1941, a state of war has existed between the United States and the Japanese Empire.

Long before you thought about writing your first argument, you learned that words had the power to affect you. Endearments and affectionate and flattering nicknames evoked good feelings about the speaker and yourself. Insulting nicknames and slurs produced dislike for the speaker and bad feelings about yourself. Perhaps you were told, "Sticks and stones may break your bones, but words will never hurt you." But even to a small child it is clear that ugly words are as painful as sticks and stones and that the injuries are sometimes more lasting.

Nowhere is the power of words more obvious and more familiar than in advertising, where the success of a product may depend on the feelings that certain words produce in the prospective buyer. Even the names of products may have emotive significance. In recent years a new industry, composed of consultants who supply names for products, has emerged. Although most manufacturers agree that a good name won't save a poor product, they also recognize that the right name can catch the attention of the public and persuade people to buy a product at least once. According to an article in the *Wall Street Journal,* a product name not only should be memorable but also should "remind people of emotional or physical experiences."[1]

PRACTICE

Careful thought and extensive research go into the naming of automobiles, a "big ticket" item for most consumers. What reasoning might have gone into the naming of these models, old and new?

Aspen
Colorado
Dart
Eclipse
Electra
Grand Prix
Impala
Infinity
Jaguar
Liberty
Malibu
Matrix
Mustang
Nova
Odyssey
Quest

[1] *Wall Street Journal,* August 5, 1982, p. 19.

Rainier
Regal
Rendezvous
Sequoia
Taurus
Trailblazer
Viper

What response do the names Mercedes-Benz and Rolls-Royce evoke?

Even scientists recognize the power of words to attract the attention of other scientists and the public to discoveries and theories that might otherwise remain obscure. A good name can even enable the scientist to visualize a new concept. One scientist says that "a good name," such as "quark," "black hole," "big bang," "chaos," or "great attractor," "helps in communicating a theory and can have substantial impact on financing."

It is not hard to see the connection between the use of words in conversation and advertising and the use of emotive language in the more formal arguments you will be writing. Emotive language reveals your approval or disapproval, assigns praise or blame—in other words, makes a judgment about the subject. Keep in mind that unless you are writing purely factual statements, such as scientists write, you will find it hard to avoid expressing judgments. Neutrality does not come easily, even where it may be desirable, as in news stories or reports of historical events. For this reason you need to attend carefully to the statements in your argument, making sure that you have not disguised judgments as statements of fact. Of course, in attempting to prove a claim, you will not be neutral. You will be revealing your judgment about the subject, first in the selection of facts and opinions and the emphasis you give to them and second in the selection of words.

Like the choice of facts and opinions, the choice of words can be effective or ineffective in advancing your argument, moral or immoral in the honesty with which you exercise it. The following discussions offer some insights into recognizing and evaluating the use of emotive language in the arguments you read, as well as into using such language in your own arguments where it is appropriate and avoiding it where it is not.

CONNOTATION

The connotations of a word are the meanings we attach to it apart from its explicit definition. Because these added meanings derive from our feelings, connotations are one form of emotive language. For example, the word *rat* denotes or points to a kind of rodent, but the attached meanings of "selfish person," "evil-doer," "betrayer," and "traitor" reflect the feelings that have accumulated around the word.

In Chapter 5 we observed that definitions of controversial terms, such as *poverty* and *unemployment,* may vary so widely that writer and reader cannot always be sure that they are thinking of the same thing. A similar problem arises when a writer assumes that the reader shares his or her emotional response to a word. Emotive meanings originate partly in personal experience. The word *home,* defined merely as "a family's place of residence," may suggest love, warmth, and security to one person; it may suggest friction, violence, and alienation to another. The values of the groups to which we belong also influence meaning. Writers and speakers count on cultural associations when they refer to our country, our flag, and heroes and enemies we have never seen. The arguer must also be aware that some apparently neutral words trigger different responses from different groups—words such as *cult, revolution, police,* and *beauty contest.*

Various reform movements have recognized that words with unfavorable connotations have the power not only to reflect but also to shape our perceptions of things. In 2007, the NAACP went so far as to hold a "funeral for the N— word." The women's liberation movement also insisted on changes that would bring about improved attitudes toward women. The movement condemned the use of *girl* for a female over the age of eighteen and the use in news stories of descriptive adjectives that emphasized the physical appearance of women. And the homosexual community succeeded in reintroducing the word *gay,* a word current centuries ago, as a substitute for words they considered offensive. Now *queer,* a word long regarded as offensive, has been adopted as a substitute for *gay* by a new generation of gays and lesbians, although it is still considered unacceptable by many members of the homosexual community.

Members of certain occupations have invented terms to confer greater respectability on their work. The work does not change, but the workers hope that public perceptions will change if janitors are called custodians, if garbage collectors are called sanitation engineers, if undertakers are called morticians, if people who sell makeup are called cosmetologists. Events considered unpleasant or unmentionable are sometimes disguised by polite terms, called *euphemisms.* During the 1992 to 1993 recession new terms emerged that disguised, or tried to, the grim fact that thousands of people were being dismissed from their jobs: *skill-mix adjustment, workforce-imbalance correction, redundancy elimination, downsizing, indefinite idling,* even a daring *career-change opportunity.* Many people refuse to use the word *died* and choose *passed away* instead. Some psychologists and physicians use the phrase *negative patient care outcome* for what most of us would call *death.* Even when referring to their pets, some people cannot bring themselves to say *put to death* but substitute *put to sleep* or *put down.* In place of a term to describe an act of sexual intercourse, some people use *slept together* or *went to bed together* or *had an affair.*

Polite words are not always so harmless. If a euphemism disguises a shameful event or condition, it is morally irresponsible to use it to mislead the reader into believing that the shameful condition does not exist. In his powerful essay "Politics and the English Language" (p. 406) George Orwell pointed out that politicians and reporters have sometimes used terms like *pacification* or *rectification of frontiers* to conceal acts that result in torture and death for millions of people. An example of such usage was cited by a member of Amnesty International, a group monitoring human rights violations throughout the world. He objected to a news report describing camps in which the Chinese were promoting "reeducation through labor." This term, he wrote, "makes these institutions seem like a cross between Police Athletic League and Civilian Conservation Corps camps." On the contrary, he went on, the reality of "reeducation through labor" was that the victims were confined to "rather unpleasant prison camps." The details he offered about the conditions under which people lived and worked gave substance to his claim.[2]

Perhaps the most striking examples of the way that connotations influence our perceptions of reality occur when people are asked to respond to questions of poll-takers. Sociologists and students of poll-taking know that the phrasing of a question, or the choice of words, can affect the answers and even undermine the validity of the poll. In one case poll-takers first asked a selected group of people if they favored continuing the welfare system. The majority answered no. But when the poll-takers asked if they favored government aid to the poor, the majority answered yes. Although the terms *welfare* and *government aid to the poor* refer to essentially the same forms of government assistance, *welfare* has acquired for many people negative connotations of corruption and shiftless recipients.

In a *New York Times*/CBS poll conducted in January 1998, "a representative sample of Americans were asked which statement came nearer to their opinion: 'Is abortion the same thing as murdering a child, or is abortion not murder because the fetus really isn't a child?'" Thirty-eight percent chose "the fetus really isn't a child." But 58 percent, including a third of those who chose "abortion is the same thing as murdering a child," agreed that abortion "was sometimes the best course in a bad situation." The author of the report suggests an explanation of the fact that a majority of those polled seemed to have chosen "murder" as an acceptable solution to an unwanted pregnancy:

> These replies reveal, at least, a considerable moral confusion.
>
> Or maybe only verbal confusion? Should the question have asked whether abortion came closer, in the respondent's view, to "killing" rather than "murdering" a child? That would leave room for the explanation that Americans, while valuing life, are ultimately not pacifists: killing, they hold, may be justified in certain circumstances (self-defense, warfare, capital punishment).
>
> So one can challenge the wording of the question. Indeed, one can almost always challenge the wording of poll questions. . . . Poll takers

[2]Letter to the *New York Times,* August 30, 1982, p. 25.

themselves acknowledge the difficulty of wording questions and warn against relying too much on any single finding.[3]

This is also true in polls concerning rape, another highly charged subject. Dr. Neil Malamuth, a psychologist at the University of California at Los Angeles, says, "When men are asked if there is any likelihood they would force a woman to have sex against her will if they could get away with it, about half say they would. But if you ask them if they would rape a woman if they knew they could get away with it, only about 15 percent say they would." The men who change their answers aren't aware that "the only difference is in the words used to describe the same act."[4]

The wording of an argument is crucial. Because readers may interpret the words you use on the basis of feelings different from your own, you must support your word choices with definitions and with evidence that allows readers to determine how and why you made them.

SLANTING

Slanting, says one dictionary, is "interpreting or presenting in line with a special interest." The term is almost always used in a negative sense. It means that the arguer has selected facts and words with favorable or unfavorable connotations to create the impression that no alternative view exists or can be defended. For some questions it is true that no alternative view is worthy of presentation, and emotionally charged language to defend or attack a position that is clearly right or wrong would be entirely appropriate. We aren't neutral, nor should we be, about the tragic abuse of human rights anywhere in the world or even about infractions of the law such as drunk driving or vandalism, and we should use strong language to express our disapproval of these practices.

Most of your arguments, however, will concern controversial questions about which people of goodwill can argue on both sides. In such cases, your own judgments should be restrained. Slanting will suggest a prejudice—that is, a judgment made without regard to all the facts. Unfortunately, you may not always be aware of your bias or special interest; you may believe that your position is the only correct one. You may also feel the need to communicate a passionate belief about a serious problem. But if you are interested in persuading a reader to accept your belief and to act on it, you must also ask: If the reader is not sympathetic, how will he or she respond? Will he or she perceive my words as "loaded"—one-sided and prejudicial—and my view as slanted?

[3] Peter Steinfels, "Beliefs," *New York Times,* January 24, 1998, sec. A, p. 15.
[4] *New York Times,* August 29, 1989, sec. C, p. 1.

R. D. Laing, a Scottish psychiatrist, defined *prayer* in this way: "Someone is gibbering away on his knees, talking to someone who is not there."[5] This description probably reflects a sincerely held belief. Laing also clearly intended it for an audience that already agreed with him. But the phrases "gibbering away" and "someone who is not there" would be offensive to people for whom prayer is sacred.

The following remarks by one writer attacking another appeared in *Salon,* an online magazine:

> Urging the hyperbolic *Salon* columnist David Horowitz to calm down and cite facts instead of spewing insults seems as pointless as asking a dog not to defecate on the sidewalk. In either instance, the result is always and predictably the same: Somebody has to clean up a stinking pile.[6]

An audience, whether friendly or unfriendly, interested in a discussion of the issues, would probably be both embarrassed and repelled by this use of language in a serious argument.

In the mid-1980s an English environmental group, London Greenpeace, began to distribute leaflets accusing the McDonald's restaurants of a wide assortment of crimes. The leaflets said in part:

> McDollars, McGreedy, McCancer, McMurder, McDisease, McProfits, McDeadly, McHunger, McRipoff, McTorture, McWasteful, McGarbage.
>
> This leaflet is asking you to think for a moment about what lies behind McDonald's clean, bright image. It's got a lot to hide. . . .
>
> McDonald's and Burger King are two of the many U.S. corporations using lethal poisons to destroy vast areas of Central American rain forest to create grazing pastures for cattle to be sent back to the States as burgers and pet food. . . .
>
> What they don't make clear is that a diet high in fat, sugar, animal products and salt . . . and low in fiber, vitamins and minerals—which describes an average McDonald's meal—is linked with cancers of the breast and bowel, and heart disease. . . .[7]

Even readers who share the belief that McDonald's is not a reliable source of good nutrition might feel that London Greenpeace has gone too far, and that the name-calling, loaded words, and exaggeration have damaged the credibility of the attackers more than the reputation of McDonald's.

[5] "The Obvious," in David Cooper, ed., *The Dialectics of Liberation* (Penguin Books, 1968), p. 17.

[6] July 6, 2000.

[7] *New York Times,* August 6, 1995, sec. E, p. 7. In 1990 McDonald's sued the group for libel. In June 1997, after the longest libel trial in British history, the judge ruled in favor of the plaintiff, awarding McDonald's £60,000. In March 1999 an appeal partially overturned the verdict and reduced the damages awarded to McDonald's by approximately one-third.

Selection, Slanting, and Charged Language

NEWMAN P. BIRK AND GENEVIEVE B. BIRK

A. THE PRINCIPLE OF SELECTION

Before it is expressed in words, our knowledge, both inside and outside, is influenced by the principle of selection. What we know or observe depends on what we notice; that is, what we select, consciously or unconsciously, as worthy of notice or attention. As we observe, the principle of selection determines which facts we take in.

Suppose, for example, that three people, a lumberjack, an artist, and a tree surgeon, are examining a large tree in the forest. Since the tree itself is a complicated object, the number of particulars or facts about it that one could observe would be very great indeed. Which of these facts a particular observer will notice will be a matter of selection, a selection that is determined by his interests and purposes. A lumberjack might be interested in the best way to cut the tree down, cut it up, and transport it to the lumber mill. His interest would then determine his principle of selection in observing and thinking about the tree. The artist might consider painting a picture of the tree, and his purpose would furnish his principle of selection. The tree surgeon's professional interest in the physical health of the tree might establish a principle of selection for him. If each man were now required to write an exhaustive, detailed report on every thing he observed about the tree, the facts supplied by each would differ, for each would report those facts that his particular principle of selection led him to notice. . . .[1]

The principle of selection then serves as a kind of sieve or screen through which our knowledge passes before it becomes our knowledge. Since we can't notice everything about a complicated object or situation or action or state of our own consciousness, what we do notice is determined by whatever principle of selection is operating for us at the time we gain the knowledge. . . .

B. THE PRINCIPLE OF SLANTING

When we put our knowledge into words, a second process of selection, the process of slanting, takes place. Just as there is something, a rather mysterious principle of selection, which chooses for us what we will notice, and what will

[1]Of course, all three observers would probably report a good many facts in common—the height of the tree, for example, and the size of the trunk. The point we wish to make is that each observer would give us a different impression of the tree because of the different principle of selection that guided his observation. [All notes are the authors'.]

This selection first appeared in *Understanding and Using English* (1972). Together, the Birks also wrote *A Handbook of Grammar, Rhetoric, Mechanics, and Usage* (1976).

then become our knowledge, there is also a principle which operates, with or without our awareness, to select certain facts and feelings from our store of knowledge, and to choose the words and emphasis that we shall use to communicate our meaning.[2] Slanting may be defined as the process of selecting (1) knowledge—factual and attitudinal; (2) words; and (3) emphasis, to achieve the intention of the communicator. Slanting is present in some degree in all communication: one may *slant for* (favorable slanting), *slant against* (unfavorable slanting), or *slant both ways* (balanced shifting). . . .

C. SLANTING BY USE OF EMPHASIS

5 Slanting by use of the devices of emphasis is unavoidable,[3] for emphasis is simply the giving of stress to subject matter, and so indicating what is important and what is less important. In speech, for example, if we say that Socrates was *a wise old man,* we can give several slightly different meanings, one by stressing *wise,* another by stressing *old,* another by giving equal stress to *wise* and *old,* and still another by giving chief stress to *man.* Each different stress gives a different slant (favorable or unfavorable or balanced) to the statement because it conveys a different attitude toward Socrates or a different judgment of him. Connectives and word order also slant by the emphasis they give: Consider the difference in slanting or emphasis produced by *old but wise, old and wise, wise but old.* In writing, we cannot indicate subtle stresses on words as clearly as in speech, but we can achieve our emphasis and so can slant by the use of more complex patterns of word order, [by choice of connectives, by underlining heavily stressed words, and] by marks of punctuation that indicate short or long pauses and so give light or heavy emphasis. Question marks, quotation marks, and exclamation points can also contribute to slanting.[4] It is impossible either in speech or in writing to put two facts together without giving some slight emphasis or slant. For example, if we have in mind only two facts about a man, his awkwardness and his strength, we subtly slant those facts favorably or unfavorably in whatever way we may choose to join them.

More Favorable Slanting	*Less Favorable Slanting*
He is awkward and strong.	He is strong and awkward.
He is awkward but strong.	He is strong but awkward.
Although he is somewhat awkward, he is very strong.	He may be strong, but he's very awkward.

[2]Notice that the "principle of selection" is at work as *we take in* knowledge, and that slanting occurs *as we express* our knowledge in words.

[3]When emphasis is present—and we can think of no instance in the use of language in which it is not—it necessarily influences the meaning by playing a part in the favorable, unfavorable, or balanced slant of the communicator. We are likely to emphasize by voice stress, even when we answer *yes* or *no* to simple questions.

[4]Consider the slanting achieved by punctuation in the following sentences: He called the Senator an honest man? *He* called the Senator an honest man? He called the Senator an honest man! He said one more such "honest" senator would corrupt the state.

With more facts and in longer passages it is possible to maintain a delicate balance by alternating favorable emphasis and so producing a balanced effect.

All communication, then, is in some degree slanted by the *emphasis* of the communicator.

D. SLANTING BY SELECTION OF FACTS

To illustrate the technique of slanting by selection of facts, we shall examine three passages of informative writing which achieve different effects simply by the selection and emphasis of material. Each passage is made up of true statements or facts about a dog, yet the reader is given three different impressions. The first passage is an example of objective writing or balanced slanting, the second is slanted unfavorably, and the third is slanted favorably.

1. Balanced Presentation

> Our dog, Toddy, sold to us as a cocker, produces various reactions in various people. Those who come to the back door she usually growls and barks at (a milkman has said that he is afraid of her); those who come to the front door, she whines at and paws; also she tries to lick people's faces unless we have forestalled her by putting a newspaper in her mouth. (Some of our friends encourage these actions; others discourage them. Mrs. Firmly, one friend, slaps the dog with a newspaper and says, "I know how hard dogs are to train.") Toddy knows and responds to a number of words and phrases, and guests sometimes remark that she is a "very intelligent dog." She has fleas in the summer, and she sheds, at times copiously, the year round. Her blonde hairs are conspicuous when they are on people's clothing or on rugs or furniture. Her color and her large brown eyes frequently produce favorable comment. An expert on cockers would say that her ears are too short and set too high and that she is at least six pounds too heavy.

The passage above is made up of facts, verifiable facts,[5] deliberately selected and emphasized to produce a *balanced* impression. Of course not all the facts about the dog have been given—to supply *all* the facts on any subject, even such a comparatively simple one, would be an almost impossible task. Both favorable and unfavorable facts are used, however, and an effort has been made to alternate favorable and unfavorable details so that neither will receive greater emphasis by position, proportion, or grammatical structure.

[5] *Verifiable* facts are facts that can be checked and agreed upon and proved to be true by people who wish to verify them. That a particular theme received a failing grade is a verifiable fact; one needs merely to see the theme with the grade on it. That the instructor should have failed the theme is not, strictly speaking, a verifiable fact, but a matter of opinion. That women on the average live longer than men is a verifiable fact; that they live better is a matter of opinion, *a value judgment.*

2. Facts Slanted Against

> That dog put her paws on my white dress as soon as I came in the door, and she made so much noise that it was two minutes before she had quieted down enough for us to talk and hear each other. Then the gas man came and she did a great deal of barking. And her hairs are on the rug and on the furniture. If you wear a dark dress they stick to it like lint. When Mrs. Firmly came in, she actually hit the dog with a newspaper to make it stay down, and she made some remark about training dogs. I wish the Birks would take the hint or get rid of that noisy, shorteared, overweight "cocker" of theirs.

10 This unfavorably slanted version is based on the same facts, but now these facts have been selected and given a new emphasis. The speaker, using her selected facts to give her impression of the dog, is quite possibly unaware of her negative slanting.

Now for a favorably slanted version:

3. Facts Slanted For

> What a lively and responsible dog! When I walked in the door, there she was with a newspaper in her mouth, whining and standing on her hind legs and wagging her tail all at the same time. And what an intelligent dog. If you suggest going for a walk, she will get her collar from the kitchen and hand it to you, and she brings Mrs. Birk's slippers whenever Mrs. Birk says she is "tired" or mentions slippers. At a command she catches balls, rolls over, "speaks," or stands on her hind feet and twirls around. She sits up and balances a piece of bread on her nose until she is told to take it; then she tosses it up and catches it. If you are eating something, she sits up in front of you and "begs" with those big dark brown eyes set in that light, buff-colored face of hers. When I got up to go and told her I was leaving, she rolled her eyes at me and sat up like a squirrel. She certainly is a lively and intelligent dog.

Speaker 3, like Speaker 2, is selecting from the "facts" summarized in balanced version 1, and is emphasizing his facts to communicate his impression.

All three passages are examples of *reporting* (i.e., consist only of verifiable facts), yet they give three very different impressions of the same dog because of the different ways the speakers slanted the facts. Some people say that figures don't lie, and many people believe that if they have the "facts," they have the "truth." Yet if we carefully examine the ways of thought and language, we see that any knowledge that comes to us through words has been subjected to the double screening of the principle of selection and the slanting of language. . . .

Wise listeners and readers realize that the double screening that is produced by the principle of selection and by slanting takes place even when people honestly try to report the facts as they know them. (Speakers 2 and 3, for instance, probably thought of themselves as simply giving information about a dog and were not deliberately trying to mislead.)

Wise listeners and readers know too that deliberate manipulators of language, by mere selection and emphasis, can make their slanted facts appear to support almost any cause.

15 In arriving at opinions and values we cannot always be sure that the facts that sift into our minds through language are representative and relevant and true. We need to remember that much of our information about politics, governmental activities, business conditions, and foreign affairs comes to us selected and slanted. More than we realize, our opinions on these matters may depend on what newspaper we read or what news commentator we listen to. Worthwhile opinions call for knowledge of reliable facts and reasonable arguments for and against—and such opinions include beliefs about morality and truth and religion as well as about public affairs. Because complex subjects involve knowing and dealing with many facts on both sides, reliable judgments are at best difficult to arrive at. If we want to be fairminded, we must be willing to subject our opinions to continual testing by new knowledge, and must realize that after all they *are* opinions, more or less trustworthy. Their trustworthiness will depend on the representativeness of our facts, on the quality of our reasoning, and on the standard of values that we choose to apply.

We shall not give here a passage illustrating the unscrupulous slanting of facts. Such a passage would also include irrelevant facts and false statements presented as facts, along with various subtle distortions of fact. Yet to the uninformed reader the passage would be indistinguishable from a passage intended to give a fair account. If two passages (2 and 3) of casual and unintentional slanting of facts about a dog can give such contradictory impressions of a simple subject, the reader can imagine what a skilled and designing manipulation of facts and statistics could do to mislead an uninformed reader about a really complex subject. An example of such manipulation might be the account of the United States that Soviet propaganda has supplied to the average Russian. Such propaganda, however, would go beyond the mere slanting of the facts: It would clothe the selected facts in charged words and would make use of the many other devices of slanting that appear in charged language.

E. SLANTING BY USE OF CHARGED WORDS

In the passages describing the dog Toddy, we were illustrating the technique of slanting by the selection and emphasis of facts. Though the facts selected had to be expressed in words, the words chosen were as factual as possible, and it was the selection and emphasis of facts and not of words that was mainly responsible for the two distinctly different impressions of the dog. In the passages below we are demonstrating another way of slanting—by the use of charged words. This time the accounts are very similar in the facts they contain; the different impressions of the subject, Corlyn, are produced not by different facts but by the subtle selection of charged words.

The passages were written by a clever student who was told to choose as his subject a person in action, and to write two descriptions, each using the "same facts." The instructions required that one description be slanted positively and the other negatively, so that the first would make the reader favorably inclined toward the person and the action, and the second would make him unfavorably inclined.

Here is the favorably charged description. Read it carefully and form your opinion of the person before you go on to read the second description.

Corlyn

> Corlyn paused at the entrance to the room and glanced about. A well-cut black dress draped subtly about her slender form. Her long blonde hair gave her chiseled features the simple frame they required. She smiled an engaging smile as she accepted a cigarette from her escort. As he lit it for her she looked over the flame and into his eyes. Corlyn had that rare talent of making every male feel that he was the only man in the world.
>
> She took his arm and they descended the steps into the room. She walked with an effortless grace and spoke with equal ease. They each took a cup of coffee and joined a group of friends near the fire. The flickering light danced across her face and lent an ethereal quality to her beauty. The good conversation, the crackling logs, and the stimulating coffee gave her a feeling of internal warmth. Her eyes danced with each leap of the flames.

Taken by itself this passage might seem just a description of an attrac- 20
tive girl. The favorable slanting by use of charged words has been done so skillfully that it is inconspicuous. Now we turn to the unfavorably slanted description of the "same" girl in the "same" actions:

Corlyn

> Corlyn halted at the entrance to the room and looked around. A plain black dress hung on her thin frame. Her stringy bleached hair accentuated her harsh features. She smiled an inane smile as she took a cigarette from her escort. As he lit it for her she stared over the lighter and into his eyes. Corlyn had a habit of making every male feel that he was the last man on earth.
>
> She grasped his arm and they walked down the steps and into the room. Her pace was fast and ungainly, as was her speed. They each reached for some coffee and broke into a group of acquaintances near the fire. The flickering light played across her face and revealed every flaw. The loud talk, the fire, and the coffee she had gulped down made her feel hot. Her eyes grew more red with each leap of the flames.

When the reader compares these two descriptions, he can see how charged words influence the reader's attitude. One needs to read the two descriptions several times to appreciate all the subtle differences between them. Words, some rather heavily charged, others innocent-looking but lightly charged, work together to carry to the reader a judgment of a person and a situation. If the reader had seen only the first description of Corlyn, he might well have thought that he had formed his "own judgment on the basis of the facts." And the examples just given only begin to suggest the techniques that may be used in heavily charged language. For one thing, the two descriptions of Corlyn contain no really good example of the use of charged abstractions; for another, the writer was obliged by the assignment to use the same set of facts and so could not slant by selecting his material.

F. SLANTING AND CHARGED LANGUAGE

. . . When slanting the facts, or words, or emphasis, or any combination of the three *significantly influences* feelings toward, or judgments about, a subject, the language used is charged language. . . .

Of course communications vary in the amount of charge they carry and in their effect on different people; what is very favorably charged for one person may have little or no charge, or may even be adversely charged, for others. It is sometimes hard to distinguish between charged and uncharged expression. But it is safe to say that whenever we wish to convey any kind of inner knowledge—feelings, attitudes, judgments, values—we are obliged to convey that attitudinal meaning through the medium of charged language; and when we wish to understand the inside knowledge of others, we have to interpret the charged language that they choose, or are obliged to use. Charged language, then, is the natural and necessary medium for the communication of charged or attitudinal meaning. At times we have difficulty in living with it, but we should have even greater difficulty in living without it.

Some of the difficulties in living with charged language are caused by its use in dishonest propaganda, in some editorials, in many political speeches, in most advertising, in certain kinds of effusive salesmanship, and in blatantly insincere, or exaggerated, or sentimental expressions of emotion. Other difficulties are caused by the misunderstandings and misinterpretations that charged language produces. A charged phrase misinterpreted in a love letter; a charged word spoken in haste or in anger; an acrimonious argument about religion or politics or athletics or fraternities; the frustrating uncertainty produced by the effort to understand the complex attitudinal meaning in a poem or play or a short story—these troubles, all growing out of the use of charged language, may give us the feeling that Robert Louis Stevenson expressed when he said, "The battle goes sore against us to the going down of the sun. . . ."

READING AND DISCUSSION QUESTIONS

1. How do the Birks distinguish between the process of selection and the process of slanting?
2. Explain the three types of slanting described by the Birks and illustrate each with examples from your own experience.
3. According to the Birks, why is charged language unavoidable—and ultimately desirable?

WRITING SUGGESTIONS

4. Choose a printed ad and analyze the use of language, applying the Birks' terminology.
5. Choose one or more editorials or letters to the editor and show how word choice reveals a writer's attitude toward a subject.

We find slanting everywhere, not only in advertising and propaganda, where we expect to find it, but in news stories, which should be strictly neutral in their recounting of events, and in textbooks. In the field of history, for example, it is often difficult for scholars to remain impartial about significant events. Like the rest of us, they may approve or disapprove, and their choice of words will reflect their judgments.

The following passage by a distinguished Catholic historian describes the events surrounding the momentous decision by Henry VIII, king of England, to break with the Roman Catholic Church in 1534, in part because of the Pope's refusal to grant him a divorce from the Catholic princess Catherine of Aragon so that he could marry Anne Boleyn.

> The *protracted* delay in receiving an annulment was very *irritating* to the *impulsive* English king. . . . Gradually Henry's former *effusive* loyalty to Rome gave way to a settled conviction of the tyranny of the papal power, and there *rushed* to his mind the recollections of efforts of earlier English rulers to restrict that power. A few *salutary* enactments against the Church might *compel* a favorable decision from the Pope.
>
> Henry seriously opened his campaign against the Roman Church in 1531, when he *frightened* the clergy into paying a fine of over half a million dollars for violating an *obsolete* statute . . . and in the same year he *forced* the clergy to recognize himself as supreme head of the Church. . . .
>
> His *subservient* Parliament then empowered him to stop the payments of annates to the Pope and to appoint bishops in England without recourse to the papacy. *Without waiting longer* for the decision from Rome, he had Cranmer, *one of his own creatures,* whom he had just named Archbishop of Canterbury, declare his marriage null and void. . . .
>
> Yet Henry VIII encountered considerable *opposition* from the *higher clergy,* from the monks, and from many *intellectual leaders*. . . . A *popular uprising*—the Pilgrimage of Grace—was *sternly* suppressed, and such men as the *brilliant* Sir Thomas More and John Fisher, the *aged* and *saintly* bishop of Rochester, were beheaded because they retained their former belief in papal supremacy.[8] [Italics added.]

[8] Carlton J. H. Hayes, *A Political and Cultural History of Modern Europe,* vol. 1 (New York: Macmillan, 1933), pp. 172–73.

In the first paragraph the italicized words help make the following points: that Henry was rash, impulsive, and insincere and that he was intent on punishing the church (the word *salutary* means healthful or beneficial and is used sarcastically). In the second paragraph the choice of words stresses Henry's use of force and the cowardly submission of his followers. In the third paragraph the adjectives describing the opposition to Henry's campaign and those who were executed emphasize Henry's cruelty and despotism. Within the limits of this brief passage the author has offered support for his strong indictment of Henry VIII's actions, both in defining the statute as obsolete and in describing the popular opposition. In a longer exposition you would expect to find a more elaborate justification with facts and authoritative opinion from other sources.

The advocate of a position in an argument, unlike the reporter or the historian, must express a judgment, but the preceding examples demonstrate how the arguer should use language to avoid or minimize slanting and to persuade readers that he or she has come to a conclusion after careful analysis. The careful arguer must not conceal his or her judgments by presenting them as if they were statements of fact, but must offer convincing support for his or her choice of words and respect the audience's feelings and attitudes by using temperate language.

Depending on the circumstances, *exaggeration* can be defined, in the words of one writer, as "a form of lying." An essay in *Time* magazine, "Watching Out for Loaded Words," points to the danger for the arguer in relying on exaggerated language as an essential part of the argument.

> The trouble with loaded words is they tend to short-circuit thought. While they may describe something, they simultaneously try to seduce the mind into accepting a prefabricated opinion about the something described.[9]

PRACTICE

Locate specific examples of slanted language in the first of these two excerpts from the debate later in the chapter. What effect does the word choice have in the first piece? How does it compare to the word choice in the second passage, on the same topic?

> 1. Grandstanding politicians love to rail against the gun. Inanimate objects are good targets to beat up on. That way, politicians do not have to address the real problems in our society. We pay a price for this craven misdirection, though, in thousands of murders, muggings, rapes, robberies, and burglaries.
>
> Yet that is not the greatest danger we face. The Founding Fathers knew that *governments* could turn criminal. That is the principal

[9] *Time*, May 24, 1982, p. 86.

> reason they wanted every man armed: An armed citizenry militates against the development of tyranny. The Founding Fathers did not want every man armed in order to shoot a burglar, although they had nothing against doing so. The Founding Fathers did not want every man armed in order to shoot Bambi or Thumper, although they had nothing against doing so. The Founding Fathers wanted every man armed in order to shoot soldiers or police of tyrannical regimes who suppress the rights of free men. (McGrath 425)
>
> 2. Americans also have a right to defend their homes, and we need not challenge that. Nor does anyone seriously question that the Constitution protects the right of hunters to own and keep sporting guns for hunting game any more than anyone would challenge the right to own and keep fishing rods and other equipment for fishing—or to own automobiles. To "keep and bear arms" for hunting today is essentially a recreational activity and not an imperative of survival, as it was 200 years ago; "Saturday night specials" and machine guns are not recreational weapons and surely are as much in need of regulation as motor vehicles.
>
> Americans should ask themselves a few questions. The Constitution does not mention automobiles or motorboats, but the right to keep and own an automobile is beyond question; equally beyond question is the power of the state to regulate the purchase or the transfer of such vehicle and the right to license the vehicle and the driver with reasonable standards. In some places, even a bicycle must be registered, as must some household dogs. (Burger 419)

PICTURESQUE LANGUAGE

Picturesque language consists of words that produce images in the mind of the reader. Students sometimes assume that vivid picture-making language is the exclusive instrument of novelists and poets, but writers of arguments can also avail themselves of such devices to heighten the impact of their messages.

Picturesque language can do more than render a scene. It shares with other kinds of emotive language the power to express and arouse deep feelings. Like a fine painting or photograph, it can draw readers into the picture where they partake of the writer's experience as if they were also present. Such power may be used to delight, to instruct, or to horrify. In 1741 the Puritan preacher Jonathan Edwards delivered his sermon "Sinners in the Hands of an Angry God," in which people were likened to repulsive spiders hanging over the flames of Hell to be dropped into the fire whenever a wrathful God was pleased to release them. The congregation's reaction to Edwards's picture of the everlasting horrors to be suffered in the netherworld included panic, fainting, hysteria, and convulsions. Subsequently Edwards lost his pulpit in Massachusetts, in part as a consequence of his success at provoking such uncontrollable terror among his congregation.

Language as intense and vivid as Edwards's emerges from very strong emotion about a deeply felt cause. In the following paragraph, Lavina Melwani uses picturesque language to call attention to some of the problems faced daily by undocumented workers.

> The rats—bold, tenacious, and totally fearless—are what bothered him the most. Prem, who requested his last name not be used, says the rodents have the run of the old apartment he shares in Baltimore City, Maryland, with five other Nepali men, most of them undocumented. "It is impossible to have beds for six people in two rooms," he says. "So we have small roll-out beds or mattresses on the floor. There are many rats running around the apartment and it's difficult to catch them. We can't complain. The landlord doesn't care. He knows we have to live here and have no choice."[10]

The rules governing the use of picturesque language are the same as those governing other kinds of emotive language. Is the language appropriate? Is it too strong, too colorful for the purpose of the message? Does it result in slanting or distortion? What will its impact be on a hostile or indifferent audience? Will they be angered, repelled? Will they cease to read or listen if the imagery is too disturbing?

CONCRETE AND ABSTRACT LANGUAGE

Writers of argument need to be aware of another use of language—the distinction between concrete and abstract. Concrete words point to real objects and real experiences. Abstract words express qualities apart from particular things and events. *Velvety, dark red roses* is concrete; we can see, touch, and smell them. *Beauty* in the eye of the beholder is abstract; we can speak of the quality of beauty without reference to a particular object or event. *Returning money found in the street to the owner, although no one has seen the discovery* is concrete. *Honesty* is abstract. In abstracting we separate a quality shared by a number of objects or events, however different from each other the individual objects or events may be.

Writing that describes or tells a story leans heavily on concrete language. Although arguments also rely on the vividness of concrete language, they use abstract terms far more extensively than other kinds of writing. Using abstractions effectively, especially in arguments of value and policy, is important for two reasons: (1) Abstractions represent the qualities,

[10] "No Roof No Roots No Rights." *Little India*, April 12, 2006, p. 42.

characteristics, and values that the writer is explaining, defending, or attacking; and (2) they enable the writer to make generalizations about his or her data. Equally important is knowing when to avoid abstractions that obscure the message.

You should not expect abstract terms alone to carry the emotional content of your message. The effect of even the most suggestive words can be enhanced by details, examples, and anecdotes. One mode of expression is not superior to the other; both abstractions and concrete detail work together to produce clear, persuasive argument. This is especially true when the meanings assigned to abstract terms vary from reader to reader.

In establishing claims based on the support of values, for example, you may use such abstract terms as *religion, duty, freedom, peace, progress, justice, equality, democracy,* and *pursuit of happiness.* You can assume that some of these words are associated with the same ideas and emotions for almost all readers; others require further explanation. Suppose you write, "We have made great progress in the last fifty years." One dictionary defines *progress* as "a gradual betterment," another abstraction. How will you define "gradual betterment" for your readers? Can you be sure that they have in mind the same references for progress that you do? If not, misunderstandings are inevitable. You may offer examples: supersonic planes, computers, shopping malls, nuclear energy. Many of your readers will react favorably to the mention of these innovations, which to them represent progress; others, for whom these inventions represent change but not progress, will react unfavorably. You may not be able to convince all of your readers that "we have made great progress," but all of them will now understand what you mean by "progress." And intelligent disagreement is preferable to misunderstanding.

Abstractions tell us what conclusions we have arrived at; details tell us how we got there. But there are dangers in either too many details or too many abstractions. For example, a writer may present only concrete data without telling readers what conclusions are to be drawn from them. Suppose you read the following:

> To Chinese road-users, traffic police are part of the grass . . . and neither they nor the rules they're supposed to enforce are paid the least attention. . . . Ignoring traffic-lights is only one peculiarity of Chinese traffic. It's normal for a pedestrian to walk straight out into a stream of cars without so much as lifting his head; and goodness knows how many Chinese cyclists I've almost killed as they have shot blindly in front of me across busy main roads.[11]

These details would constitute no more than interesting gossip until we read, "It's not so much a sign of ignorance or recklessness . . . but of fatalism." The details of specific behavior have now acquired a significance expressed in the abstraction *fatalism.*

[11]Philip Short, "The Chinese and the Russians," *The Listener,* April 8, 1982, p. 6.

A more common problem, however, in using abstractions is omission of details. Either the writer is not a skilled observer and cannot provide the details, or he or she believes that such details are too small and quiet compared to the grand sounds made by abstract terms. These grand sounds, unfortunately, cannot compensate for the lack of clarity and liveliness. Lacking detailed support, abstract words may be misinterpreted. They may also represent ideas that are so vague as to be meaningless. Sometimes they function illegitimately as short cuts (discussed on pp. 388–93), arousing emotions but unaccompanied by good reasons for their use. The following paragraph exhibits some of these common faults. How would you translate it into clear English?

> We respectively petition, request, and entreat that due and adequate provision be made, this day and the date hereinafter subscribed, for the satisfying of these petitioners' nutritional requirements and for the organizing of such methods of allocation and distribution as may be deemed necessary and proper to assure the reception by and for said petitioners of such quantities of baked cereal products as shall, in the judgment of the aforesaid petitioners, constitute a sufficient supply thereof.[12]

If you had trouble decoding this, it was because there were almost no concrete references—the homely words *baked* and *cereal* leap out of the paragraph like English signposts in a foreign country—and too many long words or words of Latin origin when simple words would do: *requirements* instead of *needs, petition* instead of *ask*. An absence of concrete references and an excess of long Latinate words can have a depressing effect on both writer and reader. The writer may be in danger of losing the thread of the argument, the reader at a loss to discover the message.

The paragraph above, according to James B. Minor, a lawyer who teaches courses in legal drafting, is "how a federal regulation writer would probably write, 'Give us this day our daily bread.'" This brief sentence with its short, familiar words and its origin in the Lord's Prayer has a deep emotional effect. The paragraph composed by Minor deadens any emotional impact because of its preponderance of abstract terms and its lack of connection with the world of our senses.

Finally, there are the moral implications of using abstractions that conceal a disagreeable reality. George Orwell pointed them out more than sixty years ago in "Politics and the English Language." Another essayist, Joseph Wood Krutch, in criticizing the attitude that cheating "doesn't really hurt anybody," observed, "'It really doesn't hurt anybody' means it doesn't do that abstraction called society any harm." The following news story reports a proposal with which Orwell and Krutch might have agreed. His intention, says the author, is to "slow the hand of any President who might be tempted to unleash a nuclear attack."

[12]*New York Times,* May 10, 1977, p. 35.

> It has long been feared that a President could be making his fateful decision while at a "psychological distance" from the victims of a nuclear barrage; that he would be in a clean, air-conditioned room, surrounded by well-scrubbed aides, all talking in abstract terms about appropriate military responses in an international crisis, and that he might well push to the back of his mind the realization that hundreds of millions of people would be exterminated.
>
> So Roger Fisher, professor of law at Harvard University, offers a simple suggestion to make the stakes more real. He would put the codes needed to fire nuclear weapons in a little capsule, and implant the capsule next to the heart of a volunteer, who would carry a big butcher knife as he accompanied the President everywhere. If the President ever wanted to fire nuclear weapons, he would first have to kill, with his own hands, that human being.
>
> He has to look at someone and realize what death is—what an innocent death is. "It's reality brought home," says Professor Fisher.[13]

The moral lesson is clear: It is much easier to do harm if we convince ourselves that the object of the injury is only an abstraction.

SHORT CUTS

Short cuts are arguments that depend on readers' responses to words. Short cuts, like other devices we have discussed so far, are a common use of emotive language but are often mistaken for valid argument.

Although they have power to move us, these abbreviated substitutes for argument avoid the hard work necessary to provide facts, expert opinion, and analysis of warrants. Even experts, however, can be guilty of using short cuts, and the writer who consults an authority should be alert to that authority's use of language. Two of the most common uses of short cuts are clichés and slogans.

■ Clichés

A cliché is an expression or idea grown stale through overuse. Clichés in language are tired expressions that have faded like old photographs; readers no longer see anything when clichés are placed before them. Clichés include phrases like "cradle of civilization," "few and far between," "rude awakening," "follow in the footsteps of," "fly in the ointment."

But more important to recognize and avoid are clichés of thought. A cliché of thought may be likened to a formula, which one dictionary defines as "any conventional rule or method for doing something, especially when used, applied, or repeated without thought." Clichés of thought rep-

[13]*New York Times,* September 7, 1982, sec. C, p. 1.

resent ready-made answers to questions, stereotyped solutions to problems, "knee-jerk" reactions. Two writers who call these forms of expression "mass language" describe it this way: "Mass language is language which presents the reader with a response he is expected to make without giving him adequate reason for having this response."[14] These clichés of thought are often expressed in single words or phrases.

Certain cultural attitudes encourage the use of clichés. The liberal American tradition has been governed by hopeful assumptions about our ability to solve problems. A professor of communications says that "we tell our students that for every problem there must be a solution."[15] But real solutions are hard to come by. In our haste to provide them, to prove that we can be decisive, we may be tempted to produce familiar responses that resemble solutions. All reasonable solutions are worthy of consideration, but they must be defined and supported if they are to be used in a thoughtful, well-constructed argument.

Although formulas change with the times, some are unexpectedly hardy and survive long after critics have revealed their weaknesses. Overpopulation is often cited as the cause of poverty, disease, and war. It can be found in the writing of the ancient Greeks 2,500 years ago. "That perspective," says the editor of *Food Monitor,* a journal published by World Hunger Year, Inc., "is so pervasive that most Americans have simply stopped thinking about population and resort to inane clucking of tongues."[16] If the writer offering overpopulation as an explanation for poverty were to look further, he or she would discover that the explanation rested on shaky data. Singapore, the most densely populated country in the world (11,574 persons per square mile) is also one of the richest ($16,500 per capita income per year). Chad, one of the most sparsely populated (11 persons per square mile) is also one of the poorest ($190 per capita income per year).[17] Strictly defined, overpopulation may serve to explain some instances of poverty; obviously it cannot serve as a blanket to cover all or even most instances. "By repeating stock phrases," one columnist reminds us, "we lose the ability, finally, to hear what we are saying."

Slogans

I have always been rather impressed by those people who wear badges stating where they stand on certain issues. The badges have to be small, and therefore the message has to be small, concise, and without elaboration. So

[14]Richard E. Hughes and P. Albert Duhamel, *Rhetoric: Principles and Usage* (Englewood Cliffs, N.J.: Prentice-Hall, 1962), p. 161.

[15]Malcolm O. Sillars, "The New Conservatism and the Teacher of Speech," *Southern Speech Journal* 21 (1956), p. 240.

[16]Letter to the *New York Times,* October 4, 1982, sec. A, p. 18.

[17]*World Almanac and Book of Facts,* 1995 (New York: World Almanac, 1995), pp. 754, 818.

it comes out as "I hate something" or "I love something," or ban this or ban that. There isn't space for argument, and I therefore envy the badge-wearer who is so clear-cut about his or her opinions.[18]

The word *slogan* has a picturesque origin. A slogan was the war cry or rallying cry of a Scottish or Irish clan. From that early use it has come to mean a "catchword or rallying motto distinctly associated with a political party or other group" as well as a "catch phrase used to advertise a product."

Slogans, like clichés, are short, undeveloped arguments. They represent abbreviated responses to often complex questions. As a reader you need to be aware that slogans merely call attention to a problem; they cannot offer persuasive proof for a claim in a dozen words or less. As a writer you should avoid the use of slogans that evoke an emotional response "without giving [the reader] adequate reason for having this response."

Advertising slogans are the most familiar. Some of them are probably better known than nursery rhymes: "Got milk?" "L'Oréal, because I'm worth it," "Nike, just do it." Advertisements may, of course, rely for their effectiveness on more than slogans. They may also give us interesting and valuable information about products, but most advertisements give us slogans that ignore proof—short cuts substituting for argument.

The persuasive appeal of advertising slogans heavily depends on the connotations associated with products. In Chapter 7 (see p. 227, under "Appeals to Needs and Values"), we discussed the way in which advertisements promise to satisfy our needs and protect our values. Wherever evidence is scarce or nonexistent, the advertiser must persuade us through skillful choice of words and phrases (as well as pictures), especially those that produce pleasurable feelings. "Let it inspire you" is the slogan of a popular liqueur. It suggests a desirable state of being but remains suitably vague about the nature of the inspiration. Another familiar slogan—"Noxzema, clean makeup"—also emphasizes a quality that we approve of, but what is "clean" makeup? Since the advertisers are silent, we are left with warm feelings about the word and not much more.

Advertising slogans are persuasive because their witty phrasing and punchy rhythms produce an automatic yes response. We react to them as we might react to the lyrics of popular songs, and we treat them far less critically than we treat more straightforward and elaborate arguments. Still, the consequences of failing to analyze the slogans of advertisers are usually not serious. You may be tempted to buy a product because you were fascinated by a brilliant slogan, but if the product doesn't satisfy, you can abandon it without much loss. However, ignoring ideological slogans coined by political parties or special-interest groups may carry an enormous price, and the results are not so easily undone.

Ideological slogans, like advertising slogans, depend on the power of connotation, the emotional associations aroused by a word or phrase. In the

[18] Anthony Smith, "Nuclear Power—Why Not?" *The Listener,* October 22, 1981, p. 463.

1960s and 1970s, a period of well-advertised social change, slogans flourished; they appeared by the hundreds of thousands on buttons, T-shirts, and bumper stickers. One of them read, "Student Power!" To some readers of the slogan, distrustful of young people and worried about student unrest on campuses and in the streets, the suggestion was frightening. To others, mostly students, the idea of power, however undefined, was intoxicating. Notice that "Student Power!" is not an argument; it is only a claim. (It might also represent a warrant.) As a claim, for example, it might take this form: Students at this school should have the power to select the faculty. Of course, the arguer would need to provide the kinds of proof that support his or her claim, something the slogan by itself cannot do. Many people, whether they accepted or rejected the claim, supplied the rest of the argument without knowing exactly what the issues were and how a developed argument would proceed. They were accepting or rejecting the slogan largely on the basis of emotional reaction to words.

American political history is, in fact, a repository of slogans. Leaf through a history of the United States and you will come across "Tippecanoe and Tyler, too," "manifest destiny," "fifty-four forty or fight," "make the world safe for democracy," "the silent majority," "the domino theory," "the missile gap," "the window of vulnerability." Each administration tries to capture the attention and allegiance of the public by coining catchy phrases. Roosevelt's New Deal in 1932 was followed by the Square Deal and the New Frontier. Today, slogans must be carefully selected to avoid offending groups that are sensitive to the ways in which words affect their interests. In 1983 Senator John Glenn, announcing his candidacy for president, talked about bringing "old values and new horizons" to the White House. "New horizons" apparently carried positive connotations. His staff, however, worried that "old values" might suggest racism and sexism to minorities and women.

Over a period of time slogans, like clichés, can acquire a life of their own and, if they are repeated often enough, come to represent an unchanging truth we no longer need to examine. "Dangerously," says the writer quoted above, "policy makers become prisoners of the slogans they popularize."

Following are two examples. The first is part of the second inaugural address of George C. Wallace, governor of Alabama, in 1971. The second is taken from an article in the *Militia News,* the organ of a group that believed the U.S. government was engaged in a "satanic conspiracy" to disarm the American people and then enslave them. Timothy McVeigh, who blew up the Oklahoma City federal building in 1995, was influenced by the group.

> The people of the South and those who think like the South, represent the majority viewpoint within our constitutional democracy, but they are not organized and do not speak with a loud voice. Until the day arrives when the voice of the people of the South and those who think like us is, within the law, thrust into the face of the bureaucrats, only then can the

> "people's power" express itself legally and ethically and get results. . . . Too long, oh, too long, has the voice of the people been silenced by their own disruptive government—by governmental bribery in quasi-governmental handouts such as H.E.W. and others that exist in America today! An aroused people can save this nation from those evil forces who seek our destruction. The choice is yours. The hour is growing late![19]
>
> Every gun owner who is the least bit informed knows that those who are behind this conspiracy—who now have their people well placed in political office, in the courts, in the media, and in the schools, are working for the total disarming of the American people and the surrender of our nation and our sovereignty. . . . The time is at hand when men and women must decide whether they are on the side of freedom and justice, the American republic, and Almighty God, or if they are on the side of tyranny and oppression, the New World Order, and Satan.[20]

Whatever power these recommendations might have if their proposals were more clearly formulated, as they stand they are collections of slogans and loaded words. (Even the language falters: Can the voice of the people be thrust into the face of the bureaucrats?) We can visualize some of the slogans as brightly colored banners: "Dislodge Big Money!" "Power to the People!" "Save This Nation from Evil Forces!" "The Choice Is Yours!" Do all the groups mentioned share identical interests? If so, what are they? Given the vagueness of the terms, it is not surprising that arguers on opposite sides of the political spectrum—loosely characterized as liberal and conservative—sometimes resort to the same clichés and slogans: the language of populism, or a belief in conspiracies against God-fearing people, in these examples.

Slogans have numerous shortcomings as substitutes for the development of an argument. First, their brevity presents serious disadvantages. Slogans necessarily ignore exceptions or negative instances that might qualify a claim. They usually speak in absolute terms without describing the circumstances in which a principle or idea might not work. Their claims therefore seem shrill and exaggerated. In addition, brevity prevents the sloganeer from revealing how he or she arrived at conclusions.

Second, slogans may conceal unexamined warrants. When Japanese cars were beginning to compete with American cars, the slogan "Made in America by Americans" appeared on the bumpers of thousands of American-made cars. A thoughtful reader would have discovered in this slogan several implied warrants: American cars are better than Japanese cars; the American economy will improve if we buy American; patriotism can be expressed by buying American goods. If the reader were to ask a few probing questions, he or she might find these warrants unconvincing.

[19] Second Inaugural Address as governor of Alabama, January 18, 1971.

[20] Chip Berlet and Matthew N. Lyons, *Right-Wing Populism in America* (New York: Guildford Press, 2000), p. 301.

Silent warrants that express values hide in other popular and influential slogans. "Pro-life," the slogan of those who oppose abortion, assumes that the fetus is a living being entitled to the same rights as individuals already born. "Pro-choice," the slogan of those who favor abortion, suggests that the freedom of the pregnant woman to choose is the foremost or only consideration. The words *life* and *choice* have been carefully selected to reflect desirable qualities, but the words are only the beginning of the argument.

Third, although slogans may express admirable sentiments, they often fail to tell us how to achieve their objectives. They address us in the imperative mode, ordering us to take an action or refrain from it. But the means of achieving the objectives may be nonexistent or very costly. If the sloganeer cannot offer workable means for implementing his or her goals, he or she risks alienating the audience.

Sloganeering is one of the recognizable attributes of propaganda. Propaganda for both good and bad purposes is a form of slanting, of selecting language and facts to persuade an audience to take a certain action. Even a good cause may be weakened by an unsatisfactory slogan. The slogans of some organizations devoted to fundraising for people with physical handicaps have come under attack for depicting those with handicaps as helpless. According to one critic, the popular slogan "Jerry's kids" promotes the idea that Jerry Lewis is the sole support of children with muscular dystrophy. Perhaps increased sensitivity to the needs of people with disabilities will produce new words and new slogans. If you assume that your audience is sophisticated and alert, you will probably write your strongest arguments, devoid of clichés and slogans.

SAMPLE ANNOTATED ESSAY

President's Address to the Nation, September 11, 2006

GEORGE W. BUSH

Words like seared, barbarity, and murdered are examples of slanting used appropriately for the author's purpose.

Good evening. Five years ago, this date—September the 11th—was seared into America's memory. Nineteen men attacked us with a barbarity unequaled in our history. They murdered people of all colors, creeds, and nationalities—and made war upon the entire free world. Since that day, America and her allies have taken the offensive in a war unlike any we have fought before. Today, we are safer, but we are not yet safe. On this solemn night, I've asked for some of your time to discuss the nature of the threat still before us, what we are doing to protect our nation, and the building of a more hopeful Middle East that holds the key to peace for America and the world.

It is exaggeration to say that the acts described in this paragraph are distinctly American, but the concrete examples are effective for the author's purpose.

On 9/11, our nation saw the face of evil. Yet on that awful day, we also witnessed something distinctly American: ordinary citizens rising to the occasion, and responding with extraordinary acts of courage. We saw courage in office workers who were trapped on the high floors of burning skyscrapers—and called home so that their last words to their families would be of comfort and love. We saw courage in passengers aboard Flight 93, who recited the 23rd Psalm—and then charged the cockpit. And we saw courage in the Pentagon staff who made it out of the flames and smoke—and ran back in to answer cries for help. On this day, we remember the innocent who lost their lives—and we pay tribute to those who gave their lives so that others might live.

More concrete examples, with the first person I making it clear that Bush has shared moments of grief with the victims' families.

For the second time Bush refers to a more hopeful world. If the rest of the essay does not provide further explanation, this will be a cliché of thought.

For many of our citizens, the wounds of that morning are still fresh. I've met firefighters and police officers who choke up at the memory of fallen comrades. I've stood with families gathered on a grassy field in Pennsylvania, who take bittersweet pride in loved ones who refused to be victims—and gave America our first victory in the war on terror. I've sat beside young mothers with children who are now five years old—and still long for the daddies who will never cradle them in their arms. Out of this suffering, we resolve to honor every man and woman lost. And we seek their lasting memorial in a safer and more hopeful world.

Two of the strongest slanted words here are perverted and, in contrast to the reference to civilized nations, the implication that America's enemies are uncivilized.

Since the horror of 9/11, we've learned a great deal about the enemy. We have learned that they are evil and kill without mercy—but not without purpose. We have learned that they form a global network of extremists who are driven by a perverted vision of Islam—a totalitarian ideology that hates freedom, rejects tolerance, and despises all dissent. And we have learned that their goal is to build a radical Islamic empire where women are prisoners in their homes, men are beaten for missing prayer meetings, and terrorists have a safe haven

On the other hand, to have a calling carries a positive slant, suggesting a religious or at least honorable sense of duty.

to plan and launch attacks on America and other civilized nations. The war against this enemy is more than a military conflict. It is the decisive ideological struggle of the 21st century, and the calling of our generation.

The allusion to the Cold War will evoke negative memories for some, depending on their age.

The reference to the war in Iraq as one that America didn't ask for suggests that it was imposed on an unwilling nation.

Suggesting what a loss would mean for America's children is an appeal to emotion.

5 Our nation is being tested in a way that we have not been since the start of the Cold War. We saw what a handful of our enemies can do with box-cutters and plane tickets. We hear their threats to launch even more terrible attacks on our people. And we know that if they were able to get their hands on weapons of mass destruction, they would use them against us. We face an enemy determined to bring death and suffering into our homes. America did not ask for this war, and every American wishes it were over. So do I. But the war is not over—and it will not be over until either we or the extremists emerge victorious. If we do not defeat these enemies now, we will leave our children to face a Middle East overrun by terrorist states and radical dictators armed with nuclear weapons. We are in a war that will set the course for this new century—and determine the destiny of millions across the world.

To be held to account for their actions is a cliché, one that may hide uncomfortable truths, given suspicions aroused about how the U.S. questions prisoners.

For America, 9/11 was more than a tragedy— it changed the way we look at the world. On September the 11th, we resolved that we would go on the offense against our enemies, and we would not distinguish between the terrorists and those who harbor or support them. So we helped drive the Taliban from power in Afghanistan. We put al Qaeda on the run, and killed or captured most of those who planned the 9/11 attacks, including the man believed to be the mastermind, Khalid Sheik Mohammed. He and other suspected terrorists have been questioned by the Central Intelligence Agency, and they provided valuable information that has helped stop attacks in America and across the world. Now these men have been transferred to Guantanamo Bay, so they can be held to account for their actions. Osama bin Laden and other terrorists are still in hiding. Our message to them is clear: No matter how long it takes, America will find you, and we will bring you to justice.

On September the 11th, we learned that America must confront threats before they reach our shores, whether those threats come from terrorist networks or terrorist states. I'm often asked why we're in Iraq when Saddam Hussein was not responsible for the 9/11 attacks. The answer is that the regime of Saddam Hussein was a clear threat. My administration, the Congress, and the United Nations saw the threat—and after 9/11, Saddam's regime posed a risk that the world could not afford to take. The world is safer because Saddam Hussein is no longer in power. And now the challenge is to help the Iraqi people build a democracy that fulfills the dreams of the nearly 12 million Iraqis who came out to vote in free elections last December.

Another cliché of thought: a risk that the world could not afford to take.

Al Qaeda and other extremists from across the world have come to Iraq to stop the rise of a free society in the heart of the Middle East. They have joined the remnants of Saddam's regime and other armed groups to foment sectarian violence and drive us out. Our enemies in Iraq are tough and they are committed—but so are Iraqi and coalition forces. We're adapting to stay ahead of the enemy, and we are carrying out a clear plan to ensure that a democratic Iraq succeeds.

References to democracy and free elections have positive connotations for most Americans.

We're training Iraqi troops so they can defend their nation. We're helping Iraq's unity government grow in strength and serve its people. We will not leave until this work is done. Whatever mistakes have been made in Iraq, the worst mistake would be to think that if we pulled out, the terrorists would leave us alone. They will not leave us alone. They will follow us. The safety of America depends on the outcome of the battle in the streets of Baghdad. Osama bin Laden calls this fight "the Third World War"—and he says that victory for the terrorists in Iraq will mean America's "defeat and disgrace forever." If we yield Iraq to men like bin Laden, our enemies will be emboldened; they will gain a new safe haven; they will use Iraq's resources to fuel their extremist movement. We will not allow this to happen. America will stay in the fight. Iraq will be a free nation, and a strong ally in the war on terror.

The allusion to World War I and World War II by alluding to a Third World War, like the allusion to the Cold War, evokes memories, mostly negative, for older Americans.

Osama bin Laden's reference to America's defeat and disgrace forever is a verbal assault on national pride.

The primary slogan for the war in Iraq: the war on terror.

The enemy is guilty of unspeakable violence. The Iraqi people are steadfast. Our Armed Forces have exhibited skill and resolve, made great sacrifices.

10 We can be confident that our coalition will succeed because the Iraqi people have been steadfast in the face of unspeakable violence. And we can be confident in victory because of the skill and resolve of America's Armed Forces. Every one of our troops is a volunteer, and since the attacks of September the 11th, more than 1.6 million Americans have stepped forward to put on our nation's uniform. In Iraq, Afghanistan, and other fronts in the war on terror, the men and women of our military are making great sacrifices to keep us safe. Some have suffered terrible injuries—and nearly 3,000 have given their lives. America cherishes their memory. We pray for their families. And we will never back down from the work they have begun.

Appeals to Americans' need for security.

We also honor those who toil day and night to keep our homeland safe, and we are giving them the tools they need to protect our people. We've created the Department of Homeland Security. We have torn down the wall that kept law enforcement and intelligence from sharing information. We've tightened security at our airports and seaports and borders, and we've created new programs to monitor enemy bank records and phone calls. Thanks to the hard work of our law enforcement and intelligence professionals, we have broken up terrorist cells in our midst and saved American lives.

Slanted language: the enemy's ideology is hateful.

The use of the adjective legal to modify authority is loaded for those who believe Congress was rushed into passing laws that threaten Americans' right to privacy out of fear.

Five years after 9/11, our enemies have not succeeded in launching another attack on our soil, but they've not been idle. Al Qaeda and those inspired by its hateful ideology have carried out terrorist attacks in more than two dozen nations. And just last month, they were foiled in a plot to blow up passenger planes headed for the United States. They remain determined to attack America and kill our citizens—and we are determined to stop them. We'll continue to give the men and women who protect us every resource and legal authority they need to do their jobs.

In the first days after the 9/11 attacks I promised to use every element of national power to fight the terrorists, wherever we find them. One of the strongest weapons in our arsenal is the power of freedom. The terrorists fear freedom as much as they do our firepower. They are thrown into panic at the sight of an old man pulling the election lever, girls enrolling in schools, or families worshiping God in their own traditions. They know that given a choice, people will choose freedom over their extremist ideology. So their answer is to deny people this choice by raging against the forces of freedom and moderation. This struggle has been called a clash of civilizations. In truth, it is a struggle for civilization. We are fighting to maintain the way of life enjoyed by free nations. And we're fighting for the possibility that good and decent people across the Middle East can raise up societies based on freedom and tolerance and personal dignity.

Many abstractions here that are clichés of thought if not supported: power of freedom, clash of civilization, struggle for civilization, way of life enjoyed by free nations.

We are now in the early hours of this struggle between tyranny and freedom. Amid the violence, some question whether the people of the Middle East want their freedom, and whether the forces of moderation can prevail. For 60 years, these doubts guided our policies in the Middle East. And then, on a bright September morning, it became clear that the calm we saw in the Middle East was only a mirage. Years of pursuing stability to promote peace had left us with neither. So we changed our policies, and committed America's influence in the world to advancing freedom and democracy as the great alternatives to repression and radicalism.

15 With our help, the people of the Middle East are now stepping forward to claim their freedom. From Kabul to Baghdad to Beirut, there are brave men and women risking their lives each day for the same freedoms that we enjoy. And they have one question for us: Do we have the confidence to do in the Middle East what our fathers and grandfathers accomplished in Europe and Asia? By standing with democratic leaders and reformers, by giving voice to the hopes of decent men and women, we're offering a path away from radicalism. And we are enlisting the most powerful force for peace and moderation in the Middle East: the desire of millions to be free.

The references to what our fathers and grandfathers did in Europe and Asia is an additional appeal to American pride. Only those who agree with America deserve the label decent.

Across the broader Middle East, the extremists are fighting to prevent such a future. Yet America has confronted evil before, and we have defeated it—sometimes at the cost of thousands of good

Allusions to previous American victories and former presidents who led the nation during World War II and the Cold War.

men in a single battle. When Franklin Roosevelt vowed to defeat two enemies across two oceans, he could not have foreseen D-Day and Iwo Jima — but he would not have been surprised at the outcome. When Harry Truman promised American support for free peoples resisting Soviet aggression, he could not have foreseen the rise of the Berlin Wall—but he would not have been surprised to see it brought down. Throughout our history, America has seen liberty challenged, and every time, we have seen liberty triumph with sacrifice and determination.

Desert of despotism and fertile ground of liberty—picturesque language used for contrast.

At the start of this young century, America looks to the day when the people of the Middle East leave the desert of despotism for the fertile gardens of liberty, and resume their rightful place in a world of peace and prosperity. We look to the day when the nations of that region recognize their greatest resource is not the oil in the ground, but the talent and creativity of their people. We look to the day when moms and dads throughout the Middle East see a future of hope and opportunity for their children. And when that good day comes, the clouds of war will part, the appeal of radicalism will decline, and we will leave our children with a better and safer world.

On this solemn anniversary, we rededicate ourselves to this cause. Our nation has endured trials, and we face a difficult road ahead. Winning this war will require the determined efforts of a unified country, and we must put aside our differences and work together to meet the test that history has given us. We will defeat our enemies. We will protect our people. And we will lead the 21st century into a shining age of human liberty.

A specific example that carries emotional impact.

Earlier this year, I traveled to the United States Military Academy. I was there to deliver the commencement address to the first class to arrive at West Point after the attacks of September the 11th. That day I met a proud mom named RoseEllen Dowdell. She was there to watch her son, Patrick, accept his commission in the finest Army the world has ever known. A few weeks earlier, RoseEllen had watched her other son, James, graduate from the Fire Academy in New York City. On both these days, her thoughts turned to someone who was not there to share the moment: her husband, Kevin Dowdell. Kevin was one of the 343 firefighters who rushed to the burning towers of the World Trade Center on September the 11th—and never came home. His sons lost their father that day, but not the passion for service he instilled in them. Here is what RoseEllen says about her boys: "As a mother, I cross my fingers and pray all the time for their safety—but as worried as I am, I'm also proud, and I know their dad would be, too."

A creative play on the two ways that people are brought to their knees.

Our nation is blessed to have young Americans 20
like these—and we will need them. Dangerous enemies have declared their intention to destroy our way of life. They're not the first to try, and their fate will be the same as those who tried before. Nine-Eleven showed us why. The attacks were meant to bring us to our knees, and they did, but not in the way the terrorists intended. Americans united in prayer, came to the aid of neighbors in need, and resolved that our enemies would not have the last word. The spirit of our people is the source of America's strength. And we go forward with trust in that spirit, confidence in our purpose, and faith in a loving God who made us to be free.

Thank you, and may God bless you.

Writer's Guide: Choosing Your Words Carefully

1. Be sure you have avoided language with connotations that might produce a negative reaction in your audience that would weaken your argument.
2. If you have used slanted language, consider whether it will advance your argument instead of weakening it.
3. Use picturesque language where appropriate for your purposes.
4. Replace abstract language with concrete language to be more effective.
5. Edit out any clichés or slogans from your early drafts.
6. Achieve a voice that is appropriate for your subject and audience.

READINGS FOR ANALYSIS

Americans Entitled to Cheap Gas—Right?

JOAN RYAN

Over the years, Americans have taken a lot of vicious abuse for being selfish and irresponsible. We are often portrayed as a nation that wants to have its cake and eat it too, which, as any American knows, is patently untrue. We also want our ice cream and maybe some Cool Whip.

I bring this up because, once again, we are the targets of international ridicule, this time for our anger over rising gas prices. Gas is up now to about $2 a gallon around the nation. It is averaging $2.31 in California. These prices are outrageous, as indicated by the newspaper and TV-news stories quoting motorists as saying, "These prices are outrageous."

The rest of the world, however, is not sympathetic. They think that because gas is $5.22 a gallon in England, $4.24 a gallon in Tokyo, and $4.92 a gallon in France, we are being piggy for complaining about per-gallon gas prices that, even with the recent spike, are still cheaper than a Starbucks Frappuccino.

Apparently the rest of the world doesn't understand the underlying sociological reasons we react as we do to increases in gas prices. Unlike them, we drive cars the size of Paris apartments. They obviously don't realize how much gas cars like these consume! It apparently has come as something of a surprise to many of us, too.

5 When asked to rank the importance of 56 characteristics they considered when buying a new car, Americans ranked fuel economy 44th. This explains why sport utility vehicles, minivans, and light trucks accounted for 54 percent of all new cars bought last year.

"It's still more important to have the right number of cup holders than high fuel economy," said Art Spinella, director of CNW Marketing Research, which conducted the survey.

Peter Rennert sells cars at John Irish Jeep in San Rafael. He showed a gray Grand Cherokee to a woman one morning earlier this week. She took the slow stroll around the vehicle, opened the doors, checked out the cargo space, took it for a test drive.

"What kind of gas mileage does it get?" she asked Rennert. He showed her the manufacturer's sticker on the window: 17 to 21 miles per gallon highway.

"That was the last I ever heard about it," Rennert said. "People bring it up mostly because they believe they're supposed to." (The woman loved the car and said she'd be back soon with her husband to hammer out a deal.)

Joan Ryan is a columnist for the *San Francisco Chronicle,* where this column appeared on May 20, 2004.

10 To understand Americans, it is essential for the rest of the world to remember that, underneath it all, we are socially responsible beings just like they are, except we like big things and lots of them. In the United States, there are now 204 million cars and 191 million drivers, more cars than we have people to operate them. Blueberry muffins here are the size of our heads. Soda cups are big enough to harbor small children. We build houses designed on the well-known scientific practice of multiplying the number of family members by pi to reach the appropriate number of bathrooms.

If the rest of the world wants to understand us better, I recommend they see the new movie, *Supersize Me!* It's a documentary about a guy who eats nothing but McDonald's food for a month. The movie reinforces what we Americans already know and have known for years: Fast food makes us fat and unhealthy. The movies shows, too, that this knowledge makes no difference whatsoever in our behavior. We still pull up to the golden arches, breathe in that great deep-fry aroma, and order a sack of cholesterol to go.

Why? For the same reasons we buy big cars despite our heartfelt concerns about saving the environment and weaning ourselves from Middle East oil: because it makes us feel good, and because everybody else is doing it.

Across the bay in Richmond, at the ARCO station on Cutting Boulevard and Harbor Way, Sandra Currier filled up her 1998 Chevy Blazer for $42 the other day. "This is the most I've ever paid," she said of the $2.29 regular unleaded. "It's got to come down."

She is a mobile notary public from Castro Valley who sometimes has to travel as much as 200 miles in a day. She is considering charging more for her services to cover the rising price of gas, but gas is not yet expensive enough to consider trading in her Blazer for something smaller and more fuel-efficient. Maybe when it hits $2.75 a gallon, she said.

15 "I feel my daughter is safer in the SUV," Currier said. "I don't want to be lower (than everybody else on the road), looking up and getting crunched."

In other words, if everybody else downsized, she would, too. Until then, she's not going to put herself in harm's way by being the poodle on a freeway of water buffalo.

How can the rest of the world blame her? They would do the same under the same circumstances, according to another CNW survey. In Western Europe, respondents said if gas prices were low enough, they would buy SUVs and big sedans, just like the Americans.

"It is kind of amusing," Spinella said. "When we do an international wish list, it's remarkable how similar people are in the kinds of things they would like to get their hands on."

See? There it is. We could be as responsible as the rest of the world if we had the benefit they do of high gas prices. The low price of gas in the United States enables our SUV indulgences. To put this complex social dynamic in the parlance of the latest psychological research: It is not our fault.

Therefore, since this situation is not of our own making, we should 20
not have to pay higher gas prices and give up the big-car life to which we have become accustomed. That would not be right.

And if there is one thing Americans believe in, it is doing what's right.

READING AND DISCUSSION QUESTIONS

1. In the first paragraph, how does Ryan reveal her attitude toward Americans' spending habits?
2. Does Ryan offer any support for her opinion other than her own emotional response to the values of other Americans?
3. How does Ryan's choice of language help her to make her point?
4. Is Ryan's use of sarcasm and exaggeration effective?

WRITING SUGGESTIONS

5. Rewrite Ryan's article using objective language.
6. Choose another one of America's "passions" and write an essay poking gentle fun at it. (Consider, for example, Americans' consumption of fast food.)
7. Compare Ryan's use of language in this piece with that used by Varian in "The True Cost of SUVs" in Chapter 7.

$hotgun Weddings

KATHA POLLITT

What would the government have to do to convince you to get married when you otherwise wouldn't? More than pay you $80 a month, I'll bet, the amount Wisconsin's much-ballyhooed "Bridefare" pilot program offered unwed teen welfare mothers beginning in the early nineties, which is perhaps why then-Governor Tommy Thompson, now Health and Human Services Secretary,[1] was uninterested in having it properly evaluated and why you don't hear much about Bridefare today. OK, how about $100 a month? That's what West Virginia is currently offering to add to a couple's welfare benefits if they wed. But even though the state has simultaneously cut by 25 percent the checks of recipients living with adults to whom they are not married (including, in some cases, their own grown

[1]Thompson resigned on December 3, 2004.

Katha Pollitt has written about controversial moral and political issues for *The Nation*, *The New Yorker*, and the *New York Times*. This selection originally appeared in the February 4, 2002, edition of *The Nation*.

children, if you can believe that!), results have been modest: Only around 1,600 couples have applied for the bonus and presumably some of these would have married anyway. With the state's welfare budget expected to show a $90 million shortfall by 2003, the marriage bonus is likely to be quietly abolished.

Although welfare reform was sold to the public as promoting work, the Personal Responsibility and Work Opportunity Reconciliation Act of 1996 actually opens with the declaration that "marriage is the foundation of a successful society." According to Charles Murray, Robert Rector, and other right-wing ideologues, welfare enabled poor women to rely on the state instead of husbands; forcing them off the dole and into the rigors of low-wage employment would push them into marriage, restore "the family," and lift children out of poverty. That was always a silly idea. For one thing, as any single woman could have told them, it wrongly assumed that whether a woman married was only up to her; for another, it has been well documented that the men available to poor women are also poor and often (like the women) have other problems as well: In one study, 30 percent of poor single fathers were unemployed in the week before the survey and almost 40 percent had been incarcerated; drugs, drink, violence, poor health, and bad attitudes were not uncommon. Would Murray want *his* daughter to marry a guy with even one of those strikes against him? Not surprisingly, there has been no upsurge of marriage among former welfare recipients since 1996. Of all births, the proportion that are to unwed mothers has stayed roughly where it was, at 33 percent.

Since the stick of work and the carrot of cash have both proved ineffective in herding women to the altar, family values conservatives are calling for more lectures. Marriage promotion will be a hot item when welfare reform comes up for reauthorization later this year. At the federal level conservatives are calling for 10 percent of all TANF [Temporary Assistance for Needy Families] money to be set aside for promoting marriage; Utah, Arizona, and Oklahoma have already raided TANF to fund such ventures as a "healthy marriage" handbook for couples seeking a marriage license. And it's not just Republicans: Senator Joe Lieberman and Representative Ben Cardin, the ranking Democrat on the House Ways and Means Committee, are also interested in funding "family formation." In place of cash bonuses to individuals, which at least put money in the pockets of poor people, look for massive funding of faith-based marriage preparation courses (and never you mind that pesky separation of church and state), for fatherhood intervention programs, classes to instruct poor single moms in the benefits of marriage (as if they didn't know!), for self-help groups like Marriage Savers, abstinence education for kids and grownups alike and, of course, ingenious pilot projects by the dozen. There's even been a proposal to endow pro-marriage professorships at state universities—and don't forget millions of dollars for evaluation, follow-up, filing and forgetting.

There's nothing wrong with programs that aim to raise people's marital IQ—I love that journalistic evergreen about the engaged couple who take a quiz in order to qualify for a church wedding and call it off when they discover he wants seven kids and she wants to live in a tree. But remember when it was conservatives who argued against social engineering and micro-managing people's private lives and "throwing money at the problem"?

Domestic violence experts have warned that poor women may find 5
themselves pushed into marrying their abusers and staying with them—in a disturbing bit of Senate testimony, Mike McManus of Marriage Savers said domestic violence could usually be overcome with faith-based help. Is that the message women in danger should be getting? But there are even larger issues: Marriage is a deeply personal, intimate matter, involving our most private, barely articulated selves. Why should the government try to maneuver reluctant women into dubious choices just because they are poor? Even as a meal ticket wedlock is no panacea—that marriage is a cure for poverty is only true if you marry someone who isn't poor, who will share his income with you and your children, who won't divorce you later and leave you worse off than ever. The relation between poverty and marriage is virtually the opposite of what pro-marriage ideologues claim: It isn't that getting married gives feckless poor people middle-class values and stability; it's that stable middle-class people are the ones who can "afford" to be married. However marriage functioned a half-century ago, today it is a class marker. Instead of marketing marriage as a poverty program, how much better to invest in poor women—and poor men—as human beings in their own right: with education, training for high-paying jobs, housing, mental health services, really good child-care for their kids. Every TANF dollar spent on marital propaganda means a dollar less for programs that really help people.

The very fact that welfare reformers are reduced to bribing, cajoling, and guilt-tripping people into marriage should tell us something. Or have they just not hit on the right incentive? As a divorced single mother, I've given some thought to what it would take for me to marry against my own inclination in order to make America great again. Here's my offer: If the government brings Otis Redding back to life and books him to sing at my wedding, I will marry the Devil himself. And if the Devil is unavailable, my ex-husband says he's ready.

READING AND DISCUSSION QUESTIONS

1. What claim is Pollitt supporting in the essay?
2. What does Pollitt reveal about the history of welfare reform as it relates to marriage? Where does Pollitt say the money for welfare reform is going? Where should it go?
3. Where does Pollitt's word choice reveal her bias? Does her own opinion keep her from being fair?

WRITING SUGGESTIONS

4. Write an essay in which you either support or refute Pollitt's claim.
5. If a monetary marriage bonus is not enough to entice many unwed Americans to get married, what might be enough?

Politics and the English Language

GEORGE ORWELL

Most people who bother with the matter at all would admit that the English language is in a bad way, but it is generally assumed that we cannot by conscious action do anything about it. Our civilization is decadent and our language—so the argument runs—must inevitably share in the general collapse. It follows that any struggle against the abuse of language is a sentimental archaism, like preferring candles to electric light or hansom cabs to aeroplanes. Underneath this lies the half-conscious belief that language is a natural growth and not an instrument which we shape for our own purposes.

Now, it is clear that the decline of a language must ultimately have political and economic causes: It is not due simply to the bad influence of this or that individual writer. But an effect can become a cause, reinforcing the original cause and producing the same effect in an intensified form, and so on indefinitely. A man may take to drink because he feels himself to be a failure, and then fail all the more completely because he drinks. It is rather the same thing that is happening to the English language. It becomes ugly and inaccurate because our thoughts are foolish, but the slovenliness of our language makes it easier for us to have foolish thoughts. The point is that the process is reversible. Modern English, especially written English, is full of bad habits which spread by imitation and which can be avoided if one is willing to take the necessary trouble. If one gets rid of these habits one can think more clearly, and to think clearly is a necessary first step towards political regeneration: So that the fight against bad English is not frivolous and is not the exclusive concern of professional writers. I will come back to this presently, and I hope that by that time the meaning of what I have said here will have become clearer.

This essay, written shortly after World War II, develops George Orwell's claim that careless and dishonest use of language contributes to careless and dishonest thought and political corruption. Political language, he argues, is "largely the defense of the indefensible." But Orwell (1903–1950), novelist, critic, and political satirist—best known for his books *Animal Farm* (1945) and *1984* (1949)—believes that bad language habits can be reversed, and he lists rules for getting rid of some of the most offensive. This essay first appeared in *Horizon* in April 1946.

Meanwhile, here are five specimens of the English language as it is now habitually written.

These five passages have not been picked out because they are especially bad—I could have quoted far worse if I had chosen—but because they illustrate various of the mental vices from which we now suffer. They are a little below the average, but are fairly representative samples. I number them so that I can refer back to them when necessary:

> (1) I am not, indeed, sure whether it is not true to say that the Milton who once seemed not unlike a seventeenth-century Shelley had not become out of an experience ever more bitter in each year, more alien *[sic]* to the founder of that Jesuit sect which nothing could induce him to tolerate.
>
> Professor Harold Laski (Essay in *Freedom of Expression*)

> (2) Above all, we cannot play ducks and drakes with a native battery of idioms which prescribes such egregious collocations of vocables as the Basic *put up with* for *tolerate* or *put at a loss* for *bewilder.*
>
> Professor Lancelot Hogben *(Interglossa)*

> (3) On the one side we have the free personality: By definition it is not neurotic, for it has neither conflict nor dream. Its desires, such as they are, are transparent, for they are just what institutional approval keeps in the forefront of consciousness; another institutional pattern would alter their number and intensity; there is little in them that is natural, irreducible, or culturally dangerous. But *on the other side,* the social bond itself is nothing but the mutual reflection of these self-secure integrities. Recall the definition of love. Is not this the very picture of a small academic? Where is there a place in this hall of mirrors for either personality or fraternity?
>
> Essay on psychology in *Politics* (New York)

> (4) All the "best people" from the gentlemen's clubs, and all the frantic fascist captains, united in common hatred of Socialism and bestial horror of the rising tide of the mass revolutionary movement, have turned to acts of provocation, to foul incendiarism, to medieval legends of poisoned wells, to legalize their own destruction of proletarian organizations, and rouse the agitated petty-bourgeoisie to chauvinistic fervor on behalf of the fight against the revolutionary way out of the crisis.
>
> Communist pamphlet

> (5) If a new spirit *is* to be infused into this old country, there is one thorny and contentious reform which must be tackled, and that is the humanization and galvanization of the BBC. Timidity here will bespeak cancer and atrophy of the soul. The heart of Britain may be sound and of strong beat, for instance, but the British lion's roar at present is like that of Bottom in Shakespeare's *Midsummer Night's Dream*—as gentle as any sucking dove. A virile new Britain cannot continue indefinitely to be traduced in the eyes or rather ears, of the world by the effete languors of Langham Place, brazenly masquerading as "standard English." When the Voice of Britain is heard at nine o'clock, better far and infinitely less ludicrous to hear aitches honestly dropped than the present

> priggish, inflated, inhibited, school-ma'amish arch braying of blameless bashful mewing maidens!
>
> Letter in *Tribune*

Each of these passages has faults of its own, but, quite apart from avoidable ugliness, two qualities are common to all of them. The first is staleness of imagery: The other is lack of precision. The writer either has a meaning and cannot express it, or he inadvertently says something else, or he is almost indifferent as to whether his words mean anything or not. The mixture of vagueness and sheer incompetence is the most marked characteristic of modern English prose, and especially of any kind of political writing. As soon as certain topics are raised, the concrete melts into the abstract and no one seems to think of turns of speech that are not hackneyed: Prose consists less and less of *words* chosen for the sake of their meaning, and more and more of *phrases* tacked together like the sections of a prefabricated hen-house. I list below, with notes and examples, various of the tricks by means of which the work of prose-construction is habitually dodged:

Dying metaphors. A newly invented metaphor assists thought by evoking 5
a visual image, while on the other hand a metaphor which is technically "dead" (e.g., *iron resolution*) has in effect reverted to being an ordinary word and can generally be used without loss of vividness. But in between these two classes there is a huge dump of worn-out metaphors which have lost all evocative power and are merely used because they save people the trouble of inventing phrases for themselves. Examples are: *ring the changes on, take up the cudgels for, toe the line, ride roughshod over, stand shoulder to shoulder with, play into the hands of, no axe to grind, grist to the mill, fishing in troubled waters, rift within the lute, on the order of the day, Achilles' heel, swan song, hotbed.* Many of these are used without knowledge of their meaning (what is a "rift," for instance?), and incompatible metaphors are frequently mixed, a sure sign that the writer is not interested in what he is saying. Some metaphors now current have been twisted out of their original meaning without those who use them even being aware of the fact. For example, *toe the line* is sometimes written *tow the line*. Another example is *the hammer and the anvil,* now always used with the implication that the anvil gets the worst of it. In real life it is always the anvil that breaks the hammer, never the other way about: A writer who stopped to think what he was saying would be aware of this, and would avoid perverting the original phrase.

Operators or verbal false limbs. These save the trouble of picking out appropriate verbs and nouns, and at the same time pad each sentence with extra syllables which give it an appearance of symmetry. Characteristic phrases are: *render inoperative, militate against, make contact with, be sub-*

jected to, give rise to, give grounds for, have the effect of, play a leading part (role) in, make itself felt, take effect, exhibit a tendency to, serve the purpose of, etc., etc. The keynote is the elimination of simple verbs. Instead of being a single word, such as *break, stop, spoil, mend, kill,* a verb becomes a *phrase,* made up of a noun or adjective tacked on to some general-purpose verb such as *prove, serve, form, play, render.* In addition, the passive voice is wherever possible used in preference to the active, and noun constructions are used instead of gerunds (*by examination of* instead of *by examining*). The range of verbs is further cut down by means of the *-ize* and *de-* formation, and the banal statements are given an appearance of profundity by means of the *not un-* formation. Simple conjunctions and prepositions are replaced by such phrases as *with respect to, having regard to, the fact that, by dint of, in view of, in the interests of, on the hypothesis that;* and the ends of sentences are saved from anticlimax by such resounding commonplaces as *greatly to be desired, cannot be left out of account, a development to be expected in the near future, deserving of serious consideration, brought to a satisfactory conclusion,* and so on and so forth.

Pretentious diction. Words like *phenomenon, element, individual* (as noun), *objective, categorical, effective, virtual, basic, primary, promote, constitute, exhibit, exploit, utilize, eliminate, liquidate,* are used to dress up simple statements and give an air of scientific impartiality to biased judgments. Adjectives like *epoch-making, epic, historic, unforgettable, triumphant, age-old, inevitable, inexorable, veritable,* are used to dignify the sordid processes of international politics, while writing that aims at glorifying war usually takes on an archaic color, its characteristic words being: *realm, throne, chariot, mailed fist, trident, sword, shield, buckler, banner, jackboot, clarion.* Foreign words and expressions such as *cul de sac, ancien régime, deus ex machina, mutatis mutandis, status quo, gleichshaltung, weltanschauung,* are used to give an air of culture and elegance. Except for the useful abbreviations *i.e., e.g.,* and *etc.,* there is no real need for any of the hundreds of foreign phrases now current in English. Bad writers, and especially scientific, political, and sociological writers, are nearly always haunted by the notion that Latin or Greek words are grander than Saxon ones, and unnecessary words like *expedite, ameliorate, predict, extraneous, deracinated, clandestine, subaqueous,* and hundreds of others constantly gain ground from their Anglo-Saxon opposite numbers.[1] The jargon peculiar to Marxist writing (*hyena, hangman, cannibal, petty bourgeois, these gentry, lackey, flunkey, mad dog, White Guard,* etc.) consists largely of words and phrases

[1] An interesting illustration of this is the way in which the English flower names which were in use till very recently are being ousted by Greek ones, *snapdragon* becoming *antirrhinum, forget-me-not* becoming *myosotis,* etc. It is hard to see any practical reason for this change of fashion: It is probably due to an instinctive turning-away from the more homely word and a vague feeling that the Greek word is scientific. [All notes are Orwell's.]

translated from Russian, German, or French; but the normal way of coining a new word is to use a Latin or Greek root with the appropriate affix and, where necessary, the *-ize* formation. It is often easier to make up words of this kind (*deregionalize, impermissible, extramarital, nonfragmentatory,* and so forth) than to think up the English words that will cover one's meaning. The result, in general, is an increase in slovenliness and vagueness.

Meaningless words. In certain kinds of writing, particularly in art criticism and literary criticism, it is normal to come across long passages which are almost completely lacking in meaning.[2] Words like *romantic, plastic, values, human, dead, sentimental, natural, vitality,* as used in art criticism, are strictly meaningless in the sense that they not only do not point to any discoverable object, but are hardly ever expected to do so by the reader. When one critic writes, "The outstanding feature of Mr. X's work is its living quality," while another writes, "The immediately striking thing about Mr. X's work is its peculiar deadness," the reader accepts this as a simple difference of opinion. If words like *black* and *white* were involved, instead of the jargon words *dead* and *living,* he would see at once that language was being used in an improper way. Many political words are similarly abused. The word *fascism* has now no meaning except insofar as it signifies "something not desirable." The words *democracy, socialism, freedom, patriotic, realistic, justice,* have each of them several different meanings which cannot be reconciled with one another. In the case of a word like *democracy,* not only is there no agreed definition, but the attempt to make one is resisted from all sides. It is almost universally felt that when we call a country democratic we are praising it: Consequently the defenders of every kind of regime claim that it is a democracy, and fear that they might have to stop using the word if it were tied down to any one meaning. Words of this kind are often used in a consciously dishonest way. That is, the person who uses them has his own private definition, but allows his hearer to think he means something quite different. Statements like *Marshal Pétain was a true patriot, The Soviet Press is the freest in the world, The Catholic Church is opposed to persecution,* are almost always made with intent to deceive. Other words used in variable meanings, in most cases more or less dishonestly, are: *class, totalitarian, science, progressive, reactionary, bourgeois, equality.*

Now that I have made this catalog of swindles and perversions, let me give another example of the kind of writing that they lead to. This time

[2]Example: "Comfort's catholicity of perception and image, strangely Whitmanesque in range, almost the exact opposite in aesthetic compulsion, continues to evoke that trembling atmospheric accumulative hinting at a cruel, an inexorably serene timelessness. . . . Wrey Gardiner scores by aiming at simple bull's-eyes with precision. Only they are not so simple, and through this contended sadness runs more than the surface bittersweet of resignation" (*Poetry Quarterly*).

it must of its nature be an imaginary one. I am going to translate a passage of good English into modern English of the worst sort. Here is a well-known verse from Ecclesiastes:

> I returned and saw under the sun, that the race is not to the swift, nor the battle to the strong, neither yet bread to the wise, nor yet riches to men of understanding, nor yet favor to men of skill; but time and chance happeneth to them all.

Here it is in modern English:

> Objective consideration of contemporary phenomena compels the conclusion that success or failure in competitive activities exhibits no tendency to be commensurate with innate capacity, but that a considerable element of the unpredictable must invariably be taken into account.

10 This is a parody, but not a very gross one. Exhibit (3), above, for instance, contains several patches of the same kind of English. It will be seen that I have not made a full translation. The beginning and ending of the sentence follow the original meaning fairly closely, but in the middle the concrete illustrations—race, battle, bread—dissolve into the vague phrase "success or failure in competitive activities." This had to be so, because no modern writer of the kind I am discussing—no one capable of using phrases like "objective consideration of contemporary phenomena"—would ever tabulate his thoughts in that precise and detailed way. The whole tendency of modern prose is away from concreteness. Now analyze these two sentences a little more closely. The first contains forty-nine words but only sixty syllables, and all its words are those of everyday life. The second contains thirty-eight words of ninety syllables: Eighteen of its words are from Latin roots, and one from Greek. The first sentence contains six vivid images, and only one phrase ("time and chance") that could be called vague. The second contains not a single fresh, arresting phrase, and in spite of its ninety syllables it gives only a shortened version of the meaning contained in the first. Yet without a doubt it is the second kind of sentence that is gaining ground in modern English. I do not want to exaggerate. This kind of writing is not yet universal, and outcrops of simplicity will occur here and there in the worst-written page. Still, if you or I were told to write a few lines on the uncertainty of human fortunes, we should probably come much nearer to my imaginary sentence than to the one from Ecclesiastes.

As I have tried to show, modern writing at its worst does not consist in picking out words for the sake of their meaning and inventing images in order to make the meaning clearer. It consists in gumming together long strips of words which have already been set in order by someone else, and making the results presentable by sheer humbug. The attraction of this way of writing is that it is easy. It is easier—even quicker once you have the habit—to say *In my opinion it is a not unjustifiable assumption that* than to say *I think*. If you use ready-made phrases, you not only don't have to hunt about for words; you also don't have to bother with the rhythms of your sentences, since these phrases are generally so arranged as to be more or less euphonious. When you are composing in a hurry—when you are dictating to a stenographer, for instance, or making a public speech—it is natural to fall into a pretentious, Latinized style. Tags like *a consideration which we should do well to bear in mind* or *a conclusion to which all of us would readily assent* will save many a sentence from coming down with a bump. By using stale metaphors, similes, and idioms, you save much mental effort, at the cost of leaving your meaning vague, not only for your reader but for yourself. This is the significance of mixed metaphors. The sole aim of a metaphor is to call up a visual image. When these images clash—as in *The Fascist octopus has sung its swan song, the jackboot is thrown into the melting pot*—it can be taken as certain that the writer is not seeing a mental image of the objects he is naming; in other words he is not really thinking. Look again at the examples I gave at the beginning of this essay. Professor Laski (1) uses five negatives in fifty-three words. One of these is superfluous, making nonsense of the whole passage, and in addition there is the slip *alien* for akin, making further nonsense, and several avoidable pieces of clumsiness which increase the general vagueness. Professor Hogben (2) plays ducks and drakes with a battery which is able to write prescriptions, and, while disapproving of the everyday phrase *put up with*, is unwilling to look *egregious* up in the dictionary and see what it means. (3), if one takes an uncharitable attitude towards it, is simply meaningless: Probably one could work out its intended meaning by reading the whole of the article in which it occurs. In (4), the writer knows more or less what he wants to say, but an accumulation of stale phrases chokes him like tea leaves blocking a sink. In (5), words and meaning have almost parted company. People who write in this manner usually have a general emotional meaning—they dislike one thing and want to express solidarity with another—but they are not interested in the detail of what they are saying. A scrupulous writer, in every sentence that he writes, will ask himself at least four questions, thus: What am I trying to say? What words will express it? What image or idiom will make it clearer? Is this image fresh enough to have an effect? And he will probably ask himself two more: Could I put it more shortly? Have I said anything that is avoidably ugly? But you are not obliged to go to all this trouble. You can shirk it by simply throwing your mind open and letting the ready-made phrases come crowding in. They will construct your sentences for you—even think your thoughts for you, to a certain extent—and at need they will perform the important service of partially concealing your meaning even from yourself. It is at this point that the special connection between politics and the debasement of language becomes clear.

In our time it is broadly true that political writing is bad writing. Where it is not true, it will generally be found that the writer is some kind of rebel, expressing his private opinions and not a "party line." Orthodoxy, of whatever color, seems to demand a lifeless, imitative style. The political dialects to be found in pamphlets, leading articles, manifestos, White Papers, and the speeches of undersecretaries do, of course, vary from party to party, but they are all alike in that one almost never finds in them a fresh, vivid, home-made turn of speech. When one watches some tired hack on the platform mechanically repeating the familiar phrases—*bestial atrocities, iron heel, bloodstained tyranny, free peoples of the world, stand shoulder to shoulder*—one often has a curious feeling that one is not watching a live human being but some kind of dummy; a feeling which suddenly becomes stronger at moments when the light catches the speaker's spectacles and turns them into blank discs which seem to have no eyes behind them. And this is not altogether fanciful. A speaker who uses that kind of phraseology has gone some distance towards turning himself into a machine. The appropriate noises are coming out of his larynx, but his brain is not involved as it would be if he were choosing his words for himself. If the speech he is making is one that he is accustomed to make over and over again, he may be almost unconscious of what he is saying, as one is when one utters the responses in church. And this reduced state of consciousness, if not indispensable, is at any rate favorable to political conformity.

In our time, political speech and writing are largely the defense of the indefensible. Things like the continuance of British rule in India, the Russian purges and deportations, the dropping of the atom bombs on Japan, can indeed be defended, but only by arguments which are too brutal for most people to face, and which do not square with the professed aims of political parties. Thus political language has to consist largely of euphemism, question-begging, and sheer cloudy vagueness. Defenseless villages are bombarded from the air, the inhabitants driven out into the countryside, the cattle machine-gunned, the huts set on fire with incendiary bullets: This is called *pacification*. Millions of peasants are robbed of their farms and sent trudging along the roads with no more than they can carry; this is called *transfer of population* or *rectification of frontiers*. People are imprisoned for years without trial, or shot in the back of the neck, or sent to die of scurvy in Arctic lumber camps: This is called *elimination of unreliable elements*. Such phraseology is needed if one wants to name things without calling up mental pictures of them. Consider for instance some comfortable English professor defending Russian totalitarianism. He cannot say outright, "I believe in killing off your opponents when you can get good results by doing so." Probably, therefore, he will say something like this:

> While freely conceding that the Soviet régime exhibits certain features which the humanitarian may be inclined to deplore, we must, I think, agree that a certain curtailment of the right to political opposition is an

> unavoidable concomitant of transitional periods, and that the rigors which the Russian people have been called upon to undergo have been amply justified in the sphere of concrete achievement.

The inflated style is itself a kind of euphemism. A mass of Latin words fall upon the facts like soft snow, blurring the outlines and covering up all the details. The great enemy of clear language is insincerity. When there is a gap between one's real and one's declared aims, one turns as it were instinctively to long words and exhausted idioms, like a cuttlefish squirting out ink. In our age there is no such thing as "keeping out of politics." All issues are political issues, and politics itself is a mass of lies, evasions, folly, hatred, and schizophrenia. When the general atmosphere is bad, language must suffer. I should expect to find—this is a guess which I have not sufficient knowledge to verify—that the German, Russian, and Italian languages have all deteriorated in the last ten or fifteen years, as a result of dictatorship.

But if thought corrupts language, language can also corrupt thought. 15
A bad usage can spread by tradition and imitation, even among people who should and do know better. The debased language that I have been discussing is in some ways very convenient. Phrases like *a not unjustifiable assumption, leaves much to be desired, would serve no good purpose, a consideration which we should do well to bear in mind,* are a continuous temptation, a packet of aspirins always at one's elbow. Look back through this essay, and for certain you will find that I have again and again committed the very faults I am protesting against. By this morning's post I have received a pamphlet dealing with conditions in Germany. The author tells me that he "felt impelled" to write it. I open it at random, and here is almost the first sentence that I see: "(The Allies) have an opportunity not only of achieving a radical transformation of Germany's social and political structure in such a way as to avoid a nationalistic reaction in Germany itself, but at the same time of laying the foundations of a cooperative and unified Europe." You see, he "feels impelled" to write—feels, presumably, that he has something new to say—and yet his words, like cavalry horses answering the bugle, group themselves automatically into the familiar dreary pattern. This invasion of one's mind by ready-made phrases *(lay the foundations, achieve a radical transformation)* can only be prevented if one is constantly on guard against them, and every such phrase anesthetizes a portion of one's brain.

I said earlier that the decadence of our language is probably curable. Those who deny this would argue, if they produced an argument at all, that language merely reflects existing social conditions, and that we cannot influence its development by any direct tinkering with words and constructions. So far as the general tone or spirit of a language goes, this may be true, but it is not true in detail. Silly words and expressions have often disappeared, not through any evolutionary process but owing to the conscious action of a minority. Two recent examples were *explore every avenue* and *leave no stone unturned,* which were killed by the jeers of a few journalists. There is a long list of flyblown metaphors which could similarly be got rid of if enough people would interest themselves in the job; and it should also be possible to laugh the *not un-* formation out of existence,[3] to reduce the amount of Latin and Greek in the average sentence, to drive out foreign phrases and strayed scientific words, and, in general, to make pretentiousness unfashionable. But all these are minor points. The defense of the English language implies more than this, and perhaps it is best to start by saying what it does *not* imply.

To begin with it has nothing to do with archaism, with the salvaging of obsolete words and turns of speech, or with the setting up of a "standard English" which must never be departed from. On the contrary, it is especially concerned with the scrapping of every word or idiom which has outworn its usefulness. It has nothing to do with correct grammar and syntax, which are of no importance so long as one makes one's meaning clear, or with the avoidance of Americanisms, or with having what is called a "good prose style." On the other hand it is not concerned with fake simplicity and the attempt to make written English colloquial. Nor does it even imply in every case preferring the Saxon word to the Latin one, though it does imply using the fewest and shortest words that will cover one's meaning. What is above all needed is to let the meaning choose the word, and not the other way about. In prose, the worst thing one can do with words is to surrender to them. When you think of a concrete object, you think wordlessly, and then, if you want to describe the thing you have been visualizing you probably hunt about till you find the exact words that seem to fit. When you think of something abstract you are more inclined to use words from the start, and unless you make a conscious effort to prevent it, the existing dialect will come rushing in and do the job for you, at the expense of blurring or even changing your meaning. Probably it is better to put off using words as long as possible and get one's meaning as clear as one can through pictures or sensations. Afterwards one can choose—not simply *accept*—the phrases that will best cover the meaning, and then switch round and decide what impression one's words are likely to make on another person. This last effort of the mind cuts out all stale or mixed images, all prefabricated phrases, needless repetitions, and humbug and vagueness generally. But one can often be in doubt about the effect of a word or a phrase, and one needs rules that one can rely on when instinct fails. I think the following rules will cover most cases:

(i) Never use a metaphor, simile, or other figure of speech which you are used to seeing in print.

(ii) Never use a long word where a short one will do.

[3]One can cure oneself of the *not un-* formation by memorizing this sentence: *A not unblack dog was chasing a not unsmall rabbit across a not ungreen field.*

(iii) If it is possible to cut a word out, always cut it out.

(iv) Never use the passive where you can use the active.

(v) Never use a foreign phrase, a scientific word, or a jargon word if you can think of an everyday English equivalent.

(vi) Break any of these rules sooner than say anything outright barbarous.

These rules sound elementary, and so they are, but they demand a deep change in attitude in anyone who has grown used to writing in the style now fashionable. One could keep all of them and still write bad English, but one could not write the kind of stuff that I quoted in those five specimens at the beginning of this article.

I have not here been considering the literary use of language, but merely language as an instrument for expressing and not for concealing or preventing thought. Stuart Chase and others have come near to claiming that all abstract words are meaningless, and have used this as a pretext for advocating a kind of political quietism. Since you don't know what Fascism is, how can you struggle against Fascism? One need not swallow such absurdities as this, but one ought to recognize that the present political chaos is connected with the decay of language, and that one can probably bring about some improvement by starting at the verbal end. If you simplify your English, you are freed from the worst follies of orthodoxy. You cannot speak any of the necessary dialects, and when you make a stupid remark its stupidity will be obvious, even to yourself. Political language—and with variations this is true of all political parties, from Conservatives to Anarchists—is designed to make lies sound truthful and murder respectable, and to give an appearance of solidity to pure wind. One cannot change this all in a moment, but one can at least change one's own habits, and from time to time one can even, if one jeers loudly enough, send some worn-out and useless phrase—some *jackboot, Achilles' heel, hotbed, melting pot, acid test, veritable inferno,* or other lump of verbal refuse—into the dustbin where it belongs.

DISCUSSION QUESTIONS

1. Orwell disagrees with a common assumption about language. What is it? Where in the essay does he attack this assumption directly?
2. What faults do his five samples of bad language have in common? Select examples of these faults in each passage.
3. What "tricks" (para. 4) for avoiding good prose does Orwell list? Do you think that some are more dangerous or misleading than others? Explain the reasons for your answer.
4. What different reasons does Orwell suggest for the slovenliness of much political writing and speaking? What examples does he give to support these reasons? Are they persuasive?

5. How does Orwell propose that we get rid of our bad language habits? Do you think his recommendations are realistic? Can the teaching of writing in school assist in the remedy?
6. Why does Orwell urge the reader to "look back through this essay" to find "the very faults I am protesting against" (para. 15)? Can you, in fact, find any?

WRITING SUGGESTIONS

7. Choose a speech or an editorial whose meaning seems to be obscured by pretentious diction, meaningless words, euphemism, or "sheer cloudy vagueness." Point out the real meaning of the piece. If you think that its purpose is deceptive, expose the unpleasant truth that the author is concealing. Use Orwell's device, giving concrete meaning to any abstractions. (One source of speeches is a publication called *Vital Speeches of the Day*. Another is the *New York Times*, which often prints in full, or excerpts major portions of, speeches by leading figures in public life.)
8. Orwell's essay appeared before the widespread use of television. Do you think that TV makes it harder for politicians to be dishonest? Choose a particular public event—a war, a street riot, a terrorist activity, a campaign stop—and argue either for or against the claim that televised coverage makes it harder for a politician to engage in "sheer cloudy vagueness." Or does it make no difference at all? Be specific in your use of evidence.

DEBATE: Does the government have the right to regulate guns?

The Right to Bear Arms

WARREN E. BURGER

Our metropolitan centers, and some suburban communities of America, are setting new records for homicides by handguns. Many of our large centers have up to ten times the murder rate of all of Western Europe. In 1988, there were 9,000 handgun murders in America. Last year, Washington, D.C., alone had more than 400 homicides—setting a new record for our capital.

The Constitution of the United States, in its Second Amendment, guarantees a "right of the people to keep and bear arms." However, the meaning of this clause cannot be understood except by looking to the purpose,

Warren E. Burger (1907–1995) was chief justice of the United States from 1969 to 1986. This article is from the January 14, 1990, issue of *Parade* magazine.

the setting, and the objectives of the draftsmen. The first ten amendments—the Bill of Rights—were not drafted at Philadelphia in 1787; that document came two years later than the Constitution. Most of the states already had bills of rights, but the Constitution might not have been ratified in 1788 if the states had not had assurances that a national Bill of Rights would soon be added.

People of that day were apprehensive about the new "monster" national government presented to them, and this helps explain the language and purpose of the Second Amendment. A few lines after the First Amendment's guarantees—against "establishment of religion," "free exercise" of religion, free speech and free press—came a guarantee that grew out of the deep-seated fear of a "national" or "standing" army. The same First Congress that approved the right to keep and bear arms also limited the national army to 840 men; Congress in the Second Amendment then provided:

> A well regulated Militia, being necessary to the security of a free State, the right of the people to keep and bear Arms, shall not be infringed.

In the 1789 debate in Congress on James Madison's proposed Bill of Rights, Elbridge Gerry argued that a state militia was necessary:

> to prevent the establishment of a standing army, the bane of liberty. . . . Whenever governments mean to invade the rights and liberties of the people, they always attempt to destroy the militia in order to raise an army upon their ruins.

We see that the need for a state militia was the predicate of the "right" 5
guaranteed; in short, it was declared "necessary" in order to have a state military force to protect the security of the state. That Second Amendment clause must be read as though the word "because" was the opening word of the guarantee. Today, of course, the "state militia" serves a very different purpose. A huge national defense establishment has taken over the role of the militia of 200 years ago.

Some have exploited these ancient concerns, blurring sporting guns—rifles, shotguns, and even machine pistols—with all firearms, including what are now called "Saturday night specials." There is, of course, a great difference between sporting guns and handguns. Some regulation of handguns has long been accepted as imperative; laws relating to "concealed weapons" are common. That we may be "overregulated" in some areas of life has never held us back from more regulation of automobiles, airplanes, motorboats, and "concealed weapons."

Let's look at the history.

First, many of the 3.5 million people living in the thirteen original Colonies depended on wild game for food, and a good many of them required firearms for their defense from marauding Indians—and later from the French and English. Underlying all these needs was an important concept that each able-bodied man in each of the thirteen independent states had to help or defend his state.

The early opposition to the idea of national or standing armies was maintained under the Articles of Confederation; that confederation had no standing army and wanted none. The state militia—essentially a part-time citizen army, as in Switzerland today—was the only kind of "army" they wanted. From the time of the Declaration of Independence through the victory at Yorktown in 1781, George Washington, as the commander in chief of these volunteer-militia armies, had to depend upon the states to send those volunteers.

10 When a company of New Jersey militia volunteers reported for duty to Washington at Valley Forge, the men initially declined to take an oath to "the United States," maintaining, "Our country is New Jersey." Massachusetts Bay men, Virginians, and others felt the same way. To the American of the eighteenth century, his state was his country, and his freedom was defended by his militia.

The victory at Yorktown—and the ratification of the Bill of Rights a decade later—did not change people's attitudes about a national army. They had lived for years under the notion that each state would maintain its own military establishment, and the seaboard states had their own navies as well. These people, and their fathers and grandfathers before them, remembered how monarchs had used standing armies to oppress their ancestors in Europe. Americans wanted no part of this. A state militia, like a rifle and powder horn, was as much a part of life as the automobile is today; pistols were largely for officers, aristocrats—and dueling.

Against this background, it was not surprising that the provision concerning firearms emerged in very simple terms with the significant predicate—basing the right on the *necessity* for a "well regulated militia," a state army.

In the two centuries since then—with two world wars and some lesser ones—it has become clear, sadly, that we have no choice but to maintain a standing national army while still maintaining a "militia" by way of the National Guard, which can be swiftly integrated into the national defense forces.

Americans also have a right to defend their homes, and we need not challenge that. Nor does anyone seriously question that the Constitution protects the right of hunters to own and keep sporting guns for hunting game any more than anyone would challenge the right to own and keep fishing rods and other equipment for fishing—or to own automobiles. To "keep and bear arms" for hunting today is essentially a recreational activity and not an imperative of survival, as it was 200 years ago; "Saturday night specials" and machine guns are not recreational weapons and surely are as much in need of regulation as motor vehicles.

15 Americans should ask themselves a few questions. The Constitution does not mention automobiles or motorboats, but the right to keep and own an automobile is beyond question; equally beyond question is the power of the state to regulate the purchase or the transfer of such vehicle

and the right to license the vehicle and the driver with reasonable standards. In some places, even a bicycle must be registered, as must some household dogs.

If we are to stop this mindless homicidal carnage, is it unreasonable:

1. to provide that, to acquire a firearm, an application be made reciting age, residence, employment, and any prior criminal convictions?
2. to require that this application lie on the table for ten days (absent a showing for urgent need) before the license would be issued?
3. that the transfer of a firearm be made essentially as that of a motor vehicle?
4. to have a "ballistic fingerprint" of the firearm made by the manufacturer and filed with the license record so that, if a bullet is found in a victim's body, law enforcement might be helped in finding the culprit?

These are the kinds of questions the American people must answer if we are to preserve the "domestic tranquility" promised in the Constitution.

A God-Given Natural Right

ROGER D. McGRATH

I do not believe in unilateral disarmament: not for the nation; not for our citizens. Neither did the Founding Fathers. They were students of history, especially of classical antiquity. They knew the history of the Greek city-states and Rome as well as they knew the history of the American colonies. This led them to conclude that an armed citizenry is essential to the preservation of freedom and democracy. Once disarmed, populations either submit meekly to tyrants or fight in vain.

The ancient Greeks knew this. The Greek city-state of Laconia had a population that was five percent Spartan (the warrior aristocracy), one percent *perioeci* (small merchants and craftsmen), and 94 percent *helots* (serfs bound to the soil). It is no mystery how five percent of the population kept 94 percent of the people enslaved. The *helots* were kept disarmed and, if found in possession of a weapon, were put to death.

For fifteen years, Roger McGrath taught courses in the history of the American West, California, and the United States at UCLA and has also taught at California State University, Northridge. He is a captain in the Naval Detachment of the California State Military Reserve. His articles have appeared in the *Wall Street Journal, American Guardian, Chronicles,* the *New York Times,* and *Harper's,* among others, and he appears extensively in documentaries about the West and has served as a consultant for television and movies. He is the author of *Gunfighters, Highwaymen, and Vigilantes* (1984) and coauthor of *Violence in America* (1989). This article appeared in the October 2003 issue of *Chronicles.*

Meanwhile, most of the Greek city-states were bastions of democracy because they had developed strong middle classes of armed citizens known as *hoplites*. Supplying their own weapons and equipment, the *hoplites* went into battle not out of fear of punishment or in hopes of plunder and booty, as did subject peoples of the Oriental empires, but to defend their liberties and to protect hearth and home. They fought side by side with neighbors, brothers, fathers, sons, uncles, and cousins. They did their utmost to demonstrate courage, side by side with their comrades in arms. If they lost a battle to the armies of an Oriental despot, they stood to lose everything—property, freedom, democracy. A defeat for subject peoples usually meant nothing more than a change of rulers.

The ancient Romans also knew this. When Tarquin, the Etruscan king of Rome, issued an order—for the public good, for safety and security—that the Romans be disarmed, they rose in rebellion. Tarquin was driven from the city, and the early Roman Republic was established. For several hundred years, Rome was defended not by a professional army of mercenaries or subject peoples but by armed citizen-soldiers who left the farm from time to time to serve the republic. Once the system broke down, the Roman Republic was transformed into an empire similar to the despotic regimes of the East.

5 Death and destruction commonly followed disarmament. England did it to the Gaels—the Irish and Scots—and the consequences beggar description. England had been fighting in Ireland for hundreds of years by the time the English got Irish leader Patrick Sarsfield to sign the Treaty of Limerick in 1691. The treaty guaranteed all Irish full civil, religious, and property rights. In return, it required that Sarsfield and more than 20,000 of his soldiers leave Ireland for the Continent.

With the armed defenders of Ireland overseas, England began to abrogate the rights supposedly guaranteed by the treaty. Beginning in 1709, England passed the statutes that collectively became known as the Penal Laws. One of the first of these laws declared that, for public safety, no Irish Catholic could keep and bear arms. Then the Irish Catholic was denied the right to an education, to enter a profession, to hold public office, to engage in trade or commerce, to own a horse of greater value than five pounds, to purchase or lease land, to vote, to attend the worship of his choice, to send his children abroad to receive an education. By the time the last of the Penal Laws was enacted, the Irish, although they were not chattel property, in many ways had fewer rights than black slaves in America. The Irish were kept on a near starvation diet, and their life expectancy was the lowest in the Western world.

Things were not much better in the Highlands of Scotland. England had subdued the Lowlands by the fourteenth century, but the Highlands, the truly Gaelic portion of Scotland, continued to be troublesome well into the eighteenth century. A major rebellion erupted in 1715; another, in 1745. The end for the Highlanders came at the Battle of Culloden in 1746. Following the battle, the English built a series of forts across the

Highlands and passed laws for the Highlanders—who were originally Irish, of course—similar to the Penal Laws. England made it a crime for the Highlanders to wear kilts, play bagpipes, and keep and bear arms. A Highlander found with a claymore or any other kind of sword or arm was put to death. The English army, understanding that it is easier to starve a fierce enemy into submission than to fight him, eagerly slaughtered the cattle herds of the Highlands, precipitating a great starvation. Thousands of Highlanders died or fled. The English later engaged in the infamous "clearances" in which thousands more were driven from the land. Without arms, the Highlanders were helpless.

What the English did to the Irish and Scots was not lost on our Founding Fathers or on the colonists in general. More than a quarter of the colonists were Irish or Scottish or Scotch-Irish. When England tried to disarm the American colonists, all under the guise of preserving public order and peace, the colonists reacted violently. While it is rarely taught in schools today, the reason the British army marched to Lexington and Concord was to confiscate the arms caches of the local citizenry.

It is not by accident, then, that the Framers of the Constitution ensured that the government could not infringe on "the right of the people to keep and bear arms." It is important to understand that the Second Amendment grants no right to the people to keep and bear arms. This is a point misunderstood by most Americans today, even by most of those who are interested in keeping their guns.

The Second Amendment, like the First, recognizes a God-given, nat- 10
ural right of the people and guarantees that the government not interfere with the exercise of that right. Note the wording of the amendment. Nowhere does it say, "This Constitution grants the people the right to . . ." Instead, it says "the right of the people . . . shall not be infringed." The right to keep and bear arms, like that of freedom of speech, is known, constitutionally, as an inherent right. By contrast, the Sixth Amendment right to be represented by an attorney in a criminal case is a derivative right—a right that comes from the Constitution.

To understand this is critical to all arguments about guns, or about freedom of speech, or religion, or the press. These freedoms were not given to us by the Founding Fathers. They were recognized by the Founding Fathers as God-given, natural rights that existed long before the establishment of our republic. These rights are not granted to men by a benevolent government but given to man by God. They are not to be destroyed, suppressed, or even compromised. When they are, it is the duty of the citizens to rise in revolt, overthrow the government, and establish a government that will protect these unalienable rights. Sound familiar? It should. This was the philosophy of our Founding Fathers.

The most basic of the natural rights of man is the right to self-preservation, the right to self-defense. No one would deny that we have such a right. In debates at universities and at other public forums, in debates on radio, in debates on television, I have never seen anyone deny that man has a natural right to self-defense. It follows that, if man has a natural right to self-defense, then he has a right to the arms necessary for that self-defense. The right to be armed is a logical and inescapable corollary of the right to self-defense. We cannot have one without the other.

If we do not have the right to the arms necessary for self-defense, then the right of self-defense is purely theoretical—something like having freedom of the press but not being allowed access to a printing press. Can you imagine the National Rifle Association telling the *New York Times* that it has freedom of the press but it may not have printing presses, or that the *Times* can purchase only one printing press per month, or that its writers must undergo background checks by the government, or that it cannot buy ink for the presses in New York City, or that its presses have limits on their speed and capacity, or that its presses must meet certain design requirements? If any of this were suggested, the *Times* would squeal like a stuck pig, and well it should.

Some people, presumably well intentioned, argue that the right to arms (and, thus, the right to self-defense) should be compromised—compromised further than it already has been—in an effort to make society safer. Such a position is ironic on two counts.

First, many of the same people who make gun-restriction arguments, 15
such as the ACLU, would be apoplectic if it were suggested that freedom of speech be curtailed to ensure greater public safety. For example, we could have a two-week waiting period on expressing an opinion after the opinion was duly registered with a government agency. That way, the government could screen the opinion to ensure that it was politically correct.

The compromise-your-rights-for-safety argument is also ironic because the thousands of gun laws on the books—municipal, county, state, and federal—have done nothing to stop crime. In fact, they have done the opposite. The laws, for the most part, have disarmed, or made access to guns more difficult for, the law-abiding, peaceable citizen. Criminals do not turn in their guns. Murderers, rapists, and robbers do not obey gun laws. However, they do calculate the risks involved in committing crime. If they can assume that potential victims are unarmed, they are emboldened and are more likely to attack.

John Lott, in *More Guns Less Crime*, an exhaustive county-by-county study of rates of gun ownership and crime, concludes that the counties with the highest rates of gun ownership have the least crime and that those with the lowest rates of gun ownership have the most crime. For years, this has been obvious when looking at cities. Washington, D.C., and New York City, for example, with the most restrictive gun laws in the nation, have, for a generation, been cesspools of crime. Criminals there know that they can count on their victims being unarmed.

I suspect that even deeply disturbed killers, such as the teenage boys in Littleton, Colorado, understood that they could kill with impunity in the disarmed environment of the high school. The presence of a highly trained, armed security guard, with a reputation as an expert marksman, may have deterred them. If not, then the guard might have granted them their suicidal wish before they were able to commit mass murder. One or two key teachers, trained and armed, might also have made a difference. Certainly, gun laws did nothing to stop the killers. The two boys violated more than a dozen different gun laws, including one of the oldest on the books—possession of a sawed-off shotgun. Gun laws promise much and deliver little, because they affect only the law abiding, something like sheep passing resolutions requiring vegetarianism while wolves circle the flock.

I grew up in Los Angeles when gun laws were few and crime was low. Nearly everyone I knew had a 30.06, a couple of .22s, a shotgun, and a revolver or two sitting around their house. We could buy guns mail-order and pick up our ammunition at the local grocery store. A gun was a common companion to the road maps in the glove compartment of the car. Did this cause crime? In 1952, there were 81 murders in Los Angeles. In 1992, 40 years and many gun laws later, there were 1,092 murders. If the increase in murder had kept pace with the increase in population, there would have been 142 murders, a 75 percent increase. Instead, murder increased 1,350 percent. Other crimes had similar increases: robbery, 1,540 percent; auto theft, 1,100 percent.

The Los Angeles Police Department used to solve more than 90 per- 20
cent of the murders committed in the city. Today, the figure is 60 percent. Detectives complain that the caseload is too great to conduct the kind of thorough investigations that were common in the '40s and '50s. It is far worse for lesser crimes. Merchants complain that customers brazenly walk out of their stores without paying for merchandise because they know that the police will not respond (at least in a timely fashion) to a call reporting shoplifting. Cars are stolen so often, some 200 per day, that the LAPD does nothing more than list the vehicle on a "hot sheet" and wish the victim good luck.

In the '50s, if your bicycle were stolen, the police would come out to your house and take a report. Try calling the LAPD today and telling them that your bike has been stolen! The police are simply overwhelmed by the sheer volume of crime and are kept fully occupied by murder, armed robbery, and rape—occupied, that is, by the aftermath of murder, armed robbery, and rape. When police arrive at the scene of a crime, the crime has already taken place—the victim has already been murdered, robbed, or raped.

"Carjacking" has become quite common in Los Angeles, because the carjackers know that California drivers cannot legally carry loaded firearms and will nearly always be unarmed. Occasionally, carjackers make poor choices. Three such carjackers followed my friend's son, Justin, as he drove home in his new car late one night. Little did they know that Justin was a reserve police officer. They did not know that he was well armed and an expert marksman.

When Justin pulled into the family driveway and got out of his car, one of the carjackers jumped out of his own vehicle and yelled at Justin, whose back was turned, "Freeze, motherf—er!" It was exactly what Justin had expected. Justin spun about and emptied the contents of his .45 into the carjacker. The carjacker's partners sped away as fast as their car would take them, leaving their good buddy very dead on my friend's front lawn.

Not long after Justin had sent the carjacker to the great salvage yard in the sky, I read of an off-duty police officer who had a similar encounter. On his way home and wearing plainclothes, he stopped to make a phone call. While he stood talking to his wife on an outdoor public phone, two muggers rushed up to him. One of them brandished a gun and said: "Your wallet!" Instead of pulling out his wallet, the cop drew a gun and sent the mugger to the morgue.

25 The *Los Angeles Times* noted that the mugger certainly picked on the wrong person. This is the same *Los Angeles Times* that regularly editorializes against an armed citizenry and has never seen a gun law that it did not like. Somehow, the newspaper thinks that disarming peaceable, law-abiding citizens will affect criminal behavior for the better. Disarming peaceable, law-abiding citizens *will* affect criminal behavior—but for the worse. Criminals will be emboldened because their chances of picking on the wrong person will be dramatically reduced. Shouldn't the opposite be the case? Shouldn't every person be the wrong person or, at least, potentially the wrong person?

Grandstanding politicians love to rail against the gun. Inanimate objects are good targets to beat up on. That way, politicians do not have to address the real problems in our society. We pay a price for this craven misdirection, though, in thousands of murders, muggings, rapes, robberies, and burglaries.

Yet that is not the greatest danger we face. The Founding Fathers knew that *governments* could turn criminal. That is the principal reason they wanted every man armed: An armed citizenry militates against the development of tyranny. The Founding Fathers did not want every man armed in order to shoot a burglar, although they had nothing against doing so. The Founding Fathers did not want every man armed in order to shoot Bambi or Thumper, although they had nothing against doing so. The Founding Fathers wanted every man armed in order to shoot soldiers or police of tyrannical regimes who suppress the rights of free men.

When governments become criminal, they disarm the populace. Then the numbers of deaths reach the tens of thousands, the hundreds of thousands, the millions. Can't happen? Ask the Irish and the Scots, or the Armenians, the Ukrainians, the Jews, the Chinese, the Cambodians.

In the Marine Corps, I was trained never to surrender my weapon. It was good advice then, and it is good advice now. I shall put my faith not in the goodwill of governments but in an armed citizenry—a band of brothers—steeped in the ideology of the Founding Fathers and the spirit of Patrick Henry, who said: "Is life so dear or peace so sweet as to be purchased at the price of slavery and chains? I know not what course others may take, but as for me, give me liberty or give me death."

DISCUSSION QUESTIONS

1. What does Burger understand the intent of the Second Amendment to have been, in context? How has history changed the way it should now be read?
2. What analogy does Burger make between guns and automobiles? Is his point a good one?
3. What questions does Burger believe Americans should be answering if we are to stop what he calls "this mindless homicidal carnage" (para. 15)?
4. Does McGrath make use of history in the same way and for the same purpose as Burger does? Explain.
5. What does McGrath mean when he says, "It is important to understand that the Second Amendment grants no right to the people to keep and bear arms" (para. 9)?
6. What is the warrant underlying Burger's essay? McGrath's?
7. What is McGrath's response to the claim that restrictions on guns would lead to a safer society?
8. Do you detect any logical fallacies in either essay?
9. Compare the authors' use of language. Do the authors use slanted or emotive language? Short cuts? Where in McGrath's essay is there a shift in the type of language used, and why?

ASSIGNMENTS FOR CHOOSING FAIR AND PRECISE LANGUAGE

READING AND DISCUSSION QUESTIONS

1. Select one or two related bumper stickers visible in your town or city. Examine the hidden warrants on which they are based, and assess their validity.
2. For a slogan found on a bumper sticker or elsewhere, supply the evidence to support the claim in the slogan. Or find evidence that disproves the claim.
3. Examine a few periodicals from fifty or more years ago. Select either an advertising or a political slogan in one of them, and relate it to beliefs or events of the period. Or tell why the slogan is no longer relevant.
4. Discuss the origin of a cliché or slogan. Describe, as far as possible, the backgrounds and motives of its users.
5. Make up your own slogan for a cause that you support. Explain and defend your slogan.
6. Choose a cliché, and find evidence to support or refute it. *Examples:* People were much happier in the past. Mother knows best. Life used to be simpler. Money can't buy happiness.
7. Select a passage, perhaps from a textbook, written largely in abstractions, and rewrite it using simpler and more concrete language.

8. In watching television dramas about law, medicine, or criminal or medical investigation, do you find that the professional language, some of which you may not fully understand, plays a positive or negative role in your enjoyment of the show? Explain your answer.
9. Listen to a radio or television report of a sports event. Do the announcers use a kind of language, especially jargon, that would not be used in print reports? One critic thinks that sports broadcasting has had a "destructive effect . . . on ordinary American English." Is he right or wrong?
10. Whose argument about the right to bear arms do you find more convincing, Burger's or McGrath's? Explain.

WRITING SUGGESTIONS

11. Choose a popular slogan from advertising or politics. Write an essay explaining how it appeals to needs and values.
12. Write an essay explaining which argument about the right to bear arms you find most convincing, Burger's or McGrath's.
13. Write an essay explaining how picturesque language is used to advance arguments. Be sure to provide specific examples.
14. Why are short cuts a natural result of ours being a technological age?
15. Analyze a presidential or other debate using some of the terms discussed in this chapter.
16. Locate a copy of President Bush's first speech after the attacks of 9/11 and compare it to Roosevelt's after the bombing of Pearl Harbor.
17. Write an essay explaining to what extent you believe that the points that Orwell makes in "Politics and the English Language" are still valid today.

[illegible]

16. [illegible]

Part Two

Researching, Writing, and Presenting Arguments

CHAPTER 11

Planning and Researching an Argumentative Paper

The person who understands how arguments are constructed has an important advantage in today's world. Television commercials, political speeches, newspaper editorials, and magazine advertisements, as well as many communications between individuals, all draw on the principles we have examined in the preceding chapters. By now you should be fairly adept at picking out claims, support, and warrants (explicit or unstated) in these presentations. The next step is to apply your skills to writing an argument of your own on a subject of your choice or for an assignment on a topic other than those covered in this text. The process of using what you have learned will enhance your ability to analyze critically the marketing efforts with which we are all bombarded every day. Mastering the writing of arguments also gives you a valuable tool for communicating with other people in school, on the job, and even at home.

In this chapter we move through the various stages involved in preparing to write an argumentative paper: choosing a topic, locating and evaluating sources, and taking notes. We also consider the more general question of how to use the principles already discussed in order to convince a real audience. The more carefully you follow the guidelines set out here and the more thought you give to your work at each point, the better you will be able to utilize the art of argument when this course is over.

FINDING AN APPROPRIATE TOPIC

An old British recipe for jugged hare is said to begin, "First, catch your hare." To write an argumentative paper, you first must choose your topic. This is a relatively easy task for someone writing an argument as part of his or her job—a lawyer defending a client, for example, or an advertising executive presenting a campaign. For a student, however, it can be daunting. Which of the many ideas in the world worth debating would make a good subject?

Several guidelines can help you evaluate the possibilities. Perhaps your assignment limits your choices. If you have been asked to write a research paper, you obviously must find a topic on which research is available. If your assignment is more open-ended, you need a topic that is worth the time and effort you expect to invest in it. In either case, your subject should be one that interests you. Don't feel you have to write about what you know—very often finding out what you don't know will turn out to be more satisfying. You should, however, choose a subject that is familiar enough for you to argue about without fearing you're in over your head.

Invention Strategies

As a starting point, think of conversations you've had in the past few days or weeks that have involved defending a position. Is there some current political issue you're concerned about? Some dispute with friends that would make a valid paper topic? One of the best sources is controversies in the media. Keep your project in mind as you watch TV, read print or online sources, or listen to the radio. You may even run into a potential subject in your course reading assignments or classroom discussions. Fortunately for the would-be writer, nearly every human activity includes its share of disagreement.

As you consider possible topics, write them down. One that looks unlikely at first glance may suggest others or may have more appeal when you come back to it later. Further, simply putting words on paper has a way of stimulating the thought processes involved in writing. Even if your ideas are tentative, the act of converting them into phrases or sentences can often help in developing them.

Evaluating Possible Topics

Besides interesting you, your topic must interest your audience. Who is the audience? For a lawyer it is usually a judge or jury; for a columnist, anyone who reads the newspaper in which his or her column appears. For the student writer, the audience is to some extent hypothetical. You should assume that your paper is directed at readers who are reasonably intelligent and well informed, but who have no specific knowledge of the subject. It may be useful to imagine you are writing for a local or school publication—this may be the case if your paper turns out well.

Be sure, too, that you choose a topic that can be seen from more than one perspective. The purpose of an argument is to defend or refute a thesis, which means the thesis must be debatable. In evaluating a subject that looks promising, ask yourself: Can a case be made for other views? If not, you have no workable ground for building your own case.

Finally, check the scope of your thesis. Consider how long your paper will be, and whether you can do justice to your topic in that amount of space. For example, suppose you want to argue in favor of worldwide nuclear disarmament. Is this a thesis you can support persuasively in a short paper? One way to find out is by listing the potential issues or points about which arguers might disagree. Consider the thesis: "The future of the world is in danger as long as nuclear weapons exist." Obviously this statement is too general. You would have to specify what you mean by the future of the world (the continuation of human life? of all life? of the earth itself?) and exactly how nuclear weapons endanger it before the claim would hold up. You could narrow it down: "Human beings are error-prone; therefore as long as nuclear weapons exist there is the chance that a large number of people will be killed accidentally." Though this statement is more specific and includes an important warrant, it still depends on other unstated warrants: that one human being (or a small group) is in the position to discharge a nuclear weapon capable of killing a large number of people; that such a weapon could, in fact, be discharged by mistake, given current safety systems. Can you expect to show sufficient evidence for these assumptions in the space available to you?

By now it should be apparent that arguing in favor of nuclear disarmament is too broad an undertaking. A more workable approach might be to defend or refute one of the disarmament proposals under consideration by the U.S. Congress, or to show that nuclear weapons pose some specific danger (such as long-term water pollution) that is sufficient reason to strive for disarmament.

Can a thesis be too narrow? Certainly. If this is true of the one you have chosen, you probably realized it when you asked yourself whether the topic was debatable. If you can prove your point convincingly in a paragraph, or even a page, you need a broader thesis.

At this preliminary stage, don't worry if you don't know exactly how to word your thesis. It's useful to write down a few possible phrasings to be sure your topic is one you can work with, but you need not be precise. The information you unearth as you do research will help you to formulate your ideas. Also, stating a thesis in final terms is premature until you know the organization and tone of your paper. If your topic or assignment does not require research, you may want to move ahead to Chapter 12.

INITIATING RESEARCH

The success of any argument, short or long, depends in large part on the quantity and quality of the support behind it. Research, therefore, can be crucial for any argument outside your own experience. Most papers will benefit from research in the library and elsewhere because development of the claim requires facts, examples, statistics, and informed opinions that are available only from primary and secondary research sources.

Writer's Guide: Keeping Your Research on Track

1. Focus your investigation on building your argument, not merely on collecting information about the topic. Do follow any promising leads that turn up from the sources you consult, but don't be diverted into general reading that has no direct bearing on your thesis.
2. Look for at least two pieces of evidence to support each point you want to make. If you cannot find sufficient evidence, you may need to revise or abandon the point.
3. Use a variety of sources. Seek evidence from different kinds of sources (books, magazines, Web sites, government reports, even personal interviews with experts) and from different fields.
4. Be sure your sources are authoritative. We have already pointed out in Chapter 7 the necessity for examining the credentials of sources. Although it may be difficult or impossible for those outside the field to conclude that one authority is more trustworthy than another, some guidelines are available. Articles and essays in scholarly journals are probably more authoritative than articles in college newspapers or in magazines. Authors whose credentials include many publications and years of study at reputable institutions are probably more reliable than newspaper columnists and the so-called man in the street. However, we can judge reliability much more easily if we are dealing with facts and inferences than with values and emotions.
5. Don't let your sources' opinions outweigh your own. Your paper should demonstrate that the thesis and ideas you present are yours, arrived at after careful reflection and supported by research. The thesis need not be original, but your paper should be more than a collection of quotations or a report of the facts and opinions you have been reading. It should be clear to the reader that the quotations and other materials support *your* claim and that *you* have been responsible for finding and emphasizing the important issues, examining the data, and choosing between strong and weak opinions.
6. Don't ignore information that opposes the position you plan to support. Your argument is not strengthened by pretending such information does not exist. You may find that you must revise or qualify your position based on what your research reveals. Your readers may be aware of other positions on the issue and may judge you to be unreliable, careless, or dishonest if you do not acknowledge them. It is far better to fairly summarize opposing arguments and refute them than to ignore them.
7. Prepare for research by identifying potential resources and learning how they work. Make sure you know how to use the library's catalog and

other databases available either in the library or through the campus network. For each database that looks useful, explore how to execute a subject search, how to refine a search, and how to print out or download results. Make sure you know how to find books, relevant reference materials, and journals. Find out whether interlibrary loan is an option and how long it takes. If you plan to use government publications, find out if your library is a depository for federal documents. Identify relevant organizations using the *Encyclopedia of Associations* and visit their Web sites. Finally, discuss your topic with a librarian at the reference desk to make sure you haven't overlooked anything.

Writer's Guide: Why Use Sources?

1. You cannot be an authority on every subject. That means that you must turn to those who are authorities on subjects you know little about.
2. Because you may not yet have a name or credentials that are recognized for their authority, you may need to use those who are considered experts as sources of information and prestige.
3. The use of sources shows that you have taken the time to do some research on the subject at hand, including researching positions other than your own.
4. As in a court of law, the more evidence you can provide for your position, the stronger your case will be.

MAPPING RESEARCH: A SAMPLE OUTLINE

To explore a range of research activities, let's suppose that you are preparing a research paper, six to ten pages long. You have chosen to defend the following thesis: *Even though thalidomide is infamous for causing birth defects in the 1960s, it has promise as a treatment for cancer and other diseases.* To keep your material under control and give direction to your reading, you would sketch a preliminary outline, which might look like this:

Thalidomide: Changing a Drug's Reputation

I. Thalidomide's history: a promising drug but a medical nightmare
   A. Explain how drug was developed
   B. Explain the medical disaster it caused
II. New look at thalidomide: its potential to effectively treat cancer and other diseases
   A. Discuss how it first worked to treat leprosy

B. Support how it can treat cancer

C. Support how it can treat other diseases

III. Conclusion

Now you need to begin the search for the materials that will support your argument. There are two principal ways of gathering the materials—primary research and secondary research. Most writers will not want to limit themselves to one kind of research, but one method may work better than another for a particular project.

USING SOURCES: PRIMARY RESEARCH

Primary research involves looking for firsthand information. By *firsthand* we mean information taken directly from the original source, including field research (interviews, surveys, personal observations, or experiments). If your topic relates to a local issue involving your school or community, or if it focuses on a story that has never been reported by others, field research may be more valuable than anything available in the library. However, the library can be a source of firsthand information. Memoirs and letters written by witnesses to past events, photographs, contemporary news reports of historical events, or expert testimony presented at congressional hearings are all primary sources that may be available in your library. The Internet, too, can be a source of primary data. A discussion list, newsgroup, or chat room focused on your topic may give you a means to converse with activists and contact experts. Web sites of certain organizations provide documentation of their views, unfiltered by others' opinions. The text of laws, court opinions, bills, debates in Congress, environmental impact statements, and even selected declassified FBI files can be found through government-sponsored Web sites. Other sites present statistical data or the text of historical or political documents.

One of the rewards of primary research is that it often generates new information, which in turn produces new interpretations of familiar conditions. It is a favored method for anthropologists and sociologists, and most physical and natural scientists use observation and experiment at some point as essential tools in their research.

Consider the sample thesis that *even though thalidomide is infamous for causing birth defects in the 1960s, it has promise as a treatment for cancer and other diseases*. It is possible to go to primary sources in addition to or instead of consulting books. For example:

- Interview one or more physicians about current or potential uses of thalidomide.
- Interview someone locally who has had a family member affected by thalidomide.

- Read a first-person account by someone negatively affected by thalidomide use.
- Read a first-person account by someone positively affected by thalidomide use.
- Research newspaper reports from the time period regarding the birth defects caused by thalidomide before its dangers were known.
- Search the Web for reputable sources of information about thalidomide and the uses for which it is currently approved.

The information gleaned from primary research can be used directly to support your claim, or can provide a starting point for secondary research.

USING SOURCES: SECONDARY RESEARCH

Secondary research involves locating commentary on and analysis of your topic. In addition to raw evidence found through primary research, secondary sources provide a sense of how others are examining the issues and can provide useful information and analysis. Secondary sources may be written for a popular audience, ranging from news coverage, to popular explanations of research findings, to social analysis, to opinion pieces. Or they may be scholarly publications—experts presenting their research and theories to other researchers. These sources might also come in the form of analytical reports written to untangle possible courses of action, such as a report written by staff members for a congressional committee or an analysis of an issue by a think tank that wants to use the evidence it has gathered to influence public opinion.

Whatever form it may take, be sure when you use a secondary source that you consider the author's purpose and the validity of the material presented to ensure that it is useful evidence for your argument. An opinion piece published in a small-town paper, for example, may be a less impressive source for your argument than an analysis written by a former cabinet member. A description of a scientific discovery published in a magazine will carry less weight as evidence than the article written by the scientists making the discovery, presenting their research findings in a scientific journal.

The nature of your topic will determine which route you follow to find good sources. If the topic is current, you may find it more important to use articles than books and might bypass the library catalog altogether. If the topic has to do with social policy or politics, government publications may be particularly useful, though they would be unhelpful for a literary paper. If the topic relates to popular culture, the Internet may provide more information than more traditional publications. Consider what kinds of sources will be most useful as you choose your strategy. If you aren't certain which approaches fit your topic best, consult with a librarian at the reference desk.

Selecting and Searching Databases

You will most likely use one or more *databases* (online catalogs of reference materials) to locate books and articles on your topic. The library catalog is a database of books and other materials owned by the library; other databases may cover articles in popular or specialized journals and may even provide the full text of articles. Some databases may be available only in the library; others may be accessible all over campus. Here are some common features that appear in many databases.

Keyword or Subject Searching. You might have the option of searching a database by *keyword*—using the words that you think are most relevant to your search—or by subject. Typically, a keyword search will search for any occurrence of your search term in titles, notes, or the descriptive headings provided by database catalogers or indexers. The advantage to keyword searching is that you can use terms that come naturally to you to cast your net as widely as possible. The disadvantage is that there may be more than one way to express your topic and you may not capture all the relevant materials unless you use the right keywords.

With *subject searching*, you use search terms from a list of subject headings (sometimes called *descriptors*) established by the creators of the database. To make searching as efficient as possible, they choose one word or phrase to express a subject. Every time a new source is entered into the database, the indexers describe it using words from the list of subject headings: When you use the list to search the database, you retrieve every relevant source. You might find that a database lists these subject headings through a thesaurus feature. The sophisticated researcher will always pay attention to the subject headings or descriptors generally listed at the bottom of a record for clues to terms that might work best and for related terms that might be worth trying.

Searching for More Than One Concept. Most database searches allow you to combine terms using the connectors *and, or,* and *not*. These connectors (also known as *Boolean operators*) group search terms in different ways. If you search for zoos *and* animal rights, for example, the resulting list of sources will include only those that deal with both zoos and animal rights, leaving out any that deal with only one subject and not the other. If you connect terms with *or*, your list will contain sources that deal with either concept: A search for dogs *or* cats will create a list of sources that cover either animal. *Not* excludes concepts from a search. A search for animal rights *not* furs will search for the concept animal rights and then cut out any sources that deal with furs.

Limiting a Search. Most databases have some options for limiting a search by a number of variables, such as publication date, language, or format. If you find a large number of sources in a database search, you might limit your search to sources published in English in the past three years. If you need a visual aid for a presentation, you might limit a search of the library's catalog to videos, and so on.

Truncating Search Terms with Wild Cards. At times you will search for a word that has many possible endings. A wild card is a symbol that, placed at the end of a word root, allows for any possible ending for a word. For example, *animal** will allow a search for *animal* or *animals*.

Options for Saving Records. You may have the opportunity to print, download, or e-mail to yourself the citations you find in a database. Many databases have a feature for marking just the records you want so you save only those of interest.

Help Screens. Most databases offer some kind of online help that explains how to use the database effectively. If you invest five minutes getting familiar with the basics of a database, it may save you twenty minutes later.

Types of Databases

The Library Catalog. If you want to search for books, videos, or periodical publications, the library catalog is the database to search. Most libraries now have computerized catalogs, but some still have a card catalog. In either case, the type of information provided is the same. Every book in the library has an entry in the catalog that gives its author, title, publisher, date, length, and subject headings and perhaps some notes about its contents. It also gives the call number or location on the shelf and often some indication as to whether it is currently available. You can search the catalog for an author, title, subject, or keyword. Most online catalogs have ways of combining and limiting searches and for printing results. Remember when searching the catalog, though, that entries are created for whole books and not for specific parts of them. If you use too narrow search terms, you may not find a book that has a chapter that includes exactly what you are looking for. Use broad search terms, and check the subject headings for search terms that will work best. Plan to browse the shelves and examine the tables of contents of the books that you find through the catalog to see which, in fact, are most helpful for your topic.

General Periodical Databases. If you want to search for articles, you can find a number of options at your library. Most libraries have a generalized database of periodical articles that may include citations, citations with abstracts (brief summaries), or the entire text of articles. *EBSCOhost, Infotrac, Searchbank, Readers' Guide Abstracts,* and *ProQuest* are all online indexes of this type. Ask a librarian what is available in your library. These are particularly good for finding current information in fairly nonspecialized sources, though they may include some scholarly journals. If you are looking for articles published before the 1980s—say, for news accounts published when the atomic bomb was dropped on Hiroshima—you would most likely need to use a print index such as the *Readers' Guide to Periodical Literature,* which began publication in 1900.

Specialized Databases. In addition to these general databases, you may find you need to delve deeper into a particular subject area. Every academic discipline has some sort of in-depth index to its research, and though the materials they cover tend to be highly specialized, they can provide more substantial support for your claims because they tend to cover sources written by experts in their fields. These resources may be available in electronic or print form:

Art Index

Biological Abstracts (the online version is known as *Biosis*)

Business Periodicals Index

ERIC (focused on education research)

Index Medicus (*Medline* or *PubMed* online)

Modern Languages Association International Bibliography (*MLA Bibliography* online)

Psychological Abstracts (*PsychInfo* or *PsychLit* online)

Sociological Abstracts (*Sociofile* online)

Sample Online Catalog Record

You searched for the TITLE—animal rights movement

```
CALL #        Z7164.C45 M38 1994.
AUTHOR        Manzo, Bettina, 1943-
TITLE         The animal rights movement in the United States, 1975-
                1990 : an annotated bibliography / by Bettina Manzo.
IMPRINT       Metuchen, N.J. : Scarecrow Press, 1994.
PHYS DESCR    xi, 296 p. ; 23 cm.
NOTE          Includes indexes.
CONTENTS      Animal rights movement -- Activists and organizations --
                Philosophy, ethics, and religion -- Law and legislation
                --  Factory farming and vegetarianism -- Trapping and
                fur industry -- Companion animals -- Wildlife --
                Circuses, zoos, rodeos, dog
SUBJECT       Animal rights movement --United States --Bibliography.
              Animal rights --United States --Bibliography.
              Animal experimentation --United States --Bibliography.
OCLC #        30671149.
ISBN/ISSN     GB95-17241.
```

Check with a librarian to find out which specialized databases or indexes that relate to your topic are available in your library.

Database Services. In addition to individual databases, many libraries subscribe to database services that provide access to a number of databases from one search screen. *FirstSearch,* for example, provides access to a variety of subject-specific databases as well as *WorldCat,* a massive database of library catalogs. *Lexis/Nexis* is a collection of databases to over a billion texts, most of them available in full text; it is a strong source for news coverage, legal research, and business information. These may be available to you through the Web anywhere on campus. Again, a visit with a librarian will help you quickly identify what your library has available.

Encyclopedias

General and specialized encyclopedias offer quick overviews of topics and easy access to factual information. They also tend to have excellent selective bibliographies, pointing you toward useful sources. You will find a wide variety of encyclopedias in your library's reference collection; you may also have an online encyclopedia, such as *Britannica Online,* available through the Web anywhere on campus. Some specialized encyclopedias include the following:

Encyclopedia of African American History and Culture

Encyclopedia of American Social History

Encyclopedia of Bioethics

Encyclopedia of Educational Research

Encyclopedia of Hispanic Culture in the United States

Encyclopedia of International Relations

Encyclopedia of Philosophy

Encyclopedia of Sociology

Encyclopedia of the United States in the Twentieth Century

Encyclopedia of World Cultures

International Encyclopedia of Communications

McGraw-Hill Encyclopedia of Science and Technology

Political Handbook of the World

Statistical Resources

Often statistics are used as evidence in an argument. If your argument depends on establishing that one category is bigger than another, that the majority of people hold a certain opinion, or that one group is more affected by something than another group, statistics can provide the evidence you need. Of course, as with any other source, you need to be sure that your statistics are as reliable as possible and that you are reporting them responsibly.

It isn't always easy to find things counted the way you want. If you embark on a search for numbers to support your argument, be prepared to spend some time locating and interpreting data. Always read the fine print that explains how and when the data were gathered. Some sources for statistics include these:

U.S. Bureau of the Census. This government agency produces a wealth of statistical data, much of it available on CD-ROM or through the Web at www.census.gov. A handy compilation of their most useful tables is found in the one-volume annual handbook, *Statistical Abstract of the United States,* which also includes statistics from other government sources.

Other Federal Agencies. Numerous federal agencies gather statistical data. Among these are the National Center for Education Statistics, the National Center for Health Statistics, the National Bureau of Labor Statistics, and the Federal Bureau of Investigation, which annually compiles national crime statistics. One handy place to find a wide variety of federal statistics is a Web site called *FedStats* at www.fedstats.gov.

United Nations. Compilations of international data published by the United Nations include the *Demographic Yearbook* and *Statistical Yearbook*. Some statistics are also published by U.N. agencies such as the Food and Health Organization. Some are available from the U.N. Web site at www.un.org.

Opinion Polls. Several companies conduct opinion polls, and some of these are available in libraries. One such compilation is the Gallup Poll series, which summarizes public opinion polling from 1935 to the present. Other poll results are reported by the press. Search a database that covers news publications by using your topic and *polls* as keywords to help you locate some summaries of results.

Government Publications

Beyond statistics, government agencies compile and publish a wealth of information. For topics that concern public welfare, health, education, politics, foreign relations, earth sciences, the environment, or the economy, government documents may provide just the information you need.

The U.S. federal government is the largest publisher in the world. Its publications are distributed free to libraries designated as document depositories across the country. If your library is not a depository, chances are there is a regional depository somewhere nearby. Local, state, and foreign governments are also potential sources of information.

Federal documents distributed to depository libraries are indexed in *The Monthly Catalog of U.S. Government Documents,* available in many libraries as an electronic database. These include congressional documents such as hearings and committee reports, presidential papers, studies conducted by the Education Department or the Centers for Disease Control, and so on. Many government documents are available through the Internet. If you learn about a government publication through the news media, chances are you will be able to obtain a copy at the Web site of the sponsoring agency or congressional body. In fact, government publications are among the most valuable of resources available on the Web because they are rigorously controlled for content. You know you are looking at a U.S. federal government site when you see the domain suffix *.gov* in the URL.

Searching the Web

The World Wide Web is an increasingly important resource for researchers. It is particularly helpful if you are looking for information about organizations, current events, political debates, popular culture, or government-sponsored research and activities. It is not an especially good place to look for literary criticism, historical analysis, or scholarly research articles, which are still more likely to be published in traditional ways. Biologists reporting on an important experiment, for example, are more likely to submit an article about it to a prestigious journal in the field than simply post their results on the Web.

Because anyone can publish whatever they like on the Web, searching for good information can be frustrating. Search engines operate by means of automated programs that gather information about sites and match search terms to whatever is out there, regardless of quality. A search engine may locate thousands of Web documents on a topic, but most are of little relevance and dubious quality. The key is to know in advance what information you need and who might have produced it. For example, if your topic has to do with some aspect of free speech and you know that the American Civil Liberties Union is involved in the issue, a trip to the ACLU home page may provide you with a wealth of information, albeit from a particular perspective. If your state's pollution control agency just issued a report on water quality in the area, you may find the report published at their Web site or the e-mail address of someone who could send it to you. The more you know about your topic before you sit down to surf, the more likely you will use your time productively.

If you have a fairly broad topic and no specific clues about where it might be covered, you may want to start your search using a selective guide to good sites. For example, the University of Texas maintains an excellent directory to sites relating to Latin America. Subject guides that selectively list valuable sites can be found at the University of California's *Infomine* at http://infomine.ucr.edu and the *World Wide Web Virtual Library* project at www.vlib.org/Home.html. Reference librarians will also be able to point you to quality sites that relate to your topic.

If you have a fairly specific topic in mind or are looking for a particular organization or document on the Web, a search engine can help you find it. *Google* is one of the best. No matter what search engine you choose, find out how it works, how it ranks results, and how deeply it indexes Web pages. Some search engines will retrieve more results than others simply because of the way the program gathers information from sites. As with databases, there are usually ways to refine a search and improve your results. Many search engines offer an advanced search option that may provide some useful options for refining and limiting a search.

It is important to know what will not be retrieved by a search engine. Because publishing and transmitting texts on the Web is relatively easy, it is becoming more common for libraries to subscribe to databases and electronic journals that are accessed through a Web browser. You may have *Britannica Online* and *Lexis/Nexis* as options on your library's home page. However, the contents of those subscriptions will be available only to your campus community and will not be searched by general Web search engines.

EVALUATING SOURCES

When you begin studying your sources, read first to acquire general familiarity with your subject. Make sure that you are covering both sides of the question—in this case the negative as well as the positive aspects of the use of thalidomide—as well as facts and opinions from a variety of sources. In investigating this subject, you might examine data from doctors, victims of earlier thalidomide use, scientists studying the current uses of thalidomide, the manufacturer of the drug, and recent patients; their varied points of view will contribute to the strength of your claim.

As you read, look for what seem to be the major issues. They will probably be represented in all or most of your sources. Record questions as they occur to you in your reading. What went wrong when thalidomide was used in the 1960s? Why is it again receiving attention? What reasons are there for bringing back such a dangerous drug? Are there advantages that outweigh the dangers? What has changed that might make use of the drug safer today?

Evaluating Print Sources

The sources you find provide useful information that you need for your paper and help you support your claims. One key to supporting claims effectively is to make sure you have the best evidence available. It is tempting when searching a database or the Web to take the first sources that look good, print them or copy them, and not give them another thought until you are sitting down to compose your argument—only to discover that the sources aren't as valuable as they could be. Sources that looked pretty good at the beginning of your research may turn out to be less useful once you have learned more about the topic. And a source that seems interesting at first glance may turn out to be a rehash or digest of a much more valuable source, something you realize only when you sit down and look at it carefully.

To find the right stuff, be a critical thinker from the start of your research process. Scan and evaluate the references you encounter throughout your search. As you examine options in a database, choose sources that use relevant terms in their titles, seem directed to an appropriate audience, and are published in places that will look good in your Works Cited list. For example, a Senate Foreign Relations Committee report will be more impressive as a source than a comparable article in *Good Housekeeping*. An article from the scholarly journal *Foreign Affairs* will carry more clout than an article from *Reader's Digest*, even if they are on the same subject.

Skim and quickly evaluate each source that looks valuable.

- Is it relevant to your topic?
- Does it provide information you haven't found elsewhere?
- Can you learn anything about the author, and does what you learn inspire confidence?

As you begin to learn more about your topic and develop an outline, you can use sources to help direct your search. If a source mentions an organization, for example, you may use that clue to run a search on the Web for that organization's home page. If a newspaper story refers to a study published in a scientific journal, you may want to seek out that study to see the results of the research firsthand. And if you have a source that includes references to other publications, scan through them, and see which might also prove helpful to you. When you first started your research, chances are you weren't quite sure what you were looking for. Once you are familiar with your topic, you need to concentrate on finding sources that will best support the claims you want to make, and your increasing familiarity with the issue will make it easier to identify the best sources. That may mean a return trip to the library.

Once you have selected some useful sources to support your claims, make a more in-depth evaluation to be sure you have the best evidence available.

- Is it current enough? Have circumstances changed since this text was published?
- Is the author someone I want to call on as an expert witness? Does the author have the experience or credentials to make a solid argument that carries weight with my readers?

- Is it reliable information for my purposes? It may be highly opinionated, but are the basic facts it presents confirmed in other sources? Is the evidence presented in the text convincing?

These questions are not always easy to answer. In some cases, articles will include some information about the author, such as where he or she works. In other cases, no information or even an author's name is given. In that case, it may help to evaluate the publication and its reputation. If you aren't familiar with a publication and don't feel confident making your own judgment, see if it is described in Katz's *Magazines for Libraries,* which evaluates the reputation and quality of periodicals.

Evaluating Web Sources

Web sites pose challenges and offer unique opportunities for researchers, for one reason because they are part of a developing genre of writing. When evaluating a Web site, first examine what kind of site you are reading. Is the Web page selling or advertising goods or services (a business site)? Is it advocating a point of view (an advocacy site) or providing relatively neutral information, such as that found in the yellow pages (an informative or educational site)? Is the Web site addressing the interests of people in a particular organization or with common interests (an information-sharing site)? Is it reporting up-to-the-minute news (a news site) or appealing to some aspect of an individual's life and interests (a personal site)? Useful information for a research paper may be obtained from any of these kinds of Web pages, but it is helpful to know what the main purpose of the site is—and who its primary audience is—when determining how productive it will be for your research.

As you weigh the main purpose of the site, evaluate its original context. Does the site originate in a traditional medium, such as a print journal or an encyclopedia? Is the site part of an online journal, in which case its material had to go through a screening process? Or is the site the product of one individual's or organization's desire to create a Web page, which means the work may not have been screened or evaluated by any outside agency? In that case, the information may still be valuable, but you must be even more careful when evaluating it.

Answering preliminary questions like these helps you before you begin a more specific evaluation of the site's content. To find answers to many of these questions, make a brief overview of the site itself, by looking, for example, at the clues contained in the Web address. That is, *.com* in the address means a business or commercial site; *.edu,* a site sponsored by a university or college; *.k12* is a site associated with a primary or secondary school; *.gov* indicates that the federal government sponsored the site; and *.org* suggests that the site is part of a nonprofit or noncommercial group. Sites originating outside the United States have URLs that end with a two-letter country abbreviation, such as *.uk* for United Kingdom.

Although these address clues can reveal a great deal about the origins and purposes of a Web site, remember that personal Web sites may also contain some of these abbreviations. Institutions such as schools and businesses sometimes sponsor individuals' personal Web sites (which are often unscreened by the institution) as well as official institutional sites. One possible key to determining whether a Web site is a personal page, however, is to look for a tilde (~) plus a name or part of a name in the address. Finally, if you are unsure of the sponsoring organization of a page, try erasing all the information in the URL after the first slash (/) and pressing the "Enter" key. Doing so often brings you to the main page of the organization sponsoring the Web site.

Most Web sites include a way to contact the author or sponsoring organization of the site, usually through e-mail. This is often a quick and easy way to get answers to the preliminary questions. If the site contains an address or phone number as part of its contact information, this means the organization or individual is available and probably willing to stand behind the site's content. If you can't find contact information the site may not be suitable to use as a primary resource. The information is not necessarily invalid, but such clues should alert you that information found on that page needs to be verified.

For the next step—that of more closely evaluating the contents of any Web site—Web researchers generally agree on the importance of five criteria: the authority, accuracy, objectivity, currency, and coverage of the site.[1] These criteria are just as important in evaluating traditional print texts, but electronic texts require special care. To understand how these criteria work, let's look at a specific example.

Evaluating a Web Site: One Example

Assume that your observations have led you to conclude that high school students are largely apathetic about government and politics. As a likely future parent, you have decided to research ways of interesting teenagers in the political process. You hypothesize that students who take the whole cyberworld for granted as a part of everyday life might be attracted to an interactive Web site. You do a search on *Google* using different combinations of keywords, and one site you access looks promising. You want to be sure, however, that the site meets the tests of authority, accuracy, objectivity, currency, and coverage.

The site is Student Voices, designed to teach high school students about government and civic responsibility. Your first job is to evaluate the home page.

The home page design is simple but attractive, and the text is easy to read. There are a number of different features to explore, and the site is

[1] Wolfgram Memorial Library Web site.

The Student-voices.org home page

typical in that there is no set order for accessing the different links. It is clear from the buttons at the top of the page that the site is used in the context of classes because there are teacher resources as well as student ones.

Clicking on the Student Resources link leads to a useful video called *How to Use the Student Voices Web Site*. This ten-minute video introduces the resources the site offers students. The Teacher Resources page does the same for teachers. Teachers can get a password to the site that allows their students to interact with the material on the site.

The Student Resources page also includes links to a wealth of sources about government, including these:

- encyclopedia entries on the U.S. president, U.S. senators, the federal government, and state government
- official government sites, from the White House to the Library of Congress
- sources that can be used for general research and constitutional research, and for access to voting/elections information
- major newspapers from across the country and Web sites of the major television networks

The video also explains the different ways that students can use the site interactively. Going back to the home page, you can see its major divisions:

The Student-voices.org Student Resources page

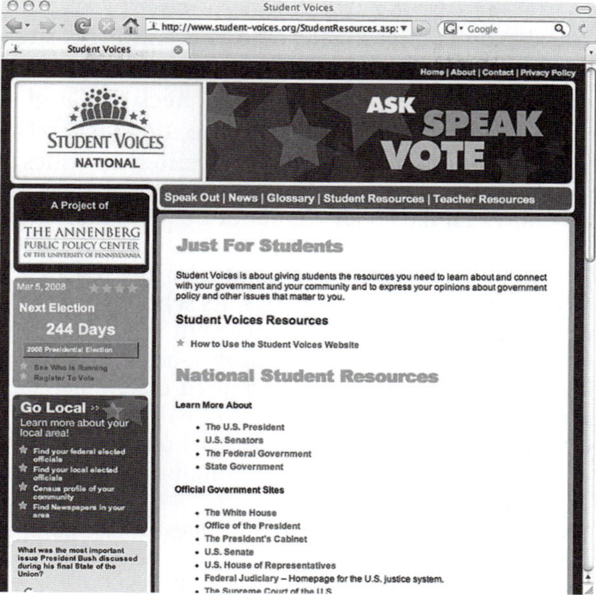

- **Speak Out** is just that—a chance for students to speak out on current political issues. Every few weeks the topic on the home page changes, and the staff of Student Voices presents a brief summary of a "hot" issue such as eminent domain, illegal aliens, or wiretapping. Students can then respond to what they read, read Speak Out on other subjects, or read more on the topic.
- **Polls.** At any given time, there is one question on which students are being polled, plus access to previous polls.
- **What's New.** Clicking on this box takes students to information about what their representatives are voting on at the time.
- **Current News.** The national political news of the day.
- **Other Voices.** Additional news of the day from a half dozen links to specific states.
- **Go Local.** These links let the students discover who their local and federal elected representatives are, what their local newspapers are, and what the census reveals about their community.
- **Next Election.** This box is updated every day to reveal how many days until the next election, who is running, and how to register to vote.
- **Photos.** These show Student Voices and related events.

The navigation bar also provides a link to a glossary of political terms.

Now that you have an overview of the site, consider whether it meets the criteria for a good source.

Authority. You decide to investigate who is behind this site. At the bottom of the home page is the information that the site is copyrighted by the Annenberg Public Policy Center. A quick check on *Google* leads you to this center's site, where you discover that the APPC is a part of the University of Pennsylvania. This is the way the center describes its mission:

> The Annenberg Public Policy Center of the University of Pennsylvania has been the premier communication policy center in the country since its founding in 1993. By conducting and releasing research, staging conferences and hosting policy discussions, its scholars have addressed the role of communication in politics, adolescent behavior, child development, health care, civics and mental health, among other important arenas. The Center's researchers have drafted materials that helped policy-makers, journalists, scholars, constituent groups and the general public better understand the role that media play in their lives and the life of the nation. The Policy Center maintains offices in Philadelphia and Washington, D.C.
>
> APPC's work has informed the policy debates around campaign finance, children's television, internet privacy, tobacco advertising and the tone of discourse in Washington. Scholars at the Policy Center have offered guidance to journalists covering difficult stories, including terrorist threats, suicide and mental health. The Center's discussions of key public policy issues have brought together industry representatives, advocates, government officials and the scholarly community. Its research has examined what messages work best to reduce the spread of HIV and drug use, how to improve candidate discourse and specific strategies for parents to use to monitor their children's media exposure. APPC has developed materials to help educators and schools do a better job of teaching youth about civic responsibility, democracy and the Constitution.
>
> To further our mission, we are launching this new web site. It is designed to give scholars, the media and the general public expanded access to the work that we began in 1993. We intend to make that complete body of research, including extensive data sets and topline surveys, available as quickly as possible. If there are any questions about materials not yet posted on the site, please contact our Philadelphia office at the number listed at the bottom of this page, or send an email to [the address shown].

The fact that the Annenberg Public Policy Center is part of a reputable university tends to give the information it presents on the site credence. There also is an e-mail address by which to reach someone at Annenberg, which also suggests credibility. The biographies of the staff at Annenberg reveal that they are scholars and journalists with substantial experience in Washington D.C.

Accuracy. Much of the information on the site is factual. The site's affiliation with a major university and its well-qualified staff make a reader inclined to accept that the facts are accurately presented. Since the site is updated daily, news does not get old, as it can with sites that are not well maintained. Those parts of the site that elicit opinion are clearly that—an invitation for students to express their opinions, right or wrong. No one under the age of thirteen is allowed to participate in Speak Out, and those between thirteen and eighteen must have parental permission to participate or to send any personally identifying information. In fact, one other project of the APPC is FactCheck.org, a site that analyzes statements made to the media and points out inaccuracies. There is a link from the home page of Student Voices to FactCheck.org.

Objectivity. Again, it is easier to maintain objectivity when dealing with facts like the outcome of a vote in the Senate or the name of a local representative. Most of the links that provide information about government are linked directly to governmental sites—the House of Representatives, the Library of Congress, and the White House, for example. They are not to sites that present partisan views of the government. The links to broad categories such as U.S. presidents are to MSN's *Encarta*. The links to newspapers are to ones that are well established and well respected, such as the *New York Times* and the *Washington Post*, but they also show a range of possible slants on controversial issues. Included in the list, for example, is the *Christian Science Monitor*.

The factual nature of much of the information on the site increases the odds that the site is objective. The purpose of the whole site is to encourage students to discuss current political issues and to form their own opinions rather than to be presented with set notions as to what the "right" answer is. For those who want to read others' views, the analyses on FactCheck.org could be a starting point.

Currency. The site is updated every day. Although the Speak Out topic remains the same for a few weeks, that schedule allows students time to respond, and the national and state news is updated daily, as are the countdown to the next election and the What's New section.

Coverage. The site covers thoroughly much of the information that students need to learn about the political process on the national, state, and local levels. They can find in one place information that would be much more difficult and time-consuming to locate without its having been brought together in one place. Hypertext works well in such a context because the multiple links put masses of information at the students' fingertips. The Student Resources add great depth to the knowledge available on the home page, where there is also a link to another project of the APPC, Justice Learning, where students can go into more depth about some of the major issues of the day, should they want or need to.

TAKING NOTES

While everyone has methods of taking notes, here are a few suggestions that should be useful to research writers who need to read materials quickly, comprehend and evaluate the sources, use them as part of a research paper assignment, and manage their time carefully. If you need more detailed help with quoting, paraphrasing, and summarizing, review pages 92–102 in Chapter 4.

When taking notes from a source, summarize instead of quoting long passages. Summarizing as you read saves time. If you feel that a direct quote is more effective than anything you could write and provides crucial support for your argument, copy the material word for word. Leave all punctuation exactly as it appears and insert ellipsis points (". . .") if you delete material. Enclose all quotations in quotation marks and copy complete information about your source, including the author's name, the title of the book or article, the journal name if appropriate, page numbers, and publishing information. If you quote an article that appears in an anthology, record complete information about the book itself.

If you aren't sure whether you will use a piece of information later, don't copy the whole passage. Instead, make a note of its bibliographic information so that you can find it again if you need it. Taking too many notes, however, is preferable to taking too few, a problem that will force you to go back to the source for missing information.

Use the note-taking process as a prewriting activity. Often when you summarize an author's ideas or write down direct quotes, you see or understand the material in new ways. Freewrite about the importance of these quotes, paraphrases, or summaries, or at least about those that seem especially important. If nothing else, take a minute to justify in writing why you chose to record the notes. Doing so will help you clarify and develop your thoughts about your argument.

Taking this prewriting step seriously will help you analyze the ideas you record from outside sources. You will then be better prepared for the more formal (and inevitable) work of summarizing, paraphrasing, and composing involved in thinking critically about your topic and writing a research paper. Maybe most important, such work will help with that moment all writers face when they realize they "know what they want to say but can't find the words to say it." Overcoming such moments does not depend on finding inspiration while writing the final draft of a paper. Instead, successfully working through this common form of writer's block depends more on the amount of prewriting and thoughtful consideration of the notes done early in the research process.

As you take notes, also remember to refer to your outline to ensure that you are acquiring sufficient data to support all the points you intend to raise. Of course, you will be revising your outline during the course of your research as issues are clarified and new ideas emerge, but the outline will serve as a rough guide throughout the writing process. Keeping close track of your outline will also prevent you from recording material that is interesting but not relevant. It may help to label your notes with the heading from the outline to which they are most relevant.

Relying on the knowledge of others is an important part of doing research; expert opinions and eloquent arguments help support your claims when your own expertise is limited. But remember, this is *your* paper. Your ideas and insights into other people's ideas are just as important as the information you uncover at the library or through reputable online sources. When writing an argument, do not simply regurgitate the words and thoughts of others in your essay. Work to achieve a balance between providing solid information from expert sources and offering your own interpretation of the argument and the evidence that supports it. You are entering an ongoing conversation on your topic, not simply recording what others have already said.

Using word-processing software can invigorate the process of note taking and of outlining. Taking notes using a computer gives you more flexibility than using pen and paper alone. For example, you can save your computer-generated notes and your comments on them in numerous places (at home, school, or work, or on a disk); you can cut and paste the text into various documents; you can add to the notes or modify them and still revert to the originals with ease.

You can also link notes to background material on the Web that may be useful once you begin writing drafts of your paper. For example, you could create links to an author's Web page or to any of his or her other works published on the Web. You could create a link to a study or an additional source cited in your notes, or you could link to the work of other researchers who support or argue against the information you recorded.

Because you can record information in any number of ways on your computer, your notes act as tools in the writing process. One of the best ways to start is to open a file for each source; enter the bibliographic information; directly type into the file a series of potentially useful quotations, paraphrases, and summaries; and add your initial ideas about the source. (For each entry, note the correct page references as you go along and indicate clearly whether you are quoting, paraphrasing, or summarizing.) You can then use the capabilities of your computer to aid you in the later stages of the writing process. For example, you can collect all your research notes into one large file in which you group like sources, evaluate whether you have too much information about one issue or one side of an argument, or examine sources that conflict with one another. You can imagine various organizational schemes for your paper based on the central themes and issues of the notes you have taken, and you can more clearly determine which quotes and summaries are essential to your paper and which may not be needed.

When you're ready to begin your first draft, the computer allows you to readily integrate material from your source notes into your research paper by cutting and pasting, thus eliminating the need to retype and reducing the chance of error. You can also combine all the bibliographic materials you have saved in separate files and then use the computer to alphabetize your sources for your final draft.

Although taking notes on the computer does not dramatically change the research process, it does highlight the fact that taking notes, prewriting, drafting a paper, and creating a Works Cited page are integrated activities that should build from one another. When you take notes from a journal, book, or Web site, you develop your note-taking abilities so that they help with the entire writing process.

DOCUMENTING YOUR RESEARCH (MLA SYSTEM)

One of the most effective ways to save yourself time and trouble when you are ready to write your research paper is to document your research as you go along. That way, when the time comes to create your Works Cited page, you will be ready to put the works you used in alphabetical order—or let your computer do it for you—and provide a list of those works at the end of your paper. Some instructors may require a bibliography, or a list of all of the works you consulted (sometimes called simply Works Consulted), but at a minimum you will need a Works Cited page. As that title indicates, the list will be only those works that you quote, paraphrase, or summarize in your paper.

Once you are fairly certain that you will use a certain source, go ahead and put it in proper bibliographic form. That way, if the citation form is complicated, you can look it up or ask your instructor before the last minute. Also, you will realize immediately if you are missing information required by the citation and can record it while the source is still at hand.

Following are examples of the citation forms you are most likely to need as you document your research. In general, for both books and magazines, information should appear in the following order: author, title, and publication information. Each item should be followed by a period. When using as a source an essay that appears in this book, follow the citation model for "Material reprinted from another source," unless your instructor indicates otherwise. Consult the *MLA Handbook for Writers of Research Papers*, Seventh Edition (New York: Modern Language Association of America, 2009) for other documentation models and a list of acceptable shortened forms of publishers.

■ Print Sources

A BOOK BY A SINGLE AUTHOR

Gubar, Susan. *Racechanges: White Skin, Black Face in American Culture*. New York: Oxford UP, 1997. Print.

THE ELEMENTS OF CITATION: BOOK (MLA)

When you cite a book using MLA style, include the following:

1 Author
2 Title and subtitle
3 City of publication
4 Publisher
5 Date of publication
6 Medium

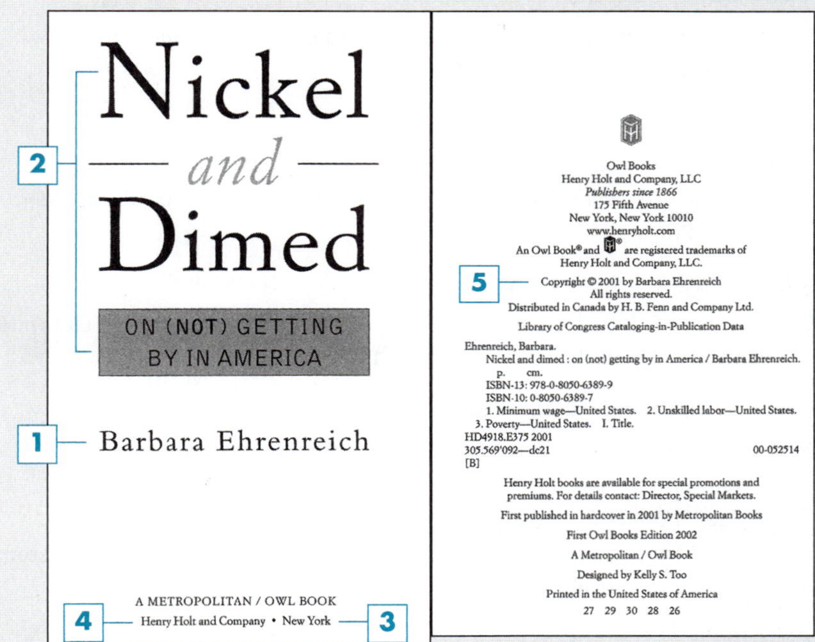

2 Nickel — *and* — Dimed

ON (NOT) GETTING BY IN AMERICA

1 Barbara Ehrenreich

A METROPOLITAN / OWL BOOK

4 Henry Holt and Company • New York 3

Owl Books
Henry Holt and Company, LLC
Publishers since 1866
175 Fifth Avenue
New York, New York 10010
www.henryholt.com

An Owl Book® and ® are registered trademarks of
Henry Holt and Company, LLC.

5 Copyright © 2001 by Barbara Ehrenreich
All rights reserved.
Distributed in Canada by H. B. Fenn and Company Ltd.

Library of Congress Cataloging-in-Publication Data

Ehrenreich, Barbara.
Nickel and dimed : on (not) getting by in America / Barbara Ehrenreich.
p. cm.
ISBN-13: 978-0-8050-6389-9
ISBN-10: 0-8050-6389-7
1. Minimum wage—United States. 2. Unskilled labor—United States.
3. Poverty—United States. I. Title.
HD4918.E375 2001
305.569'092—dc21 00-052514
[B]

Henry Holt books are available for special promotions and premiums. For details contact: Director, Special Markets.

First published in hardcover in 2001 by Metropolitan Books

First Owl Books Edition 2002

A Metropolitan / Owl Book

Designed by Kelly S. Too

Printed in the United States of America

27 29 30 28 26

Works Cited entry for a book in MLA style

1: Ehrenreich, Barbara. 2: *Nickel and Dimed: On (Not) Getting by in America.* 3: New York: 4: Holt, 5: 2001. 6: Print.

Ehrenreich, Barbara. *Nickel and Dimed: On (Not) Getting by in America.* New York: Holt, 2001. Print.

AN ANTHOLOGY OR COMPILATION

Dark, Larry, ed. *Prize Stories 1997: The O. Henry Awards.* New York: Anchor, 1997. Print.

A BOOK BY TWO AUTHORS

Alderman, Ellen, and Caroline Kennedy. *The Right to Privacy.* New York: Vintage, 1995. Print.

Note: This form is followed even for two authors with the same last name.

Ehrlich, Paul, and Anne Ehrlich. *Extinction: The Causes and Consequences of the Disappearance of Species.* New York: Random, 1981. Print.

A BOOK BY TWO OR MORE AUTHORS

Heffernan, William A., Mark Johnston, and Frank Hodgins. *Literature: Art and Artifact*. San Diego: Harcourt, 1987. Print.

If there are more than three authors, name only the first and add "et al." (meaning "and others").

A BOOK BY A CORPORATE AUTHOR

Poets & Writers, Inc. *The Writing Business: A Poets & Writers Handbook*. New York: Poets & Writers, 1985. Print.

A WORK IN AN ANTHOLOGY

Head, Bessie. "Woman from America." *Wild Women: Contemporary Short Stories by Women Celebrating Women*. Ed. Sue Thomas. Woodstock: Overlook, 1994. 45-51. Print.

AN INTRODUCTION, PREFACE, FOREWORD, OR AFTERWORD

Callahan, John F. Introduction. *Flying Home and Other Stories*. By Ralph Ellison. Ed. John F. Callahan. New York: Vintage, 1996. 1-9. Print.

MATERIAL REPRINTED FROM ANOTHER SOURCE

Diffie, Whitfield, and Susan Landau. "Privacy: Protections and Threats." *Privacy on the Line: The Politics of Wiretapping and Encryption*. Cambridge, MA: MIT P, 1998. Rpt. in *Elements of Argument: A Text and Reader*. Annette T. Rottenberg and Donna Haisty Winchell. 8th ed. Boston: Bedford/St. Martin's, 2006. 601. Print.

A MULTIVOLUME WORK

Skotheim, Robert Allen, and Michael McGiffert, eds. *Since the Civil War*. Reading: Addison, 1972. Print. Vol. 2 of *American Social Thought: Sources and Interpretations*. 2 vols. 1972.

AN EDITION OTHER THAN THE FIRST

Charters, Ann, ed. *The Story and Its Writer: An Introduction to Short Fiction*. 7th ed. Boston: Bedford/St. Martin's, 2007. Print.

A TRANSLATION

Allende, Isabel. *The House of the Spirits*. Trans. Magda Bogin. New York: Knopf, 1985. Print.

A REPUBLISHED BOOK

Weesner, Theodore. *The Car Thief*. 1972. New York: Vintage-Random, 1987. Print.

Note: The only information about original publication you need to provide is the publication date, which appears immediately after the title.

A BOOK IN A SERIES

Eady, Cornelius. *Victims of the Latest Dance Craze*. Chicago: Omnation, 1985. Print. Omnation Press Dialogues on Dance Ser. 5.

The series title goes after the publication information and the medium.

AN ARTICLE FROM A DAILY NEWSPAPER

Doctorow, E. L. "Quick Cuts: The Novel Follows Film into a World of Fewer Words." *New York Times* 15 Mar. 1999, sec. B: 1+. Print.

AN ARTICLE FROM A MAGAZINE

Schulhofer, Stephen. "Unwanted Sex." *Atlantic Monthly* Oct. 1998: 55–66. Print.

AN UNSIGNED EDITORIAL

"Medium, Message." Editorial. *Nation* 28 Mar. 1987: 383–84. Print.

ANONYMOUS WORKS

"The March Almanac." *Atlantic Monthly* Mar. 1995: 20. Print.

Citation World Atlas. Maplewood: Hammond, 1999. Print.

AN ARTICLE FROM A JOURNAL WITH SEPARATE PAGINATION FOR EACH ISSUE

Brewer, Derek. "The Battleground of Home: Versions of Fairy Tales." *Encounter* 54.4 (1980): 52–61. Print.

AN ARTICLE IN A JOURNAL WITH CONTINUOUS PAGINATION THROUGHOUT THE VOLUME

McCafferty, Janey. "The Shadders Go Away." *New England Review and Bread Loaf Quarterly* 9 (1987): 332–42. Print.

MLA style is to include the issue number after the volume number, even though the volume has continuous pagination throughout the year. In this example, there is no issue number so only the volume number is included.

A REVIEW

Walker, David. Rev. of *A Wave*, by John Ashbery. *Field* 32 (1985): 63–71. Print.

AN ARTICLE IN A REFERENCE WORK

"Bylina." *The New Princeton Encyclopedia of Poetry and Poetics*. Ed. Alex Preminger and T. V. F. Brogan. Princeton: Princeton UP, 1993. Print.

A GOVERNMENT DOCUMENT

United States. National Endowment for the Arts. *2006 Annual Report*. Washington: Office of Public Affairs, 2007. Print.

Frequently the Government Printing Office (GPO) is the publisher of federal government documents.

AN UNPUBLISHED MANUSCRIPT

Leahy, Ellen. "An Investigation of the Computerization of Information Systems in a Family Planning Program." MS thesis. U of Massachusetts, Amherst, 1990.

A LETTER TO THE EDITOR

Flannery, James W. Letter. *New York Times Book Review* 28 Feb. 1993: 34. Print.

PERSONAL CORRESPONDENCE

Bennett, David. Letter to the author. 3 Mar. 2007. TS.

Include the medium of the correspondence at the end of the entry. Use *TS* for typescript and *MS* for manuscript (for handwritten letters).

A CARTOON

Henley, Marian. "Maxine." Comic strip. *Valley Advocate* 25 Feb. 1993: 39. Print.

Electronic Sources

A WEB SITE

Heiner, Heidi Anne. *SurLaLune Fairy Tales*. Heidi Anne Heiner, 3 Sept. 2009. Web. 9 Sept. 2009. *The Celtic Connection*. The Celtic Connection, n.d. Web. 9 Sept. 2009.

Include the name of the author or editor of the Web site, when this information is available; otherwise, begin the entry with the name of the Web site in italics, followed by a period; the publisher or sponsor of the Web site (usually found near the copyright information on the site's home page) followed by a comma and the date of publication or last update. Then add the medium (Web), a period, and the date you accessed the site.

A PAGE OR ARTICLE WITHIN A WEB SITE

Goodale, Wing, and Tim Divoll. "Birds, Bats and Coastal Wind Farm Development in Maine: A Literature Review." *BioDiversity Research Institute*. BioDiversity Research Inst., 29 May 2009. Web. 25 Aug. 2009.

A BOOK AVAILABLE ON THE WEB

Kramer, Heinrich, and James Sprenger. *The Malleus Maleficarum*. Trans. Montague Summers. New York, 1971. *MalleusMaleficarum.org*. Web. 14 Dec. 2007.

In this case the book had been previously published, and information about its original publication was included at the site.

THE ELEMENTS OF CITATION: ARTICLE FROM A WEB SITE (MLA)

When you cite a brief article from a Web site using MLA style, include the following:

1 Author
2 Title of work
3 Title of Web site
4 Sponsor of site
5 Date of publication or latest update
6 Medium (Web)
7 Date of access

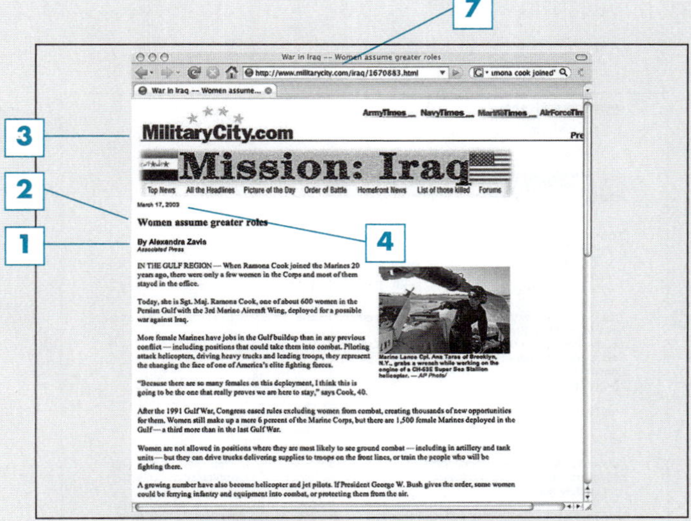

Works Cited entry for a brief article from a Web site in MLA style

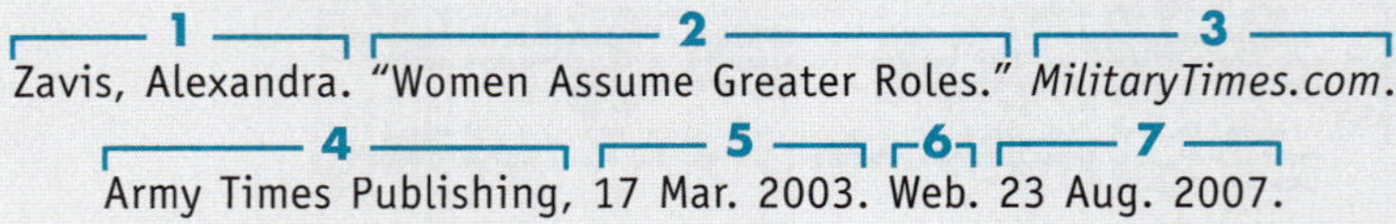
1 Zavis, Alexandra. 2 "Women Assume Greater Roles." 3 *MilitaryTimes.com*. 4 Army Times Publishing, 5 17 Mar. 2003. 6 Web. 7 23 Aug. 2007.

AN ARTICLE FROM AN ELECTRONIC JOURNAL

Minow, Mary. "Filters and the Public Library: A Legal and Policy Analysis." *First Monday* 2.12 (1997): n. pag. Web. 28 Nov. 2007.

THE ELEMENTS OF CITATION: ARTICLE FROM A DATABASE (MLA)

When you cite an article from a database using MLA style, include the following:

1 Author
2 Title of article
3 Title of periodical, volume and issue numbers
4 Date of publication
5 Inclusive pages
6 Name of database
7 Medium (Web)
8 Date of access

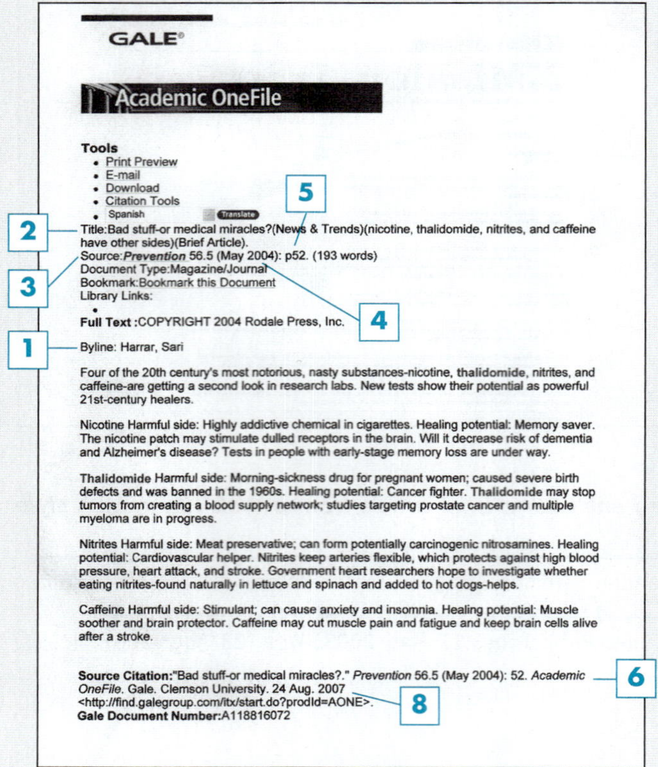

GALE®

Academic OneFile

Tools
- Print Preview
- E-mail
- Download
- Citation Tools
- Spanish Translate

Title:Bad stuff-or medical miracles?(News & Trends)(nicotine, thalidomide, nitrites, and caffeine have other sides)(Brief Article).
Source:*Prevention* 56.5 (May 2004): p52. (193 words)
Document Type:Magazine/Journal
Bookmark:Bookmark this Document
Library Links:
•
Full Text :COPYRIGHT 2004 Rodale Press, Inc.

Byline: Harrar, Sari

Four of the 20th century's most notorious, nasty substances-nicotine, thalidomide, nitrites, and caffeine-are getting a second look in research labs. New tests show their potential as powerful 21st-century healers.

Nicotine Harmful side: Highly addictive chemical in cigarettes. Healing potential: Memory saver. The nicotine patch may stimulate dulled receptors in the brain. Will it decrease risk of dementia and Alzheimer's disease? Tests in people with early-stage memory loss are under way.

Thalidomide Harmful side: Morning-sickness drug for pregnant women; caused severe birth defects and was banned in the 1960s. Healing potential: Cancer fighter. Thalidomide may stop tumors from creating a blood supply network; studies targeting prostate cancer and multiple myeloma are in progress.

Nitrites Harmful side: Meat preservative; can form potentially carcinogenic nitrosamines. Healing potential: Cardiovascular helper. Nitrites keep arteries flexible, which protects against high blood pressure, heart attack, and stroke. Government heart researchers hope to investigate whether eating nitrites-found naturally in lettuce and spinach and added to hot dogs-helps.

Caffeine Harmful side: Stimulant; can cause anxiety and insomnia. Healing potential: Muscle soother and brain protector. Caffeine may cut muscle pain and fatigue and keep brain cells alive after a stroke.

Source Citation:"Bad stuff-or medical miracles?." *Prevention* 56.5 (May 2004): 52. *Academic OneFile*. Gale. Clemson University. 24 Aug. 2007
<http://find.galegroup.com/itx/start.do?prodId=AONE>.
Gale Document Number:A118816072

Works Cited entry for an article from a database in MLA style

Harrar, Sari. [1] "Bad Stuff — or Medical Miracles?" [2] *Prevention* 56.5 [3] (2004) [4]: 52. [5]
Academic OneFile. [6] Web. [7] 24 Aug. 2007. [8]

AN ARTICLE FROM A FULL-TEXT DATABASE AVAILABLE THROUGH THE WEB

Warner, Marina. "Pity the Stepmother." *New York Times* 12 May 1991, late ed.: D17. *LexisNexis Universe.* Web. 12 Dec. 2007.

Gura, Mark. "The Gorgeous Mosaic." *School Arts* 93.2 (1993): 26–27. *General Reference Center Gold*. Web. 14 Dec. 2007.

Include the original source information and then add the name of the database in italics, the medium, and your date of access.

A REPORT FROM A DATABASE

Kassenbaum, Peter. *Cultural Awareness Training Manual and Study Guide*. 1992. *ERIC*. Web. 14 Dec. 2007.

Treat educational resources and technical reports found on a database as you would any other source from a database. Include the name of the database in italics after the publication information, and then add the medium and your date of access.

MATERIAL ACCESSED THROUGH A COMPUTER SERVICE

Boynton, Robert S. "The New Intellectuals." *Atlantic Monthly* Mar. 1995. *America Online*. Web. 3 Mar. 2007.

Treat the computer service as the database, then add the medium and your date of access. Do not include keywords or other information specific to the computer service.

A CD-ROM

Corcoran, Mary B. "Fairy Tale." *Grolier Multimedia Encyclopedia*. Danbury: Grolier, 1995. CD-ROM.

AN ARTICLE FROM A CD-ROM FULL-TEXT DATABASE

"Tribal/DNC Donations." *News from Indian Country* Dec. 1997. CD-ROM. *Ethnic Newswatch*. Stamford: SoftLine. 12 Oct. 2007.

Include the original source information and the medium of publication (CD-ROM), then add the name of the database, the publisher or vendor of the CD-ROM, and the electronic publication data, if available.

AN ARTICLE FROM AN ELECTRONIC REFERENCE WORK

"Folk Arts." *Britannica*. Encyclopaedia Britannica, 2007. Web. 14 Dec. 2007.

A PERSONAL E-MAIL COMMUNICATION

Franz, Kenneth. "Re: Species Reintroduction." Message to the author. 12 Oct. 2007. E-mail.

A POSTING TO A DISCUSSION LIST, WEB FORUM, OR NEWSGROUP

Lee, Constance. "Re: Mothers and Stepmothers." *Folklore Discussion List*. Texas A&M U, 10 Sept. 2007. Web. 24 Oct. 2008.

House, Ron. "Wind Farms: Do They Kill Birds?" *Google Groups: Rec.Animals.Wildlife*. Google, 7 Sept. 2009. Web. 14 Sept. 2009.

Treat these as short works from a Web site. Include the author of the posting and the title or subject line of the posting in quotation marks (if there is title, use the designation "Online posting" without quotation marks). Then add the name of the Web site, the sponsor of the site, the date of the posting, the medium, and your date of access.

■ Other Sources

A LECTURE

Calvino, Italo. "Right and Wrong Political Uses of Literature." Symposium on European Politics. Amherst College, Amherst. 25 Feb. 1976. Lecture.

A FILM

The Voice of the Khalam. Prod. Loretta Pauker. Perf. Leopold Senghor, Okara, Birago Diop, Rubadiri, and Francis Parkes. Contemporary Films/McGraw-Hill, 1971. Film.

Other pertinent information to give in film references, if available, is the writer and director (see model for radio/television program for style).

A TELEVISION OR RADIO PROGRAM

The Shakers: Hands to Work, Hearts to God. Narr. David McCullough. Dir. Ken Burns and Amy Stechler Burns. Writ. Amy Stechler Burns, Wendy Tilghman, and Tom Lewis. PBS. WGBY, Springfield, MA, 28 Dec. 1992. Television.

A VIDEOCASSETTE

Style Wars! Prod. Tony Silver and Henry Chalfont. New Day Films, 1985. Videocassette.

DVD

Harry Potter and the Order of the Phoenix. Prod. David Barron and David Heyman. Warner Bros., 2007. DVD.

A PERFORMANCE

Quilters: A Musical Celebration. By Molly Newman and Barbara Damashek. Dir. Joyce Devlin. Musical dir. Faith Fung. Mt. Holyoke Laboratory Theatre, South Hadley, MA. 26 Apr. 1991. Performance.

AN INTERVIEW

Hines, Gregory. Interview by D. C. Denison. *Boston Globe Magazine* 29 Mar. 1987: 2. Print.

Note: An interview conducted by the author of the paper would be documented as follows:

Hines, Gregory. Personal interview. 29 Mar. 1987.

A broadcast interview would be documented as follows:

Hines, Gregory. Interview by Charlie Rose. *Charlie Rose*. PBS. WGBH, Boston, 30 Jan. 2001. Television.

DOCUMENTING YOUR RESEARCH (APA SYSTEM)

Following are examples of the bibliographical forms you are most likely to employ if you are using the American Psychological Association (APA) system for documenting sources. If you need the format for a type of publication not listed here, consult the *Publication Manual of the American Psychological Association*, Sixth Edition (2010).

If you are used to the Modern Language Association (MLA) system for documenting sources, take a moment to notice some of the key differences. In APA style, authors and editors are listed by last name and initials(s) only, and the year comes immediately after the author's or editor's name instead of at or near the end of the entry. Titles in general are not capitalized in the conventional way. The overall structure of each entry, however, will be familiar: author, title, publication information.

Print Sources

A BOOK BY A SINGLE AUTHOR

Briggs, J. (1988). *Fire in the crucible: The alchemy of creative genius*. New York, NY: St. Martin's Press.

MULTIPLE WORKS BY THE SAME AUTHOR IN THE SAME YEAR

Gardner, H. (1982a). *Art, mind, and brain: A cognitive approach to creativity*. New York, NY: Basic Books.

Gardner, H. (1982b). *Developmental psychology: An introduction* (2nd ed.). Boston, MA: Little, Brown.

AN ANTHOLOGY OR COMPILATION

Gioseffi, D. (Ed.). (1988). *Women on war*. New York, NY: Simon & Schuster.

THE ELEMENTS OF CITATION: BOOK (APA)

When you cite a book using APA style, include the following:

1 Author

2 Date of publication

3 Title and subtitle

4 City and state of publication

5 Publisher

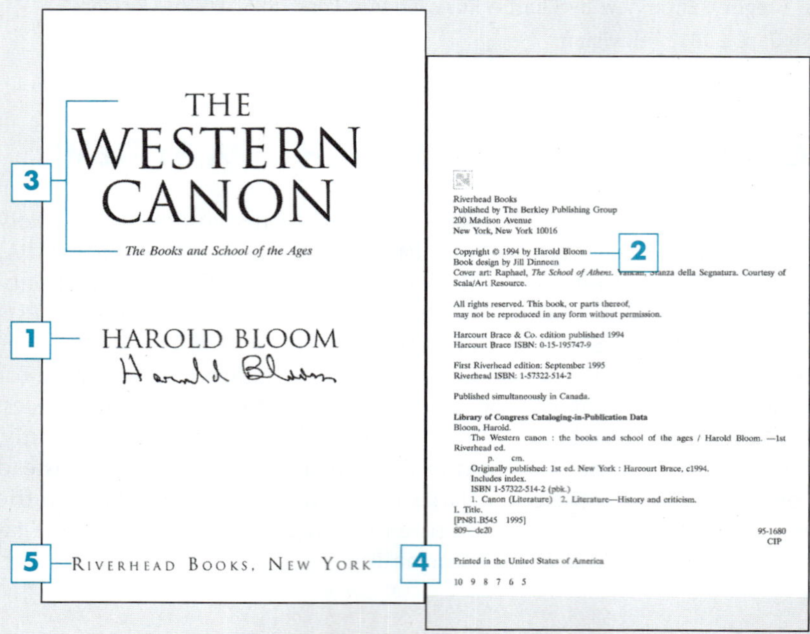

Riverhead Books
Published by The Berkley Publishing Group
200 Madison Avenue
New York, New York 10016

Copyright © 1994 by Harold Bloom
Book design by Jill Dinneen
Cover art: Raphael, *The School of Athens*. Vatican, Stanza della Segnatura. Courtesy of Scala/Art Resource.

All rights reserved. This book, or parts thereof, may not be reproduced in any form without permission.

Harcourt Brace & Co. edition published 1994
Harcourt Brace ISBN: 0-15-195747-9

First Riverhead edition: September 1995
Riverhead ISBN: 1-57322-514-2

Published simultaneously in Canada.

Library of Congress Cataloging-in-Publication Data
Bloom, Harold.
The Western canon : the books and school of the ages / Harold Bloom. —1st Riverhead ed.
p. cm.
Originally published: 1st ed. New York : Harcourt Brace, c1994.
Includes index.
ISBN 1-57322-514-2 (pbk.)
1. Canon (Literature) 2. Literature—History and criticism.
I. Title.
[PN81.B545 1995]
809—dc20 95-1680
CIP

Printed in the United States of America

10 9 8 7 6 5

Reference list entry for a book in APA style

1 — 2 — 3
Bloom, H. (1994). *The western canon: The books and school of the ages.*
4 — 5
New York, NY: Riverhead Books.

A BOOK BY TWO TO SEVEN AUTHORS OR EDITORS

Atwan, R., & Roberts, J. (Eds.). (1996). *Left, right, and center: Voices from across the political spectrum*. Boston, MA: Bedford Books.

Note: List the names of *all* the authors or editors, with an ampersand before the last one. For eight or more authors, list the first six authors followed by an ellipsis (three dots), and then list the last author's name. In these citations, there is no ampersand before the last author.

A BOOK BY A CORPORATE AUTHOR

International Advertising Association. (1977). *Controversy advertising: How advertisers present points of view on public affairs*. New York, NY: Hastings House.

A WORK IN AN ANTHOLOGY

Mukherjee, B. (1988). The colonization of the mind. In D. Gioseffi (Ed.), *Women on war* (pp. 140–142). New York, NY: Simon & Schuster.

AN INTRODUCTION, PREFACE, FOREWORD, OR AFTERWORD

Hemenway, R. (1984). Introduction. In Z. N. Hurston, *Dust tracks on a road* (pp. ix–xxxix). Urbana: University of Illinois Press.

AN EDITION OTHER THAN THE FIRST

Gumpert, G., & Cathcart, R. (Eds.). (1986). *Inter/media: Interpersonal communication in a media world* (3rd ed.). New York, NY: Oxford University Press.

A TRANSLATION

Sartre, J. P. (1962). *Literature and existentialism* (B. Frechtman, Trans.). New York, NY: Citadel Press. (Original work published 1949)

A REPUBLISHED BOOK

James, W. (1969). *The varieties of religious experience: A study in human nature*. London, England: Collier Books. (Original work published 1902)

A BOOK IN A SERIES

Berthrong, D. J. (1976). *The Cheyenne and Arapaho ordeal: Reservation and agency life in the Indian territory, 1875-1907. Vol. 136. The civilization of the American Indian series*. Norman: University of Oklahoma Press.

A MULTIVOLUME WORK

Mussen, P. H. (Ed.). (1983). *Handbook of child psychology* (4th ed., Vols. 1–4). New York, NY: Wiley.

AN ARTICLE FROM A DAILY NEWSPAPER

Hottelet, R. C. (1990, March 15). Germany: Why it can't happen again. *Christian Science Monitor*, p. 19.

AN ARTICLE FROM A PERIODICAL

Gorriti, G. A. (1989, July). How to fight the drug war. *Atlantic Monthly*, 70–76.

AN ARTICLE IN A JOURNAL WITH CONTINUOUS PAGINATION THROUGHOUT THE VOLUME

Cockburn, A. (1989). British justice, Irish victims. *The Nation, 249*, 554–555.

AN ARTICLE FROM A JOURNAL WITH SEPARATE PAGINATION FOR EACH ISSUE

Mukerji, C. (1984). Visual language in science and the exercise of power: The case of cartography in early modern Europe. *Studies in Visual Communication, 10*(3), 30–45.

AN ARTICLE IN A REFERENCE WORK

Frisby, J. P. (1990). Direct perception. In M. W. Eysenck (Ed.), *Blackwell dictionary of cognitive psychology* (pp. 95–100). Oxford, England: Basil Blackwell.

A GOVERNMENT PUBLICATION

United States Dept. of Health, Education, and Welfare. (1973). *Current ethical issues in mental health*. Washington, DC: U.S. Government Printing Office.

AN ABSTRACT

Fritz, M. (1990/1991). A comparison of social interactions using a friendship awareness activity. *Education and Training in Mental Retardation, 25,* 352–359. Abstract retrieved from *Psychological Abstracts*. (Abstract No. 11474)

When the dates of the original publication and of the abstract differ, give both dates separated by a slash.

AN ANONYMOUS WORK

The status of women: Different but the same. (1992–1993). *Zontian, 73*(3), 5.

A REVIEW

Harris, I. M. (1991). [Review of the book *Rediscovering masculinity: Reason, language, and sexuality,* by V. Seidler]. *Gender and Society, 5,* 259–261.

Give the author of the review, not the author of the book being reviewed. Use this form for a film review also. If the review has a title, place it before the bracketed material, and treat it like an article title.

A LETTER TO THE EDITOR

Pritchett, J. T., & Kellner, C. H. (1993). Comment on spontaneous seizure activity [Letter to the editor]. *Journal of Nervous and Mental Disease, 181*, 138–139.

PERSONAL CORRESPONDENCE

B. Ehrenreich (personal communication, August 7, 2007).

(B. Ehrenreich, personal communication, August 7, 2007.)

Cite all personal communications to you (such as letters, memos, e-mails, and telephone conversations) in text only, *without* listing them among the references. The phrasing of your sentences will determine which of the two above forms to use.

AN UNPUBLISHED MANUSCRIPT

McIntosh, P. (1988). *White privilege and male privilege: A personal account of coming to see correspondences through work in women's studies*. Working Paper 189. Unpublished manuscript, Wellesley College, Center for Research on Women, Wellesley, MA.

PROCEEDINGS OF A MEETING, PUBLISHED

Guerrero, R. (1972/1973). Possible effects of the periodic abstinence method. In W. A. Uricchio & M. K. Williams (Eds.), *Proceedings of a Research Conference on Natural Family Planning* (pp. 96–105). Washington, DC: Human Life Foundation.

If the date of the symposium or conference is different from the date of publication, give both, separated by a slash. If the proceedings are published annually, treat the reference like a periodical article.

Electronic Sources

AN ARTICLE FROM AN ONLINE PERIODICAL WITH A DOI

Chattopadhyay, P. (2003). Can dissimilarity lead to positive outcomes? The influence of open versus closed minds. *Journal of Organizational Behavior, 24,* 295–312. doi:10.1002/job.118

If the article duplicates the version which appeared in a print periodical, use the same basic primary journal reference. See "An Article from a Periodical." Some online articles have a "digital object identifier" (DOI.) Use the DOI at the end of the entry in place of the URL.

AN ARTICLE FROM AN ONLINE PERIODICAL WITHOUT A DOI

Riordan, V. (2001, January 1). Verbal-performance IQ discrepancies in children attending a child and adolescent psychiatry clinic. *Child and Adolescent Psychiatry On-Line*. Retrieved from http://www.priory.com/psych/iq.htm

If an article does not have a DOI, after the publication information add the exact URL for the article or the URL of the home page of the journal.

THE ELEMENTS OF CITATION: ARTICLE FROM A WEB SITE (APA)

When you cite an article from a Web site using APA style, include the following:

1 Author

2 Date of publication or most recent update

3 Title of document on Web site

4 Title of section

5 Date of access (only if content is likely to change)

6 URL of document

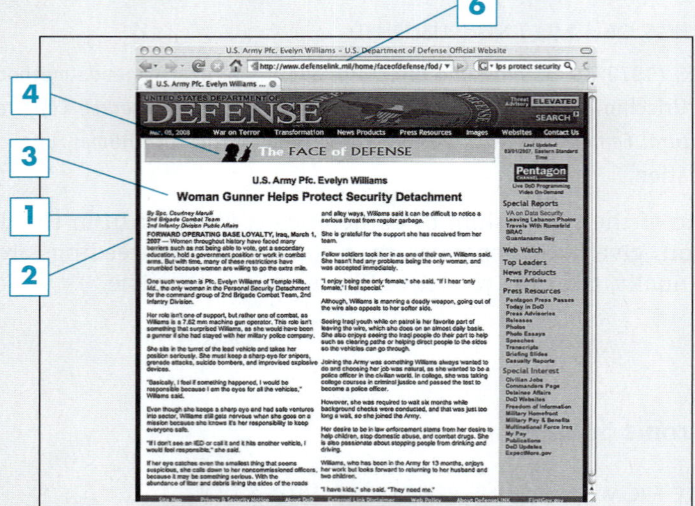

Reference list entry for a brief article from a Web site in APA style

Marulli, C. [1] (2007, March 1). [2] Woman gunner helps protect security detachment. [3] In *The Face of Defense*. [4] Retrieved from http://www.defenselink.mil/home/faceofdefense/fod/2007-03/f20070301a.html [6]

A NONPERIODICAL WEB DOCUMENT

Munro, K. (2001, February). *Changing your body image*. Retrieved from http://www.kalimunro.com/article_changing_body_image.html

In general, follow this format: author's name, the date of publication (if no publication date is available, use "n.d."), the title of the document in italics, and the source's URL.

THE ELEMENTS OF CITATION: ARTICLE FROM A DATABASE (APA)

When you cite an article from a database using APA style, include the following:

1 Author
2 Date of publication
3 Title of article
4 Name of periodical
5 Volume and issue numbers
6 Page numbers
7 DOI
8 URL for journal's home page (if no DOI)

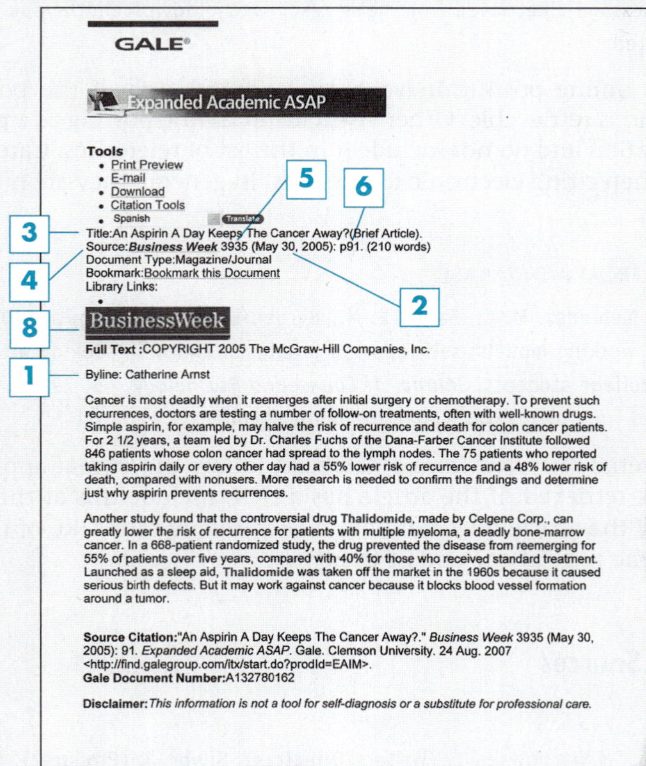

GALE®

Expanded Academic ASAP

Tools

- Print Preview
- E-mail
- Download
- Citation Tools
- Spanish Translate

Title:An Aspirin A Day Keeps The Cancer Away?(Brief Article).
Source:*Business Week* 3935 (May 30, 2005): p91. (210 words)
Document Type:Magazine/Journal
Bookmark:Bookmark this Document
Library Links:

BusinessWeek

Full Text :COPYRIGHT 2005 The McGraw-Hill Companies, Inc.

Byline: Catherine Arnst

Cancer is most deadly when it reemerges after initial surgery or chemotherapy. To prevent such recurrences, doctors are testing a number of follow-on treatments, often with well-known drugs. Simple aspirin, for example, may halve the risk of recurrence and death for colon cancer patients. For 2 1/2 years, a team led by Dr. Charles Fuchs of the Dana-Farber Cancer Institute followed 846 patients whose colon cancer had spread to the lymph nodes. The 75 patients who reported taking aspirin daily or every other day had a 55% lower risk of recurrence and a 48% lower risk of death, compared with nonusers. More research is needed to confirm the findings and determine just why aspirin prevents recurrences.

Another study found that the controversial drug Thalidomide, made by Celgene Corp., can greatly lower the risk of recurrence for patients with multiple myeloma, a deadly bone-marrow cancer. In a 668-patient randomized study, the drug prevented the disease from reemerging for 55% of patients over five years, compared with 40% for those who received standard treatment. Launched as a sleep aid, Thalidomide was taken off the market in the 1960s because it caused serious birth defects. But it may work against cancer because it blocks blood vessel formation around a tumor.

Source Citation:"An Aspirin A Day Keeps The Cancer Away?." *Business Week* 3935 (May 30, 2005): 91. *Expanded Academic ASAP*. Gale. Clemson University. 24 Aug. 2007 <http://find.galegroup.com/itx/start.do?prodId=EAIM>.
Gale Document Number:A132780162

Disclaimer: *This information is not a tool for self-diagnosis or a substitute for professional care.*

Reference list entry for an article from a database in APA style

Arnst, C. (2005, May 30). An aspirin a day keeps the cancer away? *Business Week 3935*, 91. Retrieved from http://businessweek.com/

A CHAPTER OR SECTION IN A WEB DOCUMENT

National Council of Welfare, Canada. (1998). Other issues related to poverty lines. In *A new poverty line: Yes, no or maybe?* (chap. 5). Retrieved from http://www.ncwcnbes.net/htmdocument/reportnewpovline/chap5.htm

AN E-MAIL

Do not include personal communications such as e-mails in your list of references. See "Personal Correspondence."

A MESSAGE POSTED TO A NEWSGROUP

Isaacs, K. (2008, January 20). Philosophical roots of psychology [Electronic newsgroup message]. Retrieved from news://sci.psychology.psychotherapy.moderated

Include an online posting in your reference list only if the posting is archived and is retrievable. Otherwise, cite an online posting as a personal communication and do not include it in the list of references. Care should be taken when citing electronic discussions. In general, they are not scholarly sources.

AN ARTICLE FROM A DATABASE

Lopez, F. G., Melendez, M. C., Sauer, E. M., Berger, E., & Wyssmann, J. (1998). Internal working models, self-reported problems, and help-seeking attitudes among college students. *Journal of Counseling Psychology, 45*, 79–83. Retrieved from http://www.apa.org/journals/cou

To cite material retrieved from a database, follow the format appropriate to the work retrieved. If the article has a DOI, include this at the end of the entry. If the article does not have a DOI, include the URL of the periodical's home page at the end of the entry.

Other Sources

A FILM

Wachowski, A., & Wachowski, L. (Writers/Directors). Silver, J. (Producer). (1999). *The matrix* [Motion picture]. United States: Warner Bros.

Include the name and the function of the originator or primary contributor (director or producer). Identify the work as a motion picture, or if you viewed a videocassette or DVD, include the appropriate label in brackets. Include the country of origin and the studio. If the motion picture is of limited circulation, provide the name and address of the distributor in parentheses at the end of the reference.

A TELEVISION SERIES

Jones, R. (Producer). (1990). *Exploring consciousness* [Television series]. Boston, MA: WGBH.

WRAPPING UP RESEARCH

Including Visuals in Your Paper

In this world of instantaneous Internet access to millions of documents and sites, it is easy to perceive knowledge as free for our use. The fact that information is easy to access does not relieve you of the responsibility of giving credit to those who originated the ideas expressed there. In fact, the ease with which material can be posted to the Internet makes it even more difficult to separate valid information from that which is questionable at best.

Since the Internet is a world of images as well as words, it may give you ideas for livening up your own work with all sorts of visuals. Don't forget, though, that you are obligated to give credit to the source of your visuals along with the ideas and words that you use. A graph or chart may provide just the sort of statistical support that will make a key point in your argument, and it can be easily cut and pasted or scanned into your electronic text, but you must document that graph or chart just as you would text. You should acknowledge the location where you found the visual and as much information as is provided about who produced it. If you use copyrighted graphs or charts in work that you publish either in print or electronic form, you should seek permission for their use. The same is true for photographs and other illustrations, although some books and Web sites offer images that you can use free of charge. You may be surprised to find that something as common as your school's logo is copyrighted and cannot be used on your Web page, for example, without permission.

Keeping Research under Control

How do you know when you have done enough research? If you have kept your outline updated, you have a visual record of your progress. Check this against the guidelines on pages 434–35. Is each point backed by at least two pieces of support? Do your sources represent a range of authors and of types of data? If a large proportion of your support comes from one book, or if most of your references are to newspaper articles, you probably need to keep working. On the other hand, if your notes cite five different authorities making essentially the same point, you may have collected more data than you need. It can be useful to point out that more than one authority holds a given view and to make notes of examples that are notably different from one another. But it is not necessary to take down all the passages or examples expressing the same idea.

To This Point

Before you leave the library or your primary sources and start writing, check to make sure your research is complete.

1. Does your working outline show any gaps in your argument?
2. Have you found adequate data to support your claim?
3. Have you identified the warrants linking your claim with data and ensured that these warrants too are adequately documented?
4. If you intend to quote or paraphrase sources in your paper, do your notes include exact copies of all statements you may want to use and complete references?
5. Have you answered all the relevant questions that have come up during your research?
6. Do you have enough information about your sources to document your paper?

Compiling an Annotated Bibliography

An annotated bibliography is a list of sources that includes the usual bibliographic information followed by a paragraph describing and evaluating each source. Its purpose is to provide information about each source in a bibliography so that the reader has an overview of the resources related to a given topic.

For each source in an annotated bibliography, the same bibliographic information included in a Works Cited or References list is provided, alphabetized by author. Each reference also has a short paragraph that describes the work, its main focus, and, if appropriate, the methodology used in or the style of the work. An annotation might note special features such as tables or illustrations. Usually an annotation evaluates the source by analyzing its usefulness, reliability, and overall significance for understanding the topic. An annotation might include some information on the credentials of the author or the organization that produced it.

A SAMPLE ANNOTATION USING THE MLA CITATION STYLE

Warner, Marina. "Pity the Stepmother." *New York Times* 12 May 1991, late ed.: D17. *Lexis/Nexis Universe*. Web. 12 Dec. 2007.

The author asserts that many fairy tales feature absent or cruel mothers, transformed by romantic editors such as the Grimm brothers into stepmothers because the idea of a wicked mother desecrated an ideal. She argues that figures in fairy tales should be viewed in their historical context and that social conditions often affected the way that motherhood figured in fairy tales. Warner, a novelist and author of books on the images of Joan of Arc and the Virgin Mary, writes persuasively about the social roots of a fairy-tale archetype.

APA style does not call for annotated citations.

CHAPTER 12

Writing an Argumentative Paper

Chapter 11 discusses the planning of an argumentative paper and the process involved in researching topics that require support beyond what the writer knows firsthand. This chapter discusses moving from the planning and researching stage into the actual writing of the paper.

Making a preliminary outline before you conduct any needed research gives direction to your research. If your topic requires no research, a preliminary outline helps you to organize your own thoughts on the subject. Preliminary outlines can change, however, in the process of researching and writing the paper. As you begin drafting the paper, you will need to finalize your decisions about what issues you want to raise.

Once you are satisfied that you have identified all the issues that will appear in your paper, you should begin to determine what kind of organization will be most effective for your argument. Now is the time to organize the results of your thinking into a logical and persuasive form. If you have read about your topic, answered questions, and acquired some evidence, you may already have decided on ways to approach your subject. If not, you should look closely at your outline now, recalling your purposes when you began your investigation, and develop a strategy for using the information you have gathered to achieve those purposes.

DEFINING THE ISSUES

■ Case Study: School Uniforms

To see how we raise and evaluate issues in a specific context, let's look at a controversy that has surfaced recently in many of our nation's public schools.

Some schools are considering requiring school uniforms, but that proposal has not been met with unanimous support from students or their parents.

In one particular school district, those in favor of school uniforms raised these issues:

1. Other schools that initiated a uniform requirement experienced an improvement in discipline.
2. Buying uniforms is economical for parents.
3. Wearing uniforms takes away undesirable distinctions based on social and economic class.
4. Students who wear uniforms are not distracted by what they or others are wearing.
5. A uniform requirement does away with the need for increasingly detailed dress codes.

On the other side, those who opposed school uniforms introduced the following issues:

1. Requiring uniforms does not guarantee improved discipline.
2. A uniform requirement prevents parents from buying inexpensive clothing alternatives.
3. Students have the right to express themselves through their choice of clothing.
4. A dress code can eliminate fashions that are distracting to other students without taking away the student's choice of clothing completely.
5. Some students' weight, body shape, etc., may make them uncomfortable and self-conscious in the style of uniform chosen.

You would have to understand these issues—understand the ongoing conversation—before you could argue successfully about the topic. Now let's analyze these issues, comparing their strengths and weaknesses.

1. It is clear that not all the issues in this dispute were equally important. The arguers decided, therefore, to give greater emphasis to the issues most likely to be persuasive to their audiences and less attention to those difficult to prove or narrower in their appeal. At this time in some of the communities in the district, massive layoffs had forced parents out of work. Therefore, the cost of switching to uniforms was a major concern. If parents did not have to spend money on uniforms, they could shop for the most economic alternatives or let their younger children wear clothes their older children had outgrown. Within the district, there had been few problems with fashions that were extreme enough to be a distraction to other students, and those few could be addressed with minor additions to the dress code, certainly an easy accommodation to make. To those opposed to the uniform requirement, the economic concerns seemed to outweigh the use of

uniforms as a means of establishing discipline, a goal they felt could be accomplished by other means.

2. It was also clear that, as in several of the other cases we have examined, the support on both sides consisted of both factual data and appeals to values. With regard to the factual data, each side reported evidence to prove that:

a. the wearing of uniforms leads or does not lead to a reduced number of discipline problems.
b. uniforms are or are not an economical alternative.
c. the majority of students favored or opposed wearing uniforms.
d. the majority of parents favored or opposed the uniform requirement.

The factual data were important. If opponents could prove that uniforms would place an increased financial burden on families already hurt by layoffs, the argument in favor of uniforms would be weakened. It would be weakened further if factual data from other similar districts showed no improvement in discipline.

Let us assume that the factual claims either were settled or remained in abeyance. We now turn our attention to a second set of issues, a contest over the values to be served.

3. Both sides in the dispute were concerned about the well-being of the students. Related to that, of course, was the well-being of their families. Improved discipline in the schools would benefit all students because the focus could be on education, not on policing student behavior. Beyond both of these concerns, however, were the issues of students' rights and their need to express themselves. If the majority of the students opposed uniforms, was that a strong enough concern to override the financial burden on their families? What about the minority who favored uniforms and perhaps had felt stigmatized by being unable to afford the clothes in style among their peers? In such a situation, should a vote by the students play a major role in policy decisions? Students are not allowed to hire their own teachers or to choose their manner of instruction, their courses of study, their grades, or the rules of admission. In the school community, administrators argued, the experienced are required to lead and instruct the inexperienced.

No controversy exists out of context. An outsider who entered this debate unaware of the recent layoffs, for example, would probably underestimate the weight that finances should receive in considering the uniform issue. In a different setting, a uniform requirement might raise questions about discrimination against those required by their religion to be veiled. In different cultures, students have gone to court to protect their right to wear clothing depicting the Confederate flag or making statements opposing the war in Iraq in spite of school rules against these types of displays.

Recently, a controversy over a billboard arose in a university town. An apartment complex near the university called The Reserve had designed an ad that played on its name. The left-hand side of the billboard pictured a demure young lady with the caption "Reserved." The right-hand side pictured a young lady smiling over her shoulder at the camera, dressed in low-cut jeans exposing a tattoo on her lower back. This picture, of course, was labeled "Unreserved." The billboard probably would have been accepted as a clever play on words and a catchy marketing ploy had a student not been murdered in the complex only months before, strangled with her bikini top. Members of the community were quick to judge the billboard inappropriate under the circumstances—so vocally that the billboard was taken down. The concern was that this visual might make young women at the complex the target for further sex crimes. The context influenced the response to this particular visual argument.

As you approach the writing of your argument, be mindful of the context in which the argument is taking place.

In making our way through the uniform debate, we have summarized a procedure for tackling the issues in any controversial problem.

1. Raise the relevant issues and arrange them in order of importance. Plan to devote more time and space to issues you regard as crucial.
2. Produce the strongest evidence you can to support your factual claims, knowing that the opposing side or critical readers may try to produce conflicting evidence.
3. Defend your value claims by finding support in the fundamental principles with which most people in your audience would agree.
4. Argue with yourself. Try to foresee what kinds of refutation are possible. Try to anticipate and meet the opposing arguments.
5. Consider the context in which your argument will be read and be sensitive to the concerns of your audience.

ORGANIZING THE MATERIAL

The first point to establish in organizing your material is what type of thesis you plan to present. Is your intention to make readers aware of some problem? To offer a solution to the problem? To defend a position? To refute a position held by others? The way you organize your material will depend to a great extent on your goal. With that goal in mind, look over your outline and reevaluate the relative importance of your issues. Which ones are most convincing? Which are backed up by the strongest support? Which ones relate to facts, and which concern values?

With these points in mind, let us look at various ways of organizing an argumentative paper. It would be foolish to decide in advance how many paragraphs a paper ought to have; however, you can and should choose a general strategy before you begin writing. If your thesis presents an opinion or recommends some course of action, you may choose simply to state your main idea and then defend it. If your thesis argues against an opposing view, you probably will want to mention that view and then refute it. Both these organizations introduce the thesis in the first or second paragraph (called the *thesis paragraph*). You may decide that two or more differing positions have merit and that you want to offer a compromise between or among positions. A fourth possibility is to start establishing that a problem exists and then introduce your thesis as the solution; this method is called *presenting the stock issues*. Although these four approaches sometimes overlap in practice, examining each one individually can help you structure your paper. Let's take a look at each arrangement.

Defending the Main Idea

All forms of organization will require you to defend your main idea, but one way of doing this is simple and direct. Early in the paper state the main idea that you will defend throughout your argument. You can also indicate here the two or three points you intend to develop in support of your claim; or you can raise these later as they come up. Suppose your thesis is that widespread vegetarianism would solve a number of problems. You could phrase it this way: "If the majority of people in this country adopted a vegetarian diet, we would see improvements in the economy, in the health of our people, and in moral sensitivity." You would then develop each of the claims in your list with appropriate data and warrants. Notice that the thesis statement in the first (thesis) paragraph has already outlined your organizational pattern. However, if you find that listing your two or three main ideas in the thesis leads to too much repetition later in the paper, you can introduce each one as it arises in your discussion of the topic.

Defending the main idea is effective for factual claims as well as policy claims, in which you urge the adoption of a certain policy and give the reasons for its adoption. It is most appropriate when your thesis is straightforward and can be readily supported by direct statements.

Refuting an Opposing View

Refuting an opposing view means to attack it in order to weaken, invalidate, or make it less credible to a reader. Since all arguments are dialogues or debates—even when the opponent is only imaginary—refutation of another point of view is always implicit in your arguments. As you write, keep in mind the issues that an opponent may raise. You will be looking at your own argument as an unsympathetic reader may look at it, asking yourself the same kinds of critical questions and trying to find its weaknesses in order to correct them. In this way every argument you write becomes a form of refutation.

How do you plan a refutation? Here are some general guidelines.

1. If you want to refute the argument in a specific essay or article, read the argument carefully, noting all the points with which you disagree. This advice may seem obvious, but it cannot be too strongly emphasized. If your refutation does not indicate scrupulous familiarity with your opponent's argument, he or she has the right to say, and often does, "You haven't really read what I wrote. You haven't really answered my argument."

2. If you think that your readers are sympathetic to an opposing view or are not familiar with it, summarize it at the beginning of your paper, providing enough information to give readers an understanding of exactly what you plan to refute. When you summarize, it's important to be respectful of the opposition's views. You don't want to alienate readers who might not agree with you at first.

3. If your argument is long and complex, choose only the most important points to refute. Otherwise the reader who does not have the original argument on hand may find a detailed refutation hard to follow. If the argument is short and relatively simple—a claim supported by only two or three points—you may decide to refute all of them, devoting more space to the most important ones.

4. Attack the principal elements in the argument of your opponent.
    a. Question the evidence. (See pp. 220–22 in the text.) Question whether your opponent has proved that a problem exists.
    b. Attack the warrants or assumptions that underlie the claim. (See pp. 282–83 in the text.)
    c. Attack the logic or reasoning of the opposing view. (Refer to the discussion of fallacious reasoning on pp. 337–47 in the text.)
    d. Attack the proposed solution to a problem, pointing out that it will not work.

5. Be prepared to do more than attack the opposing view. Supply evidence and good reasons in support of your own claim.

Finding the Middle Ground

Although an argument, by definition, assumes a difference of opinion, we know that opposing sides frequently find accommodation somewhere in the middle. As you mount your own argument about a controversial issue, you need not confine yourself to support of any of the differing positions. You may want to acknowledge that there is some justice on all sides and that you understand the difficulty of resolving the issue.

Consider these guidelines for an argument that offers a compromise between or among competing positions:

1. Early in your essay explain the differing positions. Make clear the major differences separating the two (or more) sides.
2. Point out, whenever possible, that the differing sides already agree to some exceptions to their stated positions. Such evidence may prove that the differences are not so extreme as their advocates insist. Several commentators, writing about the budget conflict between Democrats and Republicans in late 1998, adopted this strategy, suggesting that compromise was possible because the differences were narrower than the public believed.
3. Make clear your own moderation and sympathy, your own willingness to negotiate. An example of this attitude appears in an essay on abortion in which the author infers how Abraham Lincoln might have treated the question of abortion rights.

   > In this debate I have made my own position clear. It is a pro-life position (though it may not please all pro-lifers), and its model is Lincoln's position on slavery from 1854 until well into the Civil War: tolerate, restrict, discourage. Like Lincoln's, its touchstone is the common good of the nation, not the sovereign self. Like Lincoln's position, it accepts the legality but not the moral legitimacy of the institution that it seeks to contain. It invites argument and negotiation; it is a gambit, not a gauntlet.[1]

4. If you favor one side of the controversy, acknowledge that opposing views deserve to be considered. For example, in another essay on abortion, the author, who supports abortion rights, says,

   > Those of us who are pro-choice must come to terms with those thoughtful pro-lifers who believe that in elevating the right to privacy above all other values, the most helpless form of humanity is left unprotected and is, in fact, defined away. They deserve to have their views addressed with sympathy and moral clarity.[2]

5. Provide evidence that accepting a middle ground can offer marked advantages for the whole society. Wherever possible, show that continued polarization can result in violence, injustice, and suffering.
6. In offering a solution that finds a common ground, be as specific as possible, emphasizing the part that you are willing to play in reach-

[1] George McKenna, "On Abortion: A Lincolnian Position," *Atlantic Monthly*, September 1995, p. 68. (A gauntlet or glove is flung down in order to challenge an opponent to combat; a gambit is the opening move in a chess game, or in the words of one dictionary, "a concession that invites discussion."—EDS.)

[2] Benjamin C. Schwarz, "Judge Ginsburg's Moral Myopia," *New York Times*, July 30, 1993, sec. A, p. 27.

ing a settlement. In an essay titled "Pro-Life and Pro-Choice? Yes!" the author concludes with this:

> Must those of us who abhor abortion, then, reconcile ourselves to seeing it spread unchecked? By no means. We can refuse to practice it ourselves—or, if we are male, beseech the women who carry our children to let them be born, and promise to support them, and mean it and do it. We can counsel and preach to others; those of us who are religious can pray. . . . What we must not do is ask the state to impose our views on those who disagree.[3]

On a different subject, a debate on pornography, the author, who is opposed to free distribution of obscene material, nevertheless refuses to endorse censorship.

> I think that, by enlarging the First Amendment to protect, in effect, freedom of expression, rather than freedom of speech and of the press, the courts made a mistake. The courts have made other mistakes, but I do not know a better way of defining the interests of the community than through legislation and through the courts. So I am willing to put up with things I think are wrong in the hope that they will be corrected. I know of no alternative that would always make the right decisions.[4]

■ Presenting the Stock Issues

Presenting the stock issues, or stating the problem before the solution, is a type of organization borrowed from traditional debate format. It works for policy claims when an audience must be convinced that a need exists for changing the status quo (present conditions) and for introducing plans to solve the problem. You begin by establishing that a problem exists (need). You then propose a solution (plan), which is your thesis. Finally, you show reasons for adopting the plan (advantages). These three elements—need, plan, and advantages—are called the stock issues.

For example, suppose you wanted to argue that measures for reducing acid rain should be introduced at once. You would first have to establish a need for such measures by defining the problem and providing evidence of damage. Then you would produce your thesis, a means for improving conditions. Finally you would suggest the benefits that would follow from implementation of your plan. Notice that in this organization your thesis paragraph usually appears toward the middle of your paper, although it may also appear at the beginning.

[3] George Church, *Time,* March 6, 1995, p. 108.

[4] Ernest van den Haag, *Smashing Liberal Icons: A Collection of Debates* (Washington, D.C.: Heritage Foundation, 1981), p. 101.

Ordering Material for Emphasis

Whichever way you choose to work, you should revise your outline to reflect the order in which you intend to present your thesis and supporting ideas. Not only the placement of your thesis paragraph but also the wording and arrangement of your ideas will determine what points in your paper receive the most emphasis.

Suppose your purpose is to convince the reader that cigarette smoking is a bad habit. You might decide to concentrate on three unpleasant attributes of cigarette smoking: (1) it is unhealthy; (2) it is dirty; (3) it is expensive. Obviously, these are not equally important as possible deterrents. You would no doubt consider the first reason the most compelling, accompanied by evidence to prove the relationship between cigarette smoking and cancer, heart disease, emphysema, and other diseases. This issue, therefore, should be given greater emphasis than the others.

There are several ways to achieve emphasis. One is to make the explicit statement that you consider a certain issue the most important.

> Finally, and *most importantly,* human culture is often able to neutralize or reverse what might otherwise be genetically advantageous consequences of selfish behavior.[5]

This quotation also reveals a second way—placing the material to be emphasized in an emphatic position, either first or last in the paper. The end position, however, is generally more emphatic.

A third way to achieve emphasis is to elaborate on the material to be emphasized, treating it at greater length, offering more data and reasons for it than you give for the other issues.

Considering Scope and Audience

With a working outline in hand that indicates the order of your thesis and claims, you are almost ready to begin turning your notes into prose. First, however, it is useful to review the limits on your paper to be sure your writing time will be used to the best possible advantage.

The first limit involves scope. As mentioned earlier, your thesis should introduce a claim that can be adequately supported in the space available to you. If your research has opened up more aspects than you anticipated, you may want to narrow your thesis to one major subtopic. Or you could emphasize only the most persuasive arguments for your position (assuming these are sufficient to make your case) and omit the others. In a brief paper (three or four pages), three issues are probably all you have room to develop. On the other hand, if you suspect your thesis can be proved in one or two pages, look for ways to expand it. What additional issues might

[5] Peter Singer, *The Expanding Circle* (New York: New American Library, 1982), p. 171.

be brought in to bolster your argument? Alternatively, is there a larger issue for which your thesis could become a supporting idea?

Other limits on your paper are imposed by the need to make your points in a way that will be persuasive to an audience. The style and tone you choose depend not only on the nature of the subject but also on how you can best convince readers that you are a credible source. *Style* in this context refers to the elements of your prose—simple versus complex sentences, active versus passive verbs, metaphors, analogies, and other literary devices. *Tone* is the approach you take to your topic—solemn or humorous, detached or sympathetic. Style and tone together compose your voice as a writer.

Many students assume that every writer has only one voice. In fact, a writer typically adapts his or her voice to the material and the audience. Perhaps the easiest way to appreciate this is to think of two or three works by the same author that are written in different voices. Or compare the speeches of two different characters in the same story, novel, or film. Every writer has individual talents and inclinations that appear in most or all of his or her work. A good writer, however, is able to amplify some stylistic elements and diminish others, as well as to change tone, by choice.

It is usually appropriate in a short paper to choose an *expository* style, which emphasizes the elements of your argument rather than your personality. You may want to appeal to your readers' emotions as well as their intellects, but keep in mind that sympathy is most effectively gained when it is supported by believable evidence. If you press your point stridently, your audience is likely to be suspicious rather than receptive. If you sprinkle your prose with jokes or metaphors, you may diminish your credibility by detracting from the substance of your case. Both humor and analogy can be useful tools, but they should be used with discretion.

You can discover some helpful pointers on essay style by reading the editorials in newspapers such as the *New York Times,* the *Washington Post,* or the *Wall Street Journal.* The authors are typically addressing a mixed audience comparable to the hypothetical readers of your own paper. Though their approaches vary, each writer is attempting to portray himself or herself as an objective analyst whose argument deserves careful attention.

Again, remember your goals. You are trying to convince your audience of something; an argument is, by its nature, directed at people who may not initially agree with its thesis. Therefore, your voice as well as the claims you make must be convincing.

To This Point

The organizing steps that come between preparation and writing are often neglected. Careful planning at this stage, however, can save much time and effort later. As you prepare to start writing, you should be able to answer the following questions:

1. Is the purpose of my paper to persuade readers to accept a potentially controversial idea, to refute someone else's position, to find middle ground, or to propose a solution to a problem?
2. Can or should my solution also incorporate elements of compromise and negotiation?
3. Have I decided on an organization that is likely to accomplish this purpose?
4. Does my outline arrange my thesis and issues in an appropriate order to emphasize the most important issues?
5. Does my outline show an argument whose scope suits the needs of this paper?
6. What questions of style and tone do I need to keep in mind as I write to ensure that my argument will be persuasive?

WRITING

■ Beginning the Paper

Having found a claim you can defend and the voice you will adopt toward your audience, you must now think about how to begin. An introduction to your subject should consist of more than just the first paragraph of your paper. It should invite the reader to give attention to what you have to say. It should also point you in the direction you will take in developing your argument. You may want to begin the actual writing of your paper with the thesis paragraph. It is useful to consider the whole paragraph rather than simply the thesis statement for two reasons. First, not all theses are effectively expressed in a single sentence. Second, the rest of the paragraph will be closely related to your statement of the main idea. You may show why you have chosen this topic or why your audience will benefit from reading your paper. You may introduce your warrant, qualify your claim, and in other ways prepare for the body of your argument. Because readers will perceive the whole paragraph as a unit, it makes sense to approach it that way.

Consider first the kind of argument you intend to present. Does your paper make a factual claim? Does it address values? Does it recommend a policy or action? Is it a rebuttal of some current policy or belief? The answers to those questions will influence the way you introduce the subject.

If your thesis makes a factual claim, you may be able to summarize it in one or two opening sentences. "Whether we like it or not, money is obsolete. The currency of today is not paper or coin, but plastic." Refutations are easy to introduce in a brief statement: "Contrary to popular views on the subject, the institution of marriage is as sound today as it was a generation ago."

A thesis that defends a value is usually best preceded by an explanatory introduction. "Some wars are morally defensible" is a thesis that can be stated as a simple declarative opening sentence. However, readers who disagree may not read any further than the first line. Someone defending this claim is likely to be more persuasive if he or she first gives an example of a situation in which war is or was preferable to peace or presents the thesis less directly.

One way to keep such a thesis from alienating the audience is to phrase it as a question. "Are all wars morally indefensible?" Still better would be to prepare for the question:

> Few if any of us favor war as a solution to international problems. We are too vividly aware of the human suffering imposed by armed conflict, as well as the political and financial turmoil that inevitably result. Yet can we honestly agree that no war is ever morally defensible?

Notice that this paragraph gains appeal from use of the first person *we*. The author implies that he or she shares the readers' feelings but has good reasons for believing those feelings are not sufficient grounds for condemning all wars. Even if readers are skeptical, the conciliatory phrasing of the thesis should encourage them to continue reading.

For any subject that is highly controversial or emotionally charged, especially one that strongly condemns an existing situation or belief, you may sometimes want to express your indignation directly. Of course, you must be sure that your indignation can be justified. The author of the following introduction, a physician and writer, openly admits that he is about to make a case that may offend readers.

> Is there any polite way to introduce today's subject? I'm afraid not. It must be said plainly that the media have done about as sorry and dishonest a job of covering health news as is humanly possible, and that when the media do not fail from bias and mendacity, they fail from ignorance and laziness.[6]

If your thesis advocates a policy or makes a recommendation, it may be a good idea, as in a value claim, to provide a short background. The following paragraph introduces an argument favoring relaxation of controls in high schools.

> "Free the New York City 275,000" read a button worn by many young New Yorkers some years ago. The number was roughly the total of students enrolled in the City's high schools.
>
> The condition of un-freedom which is described was not, however, unique to the schools of one city. According to the Carnegie Commission's comprehensive study of American public education, *Crisis in the Classroom,* public schools across the country share a common characteristic,

[6]Michael Halberstam, "TV's Unhealthy Approach to Health News," *TV Guide,* September 20–26, 1980, p. 24.

> namely, "preoccupation with order and control." The result is that students find themselves the victims of "oppressive and petty rules which give their schools a repressive, almost prison-like atmosphere."[7]

There are also other ways to introduce your subject. One is to begin with an appropriate quotation.

> "Reading makes a full man, conversation makes a ready man, and writing makes an exact man." So Francis Bacon told us around 1600. Recently I have been wondering how Bacon's formula might apply to present-day college students.[8]

Or you may begin with an anecdote. In the following introduction to an article about the relation between cancer and mental attitude, the author recounts a personal experience.

> Shortly after I moved to California, a new acquaintance sat in my San Francisco living room drinking rose-hip tea and chainsmoking. Like so many residents of the Golden West, Cecil was "into" all things healthy, from jogging to *shiatsu* massage to kelp. Tobacco didn't seem to fit, but he told me confidently that there was no contradiction. "It all has to do with energy," he said. "Unless you have a lot of negative energy about smoking cigarettes, there's no way they can hurt you; you won't get cancer."[9]

Finally, you may introduce yourself as the author of the claim.

> I wish to argue an unpopular cause: the cause of the old, free elective system in the academic world, or the untrammeled right of the undergraduate to make his own mistakes.[10]

> My subject is the world of Hamlet. I do not of course mean Denmark, except as Denmark is given a body by the play; and I do not mean Elizabethan England, though this is necessarily close behind the scenes. I mean simply the imaginative environment that the play asks us to enter when we read it or go to see it.[11]

You should, however, use such introductions with care. They suggest an authority about the subject that you shouldn't attempt to assume unless you can demonstrate that you are entitled to it. Some instructors do

[7] Alan Levine and Eve Carey, *The Rights of Students* (New York: Avon Books, 1977), p. 11.

[8] William Aiken, "The Conversation on Campus Today Is, Uh . . . ," *Wall Street Journal,* May 4, 1982, p. 18.

[9] Joel Guerin, "Cancer and the Mind," *Harvard Magazine,* November–December 1978, p. 11.

[10] Howard Mumford Jones, "Undergraduates on Apron Strings," *Atlantic Monthly,* October 1955, p. 45.

[11] Maynard Mack, "The World of Hamlet," *Yale Review,* June 1952, p. 502.

not allow the use of first person in argumentative essays, so check the written guidelines for your assignments or ask your instructor.

Guidelines for Good Writing

In general, the writer of an argument follows the same rules that govern any form of expository writing. Your style should be clear and readable, your organization logical, your ideas connected by transitional phrases and sentences, your paragraphs coherent. The main difference between an argument and expository writing, as noted earlier, is the need to persuade an audience to adopt a belief or take an action. You should assume your readers will be critical rather than neutral or sympathetic. Therefore, you must be equally critical of your own work. Any apparent gap in reasoning or ambiguity in presentation is likely to weaken the argument.

As you read the essays in this book and elsewhere, you will discover that good style in argumentative writing shares several characteristics:

- variety in sentence structure: a mixture of both long and short sentences, different sentence beginnings
- rich but standard vocabulary: avoidance of specialized terms unless they are fully explained, word choice appropriate to a thoughtful argument
- use of details and examples to illustrate and clarify abstract terms, principles, and generalizations

You should take care to avoid the following:

- unnecessary repetition: making the same point without new data or interpretation
- exaggeration or stridency, which can create suspicion of your fairness and powers of observation
- short paragraphs of one or two sentences, which are common in advertising and newspaper writing to get the reader's attention but are inappropriate in a thoughtful essay

In addition to these stylistic principles, seven general points are worth keeping in mind:

1. Although *you,* like *I,* should be used judiciously, it can be found even in the treatment of weighty subjects. Here is an example from an essay by the distinguished British mathematician and philosopher, Bertrand Russell.

> Suppose you are a scientific pioneer and you make some discovery of great scientific importance and suppose you say to yourself, "I am afraid this discovery will do harm": you know that other people are likely to

> make the same discovery if they are allowed suitable opportunities for research; you must therefore, if you do not wish the discovery to become public, either discourage your sort of research or control publication by a board of censors.[12]

2. Don't pad. This point should be obvious; the word *pad* suggests the addition of unnecessary material. Many writers find it tempting, however, to enlarge a discussion even when they have little more to say. It is never wise to introduce more words into a paper that has already made its point. If the paper turns out to be shorter than you had hoped, it may mean that you have not sufficiently developed the subject or that the subject was less substantial than you thought when you selected it. Padding, which is easy to detect in its repetition and sentences empty of content, weakens the writer's credibility.

3. For any absolute generalization—a statement containing words such as *all* or *every*—consider the possibility that there may be at least one example that will weaken the generalization. Such a precaution means that you won't have to backtrack and admit that your generalization is not, after all, universal. A student who was arguing against capital punishment for the reason that all killing was wrong suddenly paused in her presentation and added, "On the other hand, if given the chance, I'd probably have been willing to kill Hitler." This admission meant that she recognized important exceptions to her rule and that she would have to qualify her generalization in some significant way.

4. When offering an explanation, especially one that is complicated or extraordinary, look first for a cause that is easier to accept, one that doesn't strain credibility. For example, years ago a great many people were bemused by reports about the mysterious Bermuda Triangle, which had apparently swallowed up ships and planes since the mid-nineteenth century. The forces at work were variously described as space-time warps, UFOs that transported earthlings to other planets, and sea monsters seeking revenge. But a careful investigation revealed familiar, natural causes. A reasonable person interested in the truth would have searched for more conventional explanations before accepting the bizarre stories of extraterrestrial creatures. He or she would also exercise caution when confronted by conspiracy theories that try to account for controversial political events, such as the assassination of John F. Kennedy.

5. Check carefully for questionable warrants. Your outline should specify your warrants. When necessary, these should be included in your paper to link claims with support. Many an argument has failed because it depended on an unstated warrant with which the reader did not agree. If you were arguing for a physical education requirement at your school, you might make a good case for all the physical and psychological benefits of

[12]"Science and Human Life," in James R. Newman, ed., *What Is Science?* (New York: Simon and Schuster, 1955), p. 12.

such a requirement. But you would certainly need to introduce and develop the warrant on which your claim was based—that it is the proper function of a college or university to provide the benefits of a physical education. Many readers would agree that physical education is valuable, but they might question the assumption that an academic institution should introduce a nonintellectual enterprise into the curriculum. At any point where you draw a controversial or tenuous conclusion, be sure your reasoning is clear and logical.

6. Avoid conclusions that are merely summaries. Summaries may be needed in long technical papers, but in brief arguments they create endings that are without force or interest. In the closing paragraph you should find a new idea that emerges naturally from the development of the whole argument.

7. Strive for a paper that is unified, coherent, and emphatic where appropriate. A *unified* paper stays focused on its goal and directs each claim, warrant, and piece of evidence toward that goal. Extraneous information or unsupported claims impair unity. *Coherence* means that all ideas are fully explained and adequately connected by transitions. To ensure coherence, give especially close attention to the beginnings and ends of your paragraphs: Is each new concept introduced in a way that shows it following naturally from the one that preceded it? *Emphasis,* as we have mentioned, is a function partly of structure and partly of language. Your most important claims should be placed where they are certain of receiving the reader's attention: key sentences at the beginning or end of a paragraph, key paragraphs at the beginning or end of your paper. Sentence structure can also be used for emphasis. If you have used several long, complex sentences, you can emphasize a significant point by stating it briefly and simply. You can also create emphasis with verbal flags, such as "The primary issue to consider . . ." or "Finally, we cannot ignore. . . ."

All clear expository prose will exhibit the qualities of unity, coherence, and emphasis. But the success of an argumentative paper is especially dependent on these qualities because the reader may have to follow a line of reasoning that is both complicated and unfamiliar. Moreover, a paper that is unified, coherent, and properly emphatic will be more readable, the first requisite of an effective argument.

THE MLA SYSTEM FOR CITING SOURCES

As you write your paper, any time that you make use of the wording or ideas of one of your sources, you must document that use. One of the simplest methods of crediting sources is the Modern Language Association (MLA) in-text system, which is used in the research paper on thalidomide in this chapter. In the text of your paper, immediately after any quotation, paraphrase, or idea you need to document, simply insert a parenthetical mention of the author's last name and the page number on which the material appears. You don't need a comma after the author's name or an abbreviation of the word *page* or *p*. For example, the following sentence appears in the thalidomide paper:

> Some of the forms of cancer that researchers believe may be treated with thalidomide are breast cancer; prostate cancer; brain cancer; and Kaposi's sarcoma, which is cancer normally found in AIDS patients (Burkholz 12).

The parenthetical reference tells the reader that the information in this sentence came from page 12 of the book or article by Burkholz that appears in the Works Cited, at the end of the paper. The complete reference on the Works Cited page provides all of the information readers need to locate the original source:

> Burkholz, Herbert. "Giving Thalidomide a Second Chance." *FDA Consumer* Sept.-Oct. 1997: 12–14. Print.

If the author's name is mentioned in the same sentence, it is also acceptable to place only the page numbers in parentheses; it is not necessary to repeat the author's name. For example,

> Burkholz reports that some of the forms of cancer that researchers believe may be treated with thalidomide are breast cancer; prostate cancer; brain cancer; and Kaposi's sarcoma, which is cancer normally found in AIDS patients (12).

Remember, though, that a major reason for using qualified sources is that they lend authority to the ideas expressed. The first time an author is cited in the paper, he should be identified by full name and by claim to authority:

> According to William A. Silverman, a specialist in neonatology who has served as professor of pediatrics at Columbia University in New York and head of intensive care at San Francisco's Children's Hospital, thalidomide was first developed in Germany back in 1954 as an antihistamine by a small, new pharmaceuticals firm, Chemie Grunenthal (404).

A last name and page number in parentheses do not carry nearly the same weight as a full name and credentials. You should save the former for subsequent citations once the author has been fully identified. If more than one sentence comes from the same source, you do not need to put parentheses after each sentence. One parenthetical citation at the end of the material from a source is enough if it is clear from the way you introduce the material where your ideas end and the source's begin.

If you are using more than one work by the same author, you will need to provide in the parentheses the title or a recognizable shortened form of the title of the particular work being cited. If the author's name is not mentioned in the sentence, you should include in parentheses the author's last name, the title, and the page number, with a comma between the author's name and the title. If both the author's name and the title of any work being cited are mentioned in the sentence, the parentheses will include only the page number. Had two works by Burkholz been listed in the Works Cited, the first example above would have looked like this:

> Some of the forms of cancer that researchers believe may be treated with thalidomide are breast cancer; prostate cancer; brain cancer; and Kaposi's sarcoma, which is cancer normally found in AIDS patients (Burkholz, "Giving" 12).

If there is more than one author, don't forget to give credit to all. Two or three authors are acknowledged by name in the parentheses if not in your own sentence: (Harmon, Livesy, and Jones 23). With four or more authors, use *et al.*, the Latin term for *and others*: (Braithwaite et al. 137).

Some sources do not name an author. To cite a work with an unknown author, give the title, or a recognizable shortened form, in the text of your paper. If the work does not have numbered pages, often the case in Web pages or nonprint sources, do not include page numbers. For example,

> In some cases Sephardic Jews, "converted" under duress, practiced Christianity openly and Judaism in secret until recently ("Search for the Buried Past").

Direct quotations should always be introduced or worked into the grammatical structure of your own sentences. If you need help introducing quotations, refer to the Writer's Guide in Chapter 4 (pp. 96–98). Remember, however, that you need to provide parenthetical documentation not only for every direct quotation but also for every paraphrase or summary. Document any words or ideas that are not your own.

As a general rule, you cannot make any changes in a quotation. Two exceptions are clearly marked when they occur. At times you may use brackets to make a slight change that does not change the meaning of the quotation. For example, a pronoun may need to be replaced by a noun in brackets to make its reference clear. Or a verb tense may be changed and bracketed to make the quotation fit more smoothly into your sentence. An ellipsis (. . .) is used when you omit a portion of the quotation that does not change the essential meaning of the quote. You do not need to use ellipses at the beginning or end of a direct quotation. If the omitted portion included the end of one sentence and the beginning of another, there should be a fourth period (. . . .).

If a quotation is more than four typed lines long, it needs to be handled as a block quotation. A block quotation is usually introduced by a sentence followed by a colon. The quotation itself is indented one inch or ten spaces from the left margin. No quotation marks are necessary since the placement on the page informs the reader that it is a quotation. The only quotation marks in a block quotation would be ones copied from the original, as in dialogue. A paragraph break within a block quotation is indented an additional five spaces. The parenthetical citation is the same as with a quotation run into your text, but the period appears before the parentheses.

With print sources in particular, you will often need to cite one work that is quoted in another or a work from an anthology. For the former, the parenthetical documentation provides name and page number of the source you actually used, preceded by the words "qtd. in":

> In the quest for evidence, Col. Patrick Toffler, Director of the United States Military Office of Institutional Research, reported that they had identified 120 physical differences. The female soldier "is, on the average, about five inches shorter than the male soldier, has half the upper body strength, lower aerobic capacity and 37 percent less muscle mass" (qtd. in Owens 35).

A work in an anthology is cited parenthetically by the name of the author of the work, not the editor of the anthology: (Simkovich 3).

The list of Works Cited includes all material you have used to write your research paper. This list appears at the end of your paper and always starts on a new page. Center the title Works Cited, double-space between the title and the first entry, and begin your list, which should be arranged alphabetically by author. Each entry should start at the left margin; indent all subsequent lines of the entry five spaces or one-half inch. Number each page, and double-space throughout.

One more point: *Content notes*, which provide additional information not readily worked into a research paper, are also indicated by superscript numbers. Content notes are included on a Notes page before the list of Works Cited.

REVISING

The final stage in writing an argumentative paper is revising. The first step is to read through what you have written for mistakes. Next, check your work against the guidelines listed under "Organizing the Material" and "Writing." Have you omitted any of the issues, warrants, or supporting evidence on your outline? Is each paragraph coherent in itself? Do your paragraphs work together to create a coherent paper? All the elements of the argument—the issues raised, the underlying assumptions, and the supporting material—should contribute to the development of the claim in your thesis statement. Any material that is interesting but irrelevant to that claim should be cut. Finally, does your paper reach a clear conclusion that reinforces your thesis?

Be sure, too, that the style and tone of your paper are appropriate for the topic and the audience. Remember that people choose to read an argument because they want the answer to a troubling question or the solution to a recurrent problem. Besides stating your thesis in a way that invites the reader to join you in your investigation, you must retain your audience's interest through a discussion that may be unfamiliar or contrary to their convictions. The outstanding qualities of argumentative prose style, therefore, are clarity and readability.

Style is obviously harder to evaluate in your own writing than organization. Your outline provides a map against which to check the structure of your paper. Clarity and readability, by comparison, are somewhat abstract qualities. Two procedures may be helpful. The first is to read two or three (or more) essays by authors whose style you admire and then turn back to your own writing. Awkward spots in your prose are sometimes easier to see if you get away from it and respond to someone else's perspective than if you simply keep rereading your own writing.

The second method is to read aloud. If you have never tried it, you are likely to be surprised at how valuable this can be. Again, start with someone else's work that you feel is clearly written, and practice until you achieve a smooth rhythmic delivery that satisfies you. And listen to what you are reading. Your objective is to absorb the patterns of English structure that characterize the clearest, most readable prose. Then read your paper aloud, and listen to the construction of your sentences. Are they also clear and readable? Do they say what you want them to say? How would they sound to a reader? According to one theory, you can learn the rhythm and phrasing of a language as you learn the rhythm and phrasing of a melody. And you will often *hear* a mistake or a clumsy construction in your writing that has escaped your eye in proofreading.

PREPARING THE MANUSCRIPT

Print your typed essay on one side of 8½-by-11-inch white computer paper, double-spacing throughout. Leave margins of 1 to 1½ inches on all sides, and indent each paragraph one-half inch or five spaces. Unless a formal outline is part of the paper, a separate title page is unnecessary. Instead, beginning about one inch from the top of the first page and flush with the left margin, type your name, the instructor's name, the course title, and the date, each on a separate line; then double-space and type the title, capitalizing the first letter of the words of the title except for articles, prepositions, and conjunctions. Double-space and type the body of the paper.

Number all pages at the top right corner, typing your last name before each page number in case pages are mislaid. If an outline is included, number its pages with lowercase roman numerals.

Writer's Guide: Checklist for Argumentative Papers

1. Present a thesis that interests both you and the audience, is debatable, and can be defended in the amount of space available.
2. Back up each statement offered in support of the thesis with enough evidence to give it credibility. Cite data from a variety of sources. Fully document all quotations and direct references to primary or secondary sources.
3. The warrants linking claims to support must be either specified or implicit in your data and line of reasoning. No claim should depend on an unstated warrant with which skeptical readers might disagree.
4. Present the thesis clearly and adequately introduce it in a thesis paragraph, indicating the purpose of the paper.
5. Organize supporting statements and data in a way that builds the argument, emphasizes your main ideas, and justifies the paper's conclusions.
6. Anticipate all possible opposing arguments and either refute or accommodate them.
7. Write in a style and tone appropriate for the topic and the intended audience. Your prose should be clear and readable.
8. Make sure your manuscript is clean, carefully proofed, and typed in an acceptable format.

Use the spell-check and grammar-check functions of your word-processing program, but keep in mind that correctness depends on context. A spell-check program will not flag a real word that is used incorrectly, such as the word *it's* used where the word *its* is needed. Also, a grammar-check function lacks the sophistication to interpret the meaning of a sentence and may flag as incorrect a group of words that is indeed correct while missing actual errors. It is ultimately up to you to proofread the paper carefully for other mistakes. Correct the errors, and reprint the pages in question.

SAMPLE RESEARCH PAPER (MLA STYLE)

The following paper, prepared in MLA style, was written for an argumentation class. A number of Suzanne's sources were articles that she accessed online via InfoTrac, so her Works Cited page offers several examples of how to document sources from databases. The Silverman article, which she accessed in the library in bound periodicals, illustrates how to cite an article from a journal. Although *FDA Consumer*, which contains Burkholz's article, is technically a government document, it is a magazine published by the FDA; thus articles from it are cited as magazine articles. The article from MayoClinic.com shows how to cite a short work from a Web site. Notice that there are a number of sources that do not have authors. These are cited parenthetically by shortened versions of the titles and alphabetized on the Works Cited page by title. The fact that online sources often have no page numbers explains why some parenthetical citations do not include page references. In some cases, there are no parentheses at all because the works are from online sources, and both authors and titles are named in the text sentences. Notice that in every case, there is enough information in the paper for a reader to find the proper source on the Works Cited page and enough information on the Works Cited page for a reader to locate the source.

Simkovich 1

Suzanne Simkovich
Ms. Carter
English 102-14
April 14, 2003

Thalidomide: Changing a Drug's Reputation

The Roman poet Ovid is commonly credited with having said, "Medicine sometimes snatches away health, sometimes gives it." He could have easily been talking about the medically controversial drug thalidomide, which has been known to do both. According to William A. Silverman, a specialist in neonatology who has served as professor of pediatrics at Columbia University in New York and head of intensive care at San Francisco's Children's Hospital, thalidomide was first developed in Germany back in 1954 as an antihistamine by a small, new pharmaceuticals firm, Chemie Grunenthal. Early hints of what was to come were ignored. Silverman gives one example:

> In the town of Stolberg, on Christmas Day in 1956, 10 months before thalidomide was placed on the market in Germany, a child was born without ears. The father, an employee of Chemie Grunenthal, had brought home samples of the new drug for his pregnant wife; years later, he learned that his daughter was the first living victim of the subsequent epidemic of thalidomide-induced infant deaths and malformations. (404)

When it was not shown to be effective as an antihistamine, doctors started to prescribe thalidomide as a sedative, and it was marketed worldwide. Many pregnant women were taking it to help with nausea and sleep. There was brief testing done on the drug, and it was proven to be safe (Silverman 404–05). Around this same time, there were an increasing number of malformed babies. Then in 1961, reports were published that linked thalidomide to these deformities (Silverman 405–06). The deformities were caused by a birth defect called phocomelia, which is one that causes deformed limbs and internal organs ("Good"). Randolph Warren, a victim of the thalidomide disaster himself

The saying is commonly attributed to Ovid, but without a source

Source's name and claim to authority used to introduce paraphrase

History of the drug

A block quotation from the same source

No quotation marks around the indented block quotation

Page number in parentheses follows period

Same source, but author not named in sentence

Shortened title for an article with no author listed

Simkovich 2

and founder and executive director of the Thalidomide Victims Association of Canada, reports that it is estimated 10,000 to 12,000 deformed babies were born to mothers who took thalidomide (40). Thalidomide was labeled a major medical disaster.

A government document in magazine form accessed through a subscription service

Although thalidomide was labeled a medical disaster, some researchers have been looking at more positive aspects of the drug, such as its ability to cure illnesses. Even though thalidomide created horrible birth defects when given to pregnant women in the sixties, it has potential to be an effective treatment in fighting cancer and other diseases since it restricts the growth of cells and lowers the production of some proteins in humans.

Transition to positive effects of drug

Many would want to know why researchers would still touch a drug that caused such horrible defects. Ricki Lewis, a contributing editor for *The Scientist*, explains that it all began in 1964, when a doctor in Israel began to use thalidomide to treat leprosy. The form of leprosy that was being treated was one which causes severe pain and eye and nerve damage, along with blindness (Elash). This doctor's success caused more research to begin into more uses of thalidomide. The Food and Drug Administration has now approved thalidomide for use in treating leprosy ("Thalidomide Maker"). This encouraged more experimentation in possible uses of the drug.

A weekly magazine accessed online

Elash's article is from a weekly magazine accessed online

No author, so cited by title

Thalidomide has properties that would make it an effective treatment for many types of cancer and other diseases. According to Karen Wright's article "Thalidomide Is Back," in the 1990s immunologist Gilla Kaplan found that thalidomide lowers TNF Alpha levels. Herbert Burkholz, a member of the Federal Drug Administration's public affairs staff, explains that when patients have cancer or a serious infection, their tumor necrosis factor (TNF) Alpha rises. It is believed that the high levels of TNF Alpha in cancer patients cause their condition to deteriorate (13). This protein, when found in moderate levels, fights infections and tumors, but in high levels causes fever, weight loss, and inflammation (Elash). Since thalidomide has the ability to lower this protein's levels, it can be an effective treatment for some illnesses (Elash). This property has made

The use of authors' names here clarifies where one author's ideas end and the other's begin

Use of thalidomide to fight cancer

Simkovich 3

thalidomide specifically effective in treating multiple myeloma, which is a malignancy of plasma cells (Lewis). In particular, thalidomide seems to be the only possible treatment for multiple myeloma. Those who were treated with thalidomide for multiple myeloma experienced an 82% success rate, with success rate meaning improvement (Lewis). Knowing this fact about thalidomide definitely will help in the fight against cancer.

In addition to its property of lowering the protein TNF Alpha, thalidomide has some other properties that are helpful in fighting cancer. The first is that thalidomide has been shown to restrict the growth of new blood vessels (Burkholz 13). In cancer patients, this would inhibit new cancer growth. Thalidomide specifically "inhibits vascular endothelial growth factor and basic fibroblast growth factor," which are factors that cause the proliferation of blood vessels that form in some types of cancer (Lewis). This property of thalidomide has also been shown effective in treating macular degeneration, which is when too many blood vessels form in the retina of the eye (Burkholz 13). Another effective quality that thalidomide has is its ability to "stimulate immune-system cells and other immunoregulators" (Wright). Thalidomide also has anti-angiogenic properties that make it effective in treating Crohn's disease ("Thalidomide: New"). These are all effective in stabilizing patients suffering from some types of cancer.

Other properties that help it fight cancer

An article from a Web site

With these astounding properties that thalidomide has, there are a variety of different illnesses that it can be used to treat. It is being used in treating Erythema nodosum leprosum, Behcet's disease, inflammatory bowel diseases, rheumatoid arthritis, sarcoidosis, aphthous ulcers in HIV infections, and systemic lupus erythematosus (von Moos), along with helping against "a potentially deadly immune system reaction in bone marrow transplant patients" (Elash). Of this extensive list, the HIV patients are helped because thalidomide helps heal lesions in the mouth and esophagus. This is helpful because these lesions normally keep patients from being able to eat (Burkholz 13). Some of the forms of cancer that researchers believe may be treated with thalidomide are breast cancer; prostate cancer;

Thalidomide's use with other diseases

Page numbers can be pinpointed with print sources

Simkovich 4

brain cancer; and Kaposi's sarcoma, which is cancer normally found in AIDS patients (Burkholz 12). Researchers are beginning to firmly believe that thalidomide can be a miracle cure for patients with some of these inoperable conditions.

Currently, the modern benefits of thalidomide keep on building. Now, forty years after it was developed, it appears to be a miracle drug due to positive results it is showing when given to patients. There still are some common side effects such as sleepiness, constipation, rash, mood changes, dry mouth, nausea, headache, increased appetite, puffiness of face and limbs, dry skin, itching, slow heart rate, irregular menstrual periods, low white blood cell count, and thyroid problems ("Thalidomide: New"). Although this seems like an extensive list of side effects, the benefits of not dying of cancer or any other illness thalidomide might be prescribed for far outweigh the discomfort. At this point, the FDA has approved thalidomide for use in treating leprosy, and for experimental use only in treating cancer and AIDS ("Thalidomide Maker"). The drug manufacturer, Celgene, and the FDA have imposed strict policies to prevent birth defects, including a program called System for Thalidomide Education and Prescribing Safety (STEPS) ("Thalidomide Maker"). Since thalidomide has some FDA approval, the use of it has become safer because it has now been taken off the underground market ("Thalidomide Maker"). Overall, there is major promise in this new drug.

Many people are currently being helped by thalidomide. The fact that the drug has a terrible history does not mean that the future will repeat the past. Today we have much safer procedures for investigating new drugs, and we work harder in restricting the uses of drugs, by creating such programs as STEPS, for example. If thalidomide had been created today, the 12,000 that were harmed by the drug probably would not have been due to more safety in drug development and use. Since more research is currently being done on thalidomide, many more than 12,000 could be helped instead of harmed. Is it not worth attempting to help people who have no other chance at life, in spite of thalidomide's dark history?

Reasons thalidomide is not the risk it once was

The essay's thesis in question form

Simkovich 5

Works Cited

Burkholz, Herbert. "Giving Thalidomide a Second Chance." *FDA Consumer* 31.6 (1997): 12–14. Print.

Elash, Anita. "Thalidomide Is Back: A Horror Drug from the '60s May Find New Cases." *MacLean's* 10 Mar. 1997: 48. *Expanded Academic ASAP*. Web. 3 Mar. 2003.

"Good Stuff." *The Economist* 17 Mar. 2001: 87–88. *Expanded Academic ASAP*. Web. 3 Mar. 2003.

Lewis, Ricki. "The Return of Thalidomide." *Scientist* 22 Jan. 2001: 5. *Expanded Academic ASAP*. Web. 3 Mar. 2003.

Silverman, William A. "The Schizophrenic Career of a 'Monster Drug.' " *Pediatrics* 110.2 (Aug. 2002): 404–06. Print.

"Thalidomide Maker Hopes Safer Drugs Follow." *Cancer Weekly Plus* 7 Sept. 1998: 8–9. *Expanded Academic ASAP*. Web. 3 Mar. 2003.

"Thalidomide: New Uses for Notorious Drug." *MayoClinic.com*. Mayo Foundation, 21 Aug. 2002. Web. 3 Apr. 2003.

von Moos, Roger, et al. "Thalidomide: From Tragedy to Promise." *Swiss Medical Weekly* 133 (2003): 77–87. *Expanded Academic ASAP*. Web. 3 Mar. 2003.

Warren, Randolph. "Living in a World with Thalidomide: A Dose of Reality." *FDA Consumer* 35.2 (2001): 40. *Expanded Academic ASAP*. Web. 3 Mar. 2003.

Wright, Karen. "Thalidomide Is Back." *Discover* Apr. 2000: 31–33. *Expanded Academic ASAP*. Web. 3 Mar. 2003.

THE APA SYSTEM FOR CITING SOURCES

Instructors in the social sciences might prefer the citation system of the American Psychological Association (APA), which is used in the paper on women in the military in this chapter. Like the MLA system, the APA system calls for a parenthetical citation in the text of the paper following any quotations from your sources. The APA only recommends that page numbers be included for paraphrases or summaries, but you should provide page numbers for these as well unless your instructor advises you that they are not necessary. In the text of your paper, immediately after any quotation, paraphrase, or idea you need to document, insert a parenthetical mention of the author's last name and the page number on which the material appears. Unlike the MLA system, the APA system also includes the year of publication in the parenthetical reference, using a comma to separate the items within the citation and using "p." or "pp." before the page number(s). Even if the source has a month of publication, only the year is included in the parenthetical citation. Here is an example:

> As of now, women are restricted from 30 percent of Army assignments and 1 percent of Air Force assignments (Baer, 2003, p. 1A).

The parenthetical reference tells the reader that the information in this sentence comes from page 1A of the 2003 work by Baer that appears on the References page at the end of the paper. The complete publication information that a reader would need to locate Baer's work will appear on the References page:

> Baer, S. (2003, March 3). In Iraq war, women would serve closer to front lines than in past. *The Baltimore Sun*, p. 1A.

If the author's name is mentioned in the same sentence in your text, the year in which the work was published follows it, in parentheses, and the page number only is placed in parentheses at the end of the sentence.

> According to Baer (2003) of the *Baltimore Sun*, as of now, women are restricted from 30 percent of Army assignments and 1 percent of Air Force assignments (p. 1A).

In the APA system, it is appropriate to include only the last name of the author unless you have more than one author with the same name in your list of references, in which case you would include the first initial of the author.

If your list of references includes more than one work written by the same author in the same year, cite the first work as "a" and the second as "b." For example, Baer's second article of 2003 would be cited in your paper like this: (Baer, 2003b).

If a work has two authors, list both in your sentence or in the parentheses, using "and" between them. In these examples from the women in combat paper, there is no page number because the source is a short work from a Web site:

> The fall 2000 suggestion from DACOWITS included a possible recruiting slogan: "A gynecologist on every aircraft carrier!" (Yoest & Yoest, 2001).
>
> Yoest and Yoest (2001) recall the fall 2000 suggestion from DACOWITS for a possible recruiting slogan: "A gynecologist on every aircraft carrier!"

If there are three to five authors, list them all by last name the first time they are referred to and, after that, by the last name of the first author and the term "et al." (meaning "and others"): (Sommers, Mylroie, Donnelly, & Hill, 2001); (Sommers et al., 2001). Also use the last name of the first author and "et al." when there are more than five authors, which is often the case in the sciences and social sciences.

If no author is given, use the name of the work where you would normally use the author's name, placing the names of short works in quotation marks and italicizing those of book-length works.

When using electronic sources, follow as much as possible the rules for parenthetical documentation of print ones. If no author's name is given, cite by the title of the work. If no date is given, use the abbreviation "n.d." instead. For a long work, if there are no page numbers, as is often the case with electronic sources, give paragraph numbers if the work has numbered paragraphs, or, if the work is divided into sections, the paragraph number within that section:

> Jamison (1999) warned about the moral issues associated with stem cell research, particularly the guilt that some parents felt about letting their children's cells be used (Parental Guilt section, para. 2).

Remember that the purpose of parenthetical documentation is to help a reader locate the information that you are citing.

At times you will need to cite one work that is quoted in another or a work from an anthology. For the former, the parenthetical documentation provides author's name, year of publication, and page number of the source you actually used, preceded by the words "as cited in":

> The female soldier "is, on the average, about five inches shorter than the male soldier, has half the upper body strength, lower aerobic capacity and 37 percent less muscle mass" (as cited in Owens, 1997, Anatomy section, para. 2).

A work in an anthology is cited parenthetically by the name of the author of the work, not the editor of the anthology.

SAMPLE RESEARCH PAPER (APA STYLE)

The following paper shows APA citations in the context of an actual text and the format for several different entries on the References page. Allison has used quotations sparingly and has instead made extensive use of summary and paraphrase. Often there is no page number in her parenthetical citations. That is because she was drawing from short online sources in which the paragraphs are not numbered but in which it is easy to find the material she refers to.

The format of the title page illustrates APA guidelines, as does the running head that is on each page and the use of lowercase Roman numerals to number each page before the first page of actual text.

Notice that Allison's thesis appears as the last sentence in her first paragraph. She carefully documents the restrictions on women that still exist in the U.S. military and argues why those restrictions are appropriate.

The Controversy over Women in Combat

Allison Mathews

English 103-13

Ms. Carter

April 7, 2003

Abstract

Women have served in the U.S. military since World War I. Although many barriers to their complete participation in all phases of military service have been broken, they are still appropriately restricted from direct ground combat assignments. Because women are held to a lower physical standard than men, men in their units cannot trust their ability to perform on the battlefield. One argument in favor of combat assignments for women has been that the lack of combat experience stands in the way of their progressing through the ranks. Such careerism, however, goes against a soldier's sworn duty, and there are ways to advance in the military other than combat service. The social and logistical problems created are an argument against women's serving in close quarters with men. Pregnancy among enlisted women is also inevitable and poses its own medical and logistical problems. Combat assignments for women would be a threat to the effectiveness and readiness of American troops.

Women in Combat 3

The Controversy over Women in Combat

Throughout the history of the military, the role of women has changed and adapted as the needs of the country have. From Molly Pitcher to Rosie the Riveter, women have always held a place in making the military what it is today. Issues have surfaced in the modern military about the current role of female service members with regard to combat assignments. Positions on submarines, small destroyers, specialized combat teams, and a handful of other assignments are restricted to men-only clubs. The factors determining why women are restricted from these assignments include physical ability, deployability, the cost effectiveness of providing the facilities that women need, and the effect on the overall readiness of the military. Women who desire these assignments, and other opponents of these restrictions, have retorted with reasons that they should be included, the foremost being women's rights and their desire to advance up the ranks of the military. However, women are rightly restricted from direct ground combat assignments to ensure the readiness of the military and the effectiveness of these combat units.

Overview of the controversy

Opposing view

Thesis

Women were first recruited, and began serving, in the military during World War I because they were needed to fill the clerical, technical, and health care jobs that were left vacant as more men were drafted. All these women, however, were discharged as soon as the war ended. The Women's Army Corps (WAC) was founded during World War II and gave women their own branch of the military. They served in the same jobs as they did in WWI but with the addition of non-combatant pilot assignments. Women did not get their permanent place in the ranks until 1948 when the Women Armed Services Integration Act was passed through Congress, allowing them to serve under the conditions that they were not to hold any rank above colonel, were limited mostly to clerical or health care jobs, and were not to make up more than 2 percent of the entire military. They were still limited to their own female only corps until 1978, when the military was fully integrated and women were

A history of women in the military from a source accessed through a subscription service

Women in Combat 4

allowed to hold any assignment that their male counterparts could except for combat roles. The rules have been relaxed over the years as women have proven themselves in combat support missions, especially in the Persian Gulf War in 1991 ("Women," 2000). They continue to push to be allowed into every job that men hold, and the effect this is having on the military is a fiery issue.

The parenthetical citation shows where paraphrase ends and her ideas begin

According to Baer (2003) of the *Baltimore Sun*, as of now, women are restricted from 30 percent of Army assignments, 38 percent of Marine assignments, and 1 percent of Air Force assignments. From the Navy, women are excluded from the special operations SEAL groups. These exclusions are from Military Occupational Specialities (MOS) "whose primary mission is ground combat" as defined by the Pentagon. They are also excluded from Navy submarines and small battleships that do not have the facilities to accommodate women (p. 1A).

Source and year included in text

Page only in parentheses

There have been many advancements for combat seeking women since the Persian Gulf War. McDonough (2003), writing for the Associated Press, reports that females are now allowed to fly combat missions in fighter jets and bombers for the Air Force and Navy. They can serve in many combat support roles such as combat Military Police companies. They can also be assigned to chemical specialist units that clean up contaminated areas on the battlefield, and to engineering units who build and repair bridges and runways in high risk areas. Women can also pilot the Army's Apache assault helicopters over the battlefield during high risk conditions, and pilot troop carrying helicopters onto the battlefield to deliver troops for a rescue mission during an assault. However, none of these MOSs are in selective special operations units such as Marine Force Recon or Army Airborne Rangers who serve as the "tip of the spear" in ground combat for missions like Operation Enduring Freedom in Afghanistan or Operation Iraqi Freedom.

Author and year in text; no page number because electronic version

The federal government and military have been under pressure from several sides on the issue of women serving in combat roles in the military. There are those that believe that all assignments, no matter how demanding of time, body, talent, and mind should be open to women as well as men. According to Gerber (2002) of the James MacGregor Burns Academy of Leadership, this is the general consensus of the Defense Advisory Committee on Women in the Services (DACOWITS). It was established in 1951 by General George Marshall but was disbanded when Secretary of Defense Donald Rumsfeld let its charter run out when it came up for renewal in 2002. However, its motives could be called into question as to whether it is rallying for the good of the military and its purposes or pushing its own platform that women should be integrated in all parts just because they believe it is deserved. Former DACOWITS Chairperson Vickie McCall even told the U.S. Air Force in Europe News Service, "You have to understand. We don't report facts, we report perception" (as cited in Yoest & Yoest, 2001). DACOWITS has often teamed up with other private women's rights activist groups that believe that the military should be an "equal opportunity employer" along with all other private and public employers.

A Web site

One source quoted in another; source with two authors

One cause of concern over women's inclusion in combat units has been the rigorous physical standards these troops must meet in training and in turn on the battlefield. Many studies have been done to prove or disprove a distinction between men's and women's physical capabilities. In the quest for evidence, Col. Patrick Toffler, Director of the United States Military Office of Institutional Research, reported that it had identified 120 physical differences (Owens, 1997, p. 40). The female soldier "is, on the average, about five inches shorter than the male soldier, has half the upper body strength, lower aerobic capacity and 37 percent less muscle mass" (as cited in Owens, 1997, p. 38). Leo (1997) reports in *U.S. News and World Report* that the way that the military accommodates for these differences is called "gender norming" and works by lowering the standards that women have to reach to pass the physical fitness tests. For instance, in the Marines, men are required to climb the length of a rope and females are only required to climb to a point below that marked with a yellow line (p. 14). These stan-

A journal paginated by issue

A magazine

dards are mostly for people to enlist in the services; so the bar is significantly raised for those that choose to compete for a MOS in special operations or combat units. Females enrolled in Army Jump School to be paratroopers are still not required to run as far or do as many pushups or sit-ups as their male counterparts. When this double standard is employed in the military, it blurs the distinction as to which soldiers actually have the physical ability to perform on the battlefield.

When there is a question as to the physical abilities of a fellow soldier in a unit, there can be no guarantee that everyone can cover your back as well as you could for them. When there is no trust in a unit, it breaks down. Take, for example, the Marine ideology that no one is left behind on the battlefield. Imagine an officer trying to motivate his troops to jump out of a helicopter in the heat of battle. Some of the soldiers may doubt a female comrade's capability to carry them to safety should they be injured, because she does not have to meet the same physical standards as her male counterparts do. The training is not only meant to prepare the troops for war combat and to show the officers that they meet the physical requirements. It is also a time to begin to build the trust that binds the troop's lives together and prove to each other they have the physical and mental toughness to accomplish the mission and bring each other back safely. How can this trust be established when male soldiers witness some female soldiers being excused from throwing live grenades in practice because they cannot throw the dummy ones far enough to keep from being blown to shreds? "The military should be the real world," said Jeanne Holm, retired two-star General of the Air Force. "The name of the game is putting together a team that fits and works together. That is the top priority, not social experimentation" (as cited in Yoest & Yoest, 2001). The military studies prove that a female body is not equipped to perform the same physical rigors as the male body; therefore, they should not be put in the position where impossible war fighting demands are put on them.

One source quoted in another

When left out of selective combat positions, there is the possibility that women cannot advance up the ranks because they would not get ample opportunity to prove themselves on the battlefield and gain combat experience. This experience goes a long way because it stands to prove that an officer has the leadership ability to command troops under fire and accomplish the mission. Experience can be gained in many ways, though, since America is not always at war. All officer career fields are necessary to the overall success of the mission, and in order to be promoted every officer must pull his or her weight. Even though the proceedings of the promotion committees are supposed to be kept private, it is no secret that combat experience weighs heavily on promotion picks (Nath, 2002). In a military that is centered on the chain of command, seniority is the most valuable commodity for any member, especially officers. The practice of officers' jockeying for promotions to further their career, stature, and income is called "careerism" (Nath, 2002). This is supposedly prohibited under the Air Force's second core value of "Service Before Self," and similar pledges in the other branches. The argument lies in the conflict between the career ambition of female officers seeking a combat MOS and the needs of a ready military to support the mission.

No page number given

The truth is, however, that the United States Armed Forces is not an "equal opportunity employer" as many other public and private organizations are. The military is not out to make a profit, or provide a ladder to corporate success. Instead, military officers swear to "support and defend the Constitution of the United States against all enemies, foreign and domestic; that I will bear the true faith and allegiance to the same" (Oath of Office, 2003). This oath states they are to uphold the best interest of the mission that the Commander in Chief charges them with. Careerism is not an option under this oath because it is only serving the individual's ambition, and not the mission of the military. Elaine Donnelly, President of the Center for Military Readiness, says, "Equal opportunity is important, but the armed forces exist to defend the country. If there is a conflict between career opportunities and military necessity, the needs of the military must come first" (as cited in "Women," 2000).

Another concern with females in combat is their deployability, or their availability to be deployed. Because the very nature of combat units is being the "tip of the spear" in battle, they are deployed and away from home much of the year and are used for an indefinite period of time during the war. Donnelly explains that "if you have a pregnancy rate and it's constant, 10 or 15%, you know that out of 500 women on a carrier at least 50 are going to be unavailable before or during the six-month deployment" (Sommers, Mylroie, Donnelly, & Hill, 2001). This pregnancy issue is not just applicable for conception before the deployment, but during deployment, as is evident on Navy aircraft carriers and destroyers that house women. Even though fraternization, defined as "sexual relationships between service members" (Nath, 2002), is illegal, many ships such as the U.S.S. *Lincoln* "report a dozen [pregnancies] a month" (Layton, 2003). In a close quarters environment, where combat units are together every hour of the day, this kind of problem distracts from the mission. Also, sailors on submarines sleep in what they call "hot beds," which are rotating shifts for sleep in the few available beds, and changing this system to accommodate separate quarters for females would not be cost effective. Also, pregnant females aboard aircraft carriers are being taken from their duty, and they must be replaced, which is a costly endeavor for the military and throws off the working relationship between service members.

First reference to source with four authors

Different parts of the same sentence cited to different sources

When men and women are put in close quarters, it is just human nature that sexual relationships will begin to develop. This fact has been proven all around the military from the pregnancies on board Naval ships all the way up to the Navy's "Tail Hook Convention," where in Las Vegas in 1991, dozens of female officers reported being openly sexually assaulted by male officers, both married and unmarried ("Women," 2000). If there was this kind of distraction within special operation ground combat units, the mission would suffer greatly because fraternization would become a huge issue, for favoritism would ensue. When the mission is not the first thing on these troops' minds, the morale, and most importantly, the trust breaks down.

Another very real barrier to the inclusion of women in these units and on small battleships and submarines is the medical needs of the female body. The fall 2000 suggestion from DACOWITS included as a possible recruiting slogan "A gynecologist on every aircraft carrier! (Yoest & Yoest, 2001). This is a possibility on every base and possibly on huge aircraft carriers, but these needs of women cannot be met in the field hospitals in the deserts of Iraq and Afghanistan where the only goal is to keep soldiers from dying long enough to get them to a base hospital. Another dilemma on 40–50 person submarines is that if a woman were to get pregnant, as is the proven trend, the vessel would have to make a risky surface to get her off to be cared for and find a replacement for her job on board. DACOWITS also suggested to "ensure an adequate supply of hygiene products during deployment" (Yoest & Yoest, 2001), which is a far cry from reality when Marines who are currently in Iraq already march with a 130-pound rucksack holding their bare living necessities. The military certainly does not have the money to cover these hygiene and medical needs when in high risk areas simply because the resources must go to fulfilling the mission.

As the way word we do battle continues to change, so will the roles of males and females; and the military will always have to come up with the best solution to accommodate these differences. As for now, the restrictions that are placed on women's assignments are based in sound reasoning. For the military's purposes, women do not have the physical abilities to fill combat oriented jobs, and the military does not have the resources to make these assignments available to them. The military needs to be aware of and most concerned with the effectiveness and readiness of its troops and figure out the best way to accomplish its mission and preserve America's freedom and sovereignty.

References

Baer, S. (2003, March 3). In Iraq war, women would serve closer to front lines than in past. *The Baltimore Sun*, p. 1A. Retrieved from http://www.baltimoresun.com

Dobbin, M. (2003, March 2). As war looms, women's role in U.S. military expands. *The Modesto Bee*, p. 3A. Retrieved from http://www.modbee.com

Gerber, R. (2002, September 23). Don't send military women to the back of the troop train. *USA Today*. Retrieved from http://www.usatoday.com

Layton, L. (2003, March 15). Navy women finding ways to adapt to a man's world. *The Washington Post*, p. A15. Retrieved from http://www.washingtonpost.com

Leo, J. (1997, August 11). A kinder, gentler army. *U.S. News and World Report, 123*(6), 14.

McDonough, S. (2003, February 10). More U.S. military women edging closer to combat positions in preparation for Iraq war. *The Associated Press*. Retrieved from http://www.ap.org/

Nath, C. (2002). *United States Air Force Leadership Studies*. Washington, DC: Air Education and Training Command, United States Air Force.

Oath of office: U.S. federal and military oath of office. Retrieved from http://www.apfn.org/apfn/oathofoffice.htm

Owens, M. (1997, Spring). Mothers in combat boots: Feminists call for women in the military. *Human Life Review, 23*(2), 35–45.

Sommers, C., Mylroie, L., Donnelly, E., & Hill, M. (2001, October 17). IWF panel: Women facing war. *Independent Women's Forum*. Retrieved from RDS Contemporary Women's Issues.

Warrior women. (2003, February 16). *The New York Times*, sect. 6, p. 23. Retrieved from http://www.nytimes.com

Women in the military. (2000, September 1). *Issues and Controversies*. Retrieved from http://www.2facts.com

Yoest, C. & Yoest, J. (2002, Winter). Booby traps at the Pentagon. *Women's Quarterly*. Retrieved from http://www.bnet.com

CHAPTER 13

Presenting an Argument Orally

You already know a good deal about the power of persuasive speech. You've not only listened to it from parents, teachers, preachers, coaches, friends, and enemies; you've practiced it yourself with varying degrees of success.

A classics scholar points out that the oratorical techniques we use today were "invented in antiquity and have been used to great effect ever since."[1] But history is not our only guide to the principles of public speaking. Much of what we know about the power of persuasive speech is knowledge based on lifelong experience—things we learn in everyday discourse with different kinds of people who respond to different appeals. Early in life you learned that you did not use the same language or the same approach to argue with your mother or your teacher as you used with your sibling or your friend. You learned, or tried to learn, how to convince people to listen to you and to trust you because you were truthful and knew what you were talking about. And perhaps equally important, if you won the argument, you wanted to make it clear that your victory would not mean hardship for the loser (no obvious gloating). Although speeches to a larger, less familiar audience will require much more preparation, many of the rules of argument that guided you in your personal encounters can be made to work for you in more public arenas.

You will often be asked to make oral presentations in your college classes. Many jobs, both professional and nonprofessional, will call for speeches to groups of fellow employees or prospective customers, to community groups, and even government officials. Wherever you live, there

[1] Mary Lefkowitz, "Classic Oratory," *New York Times*, January 24, 1999, sec. W, p. 15.

will be controversies and public meetings about schooling and political candidates, about budgets for libraries and road repairs and pet control. The ability to rise and make your case before an audience is one that you will want to cultivate as a citizen of a democracy. Great oratory is probably no longer the most powerful influence in our society, and computer networks have usurped the role of oral communication in many areas of public life. But whether it's in person or on television there is still a significant role for a live presenter, a real human being to be seen and heard.

Some of your objectives as a writer will also be relevant to you as a speaker: making the appropriate appeal to an audience, establishing your credibility, finding adequate support for your claim. But other elements of argument will be different: language, organization, and the use of visual and other aids.

Before you begin a brief examination of these elements, keep in mind the larger objectives of the speechmaker. A good introduction to the process of influencing an audience is *the motivated sequence*.[2] This outline, created by a professor of speech communication, lists the five steps that must be taken in order to motivate an audience to adopt a policy, an action, or a belief.

1. Getting attention (attention step)
2. Showing the need: describing the problem (need step)
3. Satisfying the need: presenting the solution (satisfaction step)
4. Visualizing the results (visualization step)
5. Requesting action or approval (action step)

Perhaps you noticed that these steps resemble the steps taken by advertisers. The resemblance is not accidental. According to the author of the motivated sequence, this is a description of the way "people systematically think their way through to a decision."

As you read the following discussions of audience, credibility, language, organization, support, and visual and aural aids, try to think of occasions in your own experience when you were aware of these elements in spoken argument, formal or informal.

THE AUDIENCE

Most speakers who confront a live audience already know something about the members of that audience. They may know why the audience is assembled to hear the particular speaker, their vocations, their level of education, and their familiarity with the subject. They may know whether

[2]Bruce E. Gronbeck, et al., *Principles of Speech Communication*, 13th brief ed. (New York: Longman, 1998), pp. 243–47.

the audience is friendly, hostile, or neutral to the views that the speaker will express. Analyzing the audience is an essential part of speech preparation. If speakers neglect it, both audience and speaker will suffer. At some time all of us have been trapped as members of an audience, forced to listen to a lecture, a sermon, an appeal for action when it was clear that the speaker had little or no idea what we were interested in or capable of understanding. In such situations the speaker who seems indifferent to the needs of the audience will also suffer because the audience will either cease to listen or reject his claim outright.

In college classes students who make assigned speeches on controversial topics are often encouraged to first survey the class. Questionnaires and interviews can give the speaker important clues to the things he should emphasize or avoid: They will tell him whether he should give both sides of a debatable question, introduce humor, use simpler language, and bring in visual or other aids.

But even where such specific information is not immediately available, speakers are well advised to find out as much as they can about the beliefs and attitudes of their audience from other sources. They will then be better equipped to make the kinds of appeals—to reason and to emotion—that the audience is most responsive to. For example, two young evangelists for a religious group (not students at the university) were invited to visit a speech class and present an argument for joining their group. The visitors knew that the class was learning the principles of persuasive speaking; they had no other information about the listeners. After the speech, the students in the class asked questions about some practices of the religious group which had received unfavorable media attention, but the speakers turned aside all questions, saying they did not engage in argument but were instructed only to describe the rewards of joining their group. Before some other audience, such a strategy might have been emotionally satisfying and ultimately persuasive. For this class, however, which was prepared to look for hard evidence, logic, and valid assumptions, the refusal to answer questions suggested evasion and indifference to the interests of their audience. Class evaluations of the speech revealed, to no one's surprise, that the visitors had failed to motivate their listeners.

If you know something about your audience, ask yourself what impression your clothing, gestures and bodily movements, voice, and general demeanor might convey. It might be worth pointing out here that the visitors cited above arrived dressed in dress slacks, white shirts, and ties to confront an audience in T-shirts and jeans. The fact that both speakers and listeners were the same age was not quite enough to overcome an impression of real differences. Make sure, too, that you understand the nature of the occasion—is it too solemn for humor? too formal for personal anecdotes?—and the purpose of the meeting, which can influence your choice of language and the most effective appeal.

CREDIBILITY

The evaluation of audience and the presentation of your own credibility are closely related. In other words, what can you do to persuade this particular audience that you are a reliable exponent of the views you are expressing? Credibility, as you learned in Chapter 1, is another name for *ethos* (the Greek word from which the English word *ethics* is derived) and refers to the honesty, moral character, and intellectual competence of the speaker.

Public figures, whose speeches and actions are reported in the media, can acquire (or fail to acquire) reputations for being endowed with those characteristics. And there is little doubt that a reputation for competence and honesty can incline an audience to accept an argument that would be rejected if offered by a speaker who lacks such a reputation. One study, among many that report similar results, has shown that the same speech will be rated highly by an audience that thinks the Surgeon General of the United States has delivered it but treated with much less regard if they hear it delivered by a college sophomore.

How, then, does a speaker who is unknown to the audience or who boasts only modest credentials convince his listeners that he is a responsible advocate? From the moment the speaker appears before them, members of the audience begin to make an evaluation, based on external signs, such as clothing and mannerisms. But the most significant impression of the speaker's credibility will be based on what the speaker says and how he says it. Does the speaker give evidence that he knows the subject? Does he seem to be aware of the needs and values of the audience? Especially if he is arguing an unpopular claim, does he seem modest and conciliatory?

An unknown speaker is often advised to establish his credentials in the introduction to his speech, to summarize his background and experience as proof of his right to argue the subject he has chosen. A prize-winning and widely reprinted speech by a student begins with these words:

> When you look at me, it is easy to see several similarities between us. I have two arms, two legs, a brain, and a heart just like you. These are my hands, and they are just like yours. Like you, I also have wants and desires; I am capable of love and hate. I can laugh and I can cry. Yes, I'm just like you, except for one very important fact—I am an ex-con.[3]

This is a possibly risky beginning—not everybody in the audience will be friendly to an ex-con—but it signifies that the speaker brings some authority to his subject, which is prison reform. It also attests to the speaker's honesty and may rouse sympathy among certain listeners. (To some in the

[3]Richard M. Duesterbeck, "Man's Other Society," in Wil Linkugel, R. R. Allen, and Richard Johannesen, eds., *Contemporary American Speeches* (Belmont, Calif.: Wadsworth, 1965), p. 264.

audience, the speaker's allusions to his own humanity will recall another moving defense, the famous speech by Shylock, the Jewish moneylender, in Shakespeare's *The Merchant of Venice*.)

The speaker will often use an admission of modesty as proof of an honest and unassuming character. He presents himself not as an expert but as one well aware of his limitations. Such an appeal can generate sympathy in the audience (if they believe him) and a sense of identification with the speaker.

The professor of classics quoted earlier has analyzed the speech of a former senator who defended President Clinton at his impeachment trial. She found that the speaker "made sure his audience understood that he was one of them, a friend, on their level, not above them. He denied he was a great speaker and spoke of his friendship with Mr. Clinton." As the writer points out, this confession brings to mind the speech by Mark Antony in *Julius Caesar:*

> I am no orator, as Brutus is,
> But (as you know me all) a plain blunt man
> That loves my friend; (3.2.226–28)

The similarity of these attempts at credibility, separated by almost four hundred years (to say nothing of the fact that Aristotle wrote about *ethos* 2,500 years ago) tells us a good deal about the enduring influence of *ethos* or character on the speaker's message.

ORGANIZATION

Look at the student speech on page 527. The organization of this short speech—the usual length of speeches delivered in the classroom—is easily mastered and works for all kinds of claims.

At the end of the first paragraph the speaker states what he will try to prove, that a vegetarian diet contributes to prevention of chronic diseases. In the third paragraph the speaker gives the four points that he will develop in his argument for vegetarianism. Following the development of these four topics, the conclusion urges the audience to take action, in this case, to stop eating meat.

This basic method of organizing a short speech has several virtues. First, the claim or thesis statement that appears early in a short speech, if the subject is well chosen, can engage the interest of the audience at once. Second, the list of topics guides the speaker in planning and developing his speech. Moreover, it tells the audience what to listen for as they follow the argument.

A well-planned speech has a clearly defined beginning, middle, and end. The beginning, which offers the introduction, can take a number of forms, depending on the kind of speech and its subject. Above all, the introduction must win the attention of the audience, especially if they have been required to attend, and encourage them to look forward to the rest of the speech. The authors of the motivated sequence suggest seven basic attention-getters: (1) referring to the subject or occasion, (2) using a personal reference, (3) asking a rhetorical question, (4) making a startling statement of fact or opinion, (5) using a quotation, (6) telling a humorous anecdote, (7) using an illustration.[4]

The speeches by the ex-con and the vegetarian provide examples of two of the attention-getters cited above—using a personal reference and asking a rhetorical question. In another kind of argument, a claim of fact, the student speaker uses a combination of devices to introduce her claim that culturally deprived children are capable of learning:

> In Charles Schulz's popular cartoon depiction of happiness, one of his definitions has special significance for the American school system. The drawing shows Linus, with his eyes closed in a state of supreme bliss, a broad smile across two-thirds of his face and holding a report card upon which is a big bold "A." The caption reads: "Happiness is finding out you're not so dumb after all." For once, happiness is not defined as a function of material possessions, yet even this happiness is practically unattainable for the "unteachables" of the city slums. Are these children intellectually inferior? Are they unable to learn? Are they not worth the time and the effort to teach? Unfortunately, too many people have answered "yes" to these questions and promptly dismissed the issue.[5]

The middle or body of the speech is, of course, the longest part. It will be devoted to development of the claim that appeared at the beginning. The length of the speech and the complexity of the subject will determine how much support you provide. Some points will be more important than others and should therefore receive more extended treatment. Unless the order is chronological, it makes sense for the speaker to arrange the supporting points in emphatic order, that is, the most important at the end because this may be the one that listeners will remember.

The conclusion should be brief; some rhetoricians suggest that the ending should constitute 5 percent of the total length of the speech. For speeches that contain several main points with supporting data, you may need to summarize. Or you may return to one of the attention-getters mentioned earlier. One writer recommends this as "the most obvious method" of concluding speeches, "particularly appropriate when the introduction has included a quotation, an interesting anecdote, a reference to an occasion

[4]Gronbeck et al., pp. 134–38.

[5]Carolyn Kay Geiman, "Are They Really 'Unteachables'?" in Linkugel, Allen, and Johannesen, p. 123.

or a place, an appeal to the self-interest of the audience, or a reference to a recent incident."[6]

An example of such an ending appears in a speech given by Bruce Babbitt, Secretary of the Interior, in 1996. Speaking to an audience of scientists and theologians, the Secretary defended laws that protected the environment. This is how the speech began:

> A wolf's green eyes, a sacred blue mountain, the words from Genesis, and the answers of children all reveal the religious values manifest in the 1977 Endangered Species Act.

(The children Babbitt refers to had written answers to a question posed at an "eco-expo" fair, "Why Save the Environment?")

And this is the ending of the speech:

> I conclude here tonight by affirming that those religious values remain at the heart of the Endangered Species Act, that they make themselves manifest through the green eyes of the grey wolf, through the call of the whooping crane, through the splash of the Pacific salmon, through the voices of America's children.
>
> We are living between the flood and the rainbow: between the threats to creation on the one side and God's covenant to protect life on the other.
>
> Why should we save endangered species?
>
> Let us answer this question with one voice, the voice of the child at that expo, who scrawled her answer at the very bottom of the sheet:
>
> "Because we can."[7]

The speaker must also ensure the smooth flow of his argument throughout. Coherence, or the orderly connections between ideas, is even more important in speech than in writing because the listener cannot go back to uncover these connections. The audience listens for expressions that serve as guideposts—words, phrases, and sentences to indicate which direction the argument will take. The student speech on vegetarianism uses these words among others: *next, then, finally, here, first of all, whereas, in addition, secondly, in fact, now, in conclusion.* Other expressions can also help the listener to follow the development. Each of the following examples from real speeches makes a bridge from a previous idea to a new one: "Valid factual proof, right? No, wrong!" "Consider an illustration of this misinformation." "But there is another way." "Up to this point, I've spoken only of therapy." "And so we face this new challenge." "How do we make this clear?" "Now, why is this so important?"

[6] James C. McCroskey, *An Introduction to Rhetorical Communication* (Englewood Cliffs, N.J.: Prentice-Hall, 1968), p. 204.

[7] Calvin McLeod Logue and Jean DeHart, eds., *Representative American Speeches, 1995–1996* (New York: Wilson, 1996), p. 70ff.

LANGUAGE

> It should be observed that each kind of rhetoric has its own appropriate style. That of written prose is not the same as that of spoken oratory.
>
> —Aristotle

In the end, your speech depends on the language. No matter how accurate your analysis of the audience, how appealing your presentation of self, how deep your grasp of the material, if the language does not clearly and emphatically convey your argument, the speech will probably fail. Fortunately, the effectiveness of language does not depend on long words or complex sentence structure; quite the contrary. Most speeches, especially those given by beginners to small audiences, are distinguished by an oral style that respects the rhythms of ordinary speech and sounds spontaneous.

The vocabulary you choose, like the other elements of spoken discourse we have discussed, is influenced by the kind of audience you confront. A student audience may be entertained or moved to identification with you and your message if you use the slang of your generation; an assembly of elderly church members at a funeral may not be so generous. Use words that both you and your listeners are familiar with, language that convinces the audience you are sharing your knowledge and opinions, neither speaking down to them nor over their heads. As one writer puts it, "You never want to use language that makes the audience appear ignorant or stupid."

Make sure, too, that the words you use will not be considered offensive by some members of your audience. Today we are all sensitive, sometimes hypersensitive, to terms that were once used freely if not wisely. One word, improperly used, can cause some listeners to reject the whole speech.

The short speeches you give will probably not be devoted to elaborating grand abstractions, but it is not only abstract terms that need definition. When you know your subject very well, you forget that others can be ignorant of it. Think whether the subject is one that the particular audience you are addressing is not likely to be familiar with. If this is the case, then explain even the basic terms. In one class a student who had chosen to discuss a subject about which he was extremely knowledgeable, betting on horse races, neglected to define clearly the words *exacta, subfecta, trifecta, parimutuel,* and others, leaving his audience fairly befuddled.

Wherever it is appropriate, use concrete language with details and examples that create images and cause the listener to feel as well as think. One student speaker used strong words to good effect in providing some unappetizing facts about hot dogs: "In fact, the hot dog is so adulterated with chemicals, so contaminated with bacteria, so puffy with gristle, fat, water, and lacking in protein, that it is nutritionally worthless."[8]

[8]Donovan Ochs and Anthony Winkler, *A Brief Introduction to Speech* (New York: Harcourt, Brace, Jovanovich, 1979), p. 74.

Another speech on a far more serious subject offered a personal experience with vivid details. The student speaker was a hemophiliac making a plea for blood donations.

> I remember the three long years when I couldn't even walk because repeated hemorrhages had twisted my ankles and knees to pretzel-like forms. I remember being pulled to school in a wagon while other boys rode their bikes and pushed to my table. I remember sitting in the dark empty classroom by myself during recess while the others went out in the sun to run and play. And I remember the first terrible day at the big high school when I came on crutches and built-up shoes carrying my books in a sack around my neck.[9]

As a rule, the oral style demands simpler sentences. That is because the listener must grasp the grammatical construction without the visual clues of punctuation available on the printed page. Simpler means shorter and more direct. Use subject-verb constructions without a string of phrases or clauses preceding the subject or interrupting the natural flow of the sentence. Use the active voice frequently. In addition to assuring clarity for the audience, such sentences are easier for the speaker to remember and to say. (The sentences in the paragraph above are long, but notice that the sentence elements of subject, verb, and subordinate clause are arranged in the order dictated by natural speech.)

Simpler, however, does not mean less impressive. A speech before any audience may be simply expressed without loss of emotional or intellectual power. One of the most eloquent short speeches ever delivered in this country is the surrender speech in 1877 by Chief Joseph of the Nez Percé Tribe, which clearly demonstrates the power of simple words and sentences.

> I am tired of fighting. Our chiefs are killed. Looking Glass is dead. Toohulsote is dead. The old men are all dead. It is the young men who say no and yes. He who led the young men is dead. It is cold and we have no blankets. The little children are freezing to death. My people, some of them, have run away to the hills and have no blankets, no food. No one knows where they are—perhaps they are freezing to death. I want to have time to look for my children and see how many of them I can find. Maybe I shall find them among the dead. Hear me, my chiefs. I am tired. My heart is sad and sick. From where the sun now stands I will fight no more forever.[10]

If you are in doubt about the kind of language in which you should express yourself, you might follow Lincoln's advice: "Speak so that the most lowly can understand you, and the rest will have no difficulty."

[9]Ralph Zimmerman, "Mingled Blood," in Linkugel, Allen, and Johannesen, p. 200.
[10]M. Gidley, *Kopet: A Documentary Narrative of Chief Joseph's Last Years* (Chicago: Contemporary Books, 1981), p. 31.

A popular stylistic device—repetition and balance or parallel structure—can emphasize and enrich parts of your message. Look back to the balanced sentences of the passage from the student speaker on hemophilia, sentences beginning with "I remember." Almost all inspirational speeches, including religious exhortation and political oratory, take advantage of such constructions, whose rhythms evoke an immediate emotional response. It is one of the strengths of Martin Luther King Jr.'s "I Have a Dream." (See p. 529.) Keep in mind that the ideas in parallel structures must be similar and that, for maximum effectiveness, they should be used sparingly in a short speech. Not least, the subject should be weighty enough to carry this imposing construction.

SUPPORT

The support for a claim is essentially the same for both spoken and written arguments. Factual evidence, including statistics and expert opinion, as well as appeals to needs and values, are equally important in oral presentations. But time constraints will make a difference. In a speech the amount of support that you provide will be limited to the capacity of listeners to digest and remember information that they cannot review. This means that you must choose subjects that can be supported adequately in the time allotted. The speech by Secretary Babbitt, for example, on saving the environmental protection laws, developed material on animals, national lands, water, his own history, religious tradition, and the history of environmental legislation, to name only the most important. It would have been impossible to defend his proposition in a half-hour speech. Although his subject was far more limited, the author of the argument for vegetarianism could not do full justice to his claim for lack of time. Meat-eaters would find that some of their questions remain unanswered, and even those listeners friendly to the author's claim might ask for more evidence from authoritative sources.

While both speakers and writers use logical, ethical, and emotional appeals in support of their arguments, the forms of presentation can make a significant difference. The reasoning process demanded of listeners must be relatively brief and straightforward, and the supporting evidence readily assimilated. The ethical appeal or credibility of the speaker is affected not only by what he says but by his appearance, bodily movements, and vocal expressions. And the appeal to the sympathy of the audience can be greatly enhanced by the presence of the speaker. Take the excerpt from the speech of the hemophiliac. The written descriptions of pain and heartbreak are very moving, but place yourself in the audience, looking at the victim and imagining the suffering experienced by the human body standing in front of you. No doubt the effect would be deep and long-lasting, perhaps more memorable even than the written word.

Because the human instrument is so powerful, it must be used with care. You have probably listened to speakers who used gestures and voice inflections that had been dutifully rehearsed but were obviously contrived and worked, unfortunately, to undermine rather than support the speaker's message and credibility. If you are not a gifted actor, avoid gestures, body language, and vocal expressions that are not truly felt.

Some speech theorists treat support or proofs as *nonartistic* and *artistic*. The nonartistic support—factual data, expert opinion, examples—is considered objective and verifiable. Its acceptability should not depend on the character and personality of the speaker. It is plainly different from the artistic proof, which is subjective, based on the values and attitudes of the listener, and therefore more difficult for the speaker to control. This form of support is called artistic because it includes creative strategies within the power of the speaker to manipulate. In earlier parts of this chapter we have discussed the artistic proofs, ways of establishing credibility, and recognizing the values of the audience.

PRESENTATION AIDS

■ Charts, Graphs, Handouts

Some speeches, though not all, will be enhanced by visual and other aids: charts, graphs, maps, models, objects, handouts, recordings, and computerized images. These aids, however, no matter how visually or aurally exciting, should not overwhelm your own oral presentation. The objects are not the stars of the show. They exist to make your spoken argument more persuasive.

Charts and graphs, large enough and clear enough to be seen and understood, can illuminate speeches that contain numbers of any kind, especially statistical comparisons. You can make a simple chart yourself, on paper for use with an easel or a transparency for use with a slide projector. Enlarged illustrations or a model of a complicated machine—say, the space shuttle—would help a speaker to explain its function. You already know that photographs or videos are powerful instruments of persuasion, above all in support of appeals for humanitarian aid, for both people and animals.

Court cases have been won or lost on the basis of diagrams or charts that purport to prove the innocence or guilt of a defendant. Such aids do not always speak for themselves. No matter how clear they are to the designer, they may be misinterpreted or misunderstood by a viewer. Some critics have argued that the jury in the O. J. Simpson case failed to understand the graphs of DNA relationships that experts for the prosecution displayed during the trial. Before you show any diagrams or charts of any complexity to your audience, ask friends if they find them easy to understand.

The use of a handout also requires planning. It's probably unwise to put your speech on hold while the audience reads or studies a handout that requires time and concentration. Confine the subject matter of handouts to material that can be easily grasped as you discuss or explain it.

Audio

Audio aids may also enliven a speech or even be indispensable to its success. One student played a recording of a scene from *Romeo and Juliet*, spoken by a cast of professional actors, to make a point about the relationship between the two lovers. Another student chose to define several types of popular music, including rap, goth, heavy metal, and techno. But he used only words, and the lack of any musical demonstration meant that the distinctions remained unclear.

Video

With sight, sound, and movement, a video can illustrate or reinforce the main points of a speech. A speech warning people not to drink and drive will have a much greater effect if enhanced by a video showing the tragic and often gruesome outcome of car accidents caused by drunk driving. Schools that teach driver's education frequently rely on these bone-chilling videos to show their students that getting behind the wheel is a serious responsibility, not a game. If you want to use video, check to make sure that a VCR or a DVD player and television are available to you. Most schools have an audio-visual department that manages the delivery, setup, and return of all equipment.

Multimedia

Multimedia presentation software programs enable you to combine several different media such as text, charts, sound, and still or moving pictures into one unit. In the business world, multimedia presentations are commonly used in situations where you have a limited amount of time to persuade or teach a fairly large audience. For instance, the promotion director of a leading teen magazine is trying to persuade skeptical executives that a magazine Web site would increase sales and advertising revenue. Since the magazine is sold through newsstand and subscription, some executives question whether the cost of creating and maintaining a Web site outweighs the benefits. Using multimedia presentation software, the promotion director can integrate demographic charts and graphs showing that steadily increasing numbers of teenagers surf the Web, a segment from a television news program reporting that many teens shop online (an attraction for advertisers), and downloaded pages from a competitor's Web site to demonstrate that others are already reaping the benefits of the Internet. People today are increasingly "visual" in their learning styles, and multimedia software may be the most effective aid for an important presentation.

Though effective when done well, technically complicated presentations require large amounts of time and careful planning. First you must ensure that your computer is powerful enough to adeptly handle presentation software. Then you need to familiarize yourself with the program. Most presentation software programs come equipped with helpful tutorials. If the task of creating your own presentation from scratch seems overwhelming, you can use one of the many preformatted presentation templates: You will simply need to customize the content. Robert Stephens, the founder of the Geek Squad, a Minneapolis-based business that provides on-site emergency response to computer problems, gives the following tips for multimedia presentations:

1. In case of equipment failure, always bring two of everything.
2. Back up your presentation on CD-ROM or a Zip drive.
3. Avoid live visits to the Internet. Because connections can fail or be painfully slow, and sites can move or disappear, if you must visit the Internet in your presentation, download the appropriate pages onto your hard drive ahead of time. It will still look like a live visit.
4. In the end, technology cannot replace creativity. Make sure that you are using multimedia to reinforce not replace your main points.[11]

Make sure that any necessary apparatus will be available at the right time. If you have never used the devices you need for your presentation, practice using them before the speech. Few things are more disconcerting for the speechmaker and the audience than a speaker who is fumbling with his materials, unable to find the right picture or to make a machine work.

SAMPLE PERSUASIVE SPEECH

The following speech was delivered by C. Renzi Stone to his public speaking class at the University of Oklahoma. Told to prepare a persuasive speech, Stone chose to speak about the health benefits of vegetarianism. Note his attention-grabbing introduction.

[11] Robert Stephens as paraphrased in "When Your Presentation Crashes . . . Who You Gonna Call?" by Eric Matson, *Fast Company*, February/March 1997, p. 130.

Live Longer and Healthier: Stop Eating Meat!

C. RENZI STONE

What do Steve Martin, Dustin Hoffman, Albert Einstein, Jerry Garcia, Michael Stipe, Eddie Vedder, Martina Navratilova, Carl Lewis, and 12 million other Americans all have in common? All of these well-known people were or are vegetarians. What do they know that we don't? Consuming a regimen of high-fat, high-protein flesh foods is a sure-fire prescription for disaster, like running diesel fuel through your car's gasoline engine. In the book *Why Do Vegetarians Eat Like That?* David Gabbe asserts that millions of people today are afflicted with chronic diseases that can be directly linked to the consumption of meat. Eating a vegetarian diet can help prevent many of those diseases.

In 1996, 12 million Americans identified themselves as vegetarians. That number is twice as many as in the decade before. According to a recent National Restaurant Association poll found in *Health* magazine, one in five diners say they now go out of their way to choose restaurants that serve at least a few meatless entrees. Obviously, the traditionally American trait of a meat-dominated society has subsided in recent years.

In discussing vegetarianism today, first I will tell how vegetarians are perceived in society. Next, I will introduce several studies validating my claim that a meatless diet is extraordinarily healthy. I will then show how a veggie diet can strengthen the immune system and make the meatless body a shield from unwanted diseases such as cancer and heart disease. Maintaining a strict vegetarian diet can also lead to a longer life. Finally, I will put an image into the audience's mind of a meatless society that relies on vegetables for the main course at breakfast, lunch, and dinner.

Moving to my first point, society generally holds two major misperceptions about vegetarians. First of all, society often perceives vegetarians as a radical group of people with extreme principles. In this view, vegetarians are seen as a monolithic group of people who choose to eat vegetables because they are opposed to the killing of animals for food. The second major misconception is that because vegetarians do not eat meat, they do not get the proper amounts of essential vitamins and minerals often found in meat.

Here is my response to these misconceived notions. First of all, vegetar- 5
ians are not a homogeneous group of radicals. Whereas many vegetarians in the past did join the movement on the principle that killing animals is wrong, many join the movement today mainly for its health benefits. In addition, there are many different levels of vegetarianism. Some vegetarians eat nothing but vegetables. Others don't eat red meat but do occasionally eat chicken and fish.

Secondly, contrary to popular opinion, vegetarians get more than enough vitamins and minerals in their diet and generally receive healthier nourishment than meat eaters. In fact, in an article for *Health* magazine, Peter Jaret states that vegetarians actually get larger amounts of amino acids due to the elimination of saturated fats which are often found in meat products. Studies show that the health benefits of a veggie lifestyle contribute to increased life expectancy and overall productivity.

Hopefully you now see that society's perceptions of vegetarians are outdated and just plain wrong. You are familiar with many of the problems associated with a meat-based diet, and you have heard many of the benefits of a vegetarian diet. Now try to imagine how you personally can improve your life by becoming a vegetarian.

Can you imagine a world where people retire at age eighty and lead productive lives into their early 100s? Close your eyes and think about celebrating your seventieth wedding anniversary, seeing your great-grandchildren get married, and witnessing 100 years of world events and technological innovations. David Gabbe's book refers to studies that have shown a vegetarian diet can increase your life expectancy up to fifteen years. A longer life is within your reach, and the diet you eat has a direct impact on your health and how you age.

In conclusion, vegetarianism is a healthy life choice, not a radical cult. By eliminating meat from their diet, vegetarians reap the benefits of a vegetable-based diet that helps prevent disease and increase life expectancy. People, take heed of my advice. There are many more sources of information available for those who want to take a few hours to research the benefits of the veggie lifestyle. If you don't believe my comments, discover the whole truth for yourself.

Twelve million Americans know the health benefits that come with 10
being a vegetarian. Changing your eating habits can be just as easy as making your bed in the morning. Sure, it takes a few extra minutes and some thought, but your body will thank you in the long run.

You only live once. Why not make it a long stay?

READING FOR ANALYSIS

I Have a Dream

MARTIN LUTHER KING JR.

Five score years ago, a great American, in whose symbolic shadow we stand, signed the Emancipation Proclamation. This momentous decree came as a great beacon light of hope to millions of Negro slaves who had been seared in the flames of withering injustice. It came as a joyous daybreak to end the long night of captivity.

But one hundred years later, we must face the tragic fact that the Negro is still not free. One hundred years later, the life of the Negro is still sadly crippled by the manacles of segregation and the chains of discrimination. One hundred years later, the Negro lives on a lonely island of poverty in the midst of a vast ocean of material prosperity. One hundred years later, the Negro is still languishing in the corners of American society and finds himself an exile in his own land. So we have come here today to dramatize an appalling condition.

In a sense we have come to our nation's capital to cash a check. When the architects of our republic wrote the magnificent words of the Constitution and the Declaration of Independence, they were signing a promissory note to which every American was to fall heir. This note was a promise that all men would be guaranteed the unalienable rights of life, liberty, and the pursuit of happiness.

It is obvious today that America has defaulted on this promissory note insofar as her citizens of color are concerned. Instead of honoring this sacred obligation, America has given the Negro people a bad check; a check which has come back marked "insufficient funds." But we refuse to believe that the bank of justice is bankrupt. We refuse to believe that there are insufficient funds in the great vaults of opportunity of this nation. So we have come to cash this check—a check that will give us upon demand the riches of freedom and the security of justice. We have also come to this hallowed spot to remind America of the fierce urgency of *now*. This is no time to engage in the luxury of cooling off or to take the tranquilizing drugs of gradualism. *Now* is the time to make real the promises of Democracy. *Now* is the time to rise from the dark and desolate valley of segregation to the sunlit path of racial justice. *Now* is the time to open the doors of opportunity to all of God's children. *Now* is the time to lift our nation from the quicksands of racial injustice to the solid rock of brotherhood.

In the widely reprinted "I Have a Dream" speech, Martin Luther King Jr. appears as the charismatic leader of the civil rights movement. This inspirational address was delivered on August 28, 1963, in Washington, D.C., at a demonstration by two hundred thousand people for civil rights for African Americans. From *A Testament of Hope* (1986).

5 It would be fatal for the nation to overlook the urgency of the moment and to underestimate the determination of the Negro. This sweltering summer of the Negro's legitimate discontent will not pass until there is an invigorating autumn of freedom and equality. Nineteen sixty-three is not an end, but a beginning. Those who hope that the Negro needed to blow off steam and will now be content will have a rude awakening if the nation returns to business as usual. There will be neither rest nor tranquillity in America until the Negro is granted his citizenship rights. The whirlwinds of revolt will continue to shake the foundations of our nation until the bright day of justice emerges.

But there is something that I must say to my people who stand on the warm threshold which leads into the palace of justice. In the process of gaining our rightful place we must not be guilty of wrongful deeds. Let us not seek to satisfy our thirst for freedom by drinking from the cup of bitterness and hatred. We must forever conduct our struggle on the high plane of dignity and discipline. We must not allow our creative protest to degenerate into physical violence. Again and again we must rise to the majestic heights of meeting physical force with soul force. The marvelous new militancy which has engulfed the Negro community must not lead us to a distrust of all white people, for many of our white brothers, as evidenced by their presence here today, have come to realize that their destiny is tied up with our destiny and their freedom is inextricably bound to our freedom. We cannot walk alone.

And as we walk, we must make the pledge that we shall march ahead. We cannot turn back. There are those who are asking the devotees of civil rights, "When will you be satisfied?" We can never be satisfied as long as the Negro is the victim of the unspeakable horrors of police brutality. We can never be satisfied as long as our bodies, heavy with the fatigue of travel, cannot gain lodging in the motels of the highways and the hotels of the cities. We cannot be satisfied as long as the Negro's basic mobility is from a smaller ghetto to a larger one. We can never be satisfied as long as a Negro in Mississippi cannot vote and a Negro in New York believes he has nothing for which to vote. No, no, we are not satisfied, and we will not be satisfied until justice rolls down like waters and righteousness like a mighty stream.

I am not unmindful that some of you have come here out of great trials and tribulations. Some of you have come fresh from narrow jail cells. Some of you have come from areas where your quest for freedom left you battered by the storms of persecution and staggered by the winds of police brutality. You have been the veterans of creative suffering. Continue to work with the faith that unearned suffering is redemptive.

Go back to Mississippi, go back to Alabama, go back to South Carolina, go back to Georgia, go back to Louisiana, go back to the slums and ghettos of our northern cities, knowing that somehow this situation can and will be changed. Let us not wallow in the valley of despair.

I say to you today, my friends, that in spite of the difficulties and frustrations of the moment I still have a dream. It is a dream deeply rooted in the American dream. 10

I have a dream that one day this nation will rise up and live out the true meaning of its creed: "We hold these truths to be self-evident; that all men are created equal."

I have a dream that one day on the red hills of Georgia the sons of former slaves and the sons of former slaveowners will be able to sit down together at the table of brotherhood.

I have a dream that one day even the state of Mississippi, a desert state sweltering with the heat of injustice and oppression, will be transformed into an oasis of freedom and justice.

I have a dream that my four little children will one day live in a nation where they will not be judged by the color of their skin but by the content of their character.

I have a dream today. 15

I have a dream that one day the state of Alabama, whose governor's lips are presently dripping with the words of interposition and nullification, will be transformed into a situation where little black boys and black girls will be able to join hands with little white boys and white girls and walk together as sisters and brothers.

I have a dream today.

I have a dream that one day every valley shall be exalted, every hill and mountain shall be made low, the rough places will be made plain, and the crooked places will be made straight, and the glory of the Lord shall be revealed, and all flesh shall see it together.

This is our hope. This is the faith with which I return to the South. With this faith we will be able to hew out of the mountain of despair a stone of hope. With this faith we will be able to transform the jangling discords of our nation into a beautiful symphony of brotherhood. With this faith we will be able to work together, to pray together, to struggle together, to go to jail together, to stand up for freedom together, knowing that we will be free one day.

This will be the day when all of God's children will be able to sing 20
with new meaning

My country, 'tis of thee,
Sweet land of liberty,
  Of thee I sing:
Land where my fathers died,
Land of the pilgrims' pride,
From every mountain-side
  Let freedom ring.

And if America is to be a great nation this must become true. So let freedom ring from the prodigious hilltops of New Hampshire. Let freedom ring from the mighty mountains of New York. Let freedom ring from the heightening Alleghenies of Pennsylvania!

Let freedom ring from the snowcapped Rockies of Colorado!

Let freedom ring from the curvaceous peaks of California!

But not only that; let freedom ring from Stone Mountain of Georgia!

Let freedom ring from Lookout Mountain of Tennessee! 25

Let freedom ring from every hill and molehill of Mississippi. From every mountainside, let freedom ring.

When we let freedom ring, when we let it ring from every village and every hamlet, from every state and every city, we will be able to speed up that day when all of God's children, black men and white men, Jews and Gentiles, Protestants and Catholics, will be able to join hands and sing in the words of the old Negro spiritual, "Free at last! free at last! thank God almighty, we are free at last!"

READING AND DISCUSSION QUESTIONS

1. What were the circumstances in which King delivered this speech? Of whom did the audience consist? How might the circumstances and the audience have affected decisions King made in composing the speech? Where in the speech does he most directly refer to his audience?
2. What sort of reputation had King established by the time he gave this speech in 1963? Are there ways in which he establishes his credibility through the speech itself? Explain.
3. How would you describe the organization of the speech?
4. Explain the metaphor of the check. Where else does King make use of metaphorical language?
5. How else does King's use of language lend power to his speech?
6. What allusions do you find in the speech?

WRITING SUGGESTIONS

7. Write an essay analyzing King's speech according to the elements of oral argument discussed in this chapter.
8. Write an essay analyzing King's language as a major source of the effectiveness of this historic speech.

Acknowledgments (continued from page iv)

Eric Auchard. "We're All Celebrities in Post-Privacy Age." From *Reuters.com,* June 21, 2007. Reprinted by permission of FosteReprints.

Radley Balko. "Absolutely, Government Has No Business Interfering with What You Eat." From *Time* magazine, June 7, 2004. Copyright © 2004 by Radley Balko. Reprinted by permission of the author.

Newman P. Birk and Genevieve B. Birk. "Selection, Slanting, and Charged Learning." From *Understanding and Using English.* Copyright © 1959 Newman P. Birk and Genevieve Birk. Reprinted by permission of the authors' estate.

Birmingham Post-Herald. "Eight Clergymen's Statemtent." From *The Birmingham Post-Herald,* 13 April 1963, p. 10. Copyright 1963 Martin Luther King Jr.; Copyright renewed 1991 Coretta Scott King. Reprinted by arrangement with The Heirs to the Estate of Martin Luther King Jr., c/o Writer's House as agent for the proprietor New York, NY.

Donald J. Borut. "Vital Tool of Last Resort: Opposing View: Uproar Obscures Eminent Domain's Crucial Role in Revitalizing Areas." From *USA Today,* July 10, 2006. Reprinted by permission.

Warren Burger. "The Right to Bear Arms." From *Parade* Magazine, January 14, 1990. Reprinted by permission of the Estate of Warren Burger.

Mona Charen. "The Misleading Debate on Stem Cell Research." From *Townhall.com,* August 20, 2004. Copyright © 2004 by News America Syndicate. Reprinted by permission of Mona Charen and Creator's Syndicate, Inc.

Jo Ann Citron. "Will it be Marriage or Civil Union?" From *The Gay & Lesbian Review Worldwide,* March / April 2004, v. 11 i2, p. 10(2). Copyright © 2004 Jo Ann Citron. Reprinted by permission of the author and the Gay & Lesbian Review Worldwide.

Alan M. Dershowitz. "Is There a Torturous Road to Justice?" From *The Los Angeles Times, Commentary,* November 8, 2001. Reprinted by permission of the author.

Alan M. Dershowitz. "Should We Fight Terror with Torture?" From *The Independent,* July 3, 2006. Copyright © 2007 Independent News and Media Limited. Reprinted by permission.

Roger Ebert. "Crash." From *rogerebert.com,* May 5, 2005. Reprinted by permission of Universal Press Syndicate.

Edward Jay Epstein. "Sex and the Cinema." From *Slate.com,* August 15, 2005. Reprinted by permission.

Seth Finkelstein. "Alan Dershowitz's Tortuous Torturous Argument." From *Ethical Spectacle,* February 2002. Reprinted by permission of the author.

Nathan Glazer. "Do We Need the Census Race Question?" From the *Public Interest.* Copyright © 2000. Reprinted by permission of the Public Interest.

Bernard Goldberg. "Connecting the Dots to Terrorists." From *Bias* by Bernard Goldberg. Copyright © 2002. Published by Regnery Publishing, Inc. All rights reserved. Reprinted by special permission of Regnery Publishing Inc., Washington, D.C.

Jennifer Grossman. "Food for Thought (and for Credit)." From the *New York Times,* Sept. 2, 2003, p. 23, col. 1. Copyright © 2003 by Jennifer Grossman. Reprinted by permission of the author.

Elisha Dov Hack. "College Life Versus My Moral Code." From the *New York Times,* September 9, 1997. Reprinted by permission.

Richard Hayes. "Supersize Your Child?" Originally entitled "Selective Science." From *Tompaine.com,* February 12, 2004. Copyright © 2004 by Tompaine.com. Reprinted by permission.

Chris Kapper. "Freedom to Live Trumps All!" From *Cnet.com.* Reprinted by permission of YGS Group.

Martin Luther King Jr. "Letter from Birmingham Jail" and "I Have a Dream." From *A Testament of Hope.* Copyright © 1963 by Martin Luther King Jr. Copyright renewed 1991 by Coretta Scott King. Reprinted by arrangement with the Estate of Martin Luther King Jr., c/o Writer's House, as agent for the proprietor.

Alfie Kohn. "No-Win Situations." From *Women's Sports and Fitness Magazine* (July-August 1990). Copyright © 1990. Reprinted with the author's permission. For more information, please see www.alfiekohn.org.

William Severini Kowinski. "Kids in the Mall: Growing up Controlled." From *The Malling of America* by William Severini Kowinski (Morrow, 1985). Copyright © 1985 by William Severini Kowinski. Reprinted by permission of the author.

Charles Krauthammer. "Let's Have No More Monkey Trials." From *Time* magazine,

August 8, 2005. Reprinted by permission of the publisher.

Michael Levin. "The Case for Torture." Originally published in *Newsweek*, June 7, 1982. Copyright © 1982 by Michael Levin. Reprinted by permission of the author.

Abraham Lincoln. "The Gettysburg Address." Reprinted courtesy of the Abraham Lincoln Association.

Sheryl McCarthy. "Showbiz Encourages Looser Teen Sex Habits." From *Newsday*, June 24, 2004. Copyright © 2004 by Newsday. Reprinted by permission of the publisher.

Roger D. McGrath. "A God Given Natural Right 'Shall Not Be Infringed.'" From *Chronicles*, October 2003. Copyright © 2003. Reprinted by permission of the author.

Margaret Mead. "Warfare: An Invention—Not a Biological Necessity." From *Asia*, 1940. Reprinted by permission of the Institute for Intercultural Studies.

Mark Memmott. "Disaster Photos: Newsworthy or Irresponsible?" From *USAToday.com*, August 4, 2005. Reprinted by permission of *USA Today* and the authors.

Howard Moody. "Gay Marriage Shows Why We Need to Separate Church and State." From the *Nation*, July 2004. Reprinted by permission of the publisher.

Charles Morris. "Why U.S. Health Costs Aren't Too High." From *Harvard Business Review*, February, 2007. Reprinted by permission of the Harvard Business Review.

Wesley Morris. "'Saw' Good at Tying Things in Knots." From *Boston Globe*, October 29, 2004. Reprinted by permission of the author.

Desda Moss. "'Freak Dancing': If Only It Stopped There." From *USA Today* online April 7, 2005. Reprinted by permission of the author.

Geoffrey Nunberg. "Don't Torture English to Soft-Pedal Abuse." From *www.Newsday.com*, May 24, 2004. Copyright © 2004 by Newsday, Inc. Reprinted by permission of the author.

Theodora Ooms. "Marriage-Plus." Annotated and excerpted from a special issue of *The American Prospect* on "The Politics of the American Family," April 8, 2002. Copyright © 2002 by the American Prospect. Reprinted by permission of the author.

George Orwell. "Politics and the English Language." Copyright © 1946 by Sonia Brownell Orwell and renewed 1974 by Sonia Orwell. Reprinted from his volume *Shooting An Elephant and Other Essays* by permission of Harcourt, Inc. and A. M. Heath & Co.

Orlando Patterson. "Race by the Numbers." From the *New York Times*, May 8, 2001. Copyright © 2001 by The New York Times. Reprinted by permission of the author.

Katha Pollitt. "Shotgun Weddings." From the *Nation*, February 4, 2002. Copyright © 2002 by Katha Pollitt. Reprinted by permission.

Anna Quindlen. "A New Look, an Old Battle." Published in *Newsweek*, April 9, 2001, pp. 72–73. Copyright © 2001 by Anna Quindlen. Reprinted by permission of International Creative Management, Inc.

Christopher Reeve. "Use the Body's 'Repair Kit': We Must Pursue Research on Embryonic Stem Cells." From *Time* magazine, May 1, 2000. Copyright © 2000 by Christopher Reeve. Reprinted by permission of the estate of Christopher Reeve.

Richard Rothstein. "True or False: Schools Fail Immigrants." From the *New York Times*, July 4, 2001. Copyright © 2001 the New York Times. All rights reserved. Used by permission and protected by the Copyright Laws of the United States. The printing, copying, redistribution, or retransmission of the Material without express written permission is prohibited.

Joan Ryan. "Americans Entitled to Cheap Gas—Right?" From *San Francisco Chronicle*, May 20, 2004. Copyright © 2004 by the San Francisco Chronicle. Reprinted by permission of Copyright Clearance Center.

Joe Sharkey. "Airport Screeners Could Get X-rated X-rays." From the *New York Times*, May 24, 2005. Copyright © 2005 the New York Times. All rights reserved. Used by permission and protected by the Copyright Laws of the United States. The printing, copying, redistribution, or retransmission of the Material without express written permission is prohibited.

Robert A. Sirico. "An Unjust Sacrifice." Originally published in the *New York Times*, September 30, 2000. Copyright © 2000 by the New York Times Company. Reprinted by permission.

C. Renzi Stone. "Live Longer and Healthier: Stop Eating Meat!" Reprinted by permission of the author.

Bob Sullivan. "MySpace and Sex Offenders: What's the Problem?" From *The Red Tape Chronicles*, MSNBC.com, May 29, 2007. Reprinted by permission of MSNBC.com via the Copyright Clearance Center.

Frank Thomas. "X-ray Tests Both Security, Privacy." From *USA Today*, December 26,

2006. Reprinted by permission of the publisher.

USA Today. "One Year Later, Power to Seize Property Ripe for Abuse." From *USA Today*, July 10, 2006. Reprinted by permission of the publisher.

Hal Varian. "Economic Scene: Are Bigger Vehicles Safer? It Depends." From the *New York Times*, December 18, 2003. Copyright © 2003 by the New York Times Inc. Reprinted by permission.

David Von Drehle. "It's All About Him: We Should Stop Explaining Killers on Their Terms. It's Not About Guns or culture. It's Narcissism." From *Time* magazine, Thursday, April 19, 2007. Copyright © 2007 Time Inc. Reprinted by permission. Time is a registered trademark of Time Inc. All rights reserved.

Patti Waldmeier. "Freedom of Speech and My Right to Silence at Bath Time." From *Financial Times*, Nov 10, 2003, p. 12. Copyright © 2003 by Financial Times. Reprinted by permission of the publisher.

Claudius E. Watts, III. "Single-Sex Education Benefits Men Too." From the *Wall Street Journal*, May 3, 1995. Reprinted by permission of the author.

Michael M. Weinstein. "A Reassuring Scorecard for Affirmative Action." From the *New York Times*, October 17, 2000. Reprinted by permission of PARS International.

Brian Whitaker. "The Definition of Terrorism." From the *Guardian Unlimited*, May 7, 2001. Copyright Guardian News & Media Ltd 2001. Reprinted by permission.

Barbara Dafoe Whitehead. "Parents Need Help: Restricting Access to Video Games." From *Commonweal*, January 28, 2005.

Lily Yulianti. "Praise for Student's Footage of Virginia Tech Mass Killing." From *Ohmynews.com*, April 17, 2007. Copyright © 2007 Ohmynews. Reprinted by permission of the author.

Eric Zorn. "Family a Symbol of Love and Life, but Not Politics." From the *Chicago Tribune*, May 23, 2004. Reprinted by permission.

PICTURE CREDITS

38 Photofest; **63** (top) AP Images/Dave Martin; (bottom) Chris Graythen/Getty Images; **65** AP Images/Eric Gay; **66** (top) Margaret Bourke-White/Getty Images; (bottom) Bruce Chambers/The Orange County Register; **75, 76** ©CharityUSA.com, LLC, www.thehungersite.com; **239** G. Paul Burnett/The New York Times/Redux; **448, 449** Student-Voices is a project of the Annenberg Public Policy Center; **455** Title page and copyright page from *Nickel and Dimed: On (Not) Getting By in America* written by Barbara Ehrenreich. Copyright, ©2001 by Henry Holt and Company. Reprinted by permission of Henry Holt and Company, LLC. **459** Reprinted by permission of Army Times Publishing Company; **464** Title and copyright page from *The Western Cannon: The Books and School of the Ages*, copyright ©1994 by Harold Bloom, reprinted by permission of Harcourt, Inc. **468** From www.defenselink.mil. Article by Spc. Courtney Marulli, 2nd Brigade Combat Team, 2nd Infantry Division Public Affairs. **469** From Gale. *Screen shot from Thomson/Galegroup.com Expanded Academic ASAP*. ©Gale, a part of Cengage Learning, Inc. Reproduced by permission. www.cengage .com/permissions. Article reprinted from the May 30, 2005 issue of *BusinessWeek* by permission. Copyright 2005 by The McGraw-Hill Companies.

Glossary

Abstract language: language expressing a quality apart from a specific object or event; opposite of *concrete language*

Ad hominem: "against the man"; attacking the arguer rather than the *argument* or issue

Ad populum: "to the people"; playing on the prejudices of the *audience*

Anecdotal evidence: stories or examples used to illustrate a *claim* but that do not prove it with scientific certainty

Appeal to tradition: a proposal that something should continue because it has traditionally existed or been done that way

Argument: a process of reasoning and advancing proof about issues on which conflicting views may be held; also, a statement or statements providing *support* for a *claim*

Audience: those who will hear an *argument;* more generally, those to whom a communication is addressed

Authoritative warrant: a *warrant* based on the credibility or trustworthiness of the source

Backing: the assurances on which a *warrant* or assumption is based

Begging the question: making a statement that assumes that the issue being argued has already been decided

Claim: the conclusion of an argument; what the arguer is trying to prove

Claim of fact: a *claim* that asserts something exists, has existed, or will exist, based on data that the *audience* will accept as objectively verifiable

Claim of policy: a *claim* asserting that specific courses of action should be instituted as solutions to problems

Claim of value: a *claim* that asserts some things are more or less desirable than others

Cliché: a worn-out expression or idea, no longer capable of producing a visual image or provoking thought about a subject

Concrete language: language that describes specific, generally observable, persons, places, or things; in contrast to *abstract language*

Connotation: the overtones that adhere to a word through long usage

Credibility: the audience's belief in the arguer's trustworthiness; see also *ethos*

Data: facts or figures from which a conclusion may be inferred; see *evidence*

Deduction: reasoning by which we establish that a conclusion must be true because the statements on which it is based are true; see also *syllogism*

Definition: an explanation of the meaning of a term, concept, or experience; may be used for clarification, especially of a *claim,* or as a means of developing an *argument*

Definition by negation: defining a thing by saying what it is not

Empirical evidence: *support* verifiable by experience or experiment

Enthymeme: a *syllogism* in which one of the premises is implicit

Ethos: the qualities of character, intelligence, and goodwill in an arguer that contribute to an *audience's* acceptance of the *claim*

Euphemism: a pleasant or flattering expression used in place of one that is less agreeable but possibly more accurate

Evidence: *facts* or opinions that support an issue or *claim;* may consist of *statistics,* reports of personal experience, or views of experts

Extended definition: a *definition* that uses several different methods of development

Fact: something that is believed to have objective reality; a piece of information regarded as verifiable

Factual evidence: *support* consisting of *data* that are considered objectively verifiable by the audience

Fallacy: an error of reasoning based on faulty use of *evidence* or incorrect *inference*

False analogy: assuming without sufficient proof that if objects or processes are similar in some ways, then they are similar in other ways as well

False dilemma: simplifying a complex problem into an either/or dichotomy

Faulty emotional appeals: basing an argument on feelings, especially pity or fear—often to draw attention away from the real issues or conceal another purpose

Faulty use of authority: failing to acknowledge disagreement among experts or otherwise misrepresenting the trustworthiness of sources

Hasty generalization: drawing conclusions from insufficient evidence

Induction: reasoning by which a general statement is reached on the basis of particular examples

Inference: an interpretation of the *facts*

Major premise: see *syllogism*

Minor premise: see *syllogism*

MLA: the Modern Language Association, a professional organization for college teachers of English and foreign languages

Motivational appeal: an attempt to reach an *audience* by recognizing their *needs* and *values* and how these contribute to their decision making

Motivational warrant: a type of *warrant* based on the *needs* and *values* of an *audience*

Need: in the hierarchy of Abraham Maslow, whatever is required, whether psychological, or physiological, for the survival and welfare of a human being

Non sequitur: "it does not follow"; using irrelevant proof to buttress a *claim*

Paraphrase: to restate the content of an original source in your own words

Picturesque language: words that produce images in the minds of the *audience*

Plagiarism: the use of someone else's words or ideas without adequate acknowledgment

Policy: a course of action recommended or taken to solve a problem or guide decisions

Post hoc: mistakenly inferring that because one event follows another they have a causal relation; from *post hoc ergo propter hoc* ("after this, therefore because of this"); also called "doubtful cause"

Proposition: see *claim*

Qualifier: a restriction placed on the *claim* may not always be true as stated

Quote: to repeat exactly words from a printed, electronic, or spoken source

Refutation: an attack on an opposing view to weaken it, invalidate it, or make it less credible

Reservation: a restriction placed on the *warrant* to indicate that unless certain conditions are met, the warrant may not establish a connection between the *support* and the *claim*

Slanting: selecting *facts* or words with *connotations* that favor the arguer's bias and discredit alternatives

Slippery slope: predicting without justification that one step in a process will lead unavoidably to a second, generally undesirable step

Slogan: an attention-getting expression used largely in politics or advertising to promote support of a cause or product

Statistics: information expressed in numerical form

Stipulative definition: a *definition* that makes clear that it will explore a particular area of meaning of a term or issue

Straw man: disputing a view similar to, but not the same as, that of the arguer's opponent

Style: choices in words and sentence structure that make a writer's language distinctive

Substantive warrant: a *warrant* based on beliefs about the reliability of *factual evidence*

Support: any material that serves to prove an issue or *claim;* in addition to *evidence,* it includes appeals to the *needs* and *values* of the *audience*

Syllogism: a formula of deductive *argument* consisting of three propositions: a major premise, a minor premise, and a conclusion

Thesis: the main idea of an essay

Toulmin model: a conceptual system of argument devised by the philosopher Stephen Toulmin; the terms *claim, support, warrant, backing, qualifier,* and *reservation* are adapted from this system

Two wrongs make a right: diverting attention from the issue by introducing a new point, e.g., by responding to an accusation with a counteraccusation that makes no attempt to refute the first accusation

Values: conceptions or ideas that act as standards for judging what is right or wrong, worthwhile or worthless, beautiful or ugly, good or bad

Warrant: a general principle or assumption that establishes a connection between the *support* and the *claim*

Index of Subjects

Index of Authors and Titles

Need more help with writing and research?

Re:Writing is designed to help you with important writing concerns. You'll find advice from experts, models you can rely on, and exercises that will tell you right away how you're doing. And it's all free and available any hour of the day. All of these can be accessed at bedfordstmartins.com/rewriting.

Need help with grammar problems?
Exercise Central
(bedfordstmartins.com/exercisecentral)

Want to see what papers for your other courses look like?
Model Documents Gallery
(bedfordstmartins.com/modeldocs)

Stuck somewhere in the research process? (Maybe at the beginning?)
The Bedford Research Room
(bedfordstmartins.com/researchroom)

Wondering whether a Web site is good enough to use in your paper?
Tutorial for Evaluating Online Sources
(bedfordstmartins.com/onlinesourcestutorial)

Having trouble figuring out how to cite a source?
Research and Documentation Online
(bedfordstmartins.com/resdoc)

Confused about plagiarism?
The St. Martin's Tutorial on Avoiding Plagiarism
(bedfordstmartins.com/plagiarismtutorial)

Want to get more out of your word processor?
Using Your Word Processor
(bedfordstmartins.com/wordprocessor)

Trying to improve the look of your paper?
Using Your Word Processor to Design Documents
(bedfordstmartins.com/docdesigntutorial)

Need to create slides for a presentation?
Preparing Presentation Slides Tutorial
(bedfordstmartins.com/presentationslidetutorial)

Interested in creating a Web site?
Web Design Tutorial
(bedfordstmartins.com/webdesigntutorial)